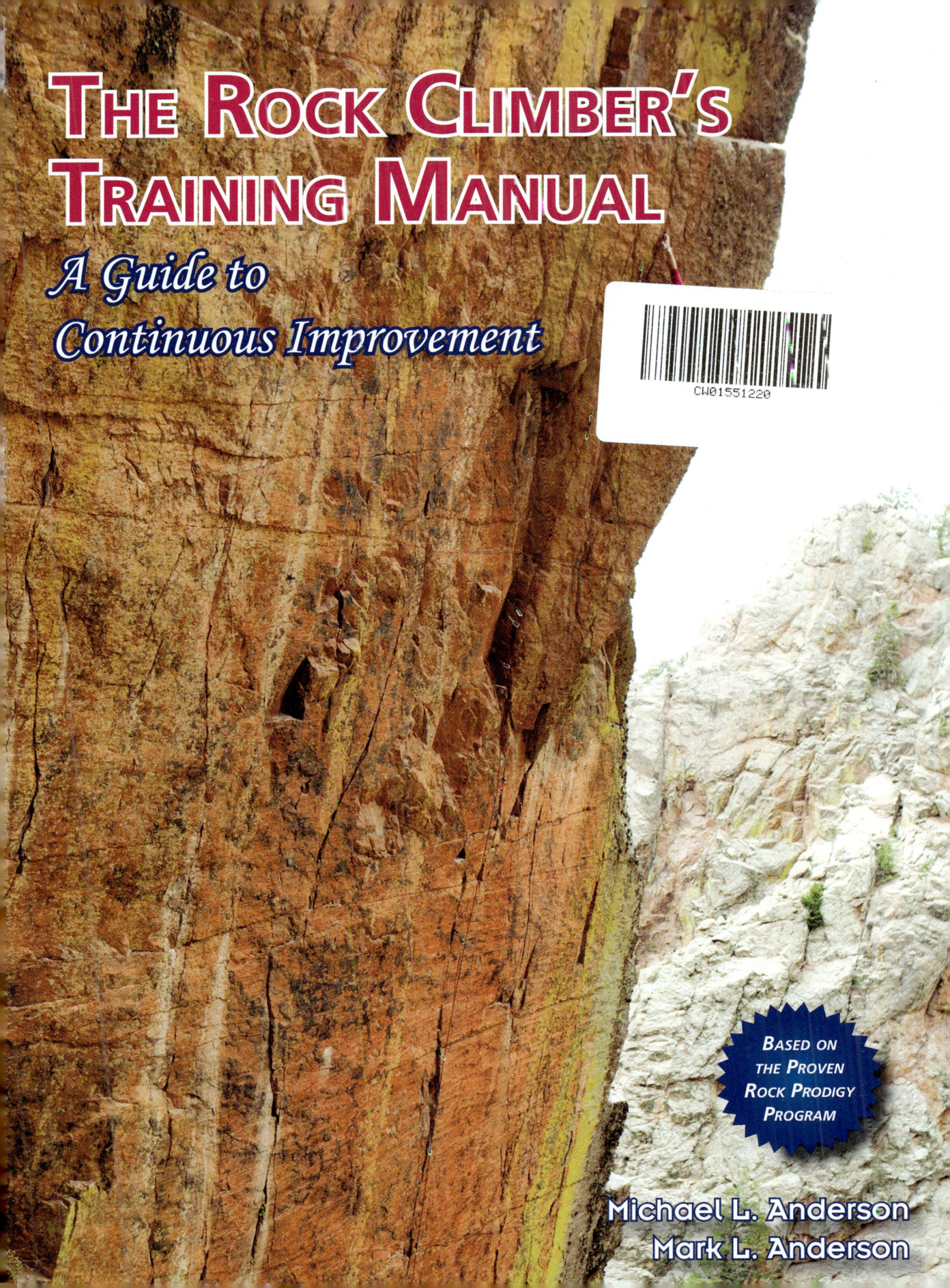

The Rock Climber's Training Manual

A Guide to Continuous Improvement

BASED ON THE PROVEN ROCK PRODIGY PROGRAM

Michael L. Anderson
Mark L. Anderson

The Rock Climber's Training Manual: A Guide to Continuous Improvement

Authors: Michael L. Anderson, PhD and Mark L. Anderson
Uncredited Photography: Mark and Mike Anderson. Training photos by Fredrik Marmsater
Cover photo: Mark Anderson on *To Bolt or Not to Be*, 5.14a, Smith Rock, OR. photo: Mike Anderson.
Opening page photo: Cody Roth getting lucky on *A Date With Death*, 5.13c, Sandias, NM. photo: Andrew Burr.
Table of Contents photo: Morgan Mcneil on *Cradle of the Deep Original*, 5.13a, Horseshoe Canyon, AR. photo: Cole Fennel.

International Standard Book Number:
ISBN 978-0-9895156-1-0

Library of Congress Catalog in Publication Data:
Library of Congress Control Number: 2013954868

Fixed Pin Publishing is continually expanding its guidebooks and loves to hear from locals about their home areas. If you have an idea for a book or a manuscript for a guide, or would like to find out more about our company, contact:

Jason Haas
Fixed Pin Publishing
P.O. Box 3481
Boulder, CO 80307
jason@fixedpin.com

Ben Schneider
Fixed Pin Publishing
P.O. Box 3481
Boulder, CO 80307
ben@fixedpin.com

WWW.FIXEDPIN.COM

WARNING:

Rock climbing is a sport with inherent danger, which may result in severe injury or death. Read and understand this warning before using this book. This is an instruction book about rock climbing, a sport with inherent risk. Do not depend solely on information from this book for your personal safety and do not allow this book to take the place of proper instruction. Employ a professional guide or instructor if you are unsure of your ability to handle any circumstances that may arise while rock climbing. The information contained within this book is a compilation of opinions and as such, is unverified. These opinions are neither facts nor promises and should not be treated as so. Rely first and foremost upon your skill, experience, conditions, and common sense rather than the opinions expressed in this book as they are all entirely subjective. If you are unwilling to assume complete responsibility for your safety, and if you (or your estate) is unwilling to never try to sue Fixed Pin Publishing if you get hurt or killed, do not use this book. Errors may exist in this book as a result of the author and/or the people with whom they consulted. Because the information was gathered from a multitude of sources, they may not have been independently verified and therefore **the publisher, or the authors, cannot guarantee the correctness of any of the information contained within this guidebook.** THE AUTHORS AND PUBLISHER EXPRESSLY DISCLAIM ANY REPRESENTATIONS AND WARRANTIES REGARDING THIS BOOK. THEY MAKE NO REPRESENTATIONS OR WARRANTIES, EXPRESSED OR IMPLIED, OF ANY KIND REGARDING THE ACCURACY OR RELIABILITY OF THE CONTENT OF THIS BOOK. THERE ARE NO WARRANTIES OF MERCHANTABILITY OR FITNESS FOR A PARTICULAR PURPOSE. THE USER ASSUMES ALL RISK ASSOCIATED WITH THE USE OF THIS BOOK AND ALL ACTIVITIES CONTAINED WITHIN IT, ESPECIALLY ROCK CLIMBING.

ACKNOWLEDGMENTS

We received tremendous assistance throughout this project, and would like to thank the following contributors: Our publisher, Jason Haas, believed in us early on, and turned our words into a book. Matt Samet edited the text and ensured it would be a consistent, readable product. Renowned climbing coach and trainer, Steve "the Chosen One" Bechtel, provided frequent technical advice, and over the years, has challenged our ideas on training, helping us refine our methods and understanding. Heather Wales-Gomez and Will Strickland provided source material and insightful feedback. We are also grateful to the many folks who took the time to review the text and provide invaluable feedback, including Jonathan Siegrist, Ryan Palo, Lamont Smith, Kris Hampton, Paige Claassen, and Tommy Caldwell.

We are forever indebted to the talented Andrew Burr, Brendan Nicholson, and Dan Brayack who contributed dozens of photographs from their spectacular collections. We are also grateful for the generous photographic contributions of Frederik Marmsater, Janelle Anderson, Bill Hatcher, Anthony Carco, Lee Hansche, Jason Haas, Keith Ladzinski, Chuck Fryberger, Peter Franzen, Rebecca Caldwell, Jason Hundhausen, Mathew Oscadal, Page Kuepper, John Borland, Cole Fennel, and Brian Mosbaugh. In addition, we appreciate all those who modeled for photos, especially Tommy Caldwell, Paige Claassen, Janelle Anderson, Kristin Yurdin, Shaun Corpron, BJ Tilden, and Jonathan Siegrist.

This work is the culmination of two climbing careers, built on the support and friendship of countless climbing partners, too numerous to list here. Thank you all for your patience. In addition, we are grateful to our parents, Marshall and Karen Anderson who taught us the value of hard work and perseverance, and instilled in us a zest for competition and adventure that has kept us motivated for all these years. Thanks also to the many friends who influenced our thoughts on training through discussion or example. In particular, this book would not have been written without the inspiration and encouragement of the Mountain Project training forum.

Finally, and most importantly, we are extremely thankful for the continued love and support of our families; Janelle, Lucas, Axel, Kate, Logan, and Amelie. We appreciate our children's understanding for the endless sessions glued to the computer. Our wives offered invaluable encouragement throughout the project, while acting as impromptu sounding boards for our ideas and frustrations. This support pales in comparison to the years of devotion they've shown putting up with our climbing obsessions; the slogs to the crag, missed vacations, and countless hours of belaying, among other sacrifices. They've kept us motivated, kept us humble, and kept things in perspective. Remember kids, it doesn't have to be "fun" to be fun!

"With clear, concise, goal-oriented prose, inspiring full-color photographs, and all the charts you'll need to get rolling on your own Rock Prodigy program, the Anderson brothers have compiled and made imminently accessible their impressive body of training lore. With proven results in their own careers, the Andersons show you how to make the most of limited training time, to time your training cycles for redpoint optimization, and to systematically improve as a rock climber. If becoming a better and stronger, more consistently performing climber is your goal, then this is the book for you!"

— Matt Samet, 5.14 first ascentionist, former editor of Climbing Magazine
and author of the Climbing Dictionary and The Crag Survival Handbook

"The Andersons understand not only the strength and technique required in training, but also the mental dedication necessary to push one's limits. Their experience as top-level athletes in the field, rather than just trainers in the gym, directly validates *The Rock Climber's Training Manual*. Even seasoned climbing veterans can benefit from understanding the science behind their performance cycle, particularly when those words of wisdom come from climbers who have self-tested, re-tested, and fine-tuned their training methods for over fifteen years."

— Paige Claassen, US National Champion and 5.14 First Ascentionist

"This is the best climbing training book ever written. It is a complete guide to success in hard rock climbing, and is a must-read for anyone serious about the sport. I don't think there is a climber in the world that wouldn't benefit from reading and applying the Rock Prodigy program."

— Steve Bechtel, Certified Strength and Conditioning Specialist, climbstrong.com

"Training is central to achieving any athletic goal. It gives an outlet for our drive, and provides the strength and technical practice we need to improve. *The Rock Climber's Training Manual* clearly lays out the details of how to train effectively to take your climbing to the next level."

— Tommy Caldwell, First Free Ascentionist of four El Cap Big Wall Free Climbs

"Whether you're a beginner or a seasoned vet, a sport climber or big waller, the Anderson brothers have been there, done that. Their training secrets are all here, laid out in a solid blend of science and anecdotal evidence, ready for you to apply to your next project. If you're searching for the path to your next level, this is where you'll find it."

— Kris Hampton, Climbing Coach, powercompanyclimbing.com

"During my early climbing years I worked on my skill and technique, but still struggled when it came time to bare down. It wasn't until I started following the Rock Prodigy program that I experienced marked improvements and since then, I've improved roughly a letter grade every six months. No other training resource has benefited more climbers, and now the Andersons have expanded and updated those concepts into a must-read for those looking to improve their climbing ability."

— Ryan Palo, Dedicated Weekend Warrior and 5.14 First Ascentionist

"*The Rock Climber's Training Manual* is an exceptional book—just flipping through the pages gets me stoked to train. I specifically like the mix of scientific and physiological explanation alongside great photographs, diagrams and suggestions that make all the data applicable to your training and climbing. I'll definitely be referencing this book during my next training period."

— Jonathan Siegrist, Professional climber, 5.14d First Ascentionist

FOREWORD

I started climbing in 1986. I wasn't an athlete and could have been best described as a founding member of the video game generation. Slow, lazy, and heavy. In high school, I became interested in climbing through a previous interest in rappelling, which was fueled not by adventure or a love of the outdoors, but by the cool gear. As a lucky coincidence, I met and started climbing with the now-legendary Steve Petro who told me I was too fat and weak to be a good climber. "What you should do," he said, "is 100 pull-ups a day." And there began my first training program. Slowly I got stronger and leaner and better at climbing.

My interest in improving my climbing continued to develop over the years, including majoring in exercise science in college and relentlessly pursuing every bit of information I could find on training for strength and conditioning. Some twenty years later, although I felt I'd pretty much figured out how to train for hard climbing, I ran across a document online called "The Making of a Rock Prodigy." It was a frank and well thought out piece about how Mike Anderson had figured out how to stop sucking at climbing.

I emailed him about the document, and Mike and I began a correspondence about training for climbing, then about big wall climbing, and eventually we became somewhat regular climbing partners.

Not much later, Mike introduced me to his brother, Mark. Mark was making regular trips to the crags near my home in Lander, and our families became fast friends. Within a few visits, I could see that Mark was every bit as serious and knowledgeable about training as his brother. In fact, Mike once told me that "Mark knows just as much about training as I do, he just applies it better." That was maybe five years ago.

Over the course of many discussions, I came to see that the Rock Prodigy plan was a living document, refined two or three times a year and discussed exhaustively between the brothers. What I saw with my own eyes was that the training program worked - not a normal attribute of many training programs.

Most climbers see a fairly steep improvement curve the first few months or couple of years that they climb. After a while, though, they plateau and then spend the rest of their career getting in and out of shape for the same old grade, never again advancing to harder routes. What fascinated me about the brothers is that both of them continued to crawl their way up the grades each year. Both Mike and Mark work full time, have families, and climb 5.14 regularly. The crazy thing is that they're still getting better!

The book you now hold in your hands is the result of years spent designing and testing training plans. It is the result of many near-misses and many successes at the crags, on big walls, and in the mountains. Never before have I met athletes as dedicated to honest self-reflection and improvement. Never before have I met climbers able to morph their vast knowledge into a useable and clear program that can be scaled to multiple performance levels.

I write articles on training for climbing, I coach climbers, and I still try to climb harder than I did when I was thirty. Over the past few years, the Anderson brothers have become my go-to B.S. detector when it comes to any fringe training ideas. They have become great advisors on redpointing hard climbs. They have become my coaches, my most valuable resource, and now they can be yours, too. Read the book, do what the book tells you to do, and you'll start creeping up the grades again.

The Rock Climber's Training Manual is an important step forward in the practice of improved climbing. The rigorous and carefully planned programs in these pages might seem too boring or restrictive compared to the "training" you normally do. But as the brothers say, "Climbing hard routes is never boring."

Steve Bechtel
Certified Strength and Conditioning Specialist
www.climbstrong.com

Table of Contents

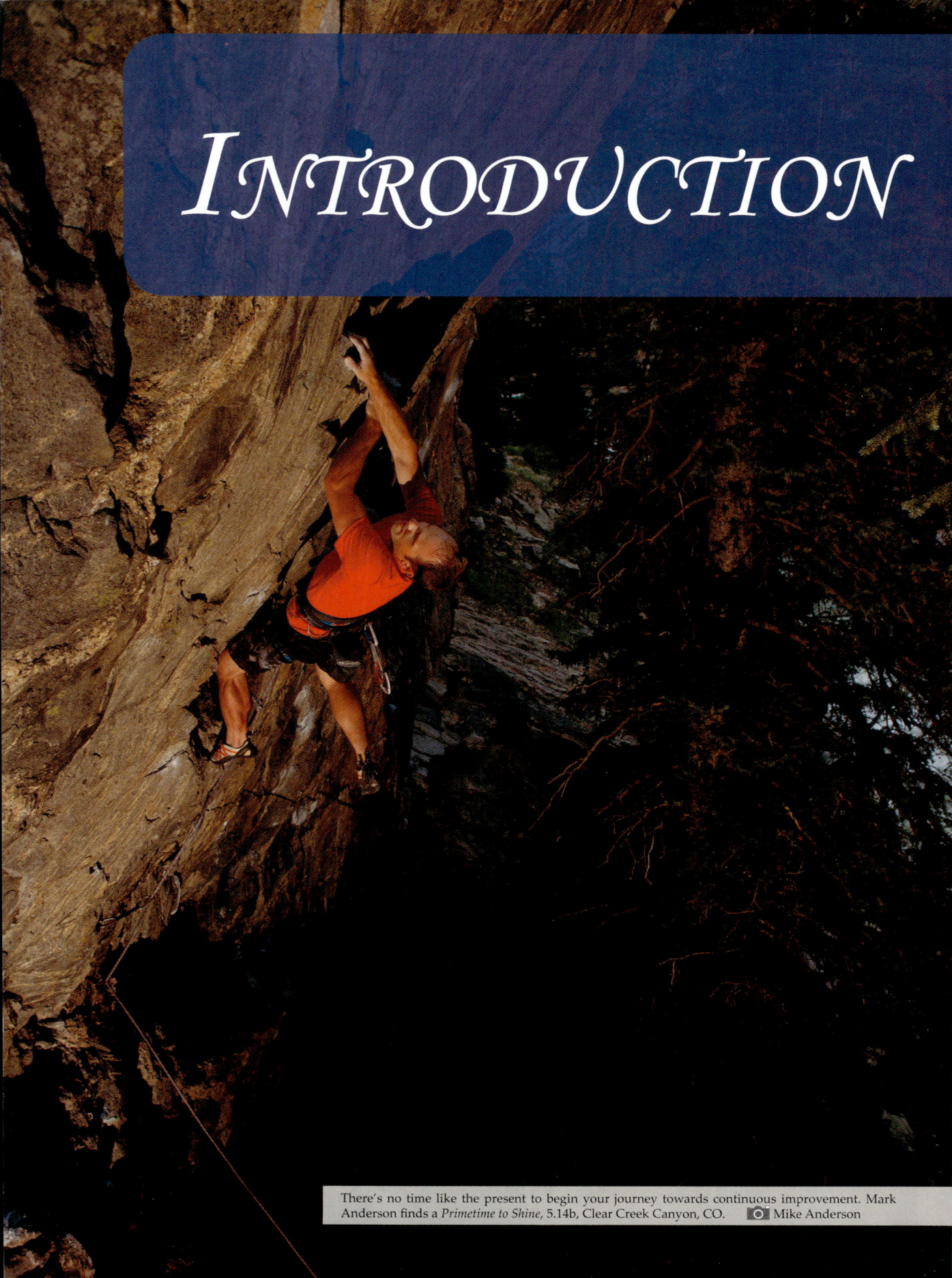

INTRODUCTION

There's no time like the present to begin your journey towards continuous improvement. Mark Anderson finds a *Primetime to Shine*, 5.14b, Clear Creek Canyon, CO. 📷 Mike Anderson

CHAPTER 1

"Whatever you can do or dream you can, begin it. Boldness has genius, power and magic in it."
— *Goethe*

There are some routes that just call to us like Homer's Sirens. A laser-cut arête, a towering line of crisp edges, an endless splitter or an epic citadel of Sierra granite. The truly beautiful lines captivate our consciousness and demand the very most from our physical abilities. These lines keep us awake at night, make our palms sweat, and occupy our attention to the exclusion of all else. And they demand to be climbed. Satisfaction can only be achieved through success. These lines require us to raise our game to new heights, literally and figuratively. But how to do so? Inspiration lies around every buttress. Hard work and commitment can be summoned for the right objective, but climbing is complex, as is the human machine, and finding the right path to reach your goals is not simple.

The Case for Training

Training Defined

So what is training anyway? In terms of climbing, and for the purposes of this book, *training* is defined as an approach to *improve climbing performance* that is *systematic, disciplined,* and *science based*. Thus, this training program is focused on the singular goal of producing improved climbing performance. Other attributes of a training program, such as how much sweat it produces or how exhausting it feels, are entirely irrelevant; only the effect on climbing performance counts. When faced with a novel training method, every climber should ask: Will this improve my climbing performance?

A training program is *systematic* when it is premeditated and organized in a logical way, leading to a defined goal. Thus, it should be designed deliberately to transform the body from a known starting point to-ward a specific, improved end point. The intensity and duration of exercises in a systematic training program can be precisely controlled and adjusted incrementally. Therefore, a systematic program is repeatable, yields predictable results, ensures adequate rest, and provides an opportunity to evaluate the training protocols used.

A training program is *disciplined* when it is executed dutifully in accordance with the plan, and diligently tracked over time. This attribute ensures that the intended benefits of the training have an opportunity to materialize, and enables evaluation and improvement of the training program in the future.

Finally, a training program is *science based* if it draws from the existing body of knowledge to design the exercises, and is inquisitive in nature. While the ultimate goal is to improve climbing performance, an ever-present, intermediate goal is to *improve the training* by following the Scientific Method: hypothesize, experiment, observe results, evaluate the hypothesis, and repeat. This is necessary because even the best training plan in a *well-studied* sport will produce different results for different athletes, so the athlete or coach must constantly evaluate and adjust the training to achieve the best results. Therefore, in climbing, a relatively new, *under-studied* sport, it is even more critical to apply the Scientific Method to adapt the training plan to best fit the needs of the athlete.

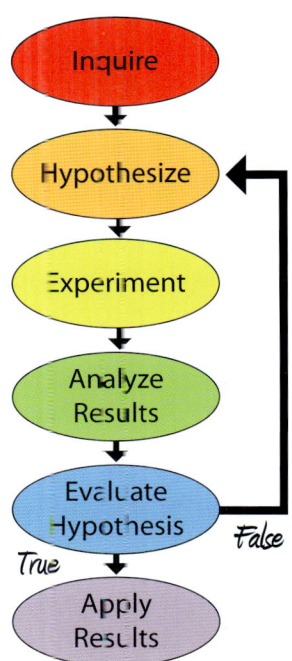

7

An athlete in *training* sets goals at the beginning of a season, then designs a specific exercise program to reach those goals. The athlete in *training* then follows this pre-planned schedule of workouts throughout the season, diligently documenting the work accomplished, specific results, and overall progress. The athlete in *training* understands the genesis of the exercises he or she is performing, how they should affect his or her body, and what changes might be made to get different results. Finally, the athlete in *training* analyzes the effectiveness of the program and, if necessary, refines it for future benefit.

DO ELITE CLIMBERS TRAIN?

Many climbers apply a spontaneous, rather than systematic, approach to their climbing. They typically adopt this approach early on and are never presented with a good reason to train systematically. This casual method is often reinforced by the impression that the most accomplished climbers follow the same easygoing approach. Be they the local honemasters, or international celebrity rock stars, it is reasonable to suppose that if the most-accomplished climbers don't need to train, then neither does anyone else. However, this argument is problematic for two reasons. First, many top climbers benefit from favorable circumstances that may not be an option for the typical climber. For example, perhaps they started climbing (or gymnastics) at a very young age, and so were able to develop tremendous finger strength during their formative years while their body was most responsive to the unusual stimuli of rock climbing. Others may simply have superior genetic gifts, or a freewheeling lifestyle that allows for more time on the rock to refine their skills. Second, and most importantly, chances are most of these accomplished climbers actually do train, though it's not always obvious. A lot may be going on "behind the scenes" between the few times a month they are *performing* at the gym or crag.

This is the case for many professional climbers. They train hard in private, but this isn't newsworthy, or terribly interesting to the public at-large, so it isn't publicized as much as their seemingly spontaneous forays to the crag where they "just climb" (...everything at the crag). There is a peculiar social norm among climbers that one should create the illusion that he or she doesn't care "too much" or try too hard. This compels many elite climbers to downplay their training, or describe it as something other than "training." Nevertheless, they are training. Dig into their blogs, or speak to them in person, and it is clear.

They may do much of their training on rock, and thus avoid tools such as finger and campus boards, but they are training in the sense that they focus on specific exercises to develop specific capabilities and overcome specific weaknesses in order to accomplish specific goals. It may be an annual three-week pilgrimage to Hueco Tanks to boost finger strength for a particularly bouldery 5.14d, or a pit stop at the Red River Gorge for some endurance work before a trip to Spain, but it *is* training. Unfortunately, most climbers lack the freedom to train in this manner. These climbers can benefit from time-efficient systematic training to achieve similar results. That is what this book offers.

THE CLIMBING ATHLETE

Climbers that are contemplating whether or not to train should consider why they climb and what they want out of it. For *recreational climbers* who climb largely for less-quantifiable reasons such as building camaraderie and visiting interesting places, training won't likely add to their fulfillment. The recreational approach is perfectly acceptable; virtually all climbers (this book's authors included) started out as recreational climbers, and even the most hardcore grade-obsessed cave troll adopts the recreational philosophy from time to time. However, other climbers consider themselves *athletes*, with climbing as their sport. Whether they clip bolts or place pro, they are driven by a desire to push themselves to their ultimate potential, and they have an unquenchable thirst for continuous improvement, like athletes in any sport. Athletes practice and train for their sport, be they cyclists, distance runners, or body builders. It doesn't matter if they are amateurs or pros—athletes train.

> *"I'm always going to try to improve and I'll always be 'that guy' who requires training, because if I don't I start to suck really bad, really fast."*
> — Sonnie Trotter[7]

Training is occasionally derided by some climbers as "trying too hard" (which is silly nonsense) or "taking the fun out of climbing." While fun is a matter of personal taste, most climbers with experience on both sides of the fence will attest that training can be fun in its own way, and nothing is more fun than crushing once-hard routes with relative ease.

Something worth doing is worth doing well, and this applies even more so to climbing because of the increased access that results from improvement. If

Rebecca Caldwell

"As a teenager I spent my evenings training in grungy garages and basements with older smelly men... and the occasional misplaced cute girl (who never stuck around that long) with the hopes that I would one day be able to ascend a more difficult 100-foot artificial wall than anyone else in the room."

— Tommy Caldwell[4]

one derived no other benefit, at a minimum, improved performance increases the pool of climbs available to choose from, and the harder lines are almost always the *best* climbs. A stroll through a typical sport crag should convince any climber that the most spectacular, highest-quality, psyche-inducing lines generally lie on the upper end of the difficulty spectrum. With hard work and training, those climbs are accessible to anyone, along with the incredible satisfaction that comes with sending a dream route. Thus by improving, not only will you be *climbing well*, you will be doing it on *better* climbs.

Improving is the obvious reason to train, and most climbers want to improve. Many climbers believe that they can improve by simply climbing as much as possible. That is true to an extent. A certain amount of improvement can be had simply through random climbing. Physically, there will be improvement so long as the volume of climbing is steadily increased (something that is hard to accomplish randomly). Technique and other less tangible factors will improve initially as well. With the availability of indoor climbing facilities and access to great sport climbing, it is possible to improve to a point without systematic training (though this still requires climbing two to three times per week). A reasonably gifted climber might reach a high level of expertise by "just climbing," but will eventually *plateau* (stop improving). For some folks, it is acceptable to reach an arbitrary grade and hover there, off into the sunset. For most, this is perpetually frustrating. So why not "just climb"? There are several reasons:

CONTINUOUS IMPROVEMENT

The first reason to train is that the best way to *ensure* steady, continuous improvement is with training. Athletes in all sports experience improvement to a point, and then eventually, long, frustrating performance plateaus in which their level of performance is constant and they don't experience any improvement. Anyone who has been climbing long enough is likely familiar with this. With a random "just climb"–type of routine, there is no way to force improvement because there is no record of what work was accomplished to reach that point, and therefore, no baseline from which to incrementally increase the load on the body in order to force adaptation. As monotonous and mundane as training can be, at least the results will not be monotonous. Improvement will come, and the training record will reflect that improvement, even if the circumstances of a given climbing season don't allow new "sends."

The knowledge that one is getting stronger can be very motivating, and can carry a climber through a number of otherwise disappointing seasons. With the "just climb" approach, the only evidence of improvement is with a "send." Imagine trying to lose weight without stepping on a scale; it would be nearly impossible to stay motivated because there would be no evidence that the sacrifices involved were paying off. Sometimes life circumstances, be they work, school, a new friend, a new baby, or even just bad weather at the crag of choice, can prevent sending, whether the climber was due for better performance or not. With a training record, the simple knowledge that gains were made during training can sustain motivation through to the next season, when there will be an opportunity to "send" again.

Often a crag's best routes are also among the hardest, inspiring us to raise our game in order to climb them. Mike Tritt stoning *Goliath*, 5.13a, at Enchanted Tower, NM. Jason Hundhausen

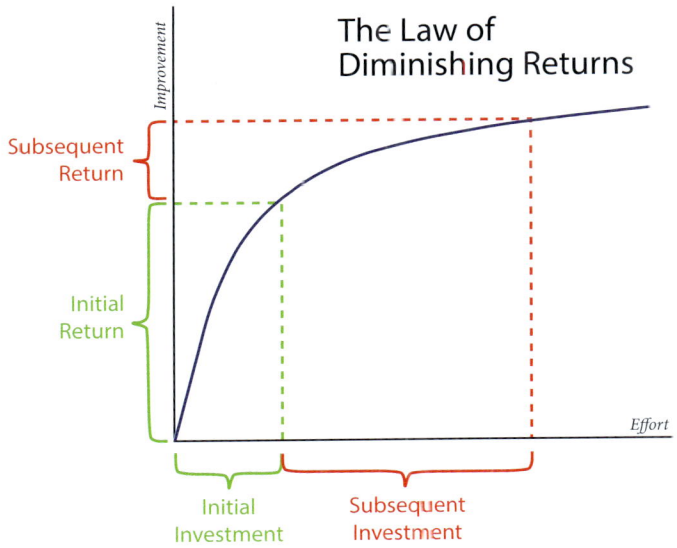

The Law of Diminishing Returns

way to measure the workload. It is virtually impossible to know if the intensity is increasing, or by how much. Unfortunately these sessions occasionally end in a wild dyno for some tweaky hold that the climber is not prepared to hold onto, then the telltale "pop" of torn connective tissue.

This spontaneous approach to improving contradicts the most fundamental rules of sport science and physical development: that the optimal way to stimulate muscular adaptation is to progressively stress it to near-failure. Furthermore, simply because a workout induces fatigue doesn't mean it will stimulate the desired physical adaptations. With random bouldering, there is no way to know when that *near-failure* point is reached, or if the desired *type* of near-failure has been achieved. However, it is always clear once that point has been exceeded (injury). The support structures of the fingers (tendons and ligaments) require up to *six years* to adapt to stress. Therefore a climber of six years is just now developing the additional ligament strength needed to handle the stress of hard climbing. Forearm muscles respond to stress in about two weeks. Therefore, within weeks of becoming a climber, the forearm muscles acquire the ability to destroy the support structure. On the other hand, a structured training regimen allows the climber to carefully and thoughtfully stress the body enough to cause the desired adaptation without stepping over the line into injury. Aside from giving up climbing for fishing, training is the best way to avoid injury!

INJURY PREVENTION

The second and most compelling reason to train is injury prevention. Stop and catch your breath—that wasn't a typo. Yes, training *prevents* injury. Here's how: Imagine two athletes lifting weights. Athlete A exercises according to no specific schedule whatsoever. He lifts whenever he has time, wherein he does one squat rep of a random weight then a couple reps of bicep curls (again at random weight, and so on), then a pull-up followed by two more squat reps, then does one max rep on triceps extensions, then does a bicep curl then one max rep on leg extension then one military press, then maxes out on bench press, then three sit-ups, etc. Suppose he does this for three straight days because it's a holiday weekend and he has the free time.

On the other hand, Athlete B goes to the weight room according to a schedule she has pre-planned that allows for hard days, easy days, and rest days. When she's in the gym she warms up each muscle group before working it, then she lifts a specified weight that is based on what she has lifted during her previous workouts plus an incremental increase (say five percent), closely monitoring her body's response to the load. Which athlete is more likely to get injured?

While this is an extreme example used to make a point, most climbers resemble Athlete A. Their typical workout is spontaneous indoor bouldering or route climbing, which is essentially a series of random exercises of various intensity and duration, sporadically involving various muscle groups. It offers few options to isolate and precisely stress the muscle (and supporting structure) to a specified amount, and there is no

REHABILITATION

Injuries might still happen from time to time, but once a climber adopts the mindset of an athlete in training, injuries will rarely hold him back for long. An athlete in training becomes an expert in listening to his body, identifying weakness, stressing weak tissue to stimulate growth, and managing rest periods to maximize recovery. Therefore, the training process of carefully applying stress to the body to maximize adaptation creates an understanding for exactly how much stress the weaker structures can handle. Training will also introduce the athlete to a variety of tools to use in the event rehabilitation becomes necessary, while providing a thorough historical strength baseline from which to develop rehabilitation plans and to track recovery. Not only does training reduce the risk of injury, it also provides a methodology and the background data necessary to facilitate recovery from injuries, should they occur. *Training* and *rehabilitation* are just two sides of the same coin.

TRAINING SAVES TIME

Finally, a third reason to train is that it simply takes less time. The systematic nature of training makes it the most efficient way to completely and thoroughly exercise. Nothing is more *inefficient*, in terms of time, than climbing an assortment of routes at the crag in hopes of fatiguing all of the relevant muscle groups in order to stimulate adaptation. If it were even possible to reach total exhaustion with this "just climb" approach, it's fair to say that it would require several more hours per session. Through systematic training, weak areas that need stimulation can be precisely identified, and the appropriate stress can be applied exactly where needed with very little wasted time and effort. Every grip position can be precisely stressed to failure in less than 90 minutes with the proper equipment and a well-designed program. Plus it can be done without a partner, at the gym or at home, any time, any day, regardless of weather, work schedules, etc. Good luck getting that at the crag! For those who don't have 40 hours per week to climb, training is by far the most time-efficient way to improve; for working adults with families, it's the *only* way to improve.

TIME VALUE OF CLIMBING ABILITY

Economists use the concept of Time Value of Money to explain the benefits of financial investment, and a similar case can be made for the benefits of training. The concept is that $100 invested today will be worth $105 a year from now, assuming an annual net interest rate of 5 percent, at which time the investor will have more buying power than he has today. There is a similar Time Value of Climbing Ability, in that *time* invested today in improving climbing ability will yield more sending-power in the future.

For example, consider a climber who consistently redpoints 5.12c in six tries, 5.12b in three tries, and onsights 5.12a about 50 percent of the time. Supposing she gets three quality redpoint attempts per climbing day, she should be able to redpoint a given 5.12c in two days of effort. If she saves a few climbing days each month to invest in following a structured training program, in a year she might be redpointing 5.12d in six tries, 5.12c in three tries, and onsighting 5.12b about 50 percent of the time. The two days she required to climb *one* 5.12c a year ago will now get her *two* 5.12c routes — more *sending-power* and a great return on her initial investment.

Many climbers skip training because they are so eager to climb every waking moment that they can't see past the routes right in front of them. However, a small up-front investment of time and effort toward training will yield improvement that will easily make up for the temporary delay in the immediate pursuit of sends. Granted, this analysis is simplistic; quality of life is not measured simply in terms of number of sends per day, and a harder send is not necessarily "better." However, taking the long view and accepting that every climber's time is limited, why not create the option that makes the most of that time? A training program that provides steady, reliable improvement is the best way to maximize climbing potential over a lifetime.

TRAINING IS FOR YOU!

Many climbers lead hectic lives, and so believe they lack the time to train due to other commitments, be they a stressful job, family, school, or other pursuit. The approach proposed here is ideal for these climbers because it offers the most *time-efficient* training program available. With the myriad climbing exercises out there, and the volume of activities going on at a local gym, it would be easy to assume training requires a lot of time, but it doesn't have to. This book describes a number of "luxury" exercises and activities so that those with extra time can strive to master their craft, but these activities are not intended for everyone. The most essential activities will be clearly identified so they can be prioritized to achieve the greatest possible benefit commensurate with the amount of time committed. The most critical exercises are *training dense*, packing a great deal of training stimulus into short time periods, yielding maximum improvement with the least cost to everyday life. What's more, most are possible to do at home, any time of day, so the lengthy commute to an elaborate climbing gym can be avoided. Those who feel that they are too busy to train may in fact be too busy *not* to train! For the very busy, what little time is available for climbing is that much more precious, and so it is that much more critical to make the most of that time.

MANY PATHS, BUT THIS ONE WORKS FOR MANY PEOPLE

When studying the training and climbing habits of elite climbers, it becomes apparent that there are many paths to success in rock climbing. If the world's 100 best climbers were asked how to train, there would be 100 unique answers. Some train like fiends, eight hours per day, seven days a week, to reach the same fitness level as those who simply "go climbing" a few days per week. The reasons for these disparities may

Family, Career, and Climbing — Is it Possible to Have It All?

In a perfect world we would all have 20-plus hours a week we could spend training, rehearsing technique in a state-of-the-art gym, or climbing outdoors on wonderful sport routes. Unfortunately, most of us can only dream of that. At the most hectic times of my life (when my kids were first born, studying for a PhD, etc.), I prioritized my training time for maximum effect. That meant leaving out many beneficial activities, but it also allowed a crucial balance. I kept up the most-critical training activities such as finger-strength training, and in so doing was able to maintain my level of performance through chaotic life events that might lead other folks to give up climbing altogether. As these events passed and I had more time, I reinstated many "luxury" training activities and, when combined with the "critical training tasks" I had maintained through the chaotic times, I saw massive improvements. While high-level climbing often involves choosing to skip out on more traditional features of life, such as a career, house, and a family, it doesn't *require* that choice. There are plenty of examples of folks who "have it all," but it *does* require hard work and careful prioritizing for efficient training.

— *Mike Anderson*

Time-efficient training makes it possible to improve despite a busy family and professional life. Mike Anderson sent his first 5.14, *God's Own Stone*, with two kids in tow and a PhD in the bag. Anthony Carco

never be known. The problem then becomes how to select a training program with so many different options that all seem—at least to some extent—to work.

Any given program is probably better than some and worse than others, with the athlete as the primary variable in determining relative success. Any program should ultimately be tailored to the individual athlete, but learning how to tailor a training program takes wisdom and experience. Thus it makes sense to start with a basic program that has a broad, proven track record of success. If it's necessary to be a genetic freak or superstar athlete simply to complete a single routine, it's probably not a good choice for most folks. Similarly, if a program depends upon superhuman (or even teenage-human) recovery

abilities to survive the workload, it's probably a worse choice. Many programs from climbing's elite prescribe loads and frequencies that would cripple the rest of us. Other programs rely on the inherent genetic talent or circumstantial advantages of the athlete, so while they work for some they are ineffective for most.

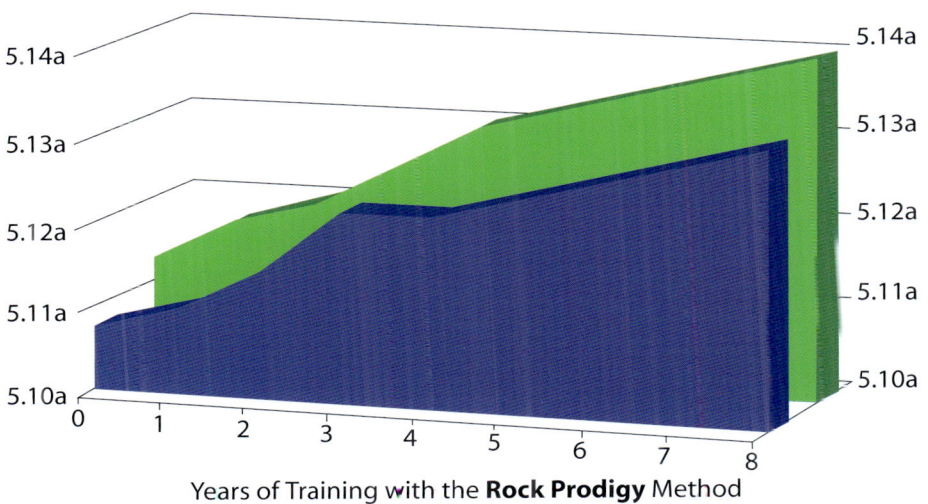

Years of Training with the **Rock Prodigy** Method

The "Wunderkind" Method

"I've never really had a problem with injuries, as my fingers are naturally strong. Then again it's probably because I did so much finger training at that critical age between 14 and 18. Finger strength is everything, and if you lay down a foundation at that age then it gives you a real advantage, both in terms of performance and avoiding injury." — Malcolm Smith[6]

A common pitfall in planning a training program is to co-opt the program of a climbing idol. Unfortunately, this strategy rarely works. The idol's methods are not necessarily incorrect, but they are specific to his or her abilities, talents, and circumstances, and do not transfer well to the general community. Consider the climbing "wunderkind." He or she starts climbing as a child, frequenting the local gym, and eventually crushes all the local testpieces. So why not mimic the training approach of the young star? *Usually* the climbing volume

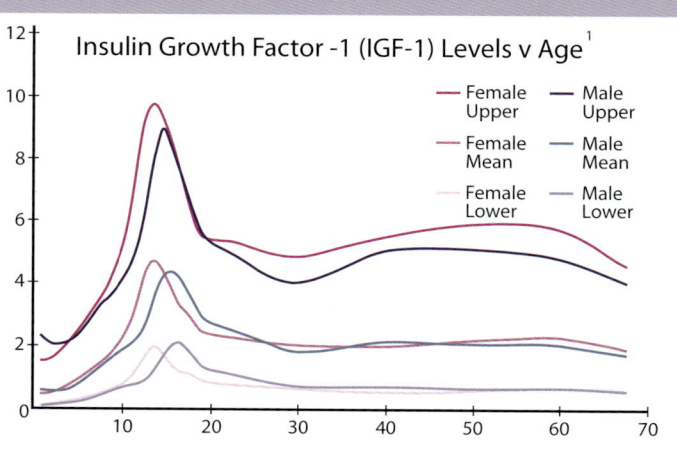

of these whippersnappers would cripple the typical adult, even young adults (those in their early twenties). The "growth spurts" that occur during and immediately after puberty permit extreme durations and intensity of exercise while facilitating rapid recovery. Adult bodies cannot handle this workload or recover as quickly. In addition to their seeming invincibility, the blessed young require relatively little stress to stimulate adaptation, so don't assume that the activities shown to stimulate growth in a teenager will produce the same effect in an adult.

It's reasonable to argue that because Adam Ondra is the greatest climber in the world, climbers should simply do as Adam did to reach the pinnacle of the sport. However, Ondra started climbing at age six, with parents who were avid climbers and could guide his development. Without a time machine, adult climbers simply cannot do what Adam did (that is, start climbing at age six). It's too late to leverage the physiological benefits of puberty to develop superhuman finger strength. While aspects of Ondra's training may be beneficial to the larger climbing community, the fundamental key to his success is not an option for the vast majority of climbers. Instead, seek a training program that is safe for adults, and works for adults. Compensate for a late start in climbing by utilizing every other advantage available, such as the heightened wisdom, patience, and perseverance that come with maturity.

The program described here may not be better than any of the others, but it has produced excellent results (often dramatic results!) for a wide variety of climbers with different athletic backgrounds, weaknesses, and abilities. It works for those who climb 5.10 and those who climb 5.14. It has continued to produce consistent improvement even for athletes who have followed the program for 10-plus years. It has propelled numerous climbers, with different genetic gifts, to the 5.14 level. It may not be the best possible program, and it's certainly not perfect, but it is one path to success that is proven to work.

PATIENCE AND PERSEVERANCE

The case for training has been made in earnest, assuming, perhaps incorrectly, that many climbers need to be convinced. On the other hand, it is possible to be *too eager* to try a new training routine. Some folks are so eager to improve that they religiously scour climber blogs for ideas, and then experiment with whatever looks promising. The danger with this approach is that whatever training was already in progress is aborted prematurely to make way for the latest "flavor of the month." Tragically, even if an effective approach comes along, these eager beavers are unlikely to no-

The Send-less Seasons

You trained your backside off all winter, making countless sacrifices, certain that they would pay off with breakthrough sends in the spring, but they never materialized. Entire seasons can pass "send-less" simply from picking the wrong project, or by squandering fitness on a route that is too easy, too hard, or otherwise fails to coincide with the training. That doesn't mean that the training activities are flawed or that the season was wasted. Improvement at such a complex sport takes time, and often, the timescales of climbing improvement don't coincide with our expectations or fit neatly into our life plan. That letter-grade jump you feel you deserve might need two or more seasons to manifest itself with a send. Nevertheless, a send-less season can be *very* productive.

I spent the entire summer season of 2011 working a single route. After weeks of training, significant sacrifices, and eight days spent on the route, I suffered a season-ending skin injury and left the project empty-handed. However, my improvements that season were clearly documented. I achieved personal bests on my hangboard, campus board, and interval circuit. Additionally, I made significant progress on a route that seemed well beyond my ability at the outset. I knew that I had reached a new level, even though the season produced no significant sends.

With new confidence and tremendous motivation, I entered my next training cycle absolutely determined to finish what I had started. Although that send-less summer season is now virtually invisible on my tick-list, it led directly to my eventual success on *Grand Ol' Opry* the following season. In the end, that "send-less season" turned out to be one of the most productive seasons of my career.

— *Mark Anderson*

Mark Anderson redpointing *Grand Ol' Opry*, 5.14c in the fall of 2011, at the Monastery, Colorado. Matthew Oscadal

tice because they don't give it time to pay off. In order to evaluate the effectiveness of an exercise, or more importantly, a training program *as a whole*, it is necessary to follow it consistently through to its conclusion. It may take multiple *seasons* to draw a fair conclusion. Yet some climbers make this mistake routinely by adopting the next training method too quickly, before the current method has had time to produce results.

The program described on these pages works best when it is followed thoroughly to completion. This cannot be overstated: *The program relies on synergies that are designed to be effective only when the program is followed in its entirety.* It is possible to cherry-pick specific workouts to achieve specific results, but if you do so, less-than-optimal results should be expected. Depending on the circumstances of a given climbing season, the program may need to be followed for multiple seasons before the improvement materializes into a personal best, but it *will* come eventually. A lot of serendipity is required to have a magical season of tangible progress, and any number of circumstances can derail it (bad weather, lack of climbing partners, crag closures, illness, etc.). When this happens, as it does from time to time, it's very hard to identify a singular root cause (such as a particular training activity), because success in climbing depends on so many variables. Don't rush to judge a training program based on one unproductive season. Every training program will yield unproductive seasons. The question is whether or not the program will eventually yield progress. For those who diligently follow the program, it has never failed to produce results *eventually*, though success requires perseverance through the occasional "bad" season. It is unrealistic to expect a letter grade of improvement every season (if that were possible, 5.19d onsights would be commonplace). Climbing is extremely difficult to master, and the longer one climbs and the longer one trains, the more difficult it is to eke out tangible improvement. Even for those following the "perfect" program, improvement still requires tremendous effort. Dramatic gains can be achieved initially with less rigor and effort, but over time, greater effort and intensity will be required to maintain improvement. Robotically following the prescribed workouts is not enough to improve indefinitely in such a complex sport. Strengths and weaknesses must be ceaselessly scrutinized, and time and effort must be applied to practicing away your weaknesses.

Furthermore, training does not remove the requirement to *try like hell* at the crag. Individual moves and routes will still be hard. Training bestows the physical and mental abilities to apply tremendous effort to such moves, and sustain that effort on a route, but it doesn't make hard moves feel easy. Finally, transferring training from plastic to rock is not trivial. Making the transition requires conscious thought, some patience, and lots of focused effort. This book will address ways to accomplish this in Chapter Three: Skill Development and in the performance chapters in Part III of the book.

> "If you are learning to climb from the guy/gal in the gym with a big university degree but little common sense, run away. You can't put a price on mileage. Try to find a teacher or coach who can offer you both: a big brain and an even bigger box of life/climbing-related experience. You won't be disappointed."
>
> — Sonnie Trotter[8]

WHY THIS PROGRAM?

Though climbing is one of the oldest and most natural sports, extreme rock climbing is a very recent development, so it has not been studied very well. As a result, there is a limited body of knowledge available to climbers, and most of what is available has merely been adapted from other, similar sports. Unfortunately, there isn't another well-studied sport that is very similar to climbing. Many theories are taken from powerlifting and middle-distance running, and recently, dance. It's not that these sports are the most closely related to climbing in terms of physical demands on the body, but rather, they are considered the most similar *among sports that have been thoroughly studied*. Researchers occasionally perform climbing-specific studies, but for the most part these studies are limited due to lack of resources and facilities, resulting in little useful new information. Thus for the time being, it is up to amateur climbing scientists to do their own informal experimentation.

Given the lack of a respected establishment to tell climbers how to train, it is wise to question sources. Whose advice should be followed? In more established sports, coaches are vetted over a long career, and the very best percolate to elite, international competitions. Expertise is not so obvious with climbing, at least not in America. Instead, climbers are self-coached, so we usually seek advice from successful climbers. This can be a big mistake, however. Douglas Hunter, a successful coach himself and the author of *The Self-Coached Climber*, has admonished people, "not to assume that an elite climber knows why he or she is elite." For example, a World Cup–level climber could probably spend the next year carving pumpkins as his "training," and he would still climb better than most, but it doesn't mean pumpkin carving is the best training. How hard someone climbs at a point in time is not enough information to evaluate the quality of his or her training. Rather, expertise should be judged based on *improvement over time*. A 5.13a climber who has been stuck at 5.13a for five or 10 years may have stumbled upon a dead end that other climbers would do well to avoid. On the other hand, a climber currently at the more modest grade of 5.12c, but who was climbing 5.11a two years ago and has been making steady progress, is probably doing something worth imitating.

Effective coaching requires three main characteristics: theoretical knowledge, practical experience, and innovative thinking. This theoretical knowledge entails an understanding of how the body works, including the biomechanics of climbing movement, the biochemical processes of muscles, and general principles for forcing physical adaptation. This knowledge and experience enable the coach to determine which mental, technical, and physical attributes need to be improved to achieve a particular goal, and which training protocols are likely to stimulate the necessary adaptation. However, this theoretical knowledge is only useful to climbers when it culminates in a practical training program that produces results on the rock.

Practical experience is perhaps the most difficult coaching trait to come by. Theoretical knowledge is plentiful, but it is not enough by itself. Theoretical knowledge is almost always based on non-climbing-specific research and relies heavily on assumptions and leaps that should not be accepted as fact until

demonstrated on actual athletes in a realistic environment (like, for example, that human muscle behaves the same as dead-rat muscle). Practical experimentation is required to determine how the body will respond to climbing-specific exercises, and whether such a response will actually improve climbing performance. The muscles used in climbing, and the constraints on them, are so unique that one can't simply transfer techniques from any sport to climbing. For example, the finger flexors are almost always used isometrically in climbing, but there is little theoretical knowledge on the best way to train isometric strength because it is rarely required by other, well-studied sports. The phenomena that cause a forearm pump are even more one of a kind. Therefore, the only way to obtain climbing-specific knowledge is through practical experimentation.

Finally, innovative thinking is critical because climbing is such a fresh sport. The exercises climbers use today such as hangboarding, campusing, and intervals were all invented within the last two decades by thoughtful climbers looking for an edge. The perfect training exercise may be yet to be discovered. The process of training innovation requires analyzing the skill or physical adaptation that must be developed, imagining an exercise that will pinpoint the weakness, and then inventing the apparatus that enables that exercise.

Training Innovations

When we first started hangboarding, the existing guidance was to put your feet on a chair to lessen the intensity or load on the fingers. This technique is highly variable, unquantifiable, and thus completely inadequate. The next suggestion was to stand in long rubber bands to subtract weight. This was a slight improvement, but still too variable and only crudely quantitative (Google "Hooke's law" for more). Instead, we developed a pulley system to remove weight precisely and accurately. Though it may seem obvious now, it wasn't at all obvious at the time, yet this simple innovation enables the development of finger strength on the most heinous (and most critical) holds, something that might never have been possible if we left our feet on the chair.

— *Mike Anderson*

With an understanding of what makes effective coaching, each climber should work to become her own great coach, which means studying the body, experimenting, and innovating. The authors started by adopting the theories of pioneers like Gullich, Neumann, and Yaniro, but since then the program has evolved through personal experimentation to test out new ideas, and thus been refined. It takes years to test new ideas on one person, but as more climbers become interested in training, collective experimentation will yield exciting new advances. Furthermore, the human body is a complex machine. Everyone is different, and everyone will respond to a specific training program differently. Therefore, it is incumbent upon each climber to be flexible. Start with the basic program, pay close attention to your body's reaction, and make corrections as needed. Try different rest periods, or different numbers of reps, sets, etc. That is how new knowledge is discovered.

THERE IS NO TIME LIKE THE PRESENT

Given the veritable heap of discarded training programs lying about, it would be easy to adopt a "wait and see" approach to training, continuing to "just climb" while waiting for the "perfect plan" to materialize. If this sounds appealing, it would be wise to reconsider. The legendary World War II General George Patton once said: "*A good plan now is better than the perfect plan next week.*" While climbing is not war, the principle applies. This book details what is, at the very

Components of Climbing Performance — A Three-Legged Stool

Overall climbing performance is a combination of physical, mental, and technical components. The relative importance of these components varies according to the demands of specific routes, and it also varies throughout a climber's career. For example, the performance of a novice gym climber is typically dominated by her technical competence, while physical and mental factors are largely irrelevant. An experienced sport climber learning to trad-climb may be limited primarily by mental factors. For an experienced climber on a steep power route, the physical component may be more limiting. Nevertheless, these components all play an important role, and a deficiency in any one component can hinder a climber's overall performance. It is helpful to think of climbing performance as the top of a stool, supported by three "pillars": physical, mental, and technical. Total climbing performance benefits the

most from growing all of the pillars in unison. It is possible to focus on one pillar while neglecting the other two, and still see an improvement in performance for a while, but that approach prevents us from reaching our true potential.

Fortunately for climbers, these components are not mutually exclusive. It is possible to construct a training program with complementary activities that benefit each of the three pillars, without ignoring the

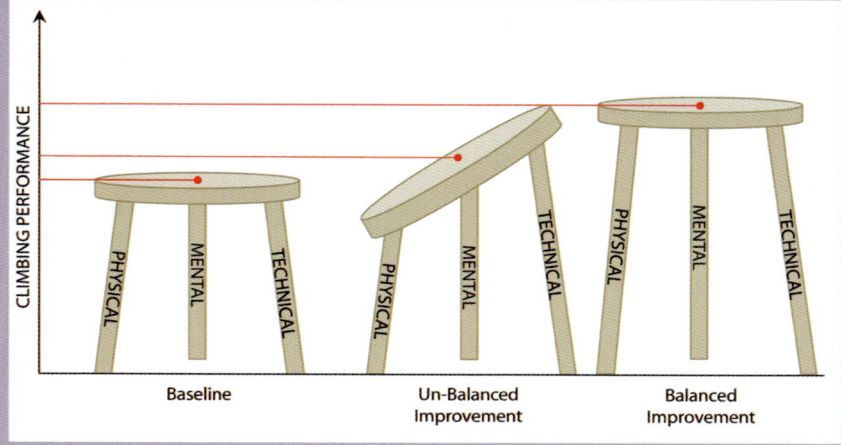

The three pillars of climbing performance. Growing all three pillars in unison is the best way to improve total climbing performance. It's difficult to reach for the stars when standing on an unbalanced platform.

others. The Rock Prodigy method is just such a training program. The program includes ample time and numerous activities that can be used to develop and improve your technical and mental climbing abilities. In Chapter Three: Skill Development, we thoroughly describe effective techniques for skill development, and how they should be integrated into the training program. In Part III: Performing, we present numerous strategies for mastering the mental aspects of performance. Utilize these methods to bring your pillars of performance into balance.

least, a "good plan." Beginning with this immediately and sticking with it will put any climber far ahead of where she might be if she waited for that perfect plan. Time is a climber's most valuable commodity, and waiting for something better squanders it. Don't wait: Start now and be all you can be, right away!

THE ROCK PRODIGY TRAINING METHOD

The program described in the following chapters was originally developed by Mike Anderson in the late 1990s, based on Neumann and Goddard's book *Performance Rock Climbing*[2] and Petro and Yaniro's training video *Fingers of Steel* [3]. Since that time, the program has evolved substantially to incorporate advances in sport science, personal experimentation, years of experience, and to broaden the applicability to climbers in different stages of development.

The Rock Prodigy training method is a form of *periodization*—a strategy for physical training in which exercises are carefully varied to avoid plateaus and create synergies that result in a *performance peak* at a predictable time (see figure below). Climbing requires diverse fitness, for example, *power* to execute extremely difficult single moves, along with *endurance* to sustain such moves. Through careful timing, the periodization of the Rock Prodigy method enables climbers to simultaneously develop a high level of each aspect of fitness. The combined effect is the performance peak: a temporary, but significant boost in climbing fitness that will enable the climber to attain never-before-seen levels of performance. The basic framework of this program is a 17-week season consisting of the following six training phases:

- Base Fitness (lasting two to four weeks)
- Strength (three to four weeks)
- Power (two to three weeks)
- Power Endurance (two to four weeks)
- Performance (three to four weeks)
- Rest (one to two weeks)

The length of each phase is designed to promote adaptation continuously up to the verge of a plateau, at which time the phase ends and a new phase begins. Phase and season length can be varied to meet the specific needs of each climber. The performance peak typically lasts six to eight weeks, during which time the athlete will climb better than ever and can plan on climbing as much as possible to reap the benefits of the season's training.

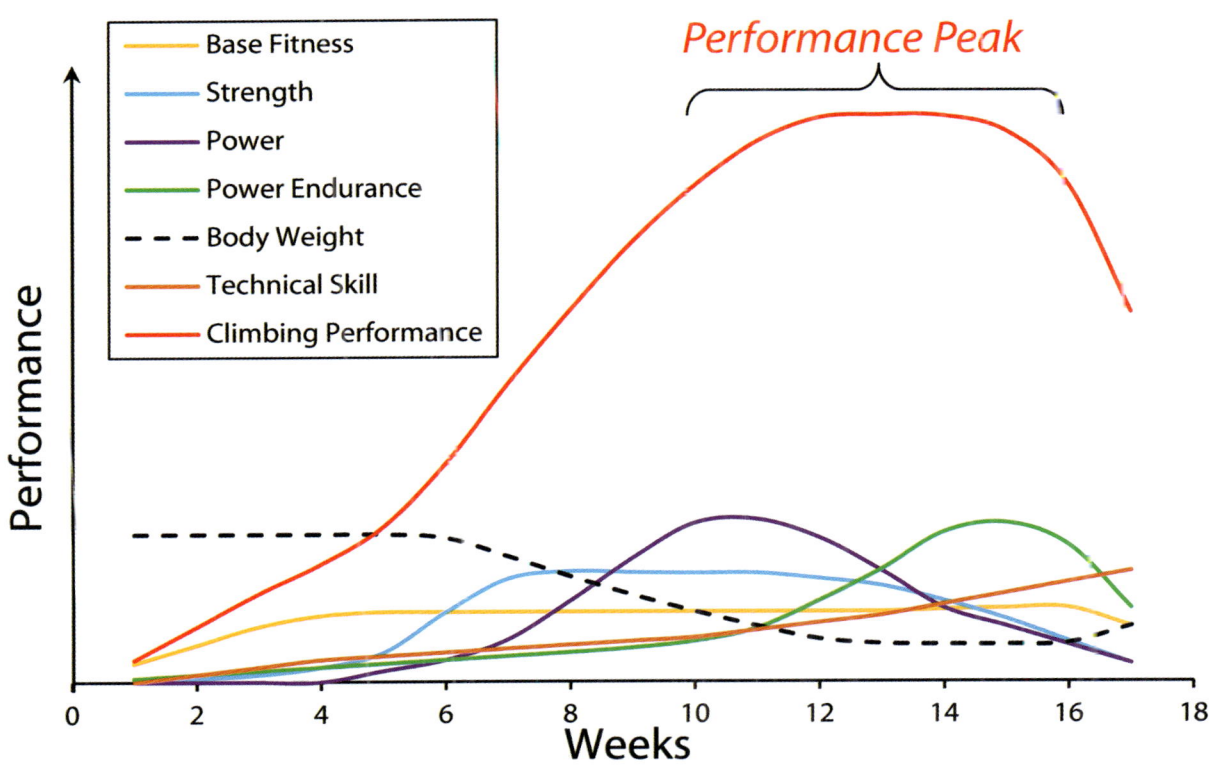

The Effects of Periodization. By timing the training of each fitness attribute, a substantial Performance Peak can be created.

THE ROUTE AHEAD...

If you're ready to raise your climbing to new heights, this book will show you how! The book's chapters are divided into three main parts:

- Part I: Taking Action
- Part II: Physical Training
- Part III: Performing

Part I: Taking Action presents techniques for setting climbing goals and strategies for achieving them through physical training and skill development. Part II: Physical Training describes how to hone your body into the ultimate climbing machine! The theoretical foundation for the Rock Prodigy program is presented, followed by detailed training instructions for developing Base Fitness, Strength, Power, and Power-Endurance. Part II also explains how and when to rest in order to prevent injuries, and how to rehabilitate injuries should they occur. Next, detailed training calendars are included that eliminate the guesswork by showing you exactly what to do and when. For more experienced climbers, instructions are provided for modifying the calendar to achieve different results. The final chapter discusses effective techniques for weight management that, when coupled with the prescribed training, will raise your climbing performance exponentially.

Once you've transformed your body into the ultimate climbing specimen, Part III: Performing takes you out to the crags. These chapters describe the cutting-edge tools, strategies, and tactics used by elite climbers to slay their dream routes. Discussions include how to select a climbing project, how to efficiently learn and rehearse the moves, how to prepare mentally and physically for the send, and how to stay focused and relaxed to realize your climbing potential. Detailed, step-by-step instructions that are both effective and time-tested are given for approaching redpoint projects and onsight attempts. Finally, the unique aspects of traditional and big-wall free climbing are discussed, along with many never-before published techniques for succeeding on these demanding adventures.

If your palms are sweating, then this is the program for you. Now is the time to rise to the occasion and take action to improve your climbing — the belay is on. So lace up your climbing shoes and get ready to send it!!!

Physical Training Theory — An Acquired Taste

Many of the chapters in Part II: Physical Training include detailed descriptions of human physiology and sports science that serve to explain the genesis of the physical training exercises described. Knowing *why* activities are prescribed will increase your confidence in the training program, and thus also increase your motivation to follow through with the training details. Also, knowing *why* gives you the understanding necessary to modify the program to fit your unique body, weaknesses, and climbing goals. In short, it empowers you to customize your training and "coach" yourself. If you're eager to start training and don't wish to wade through this theory right away, feel free to skip ahead to the juicy training details. Understanding the theory isn't required in order to succeed with this program, and it will always be waiting if you become curious at some point in the future.

QUICK-START GUIDE TO THE ROCK PRODIGY TRAINING PROGRAM

The Quick-Start Guide (See Figure on next page) is for climbers who are so eager to train that they can't bear to read this entire book first. It will get them started on the path without delay by highlighting the essential topics needed to execute the basic Rock Prodigy training program. To use the guide, start with Step One and select one of the *Seasonal Training Plans* referred to in the central circle (these plans describe *when* and *what* to train). The brief passages indicated in the steps that follow describe the training activities (how to train). Perform these exercises according to the chosen *Plan*. Refer back to the *Seasonal Training Plan* before beginning each step in the program. For full value, read the rest of the manuscript once your training is underway.

"The hardest thing is to start training; training itself is easier."

— Iker Pou[5]

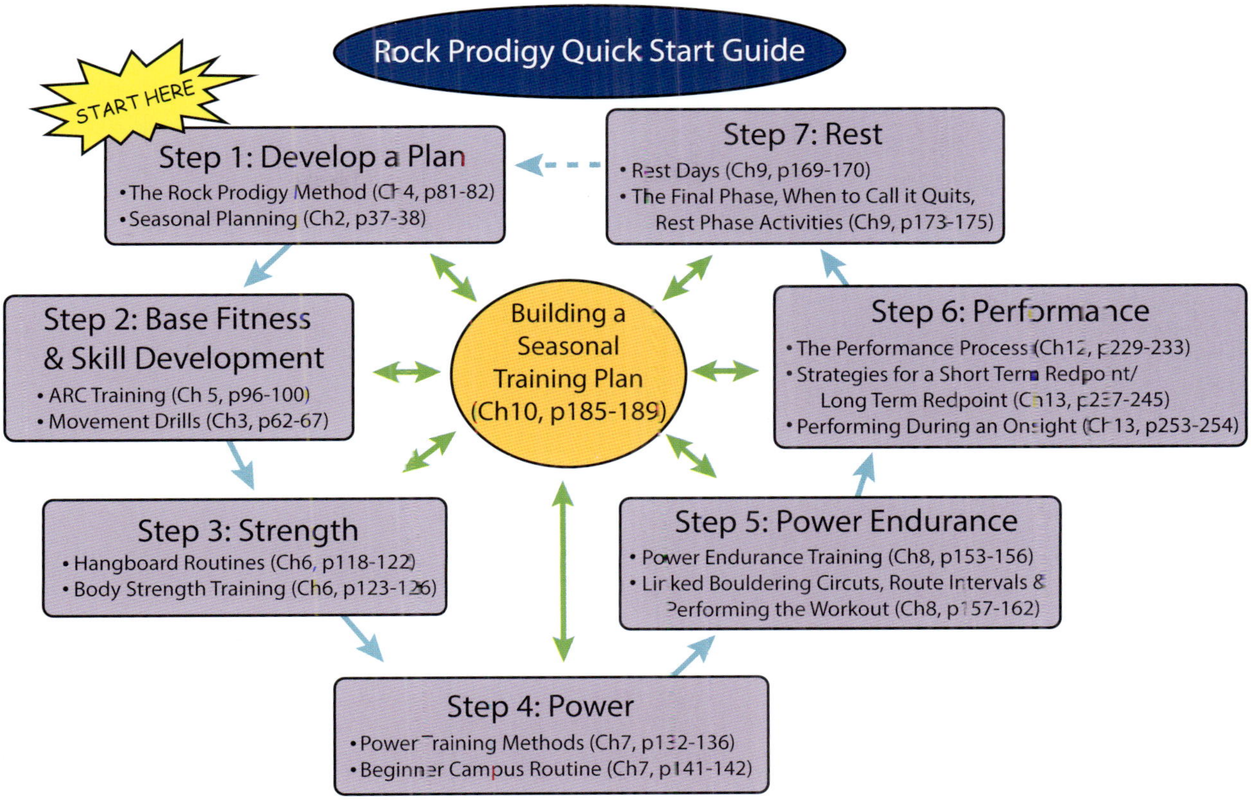

Rock Prodigy Quick Start Guide

START HERE

Step 1: Develop a Plan
• The Rock Prodigy Method (Ch 4, p81-82)
• Seasonal Planning (Ch2, p37-38)

Step 7: Rest
• Rest Days (Ch9, p169-170)
• The Final Phase, When to Call it Quits, Rest Phase Activities (Ch9, p173-175)

Step 2: Base Fitness & Skill Development
• ARC Training (Ch 5, p96-100)
• Movement Drills (Ch3, p62-67)

Building a Seasonal Training Plan (Ch10, p185-189)

Step 6: Performance
• The Performance Process (Ch12, p229-233)
• Strategies for a Short Term Redpoint/ Long Term Redpoint (Ch13, p237-245)
• Performing During an Onsight (Ch13, p253-254)

Step 3: Strength
• Hangboard Routines (Ch6, p118-122)
• Body Strength Training (Ch6, p123-126)

Step 5: Power Endurance
• Power Endurance Training (Ch8, p153-156)
• Linked Bouldering Circuits, Route Intervals & Performing the Workout (Ch8, p157-162)

Step 4: Power
• Power Training Methods (Ch7, p132-136)
• Beginner Campus Routine (Ch7, p141-142)

PROTECTING CLIMBING ACCESS SINCE 1991

ACCESS FUND

JOIN US
WWW.ACCESSFUND.ORG

Jonathan Siegrist climbs the Third Millenium (14a) at the Monastery, Colorado. Photo by: Keith Ladzinski

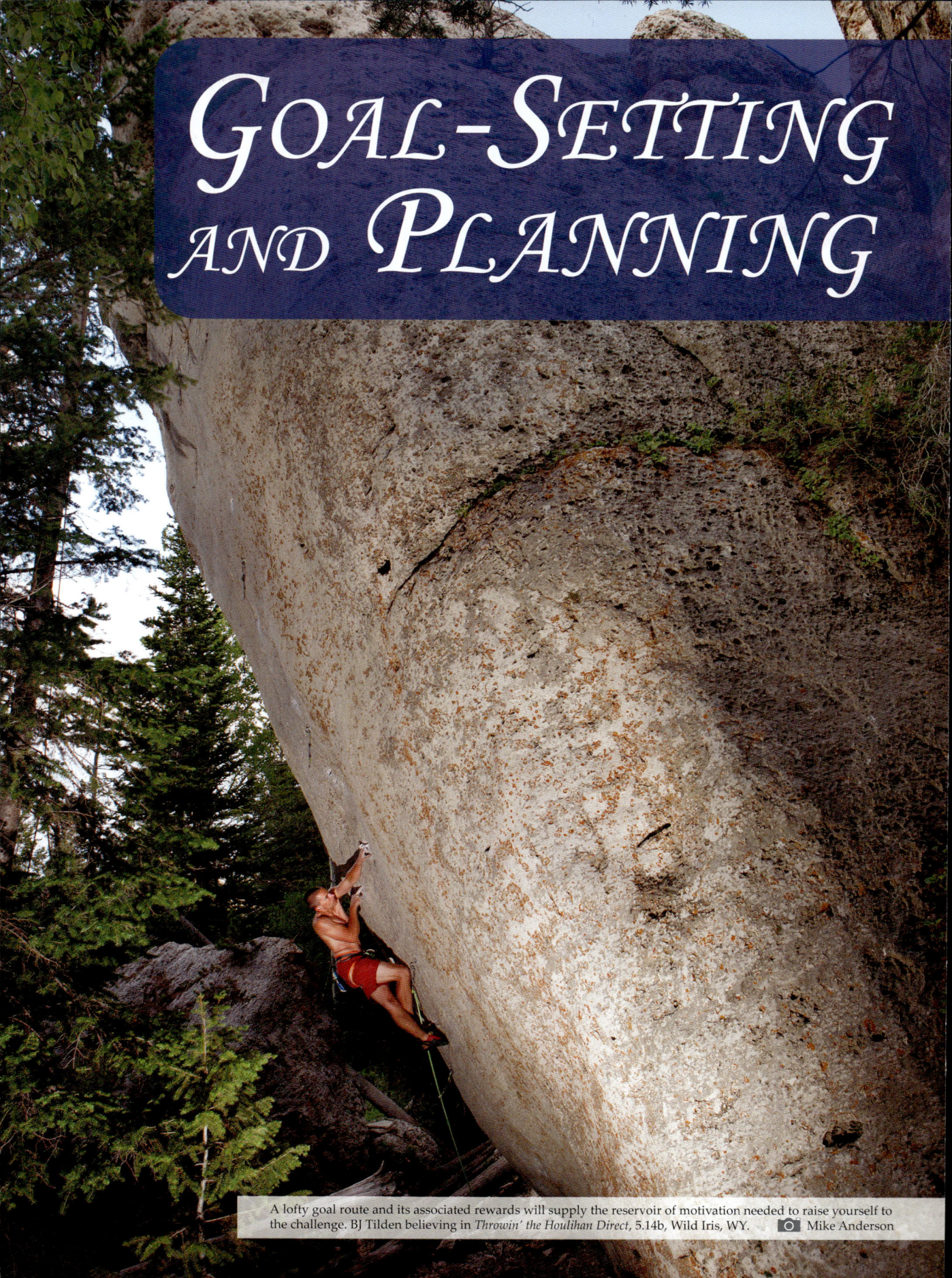

GOAL-SETTING AND PLANNING

A lofty goal route and its associated rewards will supply the reservoir of motivation needed to raise yourself to the challenge. BJ Tilden believing in *Throwin' the Houlihan Direct*, 5.14b, Wild Iris, WY. Mike Anderson

CHAPTER 2

"All men dream, but not equally. Those who dream by night in the dusty recesses of their minds, wake in the day to find that it was vanity: but the dreamers of the day are dangerous men, for they may act on their dreams with open eyes, to make them possible." — T. E. Lawrence[2]

Goal-setting has always been an essential tool in athletic pursuits, and possibly all human endeavors. Even chipmunks set out every autumn with the intention of gathering enough acorns to make it through the winter. Goal-setting is just as important in climbing. Goals create focus, steer the training plan, and provide motivation when the going gets tough.

The first step in achieving any great feat is to identify the primary objective. That's the easy part, though it presents some pitfalls as well (more on this to come). With the primary objective defined, one can identify the gaps between the desired end-state (the goal) and the present state. Next, it becomes a relative formality to lay out a plan, complete with intermediate goals, for moving from the present state to the desired end-state. With a thorough plan and the proper assortment of short-term, intermediate, and long-term goals, the climber has a framework for achieving "the impossible," and specific instructions for how to use each day to move closer and closer to his dream.

Mark Anderson nearing the summit of Denali, 2001.   ♻   Mike Anderson

This approach can and should be applied to all types of climbing, but our climbing roots in the world of mountaineering provide a great metaphor. In mountaineering, the ultimate goal is to get to the summit (and return safely), but on the big peaks this is usually accomplished through several intermediate steps. For example, a typical goal-oriented strategy for climbing Denali might be:

Main Goal:

1. Summit Denali via the *West Buttress* and return home safely

Intermediate Goals:

1. Learn to ski while pulling a sled
2. Learn to ice-climb
3. Practice camping on a glacier
4. Experience climbing above 15,000 feet
5. Experience camping and climbing in subzero temperatures
6. Organize logistics for Denali expedition
7. Climb Mt Rainier via the *Ingraham Glacier*
8. Climb a Colorado Fourteener in winter

Short-Term Goals for Achieving Intermediate Goal No. 1:

1. Procure alpine touring (AT) ski equipment
2. Practice using AT equipment on groomed trails
3. Ski up and down a 10,000-plus-foot mountain in winter conditions
4. Procure sled
5. Practice pulling sled on groomed trail
6. Practice pulling sled on backcountry trail
7. Ski downhill on backcountry trail with 40-plus-pound pack and 60-plus-pound sled

In the above example, there is a main goal, a set of intermediate goals, and a subset of short-term goals that lay the foundation for achieving the main goal. While the main goal might seem overwhelming in scope, the short-term goals are relatively attainable, could be accomplished in a single weekend, and help propel the climber directly toward achieving the main goal. Additionally, each subgoal, once attained, contributes to the climber's growing confidence, so when it comes time to take that final leap from the ski plane onto the Kahiltna Glacier, the climber will feel well-prepared for the upcoming challenges.

The Value of Goal-Setting

"I always have a goal in mind when I am training." — Jerry Moffatt[3]

Over the ten years or so that I've really focused on improving my rock climbing, I've had several great seasons, several terrible seasons, and many mediocre seasons. I've had great seasons that followed great training, subpar seasons that followed great training, and great seasons that followed subpar training. The one consistent aspect of all my great seasons was that they each started with a grand goal.

In August 2008 I decided I would go "all in" to redpoint *To Bolt or Not to Be*, an extremely technical 115-foot wall of tiny edges. Having a specific goal allowed me to tailor that season's training specifically to the route. I ordered a slew of tiny crimps for my home climbing wall, increased my emphasis on skill development, added a closed-crimp grip to my strength training routine, and built several thin, balancey boulder problems to practice on. I planned my entire season around this specific goal, arriving at Smith with fitness perfectly designed around the route. On the seventh day of work, I clipped the chains on America's most legendary sport climb.

At this point I can usually predict if a season will be "good" or "bad" based on the quality of the goals I set for the season. In my experience, training for the vague goal of "general fitness" is a surefire path to disappointment. Despite this, we are often reluctant to establish hard goals, because we are reluctant to commit to the hard work and sacrifice they require. Furthermore, any truly challenging endeavor will carry a significant risk of failure, and we are often afraid to face that demoralizing possibility. Yet while it may be risky, establishing a solid goal is almost always worth the effort it inspires. Even if superficial "success" is not realized, the personal growth experienced is in and of itself a more than sufficient return on the effort invested.

— Mark Anderson

"...To flash my enemies' routes, have them fail miserably on mine, and be the example of sexual perfection to their women."
— Todd Skinner, paraphrasing Conan the Barbarian's take on the meaning of life

THE MEANING OF LIFE

It is common to nurture a "network" of goals, including some that compete with other goals in the network, and others that are complementary. Whether it is deliberately stated or not, most people have an overarching goal to live a satisfying and joyous life (or something along those lines). This overarching goal is the genesis of many other primary goals, such as to have a loving relationship with another person, to have children, to sustain a successful career (or earn enough income to support one's chosen lifestyle), etc.

Success in climbing also supports the overarching goal, but more often than not it seems to compete with the other primary goals. To that end, any climbing goal should be considered with these other primary goals in mind, since they will directly impact each other. Furthermore, the amount of time and resources available to pursue climbing often depends directly on other, seemingly competing primary goals. For example, an otherwise unfulfilling job may produce the funds necessary to support an extended road trip. This understanding can make uninspiring tasks (like going to work on Monday) more meaningful and, ultimately, tolerable. At the same time, keep in mind that any climbing goal that significantly undermines another primary goal is self-defeating — success in climbing should *enhance* a climber's life, not degrade it. If this balance becomes disrupted to the point that climbing progress interferes with your overall happiness, you'd be wise to reconsider your priorities.

Accepting that success in climbing is only one part of a larger puzzle, how should a climber go about achieving "success in climbing"? This is a personal question with a wide variety of "correct" answers. Many climbers are entirely satisfied by simply climbing regularly with good friends in a beautiful setting. Others find this approach unfulfilling, preferring to approach rock climbing as an athletic endeavor, seeking difficult challenges and aspiring toward continuous improvement. The two approaches are hardly mutually exclusive, and many climbers will find themselves with one foot firmly in each camp.

Most climbers will cultivate a network of climbing goals that includes specific, tangible objectives like:
- To climb a 5.XX
- To climb routes A, B, C...
- To free-climb El Capitan

Along with more ambiguous goals like:
- To improve continuously
- To be able to climb the best routes at each crag
- To be a good all-around climber

These parallel sets of goals should be complementary. In most cases, the first set helps define the standard by which the second set is measured. In other words, there is no empirical way to define a "good all-around climber," but the specific goals provide insight into the climber's meaning of that term. For example, if the climber's specific goal is "to redpoint 5.13 and onsight 5.12, sport and trad," they are hinting that those are their personal thresholds for becoming "a good all-around climber." Ambiguous goals can be the basis for every other goal, but they provide little direction. Specific goals, with concrete criteria for success, are far more effective for guiding day-to-day activities. Both have their place and they should be used synergistically.

LONG-TERM GOALS

Long-term goals can be a primary source of inspiration, and area of emphasis, for many years. The quality of the goal is vital to success (both in achieving the specific goal and in directing general improvement in support of more ambiguous goals). Therefore it's important to select a good goal (or set of goals). There are several factors worth considering when making this selection: How does this particular goal fit into the larger scheme? Is this the ultimate objective, or a stepping-stone to a larger goal? Generally, it helps to start with one or more long-term goals, and work backwards from that point to establish a set of intermediate and short-term goals that support the longer goal. However, selecting an effective long-term goal is not trivial.

First consider this potential long-term goal: "I want to climb a 5.12." This goal (and its cousins, "I want to climb a 5.13, 5.14, etc.") is quite common, but it presents some significant complications. First, grades are subjective, so it can be difficult to know if the goal has *really* been achieved or not (a climber might set out to climb a sandbagged 12b just to be sure, but if she is capable of climbing a sandbagged

12b, she should probably set her sights a little higher). Instead most climbers will select a well-traveled 5.12a. Often these routes are right on the margin between the grades, and are the frequent target of downgrading. Grades are a subjective estimate of difficulty, subject to endless debate and adjustment, making them a poor choice for a specific goal.

Second, the goal lacks specifics. One of the primary purposes of goal-setting is to help define a desired end-state, in order to direct the climber's training plan. "To climb a 5.12" is too generic to provide much useful information. Will "a 5.12" require good pinch strength, improved endurance, or better gear-placing skills? The goal as written could entail anything from a 20-foot horizontal-roof deep-water solo, to a one-thousand-foot sixty-degree slab on marginal gear. These objectives require very different skillsets, and so would require very different paths to improve-

Which is More Inspiring?

This:

5.12b

or this:

Boy Prophet, 5.12b, Smith Rock, Oregon.   Mark Anderson

ment. The goal selected should be specific enough to help define the exact skillset of interest.

Finally, how motivating is the goal? Numbers have their place, but most of the time they aren't very inspiring. Climbers are inspired by stunning lines in a beautiful setting, interesting history, and the heroic characters of each generation that made the sport what it is today. The goal should be omnipresent, ready to prop the climber up at moments of weakness. It should be posted next to the hangboard, campus board, and pantry, to remind the climber what he's suffering for.

Grade thresholds can be used as goals, but they should remain in the background (with the other ambiguous goals) because they are too vague to provide specific guidance. Instead, strive to select goals that are as specific as possible, such as a particular route. Once an assortment of routes has been climbed at that grade, the climber can be satisfied that the less-specific goal ("to climb 5.12") has been achieved. The "assortment of routes at that grade" will provide the actionable specifics needed to fuel improvement.

Here's an example of an improved goal: "I want to redpoint (*Lower*) *Heinous Cling* at Smith Rock." First off, any debate about the grade becomes immediately irrelevant. The goal has nothing to do with the grade — they are totally unrelated. A goal is really just a stepping-stone to the next, bigger goal anyway, so what does the number have to do with it? The goal might even be "easier" than something the climber has already climbed, but requires a new skillset or exploits a weakness that, once improved, will provide access to other, more challenging goals.

Next, the style of ascent is defined. The original goal left some ambiguity: Would a toprope ascent, with hangs, count? The new goal makes it clear that the intent is to climb from the ground, on lead, with no hangs or falls, but rehearsal of the moves is acceptable. While a formality to some, other climbers struggle on the lead, so specifying the desired style helps define the challenge in a manner that will guide the creation of intermediate goals.

Finally, a specific route has been identified. Just a few minutes of research will provide a tremendous amount of useful information to help plan a training strategy to achieve the goal. The route is dead vertical, with many small, sharp edges, a few thin pockets, and small footholds. The route requires 60 or so feet of continuous climbing without much rest. Further research might reveal a rough number of hand movements required between rests (which will be helpful

The Power of Aspiration

"A dream that is great beyond our abilities, a mountain that is harder than we imagine possible, can make us great in our aspiration to achieve it." — Todd Skinner[4]

Todd Skinner was a big believer in dreams, establishing goals and plans to achieve them, and finally, transitioning from planning to action. His book, *Beyond the Summit*, is an outstanding resource for those looking to achieve the "impossible." Todd knew a thing or two about achieving "impossible" dreams; on no less than three occasions*, Todd succeeded on climbs that other climbers — *elite* climbers — had studied extensively and declared "impossible."

Todd believed each climber should strive for a continuum of success he referred to as the *Lifelong Ascent*. The purpose of this journey is for each person or team to achieve their *Ultimate Potential*. Ultimate Potential is not a fixed point, nor is it defined in relation to the achievement of others; it is the highest each individual could possibly hope to "ascend" in life.

For those who have their Ultimate Potential in mind, every choice becomes simple: you choose the option that will lead you closer to your Ultimate Potential. Furthermore, this construct encourages climbers to dream big, selecting goals that provide the greatest opportunity for growth, rather than "sure things" that offer the greatest odds of "success." Indeed, even the term *success* has new meaning. Success is defined by the amount of improvement and learning achieved — the quality of the process, rather than whether or not the climber stood on the summit. Truly, if the summit were the only measure of success, it would be easier (and therefore "success" more certain) to hike around the back side of the cliff.

The only possible way to reach your Ultimate Potential is to dream big. The biggest dreams inspire the biggest improvement, even if the summit is never reached. We rarely achieve beyond that which we aspire to do, so select aspirations that will inspire the best possible effort. You may be reluctant to describe your aspirations to others, and that's OK, but they should be in the back of your mind at all times. Your aspirations will propel you toward constant improvement, and fuel an indefatigable search for insights and weaknesses to address. When it's snowing outside and you don't feel like driving to the gym, your greatest aspirations provide the motivation to overcome and persevere. Think about the dream you don't dare to dream, and keep it present in your mind. The "impossible" is achieved more often than you might think.

*First free ascent of El Capitan, first free ascent of Direct Northwest Face of Half Dome, first free ascent of Trango Tower

Todd Skinner contemplating his Ultimate Potential during the first free ascent of El Capitan.　📷　Bill Hatcher

when deciding the appropriate endurance training to achieve this goal). This information can be used to determine some focus areas for training. For example:

- Crimp strength on half-pad and smaller edges
- Open-hand strength on one-pad pockets
- Footwork and balance on vertical terrain
- Lock-off endurance on vertical terrain
- Local endurance on full-pad edges
- Skin toughness on finger pads

With a specific route in mind, it's possible to identify the ideal time of year to attempt the climb. This information allows the climber to arrange for partners, request time off from work, and construct a training schedule that will maximize fitness at the perfect time. None of these critical items can be planned properly without a specific route in mind. Further guidance on selecting long-term redpoint projects is given in Chapter 13: Redpoint and Onsight Climbing.

INTERMEDIATE AND SHORT-TERM GOALS

The truly grand achievements don't happen overnight. Many take years or decades to realize. Long-term goals like these provide tremendous inspiration, but they can also be so intangible and distant that they provide little concrete direction. Intermediate goals are used to provide immediate guidance and motivation to help the climber progress toward the larger goal. One example might be a climber who just sent *Astroman* (an uber-classic, 10-pitch 5.11c crack climb in Yosemite), but aspires to one-day climb *Freerider* on El Capitan in good style. The journey from her current ability to her long-term goal may take years of hard work. The overwhelming magnitude of the long-term goal may be the larger obstacle. Where does the climber begin?

By comparing the desired end-state (the ability to free El Cap) to the current state, the climber can identify areas that need improvement and develop intermediate goals that address each area. Consider this (un-comprehensive) list of potential intermediate goals:

1. Find a willing and committed partner
2. Bivy on a big wall and haul a haul bag
3. Climb an El Cap route (mixed aid and free)
4. Redpoint a 5.10+ offwidth
5. Redpoint ten mid-5.12 granite trad pitches
6. Onsight five 5.12a granite trad pitches
7. Redpoint *The Eighth Day* (a 5.13a sport route at Rifle, CO)
8. Free *Moonlight Buttress* (a 10-pitch 5.12 crack climb at Zion, UT)

HANGBOARD LOG

Date: 04/15/13
Temp: ___ W/O #: 5
Rep Timing: 7s hang/35 rest Dressed Weight: ___ Rest Interval: 3:00

Step Up?

Y (N) Exercise 1 Grip: Large Open Edge   Notes: Warm-up

Goal:	Set:	Resistance:	#Reps:	Difficulty 1-10:	Comments:
-10	1				
0	2				
+10	3				

(Y) N Exercise 2 Grip: MR 2F Pocket   Notes: Tape Ring Finger Base

Goal:	Set:	Resistance:	#Reps:	Difficulty 1-10:	Comments:
0	1				
+10	2				
+20	3				

(Y) N Exercise 3 Grip: Small Edge   Notes: Breath!

Goal:	Set:	Resistance:	#Reps:	Difficulty 1-10:	Comments:
+10	1				
+20	2				
+30	3				

(Y) N Exercise 4 Grip: Wide Pinch   Notes: Remove All Tape

Goal:	Set:	Resistance:	#Reps:	Difficulty 1-10:	Comments:
-35	1				
-30	2				
-25	3				

Y (N) Exercise 5 Grip: IM 2F Pocket   Notes: Tape Index Finger 2nd Pad

Goal:	Set:	Resistance:	#Reps:	Difficulty 1-10:	Comments:
-30	1				
-20	2				
-10	3				

Some of these goals may be trivial (requiring only a decision to commit), while others may be multi-year endeavors in themselves. The point is to provide specific direction and break up the overwhelming long-term goal into digestible pieces that the climber can believe in. Goals can be subdivided as much as needed to create immediate tasks that seem doable, even if the resulting near-term goal is as simple as going to the climbing gym that day.

SHORT-TERM GOALS

Short-term goals are the least discussed, but perhaps most important of all goals. These are the building blocks of every other successful endeavor. Countless short-term goals are established and achieved every day, but remaining conscious of this process can be helpful when progressing through the day-to-day monotony of a training program, or while performing on the sharp end. Every day of an athlete's life should have a short-term goal, even if it is as simple as to rest (which itself may consist of multiple goals, such as eating and drinking properly, reviewing route beta, and visualizing the next performance opportunity, to list a few).

Each workout session should begin with a few short-term goals. If you're new to this process, it's helpful to write these goals down (see an example log above). The training activities described in Part II: Physical Training are presented along with goal-setting strategies for each workout, based on prior perfor-

Planning and Executing a Long-Term Goal

In 2001, we achieved a childhood dream by climbing Denali via the famed and magnificent *Cassin Ridge*. This dream arose in high school, nearly a decade before we finally set foot on the mountain. It took several years before we had the courage to deliberately vocalize this goal, and even then we were still woefully unqualified. Neither of us had traversed a glacier, climbed higher than 14,000 feet, ice-climbed, spent multiple nights snow camping, experienced subzero temperatures, planned or executed an expedition, bivied over 8,000 feet... (our lack of qualifications for such a climb could fill this page). In order to bridge the gap between our current experience and the goal, we laid out a multiyear plan, entailing a progression of intermediate goals, each of which would provide the skills and experience needed for Denali:

Intermediate Goal	Contribution to the Long-Term Goal
Step 1: Climb Mount Rainier	More altitude exposure Several nights in the snow Glacier travel experience
Step 2: Climb Moose's Tooth	Alaska Range experience Seven days of glacier living Advanced glacier-travel experience Alpine-ice and multipitch climbing experience
Step 3: Climb El Pico de Orizaba	High-altitude experience (the summit is over 18,000') Logistical planning experience for a multiweek trip
Step 4: Climb Mount Waddington	Advanced alpine, ice, and mixed experience Seven more days of glacier living in an isolated range Far more technically challenging than the *Cassin Ridge*
Step 5: Climb Grade 5 Ice	Margin for error and confidence in ice-climbing skills (expecting the *Cassin* to pose nothing harder than AI4)

It took roughly three years just to complete the intermediate goals, but once completed, we knew we were ready to give the *Cassin* a decent shot. In the end, the *Cassin* was relatively easy compared to the sum of our intermediate goals, which made the route that much more enjoyable.

While striving toward intermediate goals, it helps to keep the big picture in sight: bivy on Moose's Tooth with Denali in the upper left. 📷 Mike Anderson

mance levels. The Log Sheets provided in the Appendix can be used for recording daily training goals. At the crag, establishing goals for each attempt and each day provides improved focus and better results (see Part III: Performing for a deeper discussion on short-term goals during the Performance Phase).

The next step is easy: following through with the short-term and intermediate goals, making adjustments as necessary, until the long-term goal is realized. From the summit, with the send in the bag, the climber will have a new perspective from which to spy that next, harder goal.

DEVELOPING A PLAN OF ATTACK

With a set of goals in mind, the next step is to create a plan for achieving those goals. Goals provide tremendous inspiration and motivation, but taken by themselves they can be overwhelming and even confusing. A goal without a plan is a pipe dream. A climber's plan is the link between his current abilities or circumstances, and his goals. Like a traveler going from Point A to Point B, the plan is the road map (or GPS unit) that describes the best route.

"No plan survives first contact with the enemy." — Helmuth von Moltke, German Field Marshall[1]

This section will discuss how to develop *Long-Range Plans, Annual Plans*, and *Seasonal Plans*, with a brief introduction to weekly and day-to-day planning. When working toward long-term goals, it is best to plan in this order, but the opposite approach can be effective as well (developing individual season plans, then putting them together to develop an annual plan, and so on). Either way, as the good field marshall indicated, planning is an "iterative" process, subject to constant re-evaluation and revision once under way.

SELF-EVALUATION

Before planning for a goal, the climber's starting point must be determined. When it comes to devising the most efficient path from Point A to Point B, a well-defined starting point is just as important as a well-defined finish line. Understanding one's "starting point" comes from conducting a thorough and honest self-evaluation.

Self-evaluation is the process through which climbers identify their *strengths* and *weaknesses*. Among all the skills and abilities required for climbing, a strength is one that the climber performs well (relative to the others), while a weakness is performed relatively poorly. Since most successful ascents require a diverse set of skills, weaknesses are most often the limiting factor in climbing performance. Just as a chain is only as strong as its weakest link, if a climber cannot perform any one move on a route, failure is certain. It is tempting to only work to improve one's strengths, since these skills come naturally and are a source of

pride. However the *Law of Diminishing Returns* prevents an athlete from achieving steady improvement in one area forever. The more time spent developing a given attribute, the more difficult it becomes to improve at it. Therefore, it takes great effort to achieve modest improvement in a single strength, while modest effort can result in great improvement in a weakness. For this reason, weaknesses provide the best potential to achieve significant overall climbing improvement with the least amount of effort. That said, a well-rounded climber should strive to improve both strengths and weaknesses, but she must realize that the greatest return on training investment will come from working weaknesses.

Self-evaluation can be a humbling process, but the knowledge gained can be extremely powerful. This knowledge permits the athlete to target her efforts to the precise areas that will produce the most dramatic improvement in overall climbing performance. Unfortunately identifying one's strengths and weaknesses can be extremely difficult. Often a person's own self-image is skewed by myriad factors, ranging from personal history, to external influences, to self-esteem. Eventually it may be helpful to seek the candid assessment of third parties, but that approach has pitfalls as well. Ideally the climber should conduct her Self-Evaluation using a combination of sources.

Begin by setting aside a quiet time for simple meditation with pen and paper. Considering each style of climbing independently (sport, trad, redpoint, onsight, etc.), identify a set of three or more positive climbing experiences, and determine the attributes of these climbs. Next consider a set of disappointing climbing experiences. Some attributes to consider during this process include:

- Safety Attributes:
  - Type of protection (bolts vs. cams, etc.)
  - Frequency of protection
  - Accessibility (was the objective remote?)
  - Partners (experience, familiarity, skill level)
  - Rock (solid vs. "chossy")
- Rock Attributes:
  - Angle
  - Rock type
  - Hold types (pockets, edges, pinches, etc.)
  - Route length
  - Unusual features (arêtes, roofs, corners)
  - Friction
- Climbing Attributes:
  - Powerful vs. "pumpy"
  - Technical vs. thuggish

- Abstract Attributes:
  - Climber's attitude, expectations, mood
  - Aesthetics
  - Audience
  - Quality of "moral" support
  - Environmental conditions (cold, hot, windy, scenery, etc.)

The purpose of this exercise is to identify any attributes that are common to the positive experiences and those common to the negative. If many of the negative experiences occurred on a particular type of rock, or a particular style of climbing, these attributes might offer a clue to a particular weakness.

Climbers are often better at identifying weaknesses in others; therefore, video self-analysis can be used to reduce the bias inherent in the Self-Evaluation. While emotionally detaching from the process (easier said than done), review any available film of yourself climbing, noting moments of fluidity and moments of struggle (ideally, you'll use video from a variety of terrain and climbing styles). Consider the following attributes:

- General Physical Attributes:
  - Power
  - Endurance
  - Power-endurance
  - Finger strength
  - Core strength
  - Lock-off strength
- Technical Attributes:
  - Footwork
  - Precision
  - Efficiency/economy of effort/movement
  - Pacing
  - Breathing
  - Dynamic movement skills
  - Patience
  - Resting Ability
  - Clipping
  - Ability to "read" sequences or recall beta
- Mental Attributes:
  - Confidence
  - Courage
  - Relaxation
  - Focus
  - Hesitation

Now consider whether these attributes change depending on variations in terrain and environment. Variations to consider include:

- Route angle (slabby, vertical, overhanging, horizontal roof)
- Hold type (edges, slopers, pinches, pockets)
- Rock features (roofs, arêtes, walls, corners)
- Environmental (heat, cold, humidity, wind)
- Audience

The third method for self-evaluation is to solicit candid feedback from trusted partners as they have seen the climber at his very best and very worst, and so are in a unique position to provide valuable information. These should be partners that have observed the climber extensively and can give critical thought to this evaluation. It's easy for this exercise to devolve into an endless round of war stories, so establish some structure at the outset and be prepared to take notes. It may help to brief your partner on the process and the purpose of this exercise. Consider providing the above list of General Physical, Technical, and Mental Attributes to get the ball rolling, and reassure your evaluator that the critiques won't be taken personally.

Providing frank and earnest feedback is not easy to do, so set your partner at ease beforehand with a promise to keep this information "off the record." Avoid becoming defensive during this process. Remember, you specifically sought this criticism, and the purpose of this feedback is to stimulate improvement, so thank your evaluator for the assistance. Ask the evaluator to begin with a positive, and then alternate between descriptions of weaknesses and strengths, ending on a positive note. It may help to have the evaluator generate this list prior to the actual discussion, though usually the desired criticism must be coaxed. Keep in mind that even third-party observers have their biases. A partner with tremendous finger strength is likely to overemphasize the importance of this attribute, and so on. Don't protest or argue with the evaluator, but keep these biases in mind once the feedback session is completed.

GAP ANALYSIS

After completing these exercises, the climber should have a laundry list of strengths and weaknesses. Attempt to prioritize these lists in terms of their effect on overall climbing performance, but also consider these attributes with respect to any long-term or intermediate goals. Which physical, technical, and mental attributes will be required to achieve these goals?

What are the specific attributes of your goal climbs (rock type, hold type, steepness, length, etc.)? In many cases you'll discover that your strengths align with many of the attributes required for success, but there will probably also be some required attributes that you lack. Highlight these "gaps" between present ability and desired/required ability. These attributes should become the primary targets for improvement.

For the most challenging goals, most climbers will find that even their strengths will need improvement. Regardless, considering the overarching goal of continuous improvement, most climbers will benefit from improving all attributes (whether they belong to the physical, technical, or mental pillars of performance). Often numerous attributes can be improved concurrently, but the *Gap Analysis* allows the climber to prioritize and focus more attention on the most limiting attributes, or address the specific peculiarities of a particular goal route, such as an unusual type of handhold (monos or pinches, for example) or an unusual feature (like a horizontal roof or leaning arête).

Finally, there is a tendency during your Self-Evaluation to dwell on the negative. It never hurts to be reminded of one's strengths from time-to-time. While there may be significant need for improvement, chances are each climber possesses many positive qualities. The desire to improve, and the determination to follow through on that desire, is a tremendous strength. These traits have been the foundation of every great climbing achievement — they are more important than finger strength or technical ability — and anyone who's ventured this far can put those down in the "strengths" column. Once you make the decision to pursue continuous improvement, the sky is the limit.

THE ROUTE PYRAMID

The *Route Pyramid* is a visual representation of a climber's "resume" of single-pitch rock-climbing ascents, but more importantly, it is an approach to climbing progression that emphasizes building a broad base of experience on routes that are below the climber's maximum ability. This approach dedicates the majority of time and effort to routes that can be climbed relatively quickly (in a few attempts or after a few days of effort). The repeated pursuit of short-term projects is the best approach to long-term improvement (explained further in Chapter 3: Skill Development and Chapter 13: Redpoint and Onsight Climbing). The Route Pyramid can also be used in a number of other ways, including as a powerful gap-analysis tool. The pyramid itself is simply a stack of metaphorical build-

When considering your goal route, identify any distinctive features that can be used to steer the season's training plan. Whitney Boland pinching her way up Block Party, San Vito, Sicily 📷 Andrew Burr

ing blocks, with each block representing a successful (free) ascent. The blocks are then "stacked" in ascending rows according to difficulty as shown below.

			5.12c				
		5.12b	5.12b				
	5.12a	5.12a	5.12a	5.12a			
5.11d	5.11d	5.11d	5.11d	5.11d	5.11d	5.11d	5.11d

The classic Route Pyramid for a climber who has completed one 5.12c, two 5.12b's, four 5.12a's, and eight 5.11d's (only the top four levels of the pyramid are shown).

The purpose of the pyramid is to encourage the climber to pursue a broad foundation of experience, with relatively attainable routes, before building up toward more challenging routes. Route Pyramids can have any shape, though the conventional wisdom calls for a pyramid that obeys the function $y = 2^{(x-1)}$. In simple words, the number of ascents doubles for each step down the pyramid. This construct is arbitrary, and mathematicians will note that it quickly becomes unsustainable (climbing one 5.12c would necessitate climbing 64 5.11a's!) as shown in the Figure below.

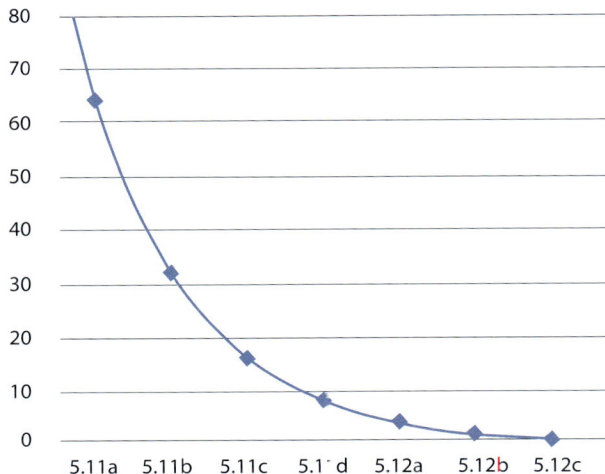

The same Route Pyramid as above, represented as a logarithmic function

To avoid this problem, climbers should primarily focus on the top four layers of the pyramid. Continue to enjoy routes of all grades, but don't feel compelled to maintain the 2-to-1 ratio between grades beyond the top several layers.

Analyzing one's Route Pyramid allows the climber to quickly identify "gaps" in the structure — areas that may require further emphasis in the future. Consider the examples at the top of the next column:

Uneven Route Pyramids

		5.12c	5.12c
		5.12b	5.12b
		5.12a	5.12a
	5.11d	5.11d	5.11d

Climber A

				5.12b			
	5.12a	5.12a	5.12a	5.12a	5.12a	5.12a	
5.11d	5.11d	5.11d	5.11d	5.11d	5.11d	5.11d	5.11d

Climber B

Climber A's Pyramid is "too steep," suggesting she favors working difficult projects. This climber might benefit from spending more time on projects she can redpoint more quickly. Climber B's Pyramid is "too wide." This might indicate that Climber B prefers a "sure thing" — a project he is almost certain to send and can complete very quickly. This climber may benefit from testing himself on more challenging projects in the future.

It can be helpful to track multiple pyramids that represent various styles of ascent (such as sport redpoint, sport onsight, trad redpoint, and trad onsight), since assembling many "blocks" in one style may not adequately prepare the climber to proceed to the next level in another style. Analyzing these pyramids separately may help to identify areas that have been neglected.

Furthermore, ascents completed many years ago may have little bearing on the climber's current abilities. For that reason, each climber should attempt to keep his pyramid "fresh," by adding new ascents at each grade level each year. It's not necessary to completely rebuild the pyramid from scratch each season (and doing so would consume the season's fitness), but consider beginning each season by adding a block to the lower one or two levels of the pyramid before beginning work on a new block for the top level.

Another benefit of maintaining a Route Pyramid is that by requiring a large volume of ascents, it necessitates climbing a wide variety of features, rock types, and styles. This diversity of experience will help sculpt a well-rounded climber, capable of succeeding on a variety of routes. Initially, it may be possible to select routes that suit the climber's strengths, but once the low-hanging fruit is consumed, the climber will be compelled to pursue routes that exploit weaknesses, thus encouraging further improvement. Climbers who struggle on particular features or rock types can construct pyramids specific to that terrain, thereby building a solid base of experience from which to improve.

Finally, the Route Pyramid concept encourages the climber to focus the bulk of his effort on routes within his ability. This enables the climber to spend most of his time actually climbing (and therefore improving), as opposed to hanging from a rope while staring at a blank patch of stone.

INTRODUCTION TO PERIODIZATION

Periodization is a strategy for physical training in which different training activities are performed in accordance with a carefully designed schedule. The purpose of this timing is to achieve a synergistic effect on overall performance that results in a *performance peak* at a predictable time. The training strategies presented in this book are designed to be implemented within the framework of a three-to-four-month periodic training plan. For the purpose of the following discussion on planning, this means that each calendar year will consist of a number of deliberately defined seasons (typically three), with each season consisting of several multiweek phases, including *Training, Performance*, and *Rest Phases*. Each phase will emphasize a particular type of physical training (such as base fitness training, strength training, power training, etc.).

Chapter 4: Foundations of Physical Training will provide much more detail on this concept and a thorough explanation of its value to climbers.

LEVELS OF PLANS

Just as an athlete establishes several layers of goals (short-term, intermediate, and long-term), it is helpful to establish several layers of plans. Each climber should have a general long-range plan that encompasses the next several years, as well as more specific plans for the current and the coming year. The next layer includes a detailed plan for the current season. Within each season, develop a plan for each individual training session or crag day. Naturally, each plan should become more detailed as the time for implementation approaches.

LONG-RANGE PLANNING

Often long-range plans are vague and ill defined. Most climbers have a general idea of where they see themselves three to five years down the road, but rarely do they have a clear idea of how to get there. Regardless of the scope, any goal is likely to go unfulfilled without a plan. The long-range plan doesn't require extensive detail, but each climber should have a rough idea of

The Long-Range Plan

Remember the climber with the long-term goal of climbing *Freerider*? Suppose she has these other long-term goals as well:

1. Climb *Freerider* in good style (a 35-pitch 5.12d in Yosemite)
2. Redpoint *Sprayathon* (a 5.13c sport route at Rifle)
3. Redpoint *Welcome to Ol' Kentuck* (a 5.13a trad pitch at the Red River Gorge)
4. Marry her fiancé (a mid-5.13 sport climber with commitment issues)

The first step is to determine how these goals relate to each other. Goals 1 and 4 are the highest priority (with a slight edge to No. 1), but goals 2 and 3 are highly complementary, both requiring the same type of fitness (power-endurance). On the other hand, the technical requirements of these goals are very different (to the extent that goal No. 2 will probably require some additional intermediate goals, such as redpointing two steeply overhanging 5.13s on limestone). Therefore, a good prioritization of these goals might be: 1, 4, 3, 2.

While Goal No. 1 is the most important, it is also the most difficult. Goal No. 3 provides a good stepping-stone toward Goal No. 1, so it could be considered an intermediate goal. Goal No. 4 competes with goals 1 and 3, but could be accomplished concurrently with some of the intermediate goals that support Goal No. 1. So a good chronological order for these goals might be: 3, 4, 1, 2.

Our hero currently redpoints most 5.12a trad pitches in two or three tries, and figures she needs to be able to redpoint 5.12d granite trad in about the same number of attempts to have a fair shot at *Freerider*, but would prefer a letter-grade buffer (so, 5.13a). Assuming a conservative improvement rate of one-half letter grade per season, she needs eight seasons (at three-four seasons a year, that's about 2.5 years) to prepare, and she wants her *Freerider* attempt to line up with ideal October conditions (*obviously*, she wants a fall wedding). With all of this information at hand, her long-range plan might look like the example shown in the calander on the opposite page (the intermediate goals are those suggested in the Intermediate and Short-Term Goals section on p. 28). Note that the "out years" will become more detailed over time.

The Long-Range Plan

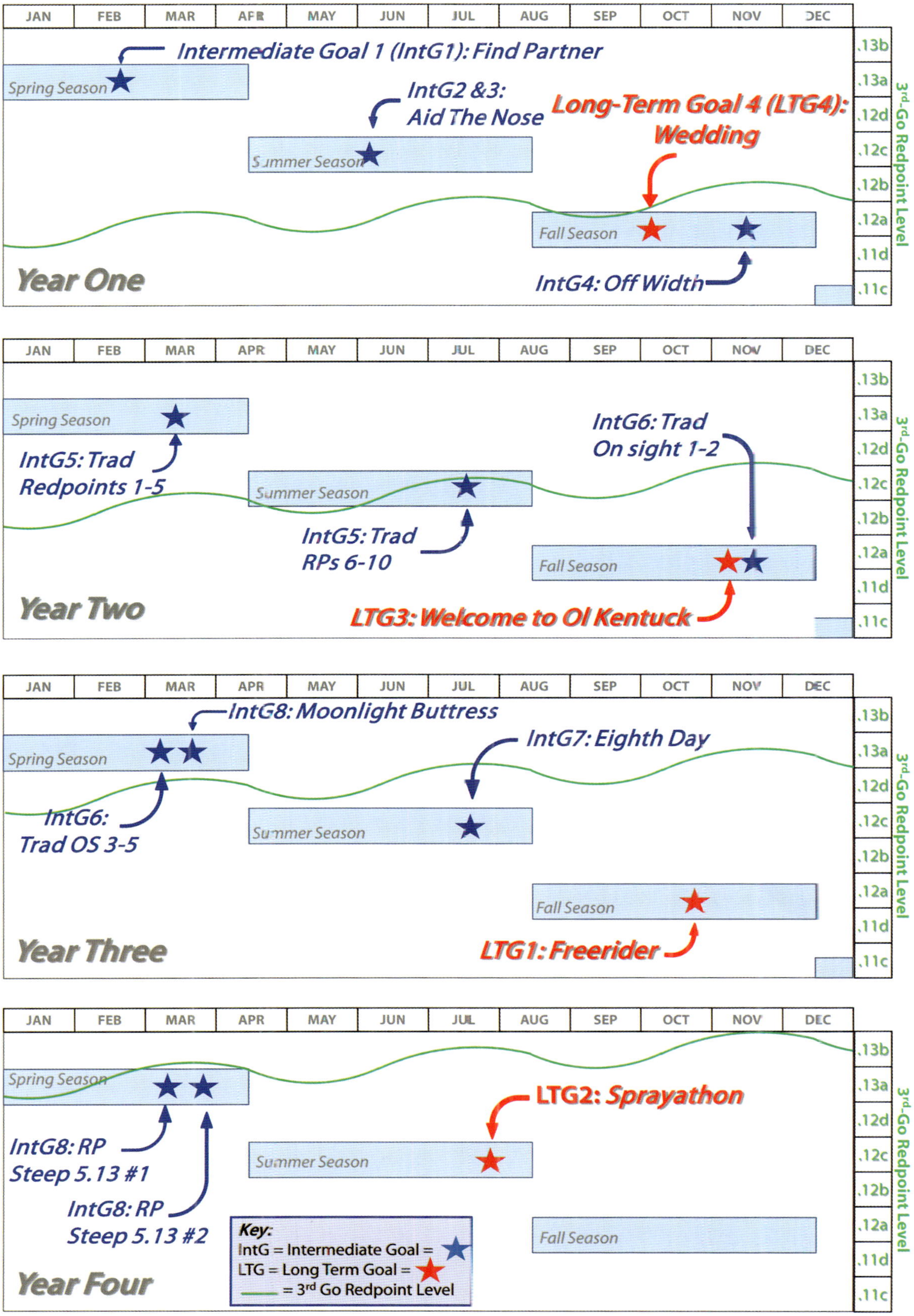

Year One

Intermediate Goal 1 (IntG1): Find Partner

IntG2 &3: Aid The Nose

Long-Term Goal 4 (LTG4): Wedding

IntG4: Off Width

Spring Season · Summer Season · Fall Season

JAN FEB MAR APR MAY JUN JUL AUG SEP OCT NOV DEC

.13b .13a .12d .12c .12b .12a .11d .11c — 3rd-Go Redpoint Level

Year Two

IntG5: Trad Redpoints 1-5

IntG5: Trad RPs 6-10

IntG6: Trad On sight 1-2

LTG3: Welcome to Ol Kentuck

Year Three

IntG8: Moonlight Buttress

IntG7: Eighth Day

IntG6: Trad OS 3-5

LTG1: Freerider

Year Four

IntG8: RP Steep 5.13 #1

IntG8: RP Steep 5.13 #2

LTG2: Sprayathon

Key:
IntG = Intermediate Goal = ★
LTG = Long Term Goal = ★
━ = 3rd Go Redpoint Level

35

how he expects his intermediate and long-term goals to fit into the big picture.

To develop a long-range plan, begin by taking an inventory of all intermediate and long-term goals. Organize these goals into a rough chronological order by considering their relative importance, attainability, and relation to each other. Intermediate goals will facilitate completion of their associated long-term goals, so they should be pursued first. Two or more competing long-term goals might be complementary in some ways, so consider if completing one long-term goal will aid completion of the other (or others), and plan to pursue them in the most logical order. During this process be mindful of other *non-climbing* goals, and how they will impact climbing goals: An impending marriage, birth of a child, or change in employment can have enormous impact on your long-range plan.

ANNUAL PLANNING

The annual-planning cycle is extremely important to climbers for several reasons: Each season offers distinctly different weather and environmental conditions, so seasons must be matched to certain goal routes (accounting for location and relative priority), such that the ideal seasons are earmarked for the most important objectives. Additionally, external factors like holidays, school calendars, and work disruptions tend to follow annual cycles, resulting in predictable periods that facilitate extra climbing or interfere with climbing. A good annual plan will consider these factors, allowing the climber to align peak fitness with optimal weather and ample free time.

The lull before the winter holiday season provides a good opportunity to take stock of the previous year and draw up a plan for the coming year. Identify any opportune periods in the coming year (such as three-day weekends, spring break, summer vacation, etc.), and then identify potential non-climbing time commitments (spouse's birthday weekend, family reunion, business trips, or end of the fiscal year for working stiffs). Lay these out on the calendar.

Next consider any long-term or intermediate goals that will be attempted during the year. Prioritize these (as explained in the Long-Range Planning section) and determine the ideal time period for executing each goal, considering environmental conditions, opportune periods, and time commitments. These time periods will define the *Performance Phases* of each season's plan. The Performance Phase is the time period during each season in which peak fitness is anticipated — the perfect time for attempting one's goal routes. Often the process of prioritizing goals will require some difficult choices, in which certain goals are eliminated or put off to the following year, in order to make room for more pressing goals.

Example three-season annual plan

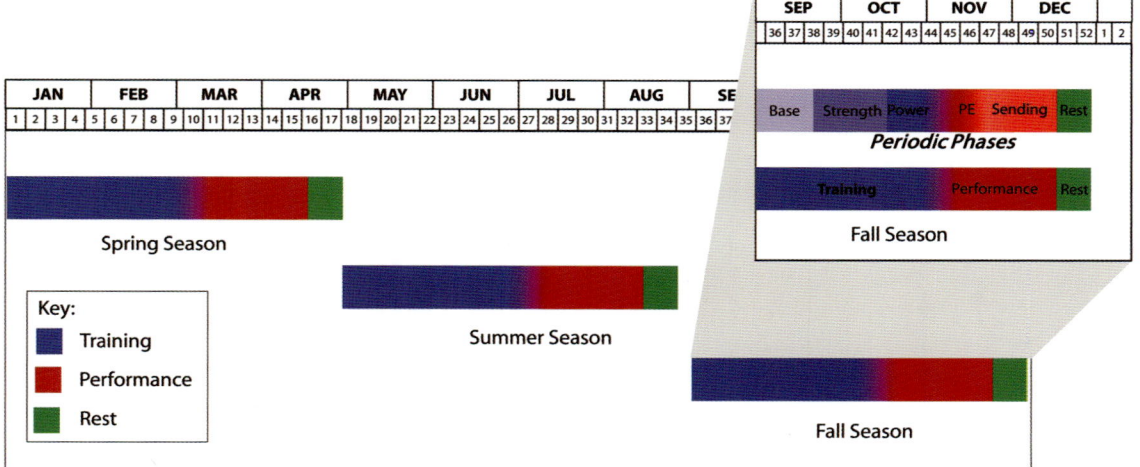

While outdoor climbing occurs throughout a season, periods of peak performance can be reliably predicted.
(Note: The seasons are not necessarily placed ideally in this example.)

During this process, consider that more powerful objectives (such as boulder problems and short, burly routes) should be scheduled earlier in the Performance Phase, when the Power Phase has recently ended and your power is maximized. Similarly, relatively endurance-oriented objectives (such as pumpy sport routes or multi-pitch efforts) should be planned for late in the Performance Phase (more on this in Chapter 10: Building a Training Plan and Other Training Considerations). Power-endurance objectives should be scheduled for the middle of the Performance Phase. Onsighting often depends more on endurance than power, but also relies heavily on technical abilities (such as movement skills and route-reading). These skills tend to be at their peak at the very end of the Performance Phase, after the climber has logged many recent days of climbing on real rock. Therefore onsight objectives should be scheduled for the very end of each Performance Phase. The Figure at the bottom of the previous page illustrates an example of a three-season annual plan.

SEASONAL PLANNING

Once the Performance Phases are identified within the annual plan, the climber should lay out a periodic training plan for each individual season (recommended seasonal training plans are provided, with extensive discussion, in Chapter 10). The purpose of the periodic training plan is to synergistically build fitness and skill to achieve a peak phase at a predetermined point in the season. This plan will entail several facets of training, including *physical training, skill development,* and *weight management* (each of these topics will be discussed in detail later in this book). Climbers with significant fear issues should also consider developing a formal plan for overcoming these issues, which is beyond the scope of this book (refer to Arno Ilgner's outstanding *The Rock Warrior's Way*).

The physical training plan will comprise the following phases of physical training, performed in this order:

- Base-Fitness (2–4 weeks)
- Strength (3–4 weeks)
- Power (2–3 weeks)
- Power-Endurance (2–4 weeks)
- Performance (3–4 weeks)
- Rest (1–2 weeks)

Variations in the prescribed phase lengths will be explained in the coming chapters. The initial climbing-specific training *volume* (a function of training intensity and training duration) will start at a modest level, gradually build through the strength phases, and then taper off as the climber progresses toward the Performance Phase. Likewise, NON-climbing specific training (such as running, cycling, power lifting, or any other form of exercise that contributes minimally to climbing performance) will taper off as the climber enters the Strength Phase, remaining minimal or non-existent through the Power and Performance Phases, then ramp back up during the Rest Phase.

Skill development will also follow a periodic schedule, with early phases emphasizing acquisition of novel skills, the middle phases emphasizing rehearsal and stress-proofing of these skills, and the performance phases requiring execution of these newly

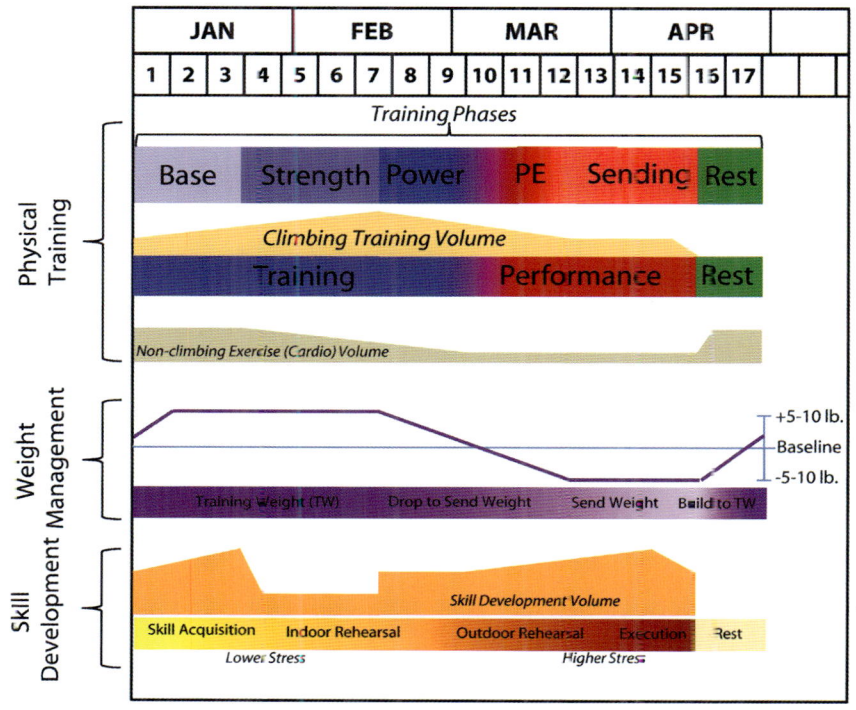

Example periodic seasonal plan

developed skills in high-stress situations. The volume of skill development will also fluctuate throughout the season, with high volume prescribed during the Base-Fitness Phase followed by a lull during the Strength Phase, before ramping back up as the climber transitions to regular outdoor climbing and performance.

Weight management should also follow a periodic schedule. Climbers should aim to reach their lowest healthy weight as they enter the Performance Phase. The Training and Rest phases do not require minimized body weight. In fact, strength training is more effective at a higher body weight. Furthermore, attempting to maintain low body weight indefinitely often leads to sickness or injury, and is not recommended. These various aspects of periodic scheduling are shown in the Figure on the previous page. Once the basic periodic schedule has been developed, you can focus on the detailed planning of each phase. Specific instructions for planning individual phases will be described in detail in Part II: Physical Training.

With a notional seasonal plan in mind, the climber should consider any specific adjustments that might be made to her plan to account for the characteristics of that season's goal routes. For example, if a particular route requires the use of an unusual body position or handhold (such as a mono, split-finger grip, or pinch) to execute the crux, or climbs a type of feature (such as a roof or arête) that is not the climber's strong suit, it may be appropriate to incorporate specific training into the plan to meet these demands. Consider the results of the Self-Evaluation and compare them against the season's planned goal routes to identify any areas that require special emphasis. With this information, you can tailor the season's training toward the demands of the goal route. Much more detail on this tactic is presented in Part II.

DAILY PLANNING

A daily plan is essential to assuring each day is spent in the most productive manner possible. At first this process may seem overwhelming and unnecessary, but with time, each climber will have a small catalogue of standard daily plans to choose from. At that point, the process of planning each day becomes a simple matter of identifying the general objective for the day (for example, to rest, to train power, or to attempt a long-term redpoint project). Certain variables will change (such as the resistance of a given strength-training exercise), but the basic framework can be recycled. The coming chapters will provide detailed instructions for planning training and crag days, complete with suggested daily training routines and schedules for each phase. Armed with these tools, the chore of planning each day becomes a simple matter of placing each training (or performance) activity on the calendar in accordance with the periodic training plan. The chart on the following page shows an example periodic training plan for a novice athlete focused on route climbing (a similar calendar will be presented in much greater detail in Chapter 10).

Phase	Week	Sunday	Monday	Tuesday	Wednesday	Thursday	Friday	Saturday
	-	Last Week of Performance Phase of Previous Season						
	-		Rest Phase of Previous Season					
	-							Day 1 — Base-Fitness (BF)
Base-Fitness Phase	1	Day 2 — Base-Fitness (BF)	Optional Aerobic Exercise (OAE)	BF	OAE	BF	OAE	BF
Base-Fitness Phase	2	BF	OAE	BF	OAE	BF	OAE	BF
Base-Fitness Phase	3	BF	OAE	BF	BF	BF	OAE	BF
Base-Fitness Phase	4	BF	OAE	BF	BF	BF	OAE	Strength
Strength Phase	5	Optional Base-Fitness (OBF)		Strength	OBF		Strength	OBF
Strength Phase	6		Strength	OBF		Strength	OBF	
Strength Phase	7	Strength	OBF		Strength			Power
Power Phase	8			Power		Power		
Power Phase	9	Power		Power			Power	
Power-Endurance	10	Power-Endurance (PE)			PE			Redpoint (RP) attempts
Power-Endurance	11	RP			PE			RP
Power-Endurance	12	RP			PE			RP
Performance	13	RP			PE			RP
Performance	14	RP			PE			RP/OS
Performance	15	RP/OS			PE			RP/OS
Rest Phase	16	RP/OS		OAE and/or Optional Cross-Training (OCT)		OAE/OCT		OAE/OCT
Rest Phase	17		OAE/OCT		OAE/OCT		OAE/OCT	First Day of Next Season

Key:

BF - Base Fitness OS - Onsight RP - Redpoint PE - Power-Endurance
OAE - Optional Aerobic Exercise OBF - Optional Base Fitness OCT - Optional Cross-Training

Example seasonal training plan showing Performance, Rest, and Training phases, with recommended activities listed for each day. Optional activities are shown in gray text. Note: This example is recommended for an athlete with limited training experience.

Executing the Plan

Creating a plan is only part of the equation. Executing it is another matter, requiring much dedication and hard work. Here are some tips for effectively executing your training plan:

1. Write Down the Training Plan. Do this at a time of rest, when far removed from the discomfort of training. Just like it's a bad idea to shop for groceries on an empty stomach, if you try to make your plan while you are training, you will be fighting the constant temptation to cut corners. Even those with a tremendous work ethic may face a related problem: biting off more than they can chew, leading to injury. Your plan will become your coach, encouraging you to persevere when the going gets tough, and requiring rest once the work is done; this coach feels no pain and has little sympathy for your suffering!

2. Stick to the Plan. As discussed above, we can't be trusted to make changes in the heat of the moment. Granted, every plan needs to be flexible to allow for unforeseen contingencies, but if you find yourself considering a change, think it over for a while, discuss it with other knowledgeable people, and make the decision at a time of rest. Over time, you'll learn to sense when the coach in you is being prudent and when he is cutting corners, but it takes honest evaluation to uncover the true motivations for changing the plan. Once your plan is set, see it through for at least one season before trying something dramatically different. If it's a good plan, you should see results in one season (unless you've been training seriously for many years already).

3. Document What You Did; Use It for Motivation. Often one of the best ways to get the most out of a workout is to have a training partner (or an entire "team" of partners) to work with. This can bring your natural competitiveness to the fight and encourage you to give it your best effort. Few of us have such a partner, and even if we do, it's rare that they are following the same plan, at the same time. The solution is to create a virtual training partner — yourself, from last week, last season, last year, or five years ago. Document the results of your training, use similar training apparatuses from season to season, and then use your previous results as motivation. Keep your training records handy during each workout. While resting between sets, flip through some previous results and see how you compare. This method never fails to motivate me to push a bit harder on the next set. Identify those magical seasons from the past, when everything "came up roses," and use the training benchmarks from those seasons as your target. If you have a training partner, but you are either geographically separated or train at different times of the day, consider sharing your results to create some friendly competition. Just remember, a rising tide lifts all boats — don't let the competition get in the way of your partnership.

— Mark Anderson

HANGBOARD PR LOG SHEET

Grip: MR 2F Pocket

Set:	Resistance:	#Reps:	Set:	Resistance:	#Reps:	Set:	Resistance:	#Reps:
1	+15	7	1			1		
2	+25	6	2			2		
3	+35	5, 6 = 5 sec	3			3		
Date	Jan 28, 2013		Date			Date		

Grip: Small Edge

Set:	Resistance:	#Reps:	Set:	Resistance:	#Reps:	Set:	Resistance:	#Reps:
1	+20	7	1	+25	7	1		
2	+30	6	2	+35	6	2		
3	+40	5	3	+45	4, 5 = 6.5 sec	3		
Date	May 15, 2013		Date	Sept 5, 2013		Date		

Grip: Mono

Set:	Resistance:	#Reps:	Set:	Resistance:	#Reps:	Set:	Resistance:	#Reps:
1	-20	7	1			1		
2	-15	6	2			2		
3	-10	5	3			3		
Date	Jan 28, 2013		Date			Date		

Grip: Wide Pinch

Set:	Resistance:	#Reps:	Set:	Resistance:	#Reps:	Set:	Resistance:	#Reps:
1	-25	7	1	-15	7	1		
2	-15	6	2	-5	6	2		
3	-5	5, 6 = 3 sec	3	+5	5 = 7.0 sec	3		
Date	May 18, 2013		Date	Sept 2, 2013		Date		

Grip: IM 2F Pocket

Set:	Resistance:	#Reps:	Set:	Resistance:	#Reps:	Set:	Resistance:	#Reps:
1	+10	7	1			1		
2	+20	6	2			2		
3	+30	5, 6 = 4 sec	3			3		
Date	Sept 2, 2013		Date			Date		

SUMMARY

- Goal-setting is an essential tool for maximizing climbing improvement.
- Goals should be well-defined and inspiring. Place photos or topos of long-term goals in your training area and use these photos for motivation.
- Short-term and intermediate goals should be established to provide stepping-stones to long-term goals. Establish daily goals for each training session, based on the results of previous workouts.
- A goal without a plan is a pipe dream. Develop a plan (the more detailed, the better) to achieve the impossible.
- Perform Self-Evaluation and Gap Analysis to identify opportunities for improvement. Route Pyramids can be used for Gap Analysis and to develop a broad repertoire of climbing abilities.
- Once a starting point and end point (goal) have been defined, develop a plan to bridge the gap. Multi-year, annual, seasonal, and daily plans can all be beneficial, but expect these plans to evolve over time.
- The Rock Prodigy training program prescribes three seventeen-week seasons per year, each consists of six phases, including Training, Performance, and Rest phases. Use the Seasonal Training Plans provided in Chapter 10, or develop your own specific plan.
- The training plan you develop will become your coach. Use it for motivation and restraint at moments of doubt.

ethan pringle

Jumbo Love, 15b

TENAYA®

SKILL DEVELOPMENT

Climbing is a complex sport that requires physical, mental, and technical capabilities. Very technical climbs, like *Darkness at Noon*, 5.13a, at Smith Rock, OR, require near-flawless movement, and are ideal for developing climbing skills. Mike Anderson

CHAPTER 3

"Sometimes I'm completely in sync with what the rock can do… some geological quirk has made it into a piece of music which, when you listen to it, makes you dance. And if you really pay attention to the dance, the harder the route gets, the more blank and featureless it is, the better and more complex is the message you get from the rock."
— Johnny Dawes[3]

INTRODUCTION

When climbers first take up the sport, there is (unfortunately and shockingly) typically very little thought put into *learning to climb*. Consider a typical first climbing experience (almost certainly in a climbing gym these days): The person will learn how to wear a harness, tie-in, and a few belay commands, and then he or she will be unleashed to "climb." These are the minimum skills needed to preserve life, and typically the only instructions provided. Sometimes the novice is accompanied by someone with more experience (but rarely *much* more) who can pass along the standard phrases such as "use your feet," which lack the nuance and context to be of much value to a total novice. Mostly what the "experienced" climber *successfully* passes on is the ultra-competitive, grade-obsessed nature of our sport, encouraging her to attempt increasingly difficult routes until every inch of vertical progress becomes a struggle. This cultural attitude will immediately and regularly hamper the novice's skill development by pressuring her to pass up teachable moments in favor of achieving immediate results, and by discouraging her from attempting to learn more fundamental skills on the most appropriate terrain.

For whatever reason, when novice climbers enter the sport, it is either assumed that they (basically) already know how to climb or the matter isn't considered at all. Perhaps the belief that the act of climbing is somewhat natural leads to this omission of instruction, just as one wouldn't expect detailed instruction from a track coach on how to run in a circle. From a skill perspective, climbing is infinitely more technically demanding than running—it is much more like basketball or gymnastics. The experience of novice climbers is thus akin to teaching a novice baller, before his first game, how to tie his sneakers but not how to make a layup! The corresponding gymnastics analogy is too dreadful to contemplate….

To make matters worse, the ability to learn new skills fades over time as the climber gains familiarity. The best opportunity to learn occurs when the climber first begins to climb, an opportunity that is often missed. A well-known sports paradox is that most athletes receive the lowest-quality coaching earliest in their career when it is most critical, and only encounter high-caliber coaching later in life (if at all) when it is least needed. (To wit, many of today's NFL quarterbacks rose to that level in part because they were shipped off at an early age to elite quarterback camps, or privately tutored by renowned coaches.)

Applying the paradox to climbing, a sport in which most athletes receive essentially *no* coaching, it's safe to assume that most climbers have a tremendous opportunity to undo numerous bad habits and replace them with good ones. This can be a daunting challenge, but facing it head-on is critical to the goal of continuous improvement. No amount of effort spent on this challenge could be considered "too much," and yet many climbers neglect it. If bad habits were immediately apparent, they could be dealt with at any time, but many do not become limiting for years, and so remain undetected or easily compensated for. Even worse, these are often overarching habits that infiltrate the climber's entire training program, sabotaging every endeavor from gym sessions to mega-redpoint projects, stifling development or even causing regression. However, for the climber who seeks to reach his potential, these overarching bad habits must eventually be replaced with overarching good habits. Before hammering away on the *specific* good habits needed for climbing (such as relaxing the grip or improving footwork), consider the likelihood that more *general* habits such as *how to acquire new skills* need to be relearned and reinforced.

The theories of motor learning and descriptions of fundamental climbing moves have been well-described in other texts (particularly the ground-breaking *Self-Coached Climber*,[5] which includes a six-chapter presentation of climbing movement and motor learning), so they won't be repeated here. These are important topics, however, and climbers are encouraged to investigate them. Rather than describing particular moves, this chapter will present climbing-specific *principles for effective skill learning* that climbers can apply broadly to skill development. Selected aspects of climbing skill are discussed, focusing on topics that are often poorly understood or regularly cited by climbers as weaknesses (such as footwork, handwork, dynamic moves, and resting). Finally, the integration of skill-development activities into a periodic training program is discussed, along with specific, easy-to-follow exercises for skill practice that enable simultaneous physical and technical progression.

GOOD HABITS FOR EFFICIENT SKILL DEVELOPMENT

The psychologist Anders Ericsson pioneered research into "deliberate practice," and one of his fundamental discoveries was that the level of mastery one attains with a skill has more to do with how one practices it than merely *how many* repetitions are performed.[4] The most effective practice obeys these principles:

- Isolate key individual components of a skill
- Perform those components repeatedly
- Incorporate expert feedback to correct deficiencies
- Gradually escalate the difficulty to attain mastery

Therefore, to maximize the benefits of practice time, it is essential to first learn *how to practice*, or more precisely, how to effectively develop and refine climbing skills. These broad principles can be applied to nearly any climbing skill-development activity, and with conscientious effort and repetition will lead to the following good *habits*:

It is essential to set-aside time for *deliberate practice* on appropriate terrain. Unfortunately, many climbers feel the need to only *train* or *perform*, inhibiting their skill development and limiting their climbing potential.

ENGAGE IN PRACTICE

The most fundamental good habit of skill development is also the most neglected: the simple act of *engaging in practice*. Climbing rhetoric itself betrays this fact—while athletes in the ball sports speak of "going to *practice*," climbers "go climbing" or "*training*." The difference between training and practice is much more than semantics. Training refers to developing the physical components of the sport: increasing strength, endurance, and flexibility. High levels of

> "*I wanted to climb as many routes as I could. And the result was that my repertoire of moves increased more and more, and the stamina, too... I gained much more self-confidence. Finally, I started to climb better and better.*"
> — Josune Bereziartu[1]

Actively *moving over rock* (not hanging on the rope) reinforces efficient climbing technique, therefore climbers should spend at least 50% of their climbing and training time *moving* over moderate terrain. Alex Honnold racking up mileage on *Logical Progression*, 5.13a, El Gigante, Mexico. Andrew Burr

fatigue, intensity, or both are required for effective training. Practice, on the other hand, is a method for gaining skill proficiency through isolation, repetition, feedback, and incremental escalation. It is meditative, requiring concentration, relaxation, moderation, analysis, and a fresh, energetic body.

Practice is critical to every skill-intensive pursuit, including nonathletic pursuits like playing an instrument or speaking a foreign language. While *training* is repetitive at times, the need to optimize physical stimulation necessitates exercises that may not be climbing specific (such as bicep curls). With *practice*

the goal is to optimize neuromuscular stimulation, so the activities used should mimic climbing as much as possible, regardless of the resulting physical stimulation. Additionally, the moves should be worked not to failure, but to perfection.

KEEP YOURSELF MOVING

To foster the best learning, practice should be carried out on appropriate terrain, which leads to the next good habit climbers should embrace: *keep yourself moving*. In climbing, a sport with an infinite number of movement possibilities, practice should consist

Practice and Training Are Not Mutually Exclusive

Novice climbers are often advised to hold off on physical training in order to focus on the higher-priority activities of skill development and movement practice. This advice assumes that the two pursuits are mutually exclusive, but they are not. Through careful planning, it is possible to carve out sufficient time for skill development within a physical training program. Engaging in shorter, but more deliberate skill-development sessions will result in far more effective practice than random climbing activities. Furthermore, most skill development is not physically taxing by design, leaving ample capacity for physical training.

For example, if a typical beginner were to climb every third day in a climbing gym, she could spend the first 30 to 60 minutes on movement drills (which double as a warm-up) and the next 30 to 60 minutes on sport-specific training. Such an approach provides ample time to acquire new skills, and ample opportunity to train in significantly less time than would be consumed by a single day of unfocused cragging. The Rock Prodigy program incorporates skill development in this complementary and synergistic way. To be successful, apply the Good Habits for Efficient Skill Development on a daily basis to make the most of each session.

primarily of simply moving smoothly over mountains of moderate terrain, aka "mileage." However, climbers often spend too much time on terrain that is too difficult for effective practice, whether bouldering at the gym or projecting at the crag. The very fundamental activity of reinforcement of efficient climbing technique occurs only when the climber is in motion, not when paralyzed by a stopper move or hanging on the end of a rope. Nevertheless, many climbers select routes that are too difficult, resulting in more time spent dangling than actually climbing. There is a time and place for the challenge of a tough climb, but it's not *every* time and *every* place. One needs look no farther than your typical novice gym climber, who may spend 45 minutes "conquering" a too-hard 30-foot route. On much easier terrain, at a humble pace of ten feet per minute, that novice might have covered nearly 500 feet, which would certainly go much further toward developing and reinforcing efficient climbing technique than struggling up one 30-foot route.

Each climber should consider what percentage of her climbing-related time (whether in the gym, at the crag, or in non-climbing-specific training exercises) is spent *moving over rock* versus doing anything else (resting, strategizing, etc.). Then, she should develop the habit of climbing more on moderate terrain, racking up mileage, and developing and reinforcing efficient movement skills. A good target is to spend more than 50 percent of your total "booted-up" climbing and training time *moving* (don't include belaying time or long rests between burns). This is especially critical for less-experienced climbers, who will benefit the most from developing fundamental, generic movement skills, rather than dissecting specific crux moves or rehearsing a particular dyno.

Not all climbing time must be set aside for practice, but the trouble is, most climbers set aside *no time* for practice. For many climbers, a simple change in attitude would yield more practice time. Warm-up and cool-down routes are ideal for practice, but only if the climber applies concentration and focus to develop specific movement skills rather than engaging in small talk with the belayer.

Learn Novel Skills in a Stress-Free Environment

The general habit of accruing mileage on moderate terrain extends beyond developing efficiency. It is also a prerequisite for learning new moves, and leads to the next good habit: *learn novel skills in a stress-free environment*. Initial learning of any complex skill is inhibited by external stress. Therefore, initial experimentation with novel moves should take place when the climber is relatively fresh, on moderate terrain, with a toprope (or close to the ground, if bouldering), to remove the stress associated with falling. Many climbers may also learn better in private, or in the company of a single supportive companion or coach. Large crowds of onlookers will make some climbers self-conscious, reducing their willingness to attempt fundamental moves or ask basic questions. The ego's desire to perform in front of an audience is not conducive to this initial learning. As the climber progresses, external stresses should be incrementally increased to make the skill more challenging to execute. This *stress-proofing* process is described in detail at the end of this chapter.

Select Appropriate Projects

The habit of keeping yourself moving also applies to the goal routes and boulder problems climbers pursue. This is the next good habit of skill development: *select appropriate projects*. The start-to-finish process of attempting a difficult route and seeing it through to a redpoint is a tremendously valuable learning experience for a climber, so it should occur as often as possible. Unfortunately, climbers often select projects that are slightly too hard and consume one or more entire climbing seasons. A good habit is to spend the majority of the peak climbing season working on routes that can be successfully redpointed in about four climbing days. Such routes are difficult enough to present the climber with the familiar challenges of deciphering difficult moves, dealing with fatigue throughout the climb, planning and executing the projecting process, and coping with the mental stress of sending. Completing four or more such projects in a single season will have an additive effect on the learning and confidence of the climber, while a single, too-hard mega-project that consumes an entire season or more will, at best, yield only one such learning experience, and at worst can be detrimental to the climber's confidence. Mega-projects have their place (when a "dream route" is within reach, for example), and they offer unique learning opportunities, but from a movement/skill-acquisition perspective, mega-projects offer diminishing returns as the process unfolds. Usually after four or five days the moves are well-known and success hinges on other factors, so make it a habit to select shorter projects as the rule, not the exception.

> *"The essence of climbing technique hinges on having a keen sense of body awareness. Experience plays a critical role, but the focus of attention is paramount."* — Lynn Hill[8]

PAY ATTENTION

Simply accruing mileage on moderate terrain will improve many climbers' technique, but that time investment can yield much more improvement if the climber learns to *pay attention* while doing so. Effective practice is more than just robotically going through the motions. Be it spontaneous climbing or specific movement drills, there are subtleties involved in every climbing movement. These subtleties are not always natural, so the body must be consciously directed to perform them while the mind meticulously evaluates the execution and provides feedback. Some moves should be broken down into parts to isolate and rehearse key subtleties. It is only through controlled, escalating repetition with feedback (practice) that these subtleties become habitual, and executed without conscious effort.

Too often climbers perform movement drills without adequately focusing on the correct details. For example, the ubiquitous "silent feet" drill has the climber place his feet on the holds silently. The purpose of the drill is to teach accurate foot placement on holds, but the metric for successful accomplishment (sound) is not the best evaluation of this learning objective, as a silent placement could be way off target, or a loud jab could be a bull's-eye. Therefore, the climber can only expect to learn the desired skill (accurate foot control) if he focuses not just on being quiet, but also on being accurate, and evaluates his performance based on accuracy rather than noise.

Every drill has one or more specific purposes that the practicing climber should understand and pay attention to as the drill is performed. Even other training activities, be they mileage climbing, warming up, endurance workouts, or bouldering sessions, can be greatly enhanced by focusing on a few key learning objectives: skills such as proper breathing, initiating movement in the lower body, etc. (many more will be listed below). High-volume climbing on moderate terrain is a brute-force way to develop more-efficient climbing technique, but with an attentive, meditative mindset, it becomes a scalpel; it becomes *practice*. So pay attention!

FREQUENTLY REPEAT NOVEL AND DIFFICULT SEQUENCES

With practice being the best-known process for developing new skills, and that process consisting of rehearsing novel skills until they are mastered, it is a sad irony that the most novel skills climbers apply in their athletic careers are often never repeated. These are the limit climbing routes and boulder problems that drive our obsession, and oddly, climbers tend to work like hell to make that redpoint but then never climb it again. This is understandable for a faraway route, but this often occurs with local and indoor boulder problems as well. While one ascent indicates some level of proficiency with a given problem, it rarely equals mastery of it; therefore, climbers should make it a habit to *frequently repeat novel and difficult sequences*. This approach is a given in gymnastics. A gymnast would

Matt Segal paying attention to his footwork on *Stingray*, 5.12c, Henry Mountains, UT. ◯ Brendan Nicholson

Good Habits for Skill Development

- Engage in practice
- Keep yourself moving
  - Learn novel skills in a stress-free environment
  - Select appropriate projects
- Pay attention
- Frequently repeat novel and difficult sequences
- Practice drills that target specific weaknesses

not move on from a routine after the first time she sketched her way through it; instead she rehearses it beyond the point of perfection, to the point that it can be performed perfectly *in competition*, under tremendous stress and scrutiny. It is appropriate, then, that the legendary "father of modern bouldering" and former gymnast John Gill was known for repeating and refining his boulder problems until he could execute them in perfect control, without a hint of desperation. In training especially, hard problems that are successfully climbed should become part of the climber's routine, and oft repeated. Pay attention to the subtleties of the route's movement, trying to identify the key elements that make each move easier or harder. Refine these subtleties by emphasizing them with each attempt. Experiment with variations in subtle movements, body positions, or alternate sequences, and try to apply novel techniques to the problem. With such focused practice, a once-limit boulder problem

may become routine, and that once-awkward move will assimilate into the climber's repertoire. This process of "learning-down" a once-desperate sequence will transmit the critical lesson that well-executed movement does indeed make climbing "easier."

Practice Drills that Target Specific Weaknesses

The final good habit for effectively developing movement skills is to *practice drills that target specific weaknesses*. We addressed identifying strengths and weaknesses in detail in Chapter Two: Goal-Setting and Planning, while the tools for eliminating technical weaknesses follow in this chapter. Just as physical training is planned out in advance to address specific physical weaknesses (such as finger strength), so too does it go with skill development. Recognizing a weakness is the hardest part, but it may be equally difficult

Observation and Imitation

Every climber, novice or expert, should seek to constantly increase his repertoire of climbing moves. Unfortunately, there is no comprehensive "library of climbing movements" to consult, so uncovering new moves can be challenging. Observing other climbers is a great way to identify new movements to add to your quiver. Here are some methods for tapping into your "inner stalker" to augment your movement skills:

Observe other climbers. This is most easily done at a climbing gym, with good lighting and a high density of climbers. For the best results, go to the gym on your rest day, when you can give 100 percent attention to observing others. Identify the more skilled climbers and note how they move, but also pay attention to others. Often a less powerful climber will discover a more efficient sequence out of necessity. Rarely does the strongest climber have the best technique. Take note of new techniques and the problems or routes on which they were applied, and then attempt these climbs on your next gym visit.

Observe elite climbers on video. The proliferation of high-quality climbing films and online videos makes it easy to watch your heroes in action and analyze their movement. Identify novel moves and make a note to try them in your next practice session.

Use video feedback. Any new skill-acquisition process relies on good feedback. Ideally, this can be achieved with a dedicated training partner, but if no such partner is available, a video camera and a cheap tripod can suffice. Film yourself on technically challenging terrain, and then analyze your performance on the next rest day. Are you committing to the most efficient technical solution, or are you attempting to compensate with extra power? This approach works best for stress-proofing skills that are already in your quiver, though not yet perfected. However, sometimes the third-person perspective will allow you to "see" a sequence that was not evident while on the sharp end.

Get the beta. In this Internet age, it seems every route, boulder problem, or plastic gym sequence ever climbed is on video somewhere. Attempt your goal project a few times first (without peeking online), and then review any existing beta (either on video or by watching or talking to other suitors) and note the differences between your sequence and those of others. Are there moves you hadn't considered? If you find yourself avoiding a particular type of move that seems obvious to others, consider the reasons. Are you masking a technical weakness that needs further attention?

Learn from the masters. If all else fails, it never hurts to take a trip to the zoo and observe the monkeys. These magnificent animals have been climbing 16 hours a day for their entire lives, and they really know how to move. Note how rarely they bend their elbows, how they utilize momentum constantly, and how they plan movements far in advance. Also, note that monkeys *never* use a crimp grip.

to design an appropriate drill to address it. Numerous drills are suggested below, but climbers may need to develop their own. Just as in physical training, devise drills that isolate the key components of the skill and provide feedback for proper execution. These drills should then be performed repeatedly and progressively, as described in the *Progressive Practice* section at the end of the chapter. In general, use the habits discussed above when implementing specific drills.

FOOTWORK

In climbing, mastery of footwork has numerous benefits. For example, foot precision enables the climber to place his or her toes on the best features of a foothold, allowing the feet to support more of the climber's weight (thus reducing the loads and fatigue placed on the upper body). Footwork is often cited as the most important technique to develop, and most climbers consider it a weakness, yet how to develop good footwork remains a mystery to many. Climbers are not born with this weakness; it arises over time from neglect as other skills develop and soon out-

pace footwork. To a large extent, climbers aren't to blame for this—the nature of climbing and the training environment facilitate this neglect. First, the fact that climbing proceeds upward and the hands lead this motion predisposes climbers to focus primarily on their hands while neglecting what the feet are doing. Second, the size and shape of artificial climbing holds are a poor representation of real rock, providing poor feedback to climbers about the quality of their footwork. These factors pervade climbing, so overcoming them requires deliberate action and persistence.

OVERCOMING THE HAND BIAS
PRACTICE DOWNCLIMBING

Moving upward, as climbers do, means the hands lead the way, guided closely by the eyes, which are nearby. This naturally results in tunnel vision, with an overemphasis on hand movements to the exclusion of the rest of the body, specifically the hips, legs, and feet. A straightforward approach to breaking this habit is to practice downclimbing more often. The feet and legs lead the way when downclimbing, requiring the climber to deliberately select footholds, guide her toes to the holds, and apply weight to the footholds. Downclimbing can easily be incorporated into existing training by descending from boulder problems, downclimbing warm-up and cool-down routes, and within endurance workouts (described in Chapter Five: Base Fitness and Chapter Eight: Power-Endurance).

Most climbers understand footwork is a critical skill, yet are unsure how to develop it. Fred Gomez demonstrates a few effective techniques for developing footwork on *Rude Boys*, 5.13c, Smith Rock, OR.
Mark Anderson

Down-climbing forces the climber to pay attention to their feet, and is a great way to practice footwork.

"When I first started climbing, my focus was polarized on clutching the hand-holds and I didn't pay much attention to how I placed my feet or hands. Over time, I began to understand the finer aspects of how to apply force on a given-shaped hold." — Lynn Hill[8]

EMPHASIZE FOOT SEQUENCES

This exclusive focus on the hands applies to sequence problem-solving as well, in which climbers routinely neglect the contribution of their feet to the solution. This under-analysis leaves climbers with nothing better to do than to simply use the *largest* footholds nearby, lacking any better ideas. Often, the best foothold is the hold that is in the correct *location*, not simply the largest. The correct location is that which permits the optimal body positions and movement from one position to the next. To overcome this, climbers must make a conscious effort to contemplate the optimal foot positions, which may not coincide with any foothold — a smear may be the best choice.

COMPENSATING FOR CLIMBING GYMS

A wide-ranging root cause of poor footwork among modern climbers is the nature of modern climbing gyms. In particular, route-setting and the size and shape of artificial climbing holds encourage bad footwork habits. In the gym, sloppy footwork is not penalized like it is outdoors, so climbers miss out on this critical feedback. Since climbers spend so much time climbing on manmade walls, it is easy to develop the habit of sloppy footwork. The following practices will help reverse this habit:

VARY ROUTE-SETTING "RULES" FOR FOOTHOLD USE

The way footholds are incorporated by human route-setters can also bias footwork practice, so climbers must be cognizant of these biases and compensate for them. An "open feet" policy does not force the use of specific holds; therefore, it would not be appropriate for developing proficiency with poor footholds. On the other hand, such a policy is appropriate for developing the feel for optimal foot location because it gives the climber more choices with which to experiment. A "tracking only" policy, in which the hands and feet are restricted to specifically designated holds (usually designated with only the hand movements in mind), tends to force large foot movements that are not often reflective of rock climbs. Furthermore, the handholds used are typically much larger than most footholds found on rock. Therefore, unless the setter takes extra care to add numerous appropriately sized footholds, the "tracking only" policy has little application to rock climbing and will not improve footwork. Smearing anywhere on the wall should always be "fair game." Ideally, each climber would use a variety of these methods to ensure exposure to a variety of practice scenarios. If this is not the case at a given gym, bend the "rules" as necessary to provide the appropriate variety of footwork-improvement opportunities.

PRACTICE ON TINY FOOTHOLDS

Compared to natural footholds, artificial holds are much larger, higher profile, and demand very little precision to mount and minimal body tension to maintain. Therefore, *always practice climbing on tiny footholds*. This policy is easy to follow outdoors, so it mostly applies to gym climbing. Climbers should ignore the demands of the route-setter and be their own master, restricting themselves to the smallest foot "chips" and/or natural features embedded in the wall. If these are not available, sub-features of larger holds may be used, such as a smaller edge or ripple, or even the bolt hole. This policy can and should be applied to all training activities, from low-intensity mileage sessions to endurance training to bouldering sessions. For those with home walls, invest in buckets of screw-on footholds and spray them all over the wall. Vary the orientation of the holds so that the best surface is not always available to the climber.

Climbing gyms are great for training, but can be less than ideal for skill development, especially footwork. In the gym, limit yourself to tiny footholds, such as these screw-on "chips", or "jibs"

WEAR GOOD SHOES

Another simple policy that will effortlessly improve footwork is to *wear good, tight-fitting climbing shoes* when practicing footwork (i.e., *always*). For their non-performance climbing days, many climbers use "training shoes" like an old, blown-out or resoled pair of shoes that are more comfortable. Such shoes are also sloppier, so they do not provide precise feedback to the climber on the quality of foot placements. Furthermore, these old, comfy shoes don't penalize the climber for clumsy foot placement the way tight-fitting shoes do (like when a climber over-aggressively smacks his toe into the wall — ouch!). For some, the added expense of good-quality shoes may be enough to promote more care with foot placement.

Overall, artificial climbing gyms are a tremendous asset to climbers and are largely responsible for the gains in climbing performance seen over the last two decades. However, a few peculiarities have caused a corresponding drop-off in footwork. The three policies detailed above (vary route setting "rules" for foothold use, practice on tiny footholds, and wear good shoes) are fairly painless, transparent steps climbers can take to replace the sloppy footwork habits inadvertently encouraged by artificial gyms.

FOOT-PLACEMENT GUIDELINES

In addition to the general policies listed above, several more deliberate steps are available to improve the climber's foot-placement precision and get the most out of footholds. These drills require concentration to perform correctly before they become habitual, so they should be deliberately practiced during targeted sessions set aside for just this purpose, when the climber is not distracted by other objectives.

MAKE MANY FOOT MOVEMENTS

While not a hard-and-fast rule, in general, the feet should move between holds more frequently than the hands. That is to say, for every hand movement, a technically skilled climber will make two or three foot movements. The reason for this is that large foot movements, or highsteps, are generally less precise and require that the climber push his center of mass (COM) out away from the wall to reach the higher foothold. As this happens, the load increases on the climber's upper body while the direction of pull on the holds rotates outward, reducing the mechanical advantage and further straining the fingers. In addition, the resulting highstep position makes it difficult to fully weight the foot and prevents the climber from

The protruding, "pinch-able" holds typical of climbing gyms encourage the bad habit of over-high-stepping. Instead, make many smaller foot movements when you are practicing in the gym.

initiating the next move in the lower body, which is most efficient.

On the other hand, small foot movements keep the climber's COM close to the rock throughout the movement, maintaining the optimal direction of pull on the handholds. Furthermore, with the feet on lower holds, it is easier to apply more weight to them, and most efficiently initiate the next moves from the lower body. Gym routes encourage the bad habit of overly highstepping because they tend to lack intermediate footholds, they use protruding handholds that can often be pinched (allowing a more outward direction of pull), and the large footholds demand less precision to mount. This makes highsteps easier in a gym than they would be on the rock, encouraging their overuse. Therefore, during practice, seek to make approximately three foot movements for every one hand movement (actual outdoor routes may dictate a different ratio), even if this requires smearing, and resist the urge to pinch every hold in the gym.

MONITOR FOOT PLACEMENT

Another good foot-placement practice is to "pick a target and watch it land." This means the climber should deliberately select not just the foothold, but also the precise desired toe location (target), then maintain eye contact with the hold as the toe is placed. It is common for climbers of all abilities to make foot movements without visually verifying the placement, relying instead on *proprioceptive* feedback (spatial

Upward progress on slab climbs relies mostly on friction between the shoe and rock. Weighting the feet and initiating moves in the lower body are mandatory skills. Tommy Caldwell waltzes up *Dancing in the Light*, 5.11b, Squamish, B.C.   📷 Andrew Burr

awareness and touch) to hit the right spot. However, making the most out of small, technical footholds can require millimeter-level accuracy, which is extremely difficult to achieve proprioceptively on the first try. Therefore, when placing the feet, especially on small, technical holds, closely watch the movement as it occurs, and don't look away until the toe has hit the target (a well-positioned partner can provide the best feedback). This process can be very easily drilled during all types of climbing activities.

BLINKING DRILL

Placing the feet on holds proprioceptively may be required in some situations—specifically on steep, strenuous terrain that must be climbed quickly, and when large, forgiving footholds are available. Therefore, it is also helpful to practice proprioceptive foot placement with the *Blinking Drill*, performed by spotting the foothold with eyes open, then closing the eyes as the foot is placed on the hold, and so on. Though the overall purpose is to allow the climber to move faster, it is not necessary or desirable to climb fast when performing the drill. Instead, the climber should select the foothold, carefully memorize its spatial location before blinking, and then carefully move to the hold. He should then observe the tactile feedback from his

toes to assess the placement quality and make necessary adjustments. Once the placement is "finalized," assess the quality of the placement with open eyes. With practice, the climber should be able to perform this operation more quickly, enabling faster climbing when it counts.

WEIGHT FOOTHOLDS

Precise foot placement is just the first step in properly utilizing the feet, yet many climbers focus on other things once their toes have landed (and sometimes sooner). Most footholds rely on friction between the shoe and the rock to maintain the foot placement, thus shoe manufacturers' closely guarded rubber formulas. The friction force that supports the foot depends not only on the properties of the rubber, but also on the pressure applied to the rock through the foot (called the *normal force*). Therefore, it is critical to develop the habit of pushing the foot into the hold and maintaining that pressure as consistently as possible throughout the move. This can require considerable core strength in some situations, so regular practice is essential. At the point of contact between rubber and rock, increase the mating surface by "wrapping" the toes around the hold as much as possible. Then, strive to keep the surfaces mated to each other with-

Habits of Good Footwork

Overcoming the Hand Bias
- Practice downclimbing
- Emphasize foot sequences

Compensating for Climbing Gyms
- Vary route-setting "rules" for foothold use
- Practice on tiny footholds
- Wear good shoes

Foot-Placement Guidelines
- Make many foot movements
- Select the target and watch the toe land—monitor foot placement
- Use the Blinking Drill to practice autonomous foot placement
- Maintain gradual, consistent pressure on the foothold throughout its use
- Seek out and master technical face and slab climbs

she inches up the face, thus providing ample repetition of these delicate processes. Pockets and other small footholds demand very precise placement and careful application of pressure to remain engaged on the hold. The toughest face cruxes will demand the careful distribution of weight across the hand- and footholds, teaching the climber to sense how much each hold can bear, and training her to apply the correct load. These critical skills cannot be obtained any other way.

out slippage or rotation. This demands flexing at the ankle and forefoot as the body moves up on the hold. Throughout the movement, concentrate on maintaining a constant force on the foothold, as overloading or underloading it will alter the friction-force interaction, possibly leading to a foot slip.

TECHNICAL FACE AND SLAB CLIMBING

Finally, a great step climbers can take to hone their footwork is to seek out and master technical face and slab climbs. These routes *demand* excellent footwork, and thus provide expert feedback to the climber. As a result, the climber can't help but to practice precise footwork, or walk away in disgust. Slab climbs (routes that are less than vertical) should be sufficiently difficult that they rely on very small friction holds. These demand very precise foot placements, and will not tolerate large variations in the magnitude and direction of the force applied by the foot as the climber moves past the hold. They also force the climber to put weight on his feet and initiate movement in the lower body. Thus, on slab climbs the climber is required to pay attention to these details and reinforce them as habits.

Technical face climbs are those in the realm of vertical, with tiny holds, especially pockets. These routes require the climber to hold her center of mass close to the rock in order to get purchase on the tiny handholds, forcing many small foot movements, with limited ability to lean out and spy holds. The numerous foot movements force the climber to carefully weight and unweight each hold, shifting balance around as

The tiny, insecure holds common to vertical face climbs demand precision and force the climber to stay close to the rock, preventing large high-steps. Tara Brouwer hugging *Sister of Mercy*, 5.12b, Penitente Canyon, CO. Mike Anderson

"I concentrate especially hard on my hands. I take time to feel the holds, not only to find the best way to grab them, but also to find out what is the best way to put my feet on them later." — François Legrand[7]

HANDWORK

Few would argue that the connection between the hands and the rock is critical to difficult climbing, so learning how to get the most from this interface is fundamental to improving a climber's technical skills. Every climber should have a basic working knowledge of the various hand positions, including but not limited to: the open grip, crimp grip (including the closed crimp and semi-closed crimp), pinch, sidepull, gaston, false grip, mantel, and undercling. If unfamiliar with these grip positions, refer to Craig Luebben's *Rock Climbing: Mastering Basic Skills* or similar texts.[6]

There are an infinite variety of handholds, and few are exactly alike. Although training tools and gym holds are generally ergonomically shaped with smooth contours, real rock rarely is. Handholds are often highly irregular, requiring precise placement of each individual finger to gain the most purchase on the hold. In some cases, fingers need to be applied in a particular sequence for maximum benefit.

Determining the most effective way to grasp a hold requires a combination of visual and tactile feedback. Various factors come into play depending on the hold type, but with practice, an experienced climber will be able to regularly select the proper hand configuration onsight. This section will provide a variety of options to consider when determining how best to grasp a hold in the real world. Experiment with these suggestions on the rock to get the most out of each handhold.

EDGES

Most edges are not perfectly flat, are not parallel with the ground, and vary in depth. Generally the most important factor is depth, so the primary aim should be to get the two strongest fingers (the middle and ring) on the deepest part of the hold. Next consider the angle of pull, which is usually the direction the forearm is pointing. All else being equal, the part of the edge perpendicular to the angle of pull will provide the best grip. For irregularly shaped edges, split grips or finger stacks may be useful to get the most out of the hold.

Consider different hand positions such as a closed crimp, semi-closed crimp, or open grip. Often the geometry of the hold will dictate a particular hand position. Perfectly flat holds will require a closed or semi-closed crimp, whereas one may benefit from the use of an open grip on certain convex, arcing edges. Often by initially grasping an edge in an open position and then "rolling it up" into a closed crimp, it's possible to maximize skin contact to get a smidgen of extra purchase. Realize, however, that this is hellish on the skin and can cause tendon and ligament injury when performed under heavy load.

POCKETS

Pockets are almost always positive in one direction, but the majority of the time that direction is not straight down. As a result, most pockets will provide a better grip when used as a sidepull, gaston, or undercling. In some cases it may make sense to use a single pocket in two or three different positions as you move past it. Poke around to determine the depth of the pocket, and note any unusual features inside the cavity or on the lip that might provide extra grip. Test the pocket with every finger (or combination of fingers) to determine which finger or set of fingers provides the best grip (for example, for a two-finger pocket, consider index-middle, middle-ring, and ring-pinkie). Often deep pockets will feel better if the fingers are *not* stuffed all the way in. For highly irregular pockets, it may be necessary to insert fingers sequentially to get the best grip.

Occasionally, the position of the inactive fingers can affect how secure or "tweaky" a given pocket feels. For two-finger pockets that use index-middle, it usually feels best to curl the ring and pinkie fingers down into a fist. However, some shallow middle-ring two-finger pockets feel better with the pinkie extended. It may be possible to scum the inactive fingers on knobs or rough patches adjacent to the pocket. In extreme situations, it may make sense to wrap or stack a free finger over one of the fingers in the pocket (as for a closed crimp), but be wary of injury when attempting this.

Finally, pockets present unique injury risks that are worth discussing. First, pockets should almost always be grasped with an open grip, except where it's possible to fit three or more fingers into the pocket. Crimp positions place severe amounts of stress on the *proximal interphalangeal* (PIP — the big knuckle) joints of the fingers used, so climbers shouldn't use these grips unless they have adequately trained them. As with fingerlocks, the collateral ligaments of the

Pockets of Subtlety

On the milky-white limestone in the backwoods of the Rockies is a magnificent pocketed testpiece. The "business" starts immediately with a brutal V9 boulder problem that leads into a 40-foot face-climbing gauntlet of tweaky, tenuous sequences, culminating in the redpoint crux: a long windmill move off a sloping two-finger pocket. On two trips spread over a year, I fell on this move repeatedly on redpoint as I slipped out of that pocket mid-windmill. My frustration was compounded by my ability to nail the move every time off the hang. One burn, while groping that pocket and experimenting with different grip positions, I noticed that if I rotated the grip clockwise slightly, toward a sidepull, the friction was just a smidgen better, the pocket's geometry made the grip just a little more positive, and I was able to get an ever-so-slight dime-edge thumb catch. These miniscule differences were imperceptible to the eye, but the fingers knew.... When you are on a route right at your limit, little details like this can be the tipping point that makes or breaks a send. That was the case this time, and I sent the route on my next go.

— *Mike Anderson*

finger joints are at risk during big moves off "locker" pockets. Take care when moving past pockets to limit the torsional (twisting) forces on these joints. Ideally, the fingers will have enough room to rotate freely in the pocket as the angle of pull changes.

SLOPERS

Two factors generally determine the best way to grasp a sloper: the friction and steepness of the contact surface. The first order of business is to locate the most positive point on the hold. This is almost always the best place to grasp the sloper, unless it is more slippery than another area that is only slightly steeper (which may be the case on well-traveled routes with polished handholds). Experiment with different areas to determine which spot provides the most secure grip; usually, feeling around for the various options with your hand is the best way to determine how to

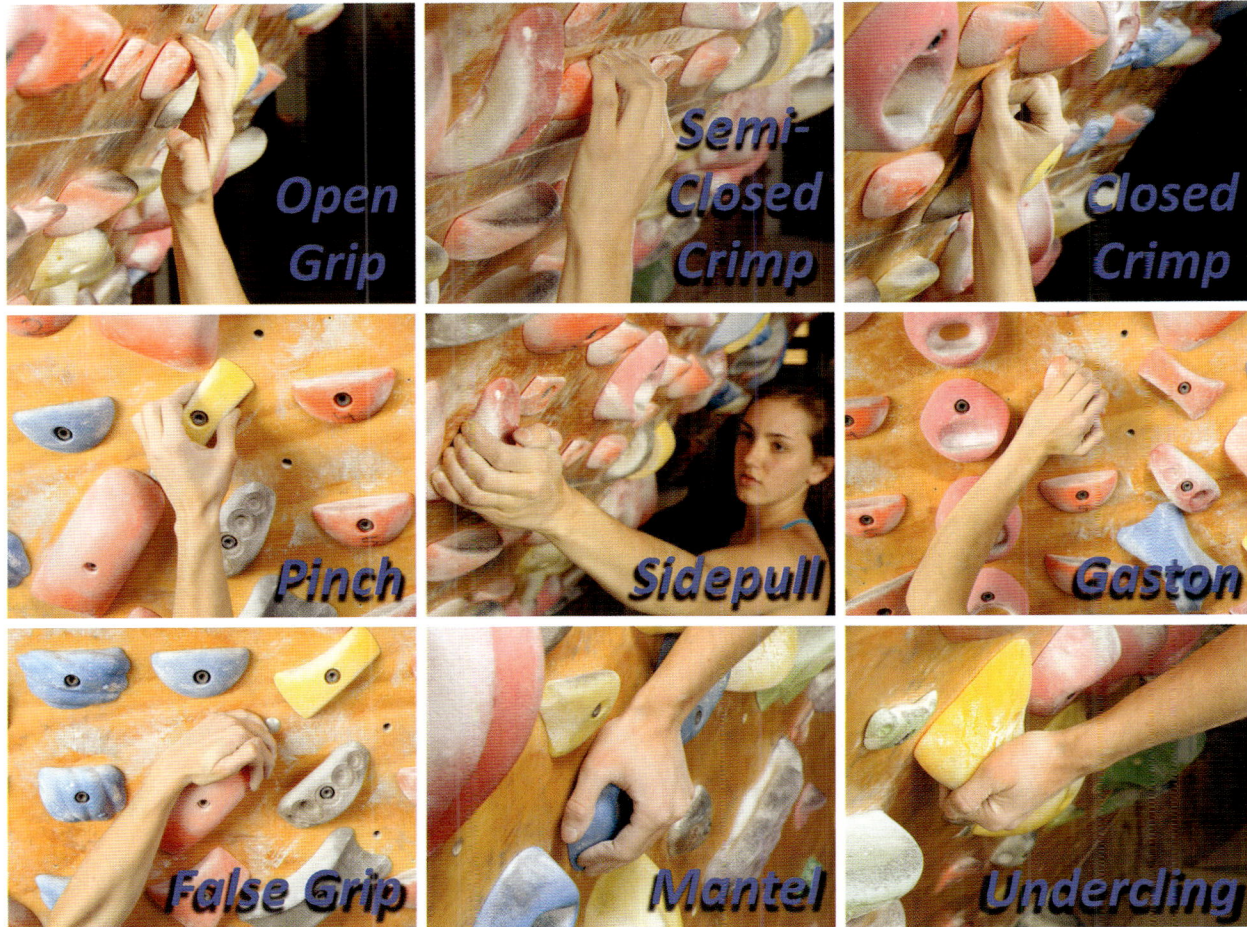

Open Grip · Semi-Closed Crimp · Closed Crimp · Pinch · Sidepull · Gaston · False Grip · Mantel · Undercling

best grip a sloper. Often large slopers will have irregularities on their surface that can be exploited for additional staying power. Align these irregularities with a finger-pad or skin ripple.

PINCHES

Most pinches vary in depth and width to some degree. Pinch strength typically varies depending on the width of the pinch involved, so experiment with different grip points. Look for irregularities in the surface of the hold, where extra friction can be utilized, or areas that are more positive, and thus allow for more outward pull. Occasionally, altering body positions can transform a desperate pinch hold into a more favorable sidepull, sloper, or gaston, so consider the alternatives to pinching.

THUMBS

After the head, thumbs are perhaps the appendage most underutilized by climbers. Nearly every hold offers a thumb catch (not that a thumb catch should always be used, but it should at least be considered). Thumbs can also wrap over the side or corner of an edge, or protruding knobs near edges, pockets, or slopers. Thumbs can be used to gaston vertical edges or pockets that are too distant for a traditional gaston, or to undercling ("gasto-cling") distant overlaps.

Finally, as discussed in the footwork section, most modern gyms are not intended to realistically represent outdoor climbing. Gyms have a disproportionate amount of slopers and pinches, so be mindful of the type of holds chosen to train and practice on. Ideally, these holds would mimic the type of holds found on performance objectives. A few hold manufacturers still make irregularly shaped plastic holds, so consider finding such grips, to practice quick identification and selection of ideal hand positions. If all this hand-placement discussion sounds like nonsense, consider that elite competition climbers memorize artificial holds from the top manufacturers in order to quickly identify them from the ground, thus ensuring optimal hand placement upon initial contact. Paying attention to every weakness the rock has to offer and learning how best to exploit them can spell the difference between success and failure.

Tips for Better Handwork

- Experiment with various grip positions to find the right fit
- Use the deepest and/or most positive aspects of edges and pinches
- Consider injury risks when evaluating the best use of pockets
- Slopers are rarely uniform; identify the spots that are more positive or offer better friction
- Consider using pinches as sidepulls or gastons
- Get the thumbs involved with catches, wraps, and distant "gasto-clings"

Thumbs can be employed to exploit distant features, such as to gaston vertical edges and pockets, or to undercling distant overlaps. Zak Roper sticking a dynamic "thumb-er-cling" on his project at the New River Gorge. Dan Brayack

physical location of stimulation in the body, but also to the *method* of training, including exercise intensity, duration, range of motion, and rest periods. For example, performing pull-ups will have a greater effect on the climber's ability to perform more pull-ups, and less effect on their ability to perform a lock-off (and vice versa). This sweeping principle will be referenced repeatedly in the chapters that follow, as it affects many aspects of training and is of vital importance to climbers. Climbing terrain offers infinite variation, giving climbers ample opportunity to train in ways that are NOT specific to their goals. Therefore, astute climbers will select training activities and terrain wisely to ensure the physical adaptations achieved are specific (or relevant) to their climbing aspirations.

OVERLOAD

Training stress must exceed the body's baseline capability in order to stimulate physical adaptation. In other words, training activities must exceed the athlete's "comfort zone." The body is prepared to handle a level of stress that is typical for the activities it routinely performs. It is necessary to exceed

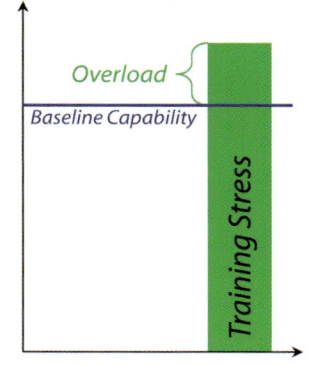

Overload is training stress that exceeds the athlete's baseline capability; it is essential to forcing adaptation.

that typical level of routine stress to cause improvement. A climber who performs 10 body-weight pull-ups every day would need to increase this training stress (by increasing the number of pull-ups, increasing the resistance, or a combination of the two) to foster improvement in pull-up ability. Overload is difficult to achieve without the ability to *quantify* (or measure) the training load. This is a significant problem for climbers, since many climbing activities are extremely difficult to quantify accurately.

RECOVERY

The act of training (particularly when overload is applied) actually makes the body weaker, causing *microtrauma* to the muscles and connective tissues trained. Each training event must be followed by a period of rest, allowing the body to repair damaged tissues and replenish energy supplies (see figure in next column). The initial period of rest allows the body to return to its baseline capability. If sufficient training stimulus has been applied, additional rest will permit the body

Erin Drasler on *Better Eat Your Wheaties*, V8, Hueco Tanks, TX
📷 Dan Brayack

to *adapt*, achieving an improved baseline capability slightly above the previous baseline. This process is known as *super-compensation*. Climbers are notorious for climbing too much and resting too little. Heed the wise words of the legendary "father of modern bouldering" John Gill:

"Be sure to have frequent rest days, and don't overstress those small tendons. Gain your strength gradually and safely."

REVERSIBILITY

Physical adaptations achieved through training are *reversible*, meaning they can be lost just as easily as they are gained. (Generally, the more difficult it is to achieve a physical adaptation, the longer it takes to lose it, and vice versa.) Once initial recovery and super-compensation periods are complete, further rest causes

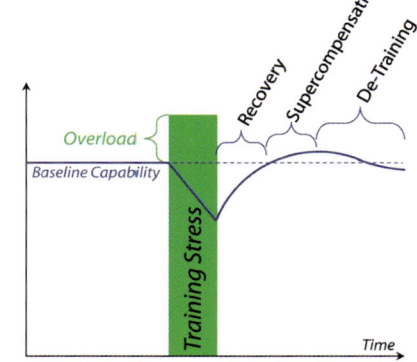

Super-compensation as a result of Overload and Recovery. Note: diagram not to scale.

DYNAMIC MOVEMENT

Other texts such as *The Self-Coached Climber* go into extensive detail on the topic of dynamic movement, so this discussion is limited to practical approaches for incorporating dynamic-movement practice into a periodic training routine. Mastering dynamic movement has tremendous advantages. Many climbers think dynos only apply to the most difficult crux moves, but with improved skills, dynos can have much broader application. Consider Basque climbing legend Josune Bereziartu (the first woman to climb 5.14b, 5.14c, and 5.14d), who has perfected her movement and confidence to the point that virtually every movement she makes is a deadpoint, thus sparing tremendous

Girl Power

I remember watching my husband, Mike, effortlessly float up and down the campus board, and I was quite sure that I would never be able to do such magic. Nevertheless, Mike insisted that I try it, and I relented. I remember grabbing the campus rungs the first time and staring straight up. What had I agreed to? I felt like a ton of bricks, and I struggled to let go of that first rung as my mind fought to maintain control. Mike took off some weight with a power spot, just enough that I could bump my right hand to the next rung. Then my left, followed by the right, and so on—all the way up the ladder I went. It was awesome! I was pretty sure Mike carried me to the top, but he insisted that he only helped a little. Campusing was possible; now it was on!

With each attempt, I grew stronger and more confident. I required less assistance each workout and made tangible progress both in training and on the rock. My movements became more precise and I gained the ability to "explode." Soon I was able to campus alone. More importantly, my climbing changed. My confidence skyrocketed, I could deadpoint much better, and my new "go for it" attitude made me more decisive and explosive. I used to waste a lot of time on routes hesitating, wasting precious energy. This hesitation allowed my mind to wander to negative self-talk, which was very harmful to my climbing.

Learning to make quick and decisive movements on the campus board brought me a new focus in climbing. Finally, I had unlocked new levels of confidence! A whole new world opened up, and climbing became much more fun.

— *Janelle Anderson*

amounts of energy throughout the course of a long ascent.

For many, climbing dynamically is a psychological challenge motivated by the reluctance to relinquish control on the rock. This manifests in a fear of letting go and a desire to remain static in every movement. The campus board (discussed in detail in Chapter Seven: Power) is arguably the best tonic for this condition, as dynoing is nearly impossible to avoid on a campus board. As with all skill development once a weakness has been identified, practice the new skill in a consequence-free environment, and gradually stress-proof the new technique. Establishing a safe landing zone is the first step to executing any dyno, so take the time to ensure a good distribution of crashpads, spotters, or a safe belay. Using a *power spot* (where the spotter assists the climber through a difficult move by pushing gently around the lower back) can be extremely helpful for timid dynamic climbers.

Many climbers struggle on dynamic moves because of a reluctance to relinquish control of their body. The Campus board is a great *practice* tool for overcoming such hesitation.

When executing difficult dynos, consider the role of the trailing hand as well as the moving hand. Aaron Parlier checks his swing on *Pocket Rocket*, V6, Joe's Valley, UT. ◉ Dan Brayack

ing hand, and the path of the hips throughout the dyno. Often the key to a difficult, foot-cutting dyno is controlling the swing of the body away from the wall. The trailing hand is the key to controlling this motion, so focus on pressing the lower hand into an effective mantel position as your center of mass rises. Extend the lower arm as the hips move away from the wall to allow consistent pressure on the lower hold, and practice slowly and gradually reducing the outward momentum, thus avoiding jerky decelerations. In addition, the forces applied through the feet (and the timing thereof) in the moments before they cut loose may be critical to controlling the swing, so consider their role as well.

REST TECHNIQUES

Resting is an essential skill, and it's a good idea to experiment with rests before one is desperately needed. In climbing, rests are used to alleviate the load on the forearm flexors allowing them to de-pump. Any body position that permits a relaxed grip can be a rest, and this provides a lot of possibilities, many of which will be described here. When first arriving at a rest, spend some time exploring the possibilities (various hand positions, hidden holds, thumb catches, scumming other body parts, etc.). Within the first minute or so, the climber should pick the best, most relaxing option and commit to it.

The campus board is also a valuable practice tool for more advanced dynoers, who will find it helpful for perfecting their deadpoint skills. The smooth rungs encourage a "go for it" mentality, and the ability to progressively increase the distance between holds allows climbers to methodically escalate the movement difficulty, making for ideal practice.

Bouldering is also an excellent platform for climbers of all abilities seeking to practice their dynamic skills, provided problems are set in a manner that mandates dynamic movement. Bouldering allows for much more complicated application of dynamic movement, requiring coordination across the entire body in multiple planes and axes of travel.

When executing a difficult dyno, most climbers focus on the moving hand, and the force and movement required by that hand to reach and latch the finishing hold. Yet you should also consider the forces and motion required to generate upward momentum from the lower body before the leading hand releases from the starting hold, consider the role of the trail-

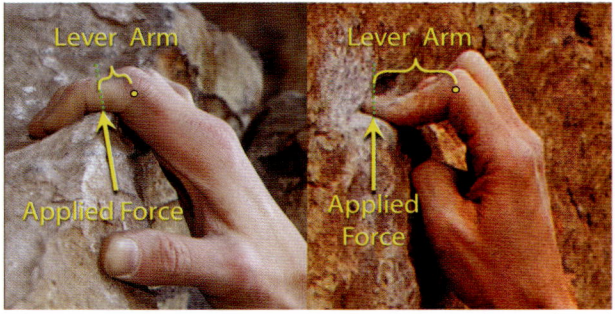

Positive "jug" holds make good rests because they provide a mechanical advantage. The supporting force of the rock is applied closer to the finger joints rather than the finger tips, which shortens the lever arm, and reduces the *moment* on the joint. This translates into a lower force that must be applied by the finger flexor muscles to hang onto the hold.

Continually groping around is less restful, and there is a learning curve that improves a singular resting position with practice; shifting around prevents this beneficial adaptation.

Practicing various rest positions in advance will make for quicker recognition of the optimal positions when climbing, improving the quality of recovery. Remember, the point of resting is to permit a relaxed grip so that the forearms can de-pump, and this does not happen automatically—it must be consciously directed. Once established in the rest, deliberately shift weight to the feet as much as possible, and then gradually loosen the grip of each hand as much as possible, carefully observing for slippage.

A large hold, or jug, is always a good rest. On steep terrain, a jug gives the climber an improved mechanical advantage by allowing him to apply force to the hold closer to the proximal joints of the fingers rather than the fingertips. This requires less force to be applied by the forearm flexors, permitting a relaxed grip. Thus, the best rest will be had by contacting the lip of the hold as close to the forearms as possible, which could mean hanging off the palm of the hand by bending the arm at the wrist. On very positive jugs, the protruding bone at the base of the hand (the *pisiform*) can be "hooked" over the lip or even slotted be-

An uncommon, but effective rest is to "stem" between a low foothold and high hand hold, such as the lip of an overhang.

On very positive jugs, the protruding bone at the base of the hand (the pisiform) can be "hooked" over the lip, or slotted behind deep flakes. ⭕ Mike Anderson

hind deep flakes. This simultaneously holds the body close to the rock and relieves the forearms, providing a great rest. On steep terrain, the climber should hang with straight arms and rotate the hips with a backstep to bring the center of mass closer to the rock, improving the direction of pull. For large holds on less-steep terrain, it may be more restful to mantel onto the hold and *stand* on it (while leaning into the wall), versus hanging off it by the arms.

Body parts can often be wedged into cracks or pockets, providing an excellent rest. Experienced crack climbers know this, and are always on the lookout for hand jams and fingerlocks during difficult sport climbs. For those who aren't crack climbers, seek instruction from an experienced crack master while experimenting with different jams close to the ground. The nuances of jamming are best learned through personal experimentation, and not during a difficult climb. The portions of the crack that form natural constrictions will offer the best jams, and the climber should seek to rest on his skeleton with a relaxed grip, not the finger-pads. Good jams can be painful, so pain (or lack thereof) is not a good indicator of a jam's quality. Athletic tape is often used to reduce pain and get the most out of a jam. Foot, knee, arm, and even head jams are possible, so cast a wide net. The time spent exploring the possibilities will not be in vain.

The legs are critical to any rest, by supporting whatever load is shed by the arms, but the legs and feet can be loaded in multiple unusual ways. Besides standing directly over them, the next most common use for the feet is the heel hook. It is best performed on a large, positive jug, but it doesn't have to be. Generally, the higher the hook, the greater the load it can bear. Heel-toe cams, calf hooks, or sideways slotted heel hooks are even better because these improve the mechanical advantage, allowing more weight transfer to the lower body. This is similar to the way a positive jug is less taxing for the forearms. A double-heel-hook "bat hang" looks impressive, but is often not very restful or worth the effort to get into.

Other leg rests include stems and kneebars. Stems are best used in corner systems, which allow the climber to lean in over the feet. Climbers should try to position their center of mass over the imaginary line formed between the two feet, or as near as possible. Sometimes this can be accomplished by crouch-

The "foot-squat" is an excellent rest that is possible with a protruding foothold or ledge on lower-angled terrain. The climber plants one foot on the protruding hold and squats down on it while flagging the other foot as low as possible to balance her center of mass over the high foot.

Mike Anderson

ing low and using backsteps or drop-knees to lower the center of mass. During a stem, the feet do not have to be level with each other, nor should stems be limited to the feet. It is often possible to stem with the feet on a low foothold and the hands pushing off the lip of an overhang, or use the heel of one hand opposed to the opposite foot. Here again, the goal is to get the center of mass hovered over the base of support formed between the feet and hand (or shoulder blade or head).

A kneebar is a type of jam utilizing the entire lower leg. Ankle flexion is necessary to adjust the size of the jam and apply the opposing pressure that locks it in place. The quality of the kneebar depends on the geometry of the rock and the climber. Generally, the best kneebars are a tight fit with a positive knee catch and foothold, and require little effort to maintain. Kneebars that don't fit tightly will require significant calf flexion and can be very strenuous. Kneebars with poor footholds or insecure knee catches will require more concentration and physical effort to maintain, and will also be less restful. A sticky-rubber kneepad improves the holding power between the rock and knee, and can improve an otherwise poor kneebar. They also improve the level of comfort.

Finally, a great rest position that is often overlooked is the foot-squat. This is used on less-steep terrain, or in a cave feature with a large foothold. The climber plants one foot on the hold, dangles the other foot lower than the first, and then squats down over the engaged foot as low as possible in an attempt to balance his center of mass over the foothold. In a cave or scoop, a hand can sometimes push off the lip of the cave to lock the climber in place. When this isn't possible, the lower dangling foot can be flagged (pressed into the wall), resisting gravity's pull on the climber away from the rock. With an adequate positive high foothold, this hooking action can provide a no-hands rest.

> "I feel that the best way to gain strength in training is to do it on plastic. But you must be aware that you need time to transfer the results of those workouts to natural rock."
> — Josune Bereziartu[2]

The Beta Trap

"Bachar reckoned he had got this trait from John Gill: never tell anyone how to do a problem. Let them figure it out, because it's part of the problem." — Jerry Moffat[9]

Discovering the solution to a puzzling sequence can be extremely satisfying, but these days it's very easy to bum the beta from a buddy or find it on YouTube rather than figure it out for yourself. Borrowing beta is most certainly the fastest way to dispatch a project, but it is a crutch that, if used too often, will develop into a significant weakness. It's possible to navigate a climbing career for some time by relying on borrowed beta, but eventually the beta well will dry up. Be it a difficult onsight, a first ascent, or simply a route off the beaten path, at some point every dedicated climber will face a confounding crux with only his wits to solve it. Furthermore, each climber has unique attributes: physical (height, wingspan, ape index, and finger size), psychological, and physiological (strength, power, endurance, flexibility, technique). Therefore, one climber's beta may not suit another. Don't make the crux harder than necessary by forcing a sequence that was developed by another climber.

Deciphering complex sequences is a skill that requires practice. It can also be great fun and extremely satisfying. Take the time to work out the beta on your own (most of the time) in order to ensure that this skill is available when you need it most. Once you *think* you have it worked out, you can still go to YouTube for a second opinion.

As John Bachar said, figuring out the beta is part of the problem—a part of what makes a problem hard, for sure, but also a part of what makes it fun and rewarding. Welcome the opportunity to discover your own solution from time to time, and don't be ashamed to feel that much more proud when you send.

Heel-toe cams, calf hooks, or sideways slotted heel hooks (shown here) make great rests because they transfwer more weight to the lower body. Rob Pizem taking it free and easy during the FFA of the *Wiggins Route* 5.12, UT. 📷 Andrew Burr

PROGRESSIVE PRACTICE

For optimum learning of any new skill, the practice activities should be repetitive and progressive, which is to say, the activities increase in difficulty as the proficiency increases. In terms of climbing, this progression can be accomplished by proceeding toward more real-world climbing situations, an environment inherently more challenging than the controlled arena of the initial skill-acquisition setting. In general, a progression toward realistic climbing scenarios can proceed as shown in the accompanying figure, with increasing difficulty arising from one of several sources: the activity type, intensity, climbing situation, audience, or various combinations thereof.

For example, a climber seeking more precise footwork begins with the Precision Feet drill performed as practice during low-intensity bouldering traverses. Over time, his footwork improves during these sessions, but it may not be evident in his climbing yet, so he includes this drill in indoor toproping sessions, both low and medium intensity. As his footwork improves in these domains, he includes the drill during power-endurance training sessions that are performed by bouldering in a gym. He may also include the drill during warm-up or non-limit climbing routes on rock. As he gains further proficiency, he includes the drill in indoor limit (high-intensity) bouldering sessions, or route-lapping endurance-training sessions outdoors.

These transitions from one combination of activities to another provide a logical transition that draws the newly acquired skills deeper into the climber's repertoire. These are incremental steps that are attainable and enable the climber to build on past success and familiarity with the skill. Over time, this process brings the skill up to a level of proficiency and familiarity where it could actually be used when it counts — on limit climbs on real rock.

To further illustrate this process, the training calendars presented in Chapter Ten: Building a Training Plan and Other Training Considerations include recommendations for planning practice, progressing from Skill Acquisition, to Skill Practice, and finally to Stress-Proofing. This demonstrates how practice activities can be premeditated and integrated into the physical training plan for a given season to create a progressive skill-development plan. As discussed in Chapter Two: Goal-Setting and Planning, at the beginning of each season, the climber should clearly identify a limited number of skill-development goals and plan how they will be reached, using the calendar as a template. It is best to focus on only a few key goals each season, so that adequate attention can be applied to each skill. Planning to work on "everything" guarantees that the climber will improve at nothing.

MOVEMENT DRILLS

Numerous movement drills are suggested below that may be incorporated into practice sessions. They are categorized according to aspects of climbing skill, and should be selected to address a specific skill or weakness. After identifying a technical weakness, select the appropriate drill. Don't try to accomplish too many drills in a given practice session—select no more than three emphasis areas for each session, and concentrate on those.

Drills should initially be performed on moderate terrain, with the primary goal of *learning*. Therefore, drilling climbers shouldn't feel pressure to send, only to learn effectively. Falling, or otherwise failing at a drill is a part of the learning process, and should be common. If possible, seek a quiet time for this practice (a quiet corner of the gym, or off-peak hours), away from distractions. For the best results, drills should be revisited, and as skills improve, the difficulty can be increased progressively as described above in Progressive Practice.

Skill development should be progressive, just like physical training, progressing toward realistic outdoor climbing along these four attributes.

General Climbing-Efficiency Drills

Beginner Drills

Name	Setting & Description	Feedback	Progression	Focus on…
Straight Arms Objective: Reduce reliance on upper body	While traversing an indoor circuit, attempt to keep the elbows virtually locked, by hanging with straight arms and a low center of gravity. Utilize flags, backsteps, and crosses to maintain straight arms while traversing across the wall.	Elbow bend. Also, note the amount of hip and leg movement needed to keep arms straight	Smaller holds, faster pace, and/or incorporate more vertical (up or down) movements in the circuit	Focus on adjusting foot and hip positioning to permit longer movements with minimal elbow flexion.

Intermediate Drills

Name	Setting & Description	Feedback	Progression	Focus on…
Rest Practice Objective: Experiment with novel rests	While traversing an indoor circuit or climbing an outdoor warm-up, seek and practice novel rest stances, especially "no-hands" or other easy stances involving stems, kneebars, drop-knees, jams, thumb wraps, etc.	Quality of forearm recovery, level of relaxation and calm, reductions in breathing and heart rate	Steeper terrain, more difficult terrain, more strenuous rests	Focus on quickly finding the best rest position, and then settling into it and progressively relaxing all muscles not needed for the rest. Slow your breathing and concentrate on relaxing the forearms.
Speed Climbing Objective: Increase climbing pace	While toproping a familiar route indoors or out, climb as fast as you can. Time yourself and try to improve each attempt. Mentally rehearse the route beforehand to speed yourself up. Efficiency is not critical, so go "all out." The goal is to extend your range of climbing pace so that you can climb faster when appropriate.	Ascent time, which can be compared with your partner's	More difficult terrain, and more technical routes	Focus on moving continuously. Don't analyze every move; just make a decision quickly and commit to it. The route should be easy enough that it isn't necessary to nail the sequence perfectly.

Advanced Drills

Name	Setting & Description	Feedback	Progression	Focus on…
Finding Calm Objective: Maintaining calm through strenuous moves	While ARC'ing (boulder or TR), plan a course that incorporates several dynamic moves. Consciously pause after each dyno to restart breathing with slow, deep breaths. Deliberately relax the grip, shift weight onto the feet, and if possible shake out.	Have a partner monitor your breathing and provide feedback	Incorporate with progressively more realistic climbing situations	Focus on your thoughts and feelings during and immediately after dynos or strenuous moves. Try to identify the moment that breathing stops or you tense up. Practice overcoming this response.
Movement Perfection Objective: Perfect a complex sequence	While bouldering indoors or outside, select a problem near your flash level and repeatedly climb the problem over several sessions, attempting to complete it as efficiently/effortlessly as possible. This drill can span seasons or years for some problems.	Partner's observation and personal evaluation of effort. Monitor for breathing and check for grunting.	Increase the difficulty of sequences/problems used, increase climbing pace	Focus on deadpointing dynamic moves, grip control, climbing with good "flow," maximizing lower-body contribution, and eliminating points of hesitation.
Momentum Climbing Objective: Develop a flowing, dynamic style	While toproping or bouldering on moderate terrain, attempt to climb the route in one continuous movement. Try to minimize any pause in motion. Use a well-known route, at first, and mentally rehearse the sequences before beginning. As you progress, attempt this drill on lesser-known routes.	Partner's observation and personal evaluation of effort required.	Steeper, more difficult terrain. Attempt this drill with higher states of fatigue or on lesser-known routes	Focus on propelling your ascent with your legs, using your arms mostly as "guides," as if you were hiking up a steep slope. Imagine yourself flowing like water or dancing a continuous choreography.

Lower-Body Involvement Drills

Beginner Drills

Name	Setting & Description	Feedback	Progression	Focus on...
Stutter Step Objective: Encourage many foot moves and reduce highstepping	While boulder traversing or toproping, the climber will make three foot movements for every one hand movement. Foot moves should be small and should allow the climber to fully weight his feet. If in a climbing gym, avoid pinching the handholds, which makes them unrealistically "positive."	Feeling of weighted feet, and initiating movements from the lower body	Steeper terrain, more difficult terrain, perform faster	Focus on keeping the COM close to the rock throughout the entirety of the movement. Initiate movement in the lower body by pressing with the toes, feet, and legs.
Thumbs Only Objective: Thumb use, and engaging the lower body	While toproping a moderate, just-under-vertical route, attempt to climb using only the thumbs (and feet). Use a well-featured route and make small foot movements. Attempt to maintain smooth, flowing movement, which requires significant effort and control from the lower body. This drill can also be done with "two fingers only."	Smooth movement	Steeper terrain, longer reaches between holds (above the shoulders), faster climbing pace	Focus on adjusting body position to maximize lower body contribution (moving hips side-to-side to distribute weight over footholds). Note how the distribution evolves through each move.

Intermediate Drills

Name	Setting & Description	Feedback	Progression	Focus on...
Downclimbing Objective: Overcome the hand bias	On any terrain, indoors or out, climb down in addition to climbing up. Deliberately select footholds, guide your feet to them, and don't look away until they "land." Balance your body before moving the leading foot, and avoid large foot movements.	Feel the pressure placed on the footholds and how your lower body supports your weight	Steeper terrain, more difficult routes	Focus on maximizing weight on your feet and relaxing your grip accordingly. Your focus on footholds should be increased, but also ensure that you are weighting them fully.

Advanced Drills

Name	Setting & Description	Feedback	Progression	Focus on...
Toeing Hard Objective: Maximizing weight on feet	On moderate terrain, attempt long reaches while concentrating on maximizing foot force throughout. The mind will try to focus exclusively on guiding the reaching hand, but also focus on the opposing foot, which drives the movement. Simultaneously guiding hands and feet in different tasks is difficult but critical.	Feeling of foot pressure through the move	Use longer reaches and dynos, less-positive feet, steeper terrain, and target handholds that require more focus to hit (i.e., pockets)	Focus on maintaining steady force on the footholds throughout the move. As the handhold nears, it will distract you, but stay focused on the feet.
Pulling Feet Objective: Improve efficiency on steep terrain	While toproping on steep terrain with positive footholds, deliberately pull with your feet to keep your COM close to the wall. Make careful toe placements in the incut part of the hold, like fingers for max pulling power. Experiment with pulling and pushing in unison. Try it on a traverse as well, pulling with the leading foot.	Feeling of foot pressure through the move	Use less-positive footholds to increase the complexity of required force application	Focus on applying the foot force in the best possible direction (not necessarily straight down) to hold yourself close to the wall. Feel the force applied by the foot and how its direction evolves as you move.

Target Campusing is an advanced drill for developing dynamic accuracy. Here the climber has marked out a "target" for his left hand and is campusing to it.

The Foot Stab Drill is a straight-forward way to practice precise foot movements. Simply pick a target on the wall and practice touching it with your toe.

The Pulling Feet Drill promotes keeping your COM close to the wall on steep terrain by pulling in on positive footholds.

Footwork Drills

Beginner Drills

Name	Setting & Description	Feedback	Progression	Focus on...
Precision Feet Objective: Precise Footwork	While boulder traversing or toproping, make careful and precise foot placements. Select the bull's-eye on each foothold deliberately, and don't look away until your foot has reached the target. Take your time initially, then speed up as you gain proficiency. Sound provides immediate feedback, but toe accuracy is the ultimate goal, so focus on that.	Sound and feel can indicate precision; have a "referee" ensure you don't look away too soon.	Combine with Blinking Drill, training exercises (PE, Limit Bouldering)	Focus on controlling the movement of the foot toward the hold; bull's-eye on the first shot. Maintain concentration until each foot is placed correctly. Don't think ahead to the next move before completing the current move.
Foot Stab Objective: Improve foot coordination	While standing near any wall with distinguishable features (not while climbing), stand on one leg, then pick out precise "targets" on the wall to aim for and touch with the toe of the free leg. Can be performed statically or dynamically.	Precise placement of toe on target; balance	Smaller targets, more distant, off-balance points. Perform from a hanging position, while climbing, and/or attempt "foot dynos"	Focus on accuracy, maintaining balance throughout the rep, moving decisively, and focusing the eyes on the target prior to movement.

Intermediate Drills

Name	Setting & Description	Feedback	Progression	Focus on...
Blinking Drill Objective: Develop proprioceptive foot control	While bouldering or toproping, visually identify the desired foothold, memorize its spatial location, and then close your eyes while guiding your foot to the hold, making any necessary adjustments by feel. Open your eyes to assess your performance, spot the next hold, and so on. Can also be performed with hand movements.	Toe feel and visual assessment of placement	Perform faster, move the hips simultaneously with foot movements	Focus on visualizing the location of the foothold, how it feels to gain the hold, and assessing the quality of a foothold and foot placement by feel.
Jibs Only Objective: Practice using rock-like footholds	While bouldering or toproping indoors, restrict footholds to only screw-on holds (aka "jibs"), smears, molded features, or empty bolt holes (divots or ripples on larger holds can also be used).	Toe feel and strain on arms	Steeper terrain, more difficult terrain, faster climbing pace, smaller footholds, polished footholds	Focus on applying as much weight as possible to small footholds, despite any natural reluctance to trust them. Experiment with relaxing the hand's grip until the point of slipping, and then note where that point is.

Advanced Drills

Name	Setting & Description	Feedback	Progression	Focus on...
Glue Feet Objective: Reducing foot slips	On any climbing terrain, climb as though your toes become "frozen" to the wall as soon as they land on the foothold (no pivoting, rotating, or sliding allowed). As you move past the hold, flex at the ankle and forefoot to avoid pivoting on the hold.	Have a partner observe and correct you. Note the "feel" of a properly "glued" foot	Slopier footholds, longer movements, and traversing moves will all increase the difficulty	Focus on establishing a wide contact area between the shoe and hold, and try to maintain that contact area throughout the hold's use. Doing so maximizes holding power and prevents slips.

Dynamic Movement Drills

Beginner Drills

Name	Setting & Description	Feedback	Progression	Focus on...
Two Points of Contact Objective: Climb more dynamically	While climbing on any terrain, remove one foot from the wall (let it dangle) before and during every hand movement. This will ensure you keep only two points of contact (at most) with the rock, and will force a more-dynamic climbing style. It is permissible to have both feet on the wall, just not while reaching with a hand.	Have a partner "referee" this drill	Performing this drill on more-technical and less-steep routes will be more difficult	Focus on selecting footholds that allow smooth, flowing movement. Note how various foothold locations change the body's motion during hand reaches.
One-Arm Traverse Objective: Climb more dynamically	While boulder-traversing on not-so-steep terrain with plenty of holds, climb with only one arm. After completing the traverse, try it again with the other arm. Use big holds, as this drill can be very pumpy.	Observe the effects of dynoing to various hold locations relative to the feet	Steeper terrain, longer reaches, combine with other drills	Focus on involving your entire body in the dyno, not just stabbing your hand to the next hold while your COM stands still. Your body should be moving toward the next static position as the hand is moving.

Intermediate Drills

Name	Setting & Description	Feedback	Progression	Focus on...
Blind Dynos Objective: Proprioceptive movement skills	While bouldering, select a group of handholds that allow you to repeatedly dyno back and forth without moving your feet. Practice these dynos several times, then try it with your eyes closed, using proprioceptive awareness to guide your hands to the hold.	Latching the dynos; note how well you remember the holds' locations and paint a picture in your mind	Increase distance and steepness. Dynos that require hip and COM movement are much harder. Combine with other dyno drills.	Focus on remaining relaxed throughout the movement (which can be somewhat frightening). This drill improves your ability to grab holds without deliberate guidance, enabling faster climbing.
Pocket Dynos Objective: Improve dyno accuracy	On a gym or home wall, set some simple boulder problems that require dynos to tight pockets (may be one-, two-, three-, or four-finger pockets). Rehearse the dynos several times in a session, and perform the drill frequently to develop accuracy.	Catching the hold	Increase the length of the dyno and/or wall steepness. Longer dynos that require the hips and COM to move are much more difficult	Focus on deliberately guiding your fingers into the pocket opening, and hitting it at the deadpoint. Observe the contributions from the other limbs in controlling your movement into the pocket.

Advanced Drills

Name	Setting & Description	Feedback	Progression	Focus on...
Target Campusing Objective: Improve dyno accuracy	On a campus board, use masking tape (or a tick mark) to create "targets" on specified rungs (place the tape on either side of the aim point to create a "virtual pocket"). While campusing, try to hit the targets.	Hitting the target; have a "referee" ensure you don't look away before hitting the target	Reduce the target size, and/or campus farther. Replace the tape boundaries with a dowel or pencil to raise the stakes	Focus on deliberately guiding your fingers to the target and watch your hand land on the hold. This drill will require more body control than a typical campus workout, and can be quite difficult as the gaps increase.
Deadpoints Objective: Improve deadpoint skills	On a gym or home wall, set boulder-problem dynos with non-positive target holds (slopers, pinches). Latching these holds will require precise deadpoints. Rehearse the dynos repeatedly. An entire route or traverse can be constructed with such moves.	The climber and a partner can observe the overshoot, and how far the COM falls before settling on the hold	Increase distance and steepness, and use less-positive target holds. Dynos that require hip and COM movement are much harder.	Focus on initiating the dyno from the lower body while employing the minimum amount of force to not overshoot (such lower-body control is difficult to execute). Use the trailing hand to control the flight.

SUMMARY

- Rock climbing is among the most technical, skill-dependent sports, yet as beginners, climbers often receive little and/or poor instruction in climbing movement technique. As a result climbers often develop bad habits, requiring extra effort to overwrite them with good habits.
- Apply the *Good Habits for Efficient Skill Development* to daily training and practice sessions. Deliberate practice is the best way to acquire new skills and perfect existing ones.
- Climbers should strive to maximize their time spent *moving over rock*, which often means spending more time on less-difficult terrain, whether training or on goal routes, indoors or outdoors.
- Modern climbing gyms are a wonderful development, but certain of their characteristics encourage sloppy footwork. Use the recommended footwork policies and practice drills to overcome these biases.
- Handwork is an essential skill to getting the most out of a climber's fitness. Experiment with each grip position to find the best fit for a given hold.
- Dynamic movement often makes climbing more efficient, and is a must on some crux moves. The campus board is a great tool for overcoming inhibitions to dynoing.
- Resting is another oft-overlooked skill that is critical to route-climbing success. Be creative, and practice novel rest techniques well before they are needed on redpoint.
- Just like physical training, skill development should be progressive. Several aspects of movement practice can be adjusted to increase the relative difficulty of a particular drill. Use these "controls" to progress the practice toward realistic climbing scenarios.

METOLIUS ✱ TRAINING

FOUNDATIONS OF PHYSICAL TRAINING

Alex Honnold drinking in *Orange Crush*, 5.13b, Little Cottonwood Canyon, UT   Andrew Burr

CHAPTER 4

"I was so interested in the theory of training that I used to translate different articles about training from French and English as well. But of course at the beginning it was pretty instinctive. I tried to transfer training methods from other individual sports or programs to climbing."

— *Josune Bereziartu*[12]

INTRODUCTION

Ultimately, climbing is a physical act. Mental exercises like meditation and rehearsal, while important, will only take a climber so far. Eventually the hands and feet grasp stone, and the vertical dance begins. This dance requires strength to resist the pull of gravity, power to move dynamically, and endurance to overcome fatigue. Every climber on the path to continuous improvement will inevitably reach the point at which these physical attributes become a limiting factor.

Part II: Physical Training will discuss detailed, recommended approaches for improving each of these attributes, as well as the physiological basis for these recommendations. This chapter will explain basic training principles for athletes and how they can be applied to climbing training, as well as the framework for organizing the training methods that follow. The methods described will allow any climber to begin the process of achieving her potential.

PRINCIPLES OF EFFECTIVE PHYSICAL TRAINING

As detailed in Chapter 1: Introduction, *training* is defined as a systematic, disciplined, science-based approach to improving climbing performance. Athletes, coaches, and scientists have studied various training approaches for more than a century. Experience and experimentation have produced a number of principles that apply broadly to nearly every successful

Author's Note on Physiology

Each of the chapters in Part II: Physical Training includes extensive discussions on human physiology. It is our belief that a solid understanding of *why* a particular exercise is used can be very helpful to many athletes, because such knowledge builds confidence in the training program and encourages the athlete to commit to it. Just as a climber would be leery of committing to a long runout on bad rock if he thought he was off-route, it can be difficult to commit to a training program when you doubt its efficacy.

On the other hand, many athletes are willing to "buy in" without exhaustive explanations. These athletes may find the discussions on physiology tedious, excessive, or downright boring (while a small minority may even find them lacking in sufficient detail). It is not necessary to follow (or even read) the sections on muscle physiology. If you find yourself disinterested, feel free to use the "Quick-Start Guide to the Rock Prodigy Training Program" at the end of Chapter 1: Introduction to skip ahead to the juicy training details. The physiology will still be there waiting if you have questions down the road.

method of physical training. Training programs developed with these principles in mind stand the best chance of producing good results come performance time. Note that most of these principles apply to skill development as well as to physical training.

SPECIFICITY

An athlete will primarily achieve physical adaptations in the systems that are stimulated by the training activity. For example, performing bicep curls with the left arm will increase strength in the left bicep, but not in the right bicep. This principle applies not only to the

the body to weaken gradually. If an athlete becomes sedentary for an extended period of time, the body will revert back to untrained levels of fitness. This is known as *de-training*. While de-training should be avoided generally, there are some advantages. For example, the only way to convert "slow-twitch" muscle fibers to "fast-twitch" is through de-training, an important consideration for power athletes like boulderers (more on this to come).

REGULARITY

Training must be performed repeatedly at reasonable time intervals. While a single training session may cause some short-term improvements, those improvements will soon recede (see "Reversibility," above). The ideal training frequency depends on many factors, including the training activity performed, the capacity of the athlete, and the desired adaptation. Low-intensity activities may be performed daily (or even two or three times a day in the case of elite endurance athletes), while higher-intensity activities (such as high-resistance weightlifting) may be performed as infrequently as once every three or four days. Climbers who wish to improve continuously must climb or train multiple times per week, at regular intervals, regardless of their goals or experience. *Simply climbing on the weekends is not sufficient.*

PROGRESSION

Training stress must gradually increase over the course of the training program. This principle is essentially the coordinated application of the overload and regularity principles (see figure below). Assuming adequate recovery, overloading the body will cause a slightly improved baseline capability, so training stress must be increased by a slight increment to overload the body during the next training event(s). Performing 10 pull-ups every other day will only train the body to maintain the ability to perform 10 pull-ups. On the other hand, regularly applied *progressive* overload

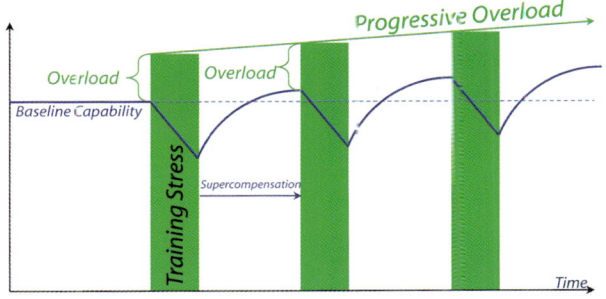

Progression as a result of correct application of Overload, Recovery, and Regularity. Note: diagram not to scale.

will gradually improve the body's capabilities over the previous baseline level. This approach can be repeated many times over to achieve significant improvements over time. Climbing grades provide a convenient way to track this progression, so it may seem logical to simply attempt harder and harder routes as a means to force improvement. However, "grade chasing" is an inefficient way to pursue continuous improvement in the long run. For that, one needs a structured training program.

VARIATION

It would be nice if athletes merely had to apply the above principles indefinitely to achieve infinite improvement. Unfortunately, the body will eventually become resistant to the same, repeated training stimulus, resulting in the dreaded performance plateau. For this reason, athletes must vary training activities periodically in order to stimulate further physical adaptation. This principle has been distorted somewhat (by recent training fads touting "muscle confusion") to suggest that athletes should never perform the same activity more than once. In reality, an athlete can progressively perform a given training activity for many consecutive weeks before improvement stagnates; in fact, doing so is the best way to ensure the principles of overload and progression are achieved. Furthermore, training should be varied to avoid mental fatigue (boredom) that ultimately results in declining motivation. Climbers often apply this intuitive principle by varying the style of climbing to follow the seasons (from bouldering to sport climbing, and to trad, multipitch, and ice climbing).

INDIVIDUALIZATION

Every person is different, so every body (and everybody) will respond differently to training. Therefore, a training program that works wonders for one athlete may be harmful to another. Each training program should be tailored to the individual athlete. Unfortunately, effective tailoring requires an observant and skilled coach or extensive personal experience. To apply this principle, most novice athletes should begin with a basic training program that applies broadly to many athletes (such as the Rock Prodigy program presented in the following chapters), and then make subtle changes over time as their experience and knowledge grow. The challenge of personalizing a *climbing* training plan is further complicated since goals (and the capabilities needed to achieve them) can vary dramatically between climbers, or even between seasons for the same climber. Even identical twins may need to individualize their training routines significantly if they are pursuing different climbing goals. As experience and ability grow, it will eventually be incumbent upon each climber to tailor the program provided in the following chapters to his or her specific goals.

TRANSFER

Train in a manner that replicates the conditions of performance to the greatest extent possible. This principle is similar to specificity, which is particular to physical adaptions within the body. Transfer, on the other hand, refers primarily to external performance factors such as time of day, environmental conditions, audience, etc. For example, climbers should train at the same temperature that they intend to perform at. While these factors may seem trivial, they are not. For example, studies have demonstrated significant improvements when the performance occurs at the same time of day as the preceding training sessions[4]. Often climbers have little control over the external conditions surrounding an important performance, so they should instead adjust the training conditions to ensure the best transfer.

CONTRIBUTING FACTORS

In addition to the nine general Principles of Effective Physical Training, the following factors contribute significantly to the successful execution of any training program:

QUANTIFICATION

The ability to measure or *quantify* training stress is critical to the principles of overload and progression. It is extremely difficult to ensure that the applied training stress exceeds baseline capabilities if the baseline capability cannot be defined, or the increment of *additional* stress (to achieve overload) cannot be measured. The same problem applies to the principle of progression. Often climbers attempt to overcome this problem through "feel" and intuition, but these methods are too easily sabotaged by the mind. An improved approach is to utilize training tools that allow climbers to precisely quantify (and therefore control) the training stress applied.

DOCUMENTATION

Related to quantification, collecting data on one's training and performance activities, recording that data, and analyzing it for future use is essential to the principles of overload and progression, as well as to recovery, regularity, variation, individualization, and transfer. While developing an initial training plan

can be overwhelming, once it's documented, creating future plans becomes much easier. Climbers who record their response to specific exercises can easily make slight adjustments to ensuing training plans, to approach ideal training exercises, frequencies, and loads. The training log sheets provided in the back of the book should simplify this process.

INTENSITY

Two primary parameters are used to measure training stress: *intensity* and *duration*. Intensity is the level of effort that must be applied to complete a given exercise. For some exercises, intensity is easily quantified in terms of the resistance used (for example, the load applied during a lifting exercise—weightlifters often track intensity as a percentage of "one-rep-maximum"). For other exercises, intensity cannot be easily quantified, but it can be qualitatively estimated. In other words, a subjective evaluation can be made of *how hard* an individual repetition *feels*, and that estimate of intensity can be documented. While this method is not perfect, each climber should at least be able to roughly define and track the intensity of a

In the case of weighted dead hangs, intensity is simply the quantity of weight applied (body weight, plus any weight added, or minus any weight removed). 📷 Fred Marmsater

given training activity relative to other types of training, as well as the relative intensity of a given workout compared to past workouts of the same type. A good rule of thumb for climbers is, the harder one must pull on the holds in question, the more *intense* the movement. Training must be performed at the proper intensity in order to achieve the desired adaptation; more intensity is not always better! The following chapters will prescribe the proper intensity for the exercises presented.

DURATION

This is quite simply a quantitative measure of the time required to complete a training activity, and can apply to specific repetitions or to entire sets of repetitions. The principle of specificity suggests that climbers should pay special attention to the duration of exercises when training, in order to achieve the desired adaptations and meet their goals. Factors that will determine the specific adaptation to training include the total time required to complete a training activity, as well as the *Time-Under-Tension* (TUT), which is essentially the amount of time actually spent hanging from holds (for example, if a climber spends two minutes hanging from a jug rest, shaking hands in alternating fashion, each hand may only grasp the hold for 60 seconds or so TUT). In addition, since climbing performances are usually not time defined, tracking the number of movements (or vertical feet ascended) is also beneficial.

VOLUME

This measure is the product of intensity and duration. When tracking overload, progression, regularity, and recovery, *volume* is the most relevant metric. An increase in either the intensity *or* duration of a training activity will increase volume. Simultaneously increasing intensity *and* duration exponentially increases volume. In other words, doubling the intensity and duration results in *quadrupled* volume. Volume must be tracked carefully, and steadily increased to achieve appropriate progression throughout a training program.

ISOLATION

Muscles and their supporting structures can be trained most effectively when the principles of overload and progression are applied directly and individually to the component parts. This is because complex movements, requiring the use of many muscle groups, are limited by the weakest component required to complete the movement, so the exercise often ends well before the strongest muscles involved are overloaded. Isolation, on the other hand, allows the athlete to specifically target and improve each link (weak *and* strong). A relevant counterexample is the fingertip pull-up. Which muscles are trained to the point of overload? The latissimus dorsi, biceps, or finger flexors could be the weak link, and it is very unlikely that all three muscle groups reach overload at the same intensity and duration. Instead, it is better to isolate the finger flexors with "dead hangs" on the fingertip edge, isolate the lats with pull-ups on a bar, and isolate the biceps with dumbbell curls.

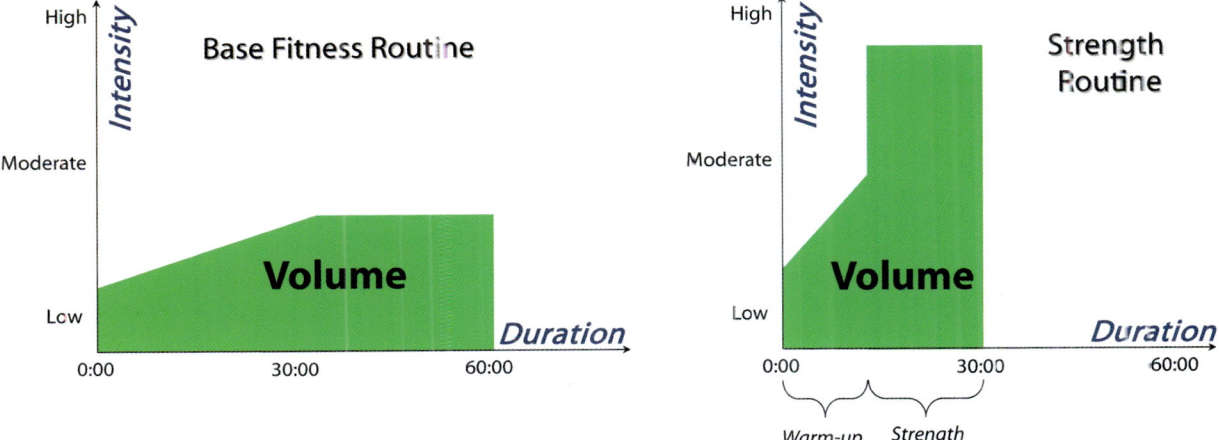

Volume is the "area under the curve" plotting intensity vs. duration. Two different examples are shown. The chart on the left describes a Base-Fitness Phase exercise, beginning with a low-intensity warm-up that gradually increases in intensity. Once the target training intensity is achieved, it is sustained while duration continues to increase. The chart on the right describes a Strength Phase exercise, beginning with a warm-up activity. While the strength routine lasts half as long, the total volume is identical to that of the much longer endurance routine.

Isolation vs. Complex Movements

Yet another in the unending parade of fitness fads is the preference for "complex movements" in strength training. The reasons for this are primarily that, first, complex movements are more specific to the way athletes perform in competition (running, jumping, etc.), and second, complex movements require the use of many muscle groups, thus creating high levels of "metabolic stress" (a key stimulator of muscle growth). However, much of this new obsession is fueled by the "bigger, faster, stronger" mentality valued by those training for team sports. Football players are keen to add mass in addition to strength, so anything that stimulates lots of muscle growth is championed.

Climbing, on the other hand, is all about strength-to-weight ratio. Remaining light is every bit as important as getting stronger. The ability to isolate specific muscle groups (those most critical to climbing performance) allows climbers to achieve overload precisely where it is desired, and limit growth where it may be harmful. As for metabolic stress, climbers easily achieve high metabolic stress where it is wanted—in the forearm muscles—without the use of complex movements. Also, the infinite variability of climbing terrain makes it essential that each link in the chain (including the strong links) is trained as effectively as possible. One move may involve a short reach from a tiny edge, where finger strength is the limiting factor. The next move may be a huge span from an enormous jug, where lock-off strength is emphasized. Training muscle groups individually ensures that each strength is at its best when it comes time to perform on the stone.

HOW TO TRAIN

Not everybody knows *how* to train. *It is one thing to follow a program with step-by-step instructions, but it is another to perform the activities in a manner that gets results. Even the best training program will fail if it is not implemented correctly.* Simply going through the motions, utilizing intensity levels that aren't challenging, or failing to face weaknesses is a waste of time. Owing to the principle of individualization, athletic training requires a certain amount of subjectivity. Each athlete must gauge for himself the relative intensity of his work output, and make adjustments to apply the desired training stress. Successful training requires constant excursions beyond the comfort zone, a good deal of temporary suffering, and large quantities of hard work.

> "I think it's desire that gets results. People are often unwilling to acknowledge or give credit to hard work, seeming to prefer talent, even if it's wasted." — Jerry Moffatt[6]

HARD WORK

Effective training requires hard work, and lots of it. This often comes in the form of dedication to a some-times-monotonous schedule, perseverance in the face of physical discomfort, and discipline to follow through despite ephemeral inconveniences like an early wake-up time or unpleasant training conditions.

Hard work is an essential part of every effective training program.
Dan Brayack

A penchant for hard work is not a character trait one is born with; it must instead be learned. Climbers with general athletic backgrounds are often at an advantage in this area, having learned how to work hard in a controlled environment, under the supervision of experienced motivators. A good coach, inspiring teammates, and healthy competition are good tools for developing a solid work ethic. These things are harder to come by in the sport of climbing, but the same basic approaches can be applied. Identify other climbers who perform at a high level and observe their work habits. While there are many paths to climbing success, they all involve hard work, and the best climbers all know how to work hard. Some may feign disinterest, but they all apply tremendous effort at the moment of truth.

Discomfort is a common barrier to hard work. Usually, hard work is unpleasant (in fact, any of the seven dwarfs still able to whistle could probably work a little bit harder). In addition to the obvious aversion to pain and suffering that tempts climbers to give less than their best, athletes are also encouraged to "listen to their body" or "back off at the first sign of injury." These pieces of advice, while fundamental and neces-

sary, create a murky line that athletes are reluctant to cross for fear of injury or wasted effort. The solution to this conundrum is for each athlete to incrementally push ever so slightly beyond her comfort zone, monitor the effects, and then analyze the results. If all goes well, the athlete can push that much further beyond her previous limits the next time around. Though it may sound complicated, this is relatively straightforward to do with diligent application of the previously discussed training principles and contributing factors. This methodical approach to progressive overload is the essence of this training program.

> "I can definitely be a work-aholic in certain ways. People who aren't climbers a lot of times look at me and they're like 'you just play all the time for your job' but I think if anybody were to really be able to experience exactly what I do, they'd be able to see that you have to get serious about it, and you have to be obsessive, and you have to really work hard."
> — Tommy Caldwell[13]

Too Hard or Not Hard Enough?

As discussed above, the intensity of a given training activity will determine how much effort must be applied, or how "hard" you must try to complete a repetition. You may already be performing the perfect training activity, but if the intensity is wrong, you won't get the proper results. Effort levels vary greatly between climbers, and many just plain don't know how much effort to apply, often because they don't realize how much they are truly capable of.

Of course, there is potential for exercises to be too intense, especially when recovering from injury, but the opposite problem is far more common, particularly among those who have little experience with organized sports. If you've never really pushed your body to the limit, you will have trouble knowing just how much effort to put into a workout. Not all discomfort is bad, and it's worth the sacrifice for each climber to discover the difference between good pain and bad. Here are some ways to help achieve the best possible training intensity:

- Prepare for important training days as you would for high-stakes performance days (like the last day of a road trip). Get proper sleep, visualize the activity in advance, and use a reliable routine to "get psyched" for the activity. This will get you in the proper mindset to apply the best possible effort to the training routine.
- Document the results of each workout, then use those records to create a "virtual training partner" in the future. Competition can bring out the best in everyone. Try to outdo your training partner each workout.
- Adjust your training intensity upward to the point that it becomes at least slightly unpleasant. Obviously, if every moment of every workout is miserable, the program will be unsustainable, but at key moments—like the last few repetitions of each exercise—things should feel uncomfortable. Sharp pains or chronic aches that persist many hours after exercise are not "good pain," though feelings of nausea, slight dizziness, or fleeting muscle aches are symptoms of extraordinarily good effort, and should be sought from time to time.

Motivation and Effort

I went to school at the Air Force Academy, so I spent four years immersed in a process that takes people from across America and demands intense levels of hard work out of them. For those of us who had competitive sporting backgrounds, the physical training (PT) was tough but familiar. For those who didn't, the PT was *life changing*. They learned that the body is capable of much more than the mind wants to allow. While they certainly had exercised before, they always backed off at the onset of discomfort. Though this "breaking-in" process is often portrayed by Hollywood as cruel and demeaning, it isn't in real life (at least not these days). While yelling still occurs, the motivation is positive, based primarily in a strong sense of team (and competition with peer units), cultivating a desire to perform on behalf of your teammates and not let them down. This environment of intense competition and encouragement from comrades creates high arousal, and never-before-seen levels of effort. Many "average Joes" learn that they can put out a lot more than they realized. The military's generations-old method has awakened the potential and confidence of millions of soldiers over the years.

While these methods are impractical for every workout, once a person experiences his true capabilities a few times, he will be able to recall that level of effort at will. As climbers, we rely on inspiration and motivation to push past these mental barriers, but these may not be enough for an aspiring athlete with limited sports experience. If this sounds like you, and enlisting in the military isn't already on your "to-do" list, consider enrolling in a "boot camp"-style exercise class at a local health club, or try a few sessions of CrossFit to experience the power of external motivation.

— *Mike Anderson*

FOCUS

Mindlessly going through the motions of a training program will not produce the desired outcome. An athlete must be "present," living in the moment and keenly motivated to apply the best effort to every repetition, set, and exercise as often as possible. To do this requires a high degree of focus, applied on a daily basis. It's often easy for climbers to "get psyched" for a hard onsight or redpoint attempt, because the rewards are tangible and close at hand. This same mentality must be applied to daily training activities to achieve the best results. Each day in the gym is an-

Difficult climbing requires focus. Sonnie Trotter in the zone on *Iconoclast*, 5.13a, Joshua Tree, CA.   Andrew Burr

other opportunity to get better. What will be done with that opportunity? Will it be squandered in favor of a few moments of forgettable conversation about the weather?

With training cycles that last for months, often involving several weeks of training on plastic, maintaining this focus can be a significant challenge. Regardless, the effort and attention given to each workout (even those completed months before booting up below a project) have as much bearing on the eventual outcome as the effort put into the redpoint attempt.

Although the constant need to cultivate and sustain focus can be draining, it is a skill that improves with practice. Regularly executing this process can make it much easier to manifest that vital focus when it comes time to perform on the rock. Here are some strategies for applying proper focus to your day-to-day training activities:

- Eliminate external distractions by setting aside time dedicated solely to training. If possible, train in an isolated location away from distracting bystanders, and turn off any potentially distracting electronic devices.
- Select appropriate music, which can be helpful for achieving the proper state of arousal and intensity. Avoid radio, or other sources of noise that you can't control.
- Place photos of goal routes or inspirational messages nearby. If attention wanders unproductively, focus in on the photo of the goal route, visualize booting up at the base, and imagine the desires and anxieties that will accompany that process. Does that climber in your mind's eye believe he trained hard enough? Use the next exercise to ensure that the answer is "yes" when the actual redpoint day comes.
- Use controlled breathing. Begin breathing steadily and deeply before beginning the training activity, then maintain it throughout the activity. Practicing good breathing while training will make your breathing more reliable during performance.
- Utilize a consistent routine to prepare for training activities. This may include performing tasks (like booting up) in a consistent order, training at a certain time of day, or always listening to the same song during your warm-up.
- Keep your eyes focused on the task at hand. Vision can steer mental processes, so keep your eyes fixed on training tools, log sheets, timers, or other objects relevant to the training activity.

METHODS OF SYSTEMATIC TRAINING

Athletes and coaches have designed many different methods of systematic physical training. This section will discuss some of these methods and their relative potential with respect to climbing training. All of these methods have their advantages, and an optimal climbing training program will borrow elements from each of these methods.

PROGRESSIVE RESISTANCE TRAINING (PRT)

Perhaps the oldest method of systematic training, PRT involves regularly performing a consistent set of exercises indefinitely, gradually increasing the volume (by increasing the number of repetitions and/or resistance) as the body adapts to training stress. The problem with PRT is that it lacks variability and the body eventually plateaus, failing to adapt or improve in response to further training stress. The majority of climbers unwittingly follow this approach, visiting the gym or crag on a regular basis and informally increasing training volume by climbing more pitches or attempting more-difficult routes (assuming they improve; however, improvements in technique and efficiency may result in reduced intensity and duration over time, thus causing regression). All successful athletes utilize this method to some extent, though usually as one element of a more comprehensive training program.

AUTO-REGULATORY PROGRESSIVE RESISTANCE TRAINING (APRT)

This new buzzword is a more deliberate method of "training to failure." Training to failure has been around for centuries, but its latest manifestation is now the hot fad in strength training. The concept is exceedingly simple: the athlete (or a coach) adjusts the training volume during the workout in order to increase the likelihood of achieving the desired amounts of intensity and duration. For example, if the athlete does not reach failure at the end of the pre-planned number of sets/repetitions, he would add more resistance and perform another set. If the athlete is unable to complete the prescription, he would reduce the resistance for the next workout. A recent study demonstrated substantially better results for this approach compared to classic PRT.[5] This approach is highly recommended when performing the routines described in the following chapters.

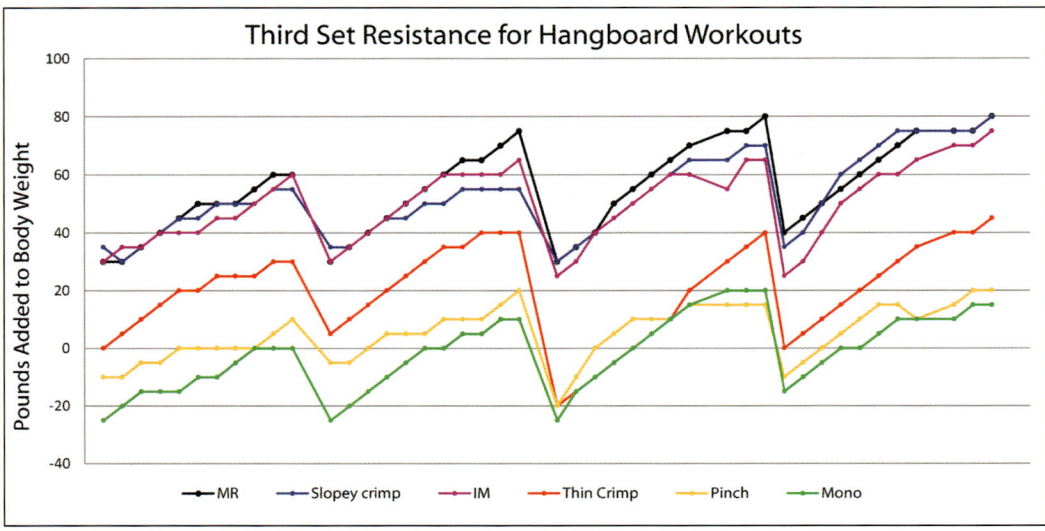

The results of Auto-Regulatory PRT while training finger strength on a hangboard. Each color of line indicates a different grip position, and each dot indicates the amount of resistance used (for the given grip) during each workout. Note that the intensity is increased between workouts, resulting in significant strength gains over the season.

SPLIT TRAINING

Used by advanced athletes training with very high volumes, to spread that volume over multiple training days. For example, if a given training program demands performing 12 exercises (each with multiple sets), the athlete might perform the first four exercises on Day 1, the next four on Day 2, and the final four on Day 3. On Day 4 the cycle would repeat, with the athlete performing the first four exercises again. This approach works best when training diverse attributes, so that one attribute (such as a particular muscle group) can recover while the other is trained. Weightlifters often use this method by focusing on their upper body, core, and lower body in turn. Climbers can utilize this method in various ways, such as performing forearm and upper-arm training on Day 1, core-muscle training and Skill Development on Day 2, and Mental Training on Day 3.

LINEAR PERIODIZATION (LP)

As discussed in Chapter 2: Goal-Setting and Planning, periodization is a method that utilizes the basic concept of PRT while also varying the training activities to avoid training plateaus. Volume is steadily reduced over the course of a pre-defined season (usually around three to four months), while intensity is gradually increased, resulting in a performance peak at the end of the season. The season is sometimes referred to as a macro-cycle, and a given phase within the macro-cycle is known as a meso-cycle. This approach has many advan-

tages, not the least of which is that numerous studies agree it produces significantly superior results to other methods [1,3,7,8,9,10,11]. Another significant advantage to climbers is that LP provides a framework for systematically training all of the many physical attributes (endurance, strength, power, skill) that contribute to climbing performance. A well-designed periodic training program can produce a synergistic culmination of these attributes, resulting in a towering performance peak lasting many weeks.

NON-LINEAR PERIODIZATION (NLP)

This method applies LP concepts to a shorter time period (usually one to two weeks) known as a micro-cycle. This method was developed for athletes whose sports demand near-peak performance throughout a long season, such as basketball players training for an 82-game season (versus those who train for many weeks to build up to a single event at the end of the season, like the Olympics). Each phase or type of training is performed within the micro-cycle, while volume and intensity are adjusted to create a mini-peak. For example, on Day 1 the athlete might train Base-Fitness, on Day 3: Strength, Day 6: Power, and Day 8: Power-Endurance, culminating in a performance on Day 10. Similarly, multiple types of training can be performed in a single day. The Rock Prodigy program borrows from this concept, beginning the macro-cycle with a classic LP approach (which is known to produce better long-term improvement than NLP), while incorporating a nonlinear approach during the Performance Phases.

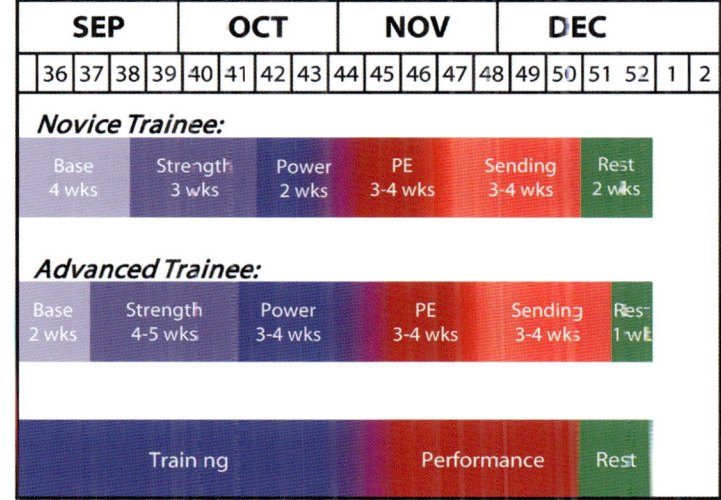

Climbers with little control over their performance schedule, such as those training for a spread-out comp season, may benefit from Non-Linear Periodization. Daniel Woods on his way to the 2013 Sport Climbing National Title. 📷 Page Knepper

THE ROCK PRODIGY TRAINING METHOD

As discussed in Chapter 1: Introduction, the Rock Prodigy training method combines various attributes of the systematic training methods described above, while dutifully adhering to the Principles of Effective Physical Training. The intent is to maximize aspects of each method that are most useful to climbers. The basic framework of this program is a linearly periodic macro-cycle consisting of the following six phases:

- Base-Fitness (lasting two to four weeks)
- Strength (three to four weeks)
- Power (two to three weeks)
- Power-Endurance (two to four weeks)
- Performance (three to four weeks)
- Rest (one to two weeks)

The length of each phase is designed to promote adaptation continuously up to the verge of plateau, at which time the phase ends and a new phase begins. Phases can be varied to individualize the program in order to address specific goals or weaknesses. A typical macro-cycle will last 17 to 18 weeks,

SEP				OCT				NOV				DEC					
36	37	38	39	40	41	42	43	44	45	46	47	48	49	50	51	52	1	2

Novice Trainee:

Base 4 wks	Strength 3 wks	Power 2 wks	PE 3-4 wks	Sending 3-4 wks	Rest 2 wks

Advanced Trainee:

Base 2 wks	Strength 4-5 wks	Power 3-4 wks	PE 3-4 wks	Sending 3-4 wks	Rest 1 wk

Training	Performance	Rest

Example macro-cycles for novice and advanced climbers. Phase lengths can and should be manipulated depending on the climber's training experience, ability, and goals. Relatively novice climbers generally benefit more from skill-development training while improving strength and power relatively quickly, so increasing the length of the skill-intensive phases (Base-Fitness, Power-Endurance, Performance) and reducing the length of the Strength and Power phases would be appropriate. Advanced climbers generally need to spend more time training strength and power to force continued adaptation.

allowing for three "seasons" per year. Shorter seasons are also possible, but usually require reducing or eliminating one or more of the six Training Phases.

Within each Training Phase (or meso-cycle), progressive resistance training is used to force physical adaptation, and auto-regulation is encouraged to ensure overload is achieved in each exercise. Split Training is used to address the various attributes affecting climbing performance. During the Performance Phases (Power-Endurance and Performance), nonlinear periodization is incorporated by utilizing multiple types of training each day (for example, warming up with a skill-focused Base-Fitness exercise, performing strength/power bouldering exercises, and then finishing with a power-endurance-oriented linked bouldering circuit). This program has been utilized by many climbers over more than a decade, and the results are indisputable.

Each of the following chapters will describe an individual Training Phase in detail, finishing with an assortment of prescriptive routines to suit climbers with various levels of training experience. Chapter 10: Building a Training Plan and Other Training Considerations will present several detailed schedules, geared toward climbers of different abilities, describing precisely how to integrate all of these routines into a comprehensive periodic training program. Refer back to Chapter 10 and Chapter 2: Goal-Setting and Planning as necessary to develop an individualized training schedule.

Finger Strength, First and Foremost

"Fingers, fingers, fingers. No world-class climber has weak fingers, but many can get away with weak bodies and weak shoulders. Make finger strength the number-one priority in your training, work on your weaknesses, and never drink on an empty stomach." — Malcolm Smith[14]

The Rock Prodigy training method prioritizes training for finger strength and endurance over other physical attributes (such as core, pulling, or shoulder strength/power/endurance). Observing many climbers over many years, and at many crags around the world, has led us to the conclusion that finger strength and endurance are the primary physical limiters for most climbers. While the relative criticality of the fingers may vary depending on the climber's preferred crags and/or climbing style, it is our observation that it is the rare climber indeed who couldn't benefit from stronger fingers.

While the fingers are the primary *physical* limiter in climbing performance, their importance relative to technical and mental attributes may never be settled. For some moves, finger strength is absolutely everything; no amount of technique or tenacity will get you past an overhanging mono in an otherwise blank wall if you lack the finger strength. Other moves can be finessed, or overcome through strong will. Often the relative value of finger strength depends on the strengths, weaknesses, and goals of each individual climber. However, even when finger strength is not a limiting factor, improving finger strength has tremendous benefits over the course of your career.

Eventually (and quickly), every climber will progress to the point that the fundamental strength to pull on the holds becomes limiting. Furthermore, it takes many years of diligent effort to develop strong fingers, so it makes sense to begin addressing this inevitable weakness as early as possible. In the meantime, climbers can simultaneously develop the technical and mental elements of climbing performance (detailed training suggestions for these other attributes are included in Chapter 3: Skill Development and Part III: Performing). Wise climbers will endeavor to improve all of these areas, but finger strength is generally given preference in the text, as we believe most climbers will ultimately want to prioritize it in their own training. Other outstanding resources like *The Self-Coached Climber* and *The Rock Warrior's Way* are better suited to comprehensively address the other elements of climbing performance.

SUMMARY

- The nine Principles of Effective Physical Training should be considered when designing any training program. These principles are: specificity, overload, recovery, reversibility, regularity, progression, variation, individualization, and transfer.
- Several contributing factors help enable effective training. These include: quantification, documentation, intensity, duration, volume, and isolation.
- Effective training requires hard work and focus. Both of these traits can be developed through practice and attention.
- There are numerous basic methods of physical training, including various forms of periodization and progressive resistance training.
- The Rock Prodigy training method incorporates elements of various time-tested training strategies to produce a synergistic performance peak at a predictable point in each climbing season.
- Physical, mental, and technical abilities all contribute significantly to climbing performance; however, the latter two have been covered exhaustively by other texts. This book focuses largely on finger strength because it has never been comprehensively described before yet is a primary determinant of climbing ability that all climbers could benefit from improving.

Certain moves demand brute finger strength. Sooner or later, every climber on the path of continuous improvement will run into such a move. Ryan Palo bearing down on *Disposable Hero*, 5.13b, Smith Rock, OR. 📷 Peter Franzen

BASE FITNESS

Long endurance climbs, like those at Maple Canyon, UT, require a high level of Base Fitness. Steve Bechtel on *Toxic Turkey*, 5.13c. Janelle Anderson

CHAPTER 5

"At the start of any training regime it's important to get into shape by doing low-intensity, high-volume workouts." — Ben Moon[13]

INTRODUCTION

In nearly every sport, athletes begin their training by establishing a training foundation, which gradually prepares the body for the work to follow in the coming training phases. This base-building phase provides a transition between the active rest period and more intense training activities by gradually exposing the body to a moderate version of the training stress to come. In climbing, this is generally accomplished by climbing at low intensity and long duration, and is often described as "climbing mileage," that is, racking up thousands of vertical feet of climbing. With the critical role that technical skill plays in climbing, these sessions have the added importance of providing an opportunity to learn and refine technique. For grade-obsessed sport climbers, these training sessions also provide an excuse to broaden one's horizons on invigorating, lengthier, moderate climbs.

In route climbing, the difference between success and failure often hinges on the climber's ability to prevent or accommodate mounting fatigue in the muscles of the forearms. To understand how to best train the body to improve these abilities, it is helpful to understand muscle function, metabolic energy pathways, muscle fatigue, and how muscles adapt to training. Therefore, the next several sections will focus on these general physiology topics. If you're not interested in these, skip to the "Aerobic Restoration and Capillarity Training" section on p96.

MUSCLE FUNCTION

Besides laying a foundation for a training cycle, mileage training establishes the athlete's level of *base-fitness* — the capacity to fuel muscle contractions for sustained activity. Climbing movement requires muscle contractions, and these require energy. In climbing, even *not moving* requires energy (to hang from small handholds). Climbers rely on three metabolic pathways to provide energy for muscular contractions by converting food energy available in the blood (or stored in fat or muscle) into a useable form; these three pathways are discussed starting on p88 in the "Muscle Cell Metabolic Energy Pathways" section. Because of the geometric constraints of the forearms, and the high relative demands placed on them, climbing performance is often limited by the capacity of these metabolic pathways in the forearms themselves. The limitations of these pathways are manifested as a forearm "pump."

Muscles create joint movement, so they are fundamental to sports performance. Skeletal muscles undergo three types of contractions:

- *Concentric* (muscle shortens during contraction)
- *Eccentric* (muscle lengthens during contraction)
- *Isometric* (muscle length remains fixed during contraction)

Isometric contractions are used by the forearm muscles to grasp handholds, and are thus critical in climbing. Isometric grip strength and endurance is often a limiting factor for many climbers and on many climbs.

Skeletal muscles are composed of *blood vessels* and *muscle fibers*, and are attached by tendons to the bones (see Figure on the next page). A muscle fiber is actually a long, tubular cell composed of numerous *myofibrils*, which are the smallest individual contractile units in the muscle. Myofibrils are segmented into

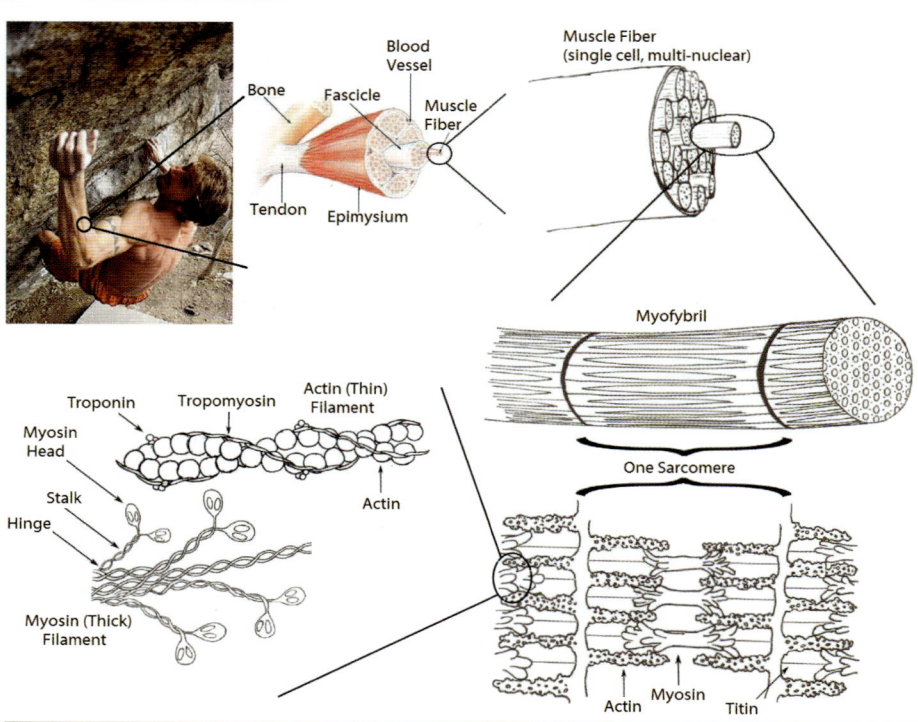

Human skeletal muscle (adapted from "Skeletal Muscle" © 2005 under a Creative Commons Attribution-ShareAlike license: creativecommons.org/licenses/by-sa/3.0/ photo: Brendan Nicholson

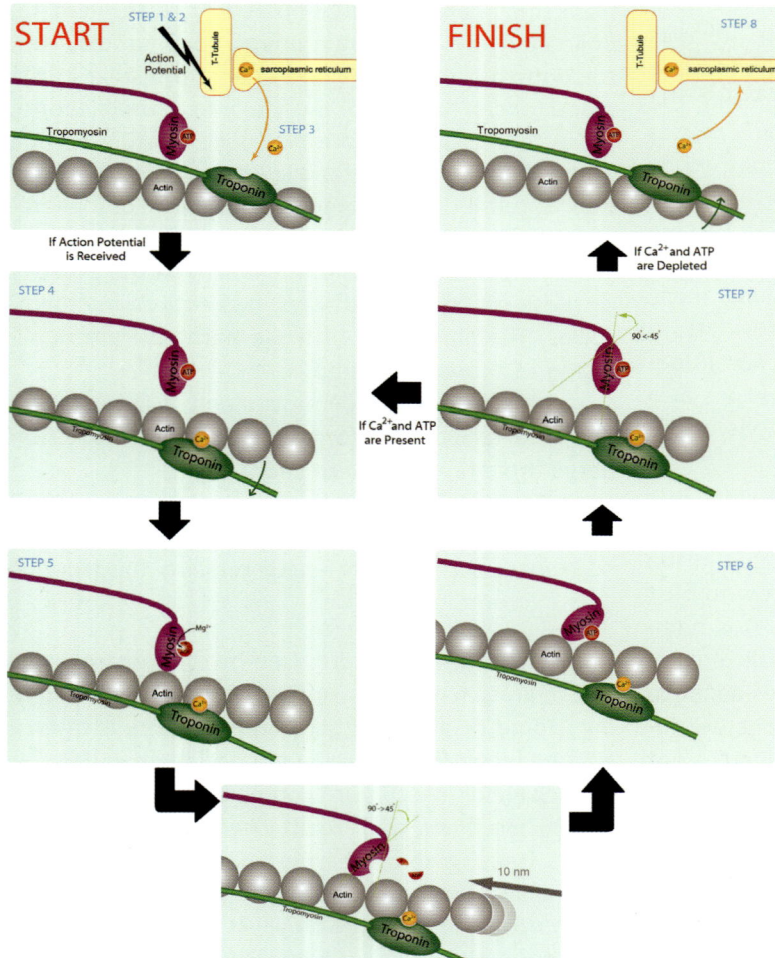

Muscle Function Glossary:
ADP - adenosine diphosphate
AP - action potential
ATP - adenosine triphosphate
Ca^{2+} - calcium ion(s)
H^+ - hydrogen ion(s), or "proton"
Mg^{2+} - magnesium ion(s)
MSS - maximum steady state
PCr - creatine phosophate
P_i - inorganic phosphate
ROS - reactive oxygen species
SR - sarcoplasmic reticulum

Illustration of muscle contraction (adapted from "Molecular Mechanism of Muscle Function" © 2007 by Hank van Helvete, used under a Creative Commons Attribution-ShareAlike license: creativecommons.org/licenses/by-sa/3.0/

Muscle Contractions

The process of initiating and sustaining muscle contractions is complex, with many moving parts. However, this complexity provides numerous controls to delay fatigue and prevent permanent muscle damage. Muscles contract in several steps (refer to the Figure on the previous page):

1. A contraction command originates in the brain, generating an electrical signal called an *action potential* (AP) that is propagated to the muscle by a *motor neuron*.

2. The motor neuron releases a molecule, *acetylcholine*, which travels across the *neuromuscular junction* to the muscle cell, thus transmitting the AP to the muscle.

3. The AP propagates through the muscle cell along *transverse tubules* (T-tubules) to the *sarcoplasmic reticulum* (SR), which contains stored *calcium ions* (Ca^{2+}). The AP stimulates release of Ca^{2+} ions from the SR, ions which then diffuse into the *cytoplasm* (the fluid within the muscle cells) and surround the *myofibrils* (made up of actin and myosin).

4. The Ca^{2+} ions control the myofibrils and stimulate contractions through a protein called *tropomyosin* that resides on the actin thin filaments. Normally, the tropomyosin prevents myosin from binding to the actin, but when Ca^{2+} ions are released from the SR, they bind to *troponin C* receptors on the tropomyosin, which moves it out of the way.

5. The myosin heads (which are preloaded with *adenosine triphosphate* [ATP] — the primary energy source for muscle movement) are now able to attach to the recently uncovered binding sites on the actin thin filaments. This process requires *ATP hydrolysis* (ATPase), in which the ATP releases energy while splitting into *adenosine diphosphate* (ADP), *inorganic phosphate* (P_i), and *hydrogen ions* (H^+), all of which are important elements of fatigue. When the P_i and ADP are released, the myosin head rotates, pulling on and moving the actin approximately 10 nanometers.

6. ATP available in the cytoplasm then binds to the myosin head, replacing the ADP and releasing the myosin head from the actin binding site.

7. The iterative process of *cross-bridging cycling* is thus initiated (steps 5 and 6). As long as Ca^{2+} ions and ATP are present in the cytoplasm, the myosin heads will repeatedly attach, pull, detach, and re-attach as they inch along the actin fiber like a ratchet, shortening the sarcomere.

8. Throughout this process, Ca^{2+} ions are actively pumped back into the SR (a process which also requires ATP). The SR will continue to release Ca^{2+} ions as long as an AP is present, and the contraction will persist. When the AP is turned off, the Ca^{2+} pumps will clear the cytoplasm of Ca^{2+} ions, and the tropomyosin will move back into the blocking position, preventing further cross-bridge cycling.

sarcomeres, forming a long chain from one end of the muscle to the other. The sarcomeres are the contracting elements of the cell, shortening, lengthening, or resisting motion, as directed by the nervous system through *motor neurons*. Sarcomeres contain bundles of long, thin proteins called *actin* (thin filament) and *myosin* (thick filament) that interact in a complex electrochemical process to create contractions.

This electrochemical process begins in the central nervous system and acts on the musculoskeletal system, but is supported by many other systems that provide numerous chemical ingredients. The process is complex, involving many components in several steps. This complexity lends robustness, with numerous controls to delay fatigue and prevent permanent muscle damage. A muscle contraction is initiated by an *action potential* (AP) from the nervous system that is transmitted to the motor neurons, which activate the myofibrils and sarcomeres. This initiates the process of *cross-bridge cycling* in which *adenosine triphosphate* (ATP) provides energy for myosin thick filaments to attach to actin thin filaments and pull them along, 10 nanometers at a time. In the case of a concentric contraction, this ratcheting process shortens the sarcomere, and thus the entire myofibril chain; this then shortens the muscle. As long as the nervous system requests it, and the necessary metabolic components (such as ATP) are available, the contraction will continue. More details are provided in the above sidebar.

MUSCLE CELL METABOLIC ENERGY PATHWAYS

Large quantities of ATP are needed to power sustained muscle activity, and the human body has robust and redundant processes to provide it. ATP is produced from biological fuels, including sugar (carbohydrates), amino acids (protein), and fatty acids (fat). Sugar, in the form of blood glucose, is by far the preferred fuel. Digested carbohydrates enter the bloodstream as glucose, an energy-dense sugar, which is either used immediately, or converted to *glycogen* for storage in the muscle cells through the *glycogenesis* process.

GLYCOLYTIC PATHWAY

Glucose and glycogen are eventually converted to ATP and *pyruvate* molecules through the complex process of glycolysis (the heart of the glycolytic energy pathway). Glycolysis is a ten-step process with several variations, but generally, it is an anaerobic process (not requiring oxygen) that quickly produces a modest amount of ATP: two ATP molecules per molecule of glucose. A consequence of glycolysis is that, in addition to ATP, it produces a number of by-products that contribute to muscle fatigue, including *hydrogen ions* (H^+) and the molecule *nicotinamide adenine dinucleotide* (NADH). However, when possible, these by-products are consumed by *aerobic respiration* to produce even more ATP while simultaneously recycling these waste products. This glycolytic energy pathway is a key contributor to performance on power-endurance climbs (those with sustained sections of very difficult moves). Chapter Eight: Power-Endurance will introduce training methods to improve glycolytic metabolism.

AEROBIC RESPIRATION PATHWAY

Aerobic respiration occurs inside the *mitochondria* (an energy-supplying organelle found in many cells), and is the general process of oxidizing pyruvate in the "Krebs" cycle. Aerobic respiration picks up where glycolysis leaves off, by using the products of glycolysis as its primary fuel (in addition to oxygen). Aerobic respiration is much more productive than glycolysis, producing roughly 28 ATP molecules per molecule of glucose, above and beyond the two generated during glycolysis. More importantly, the ATP is produced largely by metabolizing the waste products NADH, H^+, and inorganic phosphate (P_i) through a process called *oxidative phosphorylation*. During moderate-intensity, steady-state exercise, aerobic respiration completely consumes these otherwise harmful *metabolites* (harmful by-products of cellular energy metabolism), allowing exercise to continue as long as glucose is available. The *Maximum Steady State* (MSS – described in detail in "Capillarization and the Maximum Steady State") is the highest level of intensity at which a muscle can continue to function aerobically, and thus, indefinitely. Climbing *below* the MSS typically does not cause a significant forearm pump and can be sustained for many minutes. Climbing continuously *above* the MSS will result in a debilitating pump within a few minutes. This process makes continuous endurance feats (like running a marathon) possible. The aerobic energy pathway is used continuously, in all aspects of climbing, to provide ATP and recycle waste, but can be especially critical to success during onsights, very long, sustained redpoints, and long multipitch climbs.

PHOSPHAGEN PATHWAY

The *phosphagen* system is the third and final method for producing ATP for muscle activity. It delivers ATP almost immediately, and provides the supply needed for the first few seconds of a muscle contraction. ATP is produced in a reaction called *creatine kinase*, in which readily available creatine phosphate (PCr), ADP, and H^+ react in one step to produce ATP and creatine. The stores of PCr are quickly depleted, however, and ATP production must be replaced by aerobic respiration or glycolysis. (Creatine supplementation is used by some athletes because it boosts phosphagenic ATP production, thus improving high-intensity, short-term [<10 sec] performance, but it has no known enhancing effect on longer-term efforts.) By enabling maximum force production, the phosphagen pathway is critical to bouldering, and to performing bouldery moves on routes.

ATP: ENERGY FOR MUSCLE CONTRACTIONS

Before discussing the pros and cons of each metabolic energy pathway, it is necessary to briefly mention how ATP is used. Once ATP is produced in the muscle cells by one of the three metabolic systems, it is available for use by the myosin heads to power muscle contrac-

Metabolic Pathway	ATP Production Rate (mmol ATP/s)
Anaerobic	
Phosphagen	2.4
Glycolytic	1.3
Aerobic	
Aerobic Respiration (carbohydrate)	0.7
Aerobic Respiration (fat)	0.3

ATP Production via the various Metabolic Energy Pathways.[8]

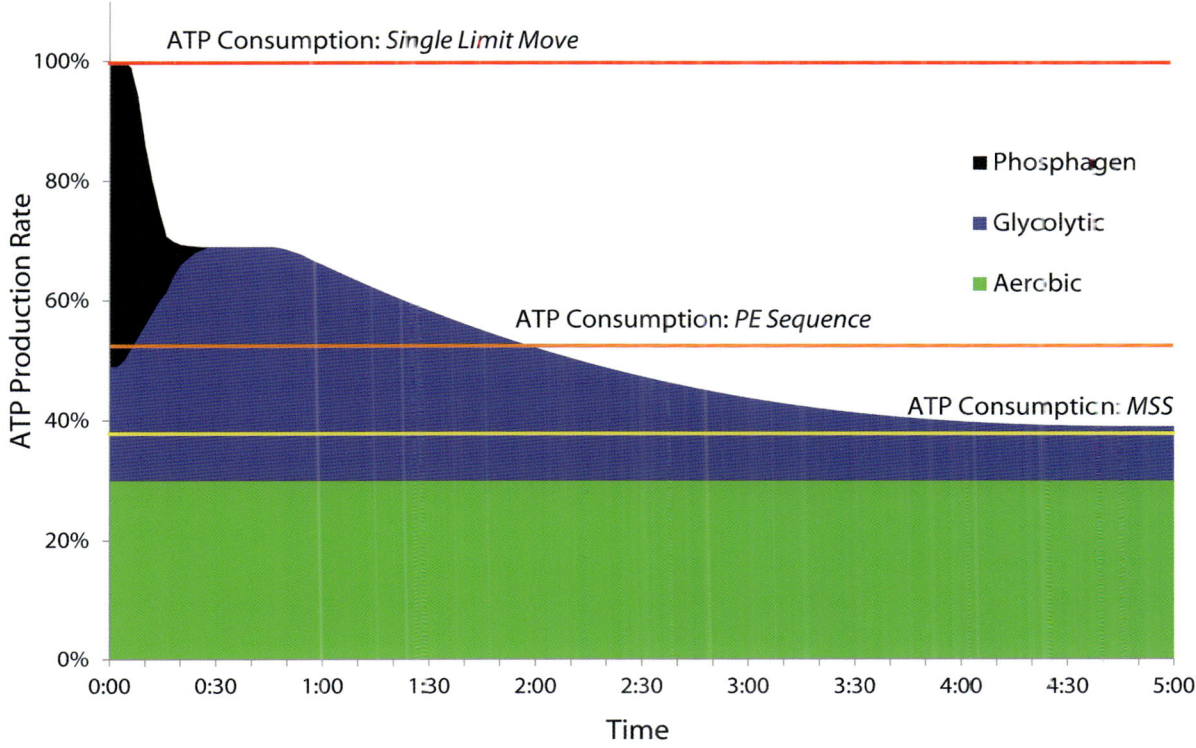

Relative Contributions of the Metabolic Energy Pathways to ATP Production

Relative Contributions of the Metabolic Energy Pathways to ATP Production. All three systems function simultaneously, at first. The Phosphagen Pathway is necessary for executing the most difficult moves, but it can only be sustained for a dozen or so seconds. The Glycolytic Pathway produces ATP rapidly, but can only sustain that production for one to three minutes. Aerobic respiration can produce ATP indefinitely, but at a slower rate. Various climbing activities consume ATP at different rates (shown notionally). Limit moves require tremendous amounts of ATP, so can only be performed until the Phosphagen Pathway is exhausted, which takes only a few seconds. Power-endurance sequences can be performed until the Glycolytic Pathway is exhausted, which takes another two minutes or so. Climbing at or below the Maximum Steady State can continue for dozens of minutes.

tions. (ATP has other uses as well, including transporting molecules across cell membranes and powering certain steps of glycolysis and aerobic respiration.) The mechanical work performed by the myosin head as it tugs on the actin filament is powered by the release of energy that accompanies *ATP hydrolysis* (aka ATPase). ATP hydrolysis is a reaction between ATP and water that yields the by-products P_i, H^+, and *adenosine diphosphate* (ADP), along with the release of energy. Muscles cannot function without ATP hydrolysis, yet the three by-products are largely responsible for muscle fatigue. Therefore, the rate at which ATP is consumed (and these waste products are produced), along with the ability of the muscle cells to deal with these waste products, largely determines how long muscle activity can continue.

This is why the metabolic energy pathways are critical: because each produces ATP and handles the associated waste products differently. However, keep in mind that all three pathways function simultaneous-

ly, but to varying degrees, depending on the climbing intensity. The relative contribution of each pathway to the total supply of ATP determines the sustainability of the climbing activity. The figure above illustrates how each pathway contributes to ATP production.

Mitochondrial aerobic respiration is the body's preferred choice for producing ATP during exercise. It consumes all of the by-products of ATP hydrolysis at the same rate as they are produced; therefore, these detrimental metabolites do not accumulate in the blood and muscle cells, they do not interfere with muscle function, and thus fatigue does not ensue. Unfortunately, aerobic respiration is also the *slowest* form of ATP production (see Table on the previous page). Therefore, as climbing intensity increases, the muscles consume ATP faster than it is produced *aerobically*. In response, the cells produce ATP faster through increased use of the unsustainable *anaerobic* glycolytic energy pathway (initiating the countdown to fatigue).

Lactic Acid...Not Guilty!

For nearly 80 years, the mainstream explanation for muscle fatigue was the familiar "burn" of lactic acid accumulation (or lactic acidosis) in the muscle cells. While exercise is closely correlated with a decrease in blood pH (making the blood more acidic), no evidence for a cause-and-effect relationship between lactic acidosis and muscle fatigue has ever been discovered.[8] The lactic acid *theory* of fatigue has since been roundly rejected by medical science, and technically, "lactic acid" is not produced by the human body — rather, sodium lactate (or just lactate) is. Lactate is a natural by-product of glycolysis, and it does not cause acidosis, or muscle fatigue.[1] Acidosis is caused by the excess hydrogen ions (H^+) released during ATP hydrolysis (the breakdown of ATP into free energy, ADP, P_i, and H^+). While lactate production does correlate with increased acidity in the blood, the lactate is a *result* of the acidity, not a cause of it, and the lactate actually helps to buffer (remove) excess H^+, reducing acidity and permitting exercise to continue longer than it would otherwise.

Despite the fact that acidosis has been closely correlated with muscle fatigue, it's currently not clear how or if acidosis causes fatigue.[10] One hypothesis supported by limited experimental evidence is that lowered pH interferes with the binding of Ca^{2+} to troponin C on the actin thin filament, thus reducing force production (but only slightly).[10] Acidity has also been implicated in the slowing of relaxation that occurs with muscle fatigue.[1]

Inorganic phosphate (P_i), however, is also a by-product of ATP hydrolysis, and it is well-known to cause muscle fatigue and reduce force production. Increased concentrations of P_i encourage the muscle cells to use the weaker of two possible actin-myosin cross-bridge states, thus reducing the force output of the muscle.[10] Further, increased P_i levels inhibit the release of Ca^{2+} from the sarcoplasmic reticulum (needed for cross-bridging between the actin and myosin filaments). Therefore, the presence of excess P_i inhibits force production in two ways: 1) It reduces the number of actin-myosin cross-bridges, and 2) It reduces the strength of those bridges.

"Excess Inorganic Phosphate Bath" just doesn't have the same ring to it. Rachel Avallone pumping out on *Lactic Acid Bath*, 5.12d, at the New River Gorge, WV. Dan Brayack

While glycolysis is less *efficient* at producing ATP (only two ATP per molecule of glucose) than aerobic respiration, it is much *faster*. Glycolysis produces ATP at nearly twice the rate of aerobic respiration, doubling the amount of ATP available but also doubling the production of fatigue-causing waste products. Further, glycolysis itself produces excess protons (H^+) in addition to those produced by ATP hydrolysis. The mitochondria still recycle as much of these harmful by-products as they can through aerobic respiration, but these efforts will eventually be outpaced by production. If physical activity continues, these waste products will accumulate and cause muscle fatigue.

MUSCLE FATIGUE

Muscle fatigue can result in reduced force production, reduced contraction speed, reduced relaxation speed, or a combination of all three. All of these manifestations contribute to an overall decline in power: the muscle's ability to produce a large force quickly. In rock climbing, muscular power is fundamental to performing dynamic movements, and thus to negotiating difficult cruxes. When muscles perform continuous maximum contractions (such as gripping a tenuous handhold), force production declines rapidly (within five to ten seconds), but recovers rapidly as well (one to two seconds). Of course, this exertion/recovery cycle cannot proceed indefinitely, and fatigue will build within a few repetitions.

Sustained rock climbs demand that climbing muscles (in the forearms especially) contract and relax repeatedly, but often at considerably less than maximum force. Running and cycling tax muscles similarly. The force required and the *duty cycle* of these contractions are critical factors in determining how long the effort can be sustained. The duty cycle is the ratio of contraction time to rest time (a two-second contraction with a one-second rest is a duty cycle of 2:1). Running and cycling have low force requirements and low duty cycles (less than one), so these activities

Muscle Fiber Types

Each muscle is composed of many *motor units*, each consisting of many individual muscle fibers. Currently, there are seven known muscle-fiber types in humans, and these form a spectrum ranging from high-fatigue-resistance fibers that contract slowly, to low-fatigue-resistance fibers that contract quickly. Classic models only recognized three fiber types, and for pragmatic purposes, the four newcomers are still grouped with the original three categories most of the time:

- *Type I* fibers are *slow twitch* (meaning they contract slowly) but they are well-equipped for aerobic respiration, allowing them to sustain longer-duration activities. These fibers take two to three times as long to contract as the so-called *fast-twitch* fibers.
- *Type IIa* are one of two primary types of *fast-twitch* fibers (meaning they contract quickly). Type IIa fibers contract relatively quickly, but are also somewhat fatigue-resistant.
- *Type IIb* (aka *Type IIx/d*) are the fastest contracting fibers, but they fatigue quickly. De-training can cause the conversion of Type IIa fibers to Type IIb.

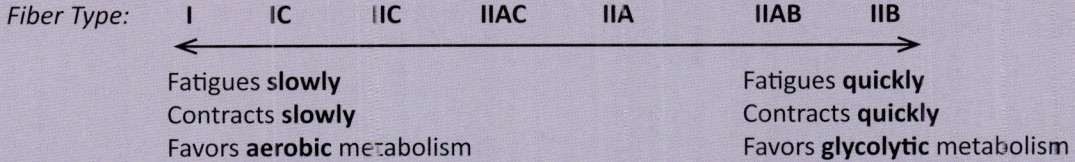

Fiber Type:	I	IC	IIC	IIAC	IIA	IIAB	IIB

Fatigues **slowly**　　　　　　　　　　Fatigues **quickly**
Contracts **slowly**　　　　　　　　　Contracts **quickly**
Favors **aerobic** metabolism　　　Favors **glycolytic** metabolism

The relative distribution of these muscle-fiber types varies by individual and muscle group (and this distribution *can* vary between muscle group), so to some extent an athlete's propensity toward endurance or power-oriented activities is genetically predetermined. Fortunately for athletes, it is possible to train intermediate-twitch Type IIa fibers to behave more like faster-twitch Type IIb fibers and vice versa (it also may be possible to convert Type I to Type II, but clinical evidence is lacking). Furthermore, it is possible to train Type I fibers to contract more quickly while retaining other "slow-twitch" characteristics (such as fatigue resistance). Therefore, while you may be predisposed toward a particular type of climbing (i.e., power moves versus endurance routes), there is significant potential to train your muscles to behave in a way that suits your individual goals, regardless of genetics.[9]

Causes of Muscle Fatigue

Given the complex system of systems involved in muscle contractions, there are numerous failure points that can cause fatigue. Several fatigue modes have been discovered, but it is difficult to implicate a specific mode (or modes) of fatigue for a given activity.[1] Exercise variables such as load, duty cycle, and duration factor into how fatigue develops. In cyclic activities (such as climbing), fatigue develops in three phases as shown in the Figure below. In phase one there is a rapid decline in force production of 10 to 20 percent, caused by reduced effectiveness in cross-bridge cycling as PCr is depleted. Phase two incurs a more gradual decline in force, and its length depends on the effectiveness of aerobic respiration. Finally, in phase three, muscle performance declines rapidly as Ca^{2+} function is impaired by accumulating metabolites. The most relevant fatigue modes for climbing are:

ATP Depletion: During cruxy climbing, fast-twitch fibers consume ATP rapidly. The phosphagen system supplies this ATP for the first few seconds, but as PCr is depleted, the cells must turn to slower glycolysis, which is soon outpaced by demand, and ATP levels decline in the cytoplasm. When the SR senses this shortage, Ca^{2+} ion release is intentionally reduced to prevent cell damage, and the muscle can't generate as much force (dietary creatine delays this fatigue by one to two seconds, but the associated weight gain may be detrimental for climbers).

Metabolite Accumulation: During power-endurance climbing efforts, fast-twitch fibers are recruited and loaded cyclically, and the metabolites P_i, H^+, ADP, and Mg^{2+} (magnesium ions) accumulate quickly. Other metabolites called *reactive oxygen species* (ROS aka *free radicals*) arise very gradually from mitochondrial respiration. Generally, all of these metabolites prevent Ca^{2+} ions from doing their job. Therefore, a climber's ability to deal with accumulating metabolites is critical to performance. Mitochondria perform this cleanup function in the cells, so any training that promotes mitochondrial performance is very beneficial.

Glycogen Depletion: It's possible to cause fatigue by depleting the body's glycogen reserves, but it takes a long time, so the exercise would have to be relatively easy. Therefore, it is difficult to *climb* into "glycogen debt" (although the Nose-in-a-Day or 24 Hours of Horseshoe Hell would be potential cases). Limit climbs will incur faster-developing fatigue modes (such as metabolite accumulation) that cause failure well before glycogen runs out. However, glycogen depletion *does* contribute to fatigue in higher-intensity activity such as cruxy climbing, by reducing force output over time. Reduced Ca^{2+} ion output by the SR is the likely culprit.

Neuromuscular Action Potential Disruption: The electrochemical channels that are used to stimulate muscle contractions can de-polarize with use (like a worn-out magnet). This fatigue mode mostly affects continuous maximum contractions. Muscles can overcome this, but only if thoroughly stimulated (through use). Therefore, a warm-up that includes significant, near-maximal exercises is required to get the muscles "firing on all cylinders."

Development of muscle fatigue showing that as the muscle is fatigued by cyclic sub-maximal loading, its potential to produce a single maximum-force contraction declines.[1] For example, if the fatiguing activity were a pumpy climb, the top figure indicates that three minutes into the climb, the climber would only be able to perform moves requiring about 80 percent or less of her maximum strength. The bottom figure shows the effect of increasing the muscle's maximum strength by 20 percent. The same hold that required 80 percent of maximum strength can now be held with only 65 percent of maximum strength, so it can still be used six or more minutes into the climb. The apparent effect is an increase in endurance.

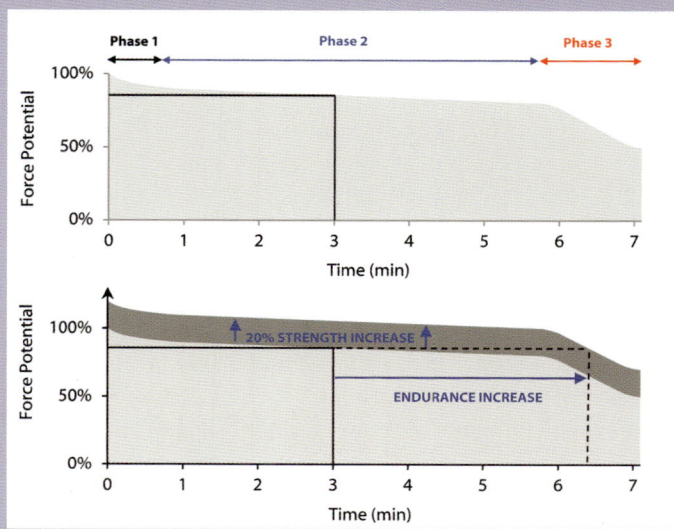

can be sustained for long periods. Climbing, on the other hand, will always have a duty cycle of greater than one (assuming that one hand contacts the rock at all times). Sub-maximal, repeated contractions can be sustained much longer than continuous maximal contractions, but once fatigued by this cyclic loading, recovery takes longer: five to ten minutes for initial recovery, and as much as 30 minutes to two hours to regain maximum strength. In general, the lower the load, the longer the effort can be sustained, but also the longer recovery will take. This is known as "low-frequency fatigue" and can linger for days. Therefore, long bouts of fatiguing, low-intensity climbing can dig a deep hole that requires days to "climb" out of.

Fatigue at the muscle cellular level arises through the accumulation of by-products from ATP metabolism. These metabolites interfere with numerous steps in the muscle contraction process, as described in the adjacent sidebar.

The three processes for producing ATP are not mutually exclusive — their relative contribution to a given muscle contraction or exercise effort varies as contractions progress and metabolic conditions change within the cell. The muscle fiber type also affects the relative reliance on any one system. So-called *fast-twitch* fibers use ATP more quickly than *slow-twitch* fibers; therefore, they lean heavily on glycolysis to produce ATP very quickly. Slow-twitch fibers have higher concentrations of mitochondria, and are better at utilizing aerobic respiration; therefore, slow-twitch fibers are *fatigue-resistant*. As a consequence, when a climber attempts difficult moves requiring high muscular force and/or power output, the more powerful fast-twitch muscle fibers will be recruited for the task. However, these fibers lack sufficient mitochondrial aerobic respiration, so fatigue will develop quickly. These muscle characteristics have profound implications on how climbers should best train for their sport, and they impact all physiological aspects of climbing performance: strength, power, and endurance.

MUSCLE CHARACTERISTICS AND THEIR IMPLICATIONS FOR CLIMBING TRAINING

Muscle cells have several fatigue mechanisms that are triggered by different conditions within the cells. Therefore, the fatigue mechanism is specific to the activity being performed.[3] So when training to increase fatigue *resistance* in climbing, it is critical to create the right type of fatigue in order to yield the desired adaptations. That is, the training must be *climbing specific* in order to develop muscular endurance that is rele-

vant to climbing. For best results, the training should be tailored to mimic specific aspects of the *goal route*, such as the muscle loads (hold type), duty cycle, and total-effort duration. Specific training will achieve the most-applicable improvements to muscle performance, best preparing the climber for his goal route. Another effect of the muscles' versatility is that climbers can improve their endurance by training for strength. Relatively high-force contractions recruit more fast-twitch fibers, which produce more force but fatigue more quickly. By training to increase maximum strength, a given climbing move will require a relatively lower percentage of that maximum strength, and thus relatively fewer fast-twitch fibers.[1] Instead, the more fatigue-resistant slow-twitch fibers can support more of the workload, resulting in less fatigue. Over the course of an entire climb, the increased use of slow-twitch fibers delays the accumulation of fatigue significantly. In short, strength training improves muscular endurance, which is one reason it should be central to any climbing training program.

Another important ramification for training is the ability of all fibers (including fast-twitch) to respond to endurance training by adding mitochondria. This adaptation does not impair the fibers' fast-twitch performance, but does allow them to perform longer before fatiguing.[9] Therefore, climbers should train to increase the strength and quantity of fast-twitch fibers, while also improving their fatigue resistance. Thus, high-intensity power training *and* endurance training are both beneficial and necessary for optimizing overall climbing performance.

Finally, it is essential to emphasize the critical importance of mitochondria in the performance of all types of muscle fibers (slow and fast). Regardless of the duration or intensity of the activity (whether bouldering or enduro-climbing), mitochondria are involved in clearing waste and efficiently providing ATP. Their presence and effectiveness will prolong optimal muscular performance during any climbing activity. The quantity and capacity of mitochondria can be increased by moderate-intensity "threshold" training, which will benefit all aspects of climbing performance.[9]

THE FOREARM PUMP

One unfortunate but consequential feature of skeletal muscles is that high-force contractions restrict blood flow to the contracting muscle. Muscles are infused with small capillaries to supply necessary fuel, but as the sarcomeres contract, they also widen (easily ob-

High force contractions in the forearm muscles occlude blood flow, eventually resulting in the dreaded foream pump. Janelle Anderson on *Jesus Wept*, 5.12d, Red River Gorge, KY.   📷 Mike Anderson

served in a flexing bicep), constricting the surrounding capillaries. This *blood-flow occlusion* has long been suspected by climbers, and recent research has verified it. Studies have shown that circulation in the forearms is severely reduced or eliminated during intense contractions (50 to 70 percent of maximum strength or greater).[2, 3, 5, 6] To make matters worse, one study has shown that raising the arms above the head during moderate, repetitive isometric hand contractions reduces local blood pressure and hastens fatigue (suggesting climbers should alternate shaking out above and below their heads to promote blood flow in and out of the forearm muscles).[11] Blood flow provides the essential fuels of oxygen, glucose, and ATP for aerobic and anaerobic respiration, and it removes the fatigue-inducing metabolic waste products, along with CO_2.[1, 3] Muscles fatigue more rapidly when blood flow is occluded, whether the fatiguing exercises are high-intensity maximal contractions (cruxy climbing) or endurance activities (enduro-climbing).

In climbing, blood-flow occlusion is especially problematic. During difficult climbing, blood flow to the forearm muscles is severely reduced. Furthermore, to handle the strenuous moves, less efficient metabolic pathways are employed to rapidly produce ATP. As a result, metabolites from ATP hydrolysis and glycolysis quickly accumulate, while much-needed

blood glucose and oxygen "reinforcements" are prevented from entering the muscle tissue. This problem is compounded by the muscle's growing inability to *stop* contracting. The myosin heads require ATP to release from the actin binding sites (step six of muscle contraction), so as ATP is depleted, some fibers may be unable to relax, perpetuating blood-flow occlusion. This vicious cycle is well-known to climbers as the dreaded forearm pump, which reduces strength, speed of contraction/release, and coordination, all greatly impairing climbing performance.

Climbing typically loads the forearm muscles cyclically with five-to-ten-second periods of high-intensity, blood-occluding isometric contractions, separated by brief (~ one second) rests with resumed blood flow (shaking out permits a longer rest). Therefore, a long, sustained pitch of hard climbing can be thought of as an ebb and flow between mounting muscle fatigue and recovery. Each contraction draws the climber closer to failure, while each release provides a brief retreat from it. Assuming the climber can do the moves, success on a difficult climb may then depend on his ability to repeatedly, briefly, and consistently recover between handholds.

Muscular Recovery from Fatiguing Exercise

The recovery of muscle performance following fatiguing exercise has interesting characteristics that inform climbing training. When muscles perform short-duration, maximum-force contractions (like repetitive weightlifting), strength recovers very quickly (almost completely in only a couple of seconds). Generally, the longer the length of continuous contraction, the longer recovery takes. Fatigue caused by repetitive, sub-maximal contractions, like those required for route climbing, requires much longer recovery in general, but also depends on the level of effort and duration of activity. Relatively easy moves that can be sustained longer require more recovery time than harder moves that cause fatigue quickly. This is why climbers typically rest longer after pumping off a long route (with many, relatively easier moves) than after failing on a boulder problem (with fewer, more difficult moves).

While a substantial amount of recovery occurs in the minutes and hours immediately following fatiguing climbing, there is a component of fatigue that lingers for many hours or days. This fatigue is not a result of reduced ATP or the accumulation of metabolites (these return to normal levels in 15 to 60 minutes). Instead, it results from a breakdown in the neuromuscular excitation process that stimulates the SR to release Ca^{2+} (needed for cross-bridge cycling). This impairment persists for many hours or days after intense exercise.[1] These characteristics of muscle recovery can be used to plan rest cycles to optimize climbing performance. At the Red River Gorge, it is not unheard of to rest for up to two hours between attempts on long, sustained routes, whereas the roped-bouldering routes of Wyoming's Wild Iris may require only 20 minutes of rest between burns. Furthermore, more rest may be required between climbing days filled with long, pumpy climbing.

RECOVERING FROM A FOREARM PUMP

Recovery from fatigue is severely hindered by occluded blood flow. Regardless of the intensity and duration of the climbing activity, it can be sustained longer and stronger with improved blood flow. Blood flow to the forearms during a climb can be improved through two primary mechanisms: The first is to reduce the percentage of maximum contraction used to complete the move. This can further be accomplished in two ways: First, by increasing the climber's maximum finger strength (Chapter Six: Strength) so that, for any given move, a lower percentage of maximum effort is required (See Figure on p92); and second, by improving grip control (Chapter Three: Skill Development) so that the bare minimum amount of force is applied to each hold.

The second primary mechanism for increasing blood flow to the forearms is to improve the capillary network throughout the forearm muscles, or *capillarization*. Oxygen enters the muscle fibers passively through diffusion. Therefore, blood must be positioned very near the muscle fibers for the best transportation of this critical fuel. Through proper training, it is possible to increase the quantity of capillaries, as well as their size, thus increasing blood flow oxygen delivery, and waste removal.

CAPILLARIZATION AND THE MAXIMUM STEADY STATE

Recall that the aerobic energy pathway can function indefinitely, as long as glucose is available. The highest level of intensity at which a muscle can continue to function aerobically, and thus, indefinitely, is called the *Maximum Steady State* (MSS; aka aerobic threshold, anaerobic threshold, or lactic threshold). The level of capillarization within a muscle is a key determiner of the MSS. Climbing at an intensity level above the MSS relies sufficiently on anaerobic respiration (glycolytic and/or phosphagen) that such effort becomes unsustainable, ultimately resulting in fatigue and eventual muscle failure. In endurance sports, it is often said that the MSS is the singlemost important determinant of performance, and so the majority of training activities are geared toward improving it.

In climbing, the importance of the MSS varies depending on the goals of the climber, i.e., the characteristics of the routes the climber attempts. The more sustained the climb, the more important MSS will be, but as described previously, *all climbing activities will benefit from improved capacity for aerobic respiration within the muscle fibers*. However, this characteristic must be specific to the muscles used (mostly the forearms) for it to be relevant to climbing. The whole body's systemic capacity for aerobic respiration is largely irrelevant in rock climbing, while the aerobic capacity of the muscle cells within the forearm is of utmost importance. Therefore, training must be properly tailored to the demands of climbing to improve local capillarity of the forearms in order to raise their MSS. Fortunately, this type of training has long-lasting effects, and investments in improving capillarity will pay dividends for years.

AEROBIC RESTORATION AND CAPILLARITY TRAINING

For rock climbing, the most practical method for improving capillarization in the forearms and raising the MSS is "aerobic respiration and capillarity" (ARC) training.[4] This consists of climbing for long, sustained periods as close as possible to the MSS. This is best performed by climbing on vertical to slightly overhanging terrain that places a steady load on the forearms so that a moderate, but sustainable pump ensues for upwards of 30 minutes. (Interval training is also beneficial for improving endurance, and is discussed in Chapter Eight: Power-Endurance.) In climbing, ARC training is used to:

"...I started to learn the value of recovery. With Bachar's influence, this would often involve 'active rest.' Not total rest, but days of doing the activity at a much-reduced level. For a sprinter, on a rest day, you would go out and do a bit of a jog. As a climber, I would go on easy soloing circuits. It keeps coordination and flow intact."
— Jerry Moffatt[7]

- Develop a foundation of muscular fitness to prepare for more-intense training
- Improve local forearm capillarity for improved aerobic energy metabolism
- Improve grip control (to prevent "over-gripping") and pump-management skills
- Aid recovery from intense training and performance efforts
- Acquire and practice new movement skills and techniques

BOHICA at the Red River Gorge, KY is a classic endurance route that rewards those with a high MSS – though rated 5.13b, most of the moves are 5.11 to 5.12-, so climbers who can ARC at the 5.12- level will cruise this commanding line, just like Greg Kerzhner. Dan Brayack

Because of the moderate intensity, ARC training gradually develops muscular fitness in all of the prime movers needed for climbing. This provides a gradual introduction to the more-intense activities that will be introduced later in the training cycle, stimulating modest adaptations to prepare the body for the upcoming additional stress. More importantly, this training establishes the base level of fitness that each climbing performance relies on, and off which other performance characteristics (strength, power, and power-endurance) build. Therefore, Base-Fitness training is an integral part of any training program.

The major goal of ARC training is to improve the forearm muscles' local ability to utilize aerobic energy metabolism, and thus reduce reliance on the other two, less-efficient processes (glycolytic and phosphagen systems). Another way to illustrate this is in terms of quantifiable climbing performance. For example, imagine a pumpy route that is composed of several 5.10 cruxes with few rests; this would be rated 5.11. A climber whose MSS is right at 5.10 (he can climb 5.10 moves uninterrupted for half an hour without getting tired) would be able to redpoint this climb easily because he would never need to rely on the less-efficient metabolic pathways. Now imagine he tries a 5.12 route that is packed with 5.11 cruxes. These will push him beyond his MSS, leading him to get pumped and possibly fail on the route. If he raised his MSS through ARC training to the 5.11 level, he would be able to climb this second route easily.

Improvement in your ability to utilize local aerobic metabolism directly enhances the ability to hold onto small holds longer, delay the onset of a pump, climb more-difficult moves while pumped, and recover from difficult moves more quickly. This is how the superstars onsight 5.14, or free a Grade VI big wall in a day; their MSS is so high that they can accomplish these feats while climbing aerobically. While aerobic climbing capacity benefits all aspects of performance, it is absolutely critical on certain types of routes, especially onsights and long, pumpy redpoints.

Proper ARC training requires careful moderation of forearm effort in order to maintain muscular exertion right at the MSS. This attention to hand-grip control is extremely valuable in difficult climbing as well, and will spell the difference between success and failure on routes of all kinds. Therefore, ARCing provides a great opportunity to hone this essential skill. The ability to manage a mounting pump throughout a climb is related to grip control, and is also essential to proper ARC training. The ARCing climber will quickly develop the ability to pace climbing sessions, time rests, and modulate effort throughout a climb to keep the pump in control.

Another critical purpose of ARCing is to speed recovery between workouts or taxing climbing days. Blood flow through skeletal muscle is stimulated by muscle contractions, through a system called the "skeletal muscle pump" (not to be confused with the climbing "pump"). The cyclic contraction of a muscle helps to transfer blood from capillaries to the veins so it can be transported back to the lungs for re-oxygenation. This process helps remove waste products and supply the muscle with fuel and other raw materials to rebuild muscle tissue after a hard workout. Inactivity causes blood to pool, and deprives the muscle of essential nutrients. ARCing provides the perfect stimulus for increased blood flow, as well as improved recovery. This "flushing" effect can be clearly felt after a hard climbing day.

Finally, ARC training is the perfect venue for learning and practicing novel climbing movements and techniques. The relatively low level of intensity permits the climber to concentrate on the subtleties of climbing technique, and to explore novel move-

Boulder-traversing in a gym is the simplest way to perform AEC training, and provides an opportunity for learning and reinforcing new techniques.

The Lost Art of ARC

ARCing may be one of the most derided forms of climbing training because it is hard to see the connection between the effort and tangible results. Many feel that because ARCing feels "easy" it must not be helping; "no pain, no gain," right? Not necessarily.

Early in my career as a climbing athlete (the point at which I started dedicated training), I ARC'd a lot. I did long (four-to-six-week) phases of dedicated ARC training, three sets a day, five days per week. At the time, it wasn't clear that these sessions had any direct benefit. I was improving at climbing, but I attributed those gains to other training activities. (Part of this conclusion resulted from the routes I was climbing: They were short and bouldery, and rarely had any endurance component.) Years later, I'm convinced that the time I spent ARCing had tremendous value, and it comes down to technique. In my career, I've managed to climb several highly technical routes. According to others, I have relatively precise footwork, smooth, accurate movement, and little wasted effort. I didn't start out this way; it came from hours upon hours of moderate climbing. Furthermore, this was pre-iPod, so I had nothing better to think about than dialing in my movement skills.

Fast-forward ten years, and now I climb extensively on steeper, more sustained routes, especially at the Red River Gorge, where much of the climbing is done at or very near the MSS, with brief excursions beyond the MSS. Therefore, the ability to raise my MSS through ARC training has had tremendous physical benefit, in addition to the technical benefits such as improved grip control and relaxation. A great example of the power of ARCing is the Motherlode's premier route, *Transworld Depravity*. *Transworld* has three distinct cruxes, each slightly easier than the last, separated by more-moderate but pumpy climbing. I decided to ARC (climb below my MSS) between the cruxes, and suppress the pump until I hit each crux, where I expected the pump to build. As I finished each crux and arrived at more-moderate terrain, the skills and physical adaptations I'd developed through ARCing would enable me to recover from the crux, clear out the pump, and set up for the next crux. I had to focus intensely to stay relaxed, control the pump, and keep climbing, but the ARCing paid off, and I redpointed *Transworld* in a quick four days of work. At the Red, raising my MSS corresponded directly to an increase in high-end climbing performance.

— *Mike Anderson*

Mike Anderson ARCing his way up *Transworld Depravity*, 5.14a, at the Motherlode, Red River Gorge, KY.　Janelle Anderson

ments while still achieving physical training goals. The duration of ARC sets provides ample time for repetitive practice of new techniques.

When properly performed, ARC training causes three key adaptations in the muscles of the forearm:

1. Increased blood *flow* increases shear stress on the capillary walls and stimulates capillary growth. Increased blood *pressure* stimulates cross-sectional growth of blood *arterioles* (the blood vessels that feed into the capillaries). This growth can occur after as little as two weeks of training, and will improve blood flow in the forearms while climbing.[12]
2. Stimulates the release of a protein (VEGF) that initiates *angiogenesis*, or capillary growth (training at altitude can stimulate similar adaptations).
3. Stimulates increases in the quantity, size, and capacity of mitochondria in the affected muscle cells, which improves the muscles' ability to utilize aerobic respiration to the maximum extent possible, during all aspects of climbing performance.

PERFORMING ARC TRAINING

An ARC workout involves sustained climbing, usually in a climbing gym, right at the MSS. A single set typically consists of climbing, without a break, for 20 to 45 minutes straight. Up to three sets can be completed in a single ARC workout. The goal is to continuously climb at the MSS: the level of intensity that taxes the muscles of the forearms such that aerobic respiration of the muscle cells can just barely meet the energetic demands for ATP. This level of effort will stimulate desired adaptations, which are dependent on high blood flow through the capillaries. Climbing on terrain that is too difficult, above the MSS, will occlude blood flow, preventing this necessary stimulus. The volume of ARC training completed determines the level of improvement achieved, so the more ARC training, the better (barring injury).

FOCUS AND INTENSITY

Since climbers are not equipped with an "ATP consumption gauge," we must use subjective indicators to judge the correct level of effort — mainly, the level of forearm pump. The key to performing the workout properly (thus stimulating the proper adaptations) is to modulate the difficulty of moves in order to maintain the level of muscular effort right at, or below, the MSS. Begin with more difficult climbing to build to a moderate pump, and then adjust the difficulty as needed to maintain the pump. Constant focus is necessary throughout each set to assess and control

the level of intensity. Pay close attention to the body's feedback, and adjust the terrain and hold selection as necessary. Here are some tips for maintaining proper focus and intensity:

- ARCing must be done by *feel*; with practice, the feel of a strenuous but sustainable pump will become second nature. A good ARC session should have the climber breathing heavily and lightly sweating after the first 10 minutes or so.
- Most climbers will spend the majority of each set on vertical to just slightly overhanging terrain.
- Each set should last at least 20 minutes; therefore, develop and maintain the level of pump that can be sustained for that duration. It should be as severe as is tolerable short of falling off or flailing. That said, the goal is NOT to pump off the wall just as the clock strikes midnight. With varied terrain and an assortment of holds, you should be able to modulate the grip size, angle, and movement difficulty as needed to "dial in" the perfect pump.
- If the level of pump is too great, blood flow will be occluded, preventing the beneficial adaptations stimulated by high blood flow and high blood pressure.
- Every move in an ARC set doesn't have to be of equal difficulty. It is acceptable to climb a short series of hard moves followed by an easier set of moves to recover. For example, a climber could alternate between short stints of small and large footholds, if the gym's walls are too steep to use small footholds exclusively. This works well for practicing specific movements that are slightly too hard for ARCing.
- If a severe pump develops, the moves are too difficult; if no pump, sweating, or heavy breathing develops then the moves are too easy.
- Effective training is always progressive, so expect to *slightly* increase the intensity of the ARC sessions over the course of the phase. Progress is gradual but persistent, so don't expect meteoric gains right away.
- Once the correct level of effort is determined, add in movement practice, breathing, and other skills discussed in Chapter Three: Skill Development to create a workout that is equal parts physical training and skill practice.

ARC sessions provide a great opportunity to discover and practice novel rest positions.

- Emphasize smaller footholds to increase climbing specificity.
- A fun challenge is to locate increasingly improbable and awkward rest positions while ARCing. Look for unlikely stems, highsteps, mantels, heel hooks, etc. (refer to Chapter Three: Skill Development). Avoid easy rests that unweight the arms, practicing active rests instead (those that require alternating hands and labored breathing). This practice will be much appreciated when the Performance Phase rolls around.
- In the gym, ARCing should not be limited to designated (taped) routes; utilize all the available holds and features to modulate intensity and specificity.
- ARCing can be difficult to accomplish in a crowded public climbing gym, so try to visit the gym at an off-peak time. Treadwalls or auto-belay systems can be great tools for ARCing, if available.
- If a dedicated training partner is available, consecutive up-down-up-etc. sessions on toprope can help spice up the monotony of ARCing.

- ARC-leading in a gym is one of the ultimate forms of training, creating physical, technical, and mental gains. Tie in, and up and down-climb (unclipping while downclimbing so you can climb back up a different route) on a lead wall for 30 minutes, then swap roles with the belayer. This provides critical practice for relaxed lead climbing, clipping, resting, etc., and is the perfect opportunity to "stress-proof" new movement techniques. These workouts should be scheduled late in the Base-Fitness Phase.
- ARC training is not a mutually exclusive workout; nothing has to be replaced in order to include it in a training program. It can be performed at the end of a workout, or the day after a hard workout.
- The total sum of ARCing time determines improvement, not the duration of individual sets. I.e., three sets of 30 minutes will theoretically produce the same effect as two sets of 45 minutes. Many climbers find it easier to maintain focus and intensity through a greater number of shorter sets as opposed to two mega-sets.
- Too much ARCing can lead to tendonitis in the fingers. Pay attention to signs of overuse, and plan adequate rest.

"In general, endurance work is all about volume, so if you've got the time, then the best place to get fit is at the crag, simply by putting the mileage in." — Ben Moon[13]

OUTDOOR MILEAGE TRAINING

While the typical Base-Fitness workout is performed by ARCing in a climbing gym, it is beneficial to perform these workouts outside on occasion. In terms of skill development, outdoor routes are preferred, as they provide a more realistic practice environment. Throughout the training season, indoor ARC workouts may be substituted with Outdoor Mileage (OM) days in which six to twelve "moderate" routes or pitches are climbed out at the crags. These routes should be approximately one to two full number grades below the climber's maximum onsight ability; they should not require rehearsal or "all-out" efforts to complete, but they should be moderately fatiguing — just like ARCing. Apply the guidelines of ARC training (described previously) to these routes, concentrating on

> "A lot of the time when you're climbing, John [Bachar] explained, you really want to be letting go of holds, not gripping them harder. Find ways of applying just the right amount of force to a hold, he suggested, instead of wasting lots of energy. Relax the entire body. Flow." — Jerry Moffatt[7]

details such as breathing, grip control, movement, etc. Try to create continuous ARC "sets" of 20 to 45 minutes, which may require fast climbers to climb multiple pitches back-to-back. Think of OM workouts as simply ARCing on a rope, outside. Finally, OM days should be fun. This is the opportunity to spend a stress-free day at the crag with friends, ticking off enjoyable classics or conquering that multipitch route you've been meaning to climb.

SKILL DEVELOPMENT WITH BASE-FITNESS TRAINING

The moderate intensity of Base-Fitness training makes it ideal for practicing climbing movement, including acquiring new skills and rehearsing and refining existing skills. Chapter Three: Skill Development covers this topic in detail, suggesting many drills that can be accomplished to develop and rehearse critical climbing skills. Many of these should be performed during ARC workouts, but there are a few guidelines to keep in mind:

- Correctly performing technique drills requires concentrating on the drill itself, but don't forget to pay attention to the level of physical exertion. Maintain proper intensity to achieve the correct ARC training effect. Climbers new to ARC training should wait to incorporate technique drills for a few sessions until they have found suitable terrain and determined the right level of effort to reach their MSS.

- It is best to concentrate on only a few techniques and/or drills in a given session. This allows the climber to remain mindful of the key focus areas of each drill and perform them correctly.

- Specific techniques and drills should be progressively revisited in subsequent ARC sessions throughout a season, as suggested in the calendar in the Figure below.

- A major technical goal of ARC training is to learn to climb relaxed and remain calm, regardless of the mounting fatigue or tactical errors on a route. Listening to mellow, soothing music while ARCing may help encourage this mindset.

SCHEDULING BASE-FITNESS TRAINING

A typical Base-Fitness workout is two or three 30-minute continuous climbing sessions, or "sets," with 10 minutes of rest between each set (bring your MP3 player!). Again, the total duration of MSS climbing is more important than how the sets are split up; therefore, aim for a total of 60 to 90 minutes of climbing time in an ARC or OM workout, with at least 20 min-

Sunday	Monday	Tuesday	Wednesday	Thursday	Friday	Saturday
Rest Phase of Previous Season						Sa Day 1 *Outdoor Mileage (OM), 6 mod pitches *Skill acquisition
Su Day 2 *OM, 4 mod pitches *Skill acquisition	Mo 3 *Optional Aerobic Exercise (OAE)	Tu 4 *ARC 1: 2 x 20 min *Skill acquisition	We 5 *OAE	Th 6 *ARC 2: 2 x 25 min *Skill acquisition	Fr 7 *OAE	Sa 8 *OM, 7 mod pitches *Skill acquisition
Su 9 *OM, 5 mod pitches *Skill acquisition	Mo 10 *OAE	Tu 11 *ARC 3: 2 x 30 min *Skill practice	We 12 *OAE	Th 13 *ARC 4: 2 x 30 min *Skill practice	Fr 14 *OAE	Sa 15 *OM, 8 mod pitches *Skill practice
Su 16 *OM, 6 mod pitches *Skill practice	Mo 17 *OAE	Tu 18 *ARC 5: 3 x 25 min *Skill practice	We 19 *ARC 6: 3 x 25 min *Skill practice	Th 20 *ARC 7: 2 x 25 min *Stress-proofing	Fr 21 *OAE	Sa 22 *OM, 10 mod pitches *Stress-proofing
Su 23 *OM, 8 mod pitches *Stress-proofing	Mo 24 *OAE	Tu 25 *ARC 8: 3 x 30 min *Stress-proofing	We 26 *ARC 9: 3 x 30 min *Stress-proofing	Th 27 *ARC 10: 2 x 30m *Stress-proofing	Fr 28 *OAE	Sa 29

A typical Base-Fitness schedule for a novice climber, consisting of indoor ARC sessions and Outdoor Mileage sessions. Notice that the volume of ARC training increases throughout the phase, and Skill Development activities are specified and also progress from acquisition, to practice, to stress-proofing.

Key:
ARC – Aerobic Restoration and Capillarity Training
OM – Outdoor Mileage
OAE – Optional Aerobic Exercise

utes of continuous climbing per set. A typical four-week Base-Fitness training schedule for a novice climber is shown on p101.

ARC training is not very intense, so the climber does not need to be completely rested, or "fresh," to ARC. Therefore, ARC workouts can be scheduled the day after intense training days (such as strength work-outs), though typically you'd perform at a reduced volume (two 20-to-30-minute sets, or one 45-minute set). This works particularly well when two rest days are taken between intense workouts. For example, a typical three-week Strength Phase schedule for a novice climber that includes optional, supplemental Base-Fitness workouts is:

Sunday	Monday	Tuesday	Wednesday	Thursday	Friday	Saturday
Su 23	Mo 24	Tu 25	We 26	Th 27	Fr 28	Sa 29 *Hangboard (HB) 1 *Supplemental Ex
		Last Week of Base-Fitness Phase				
Su 30 *Optional OM, 4p *OAE *Skin care	Mo 31 *OAE	Tu 32 *HB 2 *SE	We 33 *Opt ARC: 2x20 min *OAE *Skin care	Th 34 *OAE	Fr 35 *HB3 *SE	Sa 36 *Optional OM, 4p *OAE *Skin care
Su 37 *OAE	Mo 38 *HB 4 *SE	Tu 39 *Opt ARC: 2x20 min *OAE *Skin care	We 40 *OAE	Th 41 *HB5 *SE	Fr 42 *Opt ARC: 2x20 min *OAE *Skin care	Sa 43 *OAE
Su 44 *HB6 *SE	Mo 45 *Opt ARC 1 x 30min (Begin Tapering) *Skin care	Tu 46	We 47 *HB7 *SE	Th 48 *Skin care	Fr 49	Sa 50

A typical Strength Phase schedule for a novice climber, which includes supplemental Base-Fitness training (indoor ARC sessions and Outdoor Mileage sessions). These workouts are optional during the Strength Phase, so they are shown in grey text. Notice that the volume of ARC training is lower than it is during the Base-Fitness Phase, and tapers near the end of the phase.

Key:
ARC – Aerobic Restoration and Capillarity Training
OM – Outdoor Mileage
OAE – Optional Aerobic Exercise
HB - Hangboard Excercise

In the above example, the Base-Fitness work-outs (ARC or OM) can be completed the day after strength training because they are not very intense, so the fatigue of Day 32 will not impair Day 33's ARC workout. Further, because Day 34 is a rest day, there is plenty of time for the body to recover from any lingering fatigue caused by the ARC workout on Day 33, before strength training again on Day 35. As an added benefit, the ARC workout will aid recovery from Day 32's strength workout by encouraging blood flow through the climbing-relevant muscles, improving the climber's performance on Day 35.

In addition to entire workouts consisting of multiple ARC sets, it can be beneficial to incorporate one or more ARC sets into other workouts or climbing days. For example, 20 to 30 minutes of ARCing may be performed at the beginning of a strength workout as part of the warm-up, or a 30-minute ARC set may be done at the end of a climbing day as a cooldown (many climbers end a day with "laps" on a moderate route, which creates a similar effect). This "modularity" is a great feature of ARC training; ARCing can thus be squeezed into a training program in many different ways, without interfering with other forms of training.

In the periodic Rock Prodigy program, dedicated ARCing is scheduled at the start of each climbing season in a two-to-four-week phase that prepares the climber for the more-intense training activities to come. After this initial phase, ARC workouts can be included occasionally within the Strength and Power-Endurance phases (at a reduced volume, as described above). ARC workouts performed in the latter phases are supplemental and should be reduced or eliminated if they interfere with the primary workouts of that phase. Interference might include inadequate recovery between workouts, signs of impending overuse injury, excessive skin wear, or insufficient time to accommodate all of the weekly training activities.

SUMMARY

- Building a training base prepares the climber for more-intense training and establishes the baseline for further muscular performance.
- Muscle function is complex, with many redundant adaptable systems that can be trained, as desired, to permit sustained activity and/or increased force production.
- There are three metabolic energy pathways that the muscles use to varying degrees to provide fuel for muscular contractions. The more the muscles use aerobic respiration, the longer climbing can be sustained.
- Muscle fatigue is specific to the activity, so endurance training must be specific to the climber's goals.
- Because of the importance of aerobic respiration, all climbing disciplines will benefit from Base-Fitness training, which improves mitochondrial density and performance.
- A forearm pump results from occluded blood flow in the forearms, limiting the delivery of fuel and removal of waste. Increasing strength, controlling grip effort while climbing, and improving local forearm capillarity will all help to delay the onset of a pump.
- Local muscular capillarity and aerobic efficiency are increased through aerobic restoration and capillarity (ARC) training.
- ARC training must be performed at the correct intensity to achieve the desired results. ARCing above the MSS will occlude blood flow, preventing the necessary training stimulus.
- ARC training has several other benefits, including facilitating skill development, accelerating recovery, and improving grip control.

Climbing long, sustained multipitch routes, such as *La Fiesta del Biceps*, 7a, at Riglos, Spain, is a brilliant way to perform Base-Fitness training.
Andrew Burr

STRENGTH

Many outstanding routes, such as the iconic *Chain Reaction*, 5.12c, Smith Rock, OR, require substantial finger strength. The legendary Alan Watts returns to the catalyst of American sport climbing, 30 years after the first ascent. Mike Anderson

CHAPTER 6

"Because your fingers are the link to the rock, finger strength is probably the most important strength you can have. Your fingers can never be strong enough." — *Jerry Moffat*[12]

INTRODUCTION

Every climber could use greater strength. Finger strength in particular can overcome many other weaknesses. While technical skill plays a tremendous role in every climber's career, those that continue to improve will inevitably reach the point where finger strength is a weak link, if not *the* limiting factor. While some routes can be finessed, there are certain routes — including countless legendary routes like *Chain Reaction*, *Quinsana Plus*, or *The Beast*, to name a few — that simply cannot be climbed without a decent serving of brute force. Flawless movement and perfect balance will only take a climber so far; eventually, it becomes necessary to squeeze like an ape on miniscule holds.

Furthermore, unlike other physiological elements of performance, improving strength kills two birds with one stone. Obviously, greater strength imparts the ability to perform more-difficult individual moves, but as explained in the previous chapter, increased strength improves endurance as well. By raising one's strength ceiling, a move that previously may have required 80 percent effort might only require 70 percent effort in the future, resulting in less fatigue over a sequence of moves.

Unfortunately, strength gains are not realized "overnight"; however, the gains that *are* made build from one season to the next, and year-to-year, making impressive strength gains possible over the course of a career. While muscles respond to training within a matter of weeks, it takes many years for the critical connective tissue supporting those muscles to adapt to the increased forces that stronger muscles will impart. Regardless of the climber's preferred style, finger strength will inevitably become central to his or her quest for continuous improvement, so climbers should constantly be working to improve it.

Proven finger-strength training methodologies are surprisingly scarce, considering climbers' universal desire for stronger fingers. The Olympic sports have perfected methods for increasing strength in the large muscle groups, but the fingers are much more fragile, and climbers use them in unique ways. For this reason, practices for strengthening the quadriceps or biceps may wreak havoc on the fingers. Instead, climbers must develop their own training approaches, through theory, logic, and trial and error — the way this program was developed. As a result of this strong foundation, the Rock Prodigy program has produced tremendous finger-strength gains in a wide variety of climbers, and is a great starting point for anyone seeking continuous improvement.

FORCE PRODUCTION

As discussed in Chapter Five: Base-Fitness, muscles produce force when the motor units within the muscle contract. That contraction is caused by the tensing action of the sarcomeres within the muscle fiber. The amount of force generated by a motor unit during a contraction is a function of the number of cross-bridges within the sarcomere, and the number and size of sarcomeres acting in parallel.[14] The greater the cross-sectional area (CSA) of parallel sarcomeres in a motor unit, the greater potential force generation.[14]

Force production is complicated further because not all motor units respond effectively during a given contraction. Initially, only the smallest (and therefore weakest) motor units are activated. As the duration of contraction grows, increasingly larger (and there-

Moves like this place abnormal stress on the fingers. Prepare your fingers for such stress through a structured strength training program. Chris Weidner wrangling *Horse Lattitudes*, 5.14a, Virgin River Gorge, UT.   📷 Andrew Burr

fore stronger) motor units are *recruited* to assist.[14] Depending on the nature of the contraction, some motor units may activate too slowly to contribute to the effort, and others may not activate at all. Thus the amount of force generated by a given muscle during a contraction depends on the number of active motor units, as well as the sarcomere CSA of those motor units.

Considering these two primary contributors to muscular-force production, there are essentially two fundamental ways to increase the strength of a given muscle:

- Increase the cross-sectional area of the muscle
- Improve motor-unit activation

Climbers should work to improve both. In practice, these two factors are closely intertwined, such that any effort to improve one will likely impact the other.

HYPERTROPHY

Hypertrophy is the volumetric increase of a particular organ or tissue. In strength training, this term is used to describe growth in muscle-tissue volume, and it is the primary method of increasing the cross-sectional area of the muscle. In extreme cases, *hyperplasia* (splitting of cells to increase the total number of mus-

cle cells) can occur, though strength training has not been shown to cause hyperplasia in human skeletal muscle without the use of artificially injected growth hormones.[5]

Hypertrophy can be further categorized as *sarcomere hypertrophy* and *sarcoplasmic hypertrophy*. These classifications refer to growth of those respective tissues within the muscle cells. The sarcomeres are the fundamental force-generating tissues within the muscle, and the sarcoplasm is the tissue that stores energy for use by the sarcomeres. While the sarcomeres contain the contractile proteins of the muscle tissue, the sarcoplasm is critical to fueling the muscles (and delaying fatigue) during sustained climbing, so both are important to climbers.[5]

Any increase in muscle volume will come with a corresponding increase in mass. Hypertrophy is the primary objective in bodybuilding, where muscle *size* is the ultimate goal, and body weight and strength are irrelevant. However, climbing performance is ultimately a matter of strength-to-weight ratio, so it is wise to consider whether an increase in the strength (and size) of a particular muscle group is worth the resultant weight gain. For this reason, many climbers are reluctant to embrace hypertrophy. Each muscle group should be considered individually. Except in extreme cases, any hypertrophy below the waist is unlikely to improve performance. On the flip side, the forearm muscles are relatively small yet their contribution to climbing performance is enormous. Forearm strength is quite literally "worth its weight in gold," so hypertrophy in these muscles should be embraced.

Desirability of Hypertrophy:

Highly Undesirable		Neutral		Highly Desirable
Lower Legs	Back	Shoulders		Forearms
Upper Legs		Abdominals		
		Upper Arms		

In reality, significant hypertrophy is difficult to achieve. The muscle-bound beasts at Gold's Gym are training several hours every day, and consuming massive amounts of calories (4,000 or more per day!) to fuel their muscular growth. That said, some people achieve hypertrophy more easily than others, and this may not be consistent across muscle groups. Women, prepubescent children, and middle-aged or older men will have difficulty achieving significant hypertrophy.[4] Fortunately, hypertrophy is only one part of the strength-gain equation. Strength can be increased effectively through other mechanisms.

"I wanted to build up my physique. For the levels of difficulty in climbing these days, this approach would not be very effective if you want to be only a climber. Big muscles are not required. Good genetics is. Lightness is a blessing." — John Gill[19]

NEUROLOGICAL ADAPTATIONS

Muscle contractions are initiated when the brain signals the motor neurons. Each motor neuron controls a single motor unit, which may consist of one or more individual muscle fibers.[14] The motor neuron creates an action potential, which causes a mechanical response in the motor unit known as a *twitch*. A single motor-unit twitch is quite brief (on the order of 0.1 seconds), so the neural system sustains muscle contractions by activating many neurons in a continuous fashion, and by repeatedly activating the same neurons. Force production builds as more and more motor units cycle on and off. Additionally, as a particular motor neuron receives a cascade of consecutive signals, the high frequency of activation produces a synergistic effect that results in increased fiber tension.[14] The neurological system also produces feedback signals that are used to regulate motion and protect the

Skinny Legs

At a certain point — the point where your goal routes start to overhang — climbing performance depends heavily on strength-to-weight ratio. This can be improved through proper diet (see Chapter Eleven: Weight Management), but many climbers could also benefit from reducing unhelpful muscle mass. The legs are a good place to look for several pounds of lazy, free-loading muscle (muscle that does not contribute significantly to rock-climbing performance). Granted, leg muscles do have a role to play in pushing out highsteps and such, but the science shows that de-training actually improves muscular power — which is why endurance athletes have no hops!

The solution to excess leg muscle is exceedingly simple. Stop using your legs! If you currently engage in any form of regular leg-training (such as running, biking, tele-skiing, step aerobics, speed skating, rowing, weight-lifting, P90X, Crossfit, etc.), all you need do is stop. If this sounds undesirable or unbelievable, try it for at least a couple of months to see what happens. You might be pleasantly surprised by the results, and you can always go back to your cross-training if you discover you can't live without it. Muscles "in training" for extended aerobic efforts can store as much as five pounds of useless (to climbing) glucose and water alone, so even if you are reluctant to downsize your sexy quads, simply laying off the treadmill for a few weeks can save precious pounds.

For those who want the best of both worlds, you can resume your aerobic passion periodically and still reap the benefits of skinny legs. Get your fill of these activities early in each training cycle, allowing plenty of time to slim down for peak climbing phases (refer to Chapter Ten: Building a Training Plan and Other Training Considerations). For example, I "got skinny" for the summer 2011 season, then as my Performance Phase was winding down I began training for a 450-mile bike trip in early August. I spent the rest of August and September training to climb, and by early October I was lean and mean and sent the hardest route of my career.
— *Mark Anderson*

muscle from generating so much force that it would damage the muscle or supporting tissue.

These neural processes are quite inefficient in "untrained" individuals. Significant strength gains can be achieved simply by "teaching" the neural system to be more efficient through "practice." These adaptations occur much more quickly than hypertrophy (which requires tissue growth) and account for most of an athlete's gains during the first several weeks of strength training.[4, 13] Furthermore, these gains don't increase body weight.

Force production can be increased by commanding more motor units to activate simultaneously (also known as recruitment — see Chapter Seven: Power) and by increasing the frequency with which a single motor unit is activated.[1] Furthermore, progressive training can reduce the neural system's contraction inhibitions, allowing well-trained individuals to generate even more force by minimizing the muscle's intrinsic margin of safety.[1, 4] These strength gains are distinct from those achieved through recruitment. This particular adaptation to strength training is typically responsible for the gains experienced by women and adolescents (who lack the necessary hormones for significant hypertrophy). Most climbers likely experience similar adaptations, since they do not consume enough calories for significant hypertrophy.

INCREASING STRENGTH

As discussed in Chapter Four: Foundations of Physical Training, the fundamental method for stimulating muscular adaptation is through the cycle of overload, recovery, and super-compensation. As the body adapts, the training stress applied must increase in order to force further adaptation.

These principles hold true for both hypertrophic and neural adaptations. However, research shows that neural adaptations occur much more quickly than hypertrophy in the muscles.[4, 13] Some studies indicate hypertrophy may not *begin* until eight or more weeks after stimulation.[11] Often the Strength Phase will end before hypertrophy occurs (though the hypertrophy will often manifest itself later in the macro-cycle). On the other hand, neurological adaptations can occur in a matter of several days, but these gains generally plateau after a few weeks. Therefore, rather than pushing through this multi-week plateau, waiting for hypertrophy gains, climbers should transition to the next training phase after about three to four weeks of strength training.

An effective strength-training program requires progressive overload. In other words, the training volume must exceed the body's baseline capability, and must continuously increase from one workout to the next. During strength training this is best accom-

plished by steadily increasing resistance. Periodically applying a constant, comfortable load only trains the muscles to maintain their current level of strength. *Increasing* strength requires the athlete to consistently push right up against their physical limits, and then incrementally increase that resistance over time.

The only guaranteed way to ensure overload *and* progression between workouts is to carefully quantify the resistance used. Then the athlete can establish her baseline strength and carefully control the resistance to create predictable, incremental increases in training stress. To do this reliably, the athlete must:

- Use training exercises with controllable and quantifiable resistance
- Document the results of every exercise and workout
- Use the recorded data to incrementally increase the resistance

Athletes have long achieved these three objectives with carefully planned weightlifting programs. Unfortunately, these programs are not specific to climbing. For this reason, climbers have developed unique, sport-specific training tools such as the *hangboard* (described later), which is used in the Rock Prodigy program to conduct controlled, quantifiable, progressive strength training.

CONTRACTION TYPES AND STRENGTH TRAINING

As discussed in Chapter Five: Base-Fitness, skeletal muscles undergo three types of muscular contractions:

- *Concentric* (muscle shortens during contraction)
- *Eccentric* (muscle lengthens during contraction)
- *Isometric* (muscle length remains fixed during contraction)

The first two contraction types are considered *isotonic contractions*, since the muscle fibers move with respect to each other. A typical strength-training exercise for a weightlifter involves a cycle of all three contractions (during a bicep curl, the athlete lifts the weight with a concentric contraction, pauses at the top with a brief isometric contraction, then lowers the weight with an eccentric contraction).

Weightlifters emphasize isotonic contractions because they cause greater strength and size gains *throughout the range of motion* of a given joint.[9, 10, 17] Most athletes seek strength gains throughout the range of motion, and many "ball sport" athletes are all too happy to add size as well. A great deal of experimental effort has been applied to maximizing the effectiveness of isotonic strength training.

On the other hand, isometric contractions have not been studied much, as they are considered less applicable to the Olympic and big-money sports. That said, some clinical data exists, and it shows that isometric contractions are vastly superior to isotonic contractions for increasing strength *at a specific joint angle*. One study in particular showed a 20 percent increase in max strength when isometric contractions were used, compared to an 11 percent increase for isotonic contractions.[8] Therefore, athletes should train isometrically if their sport primarily requires isometric contractions at a *consistent, fixed joint position*. In climbing, the fingers are almost always used isometrically, and the required joint angles are easy to predict. The catch is, the strength gained does not transfer well to other joint angles.[9, 10, 17] The bottom line for climbers is: Isometric finger-strength training is superior to isotonic training, but in order for it to be effective, *climbers must train at the precise joint angles they need to strengthen*.

Fortunately, climbers use a relatively small number of fixed hand positions for rock climbing. These hand positions are easily identified, repeatable, and for the vast majority of climbing movements, these finger positions remain more or less static (or isometric, as far as the muscles are concerned).

Of course, some climbs require the forearm muscles to contract isotonically, such as the eccentric stretch-lengthening that occurs when latching an extreme dyno, or when "rolling up" from an open crimp to a closed crimp. Furthermore, isometric contractions have little to no effect on muscle-contraction speed, which is a critical component of dynamic movement.[8, 18] This is a significant problem for climbers, so isomet-

Heavy Finger Rolls

Heavy finger rolls are an isotonic finger exercise often considered for finger-strength training. A heavily loaded barbell is grasped with two hands, with the arms hanging straight down. A repetition consists of eccentrically uncurling the fingers, allowing the bar to slowly "roll" down until the fingers are almost completely extended, and then concentrically curling the fingers back up to form a fist around the bar. Since these contractions are isotonic, they *should* produce more hypertrophy than isometric contractions. Limited experimentation has shown that this may be true; however, there appears to be no net improvement in functional strength (as it pertains to rock climbing).

The authors (and other similarly minded climbers) have experimented extensively with the use of heavy finger rolls, including using them as a precursor to the Strength and Power phases described in this chapter and the next. Our conclusion is that heavy finger rolls are not sufficiently sport specific to produce hypertrophy or strength gains that are relevant to rock climbers. The specific shortcoming is not known, but one theory is that none of the joint angles utilized during a heavy finger roll repetition are used in climbing. Furthermore, while the contractions are isotonic, they occur too slowly to have any practical effect on contact strength. Skip the heavy finger rolls, and stick to sport-specific training that produces results *on the rock*.

ric finger-strength training alone is not sufficient. Dynamic training is also essential, but it must be sport specific and complement the larger training program (Chapter Seven: Power describes such training). That said, isometric training of the most common grip positions is the ideal way for climbers to begin finger strength training.

So far this discussion has considered only finger-strength training, but shoulders, upper arms, chest, back, abdominals, and other "core" muscle groups also play an important role in climbing performance. Each climber should consider his own strengths and weaknesses with respect to his goals when deciding which muscle groups require additional strength, which groups only require strength maintenance, and which might even be worth de-training in the interest of improving the climber's strength-to-weight ratio. Most climbers will have limited training time and/or

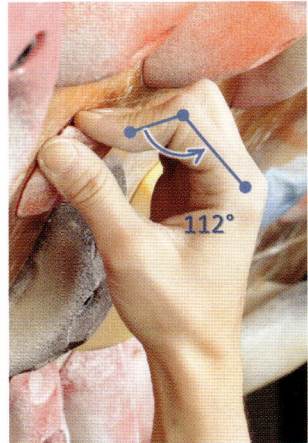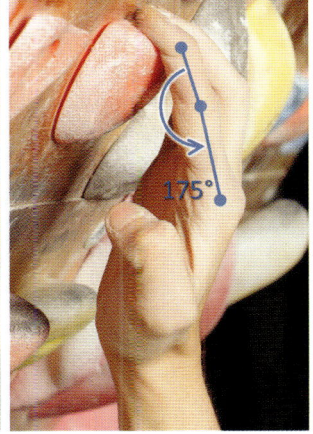

112°   175°

Open grip strength gains achieved through isometric training do not transfer well to the crimp grip because the PIP joint angle differs significantly between these grips.

energy, so it makes sense to prioritize these areas and focus attention on those that are the most limiting. Generally, these muscle groups should be trained isotonically since climbers use them in a wide variety of positions. However, "pull muscles" and core muscles are often used isometrically (for example, during lock-offs or flagging moves), so climbers may benefit from training these muscle groups isometrically.

- Favor Isotonic Contractions for:
  - Pull exercises
  - Push exercises
  - Shoulder exercises
  - Core exercises
  - Pinch grips*
- Favor Isometric Contractions for:
  - Most finger grips
  - Lock-offs
  - Goal-route specific crux positions where joint angle is known

Pinches are unique from most grips in that their width varies drastically from one hold to the next, varying the joint angles used by the thumb and fingers. Ideally, climbers would train this entire range of motion, either by performing isotonic contractions, or isometric contractions using multiple pinch grips of varying width that span the range of motion.

For movements that are executed both isotonically and isometrically while climbing (such as pull-ups and lock-offs), a compromise between both training approaches can be used. For example, the climber can execute a normal pull-up, then lock-off at the top of the repetition for several counts before descending. The same approach can be applied to core exercises such as hanging leg-lifts.

Set and Repetition Ranges

Weightlifters achieve progressive overload by performing one or more sets, each consisting of a certain number of repetitions. Climbers should follow a similar approach. There are an infinite number of possible set and repetition combinations, and the debate rages endlessly as to which protocol is ideal for achieving this or that result. In fact, one analysis suggests that numbers of sets and reps are completely irrelevant, so long as the resistance is sufficient to cause failure by the end of the prescribed protocol.[7] Any authority claiming to know with certainty what is ideal should be viewed with extreme skepticism. That said, there is tremendous anecdotal evidence (backed by decades of practical experience) suggesting that certain *ranges* of sets and repetitions are *generally* more effective than others at producing certain results. For the sake of this discussion, unless otherwise stated, assume that resistance should be adjusted such that the prescribed number of repetitions can just barely be completed before fatigue sets in.

Any prescription will vary depending on the goal. Power training seeks to achieve recruitment over hypertrophy, and generally calls for fewer repetitions. Even when hypertrophy is desired, adjusting the number of repetitions may affect the *type* of hypertrophy achieved. Some have theorized that it may be possible to favor sarcomere or "functional" hypertrophy (growth of the contractile units of the muscle) over sarcoplasmic hypertrophy (growth of the energy storage fluids and non-contractile tissues) in order to maximize strength gains while minimizing size/weight gain, or vice versa by varying set/rep ranges, although the scientific data remains inconclusive. However, practical experience in the weightlifting community suggests that it is indeed possible to emphasize strength gains over size gains by limiting the number of repetitions (and vice versa). Furthermore, maintaining low rep ranges can increase the likelihood that the more powerful fast-twitch fibers are stimulated to strengthen.

The number of sets the athlete performs should depend on the training objective. Experience shows it is beneficial to perform more repetitions (with correspondingly lower resistance) in the early sets, and then steadily reduce the number of reps (while increasing resistance) for each subsequent set. This approach provides a progressive warm-up for the most intense repetitions. For example, the first set of an exercise might consist of 12 reps, then the second set

Desired Adaptation	Number of Sets	Number of Repetitions	Rest Between Sets
Power	1-3	3-5	3-5 minutes
"Functional" Hypertrophy	3-4	6-8	3-5 minutes
"Non-Functional" Hyp.	3-4	8-12	1-3 minutes
Strength-Endurance	2-4	12-20	30 sec – 1 minute

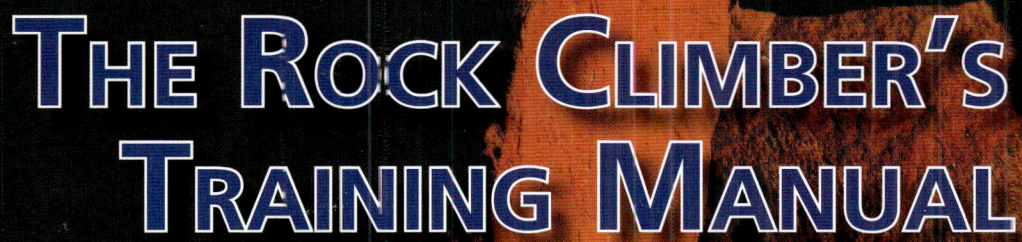

A Guide to Continuous Improvement

Seasonal Training Plan

Example

Week	Sunday	Monday	Tuesday	Wednesday	Thursday	Friday	Saturday
	ARC #5 29 3 x 30 min	ARC#6 30 3 x 25min	ARC#7 31 2 x 25 min	2013 1 January 1-hr hike	Hangboard 1 2 HB1, Completed 6 of 8 grips	Outdoor Mileage 3 4 x 5.10 at Shelf	15-mile MTB 4
	HB#2 5 HB2, Completed 7 of 8 grips	ARC#8 6 **TODAY**	7	HB#3 8	9	10	HB#4 11

Record your plan before each workout

Record what you did after each workout

Week	Sunday	Monday	Tuesday	Wednesday	Thursday	Friday	Saturday
1							
2							
3							
4							

Week	Sunday	Monday	Tuesday	Wednesday	Thursday	Friday	Saturday
5							
6							
7							
8							
9							
10							
11							

Week	Sunday	Monday	Tuesday	Wednesday	Thursday	Friday	Saturday
12							
13							
14							
15							
16							
17							
18							

The Rock Climber's Training Manual
Aerobic Restoration and Capillarity (ARC) Log

Date: ____/____/_____   W/O#: _____
Location: _____
Description of Terrain: _____
_____
Approximate Difficulty: _____
SET: Duration: Comments:
____   _____   _____
____   _____   _____

Date: ____/____/_____   W/O#: _____
Location: _____
Description of Terrain: _____
_____
Approx. Difficulty: _____
SET: Duration: Comments:
____   _____   _____
____   _____   _____

Date: ____/____/_____   W/O#: _____
Location: _____
Description of Terrain: _____
_____
Approx. Difficulty: _____
SET: Duration: Comments:
____   _____   _____
____   _____   _____

Date: ____/____/_____   W/O#: _____
Location: _____
Description of Terrain: _____
_____
Approx. Difficulty: _____
SET: Duration: Comments:
____   _____   _____
____   _____   _____

Date: ____/____/_____   W/O#: _____
Location: _____
Description of Terrain: _____
_____
Approx. Difficulty: _____
SET: Duration: Comments:
____   _____   _____
____   _____   _____

Date: ____/____/_____   W/O#: _____
Location: _____
Description of Terrain: _____
_____
Approx. Difficulty: _____
SET: Duration: Comments:
____   _____   _____
____   _____   _____

Date: ____/____/_____   W/O#: _____
Location: _____
Description of Terrain: _____
_____
Approx. Difficulty: _____
SET: Duration: Comments:
____   _____   _____
____   _____   _____

Date: ____/____/_____   W/O#: _____
Location: _____
Description of Terrain: _____
_____
Approx. Difficulty: _____
SET: Duration: Comments:
____   _____   _____
____   _____   _____

Date: ____/____/_____   W/O#: _____
Location: _____
Description of Terrain: _____
_____
Approx. Difficulty: _____
SET: Duration: Comments:
____   _____   _____
____   _____   _____

Date: ____/____/_____   W/O#: _____
Location: _____
Description of Terrain: _____
_____
Approx. Difficulty: _____
SET: Duration: Comments:
____   _____   _____
____   _____   _____

The Rock Climber's Training Manual
Outdoor Mileage (OM) Log

Date: ____/____/_____   Crag:_____
Description: _____
Route Name: Grade: Route Name: Grade:
_____   ____   _____   ____
_____   ____   _____   ____
_____   ____   _____   ____
_____   ____   _____   ____
_____   ____   _____   ____
Total Climbing Time: _____
Comments: _____

Date: ____/____/_____   Crag:_____
Description: _____
Route Name: Grade: Route Name: Grade
_____   ____   _____   ____
_____   ____   _____   ____
_____   ____   _____   ____
_____   ____   _____   ____
_____   ____   _____   ____
Total Climbing Time: _____
Comments: _____

Date: ____/____/_____   Crag:_____
Description: _____
Route Name: Grade: Route Name: Grade:
_____   ____   _____   ____
_____   ____   _____   ____
_____   ____   _____   ____
_____   ____   _____   ____
_____   ____   _____   ____
Total Climbing Time: _____
Comments: _____
_____

Date: ____/____/_____   Crag:_____
Description: _____
Route Name: Grade: Route Name: Grade:
_____   ____   _____   ____
_____   ____   _____   ____
_____   ____   _____   ____
_____   ____   _____   ____
_____   ____   _____   ____
Total Climbing Time: _____
Comments: _____
_____

Date: ____/____/_____   Crag:_____
Description: _____
Route Name: Grade: Route Name: Grade:
_____   ____   _____   ____
_____   ____   _____   ____
_____   ____   _____   ____
_____   ____   _____   ____
_____   ____   _____   ____
Total Climbing Time: _____
Comments: _____

Date: ____/____/_____   Crag:_____
Description: _____
Route Name: Grade: Route Name: Grade:
_____   ____   _____   ____
_____   ____   _____   ____
_____   ____   _____   ____
_____   ____   _____   ____
_____   ____   _____   ____
Total Climbing Time: _____
Comments: _____

Date: ____/____/_____   Crag:_____
Description: _____
Route Name: Grade: Route Name: Grade:
_____   ____   _____   ____
_____   ____   _____   ____
_____   ____   _____   ____
_____   ____   _____   ____
_____   ____   _____   ____
Total Climbing Time: _____
Comments: _____

Date: ____/____/_____   Crag:_____
Description: _____
Route Name: Grade: Route Name: Grade:
_____   ____   _____   ____
_____   ____   _____   ____
_____   ____   _____   ____
_____   ____   _____   ____
_____   ____   _____   ____
Total Climbing Time: _____
Comments: _____

The Rock Climber's Training Manual
Hangboard Log

Date: ____/____/_____ W/O #:_____ Rep Duration (sec): _____

Temp/Humidity: _____ Weight:_____ Rest Duration (sec): _____

Step Up?	Exercise 1 Grip:_____				Notes:_____
	Goal:	Set:	Resistance:	#Reps:	Comments:
	_____	1	_____	____	_____
Y / N	_____	2	_____	____	_____
	_____	3	_____	____	_____

Step Up?	Exercise 2 Grip:_____				N:_____
	_____	1	_____	____	_____
Y / N	_____	2	_____	____	_____
	_____	3	_____	____	_____

Step Up?	Exercise 3 Grip:_____				N:_____
	_____	1	_____	____	_____
Y / N	_____	2	_____	____	_____
	_____	3	_____	____	_____

Step Up?	Exercise4 Grip:_____				N:_____
	_____	1	_____	____	_____
Y / N	_____	2	_____	____	_____
	_____	3	_____	____	_____

Step Up?	Exercise 5 Grip:_____				N:_____
	_____	1	_____	____	_____
Y / N	_____	2	_____	____	_____
	_____	3	_____	____	_____

Step Up?	Exercise 6 Grip:_____				N:_____
	_____	1	_____	____	_____
Y / N	_____	2	_____	____	_____
	_____	3	_____	____	_____

Step Up?	Exercise 7 Grip:_____				N:_____
	_____	1	_____	____	_____
Y / N	_____	2	_____	____	_____
	_____	3	_____	____	_____

Step Up?	Exercise 8 Grip:_____				N:_____
	_____	1	_____	____	_____
Y / N	_____	2	_____	____	_____
	_____	3	_____	____	_____

Step Up?	Exercise 9 Grip:_____				N:_____
Y / N	_____	1	_____	____	_____

Step Up?	Exercise 10 Grip:_____				N:_____
Y / N	_____	1	_____	____	_____

The Rock Climber's Training Manual
Hangboard Log

Date: ____/____/_____   W/O #:_____   Rep Duration (sec): _____
Temp/Humidity: _____   Weight:_____   Rest Duration (sec): _____

Step Up?					

Exercise 1 Grip:_____   Notes:_____

	Goal:	Set:	Resistance:	#Reps:	Comments:
	_____	1	_____	_____	_____
Y / N	_____	2	_____	_____	_____
	_____	3	_____	_____	_____

Exercise 2 Grip:_____   N:_____

		1	_____	_____	_____
Y / N	_____	2	_____	_____	_____
	_____	3	_____	_____	_____

Exercise 3 Grip:_____   N:_____

		1	_____	_____	_____
Y / N	_____	2	_____	_____	_____
	_____	3	_____	_____	_____

Exercise4 Grip:_____   N:_____

		1	_____	_____	_____
Y / N	_____	2	_____	_____	_____
	_____	3	_____	_____	_____

Exercise 5 Grip:_____   N:_____

		1	_____	_____	_____
Y / N	_____	2	_____	_____	_____
	_____	3	_____	_____	_____

Exercise 6 Grip:_____   N:_____

		1	_____	_____	_____
Y / N	_____	2	_____	_____	_____
	_____	3	_____	_____	_____

Exercise 7 Grip:_____   N:_____

		1	_____	_____	_____
Y / N	_____	2	_____	_____	_____
	_____	3	_____	_____	_____

Exercise 8 Grip:_____   N:_____

		1	_____	_____	_____
Y / N	_____	2	_____	_____	_____
	_____	3	_____	_____	_____

Exercise 9 Grip:_____   N:_____

		1	_____	_____	_____
Y / N	_____				

Exercise 10 Grip:_____   N:_____

		1	_____	_____	_____
Y / N	_____				

The Rock Climber's Training Manual
Hangboard Log

Date: ____/____/_____ W/O #:_____ Rep Duration (sec): _____
Temp/Humidity: _____ Weight:_____ Rest Duration (sec): _____

Step Up?	Exercise 1 Grip:_____			Notes:_____
	Goal:	Set:	Resistance:	#Reps:	Comments:
	_____	1	_____	_____	_____
Y / N	_____	2	_____	_____	_____
	_____	3	_____	_____	_____

Exercise 2 Grip:_____ N:_____
Step Up?	Goal:	Set:	Resistance:	#Reps:	Comments:
	_____	1	_____	_____	_____
Y / N	_____	2	_____	_____	_____
	_____	3	_____	_____	_____

Exercise 3 Grip:_____ N:_____
Step Up?	Goal:	Set:	Resistance:	#Reps:	Comments:
	_____	1	_____	_____	_____
Y / N	_____	2	_____	_____	_____
	_____	3	_____	_____	_____

Exercise4 Grip:_____ N:_____
Step Up?	Goal:	Set:	Resistance:	#Reps:	Comments:
	_____	1	_____	_____	_____
Y / N	_____	2	_____	_____	_____
	_____	3	_____	_____	_____

Exercise 5 Grip:_____ N:_____
Step Up?	Goal:	Set:	Resistance:	#Reps:	Comments:
	_____	1	_____	_____	_____
Y / N	_____	2	_____	_____	_____
	_____	3	_____	_____	_____

Exercise 6 Grip:_____ N:_____
Step Up?	Goal:	Set:	Resistance:	#Reps:	Comments:
	_____	1	_____	_____	_____
Y / N	_____	2	_____	_____	_____
	_____	3	_____	_____	_____

Exercise 7 Grip:_____ N:_____
Step Up?	Goal:	Set:	Resistance:	#Reps:	Comments:
	_____	1	_____	_____	_____
Y / N	_____	2	_____	_____	_____
	_____	3	_____	_____	_____

Exercise 8 Grip:_____ N:_____
Step Up?	Goal:	Set:	Resistance:	#Reps:	Comments:
	_____	1	_____	_____	_____
Y / N	_____	2	_____	_____	_____
	_____	3	_____	_____	_____

Exercise 9 Grip:_____ N:_____
Step Up?	Goal:	Set:	Resistance:	#Reps:	Comments:
Y / N	_____	1	_____	_____	_____

Exercise 10 Grip:_____ N:_____
Step Up?	Goal:	Set:	Resistance:	#Reps:	Comments:
Y / N	_____	1	_____	_____	_____

Date: ____/____/_____ W/O #:_____ Rep Duration (sec): _____
Temp/Humidity: _____ Weight:_____ Rest Duration (sec): _____

Step Up?		Goal:	Set:	Resistance:	#Reps:	Notes: / Comments:

Exercise 1 Grip:_____ Notes:_____

Step Up?	Goal	Set	Resistance	#Reps	Comments
	_____	1	_____	_____	_____
Y / N	_____	2	_____	_____	_____
	_____	3	_____	_____	_____

Exercise 2 Grip:_____ N:_____

	_____	1	_____	_____	_____
Y / N	_____	2	_____	_____	_____
	_____	3	_____	_____	_____

Exercise 3 Grip:_____ N:_____

	_____	1	_____	_____	_____
Y / N	_____	2	_____	_____	_____
	_____	3	_____	_____	_____

Exercise4 Grip:_____ N:_____

	_____	1	_____	_____	_____
Y / N	_____	2	_____	_____	_____
	_____	3	_____	_____	_____

Exercise 5 Grip:_____ N:_____

	_____	1	_____	_____	_____
Y / N	_____	2	_____	_____	_____
	_____	3	_____	_____	_____

Exercise 6 Grip:_____ N:_____

	_____	1	_____	_____	_____
Y / N	_____	2	_____	_____	_____
	_____	3	_____	_____	_____

Exercise 7 Grip:_____ N:_____

	_____	1	_____	_____	_____
Y / N	_____	2	_____	_____	_____
	_____	3	_____	_____	_____

Exercise 8 Grip:_____ N:_____

	_____	1	_____	_____	_____
Y / N	_____	2	_____	_____	_____
	_____	3	_____	_____	_____

Exercise 9 Grip:_____ N:_____

Y / N	_____	1	_____	_____	_____

Exercise 10 Grip:_____ N:_____

Y / N	_____	1	_____	_____	_____

Date: ____/____/_____   W/O #:_____   Rep Duration (sec): _____
Temp/Humidity: _____   Weight:_____   Rest Duration (sec): _____

| Step Up? | Exercise 1 Grip:_____ | | | Notes:_____ |

Exercise 1 Grip:

Step Up?	Goal:	Set:	Resistance:	#Reps:	Comments:
	_____	1	_____		_____
Y / N	_____	2	_____		_____
	_____	3	_____		_____

Exercise 2 Grip:_____   N:_____

Y / N	_____	1	_____		_____
	_____	2	_____		_____
	_____	3	_____		_____

Exercise 3 Grip:_____   N:_____

Y / N	_____	1	_____		_____
	_____	2	_____		_____
	_____	3	_____		_____

Exercise4 Grip:_____   N:_____

Y / N	_____	1	_____		_____
	_____	2	_____		_____
	_____	3	_____		_____

Exercise 5 Grip:_____   N:_____

Y / N	_____	1	_____		_____
	_____	2	_____		_____
	_____	3	_____		_____

Exercise 6 Grip:_____   N:_____

Y / N	_____	1	_____		_____
	_____	2	_____		_____
	_____	3	_____		_____

Exercise 7 Grip:_____   N:_____

Y / N	_____	1	_____		_____
	_____	2	_____		_____
	_____	3	_____		_____

Exercise 8 Grip:_____   N:_____

Y / N	_____	1	_____		_____
	_____	2	_____		_____
	_____	3	_____		_____

Exercise 9 Grip:_____   N:_____

Y / N	_____	1	_____		_____

Exercise 10 Grip:_____   N:_____

Y / N	_____	1	_____		_____

Date: ____/____/_____   W/O #:_____   Rep Duration (sec): _____
Temp/Humidity: _____   Weight:_____   Rest Duration (sec): _____

Step Up?					

Exercise 1 Grip:_____   Notes:_____

	Goal:	Set:	Resistance:	#Reps:	Comments:
	_____	1	_____	_____	_____
Y / N	_____	2	_____	_____	_____
	_____	3	_____	_____	_____

Exercise 2 Grip:_____   N:_____

		1			
Y / N		2			
		3			

Exercise 3 Grip:_____   N:_____

		1			
Y / N		2			
		3			

Exercise4 Grip:_____   N:_____

		1			
Y / N		2			
		3			

Exercise 5 Grip:_____   N:_____

		1			
Y / N		2			
		3			

Exercise 6 Grip:_____   N:_____

		1			
Y / N		2			
		3			

Exercise 7 Grip:_____   N:_____

		1			
Y / N		2			
		3			

Exercise 8 Grip:_____   N:_____

		1			
Y / N		2			
		3			

Exercise 9 Grip:_____   N:_____

Y / N		1			

Exercise 10 Grip:_____   N:_____

Y / N		1			

The Rock Climber's Training Manual
Hangboard Log

Date: ____/____/_____ W/O #:_____ Rep Duration (sec): _____
Temp/Humidity: _____ Weight:_____ Rest Duration (sec): _____

Step Up?	Exercise 1 Grip:_____				Notes:_____
	Goal:	Set:	Resistance:	#Reps:	Comments:
	_____	1	_____	_____	_____
Y / N	_____	2	_____	_____	_____
	_____	3	_____	_____	_____

Step Up?	Exercise 2 Grip:_____				N:_____
	_____	1	_____	_____	_____
Y / N	_____	2	_____	_____	_____
	_____	3	_____	_____	_____

Step Up?	Exercise 3 Grip:_____				N:_____
	_____	1	_____	_____	_____
Y / N	_____	2	_____	_____	_____
	_____	3	_____	_____	_____

Step Up?	Exercise4 Grip:_____				N:_____
	_____	1	_____	_____	_____
Y / N	_____	2	_____	_____	_____
	_____	3	_____	_____	_____

Step Up?	Exercise 5 Grip:_____				N:_____
	_____	1	_____	_____	_____
Y / N	_____	2	_____	_____	_____
	_____	3	_____	_____	_____

Step Up?	Exercise 6 Grip:_____				N:_____
	_____	1	_____	_____	_____
Y / N	_____	2	_____	_____	_____
	_____	3	_____	_____	_____

Step Up?	Exercise 7 Grip:_____				N:_____
	_____	1	_____	_____	_____
Y / N	_____	2	_____	_____	_____
	_____	3	_____	_____	_____

Step Up?	Exercise 8 Grip:_____				N:_____
	_____	1	_____	_____	_____
Y / N	_____	2	_____	_____	_____
	_____	3	_____	_____	_____

Step Up?	Exercise 9 Grip:_____				N:_____
Y / N	_____	1	_____	_____	_____

Step Up?	Exercise 10 Grip:_____				N:_____
Y / N	_____	1	_____	_____	_____

The Rock Climber's Training Manual
Hangboard Log

Date: ____/____/_____ W/O #:_____ Rep Duration (sec): _____
Temp/Humidity: _____ Weight:_____ Rest Duration (sec): _____

Step Up?	Exercise 1 Grip:_____				Notes:_____
	Goal:	Set:	Resistance:	#Reps:	Comments:
	_____	1	_____	_____	_____
Y / N	_____	2	_____	_____	_____
	_____	3	_____	_____	_____

Step Up?	Exercise 2 Grip:_____				N:_____
	_____	1	_____	_____	_____
Y / N	_____	2	_____	_____	_____
	_____	3	_____	_____	_____

Step Up?	Exercise 3 Grip:_____				N:_____
	_____	1	_____	_____	_____
Y / N	_____	2	_____	_____	_____
	_____	3	_____	_____	_____

Step Up?	Exercise4 Grip:_____				N:_____
	_____	1	_____	_____	_____
Y / N	_____	2	_____	_____	_____
	_____	3	_____	_____	_____

Step Up?	Exercise 5 Grip:_____				N:_____
	_____	1	_____	_____	_____
Y / N	_____	2	_____	_____	_____
	_____	3	_____	_____	_____

Step Up?	Exercise 6 Grip:_____				N:_____
	_____	1	_____	_____	_____
Y / N	_____	2	_____	_____	_____
	_____	3	_____	_____	_____

Step Up?	Exercise 7 Grip:_____				N:_____
	_____	1	_____	_____	_____
Y / N	_____	2	_____	_____	_____
	_____	3	_____	_____	_____

Step Up?	Exercise 8 Grip:_____				N:_____
	_____	1	_____	_____	_____
Y / N	_____	2	_____	_____	_____
	_____	3	_____	_____	_____

Step Up?	Exercise 9 Grip:_____				N:_____
Y / N	_____	1	_____	_____	_____

Step Up?	Exercise 10 Grip:_____				N:_____
Y / N	_____	1	_____	_____	_____

Date: ____/____/_____   W/O #:_____   Rep Duration (sec): _____
Temp/Humidity: _____   Weight:_____   Rest Duration (sec): _____

Step Up?	Exercise 1 Grip:_____				Notes:_____
	Goal:	Set:	Resistance:	#Reps:	Comments:
	_____	1	_____	_____	_____
Y / N	_____	2	_____	_____	_____
	_____	3	_____	_____	_____

Step Up?	Exercise 2 Grip:_____				N:_____
	_____	1	_____	_____	_____
Y / N	_____	2	_____	_____	_____
	_____	3	_____	_____	_____

Step Up?	Exercise 3 Grip:_____				N:_____
	_____	1	_____	_____	_____
Y / N	_____	2	_____	_____	_____
	_____	3	_____	_____	_____

Step Up?	Exercise4 Grip:_____				N:_____
	_____	1	_____	_____	_____
Y / N	_____	2	_____	_____	_____
	_____	3	_____	_____	_____

Step Up?	Exercise 5 Grip:_____				N:_____
	_____	1	_____	_____	_____
Y / N	_____	2	_____	_____	_____
	_____	3	_____	_____	_____

Step Up?	Exercise 6 Grip:_____				N:_____
	_____	1	_____	_____	_____
Y / N	_____	2	_____	_____	_____
	_____	3	_____	_____	_____

Step Up?	Exercise 7 Grip:_____				N:_____
	_____	1	_____	_____	_____
Y / N	_____	2	_____	_____	_____
	_____	3	_____	_____	_____

Step Up?	Exercise 8 Grip:_____				N:_____
	_____	1	_____	_____	_____
Y / N	_____	2	_____	_____	_____
	_____	3	_____	_____	_____

Step Up?	Exercise 9 Grip:_____				N:_____
Y / N	_____	1	_____	_____	_____

Step Up?	Exercise 10 Grip:_____				N:_____
Y / N	_____	1	_____	_____	

The Rock Climber's Training Manual
Hangboard Log

Date: _____/_____/_____   W/O #:_____   Rep Duration (sec): _____

Temp/Humidity: _____   Weight:_____   Rest Duration (sec): _____

Step Up?	Exercise 1 Grip:_____				Notes:_____
	Goal:	Set:	Resistance:	#Reps:	Comments:
	_____	1	_____	_____	_____
Y / N	_____	2	_____	_____	_____
	_____	3	_____	_____	_____

Step Up?	Exercise 2 Grip:_____				N:_____
	_____	1	_____	_____	_____
Y / N	_____	2	_____	_____	_____
	_____	3	_____	_____	_____

Step Up?	Exercise 3 Grip:_____				N:_____
	_____	1	_____	_____	_____
Y / N	_____	2	_____	_____	_____
	_____	3	_____	_____	_____

Step Up?	Exercise4 Grip:_____				N:_____
	_____	1	_____	_____	_____
Y / N	_____	2	_____	_____	_____
	_____	3	_____	_____	_____

Step Up?	Exercise 5 Grip:_____				N:_____
	_____	1	_____	_____	_____
Y / N	_____	2	_____	_____	_____
	_____	3	_____	_____	_____

Step Up?	Exercise 6 Grip:_____				N:_____
	_____	1	_____	_____	_____
Y / N	_____	2	_____	_____	_____
	_____	3	_____	_____	_____

Step Up?	Exercise 7 Grip:_____				N:_____
	_____	1	_____	_____	_____
Y / N	_____	2	_____	_____	_____
	_____	3	_____	_____	_____

Step Up?	Exercise 8 Grip:_____				N:_____
	_____	1	_____	_____	_____
Y / N	_____	2	_____	_____	_____
	_____	3	_____	_____	_____

Step Up?	Exercise 9 Grip:_____				N:_____
Y / N	_____	1	_____	_____	_____

Step Up?	Exercise 10 Grip:_____				N:_____
Y / N	_____	1	_____	_____	_____

The Rock Climber's Training Manual
Campus Log

Campus Board Configuration:

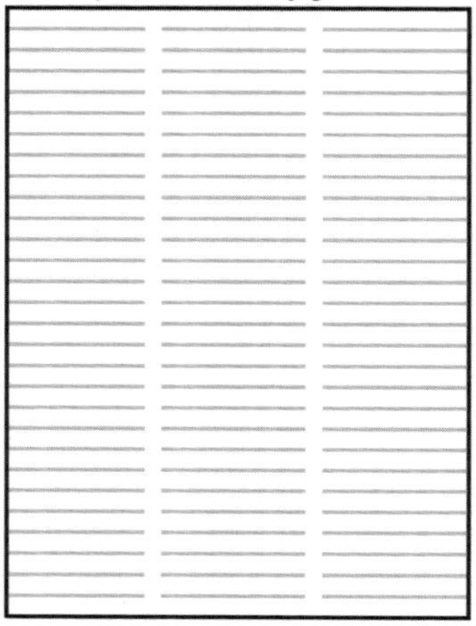

Date: _____ / _____ / _____

W/O # _____

Warmup Boulder Ladder Summary/Notes:

R = Right Hand, L = Left Hand, B = Both Hands

Rungs Used (circle):

Set 1:   L M S _____

Set 2:   L M S _____

Set 3:   L M S _____

Set 4:   L M S _____

Set 5:   L M S _____

Set 6:   L M S _____

Set 7:   L M S _____

Set 8:   L M S _____

Set 9:   L M S _____

Set 10: L M S _____

Set 11: L M S _____

Set 12: L M S _____

Set 13: L M S _____

Set 14: L M S _____

Set 15: L M S _____

Set 16: L M S _____

Set 17: L M S _____

Set 18: L M S _____

Limit Bouldering (LB) Log

Date: ____/____/________ Location: ________________________
WBL Description: ____________________ # Problems Attempted: ________ Duration: ________
Problem Description: Grade: # of attempts: Comments:

Total Climbing Time: __________ General Comments: ________________________

Date: ____/____/________ Location: ________________________
WBL Description: ____________________ # Problems Attempted: ________ Duration: ________
Problem Description: Grade: # of attempts: Comments:

Total Climbing Time: __________ General Comments: ________________________

Date: ____/____/________ Location: ________________________
WBL Description: ____________________ # Problems Attempted: ________ Duration: ________
Problem Description: Grade: # of attempts: Comments:

Total Climbing Time: __________ General Comments: ________________________

Date: ____/____/________ Location: ________________________
WBL Description: ____________________ # Problems Attempted: ________ Duration: ________
Problem Description: Grade: # of attempts: Comments:

Total Climbing Time: __________ General Comments: ________________________

The Rock Climber's Training Manual

Campus Log

Campus Board Configuration:

Rungs Used (circle):

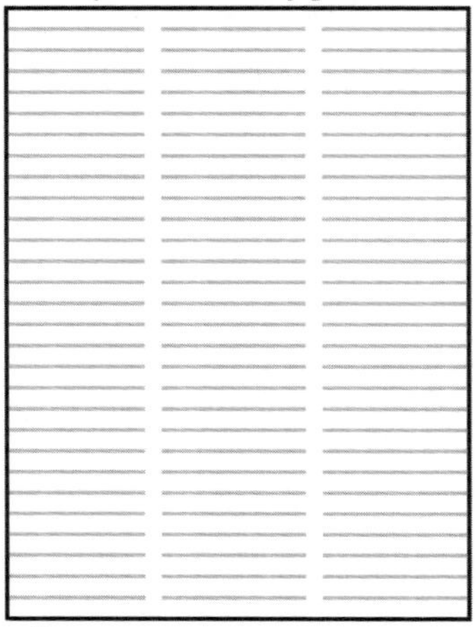

Date: ____ / ____ / ____

W/O # ____________

Warmup Boulder Ladder Summary/Notes:

R = Right Hand, L = Left Hand, B = Both Hands

Set 1: L M S ____________________

Set 2: L M S ____________________

Set 3: L M S ____________________

Set 4: L M S ____________________

Set 5: L M S ____________________

Set 6: L M S ____________________

Set 7: L M S ____________________

Set 8: L M S ____________________

Set 9: L M S ____________________

Set 10: L M S ____________________

Set 11: L M S ____________________

Set 12: L M S ____________________

Set 13: L M S ____________________

Set 14: L M S ____________________

Set 15: L M S ____________________

Set 16: L M S ____________________

Set 17: L M S ____________________

Set 18: L M S ____________________

Campus Board Configuration:

Date: _____ / _____ / _____

W/O # _____

Warmup Boulder Ladder Summary/Notes:

Rungs Used (circle):

R = Right Hand, L = Left Hand, B = Both Hands

Set 1: L M S _____

Set 2: L M S _____

Set 3: L M S _____

Set 4: L M S _____

Set 5: L M S _____

Set 6: L M S _____

Set 7: L M S _____

Set 8: L M S _____

Set 9: L M S _____

Set 10: L M S _____

Set 11: L M S _____

Set 12: L M S _____

Set 13: L M S _____

Set 14: L M S _____

Set 15: L M S _____

Set 16: L M S _____

Set 17: L M S _____

Set 18: L M S _____

The Rock Climber's Training Manual
Campus Log

Campus Board Configuration:

Date: _____ / _____ / _____

W/O # _____

Warmup Boulder Ladder Summary/Notes:

Rungs
Used (circle):

R = Right Hand, L = Left Hand, B = Both Hands

Set 1:   L M S _____

Set 2:   L M S _____

Set 3:   L M S _____

Set 4:   L M S _____

Set 5:   L M S _____

Set 6:   L M S _____

Set 7:   L M S _____

Set 8:   L M S _____

Set 9:   L M S _____

Set 10:   L M S _____

Set 11:   L M S _____

Set 12:   L M S _____

Set 13:   L M S _____

Set 14:   L M S _____

Set 15:   L M S _____

Set 16:   L M S _____

Set 17:   L M S _____

Set 18:   L M S _____

Campus Board Configuration:

Date: _____ / _____ / _____

W/O # _____

Warmup Boulder Ladder Summary/Notes:

*Rungs
Used (circle):*

R = Right Hand, L = Left Hand, B = Both Hands

Set 1: L M S _____

Set 2: L M S _____

Set 3: L M S _____

Set 4: L M S _____

Set 5: L M S _____

Set 6: L M S _____

Set 7: L M S _____

Set 8: L M S _____

Set 9: L M S _____

Set 10: L M S _____

Set 11: L M S _____

Set 12: L M S _____

Set 13: L M S _____

Set 14: L M S _____

Set 15: L M S _____

Set 16: L M S _____

Set 17: L M S _____

Set 18: L M S _____

Date: ____/____/_____   Location:_____

WBL Description: _____   # Problems Attempted:_____   Duration:_____

Problem Description: **Grade:**   **# of attempts:**   **Comments:**

_____

_____

_____

_____

_____

_____

Total Climbing Time: _____   General Comments:_____

Date: ____/____/_____   Location:_____

WBL Description: _____   # Problems Attempted:_____   Duration:_____

Problem Description: **Grade:**   **# of attempts:**   **Comments:**

_____

_____

_____

_____

_____

_____

Total Climbing Time: _____   General Comments:_____

Date: ____/____/_____   Location:_____

WBL Description: _____   # Problems Attempted:_____   Duration:_____

Problem Description: **Grade:**   **# of attempts:**   **Comments:**

_____

_____

_____

_____

_____

_____

Total Climbing Time: _____   General Comments:_____

Date: ____/____/_____   Location:_____

WBL Description: _____   # Problems Attempted:_____   Duration:_____

Problem Description: **Grade:**   **# of attempts:**   **Comments:**

_____

_____

_____

_____

_____

_____

Total Climbing Time: _____   General Comments:_____

The Rock Climber's Training Manual

Campus Log

Campus Board Configuration:

Date: ______/______/______

W/O # ____________

Warmup Boulder Ladder Summary/Notes:

Rungs Used (circle):

R = Right Hand, L = Left Hand, B = Both Hands

Set 1: L M S ____________________

Set 2: L M S ____________________

Set 3: L M S ____________________

Set 4: L M S ____________________

Set 5: L M S ____________________

Set 6: L M S ____________________

Set 7: L M S ____________________

Set 8: L M S ____________________

Set 9: L M S ____________________

Set 10: L M S ____________________

Set 11: L M S ____________________

Set 12: L M S ____________________

Set 13: L M S ____________________

Set 14: L M S ____________________

Set 15: L M S ____________________

Set 16: L M S ____________________

Set 17: L M S ____________________

Set 18: L M S ____________________

The Rock Climber's Training Manual
Campus Log

Campus Board Configuration:

Date: _____ / _____ / _____

W/O # _____

Warmup Boulder Ladder Summary/Notes:

Rungs
Used (circle):

R = Right Hand, L = Left Hand, B = Both Hands

Set 1:   L M S _____

Set 2:   L M S _____

Set 3:   L M S _____

Set 4:   L M S _____

Set 5:   L M S _____

Set 6:   L M S _____

Set 7:   L M S _____

Set 8:   L M S _____

Set 9:   L M S _____

Set 10:   L M S _____

Set 11:   L M S _____

Set 12:   L M S _____

Set 13:   L M S _____

Set 14:   L M S _____

Set 15:   L M S _____

Set 16:   L M S _____

Set 17:   L M S _____

Set 18:   L M S _____

Linked Bouldering Circuit (LBC)/Route Interval Training Log

Date: ___ / ___ / ___   Location: _____   Previous W/O: ___ / ___ / ___ , _____

                                                              (Date)   (Description)

Description of Warm-Up: _____

_____

_____

Description of LBC/Interval Route (*length, # of hand moves, steepness, difficulty*):

_____

_____

_____

_____

SET #1: Sent? **Y / N**   If No, Fell on Move #: _____   **Total Set Time:** _____

Comments: _____

_____   **Rest Between Sets:** _____

SET #2: Sent? **Y / N**   If No, Fell on Move #: _____   **Total Set Time:** _____

Comments: _____

_____   **Rest Between Sets:** _____

SET #3: Sent? **Y / N**   If No, Fell on Move #: _____   **Total Set Time:** _____

Comments: _____

_____   **Rest Between Sets:** _____

SET #4: Sent? **Y / N**   If No, Fell on Move #: _____   **Total Set Time:** _____

Comments: _____

_____   **Rest Between Sets:** _____

SET #5: Sent? **Y / N**   If No, Fell on Move #: _____   **Total Set Time:** _____

Comments: _____

_____   **Rest Between Sets:** _____

SET #6: Sent? **Y / N**   If No, Fell on Move #: _____   **Total Set Time:** _____

Comments: _____

_____   **Rest Between Sets:** _____

SET #7: Sent? **Y / N**   If No, Fell on Move #: _____   **Total Set Time:** _____

Comments: _____

_____   **Rest Between Sets:** _____

SET #8: Sent? **Y / N**   If No, Fell on Move #: _____   **Total Set Time:** _____

Comments: _____

_____   **Rest Between Sets:** _____

Linked Bouldering Circuit (LBC)/Route Interval Training Log

Date: ___/___/___ Location: _____ Previous W/O: ___/___/___, _____
                                                          (Date)   (Description)

Description of Warm-Up: _____

_____

_____

Description of LBC/Interval Route (*length, # of hand moves, steepness, difficulty*):

_____

_____

_____

_____

SET #1: Sent? **Y / N** If No, Fell on Move #: _____ **Total Set Time:** _____

Comments: _____

_____ **Rest Between Sets:** _____

SET #2: Sent? **Y / N** If No, Fell on Move #: _____ **Total Set Time:** _____

Comments: _____

_____ **Rest Between Sets:** _____

SET #3: Sent? **Y / N** If No, Fell on Move #: _____ **Total Set Time:** _____

Comments: _____

_____ **Rest Between Sets:** _____

SET #4: Sent? **Y / N** If No, Fell on Move #: _____ **Total Set Time:** _____

Comments: _____

_____ **Rest Between Sets:** _____

SET #5: Sent? **Y / N** If No, Fell on Move #: _____ **Total Set Time:** _____

Comments: _____

_____ **Rest Between Sets:** _____

SET #6: Sent? **Y / N** If No, Fell on Move #: _____ **Total Set Time:** _____

Comments: _____

_____ **Rest Between Sets:** _____

SET #7: Sent? **Y / N** If No, Fell on Move #: _____ **Total Set Time:** _____

Comments: _____

_____ **Rest Between Sets:** _____

SET #8: Sent? **Y / N** If No, Fell on Move #: _____ **Total Set Time:** _____

Comments: _____

_____ **Rest Between Sets:** _____

Linked Bouldering Circuit (LBC)/Route Interval Training Log

Date: ___/___/___ Location: _____ Previous W/O: ___/___/___, _____

(Date)   (Description)

Description of Warm-Up: _____

_____

_____

Description of LBC/Interval Route (*length, # of hand moves, steepness, difficulty*):

_____

_____

_____

_____

SET #1: Sent? **Y / N** If No, Fell on Move #: _____ **Total Set Time:** _____

Comments: _____

_____ **Rest Between Sets:** _____

SET #2: Sent? **Y / N** If No, Fell on Move #: _____ **Total Set Time:** _____

Comments: _____

_____ **Rest Between Sets:** _____

SET #3: Sent? **Y / N** If No, Fell on Move #: _____ **Total Set Time:** _____

Comments: _____

_____ **Rest Between Sets:** _____

SET #4: Sent? **Y / N** If No, Fell on Move #: _____ **Total Set Time:** _____

Comments: _____

_____ **Rest Between Sets:** _____

SET #5: Sent? **Y / N** If No, Fell on Move #: _____ **Total Set Time:** _____

Comments: _____

_____ **Rest Between Sets:** _____

SET #6: Sent? **Y / N** If No, Fell on Move #: _____ **Total Set Time:** _____

Comments: _____

_____ **Rest Between Sets:** _____

SET #7: Sent? **Y / N** If No, Fell on Move #: _____ **Total Set Time:** _____

Comments: _____

_____ **Rest Between Sets:** _____

SET #8: Sent? **Y / N** If No, Fell on Move #: _____ **Total Set Time:** _____

Comments: _____

_____ **Rest Between Sets:** _____

The Rock Climber's Training Manual
Linked Bouldering Circuit (LBC)/Route Interval Training Log

Date: ___/___/___ Location: _____ Previous W/O: ___/___/___, _____
                                                            (Date)   (Description)

Description of Warm-Up: _____
_____
_____

Description of LBC/Interval Route (*length, # of hand moves, steepness, difficulty*):

_____
_____
_____
_____

SET #1: Sent? **Y / N** If No, Fell on Move #: _____   **Total Set Time:** _____
Comments: _____
_____ **Rest Between Sets:** _____

SET #2: Sent? **Y / N** If No, Fell on Move #: _____   **Total Set Time:** _____
Comments: _____
_____ **Rest Between Sets:** _____

SET #3: Sent? **Y / N** If No, Fell on Move #: _____   **Total Set Time:** _____
Comments: _____
_____ **Rest Between Sets:** _____

SET #4: Sent? **Y / N** If No, Fell on Move #: _____   **Total Set Time:** _____
Comments: _____
_____ **Rest Between Sets:** _____

SET #5: Sent? **Y / N** If No, Fell on Move #: _____   **Total Set Time:** _____
Comments: _____
_____ **Rest Between Sets:** _____

SET #6: Sent? **Y / N** If No, Fell on Move #: _____   **Total Set Time:** _____
Comments: _____
_____ **Rest Between Sets:** _____

SET #7: Sent? **Y / N** If No, Fell on Move #: _____   **Total Set Time:** _____
Comments: _____
_____ **Rest Between Sets:** _____

SET #8: Sent? **Y / N** If No, Fell on Move #: _____   **Total Set Time:** _____
Comments: _____
_____ **Rest Between Sets:** _____

Linked Bouldering Circuit (LBC)/Route Interval Training Log

Date: ___/___/___ Location: _____ Previous W/O: ___/___/___, _____
                                                              (Date)   (Description)

Description of Warm-Up: _____

_____

_____

Description of LBC/Interval Route (*length, # of hand moves, steepness, difficulty*):

_____

_____

_____

_____

SET #1: Sent? **Y / N** If No, Fell on Move #: _____   **Total Set Time:** _____

Comments: _____

_____   **Rest Between Sets:** _____

SET #2: Sent? **Y / N** If No, Fell on Move #: _____   **Total Set Time:** _____

Comments: _____

_____   **Rest Between Sets:** _____

SET #3: Sent? **Y / N** If No, Fell on Move #: _____   **Total Set Time:** _____

Comments: _____

_____   **Rest Between Sets:** _____

SET #4: Sent? **Y / N** If No, Fell on Move #: _____   **Total Set Time:** _____

Comments: _____

_____   **Rest Between Sets:** _____

SET #5: Sent? **Y / N** If No, Fell on Move #: _____   **Total Set Time:** _____

Comments: _____

_____   **Rest Between Sets:** _____

SET #6: Sent? **Y / N** If No, Fell on Move #: _____   **Total Set Time:** _____

Comments: _____

_____   **Rest Between Sets:** _____

SET #7: Sent? **Y / N** If No, Fell on Move #: _____   **Total Set Time:** _____

Comments: _____

_____   **Rest Between Sets:** _____

SET #8: Sent? **Y / N** If No, Fell on Move #: _____   **Total Set Time:** _____

Comments: _____

_____   **Rest Between Sets:** _____

Linked Bouldering Circuit (LBC)/Route Interval Training Log

Date: ___/___/___ Location: _____ Previous W/O: ___/___/___, _____

(Date)   (Description)

Description of Warm-Up: _____

_____

_____

Description of LBC/Interval Route (*length, # of hand moves, steepness, difficulty*):

_____

_____

_____

_____

SET #1: Sent? **Y / N** If No, Fell on Move #: _____   **Total Set Time:** _____

Comments: _____

_____ **Rest Between Sets:** _____

SET #2: Sent? **Y / N** If No, Fell on Move #: _____   **Total Set Time:** _____

Comments: _____

_____ **Rest Between Sets:** _____

SET #3: Sent? **Y / N** If No, Fell on Move #: _____   **Total Set Time:** _____

Comments: _____

_____ **Rest Between Sets:** _____

SET #4: Sent? **Y / N** If No, Fell on Move #: _____   **Total Set Time:** _____

Comments: _____

_____ **Rest Between Sets:** _____

SET #5: Sent? **Y / N** If No, Fell on Move #: _____   **Total Set Time:** _____

Comments: _____

_____ **Rest Between Sets:** _____

SET #6: Sent? **Y / N** If No, Fell on Move #: _____   **Total Set Time:** _____

Comments: _____

_____ **Rest Between Sets:** _____

SET #7: Sent? **Y / N** If No, Fell on Move #: _____   **Total Set Time:** _____

Comments: _____

_____ **Rest Between Sets:** _____

SET #8: Sent? **Y / N** If No, Fell on Move #: _____   **Total Set Time:** _____

Comments: _____

_____ **Rest Between Sets:** _____

The Rock Climber's Training Manual
Supplemental Exercise Log

Date	Set #	Exercise (e.g. "Shoulder Press", "Leg Lifts", etc.)					
		Front -Lateral	Leg Lifts	Bicep Curls	Shoulder Press	*Example*	-
1 Jan 2014	1	10# 6 reps	12	30# R:8 L:7	25#, 8	-	-
" "	2	" " 8 reps	14	35# R:6 L:4	30#, 6	-	-

Date	Set #	Exercise				

The Rock Climber's Training Manual
Hangboard Personal Record Log

	Set:	Resistance:	#Reps:		Set:	Resistance:	#Reps:		Set:	Resistance:	#Reps:
Grip: _____	1 2 3	_____ _____ _____	_____ _____ _____		1 2 3	_____ _____ _____	_____ _____ _____		1 2 3	_____ _____ _____	_____ _____ _____
	Date: _____				Date: _____				Date: _____		
Grip: _____	1 2 3	_____ _____ _____	_____ _____ _____		1 2 3	_____ _____ _____	_____ _____ _____		1 2 3	_____ _____ _____	_____ _____ _____
	Date: _____				Date: _____				Date: _____		
Grip: _____	1 2 3	_____ _____ _____	_____ _____ _____		1 2 3	_____ _____ _____	_____ _____ _____		1 2 3	_____ _____ _____	_____ _____ _____
	Date: _____				Date: _____				Date: _____		
Grip: _____	1 2 3	_____ _____ _____	_____ _____ _____		1 2 3	_____ _____ _____	_____ _____ _____		1 2 3	_____ _____ _____	_____ _____ _____
	Date: _____				Date: _____				Date: _____		
Grip: _____	1 2 3	_____ _____ _____	_____ _____ _____		1 2 3	_____ _____ _____	_____ _____ _____		1 2 3	_____ _____ _____	_____ _____ _____
	Date: _____				Date: _____				Date: _____		
Grip: _____	1 2 3	_____ _____ _____	_____ _____ _____		1 2 3	_____ _____ _____	_____ _____ _____		1 2 3	_____ _____ _____	_____ _____ _____
	Date: _____				Date: _____				Date: _____		
Grip: _____	1 2 3	_____ _____ _____	_____ _____ _____		1 2 3	_____ _____ _____	_____ _____ _____		1 2 3	_____ _____ _____	_____ _____ _____
	Date: _____				Date: _____				Date: _____		
Grip: _____	1 2 3	_____ _____ _____	_____ _____ _____		1 2 3	_____ _____ _____	_____ _____ _____		1 2 3	_____ _____ _____	_____ _____ _____
	Date: _____				Date: _____				Date: _____		
Grip: _____	1	_____	_____		1	_____	_____		1	_____	_____
	Date: _____				Date: _____				Date: _____		
Grip: _____	1	_____	_____		1	_____	_____		1	_____	_____
	Date: _____				Date: _____				Date: _____		

The Rock Climber's Training Manual Logbook

The Official Data Tracker for the Rock Prodigy Training Program

You might be a veteran of physical training and conditioning or you might be brand new to the concept. Either way this logbook will help you continue to improve by helping you stay organized and easily chart your progress each week. All the logs and charts needed for one training season are included in this free logbook, making it easy to visually see your growth and accomplishments throughout the season.

Did you find this complimentary book helpful? Want another one for your next season?

Re-order Three-Season Logbooks online at www.fixedpin.com

WWW.FIXEDPIN.COM

10 reps, and the third set, eight reps. For isotonic contractions, the set/repetition protocols listed on the bottom of the previous page are recommended (note: Power and "Functional" Hypertrophy are most applicable to climbing).[3, 5, 6, 15, 16]

As mentioned earlier, isometric contractions have not been studied as thoroughly as isotonic contractions, so less is known about how to optimize isometric training. That said, the limited research has produced a few noteworthy conclusions. It is up to climbers to build on this information through trial and error.

- Multiple "brief" repetitions at high resistance are significantly better (~ 66 percent better) at improving strength than using a single repetition of "long" (~ one minute) duration at lower resistance.[18]
- Strength gains occur within (roughly) 15 degrees of the joint angle that is trained, so climbers should carefully consider which grip positions to train.[8, 9, 10, 17]
- Repetitions should last from three to 10 seconds.[9]
- After a brief force peak, "high-frequency fatigue" will set in approximately six or seven seconds into the contraction, and if rest is received, the muscle recovers in about two seconds.[2]
- Sets of isometric exercises should total approximately 15-20 repetitions.[7]

As with any physical training, the most improvement will occur in the vicinity of the rep number and duration that is trained, with some translation to adjacent rep numbers and durations; therefore, specificity is critical.[3, 6, 16] That is, if the athlete expects to execute a single isometric contraction followed by a minute or more of rest, then it would make sense to train with sets of a single rep (and so on). On the other hand, if the athlete expects to perform repeated isometric contractions with only a few seconds rest in between, then the protocol should be designed as such. The finger-strength training routines described below were based on these principles, but have since been thoroughly tested and refined to optimize their effectiveness. They are not perfect, but they should provide even the best-trained athletes with a great starting point.

"I do yoga, and I hang on my finger-board a lot. It works better than the gym." — Sonnie Trotter[20]

FINGER-STRENGTH TRAINING

The *hangboard* (aka *fingerboard*) is a sport-specific tool developed for the exact purpose of improving finger strength in climbers. There are myriad other tools available, including the Campus Board (discussed in Chapter Seven: Power), system board, and a plethora of gimmick devices (which non-climber relatives often consider to be the ideal Christmas gift), but the hangboard is hands down the best tool for isometric finger-strength training.

Nearly every aspect of hangboard training can be carefully controlled by the athlete to produce the desired results. It is easy to isolate sport-specific grip positions on a hangboard and train them to failure. The resistance can be precisely controlled, allowing the climber to push right up against her physical limits while minimizing the risk of injury. Training results can be accurately quantified, allowing steady and predictable increases in resistance from workout to workout, ensuring that the goal of progressive overload is achieved. Finally, hangboard equipment is relatively small and portable, allowing virtually anyone to utilize this training method regardless of their proximity to climbing facilities.

Most climbing gyms have one or more hangboards already installed that novice hangboarders can "test-drive" in order to learn the basics of hangboarding and experiment with different features. Unfortunately most of these boards are in poor condition, and the ceaseless distractions of the climbing gym make it difficult to train in a consistent manner. As a result, most climbers eventually opt to install their own hangboard at home.

Example hangboard installation in a climber's home.

HANGBOARD SELECTION AND CONFIGURATION

A good hangboard-training setup includes one or more hangboards secured to a solid structure at a height that allows the athlete to reach all of the holds from ground level (or a secure platform). If all goes well, it will eventually be necessary to hang from very tiny holds with significant amounts of additional weight, so the holds need to be easy to reach statically. Generally, if the lowest holds are placed just at arm's reach, the highest holds will be too high, so consider creating a makeshift platform out of 2x6s or similar materials to make it easy to reach the highest holds. This platform must be sturdy enough to support the climber in the event she drops suddenly from the hangboard with weight added.

Selecting the proper hangboard is not easy, and many climbers may evolve their choice of hangboard(s) over time as they progress and refine their needs. It is essential to feel a prospective hangboard before purchasing it — therefore, a hangboard should not be selected over the Internet. Each grip should be ergonomically shaped and comfortable. If something feels "off" from the comfort of a retail store, imagine how bad it will feel when hanging free with 50 pounds added! Avoid heavily textured boards (sanding a rough board with high-grit sandpaper may help). Ensure the lower row of grips does not interfere with the ability to ergonomically grasp the higher row of grips (for example, pockets should generally be placed on the bottom row so that the unused fingers have room to curl toward the palm without contacting the board). Most boards are too narrow, putting unneeded stress on the shoulders and elbows. In this case, it may help to cut the board in half down the center line and spread the two halves of the board a few inches, remounting them on a piece of lumber (this may void the warranty!).

Example Hangboard Log Sheet. Use this to establish training goals for each workout and document your results.

Hangboard grips should provide sufficient clearance for inactive fingers. The grip shown interferes with the climber's index finger, possibly resulting in injury or skin irritation after extended use.

Hangboard Log

Date: 15 January 2012   W/O #: 5
Temp: 58 deg   Dressed Weight: 152 lb.
Rep Timing: 7s hang/3s rest   Rest Interval: 3:00

Step Up?

Y (N)   Exercise 1 Grip: Large Open Edge   Notes: Warm-up

Goal:	Set:	Resistance:	#Reps:	Difficulty 1-10:	Comments:
-10	1	-10	7	1	Easy
-	2	-	-		
+10	3	+10	5	2	Not too bad, but not easy

(Y) N   Exercise 2 Grip: MR 2F Pocket   N: tape ring finger base

Goal:	Set:	Resistance:	#Reps:	Difficulty:	Comments:
0	1	0	7	4	Not too bad
+10	2	+10	6	6	Kinda hard
+20	3	+20	(6)	7	Hard but not to failure

(Y) N   Exercise 3 Grip: Small Edge   N: Breath!

Goal:	Set:	Resistance:	#Reps:	Difficulty:	Comments:
+10	1	+10	7	6	Hard for 1st set
+20	2	+20	5	8	To failure; #5 = 4 seconds
+30	3	(+20)	5	9	To failure; #5 = 6 s, good recovery

(Y) N   Exercise 4 Grip: Mono   N: tape middle finger 2nd pad

Goal:	Set:	Resistance:	#Reps:	Difficulty:	Comments:
-35	1	-35	7	3	Fairly easy
-30	2	-30	6	6	Kinda hard
-25	3	-25	5	7	Hard at end but coulda done more

Y (N)   Exercise 5 Grip: Wide Pinch   N: Remove all tape

Goal:	Set:	Resistance:	#Reps:	Difficulty:	Comments:
-30	1	-30	7	6	Pumpy at end
-20	2	-20	6	7	Hard!
-10	3	-10	5	8	Barely did em all; great effort!

Y (N)   Exercise 6 Grip: IM 2F Pocket   N: tape index finger 2nd pad

Goal:	Set:	Resistance:	#Reps:	Difficulty:	Comments:
0	1	0	7	4	Not too bad
+10	2	+10	6	5	Pumpy at end
+20	3	+20	(6)	7	To failure; 1-5 good, 6 = 5 seconds

(Y) N   Exercise 7 Grip: Narrow Pinch   N: Remove all tape

Goal:	Set:	Resistance:	#Reps:	Difficulty:	Comments:
-35	1	-35	7	4	Not too bad
-25	2	-25	6	6	Pretty hard
-15	3	-15	(6)	7	Hard but not quite to failure

Y N   Exercise 8 Grip: _____   N: _____

Goal:	Set:	Resistance:	#Reps:	Difficulty:	Comments:
	1				
	2				
	3				

The Perfect Hangboard

Effective training requires the right tool. The challenge is finding a board that is designed for elite finger strength training – that is, a board that includes all critical grip positions, is ergonomically shaped for limit training, and fits your body, in terms of shoulder width and finger/hand size. This allows you to push yourself on every rep free of pain, and without courting injury. The traditional "one-size-fits-all" hangboard doesn't account for body size variation, forcing many climbers to awkwardly contort themselves onto a board. To alleviate this, we worked with Trango to create the Rock Prodigy Training Center (RPTC—pictured on the right). This board was designed deliberately for elite finger strength training, with ergonomics and functionality at the forefront. It consists of two halves that can be spaced to match the shoulder-width of each user, and a multitude of grips to fit various hand sizes. The RPTC isn't perfect, but connoisseurs agree it's the best training board on the market.

Recommended hangboards:
- Rock Prodigy Training Center (RPTC) by Trango
- Power Station by Eldorado Climbing Walls
- Nicros NexGen™
- Metolius Simulator

The board should be installed in an area that is isolated from distractions (so the climber can focus on training) and where environmental conditions such as temperature and humidity can be somewhat controlled. To maximize strength gains, it is essential to document the results of each workout. At a bare minimum, record:

- Grip positions used
- Goal resistance for each set (usually in terms of weight added or weight removed)
- Actual resistance for each set
- Number of repetitions, or partial repetitions, completed for each set
- Rest taken between repetitions and sets

In addition, more-obsessive training fiends will also want to record:
- Body weight (including clothing, harness, etc.)
- Temperature
- Humidity
- Comments on how each set felt
- Any other information that helps reconstruct the quality of the workout.

The data collected will be critical in establishing goal resistance for future workouts, and it can be extremely motivating to track what is sure to be impressive progress from week to week. It is best to prepare a log sheet before the workout, such as the one shown in the Figure on the previous page, to record the results of each set as you complete it. It may also help to embed strategic reminders into the log sheet, such as "Breathe!" or "Tape middle finger here."

The following finger-strength exercises utilize two-arm "dead hangs." That is, two hands will be used on the board at all times — with each hand on the same size and type of grip for a given set — and the climber will hang with her arms in a static position throughout each rep. Elbows and shoulders should be slightly bent to avoid unnecessary strain, but you should not pull-up, lock-off, or otherwise vary your body position during the repetition. Nevertheless, the muscles of the upper arm, shoulder, and upper back should be flexed during each hang to take your weight, rather than hanging purely from the joints.

Proper deadhang posture: hands shoulder-width apart, arms slightly bent, and muscular tension through the elbows and shoulders.

Tools for Effective Hangboard Training

The following list of accessories, painstakingly developed and tested over more than a decade by hangboarding lab monkeys, will help you get the most out of your hangboard workouts:

- **Fan:** Positioned to circulate air across the surface of the hangboard.
- **Stopwatch:** Placed in the climber's field of view; used to time reps and rest periods.
- **Chalk and a toothbrush:** Placed within arm's reach and used for cleaning holds and drying hands between sets.
- **Skin-Care Kit:** Available nearby to address any skin issues that arise during the workout. Be prepared to apply preemptive tape to sensitive areas, and sand down any callouses between workouts (see Chapter Nine: Rest, Injury Prevention, and Rehabilitation for details on skin care).
- **Harness:** Should be comfortable (padded) with a load-bearing haul loop for "adding" weight (it's OK to use an old, worn-out harness for hangboarding).
- **Pulley System:** Used to "remove" weight during certain sets (see photo opposite). To install this, you'll need two pulleys, two carabiners, two or more eyebolts, and about six feet of seven- or eight-millimeter static cord. Place one eyebolt in the bottom of your hangboard's mounting board, sited such that the cord will hang straight below the centerline of the board when the pulley is attached to the eyebolt with a carabiner. The second eyebolt should be placed roughly two feet to either side of the hangboard . Attach one pulley to each eyebolt, and run the length of cord through the pulleys, with a carabiner clipped to a knot at either end of the cord. Remove weight by clipping one end of the cord to the belay loop on your harness and the other end to the amount of weight you would like to remove.
- **Weights:** Several five- and ten-pound plates available for "adding to" or "subtracting from" your body weight. Girth-hitch a sling through the holes in the plates.

Intstall a pulley system using two or more eye-bolts, two pulleys, several carabiners and a length of cord as shown to "remove" weight during hangboard workouts.

Note the platform, timer, fan, pulley system, weights, chalkbag, toothbrush, and logsheet.

Each workout will consist of a predetermined number of "exercises" or climbing-grip positions. Each exercise will consist of one, two, or three sets corresponding to the beginner, intermediate, and advanced routines, respectively. Each set will consist of five to seven repetitions of a consistent duration. A repetition begins when the legs are slowly lifted off the ground (or platform), and ends when the feet gently return to the ground. Repetitions should not involve any jerky or sudden movements. The goal is NOT to shock-load the fingers — save that for the campus board. Usually the hands will remain near the hangboard between repetitions, until the entire set is completed.

The climber should establish baseline levels of resistance (in terms of weight added or removed) for each grip position. This will probably take some trial and error to determine, and in most cases, baseline resistance will be different for each grip. Novice hangboarders should err on the side of using too *little* resistance (which will require removing 30 or more pounds for all but the juggiest of hangboards); it's much more motivating to progress quickly than regress or stagnate, and using too much resistance can have undesirable consequences. For routines with multiple sets per exercise, the resistance will typically be increased in 10-pound increments between each set of a given exercise. If every repetition of each set of a given exercise is successfully completed, increase the resistance during the next workout for each set of

that exercise by five pounds. The climber should begin each Strength Phase by returning to near baseline for each grip, then ratchet up the resistance as necessary to achieve the desired training stimulus. If your weight fluctuates substantially you should weigh in before each workout and factor that into the baseline load for each grip.

GRIP SELECTION

Experience shows that attempting to perform too many total sets diminishes the quality of the workout, so include only the most fundamental (and important) grip positions. Utilize the same grips for each workout within a training cycle so that progress can be made and tracked.

The Beginner Hangboard Routine should include one set each of eight to ten different grip positions. The following are recommended:

- Warm-up jug
- Large edge
- Medium edge
- Wide pinch
- Medium pinch
- Sloper*
- Index-middle-ring (IMR) deep three-finger pocket
- Middle-ring-pinky (MRP) deep three-finger pocket
- Middle-ring (MR) deep two-finger pocket

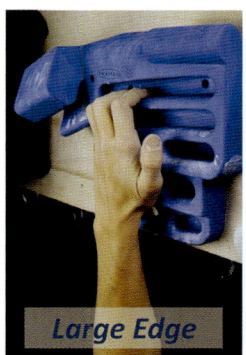
Large Edge

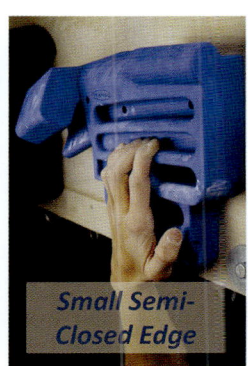
Small Semi-Closed Edge

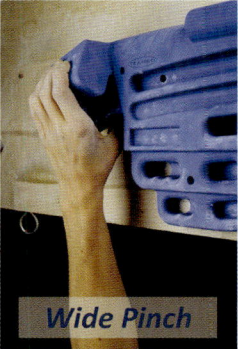
Wide Pinch

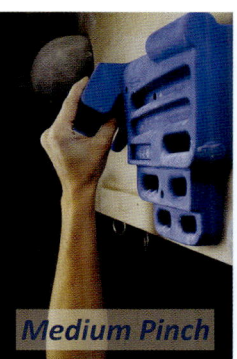
Medium Pinch

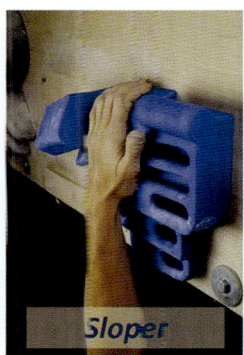
Sloper

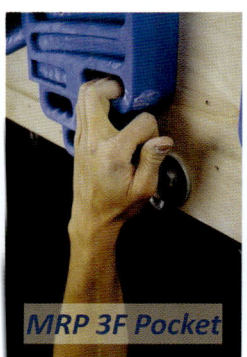
MRP 3F Pocket

IMR 3F Pocket

MR 2F Pocket

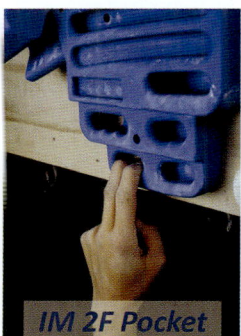
IM 2F Pocket

Mono

The Intermediate Hangboard Routine should include two sets each of five or six of the following different grip positions:

- Warm-up sloper*
- Medium open-hand edge
- Small semi-closed edge
- MR shallow two-finger pocket
- Index-middle (IM) deep two-finger pocket
- IMR *or* MRP deep three-finger pocket
- Pinch

* Sloper training with a hangboard often depends more on skin friction than strength, so many athletes find this grip position is not worth training on the hangboard. Consider leaving this grip out unless it is relevant to a particular goal route.

The Advanced Hangboard Routine should include three sets each of six or seven different grip positions. Start with the grips listed for the Intermediate Hangboard Routine, but consider replacing some of the larger grips with more advanced grips such as:

- Middle one-finger (1F) pocket
- Additional pinch grips (of differing width)
- Closed crimp**

**Training in a closed-crimp position can place tremendous strain on the finger joints, and should only be considered by extremely well-trained athletes who are capable of weighing the risks and making an informed decision.

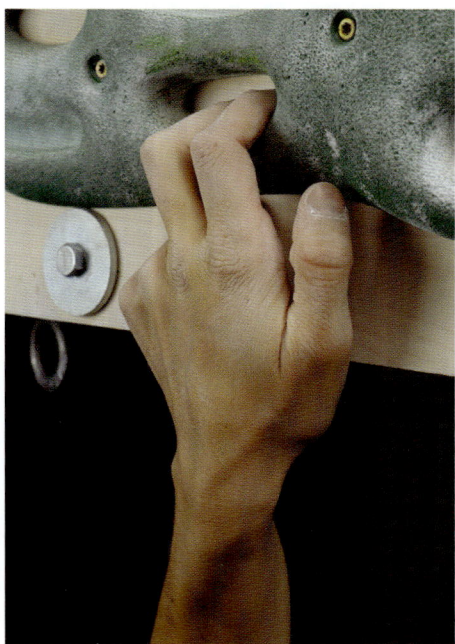

Do not use hangboard grips that unnaturally contort the fingers. This grip arrangement is a poor choice because it twists the PIP joints. Repetitive training under heavy loads with this grip will cause injury.

Risk Management and Injury Prevention

Certain grip positions are known to present a high risk of finger injury. For example, the closed-crimp position puts tremendous stress on the proximal inter-phalangeal or PIP joint (the big knuckle) of the fingers. One strategy for limiting injury risk to these joints is to avoid crimping entirely. However, we all know that when the send is in the balance we're going to bear down on that credit-card edge, regardless of the consequences.

Knowing full well that sooner or later we will apply tremendous strain to our PIP joints, should you prepare for these forces through controlled, progressive overload? Perhaps it would be better to limit the use of these threatening grips, in order to minimize the accumulation of microtrauma, hoping that this neglect will not result in acute injury when these grips are inevitably used in the heat of battle.

With only anecdotal arguments on either side, it comes down to a personal decision. I think it makes more sense to prepare my body in anticipation of a stressful event, but the choice is yours. Realize, however, that an active risk-management approach only works if the preventative training is *controlled* and *conservative*. Don't "red-line" on tweaky holds; instead listen to your body and be prepared to back off at the first sign of distress.

— *Mark Anderson*

When selecting the type and size of grips to use for hangboard training, remember the principle of specificity. Each climber should anticipate the type and size of holds he will encounter on his most important and challenging goal routes, and train on similar holds. In terms of hold *size*, one athlete's goals may dictate using relatively large holds with extra weight added, while another may need to use smaller holds with weight removed.

For those that climb primarily at a single crag, determining hold type and size should be fairly simple, as they tend to be relatively consistent across a crag. Those that visit many different crags will have more difficulty. The typical hold on a 5.12 at Rifle is much different than on a 5.12 at Smith Rock. Climbers in this situation should consider which types of routes are most valued, or represent a more-limiting weakness.

Recommended Grip Positions and Order:

Beginner Hangboard Routine
- Warm-up jug
- IMR deep 3F pocket
- Medium edge
- Medium pinch
- MR deep 2F pocket
- Large edge
- Wide pinch
- Sloper
- MRP deep 3F pocket

Intermediate Hangboard Routine
- Warm-up jug
- Large open-hand edge
- MR shallow 2F pocket
- Small semi-closed edge
- IMR deep 3F pocket
- Wide pinch
- Sloper (optional)
- Narrow pinch

Advanced Hangboard Routine
- Warm-up open-hand edge
- MR shallow 2F pocket
- Small semi-closed edge
- Middle 1F pocket
- Wide pinch
- IM deep 2F pocket
- Narrow pinch

Ideally, the selected training grips will be a bit of a stretch at first. A 5.12 climber should select hold sizes typical of the 5.13s at her favorite crag, since she will be progressing quickly through the grades once she begins training. It may be beneficial to add a specialized grip to address a particular weakness or prepare for an important goal route. Plan to stick with the selected grips for several seasons in order to track progress over time, but expect to downsize each hold every few years as strength improves.

The grips used should be ergonomically shaped and minimize skin irritation. They should not aggravate the collateral ligaments or other supporting connective tissues. This training is extremely repetitive by design, so even subtle irritation can have enormous consequences down the road. Avoid any pocket or edge that requires a finger to twist (such as fingerlocks) or imparts forces that do not align with the body's natural geometry.

Once the grip positions are identified, arrange them in a sensible order. Place the more important or basic positions earlier in the workout, but also separate like exercises as much as possible. For example, avoid arranging the two-finger pocket grips back-to-back

FOCUS AND INTENSITY

Proper hangboard training requires focus and high intensity. The first step in establishing a focused mindset is to eliminate any external distractions. Rest periods between sets will be dedicated to documenting the workout and preparing physically and mentally for the ensuing set; there will be no time for idle chitchat or checking email. If applicable, select music that elicits the proper level of arousal (generally, high arousal is preferable). Avoid any music or other external noise that may cause laughter. Seriously: A good chuckle can easily ruin a set! External motivators can help to maintain focus and proper intensity. Post photos of goal routes or inspirational messages near the hangboard, and keep a log sheet of "personal records" (PRs) handy to generate a competitive atmosphere. Aim to meet or beat those records by the end of the Strength Phase.

Progression on a Hangboard

Strength training must be progressive to be effective, meaning the volume must increase throughout the phase. In the case of hangboard training, volume can be increased in three basic ways:
- Increase duration (with longer reps or more reps)
- Increase intensity by reducing the size of the hold, thus increasing gravity's leverage on the finger flexors
- Increase intensity by increasing the weight supported by the fingers.

The durations and quantities of repetitions prescribed were selected because they are optimal for the specific physical adaptations most beneficial to climbing. It's beneficial to add an extra rep or set here and there to ensure overload is achieved within a single workout, but generally the timing prescribed in these workouts should be maintained.

The two methods of increasing intensity both have their merits. Both are specific to rock climbing, but increasing weight is far more practical. It's easier to control and quantify, while allowing for small adjustments within a workout. As strength improves, it will eventually be necessary to reduce hold size to avoid using excessive weight. Plan to downsize your holds every two to three years or so, but until then increase weight from workout to workout, and season to season, to ensure that progressive overload is attained.

> "There are no secrets to becoming strong. It's all about hard work. Beer and women will be the ruin of you."
> — Ben Moon[21]

Maintain regular, deep breathing throughout the workout. As the resistance increases, breathing becomes more critical. Take several deep breathes before each set, focus on maintaining regular breathing during each repetition, and then take a few quick deep breaths during the rest period between each rep. Vision can influence thought, so keep your eyes focused on objects that will reinforce mental focus, such as the fingers, stopwatch, or motivational photos or quotes.

Whenever you do multiple sets, training intensity should ramp up from set to set within a given exercise (grip). In the three-sets-per-grip Advanced Hangboard Routine, the first set of each exercise should require approximately 80 percent intensity — moderately difficult, requiring attention, but done completely in control. You should feel fatigued at the end of the first set, but should routinely complete all seven repetitions, and should feel confident that you could do more reps if you so desired. The second set will start out controlled and perhaps relatively casual, but the last two or three reps will feel very difficult, and on rare occasions may not all be completed. By the end of the last set, you should be breathing heavily, perhaps trembling a bit, and will have difficulty maintaining proper form. You will be giving 100 percent effort to complete the set. The last two reps of the third set should feel "in doubt," and you may even begin sliding off the hold near the end of the last few reps (avoid sliding entirely off the board, as this results in significantly increased force on the finger joints and high injury risk). Adjust the training resistance as necessary to achieve similar levels of intensity during each workout. Generally each workout in the Strength Phase will be slightly harder than the previous one.

Finally, hangboard training is hard work. The hangboard is an extremely powerful tool, but only if used correctly. Simply going through the motions, applying moderate effort, will not produce results. This is the time to buckle down and give the best possible effort to each workout. Eat right, get adequate sleep, and rest thoroughly between workouts. Prepare a supportive training environment and get psyched to push your finger strength to the next level!

HANGBOARD ROUTINES

Hangboard workouts should only be done after a *thorough* warm-up. Warm up with low-to-moderate intensity traversing for at least 20 minutes. Movements should be easy at first and then become progressively more difficult. Work through all the grip positions that will be used during the workout, increasing intensity throughout the warm-up. If practical, consider warming up at a climbing gym, then traveling home to complete the hangboard routine (try to keep the gap between the end of the warm-up and the start of your routine to 30 minutes or less).

BEGINNER HANGBOARD ROUTINE

This routine is intended for climbers who are new to hangboarding but are not necessarily "beginner" climbers. In addition to improving finger strength, the purpose of this routine is to learn the basics of effective hangboarding and identify any weak grip positions. This routine will provide a solid base of strength to build upon. Climbers should advance to the Intermediate Hangboard Routine after one to three complete training cycles.

For each exercise, complete a single set of six repetitions. The first exercise of each routine should be a "warm-up" exercise, performed on a relatively large, open-hand grip with relatively low intensity. The purpose of this exercise is to prepare the shoulders and elbows for the coming loads, so this exercise should be performed at similar loads to those planned for the ensuing workout. Rest three minutes between each set in the routine. Note that most climbers will need to *remove* weight (see "Tools for Effective Hangboard Training" sidebar) in order to complete the prescribed sets.

Example Timing for Beginner Hangboard Routine

Repetition Number	Start Time	End Time	Activity
1	0:00	0:10	Deadhang
	0:10	*0:15*	*Rest*
2	0:15	0:25	Deadhang
	0:25	*0:30*	*Rest*
3	0:30	0:40	Deadhang
	0:40	*0:45*	*Rest*
4	0:45	0:55	Deadhang
	0:55	*1:00*	*Rest*
5	1:00	1:10	Deadhang
	1:10	*1:15*	*Rest*
6	1:15	1:25	Deadhang
	1:25	*4:25*	*Rest*

A repetition is a static dead-hang of a relatively short, timed duration, followed by a brief, timed rest period. For the Beginner Hangboard Routine, a repetition is a 10-second hang followed by five seconds of rest. For example, a set of a given exercise of the Beginner Hangboard Routine would last 85 seconds and transpire as shown at the bottom of the last page.

This timing is used for several reasons. First, it loosely replicates the duty cycle typical of less-experienced climbers on the rock. Second, the relatively long repetitions permit lower intensity, limiting the risk to untrained fingers. Finally, this timing is practical, resulting in 15-second cycles that are easy to track while fatigued.

BEGINNER HANGBOARD ROUTINE

WARM-UP:

Low-intensity ARC traversing (30 - 40 minutes)
- Rehearse techniques
- Light, active stretching on the wall
- Progress through every grip that will be trained

HANGBOARD ROUTINE*:

Exercise	Grip	Set	Reps	Resistance	Total Set Time	TUT
1	Warm-up jug	1	6	Baseline	1:25	1:00
		Rest 3:00				
2	IMR 2-pad 3F pocket	1	6	Baseline	1:25	1:00
		Rest 3:00				
3	Medium edge (semi-closed)	1	6	Baseline	1:25	1:00
		Rest 3:00				
4	Medium pinch	1	6	Baseline	1:25	1:00
		Rest 3:00				
5	MR 2-pad 2F pocket	1	6	Baseline	1:25	1:00
		Rest 3:00				
6	Large open-hand edge	1	6	Baseline	1:25	1:00
		Rest 3:00				
7	Wide pinch	1	6	Baseline	1:25	1:00
		Rest 3:00				
8	Sloper	1	6	Baseline	1:25	1:00
		Rest 3:00				
9	MRP 2-pad 3F pocket	1	6	Baseline	1:25	1:00
					Total TUT:	9:00

* NOTE: *Each repetition is 10 seconds long with 5 seconds rest between repetitions within a set.*

SUPPLEMENTAL EXERCISES:
- Select two to six high-priority movements
- Complete two to four sets of each exercise

INTERMEDIATE HANGBOARD ROUTINE

WARM-UP:

Low-intensity ARC traversing (20 - 30 minutes)
- Rehearse techniques
- Light, active stretching on the wall
- Progress through every grip that will be trained

HANGBOARD ROUTINE*:

Exercise	Grip	Set	Reps	Resistance	Total Set Time	TUT
1	Warm-up jug	1	7	Baseline	1:07	0:49
	Rest 3:00					
2	Large open-hand edge	1	7	Baseline	1:07	0:49
	Rest 3:00					
	...	2	6	Baseline +10	0:57	0:42
	Rest 3:00					
3	MR 1-pad 2F pocket	1	7	Baseline	1:07	0:49
	Rest 3:00					
	...	2	6	Baseline +10	0:57	0:42
	Rest 3:00					
4	Small semi-closed crimp	1	7	Baseline	1:07	0:49
	Rest 3:00					
	...	2	6	Baseline +10	0:57	0:42
	Rest 3:00					
5	IMR 2-pad 3F pocket	1	7	Baseline	1:07	0:49
	Rest 3:00					
	...	2	6	Baseline +10	0:57	0:42
	Rest 3:00					
6	Wide Pinch	1	7	Baseline	1:07	0:49
	Rest 3:00					
	...	2	6	Baseline +10	0:57	0:42
	Rest 3:00					
7	Sloper	1	7	Baseline	1:07	0:49
	Rest 3:00					
	...	2	6	Baseline +10	0:57	0:42
	Rest 3:00					
8	Narrow pinch	1	7	Baseline	1:07	0:49
	Rest 3:00					
	...	2	6	Baseline +10	0:57	0:42
					Total TUT:	11:26

* NOTE: *Each repetition is 7 seconds long with 3 seconds rest between repetitions within a set.*

SUPPLEMENTAL EXERCISES:

- Select two to six high-priority movements
- Complete two to four sets of each exercise

INTERMEDIATE HANGBOARD ROUTINE

This routine is recommended for those with some hangboard experience and at least a year of focused training under their belt. Alternatively, training "neophytes" who consistently climb at the 5.12 level or above should consider beginning with this routine. For each exercise (or grip position), complete two sets of six or seven repetitions. These should be done in a progressive fashion as shown below:

Set	Number of Repetitions	Resistance
1	7	Baseline*
2	6	Baseline* + 10 lbs.

Note: "Baseline" is not body weight. It is whatever amount of resistance results in failure at the end of the sixth rep of the second set. For most climbers and grips, this will be much <u>less</u> than body weight.

The first exercise of each routine should be a pseudo-warm-up, performed on a relatively large, open-hand grip with relatively low intensity. The purpose of the warm-up exercise is to prepare the shoulders and elbows for the ensuing loads, so use loads that are comparable to those used throughout the workout. Rest three minutes between each set in the exercise, and three minutes between exercises. Complete both sets of one exercise before moving to the next exercise. Most climbers will need to begin each Strength Phase by *removing* weight (see "Tools for Effective Hangboard Training" sidebar) in order to complete the prescribed sets.

A repetition is a static dead-hang of a relatively short, timed duration, followed by a brief, timed rest period. For the Intermediate Hangboard Routine, a repetition is a seven-second hang followed by three seconds of rest. For example, the second set of a given exercise of the Intermediate Hangboard Routine would last 57 seconds and transpire as shown at the top of the next column.

This seven-second dead-hang/three-second rest (7/3) timing was selected after experimenting with 6/4 and 5/5 timing because it is more specific to the duty cycle used by advanced climbers during performance, it produces the right amount of metabolic stress, and it equates to the initial period of contraction in which muscles can produce maximal force (before high-frequency fatigue sets in). At first, the rest periods may seem too brief, but with practice this protocol is easy to execute. Climbers should plan to follow this routine for three to six training cycles before progressing to the Advanced Hangboard Routine.

Example Timing for Intermediate Hangboard Routine

Repetition Number	Start Time	End Time	Activity
1	0:00	0:07	Deadhang
	0:07	0:10	Rest
2	0:10	0:17	Deadhang
	0:17	0:20	Rest
3	0:20	0:27	Deadhang
	0:27	0:30	Rest
4	0:30	0:37	Deadhang
	0:37	0:40	Rest
5	0:40	0:47	Deadhang
	0:47	0:50	Rest
6	0:50	0:57	Deadhang
	0:57	4:00	Rest

ADVANCED HANGBOARD ROUTINE

The Advanced Hangboard Routine is intended for climbers with two or more years of hangboard experience. However, climbers with little training experience who consistently climb at the 5.13 level should consider transitioning to this workout more quickly — perhaps after one or two complete training cycles using the Intermediate Hangboard Routine. The grips recommended in this routine are more strenuous and the volume of exercise is much higher, so climbers should have experience with less-intense hangboard training before using this routine.

For each exercise (or grip position), complete three sets of five to seven repetitions. These should be done in a progressive fashion as shown below:

Set	Number of Repetitions	Resistance
1	7	Baseline*
2	6	Baseline* + 10 lbs.
3	5	Baseline* + 20 lbs.

* Note: "Baseline" is not body weight. It is whatever amount of resistance results in failure at the end of the fifth rep of the third set. For most climbers and grips, this will initially be <u>less</u> than body weight.*

The first exercise of each routine should be a pseudo-warm-up, performed on a relatively large, open-hand grip with relatively low intensity. Rest three minutes between each set in the exercise, and three minutes between exercises. Complete all three sets of one exercise before moving to the next exercise.

A repetition is a static dead-hang of a relatively short, timed duration, followed by a brief, timed rest period. For the Advanced Hangboard Routine, a repetition is a seven-second hang followed by three seconds of rest. For example, the second set of a given exercise of the Advanced Hangboard Routine would last 57 seconds (see "Example Timing for Intermediate Hangboard Routine," above, for a detailed explanation of this timing).

ADVANCED HANGBOARD ROUTINE

WARM-UP:

Low-intensity ARC traversing (20 - 30 minutes)
- Rehearse techniques
- Light, active stretching on the wall
- Progress through every grip that will be trained

HANGBOARD ROUTINE*:

Exercise	Grip	Set	Reps	Resistance	Total Set Time	TUT
1	Warm-up open hand edge	1	7	Baseline	1:07	0:49
	...	2	5	Baseline +20	0:47	0:35
2	MR 1-pad 2F pocket	1	7	Baseline	1:07	0:49
	...	2	6	Baseline +10	0:57	0:42
	...	3	5	Baseline +20	0:47	0:35
3	Small semi-closed crimp	1	7	Baseline	1:07	0:49
	...	2	6	Baseline +10	0:57	0:42
	...	3	5	Baseline +20	0:47	0:35
4	Middle 1-pad 1F pocket	1	7	Baseline	1:07	0:49
	...	2	6	Baseline +10	0:57	0:42
	...	3	5	Baseline +20	0:47	0:35
5	Wide pinch	1	7	Baseline	1:07	0:49
	...	2	6	Baseline +10	0:57	0:42
	...	3	5	Baseline +20	0:47	0:35
6	IM deep 2F pocket	1	7	Baseline	1:07	0:49
	...	2	6	Baseline +10	0:57	0:42
	...	3	5	Baseline +20	0:47	0:35
7	Narrow pinch	1	7	Baseline	1:07	0:49
	...	2	6	Baseline +10	0:57	0:42
	...	3	5	Baseline +20	0:47	0:35
					Total TUT:	14:00

* NOTES:
- *Each repetition is 7 seconds long with 3 seconds rest between repetitions within a set.*
- *Rest 3:00 between each set in the routine.*

SUPPLEMENTAL EXERCISES:
- Select two to six high-priority movements
- Complete two to four sets of each exercise

WHOLE-BODY STRENGTH TRAINING

At the conclusion of each hangboard routine, the climber should consume his preferred post-workout recovery foods (such as a protein bar), then perform any desired supplemental exercises. Since weaknesses vary, each climber must select the exercises that are most likely to improve his climbing, considering that time and effort is limited. These exercises should be selected to address weaknesses or to prepare for specific goal routes. Most climbers should perform at least one exercise that addresses each of the following muscle groups:

- Latissimus dorsi ("Lats") and associated pull muscles
- Shoulders
- Core

The following section describes a variety of basic exercises that have been used by climbers to improve strength in various muscle groups. Unless otherwise stated, all of these exercises should be performed slowly, in complete control, favoring good form over high load.

Once a set of exercises has been selected, consider the desired adaptation (power vs. endurance, etc.) and utilize the set/rep table below to determine the proper number of sets and reps for each exercise. Try to limit the number of exercises to six or less in order to avoid diminishing the quality of effort.

Desired Adaption	# of Sets	# of Reps	Rest Between Sets
Power	1-3	3-5	3-5 minutes
"Functional" Hypertrophy	3-4	6-8	3-5 minutes
"Non-Functional" Hyp.	3-4	8-12	1-3 minutes
Strength-Endurance	2-4	12-20	30 sec - 1 minute

PULLING-MUSCLE EXERCISES

Pull-up: Pull-ups are common exercises for climbers, though some debate their efficacy. Regardless, they can help athletes prepare for other training activities like lock-off laps and Campus Board exercises. Pull-ups primarily train the latissimus dorsi muscles, but also affect many upper-arm, back, and shoulder muscles. Pull-ups can harm elbow joints if performed incorrectly, so use controlled movements, and keep your elbows slightly bent at the low point of the movement. Healthy athletes can attempt "explosive"

pull-ups by utilizing a quick, energetic contraction to propel the body upward (as for a Campus exercise).

Pull-ups are normally performed on a still bar, but climbers should use independent, free-hanging grips (such as gymnastic rings or "Rock Rings"), which allow the hands to *supinate* (rotate, such that the palms face each other at the top of the contraction). Avoid doing pull-ups on a hangboard, which overly constrains supination. Begin from a dead-hang, pull your body upward until your chin is level with the tops of your hands, lock-off momentarily, and then lower your body back to a dead-hang position.

One-Arm Inverted Row

One-Arm Inverted Row: This exercise is a modified pull-up intended to achieve a more sport-specific body position. Use a similar free-hanging grip, but position the ring low enough that your feet can rest on the ground (or another support), such that the body is inclined to the ground at an angle of zero to 30 degrees.

Using one arm at a time, begin with a dead-hang, then raise the upper body and rotate the hips while "reaching" with the free hand, bringing the armpit of the free arm up to the ring, as if reaching for a hold. After a brief lock-off, lower the upper body until the pulling arm is nearly straight. Keeping the feet fixed and the body in a reverse-plank position throughout the repetition will help train core strength as well.

Lock-Off Laps: A lock-off is a static hang in a contracted position (such as at the apex of a pull-up), and they are a key element of climbing performance. Lock-offs can be trained using individual isometric contractions, or incorporated into an isotonic repetition with predefined "hold points." Using a combination of isotonic and isometric contractions will ensure that the entire range of motion is trained to some degree.

Lock-off laps should be performed on a 45-degree (or so) overhanging climbing wall with many footholds and a ladder of large jugs. Begin in a seated position with feet on small but positive footholds and one hand on the wall (the other hand should hang free). Pull onto the wall, and then raise the upper body until the shoulder of the active hand is adjacent to that same hand. Hold this lock-off position for two deep breaths, then grasp the next jug with the inactive hand. Step the feet up the wall, release the low hand, and then raise the upper body until the other shoulder is adjacent to the other hand. Hold this lock-off position for two deep breaths. Continue in this fashion until the top of the wall is reached (or continuing higher would be unsafe), then work down the board, locking-off each move as on the way up. Continue moving up and down the wall until the desired number of repetitions is reached. This can be an excellent power-endurance exercise when performed with body weight, and also trains functional core strength.

PUSHING-MUSCLE EXERCISES

Push-Ups: Push-ups are a great exercise for maintaining pectoral strength without adding unwanted mass. Push-ups also train deltoid and triceps muscles to a lesser extent, as well as the rectus

abdominis, obliques, and erector spinae core muscles. Begin by lying flat on the floor with the body in a plank position and palms flat on the ground, adjacent to the shoulders. Extend both arms until nearly locked to raise the chest off the ground. After a brief pause, lower the chest to within two inches or so of the ground. A dumbbell can be held between the shoulder blades to add resistance.

Shoulder Press

Shoulder Press: This exercise trains the deltoids and triceps and helps with so-called "shouldery moves" like extended gastons and overhead underclings. The shoulder press is normally performed with a dumbbell in each hand (though advanced athletes can use body weight to perform "handstand push-ups"). In a standing position, hold a dumbbell in each hand at shoulder level, with your elbows bent. Extend the dumbbells straight up until your elbows are nearly locked, allowing the palms to rotate freely. After a brief hold, lower the dumbbells back to the shoulders. When performed with free weights in a standing position, this exercise also trains core strength.

Pause 2 Breaths — *Lock-Off Laps* — *Pause 2 Breaths* — *Repeat*

Dips

Hanging Leg Raise

Dips: This exercise trains the triceps, deltoids, pectoral, latissimus dorsi, and rhomboid muscles. These are usually performed on a set of parallel bars, but in a pinch can be performed on the interior corner of a countertop (found in most kitchens). Begin with one hand on each parallel bar, with arms straight and the body suspended in a vertical plank position. Bending at the elbows and shoulder, lower the body until the armpits are level with the hands. Hold this position for one deep breath, and then raise the body back up until the elbows are nearly locked. Use a harness or weight belt to add resistance.

CORE EXERCISES

Hanging Leg Raises: There are an endless number of potential core exercises, but this one is among the most specific to climbers. These lifts isometrically train the rectus abdominis and obliques, while isotonically training the iliopsoas and other hip flexor muscles. These can be performed with specialized equipment designed to allow the athlete to hang relatively easily from the forearms, or advanced athletes can perform the more difficult version of this exercise from a pull-up bar or free-hanging rings. Beginning with the body suspended in a vertical plank position, raise your straightened legs forward to form a free-hanging pike position (beginners will want to start with knees bent, but should aim to perform this lift with legs straight). Hold this position for one deep breath, then lower the legs back to the free-hanging pike position. Alternate between extending the legs straight forward and 30 degrees or so to either side. Ankle weights can be used to increase resistance as desired.

Leg Lifts: These train similar muscle groups to hanging leg raises, but target the opposite end of the range of motion. These are much easier (but less sport-specific), so they can be a good variation for beginners. Lie flat on the floor in a reverse plank position. Keeping the legs straight at the knee joint, bend at the hips to raise the feet until they are roughly 16 inches off the floor. Hold this position for two deep breaths, then lower the feet back to the ground. Alternate between raising the legs straight up and 30 degrees or so to either side. Replace this exercise with hanging leg raises as soon as you're able.

Leg Lifts

SHOULDER EXERCISES

Lateral-to-Front Raise: These exercises are outstanding for training the deltoid and trapezius, but also train the supraspinatus and serratus anterior muscles of the back. For this reason, those with back problems should perform these only with low resistance. Begin in a standing position with arms hanging straight down, elbows slightly bent, with a dumbbell in each hand. Raise both arms straight out to the side, so that the arms are nearly straight, parallel to the ground, and

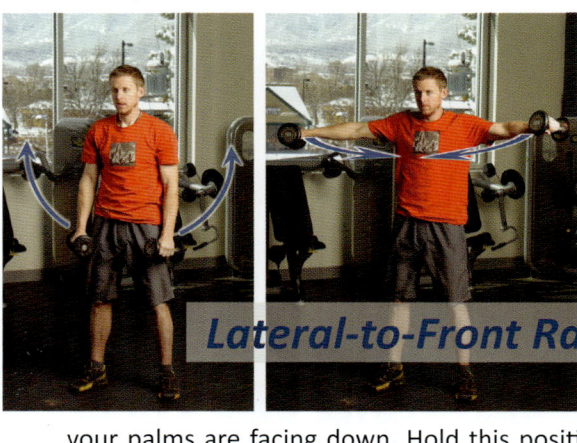

Lateral-to-Front Raise

up with arms straight down. Bending at the elbow, slowly raise the dumbbell until the hand is level with the shoulder, and then slowly lower the dumbbell back down until the elbow is nearly locked.

Shoulder Press: (Described on the previous page.)

Dips: (Described on the previous page.)

your palms are facing down. Hold this position for one deep breath. Next, keeping the arms nearly straight at the elbow joint, parallel to the ground, and palms facing down, slowly swing the arms inward until the two dumbbells are touching. Hold this position for one deep breath, and then slowly lower the dumbbells (keeping the arms nearly straight at the elbow joint) until the arms are again hanging straight down. These should be performed with relatively low weight.

Dips: (Described on the previous page.)

Shoulder Press: (Described on previous page.)

UPPER ARM EXERCISES

Bicep Curl: This exercise isolates the biceps brachii, brachialis, and brachioradialis muscles, which are critical in executing many climbing movements, including underclings and lock-offs. Grasp a dumbbell in one hand, standing straight

FREQUENCY AND REST

A properly executed hangboard routine may not feel exhausting, but will thoroughly exhaust the forearm muscles and the relatively fragile connective tissue in the fingers. Avoid any additional climbing or other finger training, and follow each hangboard workout with a relatively long rest period. Two full days (~ 70 hours) of rest are recommended between hangboard workouts. Avoid any non-climbing activity that taxes the fingers on these rest days (*light* aerobic exercise is acceptable). Some climbers will benefit from performing low-intensity ARC workouts on the day immediately following a hangboard routine. As described in Chapter Five: Base-Fitness, such workouts can speed recovery, but must be performed at a low intensity. Follow such workouts with a complete rest day, and monitor the fingers and forearms closely for signs of overtraining. Climbers primarily focused on improving strength

Key:

ARC - Aerobic Restoration and Capillarity Training	m/min - Minutes SE - Supplemental Exercises
HB - Hangboard Workout mod - Moderate	OAE - Optional Aerobic Exercise OM - Outdoor Mileage

Sunday	Monday	Tuesday	Wednesday	Thursday	Friday	Saturday
Su 23	Mo 24	Tu 25	We 26	Th 27	Fr 28	Sa 29
		Last Week of Base-Fitness Phase				*Hangboard (HB) 1 *Supplemental Ex
Su 30 *Optional OM, 4p *OAE *Skin care	Mo 31 *OAE	Tu 32 *HB 2 *SE	We 33 *Opt ARC: 2x20 min *OAE *Skin care	Th 34 *OAE	Fr 35 *HB3 *SE	Sa 36 *Optional OM, 4p *OAE *Skin care
Su 37 *OAE	Mo 38 *HB 4 *SE	Tu 39 *Opt ARC: 2x20 min *OAE *Skin care	We 40 *OAE	Th 41 *HB5 *SE	Fr 42 *Opt ARC: 2x20 min *OAE *Skin care	Sa 43 *OAE
Su 44 *HB6 *SE	Mo 45 *Opt ARC 1 x 30min (Begin Tapering) *Skin care	Tu 46	We 47 *HB7 *SE	Th 48 *Skin care	Fr 49	Sa 50

Strength Training Schedule. This example is for climbers using the Beginner Hangboard Routine, and includes optional Outdoor Mileage (OM) or ARC workouts for the days immediately following Strength Training. More advanced trainees might opt out of these supplemental workouts, while performing as many as three additional strength workouts before transitioning to the Power Phase. Any Optional Aerobic Exercise (OAE) should be gradually "tapered off" as the Strength Phase progresses.

and power should avoid supplemental ARC workouts to allow for maximum intensity during strength training. The Figure at the bottom of the previous page describes an example Strength Training schedule.

The Strength Phase should normally be positioned early in the training cycle, as it is perhaps the least sport-specific activity and the training volume is extremely high. Less-trained athletes will usually experience significant strength gains in a modest number of workouts (five to seven), so can afford to use a shorter Strength Phase in favor of more sport-specific phases that allow ample opportunity to focus on skill development (such as Base-Fitness and Power-Endurance). More-experienced athletes will notice a significant plateau in strength gains after eight or so hangboard workouts. These climbers should aim to complete at least eight (but no less than six) hangboard workouts in the Strength Phase before proceeding to the Power Phase. Very well-trained athletes may require as many as eight workouts just to regain previous strength levels, so these athletes should plan to complete 10 or more workouts per phase. Keep goals and weaknesses in mind when selecting the appropriate phase length. Those more determined to improve strength may consider a longer Strength Phase.

SUMMARY

- Physical strength is a critical attribute of climbing performance. Finger strength is the primary physical limiter for most climbers.
- Hypertrophy is the increase in muscle-fiber size. It can lead to improved strength but it increases weight, so it's not always desirable for climbers, and is difficult to achieve in the forearms anyway.
- Strength gains due to neurological adaptation occur much more quickly than hypertrophy and without any body-weight penalty, making them the best first option for climbers.
- The cycle of progressive overload, recovery, and super-compensation is the best way to increase strength while minimizing injury risk.
- Fingers primarily contract isometrically during climbing, so isometric finger-strength training should be favored. Train at the finger joint angles used during performance for the best results. Favor multiple, short repetitions over fewer, longer repetitions.
- Vary the number of sets and repetitions performed in accordance with your goals. The best transference of training to performance will occur at the set/rep ranges trained.
- The hangboard is the ideal tool for isometric finger-strength training. Take care to select a safe, useful hangboard. Select grips that are ergonomic and specific to your goal routes, both in terms of size and grip type.
- Hangboard training is most effective when performed with proper focus and intensity. Document and track each workout for best results.
- Select an appropriate hangboard routine, and perform five to ten workouts per Strength Phase, depending on your goals. Take two full rest days between workouts (low-intensity ARC or Outdoor Mileage workouts can be performed on the first rest day).
- Finish off each hangboard workout with two to six supplemental exercises, completing the specified number of sets and repetitions, according to the desired physical adaptation.

POWER

Power is the speedy application of force. Dave Graham powering through *Jaws II*, 5.15a, Rumney.   Lee Hansche

CHAPTER 7

"To give the maximum effort at the precise moment it [is] needed. This is power." — Fred Nicole[2]

Muscular power is a universal requirement in athletics and a fundamental discriminator in many sports. Generally speaking, *power* is the ability to generate a large amount of force in a short period of time. Jumping, sprinting, and explosive lifts are good examples of activities that require power. This area of athletic performance has been studied extensively to improve performance in Olympic and ball sports, and much of that knowledge can be applied to climbing. Climbers define power as the ability to quickly exert high force on a set of holds. *Climbing power* is typically needed to execute cruxy, dynamic moves between small holds. This ability is essential to all free climbers. Even on a 30-pitch big wall, success or failure can come down to a single powerful move. No aspect of climbing performance presents such a clear-cut limiting factor as a climber's power. As the great Tony Yaniro says: "If you cannot pull a single move, you have nothing to endure."[9]

Improving one's power is critical to long-term improvement. As a climber rises through the grades, the crux moves become more powerful, and though progress can be made initially with improvements to other performance aspects, eventually, he will face moves that are too powerful. The specter of getting shut down by one or two "stopper" moves on a given goal route is always waiting in the future, at a higher grade. It only takes a single, too-hard move to doom a project. In order to have a fighting chance, the climber must be able to do the moves, and the hardest moves require power.

MAXIMUM RECRUITMENT, POWER, AND CONTACT STRENGTH

Maximum recruitment, power, and *contact strength* are terms used often by climbers in training, but their actual meanings and interrelationships can be somewhat ambiguous. When skeletal muscle performs a contraction, not all motor units are contributing to that contraction in a useful way. Some motor units may contract at the wrong time, or too slowly to be effective, and some may not contract at all. Some of this is accidental, but some is intentional. Individual motor units can only sustain a contraction for a fraction of a second, so sustained muscular contractions are achieved by alternating the brief contractions of individual motor units (allowing some to rest while others work).[11] This is an elegant trade-off for meeting the various demands placed on the muscles, but it necessitates careful training to align the competing traits of endurance and maximum force production with an athlete's goals. Fortunately, understanding how human skeletal muscle adapts to external stimulation makes it possible to design effective training for all styles of climbing.

MAXIMUM RECRUITMENT

The term *recruitment* describes the proportion of active motor units contributing to a given muscular contraction. By recruiting more units, greater force can be produced. Maximum Recruitment Training (aka Max R) seeks to condition the muscle to increase the proportion of motor units activated for a given contraction. In addition, Max R training improves force production on a second front: by improving the force production of each individual motor unit. The *size*

Contact Strength: if you can't generate high force quickly, you won't be able to latch dynamic moves. Brad Gobright sticking to *The Backbone*, 5.13a, Smith Rock, OR.   Brian Mosbaugh

principle states that smaller, slow-twitch motor units tend to be activated first, and the larger and stronger fast-twitch motor units tend to be activated last. If a given contraction does not require high force production, the large motor units are never activated. Lower-intensity strength training may fail to activate the largest units. High-intensity strength training, such as Max R training, demands activation of the strongest motor units, stimulating them to adapt.[11] However, Max Recruitment is only one-half of the power equation (the force element). The other half is the speed element.

POWER

What separates *power* from *strength* is the speed or quickness of the contraction. The importance of speed in a muscular contraction is apparent to jumpers, sprinters, and other ball-sport athletes. The very hardest climbing moves usually have dynamic components as well, demanding rapid and precisely timed application of force. This is where speed becomes vital to the performance-oriented rock climber. Power is essential to both ends of any dynamic movement. First, power is needed to initiate the movement, creating upward momentum. Although usually (with good technique) the bulk of upward momentum is generated in the lower body, the fingers and upper body will experience a sudden, speed-dependent increase in load as the body moves upward, peaking when one hand leaves the rock to lunge for the next hold. In the latter half of a dynamic movement, the climber latches a target handhold, sometimes while "falling away." This requires the forearm muscles to rapidly apply a great amount of force (*power*!).

CONTACT STRENGTH

The ability to rapidly latch a hold depends on *contact strength*, a mysterious term that is often misunderstood. During any contraction, muscles do not exert peak force instantaneously; rather, it can take up to a few tenths of a second to reach peak force. This is easy to demonstrate and worth experimenting with. Once properly warmed up, grab a flat edge and slowly lift your feet off the ground, allowing the muscles time to produce maximum force. Next grab the same hold and quickly pull your feet off the ground. Notice how much more difficult it is to generate force the second time, instantly (and hang from the hold). Contact strength is the amount of force the fingers can generate during the period of initial contact with a given hold. This is critical during dynamic movements, because the fingers need to generate sufficient force as quickly as possible, during the brief instant when they first contact the target hold. If the dyno has been executed perfectly, the hold can be latched during the *deadpoint* (the point of time when the body is at the apex of flight, moving neither up nor down). Catching the hold at the deadpoint requires much less force. In most cases the climber will be falling back down onto the hold, requiring exponentially more force as he falls away. The sooner force can be generated, the less force is required.

MUSCLE FIBER TYPES

Clearly the ability to rapidly apply force is essential, as it is a fundamental component of contact strength, but how can it be improved? As discussed in Chapter 5: Base-Fitness, each muscle is composed of many motor units, each consisting of many individual muscle fibers. Currently there are seven known muscle-fiber types in humans, grouped into three categories. As you'll recall from that chapter, each fiber type behaves slightly differently. Type I fibers contract slowly, but are able to sustain longer duration activities. Type IIa and Type IIb (aka Type IIx/d) fibers are unable to sustain long contractions, but tend to be larger (and therefore stronger), and contract much more quickly than Type I fibers.

Fortunately for athletes it is possible to convert some fibers from one type to another, or to train fibers to behave like other fibers (by increasing mitochondria, glycolytic enzymes, fiber diameter, or contraction speed), so there is significant potential for climbers to train their muscles to behave in a way that suits their individual goals, regardless of genetics.[10, 11]

PLYOMETRIC TRAINING

To succeed on powerful, dynamic moves, climbers must be able to apply a great amount of muscular force in a short amount of time. This can be done by:

- Increasing muscle-fiber recruitment
- Cultivating a higher distribution of fast-twitch fibers
- Training slow-twitch fibers to contract more quickly

Fortunately, there are specific training activities that accomplish all of these. Max-recruitment training in strength athletes is well understood, and it would be relatively simple to transfer this approach to climbing by using the typical finger-training tools, with adjusted repetitions and sets to achieve the desired muscular adaptations (this approach is described later in the chapter under "Max-Recruitment Training with a Hangboard"). Unfortunately, the tools used for developing static finger strength do little to improve contraction speed; enter plyometrics.

Plyometric training was originally developed by Soviet track and field coaches in the 1960s to help train explosive power in their athletes. Early plyometrics involved activities such as jumping from an elevated box, down to the ground, then immediately springing back up onto the box. Theoretically, the landing causes an involuntary eccentric contraction in the leg muscles, which must be immediately converted to a concentric contraction in a very short period of time (ideally less than 0.2 seconds to achieve a true plyometric effect). The initial eccentric contraction experienced during landing forces a quick stretch of the muscles and tendons. As a defense mechanism against injury, the muscles involved will activate otherwise dormant muscle fibers in order to resist this stretching action, hence increasing recruitment. Additionally, if the athlete transitions immediately from the eccentric phase to the concentric, the muscle fibers involved are forced to contract very quickly, thus improving contraction speed.[12]

Plyometrics are used in climbing to improve recruitment, and more importantly, contact strength, the key to performing difficult, dynamic climbing moves, and thus hard routes or boulder problems. The challenge of applying plyometric training to climbing is that usually, finger contractions are isometric, whereas plyometric training requires the cycle of concentric to isometric to eccentric contractions. This challenge was overcome with the invention of the Campus Board.

> "On Wallstreet there is a very difficult boulder problem.... Through the winter I went to this training center in Nuremberg, and with the help of a physical education professor I worked specific muscles, training intramuscular coordination combined with reaction time so that I would be able to do the moves for this problem."
> — Wolfgang Gullich[6]

THE CAMPUS BOARD

The incomparable Wolfgang Gullich was perhaps the first climber to recognize the power of plyometrics and apply it to climbing training. Gullich's visionary adaptation of these concepts proved to be the key to his groundbreaking ascents of Wallstreet in 1987 (the world's first 5.14b) and the legendary Action Directe in 1991 (5.14d, and still one of the hardest routes in the world).

To apply plyometric methods to his training, Gullich invented the now-infamous Campus Board. Gullich installed the original board at a Nuremberg fitness club known as "The Campus Centre" (hence the name), and used this tool to help elevate his power to levels that could only be described as "futuristic."[4] The board consisted of a ladder of one-pad-deep wooden finger edges fixed to a slightly overhanging wall. Gullich's original method was to use momentum to move dynamically between these edges with feet dangling (jumping from handhold to handhold, so to speak, now known as campusing). Climbers have since developed countless variations on the basic exercise. Although the Campus Board is still the best medium for isolating plyometric movements, any difficult, dynamic movement (with or without feet on the wall) has the potential to create a plyometric effect.

POWER TRAINING METHODS

The ideal power-training exercise would increase motor-unit recruitment, increase fiber-contraction speed, and be sufficiently sport-specific to develop technical skill and specific body strength. Climbers can accomplish these objectives through a combination of the two fundamental power training methods described below: *limit bouldering* and *campusing*.

LIMIT BOULDERING

Limit bouldering is arguably the ideal method for improving power and contact strength while focusing attention on sport-specific factors like technique and body strength. Limit bouldering is climbing short boulder problems that feature one to two crux moves that are right at the climber's limit. This training activity is frequently confused with "bouldering," which entails climbing problems of any length with an emphasis on fun, camaraderie, and sending the hardest line possible. Limit bouldering, on the other hand, entails focusing on short boulder problems that emphasize one or two extremely hard moves (rather than problems that entail six to eight *pretty* hard moves, or 10 to 20 *kinda* hard moves). To improve recruitment and pow-

Limit boulder problems should feature holds that are specific to your climbing goals, and one or two dynamic moves that are right at your limit.

er, the number of repetitions must be small, and the intensity very high. Bouldering at a lower intensity is enjoyable and can be applied to other training goals, but for power training, the moves must be extremely difficult and few in number.

Limit bouldering is superior to other power-training methods because it involves the entire body in a highly sport-specific manner, it's easy to perform indoors or out, it includes skill practice, and it's fun. The downsides are that it's difficult to control and quantify (making it difficult to ensure progressive overload is achieved) and does not facilitate isolation of individual muscle groups (the forearm flexors in particular). Furthermore, it's easy to get sidetracked during limit-bouldering sessions, and it can be challenging to find suitable training terrain.

To get the most from this training, limit boulder problems should address specific weaknesses or areas of emphasis within the training plan. Utilize wall angles and hold types that are specific to your goals, be they crimps, pockets, pinches, etc. Keep in mind that the existing boulder problems in most commercial facilities emphasize big heroic moves between jugs, slopers, pinches, and other features that are not frequently encountered on real rock climbs. Likewise, the footholds are often much bigger than those found on real rock.

Emphasize hard, dynamic moves to achieve a plyometric effect and improve contact strength. Moves that require a precise deadpoint to a small target hold are ideal. If a move can be completed in three or four tries, it is not a limit move. A good limit boulder problem should take two or three *days* of effort to complete (with each session consisting of only five to ten serious attempts before fatigue prevents further progress). The moves involved should not be overly technical; the goal is to isolate recruitment and contraction speed — overly complicated moves only interfere with these objectives.

LIMIT BOULDERING ROUTINE

Like any training activity, begin with a thorough warm-up. The first phase of the warm-up should entail 10 to 30 minutes of low-intensity ARC-style traversing. Treat this period like any ARC set, focusing on efficient technique and smooth, relaxed movement. Near the end of this period do some active stretching while still on the wall.

During phase two of the warm-up, complete a progressive Warm-Up Boulder Ladder (WBL). Begin with "easy" bouldering (starting at V0, or the easiest problems available). Complete one to four boulder problems at each V-grade before progressing to the next grade (the number of problems completed at each grade depends on how many grades you need to step through, with the goal of completing the WBL in 20 to 30 minutes). Continue up the ladder until the typical boulder flash level is reached. The goal is *not* to get entrenched in an epic project during the warm-up phase. Climb a variety of problems that span multiple climbing styles. Take typical rest periods between problems (one to five minutes, increasing as the level of difficulty increases). By the end of the warm-up, you should have completed 10 to 20 problems of increasing difficulty.

At this point, the climber should feel warm, limber, and ready to crank, but she may not be warm enough to produce maximal performance. The neurological pathways that initiate motor-unit contractions require a thorough warm-up as well, so performance may continue to improve through the limit-bouldering session as these pathways perform more effectively.

Next complete 20 to 30 minutes of "hard" bouldering. Pick three to four problems harder than your flash level and work them for five to 10 minutes each. Ideally, these would be problems that require three to four attempts to climb. These problems should address certain areas of training emphasis (a weakness, or a climbing move replicating a goal route). On a good day, it should be possible to send most of these problems, but that is not the goal. It's easy to get sidetracked during this activity, so watch the clock and stay focused on the big picture.

Next, move on to the limit boulder problems. These should be carefully selected (or better, *designed*) with specific attributes. In theory, these problems will be worked throughout most or all of the Power Phase, so they should be enjoyable and specific to the season goals. Two or three problems of the correct difficulty are usually enough to last through the phase. These problems should be right at the climber's limit, and they should be powerful, with one or two extremely hard, dynamic moves that she can't do (as opposed to 10 consecutive *pretty* hard moves that result in a pump-management challenge). If necessary, consider using a power spot to work these moves initially. The crux should be low to the ground (but probably not the first move) so that the climber is fresh for each attempt at the crux, and fear is not a factor. Ideally, the crux moves will have a dynamic element, requiring precision at the end of a long reach and good contact strength to latch the finishing hold. Try to keep these problems as realistic as possible, using small footholds

A "Power Spot" can be used to train limit moves. Ask your partner to exert a small amount of upward force just above your hips, and to gradually reduce the assistance provided as you improve at the move.

that require precise footwork and core tension, and handholds that mimic specific goal routes. The set of problems selected should be diverse, covering the different styles needed to achieve all of the climber's goals.

Spend 15 minutes (or more) on each limit boulder problem. Ideally, you'll make at least four or five solid attempts, with sufficient rest to ensure maximum effort is applied to each attempt. It's not necessary to work each problem or dedicate equal time to each problem during a given session. Rest for five to 10 minutes between problems.

At some point during the limit-bouldering period power will start to wane. End the workout as soon as it's no longer possible to move explosively. There is nothing more to be gained (in terms of power) at this point. Continuing with easier problems only increases the risk of injury and the time required to recover from the workout. Finish the workout with two to four supplemental exercises (perform the set and repetition protocols listed for "Power" in the Table or p110 in Chapter 6: Strength).

The limit-bouldering routine should be tailored to the climber's ability level and training experience by adjusting the duration and intensity of the various phases of the workout. Less-experienced climbers will achieve significant physical improvements with relatively little training, and can benefit most from skill-specific training.[3] Therefore, these climbers should spend most of their time on the first few phases of the workout (ARC traversing, WBL, and, to a lesser extent, hard bouldering), striving to complete a relatively high volume of challenging movements. Since a beginner's ladder won't be quite as "tall" as an advanced climber's, beginners can perform more problems on each rung of the ladder, thus experiencing a wider variety of moves. More-advanced climbers should spend more time attempting the most difficult moves, thus applying more time to the latter part of the workout, as described in the Figure to the right.

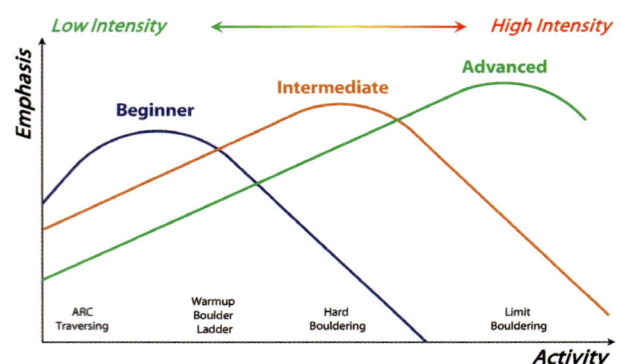

Less-experienced climbers should focus more effort on the less intense parts of the Limit Bouldering Routine, and vice versa for more-advanced climbers.

LIMIT BOULDERING ROUTINE

WARM-UP:

	Duration of Activity		
	Beginner	**Intermediate**	**Advanced**
Phase 1: Low-intensity ARC traversing • Rehearse techniques • Light, active stretching on the wall	30 min.	20 min.	10 min.
Phase 2: Warm-Up Boulder Ladder • Begin with "V-easy" • 1 to 4 problems of each grade up to flash level • No more than three attempts per problem • Increase rest periods with difficulty	30 min. 4 problems /grade	25 min. 3 problems /grade	25 min. 2 problems /grade
Phase 3: Hard Bouldering • 3 to 4 problems just above flash level • Problems should address areas of training emphasis • 3 to 4 attempts per problem	30 min. 3 problems	30 min. 4 problems	25 min. 3 problems

LIMIT BOULDERING:

	Duration of Activity		
• 2 to 4 "realistic" problems			
• Feature 1 or 2 powerful moves that you cannot do in a single session of work	**Beginner**	**Intermediate**	**Advanced**
• Dynamic cruxes, low to the ground	0 min.	30 min.	60 min.
• Four or five quality attempts per problem	0 problems	2 problems	4 problems
• Extremely high intensity and arousal			
• 2 to 5 minutes rest between attempts, 5 to 10 minutes rest between problems			

SUPPLEMENTAL EXERCISES:

• Select one to three high-priority movements
• Complete one to three sets of each exercise

The Limit Bouldering Routine includes activities of various intensity. Adjust the emphasis of Limit Bouldering sessions to your abilities.

"I like to do Campus Board, because it is very effective and you don't need a lot of time for that." — Iker Pou[1]

CAMPUS TRAINING

This dynamic style of training involves footless dynos between like holds, and is probably the best method of pure power training available to climbers due to its plyometric nature. Unlike limit bouldering, campusing is relatively easy to quantify, so climbers can track progress from workout to workout and year to year. Campusing also permits better isolation of specific grip positions than limit bouldering.

In addition to the pure power benefits of campus training, this method is very helpful for improving the intramuscular coordination required to make accurate dynamic moves. Practicing dynos, or campus, moves improves spatial awareness and motor skills, resulting in improved "aim" when launching toward a target hold. In just a few sessions it's possible to prog-

Consistent Campus Training will greatly improve inter-muscular coordination, key for moves requiring dynamic accuracy like this dyno to a pocket.

ress to a point where virtually every campus move is a "deadpoint." This accuracy translates directly to the rock, a skill element of campus training that is often overlooked. The campus board is an extremely powerful tool for teaching climbers *of all abilities and experience levels* to move with speed and accuracy.

Finally, it's well known that some climbers struggle with dynamic moves. This could be due to a general lack of aggression or a strong desire to remain "in control" on the rock. Campus training can solve these issues in short order. It demands aggressive and committing movement, in a structured, low-risk environment. Numerous climbers have corrected years of overly static movement after only a handful of short campus sessions.

With all the many benefits of campusing, it's worth noting the downsides. First, there is no doubt that campusing is much harder on the joints than other training methods, such as hangboarding. Campusing is, by its very nature, somewhat wild and out of control. A hangboard allows the climber to adjust the intensity at will, and let go the instant a repetition becomes uncomfortable. Often while campusing (or dyncing in general), the only sign of injury comes after it's too late. For that reason, it's critical to minimize the amount of time spent on the campus board, and ensure that the climber is 100 percent injury-free before beginning any campus activities. Elbows are particularly at risk, but shoulders and fingers must be healthy as well. Campus training should only be performed with an open-hand or half-crimp-grip position (index and pinkie fingers straight, middle and ring fingers bent approximately 90 degrees at the big knuckle). Do not campus with a closed crimp grip. Finally, campusing can be hard on the finger pads. Pay attention to skin health and keep workouts short and intense to limit skin degradation.

Campus training requires a thoughtfully designed Campus Board, which many gyms don't have. Fortunately building a board is relatively simple and inexpensive (see the sidebar on p136). Campusing can be done on a regular bouldering wall, systems wall, or similar wall with a series of regularly spaced, like holds, but a proper Campus Board is preferred.

A good board will have several different sizes of wooden "rungs" (plastic rungs are hard on the finger pads). Err on the side of using the smallest manageable rungs. Smaller rungs will isolate finger strength, while larger (deeper) rungs isolate the upper arms, shoulder, and back muscles. Most climbers should focus on increasing finger strength rather than big-muscle strength. The large rungs are helpful for warming up and learning the basic movements, but climbers should progress to the smallest rungs as soon as possible.

One final note: Campusing can be extremely fun, bordering on addictive, to the point that it has the potential to become a major distraction. It's not uncommon for serious campus enthusiasts to lose focus on the big picture in order to achieve a specific campus goal (like what Ben Moon calls the "ultimate expression of power," the 1-5-9 ladder). Enjoy campusing but don't get sidetracked.

The Campus Board

Campus Boards come in many shapes and sizes, and not all are created equal. A well-constructed board will make workouts more enjoyable and facilitate quick and steady progression. The board must be securely attached to a solid structure, as it will be subjected to heavy dynamic forces. There are several primary variables in Campus Board design:

- Rung type and material
- Rung size (depth)
- Rung spacing
- Board angle

Wood is the material of choice for campusing connoisseurs. It offers the right amount of friction and durability. Rungs can be flat or slightly incut, but they must be skin friendly, with a well-rounded and smooth leading edge. Each rung should be numbered so that you can record and track your training. Metolius makes three sizes of wooden campus rungs that are highly recommended (3/4", 1", and 1-1/4"-deep). They also have a free download on their website describing how to construct a board.

Rung size (or depth) can, and should, vary. Beginners can use deeper rungs, while more-advanced climbers should use shallower rungs. A good board will have a variety of rungs (usually two to three sizes) but these rungs should NOT be mixed in the same ladder.

Standard rung width is 16", allowing three distinct columns of rungs to fit side-by-side onto one four-foot-wide plywood sheet. Each rung in a single ladder should be the same size, shape, texture, and orientation. This uniformity provides the necessary repetition to isolate weaknesses and progress steadily.

Vertical spacing between rungs is a hotly debated topic. There are currently two competing standards. "Moon-spacing" (so-named for legendary climber and campus-fiend Ben Moon) is the most common outside the US, with rungs spaced 22 cm (8.66") apart *on-center* (meaning, the vertical distance from the center of one rung to the center of the next rung is 22 cm). "Metolius-spacing" is 4" on-center within a column of shallow-depth rungs, 6" on-center within a column of medium rungs, and 12" on-center within a column of large rungs. Tighter vertical spacing is preferred because it allows smaller increments of progression. If using Moon-spacing, alleviate this problem by adding "half-steps" (i.e., spacing rungs vertically at 11-cm on-center; this is still a bit wider, and therefore harder, than Metolius-spacing). Using standardized spacing allows you to compare your campus feats to others' around the world. Moon-spacing is gaining ground in the US, and will likely be the world standard moving forward.

Finally, not much thought is given to the steepness of the board, but it's an important factor. Steeper (more overhanging) boards require less vertical movement to make larger moves, meaning the effect of gravity is slightly reduced. Of course, it can be more difficult to grasp the rungs on a steeper board, since the rungs will seem more slopey. Those with experience on many boards report steeper boards are easier to use, up to a point. While there is no clear standard, 15 to 20 degrees overhanging is most common. Anything below 10 degrees increases the risk of inadvertently kicking the board, and puts extra stress on the elbows.

Start: | **1st Move:** | **2nd Move:** | **3rd Move:**
B1 | **L1 to L2** | **R1 to R2** | **L2 to L3**

Matching Ladders: *Climb the board one rung at a time, matching on every rung until reaching the top. For example, begin with both hands matched on rung No.1, then bump the left hand to rung No. 2, then bump the right hand from rung No. 1 to rung No. 2, then the left hand to rung No. 3, and so on. Alternate sets leading with each hand.*

Note: B = Both Hands; L = Left Hand; R = Right Hand; Numerals indicate Campus Rung Number

Start: | **1st Move:** | **2nd Move:** | **3rd Move:**
B1 | **L1 to L2** | **R1 to R3** | **L2 to L4**

Basic Ladders: *Climb the board one rung at a time, alternating hands, latching every rung until reaching the top. For example, begin with both hands on rung No. 1, then bump the left hand from rung No. 1 to rung No. 2, then move the right hand from rung No. 1 to rung No. 3 (without matching on rung No. 2), then move the left hand from rung No. 2 to rung No. 4, and so on, until the top of the board is reached.*

Start: | **1st Move:** | **2nd Move:** | **3rd Move:**
B1 | **R1 to R3** | **L1 to L5** | **R3 to R5**

Max Ladders: *Climb the board alternating hands, skipping as many rungs as possible. For example, start with both hands on rung No. 1, throw the right hand from rung No. 1 to rung No. 3, then, without matching, throw the left hand from rung No. 1 to rung No. 5, then match the right hand to rung No. 5. The ultimate goal is to travel as far up the board as possible in two hand moves. In this example, the climber goes from a match on rung No. 1 to a match on rung No. 5 (traveling four increments). This is the single best campus exercise for climbers. This is the most basic movement, the most specific to rock climbing, and the best for isolating individual hands.*

Start: | **1st Move:** | **2nd Move:** | **3rd Move:**
B5 | **Bump Right Hand** | **Bump RH again** | **Match**

Typewriters: *In this exercise, the climber campuses horizontally. Begin with hands matched on the left end of the board. Bump the right hand progressively farther right, without going up the board, until near failure or you run out of real estate. Then progressively bump the left hand to the right, eventually matching the left hand next to the right. Then reverse the exercise. These should be used infrequently to train for a specific move, and can be hard on the shoulders.*

CAMPUS EXERCISES

A variety of campus exercises are described below, listed in approximate order of difficulty from easiest to hardest. These should be performed with feet dangling (though it's OK to use your lower body to help generate momentum, also known as *kipping*). If these exercises are too difficult, consider using a power spot to practice the movements. Use the smallest rungs manageable to emphasize the forearm flexors.

Any of these exercises can be done in both directions — that is, going up the board or going down. Downward campusing is known as *reactive* training because it activates the muscles' inherent injury-defense mechanism to recruit otherwise dormant fibers. Theoretically, it will produce more-dramatic results, but also increases injury risk significantly, because the forces on the elbow, shoulder, and finger joints are much higher. Keep in mind that down-campusing completely eliminates what little specificity exists in campus training. For these reasons, down-campusing should be reserved for highly trained athletes looking to push just a little bit harder (as a rule of thumb, those with five or more years of campus training under their belt). The weak link in down-campusing is almost always finger strength, so it can be a good way to isolate this area if other factors prevent doing so with more basic upward movements.

- **Matching Ladders:** Climb the board one rung at a time, matching on every rung until reaching the top. For example, begin with both hands matched on rung No.1, then bump the left hand from rung No. 1 to rung No. 2, then bump the right hand from rung No. 1 to rung No. 2, then the left hand to rung No. 3, and so on. Alternate sets leading with each hand.

Two acceptable campus grip positions: open-hand with inactive pinky (L), and semi-closed crimp (R).

- **Basic Ladders:** Climb the board one rung at a time, alternating hands, latching every rung until reaching the top. For example, begin with both hands on rung No. 1, then bump the left hand from rung No. 1 to rung No. 2, then move the right hand from rung No. 1 to rung No. 3 (without matching on rung No. 2), then move the left hand from rung No. 2 to rung No. 4, and so on, until the top of the board is reached.

- **Max Ladders:** Climb the board alternating hands, skipping as many rungs as possible. For example, start with both hands on rung No. 1, throw the left hand from rung No. 1 to rung No. 5, then, without matching, throw the right hand from rung No. 1 to rung No. 9, then match the left hand to rung No. 9. The ultimate goal is to travel as far up the board as possible in two hand moves. In the above example, the climber goes from a match on rung No. 1 to a match on rung No. 9 (traveling eight increments). This is the single best campus exercise for climbers. This is the most basic movement, the most specific to rock climbing, and the best for isolating individual hands.

- **Typewriters:** In this exercise, the climber campuses horizontally. Begin with hands matched on the left end of the campus board. Bump the right hand progressively farther right, without going up the board, until near failure or until you run out of real estate. Then progressively bump the left hand to the right, eventually matching the left hand next to the right. Then reverse the exercise. These should be used infrequently to train for a specific move, and can be hard on the shoulders.

- **Max First Move:** Start matched on the first rung and throw one hand to the highest rung possible (leaving the other hand on the first rung). These are very specific to rock climbing, but also good for building the shoulder strength necessary for progressing on max ladders. Once the high rung is latched, try to match (or pass the high rung).

- **Go-Agains (aka "Bumps"):** Complete the first move of the max-ladder exercise, then continue bumping the high hand one rung at a time until failure, leaving the low hand on the first rung. This exercise can be hard on the shoulders.

Start: B3

1st Move: L3 to L5

2nd Move: L5 to L5.5

3rd Move: L5.5 to L6

Go-Agains (aka "Bumps"): *Complete the first move of the max-ladder exercise, then continue bumping the high hand one rung at a time until failure, leaving the low hand on the first rung. This exercise can be hard on the shoulders.*

Start: B2

1st Move: L1 to touch L2

2nd Move: L2 to L1

Touches: *Begin as for the first move of a max ladder, but instead of latching the high rung, simply touch the rung, then fall slowly back onto the starting rung. These work upper-arm explosive power and lock-off strength in a "negative," eccentric contraction.*

Start: B3

1st Move: B3 to B4

Double Dynos (aka "Doubles"): *Move both hands at the same time in matched double-dynamic fashion — so for each movement you'll have no contact with the board. These lack specificity, but they are also the most plyometric and are great for developing dynamic aggression, spatial awareness, and hand-eye coordination at high speeds. Additionally, doubles require a quick latch of the target rung, thus improving contact strength.*

Start: B4

1st Move: B4 to B3

Latch B3 & pull up to B4 in one continuous action

2nd Move: B3 to B4

Up-Down-Up: *A more advanced, plyometric version of the other exercises, usually done with a double dyno, but can be done with one hand fixed if doubles prove too hard. Begin on a relatively high rung, then down-campus a set increment. When the lower rung is latched, explode back up to the starting rung, striving to make the down-and-up portion one continuous movement, executed as quickly as possible. These emphasize the plyometric cycle of eccentric/concentric contraction in the upper arms, though they also significantly increase the load on the fingers.*

• **Touches:** Begin as for the first move of a max ladder, but instead of latching the high rung, simply touch the rung, then fall slowly back onto the starting rung. These work upper-arm explosive power and lock-off strength in a "negative," eccentric contraction.

• **Double Dynos (aka "Doubles"):** Move both hands at the same time in matched double-dynamic fashion — so for each movement you'll have no contact with the board. These are among the least specific campus exercises (campus expert Ben Moon dislikes doubles, citing this lack of specificity),[8] but they are also the most plyometric and are great for developing dynamic aggression, spatial awareness, and hand-eye coordination at high speeds. Additionally, doubles require a quick latch of the target rung, thus improving contact strength.

• **Up-Down-Up:** This is a more advanced plyometric version of the other exercises, and is usually done with a double dyno, but can also be done with one hand fixed if doubles prove too hard (as for max ladders). Begin on a relatively high rung, then down-campus a set increment (with a single hand or matched hands). When the lower rung is latched, explode back up to the starting rung, striving to make the down-and-up portion one continuous movement, executed as quickly as possible. These emphasize the plyometric cycle of eccentric/concentric contraction in the upper arms, though they also significantly increase the load on the fingers.

Tips for Effective Campusing

There's more to campusing than bulging back muscles and misplaced aggression. Campusing is a skill that improves with practice. Campusing with proper technique will allow you to perform better on the board, surely, but it will also help reduce injury risk and achieve the most sport-specific power gains possible. These tips will help you get the most benefit from your campus sessions:

• Dynamic movements depend on effective use of momentum. The same is true of campusing. Try to keep your center of mass moving continuously up the board, with each move flowing rhythmically into the next. Avoid pausing or adjusting between moves. This will keep the exercises plyometric.

• Keep your eyes wide open and focused on your target throughout the movement, but especially while latching the rung. Many climbers inexplicably close their eyes during dynamic movements. Use the campus board to break this undesirable habit.

• Practice deadpointing each move. At first, this will take a great deal of control and concentration, but with practice you will be able to do this on moves right at your limit. This skill transfers directly to the rock and will save your elbows and fingers tremendous strain.

• On big moves, focus on pushing with your lagging hand. Climbers are used to pulling, and once a hand drops below shoulder level, it is often forgotten. Get in the habit of pushing down with your low hand all the way through the movement.

• Twist in toward the lagging hand to get a bit of extra reach, just as when performing a dropknee or twist-lock with the feet.

To maximize reach and efficiency during extended campus moves, rotate the lagging shoulder into the board and use your triceps to push down on the low rung with the lagging hand.

- **Three-/Two-/One-Finger Campusing:** For the hardcore, any of the exercises described above can be performed with three, two, or even one finger. Campusing in this manner isolates finger strength.

A common mistake is trying to do too many different exercises on the campus board in one session. To achieve the desired power-training objective, a campus workout must be short and intense, so there isn't time to properly execute all of these exercises. Remember, these movements are supposed to be right at your physical limit. If you can do an exercise on the first attempt, it is not limiting. Instead, focus on a handful of limiting exercises and attempt them repeatedly to allow progression to occur. It should take many, many tries over multiple sessions to succeed on the most powerful movements.

movement, using momentum to flow from one move to the next. Focusing on mastering relatively easier ladders, as opposed to flailing on more difficult ones, will provide the quickest improvement. Once all of the exercises in this routine can be performed, transition to the Intermediate Campus Routine.

Campusing should only be done after a thorough warm-up. Additionally, campusing should also be done early enough in the workout that the climber still feels "explosive" and able to "pop" off of every rung. Warm-up as described for the Limit Bouldering Routine, completing a 20-minute ARC set, then a 30-minute Warm-Up Boulder Ladder, followed by 10 minutes of Hard Bouldering. Record the results of each set in a log sheet like the one shown below.

BEGINNER CAMPUS ROUTINE

Note: This training regimen is for the thoroughly healthy. Climbers with nagging injuries, particularly finger, elbow, or shoulder injuries, SHOULD NOT DO THIS! Use another training method, or consider less-intense goals until healthy. The frequency and rest associated with these workouts are critical to avoiding injury. Avoid consecutive campus workouts, and take extra rest following each campus workout.

This routine is an introduction to campus training designed for those who are new to structured campusing. This routine is focused on learning the basic movements, practicing dynamic accuracy, and overcoming inhibitions. Emphasize smooth

Use a log sheet to document your campus training sessions.

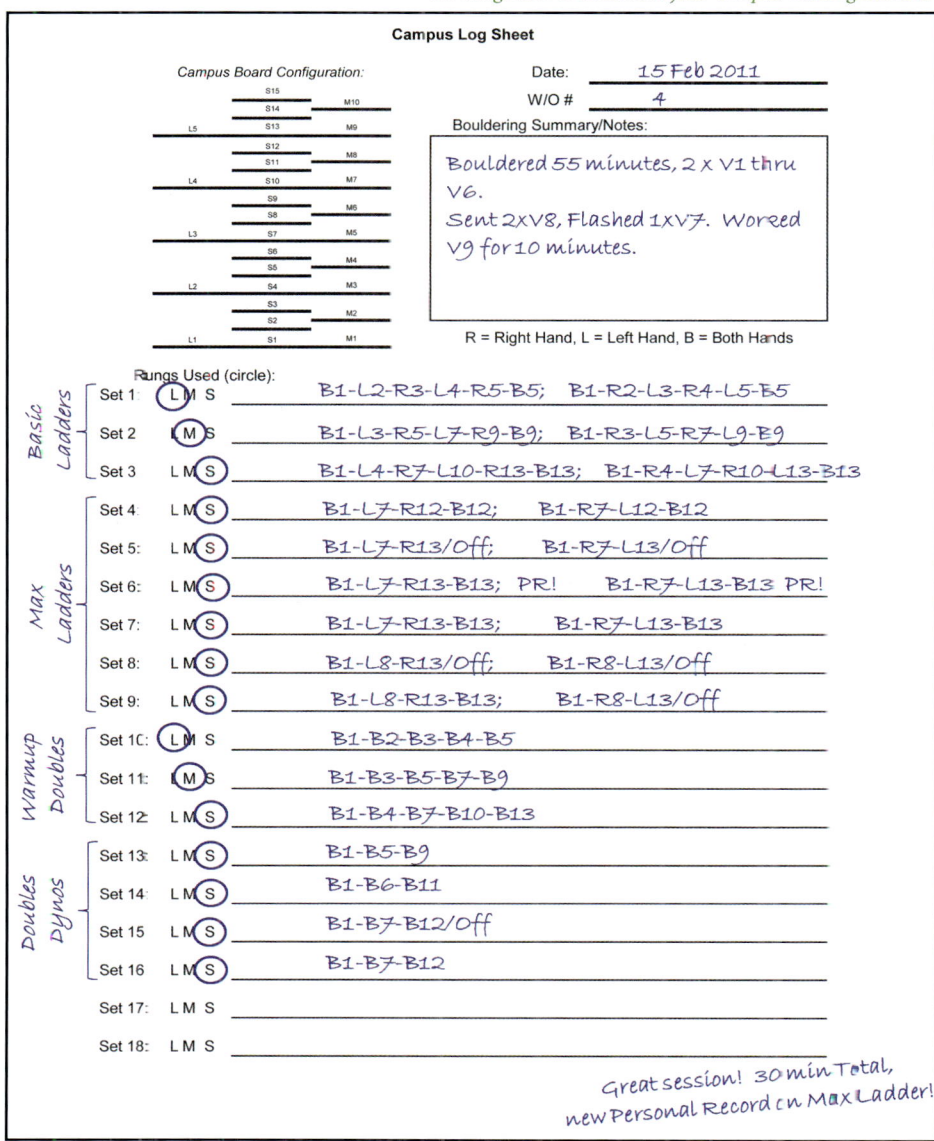

Campus Log Sheet

Campus Board Configuration:

Date: 15 Feb 2011
W/O # 4

Bouldering Summary/Notes:

Bouldered 55 minutes, 2 x V1 thru V6.
Sent 2xV8, Flashed 1xV7. Worked V9 for 10 minutes.

R = Right Hand, L = Left Hand, B = Both Hands

Rungs Used (circle):

Basic Ladders
- Set 1: (L) M S — B1-L2-R3-L4-R5-B5; B1-R2-L3-R4-L5-B5
- Set 2: (M) S — B1-L3-R5-L7-R9-B9; B1-R3-L5-R7-L9-B9
- Set 3: L M (S) — B1-L4-R7-L10-R13-B13; B1-R4-L7-R10-L13-B13

Max Ladders
- Set 4: L M (S) — B1-L7-R12-B12; B1-R7-L12-B12
- Set 5: L M (S) — B1-L7-R13/Off; B1-R7-L13/Off
- Set 6: L M (S) — B1-L7-R13-B13; PR! B1-R7-L13-B13 PR!
- Set 7: L M (S) — B1-L7-R13-B13; B1-R7-L13-B13
- Set 8: L M (S) — B1-L8-R13/Off; B1-R8-L13/Off
- Set 9: L M (S) — B1-L8-R13-B13; B1-R8-L13/Off

Warmup Doubles
- Set 10: (L) M S — B1-B2-B3-B4-B5
- Set 11: (M) S — B1-B3-B5-B7-B9
- Set 12: L M (S) — B1-B4-B7-B10-B13

Doubles Dynos
- Set 13: L M (S) — B1-B5-B9
- Set 14: L M (S) — B1-B6-B11
- Set 15: L M (S) — B1-B7-B12/Off
- Set 16: L M (S) — B1-B7-B12

- Set 17: L M S —
- Set 18: L M S —

Great session! 30 min Total, new Personal Record on Max Ladder!

BEGINNER CAMPUS ROUTINE

WARM-UP:

Phase 1: Low-intensity ARC traversing (20 Minutes)
- Rehearse techniques
- Light, active stretching on the wall

Phase 2: Warm-Up Boulder Ladder (30 Minutes)
- Begin with "V-easy," complete 1 to 3 problems of each grade up to flash level
- No more than three attempts per problem

Phase 3: Hard Bouldering (10 minutes)
- 2 "realistic" problems
- 3 to 4 quality attempts per problem
- 2 to 5 minutes rest between attempts

CAMPUS EXERCISES:

Notes:
- Assumes "**Metolius**" rung spacing or "**Moon**" half-spacing:
- Key: **B** = both hands, **L** = left hand, **R** = right hand, number indicates rung number

Matching Ladders
- Set 1: Large Rungs   B1-L2-R2-L3-R3-L4-B4
- Set 2: Large Rungs   B1-R2-L2-R3-L3-R4-B4
- Set 3: Medium Rungs   B1-L2-R2-L3-R3-L4-B4
- Set 4: Medium Rungs   B1-R2-L2-R3-L3-R4-B4

Basic Ladders
- Set 5: Large Rungs   B1-L2-R3-L4-R5-L6-B6
- Set 6: Large Rungs   B1-R2-L3-R4-L5-R6-B6
- Set 7: Medium Rungs   B1-L2-R3-L4-R5-L6-B6
- Set 8: Medium Rungs   B1-R2-L3-R4-L5-R6-B6

Max Ladders - Summon maximal effort and arousal for each attempt
- Set 9: Medium Rungs   B1-L3-R4-B4
- Set 10: Medium Rungs   B1-R3-L4-B4
- **...Repeat as necessary until successful**
- Set 11: Medium Rungs   attempt B1-L3-R5-B5
- Set 12: Medium Rungs   attempt B1-R3-L5-B5
- **...Repeat until successful, but no more than eight total sets of Max Ladders**

SUPPLEMENTAL EXERCISES:

- 2 to 4 exercises addressing specific physical weaknesses
- 1 to 3 sets each of 8 or fewer repetitions

NOTES ON BEGINNER CAMPUS ROUTINE
- Most beginners will find it difficult to use the Campus Board at first. If possible, get a power spot from a partner. Reduce the support from the power spot as you progress.
- Begin with the largest or easiest rungs, and then progress to smaller rungs. Depending on the board's rung spacing, medium rungs may be easier than large rungs, etc.
- Do not attempt max ladders until basic ladders can be performed smoothly, with good control.
- Emphasize smooth, flowing movement over attempting big moves.

INTERMEDIATE CAMPUS ROUTINE

Note: This training is for the thoroughly healthy. Climbers with nagging injuries, particularly finger, elbow, or shoulder injuries, SHOULD NOT DO THIS! Use another training method, or consider less-intense goals until healthy. The frequency and rest associated with these workouts are critical to avoiding injury. Avoid consecutive campus workouts, and take extra rest following each campus workout.

This routine is intended for climbers who can smoothly and reliably complete basic ladders without assistance. Unlike the Beginner Campus Routine, this workout includes greater emphasis on physical power, as opposed to movement skill and commitment. However, you should continue to focus on completing the moves smoothly, using momentum to flow from one move to the next. Focusing on mastering relatively easier ladders, as opposed to flailing on more-difficult ones, will provide the quickest improvement. Once all of the exercises in this routine can be performed smoothly, transition to the Advanced Campus Routine.

Campusing should only be done after a thorough warm-up. Additionally, campusing should also be done early enough in the workout that you still feel "explosive" and able to "pop" off of every rung. Warm-up as described for the Limit Bouldering Routine, completing a 15-minute ARC set, then a 30-minute Warm-Up Boulder Ladder, followed by 15 minutes of Hard Bouldering. Record the results of each set in a log sheet like the one shown in the Figure on p141.

NOTES ON INTERMEDIATE CAMPUS ROUTINE

- Campus exercises are denoted as "Baseline +X, +Y", which describes each set relative to the climber's "baseline" max ladder. The baseline max ladder is the most difficult ladder the climber can reliably execute, for example, small rungs, B1-L3-R5-B5. The next increment of difficulty would be B1-L3-R6-B6, and is denoted as "Baseline +0, +1", as shown in the figure below. This numbering refers to the rung increments spanned during each move of the ladder, relative to the climber's baseline. The first move deposits the climber's left hand on rung 3, the same rung reached during the first move of the baseline ladder, so "Baseline +0" is used to denote the first move. The second move deposits the climber on rung 6, one rung higher than the rung reached during the second move of the baseline ladder, so "+1" is used to denote the second move of this ladder. The final move of the max ladder is always a match to the rung reached during the second move, so it is omitted.

- Depending on the board's rung spacing, it may be prudent to skip a rung or two during basic ladders.

- Once warmed up, perform all sets on the smallest rungs manageable.

- Perform no more than 12 total sets of max ladders (often much less than 12 is best). Begin with a baseline max ladder, such as small rungs, B1-L3-R5-B5. Use the remaining sets to increase the spacing of the ladder. For example, attempt small rungs, B1-L3-R6-B6, etc.

- Double dynos will be difficult at first, so consider using a power spot. Do not attempt double dynos until max ladders can be performed smoothly. At first, use the largest or easiest rungs available, and do not attempt to skip any rungs.

- When performing double dynos, emphasize the plyometric cycle by latching and moving off each rung as quickly as possible.

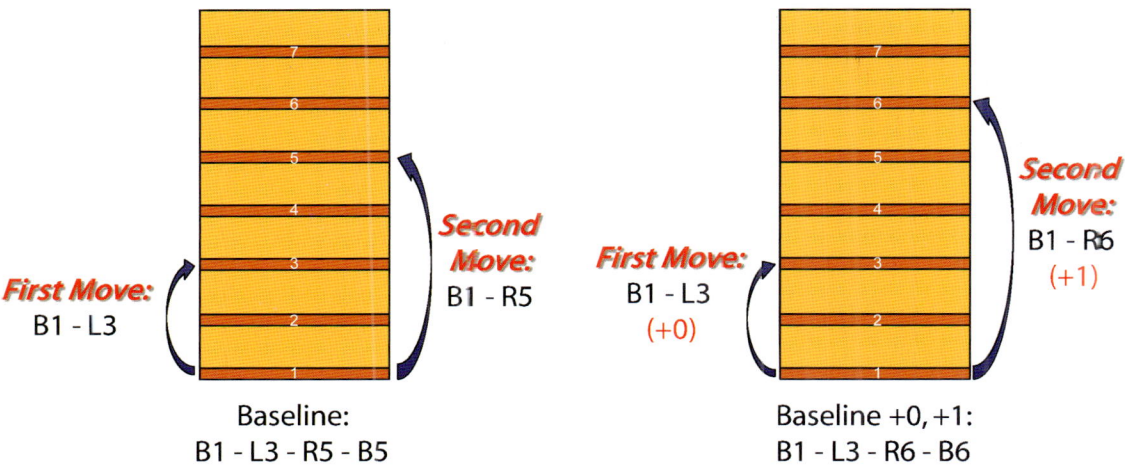

Baseline:
B1 - L3 - R5 - B5

Baseline +0, +1:
B1 - L3 - R6 - B6

INTERMEDIATE CAMPUS ROUTINE

WARM-UP:

Phase 1: Low-intensity ARC traversing (15 Minutes)
- Rehearse techniques
- Light, active stretching on the wall

Phase 2: Warm-Up Boulder Ladder (30 Minutes)
- Begin with "V-easy," complete 1 to 2 problems of each grade up to flash level
- No more than three attempts per problem

Phase 3: Hard Bouldering (15 minutes)
- 2 "realistic" problems
- 3 to 4 quality attempts per problem
- 2 to 5 minutes rest between attempts

CAMPUS EXERCISES:

- Assumes "**Metolius**" rung spacing or "**Moon**" half-spacing:
- Key: **B** = both hands, **L** = left hand, **R** = right hand, number indicates rung number

Basic Ladders
- Set 1:   Large Rungs   B1-L2-R3-L4-R5-L6-B6
- Set 2:   Large Rungs   B1-R2-L3-R4-L5-R6-B6
- Set 3:   Medium Rungs   B1-L2-R3-L4-R5-L6-B6
- Set 4:   Medium Rungs   B1-R2-L3-R4-L5-R6-B6
- Set 5:   Small Rungs   B1-L2-R3-L4-R5-L6-B6
- Set 6:   Small Rungs   B1-R2-L3-R4-L5-R6-B6

Max Ladders - Summon maximal effort and arousal for each attempt; *THIS IS WAR!*
- Set 7:   Small Rungs   Baseline Max Ladder (leading with left hand)
- Set 8:   Small Rungs   Baseline Max Ladder (leading with right hand)
- Set 9:   Small Rungs   Baseline +0, +1 Max Ladder (leading with left hand)
- Set 10: Small Rungs   Baseline +0, +1 Max Ladder (leading with right hand)
- **…Repeat until successful, but no more than 12 total sets of Max Ladders**

If successful…
- Sets 11-14: Small Rungs   Progressive Max Ladders (alternate leading hand)
- **…Repeat until successful, but no more than 12 total sets of Max Ladders**

Double Dynos
- Set 15: Medium Rungs   B1-B2-B3-B4
- Set 16: Small Rungs   B1-B3-B5 (or Baseline Double Dyno)
- Set 17: Small Rungs   Baseline +1, +1
- Set 18: Small Rungs   Baseline +1, +2
- **…Repeat above sets until successful, but no more than four total sets of Doubles**

SUPPLEMENTAL EXERCISES:

- 2 to 4 exercises addressing specific physical weaknesses
- 1 to 3 sets each of 8 or fewer repetitions

ADVANCED CAMPUS ROUTINE

WARM-UP:

Phase 1: Low-intensity ARC traversing (10 Minutes)
- Rehearse techniques
- Light, active stretching on the wall

Phase 2: Warm-Up Boulder Ladder (30 Minutes)
- Begin with "V-easy," complete 1 to 3 problems of each grade up to flash level
- No more than three attempts per problem

Phase 3: Hard Bouldering (20 minutes)
- 2 to 3 "realistic" problems
- 3 to 4 quality attempts per problem
- 2 to 5 minutes rest between attempts

CAMPUS EXERCISES:

- Assumes "**Metolius**" rung spacing or "**Moon**" half-spacing:
- Key: **B** = both hands, **L** = left hand, **R** = right hand, number indicates rung number

Warm-up Ladders
- Set 1:   Medium Rungs   B1-L3-R5-L7-R9-L10-B10
- Set 2:   Medium Rungs   B1-R3-L5-R7-L9-R10-B10
- Set 3:   Small Rungs   B1-L4-R7-L10-R13-L16-B16
- Set 4:   Small Rungs   B1-R4-L7-R10-L13-R16-B16

Max Ladders - Summon maximal effort and arousal for each attempt; *THIS IS WAR!*
- Sets 5-6: Small Rungs   Baseline Max Ladder (leading with each hand)
- Sets 7-8: Small Rungs   Baseline +0, +1 Max Ladder (leading with each hand)
- Sets 9-20: Small Rungs   Progressive Max Ladders (alternate leading hand)
- **...Repeat until successful, but no more than 16 total sets of Max Ladders**

Double Dynos
- Set 21: Medium Rungs   B1-B3-B5-B7
- Set 22: Small Rungs   Baseline Double Dyno
- Set 23: Small Rungs   Baseline +1, +1
- Sets 24-5: Small Rungs   Progressive Double Dynos
- **...Repeat above sets until successful, but no more than four total sets of Doubles**

Up-Down-Up
- Set 25: Small Rungs   B2-B1-B2
- Set 26: Small Rungs   B3-B1-B3
- Sets 27-28: Small Rungs   Progressive Up-Down-Up

SUPPLEMENTAL EXERCISES:

- 2 to 4 exercises addressing specific physical weaknesses
- 1 to 3 sets each of 8 or fewer repetitions

ADVANCED CAMPUS ROUTINE

Note: This training is for the thoroughly healthy. Climbers with nagging injuries, particularly finger, elbow, or shoulder injuries, SHOULD NOT DO THIS! Use another training method, or consider less-intense goals until healthy. The frequency and rest associated with these workouts are critical to avoiding injury. Avoid consecutive campus workouts, and take extra rest following each campus workout.

This routine is for well-trained climbers with extensive experience using the campus board. This routine introduces extremely intense reactive movements, so climbers should have approximately five years of campus training experience before attempting it. This experience is necessary to know how hard to push and when to stop.

Warm-up as described for the Limit Bouldering Routine, completing a 10-minute ARC set, then a 30-minute Warm-Up Boulder Ladder, followed by 20 minutes of Hard Bouldering. Record the results of each set in a log sheet like the one shown in the Figure on p141.

NOTES ON ADVANCED CAMPUS ROUTINE

- Up-down-ups will be very difficult initially. Use a power spot or foot dab, and perform on larger rungs before progressing to smaller rungs and larger moves.
- To get the most value out of up-down-ups, the period of transition from latch to upward motion must be as brief as possible. Favor shorter drops with a quicker transition over longer drops with a slower transition.

FOCUS AND INTENSITY

Effective power training demands high intensity. Whether bouldering or campusing, each problem or set (excluding warm-up activities) should include one or two limit moves. Such moves can only be completed with maximal effort. Summoning maximal effort many times within a single session is not trivial. It requires focus, attention, and strong motivation. Fortunately, this process becomes easier with practice, and translates directly to performance opportunities on the rock.

Approach a limit boulder problem as you might approach a cage fight. Be prepared to squeeze like hell, and expect it to hurt a little bit. Spend rest periods analyzing the previous attempt and considering opportunities for more efficient movement or better

effort. Additional rest, and encouragement from on-lookers, can help achieve the high level of arousal required for this activity.

Even more so than for the Limit Bouldering Routine (which is more technically demanding), the training intensity for campusing must be *extremely* high. Summon 100 percent effort and commitment for each attempt, and rest between attempts as much as necessary to allow 100 percent effort. Instead of a drawn-out cage fight, seek a knockout blow with one punch of maximal power. Scream and yell, don't give up, and expect it to hurt when you latch that distant rung. Olympic-style lifters report it can be helpful to get downright angry. Think of something irritating and punish the campus board. Further recommendations on achieving high arousal are provided in Chapter 15: Bouldering.

FREQUENCY AND REST

Rest intervals are extremely important for all power training. Elite power athletes in Olympic sports will routinely use work-to-rest ratios on the order of 1:20 for intense power workouts. For a max ladder set that takes about five seconds to complete, a rest period of approximately 100 seconds should be used. There really is no such thing as too much rest, so rest as long as needed to achieve maximum effort for each set.

For these exercises to be effective, the moves must be explosive. Remember that the goal is to complete the plyometric cycle of contractions, meaning that the movements *must* be explosive and you *must* "pop" from rung to rung. Do not latch a rung and hang out for a while before moving to the next. Attempt to bound steadily up the board in one continuous movement. Once fatigue begins to develop, end the workout. At that point, power no longer improves, but injury potential increases significantly, as does recovery time. As a rule of thumb, the beginner routine should include no more than 16 total sets in a single session, the intermediate routine no more than 24, and the advanced routine no more than 32. Perform far fewer sets early in the Power Phase, progressively increasing the number of sets attempted throughout the phase. Finish each workout with two to four supplemental exercises that address specific weaknesses.

"Power training is all about quality of effort so you should take as long as you need to ensure that every attempt is a good one, especially if your aim is to do the problem." — Ben Moon[5]

Sunday	Monday	Tuesday	Wednesday	Thursday	Friday	Saturday
Su 44	*Mo* 45	*Tu* 46	*We* 47	*Th* 48	*Fr* 49	*Sa* 50 *Warmup Boulder Ladder (WBL) 60m *Campus 15 min
Su 51 *Skin Care	*Mo* 52	*Tu* 53 *Limit Boulder (LB) 90 min *SE	*We* 54 *Skin Care	*Th* 55 *WBL 60 min *Campus 20 min *SE	*Fr* 56 *Skin Care	*Sa* 57 *(Optional LB Outdoors)
Su 58 *LB Outdoors	*Mo* 59 *Skin Care	*Tu* 60 *WBL 60 min *Campus 25 min *SE	*We* 61 *Skin Care	*Th* 62	*Fr* 63 *LB 90 min *SE	*Sa* 64 *Skin Care

The section labeled *Last Week of Strength Phase* spans Sunday through Friday of the first week.

Key: LB - Limit Bouldering   m/min - Minutes   SE - Supplemental Exercises   WBL - Warm-Up Boulder Ladder

Example Power Phase schedule for a novice trainee. Note that campus workouts are followed by two full rest days, whereas Limit Bouldering Routine workouts are followed by a single rest day.

Campus training should be used sparingly because it is extremely high intensity, and has limited specificity to rock climbing compared to other mutually exclusive activities like the Limit Bouldering Routine. Throughout the Power Phase, schedule four to five minutes of bouldering (including Warm-Up Boulder Ladders, Hard Bouldering, and the Limit Bouldering Routine) for every minute of campusing. For example, in one workout, a climber might do 60 minutes of bouldering and 30 minutes of campusing, then during the next workout he might do 90 minutes of bouldering only, for a total of 150 minutes of bouldering and 30 minutes of campusing over the two workouts (a 5-to-1 ratio).

These workouts are stressful to the finger, elbow, and shoulder joints, even though fatigue might not be apparent. Some coaches (in Olympic sports) theorize that since plyometric training elicits significant neurological adaptations, it can be mentally exhausting, resulting in sleepless nights and other signs of mental fatigue. Pay attention to the body's response to this training and establish rest periods accordingly. If fatigue mounts from session to session, or if explosive power can't be summoned, increase the rest period between workouts. Since a good campus routine should be relatively short by definition, many climbers will be able to get by on only one full rest day (i.e., 46 hours of rest) between workouts. The injury-prone should strongly consider two full rest days (i.e., 70 hours of rest) between workouts. Baseline Power Phases for novice and advanced trainees are shown.

The Power Phase should generally not last more than four weeks. Campus power typically wanes after three to four weeks, while bouldering ability continues to progress as movement skills and core strength improve. Once campus performance plateaus, replace it with the Limit Bouldering Routine, or proceed to the Power-Endurance Phase. The above schedule should vary based on specific climbing goals and on opportunities for outdoor bouldering (three-day weekends), etc.

Sunday	Monday	Tuesday	Wednesday	Thursday	Friday	Saturday
Su 37	*Mo* 38	*Tu* 39	*We* 40	*Th* 41	*Fr* 42 *Warmup Boulder Ladder (WBL) 60m *Campus 25m; SE	*Sa* 43 *Skin Care
Su 44	*Mo* 45 *Limit Boulder (LB) 120 min *SE	*Tu* 46 *Skin Care	*We* 47 *WBL 60 min *Campus 30 min *SE	*Th* 48 *Skin Care	*Fr* 49	*Sa* 50 *LB Outdoors
Su 51 *Skin Care	*Mo* 52 *WBL 60 min *Campus 35 min *SE	*Tu* 53 *Skin Care	*We* 54	*Th* 55 *WBL 60 min *Campus 40 min *SE	*Fr* 56 *Skin Care	*Sa* 57 *LB Outdoors (on boulders or routes)
Su 58 *Skin Care	*Mo* 59 *WBL 60 min *Campus 45 min *SE	*Tu* 60 *Skin Care	*We* 61	*Th* 62 *LB 120 min *SE	*Fr* 63 *Skin Care	*Sa* 64 PE Phase

The section labeled *Last Week of Strength Phase* spans Sunday through Thursday of the first week.

Example Power Phase schedule for an advanced trainee.

Max-Recruitment Training with a Hangboard

While not ideal, a hangboard can be used for power training; it's just a matter of varying the number and duration of reps and sets. The major drawback is the lack of dynamic movement, which prevents training the speed element of power. Also, hangboard training is less specific than preferred power-training exercises, such as the Limit Bouldering Routine, that provide a transition between the (hangboard-heavy) Strength Phase and outdoor rock climbing. Continuing on the hangboard during the Power Phase impedes this transition, so if using a hangboard for power training, include other movement-oriented activities as well. That said, the controlled environment that makes the hangboard ideal for strength training can also be leveraged to achieve significant gains in recruitment.

Max-Recruitment Hangboard Routine

This routine is similar to the hangboard routines of the Strength Phase, but with reduced numbers of repetitions and more rest to permit higher intensity efforts. Only extremely well-trained climbers should attempt this workout (those who have used the hangboard for many years or are climbing in the 5.13+ range). As with the finger-strength routines described in Chapter Six: Strength, all repetitions are static dead-hangs.

The high intensity (and therefore high amount of supplemental weight) required for this workout can create a significant logistical problem. Well-trained climbers may need to add triple-digit weight loads to achieve the desired intensity when hanging with two hands. For this reason, certain grips should be trained with one hand at a time (normally not advised). If using one-arm hangs, arrange them consecutively within the routine to maintain consistent rest periods for each hand — the routine below provides an example. Also, the higher intensity of this routine increases the importance of a thorough warm-up. Warm-up as per the Advanced Campus Routine, but end the Warm-Up Boulder Ladder one or two V-grades below your flash limit, then begin this workout.

MAX-RECRUITMENT HANGBOARD ROUTINE

WARM-UP:

Phase 1: Low-intensity ARC traversing (15 to 30 Minutes)
- Light, active stretching on the wall
- Progressively increase difficulty over last 10 minutes

Phase 2: Abbreviated Boulder Ladder (20 to 30 Minutes)
- 1 to 2 problems per grade from "V-easy" to one or two grades below flash level
- Increase rest period with difficulty

HANGBOARD ROUTINE:

Exercise	Grip	Set	Hand	Reps	Resistance	Total Set Time	TUT	Rest
1	Warm-up edge	1	Both	5	Baseline	0:45	0:25	3:00
...	...	2a	Left	3	½ Baseline +10	0:25	0:15	1:25
...	...	2b	Right	3	½ Baseline +10	0:25	0:15	3:00
2	Semi-closed crimp	1a	Left	5	½ Baseline	0:45	0:25	1:05
...	...	1b	Right	5	½ Baseline	0:45	0:25	1:15
...	...	2a	Left	4	½ Baseline +10	0:35	0:20	1:15
...	...	2b	Right	4	½ Baseline +10	0:35	0:20	1:15
...	...	3a	Left	3	½ Baseline +20	0:25	0:15	1:25
...	...	3b	Right	3	½ Baseline +20	0:25	0:15	3:00
3	Middle-ring	1a	Left	5	½ Baseline	0:45	0:25	1:05
...	...	1b	Right	5	½ Baseline	0:45	0:25	1:15
...	...	2a	Left	4	½ Baseline +10	0:35	0:20	1:15
...	...	2b	Right	4	½ Baseline +10	0:35	0:20	1:15
...	...	3a	Left	3	½ Baseline +20	0:25	0:15	1:25
...	...	3b	Right	3	½ Baseline +20	0:25	0:15	3:00
4	Closed crimp	1	Both	5	Baseline	0:45	0:25	3:00
...	...	2	Both	4	Baseline +15	0:35	0:20	3:00
...	...	3	Both	3	Baseline +30	0:25	0:15	3:00
5	Pinch	1	Both	5	Baseline	0:45	0:25	3:00
...	...	2	Both	4	Baseline +15	0:35	0:20	3:00
...	...	3	Both	3	Baseline +30	0:25	0:15	...

SUPPLEMENTAL EXERCISES:

- 2 to 4 exercises addressing specific physical weaknesses
- 1 to 3 sets each of 8 or fewer repetitions

The Max R Hangboard Routine should consist of a larger warm-up grip, followed by four to five basic grip positions (such as semi-closed crimp, middle-ring two-finger pair, closed crimp, mono, pinch). Complete three sets for each grip, with the first set consisting of five repetitions, the second four reps, and the third set consisting of three reps. Each rep comprises a five-second hang followed by five seconds of rest. Rest three minutes between each set.

Unlike the finger-strength routines described in Chapter 6: Strength, the goal is not to carry cumulative fatigue from one set to the next. The purpose of the first and second sets of each grip position is to prepare the muscles for maximal intensity on the final set. Therefore, the increment of applied load from set to set should be greater than that of the finger-strength routines (for example, if the correct load for a given grip of a finger-strength routine is "body weight" for set one, "body weight +10 pounds" for set two, and "body weight +20 pounds" for set three, the correct load for the Max R routine might be "body weight" for set one, "body weight +15 pounds" for set two, and "body weight +30 pounds" for set three).

SUMMARY

- Power is a primary determinant of climbing ability. Power is the ability to quickly exert high force on a set of holds.
- Not all motor units contribute to every muscle contraction. Recruitment describes the proportion of active motor units contributing to a given muscular contraction. Increasing recruitment results in higher force production, but does little to improve contraction speed, which is critical to latching the target hold during a dynamic movement.
- Contact strength is the amount of force the fingers can exert on a hold during the period of initial contact. The faster such force can be generated, the less force is required to latch the target hold.
- Muscle fibers can be trained to improve certain traits like contraction speed and cross-sectional area.
- Plyometric training is widely regarded as the best method for improving explosive power in all types of athletes because it 1) helps increase muscle-fiber recruitment and 2) helps train muscle fibers to contract more quickly.
- The Limit Bouldering Routine is the most climbing-specific method of training power. Limit boulder problems should be short, featuring one to two dynamic crux moves right at the climber's physical limit.
- The Campus Board is ideal for climbing-specific plyometric training. Campusing also greatly improves confidence, speed, and accuracy for dynamic movements.
- Focus on performing a few, climbing-specific campus exercises well (with smooth, flowing movement) rather than performing a plethora of exercises poorly.
- Power training must be done when the climber is fresh, and able to move explosively. Once power begins to wane, end the training activity.
- Plan adequate recovery periods between power workouts. Plan additional recovery following each campus session.

POWER-ENDURANCE

To succeed on climbs like *Quinsana Plus*, 5.13b, at the New River Gorge, WV, climbers need to be able to execute dozens of powerful moves with little rest. Climbers call this type of fitness "Power-Endurance". Dan Brayack

CHAPTER 8

"Climbing the tenth grade (5.13+) is not just a question of having sufficient power." — Wolfgang Gullich[1]

Strong, powerful muscles and expert technique will only get a climber so far. Eventually a dream route will come along that demands the ability to string together a series of difficult moves in order to claim success. The ultimate routes — those that hold the highest place of honor at each crag and occupy our dreams — all demand sustained, intense effort. This requirement to hold it together through a continuous stretch of climbing is part of a great route's draw; this type of climbing is selective, "separating the wheat from the chaff." Routes like these are the most dramatic, with long, sweeping stretches of steep, improbable stone. Such features require climbers to link long sequences of brutally difficult moves. These routes demand the very best from those who seek to climb them, making them the most sought-after routes, and the most rewarding.

This type of climbing is also unsustainable beyond a very brief stretch of time, and climbers know it. Entering into this realm is akin to playing chicken with the muscles' metabolic systems. Most climbers know that once they cross the threshold, it is a race against mounting fatigue and an incapacitating forearm pump. Fortunately, with training, it is possible to "add time" to the proverbial "pump clock," and turn those dream routes into sends.

This brand of climbing is known as *power-endurance* (PE). It is the ability to perform multiple near-maximal climbing moves without rest (in bouts lasting 30 to 180 seconds). It refers to sequences of moves that are so continuous they afford no opportunities to shake (even quickly) or chalk up. The term itself is somewhat controversial because it sounds like an oxymoron, but it is an accurate way to describe this type of training. "Power" refers to the activation of

fast-twitch muscle fibers, a component essential to this type of training that sets it apart from "regular" endurance training. Less-intense endurance training doesn't activate these fibers, and therefore, doesn't improve their endurance. Climbers rely on these fast-twitch fibers to execute difficult moves, so low-intensity endurance training alone is not sufficient for those intent on performing sequences of sustained, powerful moves. Well-executed PE training will improve the metabolic energy pathways of both slow- and fast-twitch muscle fibers, adding precious time to the pump clock and granting a temporary stay of execution when it comes time to go for the redpoint of that dream route.

MUSCLE FATIGUE

Chapter 5: Base-Fitness explained that fatigue develops within skeletal muscle for various reasons. In the case of climbing, fatigue is caused by a culmination of several critical factors, resulting in the debilitating pump that ends many redpoint attempts. A climber attempting a difficult, pumpy rock climb will encounter strenuous holds that require substantial muscular effort to hold onto, and thus a high percentage of the climber's maximum strength. Such intense contractions will:

1. Require a greater rate of ATP production to power muscle contractions.
2. Rely on fast-twitch fibers (which have reduced capacity for aerobic metabolism).
3. Restrict blood flow to the forearms.

The combination of these factors reduces the muscles' ability to utilize the most-efficient means of providing ATP energy for muscle contractions: mitochondrial aerobic respiration. As a result, muscles will turn to glycolysis, which provides ATP at a faster rate but does so by burning up glucose faster and producing more metabolic waste. Reduced blood flow prevents resupply of glucose fuel and removal of that waste, further exacerbating this problem. Within minutes, harmful metabolites accumulate in the muscles as local supplies of ATP are depleted. These events interfere with cross-bridge cycling of the actin and myosin proteins that create muscle contractions, preventing the climber from holding on. Climbers can avoid or delay this debilitating cycle through power-endurance training.

All Endurance Is Local

In single-pitch rock climbing, fatigue develops and becomes limiting *locally* much more than *systemically*. Compared to many sports, this is rather unusual. In endurance sports like running and cycling, performance is typically limited by the systemic ability of the entire body to intake and process oxygen for aerobic metabolism to fuel muscle activity. Therefore, traits like VO2 max and heart and lung function are critical (and potentially limiting) factors.

Climbers are typically limited by the performance of the forearm muscles, whose metabolic demands for fuel and oxygen are trivial compared to what the legs consume while running or cycling. Our cardiovascular system can easily provide the relatively little oxygen needed by our forearms during a climb, even without breathing heavily. Therefore, it isn't necessary or beneficial to improve systemic aerobic fitness in most cases, and time and effort spent on this is just a distraction from more-productive activities (granted, it is an enjoyable distraction for many, including the authors).

On the other hand, the local glycolytic and aerobic energy systems within our forearm muscles *will* be pushed to their limit, and quite likely determine success or failure. Effort spent on improving these systems will be rewarded. So-called cardiovascular exercise (or *cardio*, such as running, cycling, swimming, etc.) may promote recovery between climbing workouts by increasing general blood flow throughout the body. Still, it would be preferable to perform a more climbing-specific exercise such as ARC training, which promotes blood flow directly where it is needed as well as includes skill practice. Therefore, while it is advisable to perform cardio for the purpose of promoting overall health and wellness or to manage weight, don't expect it to improve your climbing directly.

EFFECTS OF ENDURANCE TRAINING

Recall that all three metabolic energy pathways (glycolytic, aerobic, and phosphagenic) are active within the muscle cells at all times; it is their relative contribution to muscle function that changes based on the intensity of the activity. Activities that require greater muscular force will require more ATP, and the muscle will first try to provide as much ATP as possible through aerobic respiration (which is sustainable indefinitely). When the limits of aerobic respiration are reached, the muscle increasingly (but not exclusively) relies on glycolysis, which doesn't require oxygen. On difficult, near-limit rock climbs, this threshold is reached very quickly, and the pump clock begins to tick.

Climbing that requires a substantial contribution from glycolysis is unsustainable, and the onset of fatigue and failure is simply a matter of time. The climber's only hope is to complete the difficult climbing before that time arrives — by reaching a rest or the end of the climb. Fortunately, the climber's ability to sustain climbing of this nature can be improved through power-endurance (PE) training.

PE training involves the use of repeated work *intervals* that simulate very intense stretches of climbing, such as route cruxes or long boulder problems. This approach was first developed by runners in the early 1900s, and has since been adopted by all endurance sports. Climbers have used this same basic method for several decades. PE training stimulates adaptations that improve the muscles' ability to perform repeated, high-intensity contractions. These adaptations primarily improve aerobic respiration within the muscle cells[3]. Aerobic respiration is always occurring in the muscle, even once the maximum steady state (MSS) is surpassed (as it is during PE climbing). Therefore, promoting mitochondrial performance is still a powerful means of improving climbing endurance because it will increase the aerobic production of ATP and removal of metabolites. As described in Chapter 5: Base-Fitness, mitochondrial function (quantity, size, and capacity) can be greatly improved through low-intensity endurance training (such as ARCing), but PE training also promotes mitochondrial function.

PE training improves the muscle cells' ability to tolerate sustained muscle contractions by promoting key enzymes in the cells. Enzymes regulate the cells' energetic processes during activity, while also triggering the development of beneficial infrastructure after exercise. PE training increases the quantity of these enzymes, which then go on to stimulate beneficial adaptations. PE training promotes enzymes that[3]:

- Increase the quantity, size, and capacity of mitochondria in the exercised muscle, thus increasing the muscle's overall capacity to use aerobic respiration.
- Improve the mitochondria's capacity to oxidize fatty acids and glucose during exercise, thus increasing the rate of ATP production.
- Shuttle nicotinamide adenine dinucleotide (NADH) into the mitochondria for oxidative phosphorylation (thus producing ATP while removing this otherwise-harmful metabolite).
- Initiate the most-efficient ATP production mechanisms at the onset of exercise rather than waiting for fatigue to occur before "kicking into high gear." Thus, PE training allows the muscle cells to anticipate the requirement for ATP when climbing, a key adaptation that delays fatigue by avoiding the use of less-efficient ATP production methods.

All of these adaptations improve the ability of the aerobic energy pathway to provide ATP for muscle function, and, in effect, raise the MSS, thus delaying the transition to glycolysis and eventual muscle fatigue. Even once the MSS is surpassed, these adaptations continue to benefit performance through improved aerobic respiration (which persists even once glycolysis assumes the leading role).

The adaptations caused by endurance training are specific to the actual muscle and fiber used, which has enormous implications for climbers. First, because each grip position uses different muscles and fibers within the forearm, it is important that the holds used in training match those of the climber's goal routes as closely as possible. This will ensure that the endurance needed for the goal route is actually developed during training. To say it plainly, performing laps on slopers in the gym will not improve the crimp endurance needed for an outdoor project, just as lapping the crag's crimpfest testpiece will do little to prepare a climber for a pinch-and-sloper-dominated competition climb.

The second consequence of the specificity of endurance-training adaptations is that low-intensity training will not recruit fast-twitch muscle fibers, so low-intensity *endurance* training will not benefit fast-twitch fibers (which are critical to difficult climbing). Therefore, it is necessary for climbers to perform both low- and high-intensity endurance training to ensure that all types of fibers are trained. Fast-twitch fibers are known to experience a fourfold (or more) increase in mitochondria as a result of endurance training, but only if the training is intense enough to recruit fast-twitch fibers[2]. Such training will, in effect, raise the MSS of the fast-twitch fibers *without reducing their power*, which is enormously beneficial on the most-difficult climbs. The low-intensity ARC training described in Chapter 5: Base-Fitness primarily benefits Type I (slow-twitch) fibers, while the exercises described in this chapter will provide the correct intensity and duration to promote endurance improvements in the Type IIa and IIb (aka IIx/d) fast-twitch fibers also.

POWER-ENDURANCE TRAINING

Power-endurance training has existed in many forms for decades, at least. The memoirs of legendary climbing heroes contain numerous accounts of punishing bouldering circuits or desperate traverses, repeated beyond the point of exhaustion and frequently revisited as training for their next revolutionary ascent. Still to this day, most climbers agree that interval training is the preferred way to develop power-endurance. Interval training can take many forms, but it generally consists of repeated bouts of climbing effort of a set duration or length, separated by timed rest periods.

The various forms of endurance training create a spectrum that encompasses many training activities, from low-intensity and long-duration sessions (like ARCing), right up to high-intensity, short-duration exercises that border on strength training. The key is to design the training protocol based on strengths, weaknesses, and goals to stimulate the desired improvement. A climber can sculpt a PE routine that lies anywhere on the endurance spectrum (Figure below), but such a routine should be deliberately designed to prepare the climber to accomplish the season's goals.

Duration		Intensity
Low-intensity, High-repetition	Moderate-intensity, Moderate-repetition	High-intensity, Low-repetition

Endurance Training Spectrum

"One of the best bouldering areas at Stoney is Minus Ten Wall, a thirty-foot-wide wall of vertical limestone, covered in small, polished fingerholds. It was possible to work out endless desperate problems on this, which trained my fingers for the style of climbing on Genesis." — Jerry Moffat[5]

SPECIFICITY OF ENDURANCE TRAINING

Since adaptations to PE training occur in individual muscle fibers, endurance training is very specific in terms of hold size and type, contraction duration, number of moves (repetitions), and total set duration. Therefore, it is critical to match the training to the climber's intended goal routes as much as possible. Fortunately, the Power-Endurance Phase directly precedes the Performance Phase, so by the time the PE Phase begins, the goal routes and their characteristics should be very clear. This should remove much of the guesswork from planning your training exercises.

With a specific route (or routes) in mind, the climber should identify the sections of the route that will push him to the limit of his power-endurance. (Some routes may not have this characteristic, and in these cases, PE training may not be a priority for *that route*.) This crux section could be the entire route, but will likely be a stretch of climbing between good rests, spanning at least a few bolts, and often including the route's hardest moves. Often, such a stretch may be

so demanding that it is not even possible to chalk up in the midst of it, and clipping the bolts may be very difficult. Count the number of movements *per hand* for this crux section and, if possible, estimate how much time it takes to climb it, accounting for the likelihood that, with practice, the sequence can be climbed more quickly. (It's likely that early in the Performance Phase, it isn't possible to "link" this entire section, so add up the durations of the links that can be climbed.) There shouldn't be any good rests in this section, but take note of any poor rests which may be simulated in training. In summary, note all of these physical characteristics of this crux section:

- Number of moves *per hand*
- Handhold size and type
- Foothold size and type
- Wall angle
- Time duration required to climb it (once the moves are rehearsed)
- Appropriate climbing pace
- Rest opportunities

If it's not possible to physically climb on the goal route (i.e., it's at a faraway crag), it may be possible to view video of other climbers on it — preferably climbers of similar ability, with similar pacing, who know the best beta! The parameters obtained during this analysis will be used to design specific PE-training exercises.

Endurance adaptations are very specific to the training activity. For best results, train on holds that mimic the size and shape of those on your goal route.

Route Analysis for PE-Training Specificity

Specificity is critical to PE training. When there is a specific goal route in mind, the best approach is to try the route and record its key characteristics. Absent a specific goal, data from a sampling of routes can be used to steer PE training. The best way to collect this data is by analyzing video footage of yourself on past redpoint projects. Here is an example:

Route	Grade	Crag	Hand Moves	Total Time (sec)	Pace (sec/move)	Route Style
Cow Reggae	13b	Wild Iris, WY	18	140	7.78	Steep, big moves, pumpy
Trench Warfare	13d	China Cave, UT	30	200	6.67	Steep, big moves, pumpy
The Heretic	13b	City of Rocks, ID	16	115	7.19	Steep, big moves
Deceivor	13d	Little River Canyon, AL	16	80	5.00	Near-vertical, bouldery, short
Before There Were Nine	13d	Independence Pass, CO	25	160	6.40	Gently overhanging, techy, many complex moves
Busload of Faith	14a	Sinks Canyon, WY	20	114	5.70	Gently overhanging, techy, many complex moves
Calypso	13d	City of Rocks, ID	26	145	5.58	Gently overhanging, techy, many complex moves

This table is meant to describe how to perform the analysis, so don't fixate on the route grades or pace, which will vary between climbers. The pace values are averages, obtained by timing the total duration of the crux section and then dividing it by the number of hand movements. Therefore, any particular move could take much more or less time.

Analyzing your climbing in this way can be very enlightening. First, notice how similar the results are. These are seven very different routes from across the country, and yet they all contain crux sections with between 16 and 26 hand moves, and I climbed them all with a consistent pace; around six seconds per hand move (once the moves were well-rehearsed). Second, it is evident that steeper routes tend to be climbed at a slower pace. This is because they have fewer, but longer moves (such as hip rotations, and large foot movements) that often require multiple foot movements per hand move. On the other hand, technical routes often have many "tic-tac" moves that can be executed quickly, with only minimal body adjustments. This may be surprising because many assume that technical routes are climbed more slowly. They may be climbed slower in terms of "vertical feet per second," but not in terms of "moves per second," which is the more-relevant measure for PE training.

If you haven't done so already, start recording some of your projecting efforts and put the footage to good use, refining your PE training for better performance.

— Mike Anderson

"I think that drive and mental strength are the factors that distinguish ordinary from extraordinary achievements. In competition, it is not the physically strongest climbers who win, but rather the mentally strongest."

— J.B. Tribout[4]

POWER-ENDURANCE TRAINING EXERCISES

Two forms of interval training exercises, each one lying on either end of the endurance spectrum, will be described below. They are *Linked Bouldering Circuits*, and *Route Intervals*. Though both exercises use repeated efforts of sustained climbing, they differ in the adaptations they seek to achieve. Therefore, they require subtle differences in execution, including distinctly different mentalities from the athlete. Linked Bouldering Circuits are used to prepare for routes requiring powerful sprints with little or no rest, where a boulderer's commitment and gymnastic attitude is required. They require higher intensity and arousal.

	Exercise	Simulates	Set Duration (minutes)	Total Hand Moves	Total Sets	Work/Rest Duty Cycle	Rest Between Workouts
High-Intensity	LBC	Long Boulder Problems	0:45 -1:30	10 - 20	6 - 8	1:2 to 1:1	48 - 72 hrs
Mid-Intensity	LBC	Bouldery "PE" Routes	1:30 - 4:00	20 - 40	4 - 6	1:2 to 1:1	48 - 72 hrs
Low-Intensity	Intervals	Pumpy, "Enduro" Routes	4:00 - 15:00	40 - 100	2 - 4	1:2 to 1:1	48 - 72 hrs

Guidelines for Power-Endurance training.

Route Intervals prepare climbers for long endurance routes with rest points, where concentration, pump management, and precise technical execution are required for success.

Ideally, PE training will be tailored to simulate a specific goal route. With a goal route in mind, select the appropriate type of PE training and use the Table above as a guide to determine the set quantities and rest periods. The driving characteristic should be the duration of the set, because muscle fatigue is more a function of time-under-tension (TUT) than number of repetitions. Therefore, the number of hand movements used in the various types of PE training may vary depending on the typical pace of the climber or the intricacy of the climbing. Analyze the goal route to determine the required duration of effort, then use the table to select the other parameters of the workout. Also, realize that high-intensity moves will generally be climbed considerably faster than moderate moves, which are subsequently faster than low-intensity moves. Therefore, there may be overlap between the various endurance categories (a 90-second high-intensity crux "sprint" may contain more hand movements than a two-minute, mid-intensity "half-sprint," etc.). The *duty cycle* is the ratio of work to rest. Initially, climbers should aim for a duty cycle of 1:2; that is, the set duration should be half the rest duration. As fitness improves, the climber should steadily reduce the work/rest ratio toward a 1:1 duty cycle, in which the rest duration is equal to the set duration.

THE LEGENDARY 4x4

The "4x4" is a prevalent training tool that has many variations, but in its fundamental form consists of a circuit of four carefully selected boulder problems climbed in immediate succession, followed by a rest period, then climbed again, and so on until the four-boulder-problem circuit has been climbed four times. 4x4s were developed by climbers in Salt Lake City in the early 1990s to train for the short, powerful routes they were developing at the nearby American Fork Canyon. Any climber who has come to grips with the desperates on the Hell Wall will understand why.

4x4s have been a popular and successful training tool for many years, but they have a clear flaw that can easily be improved: the slight rest that is obtained as the climber completes one problem then drops to

4x4s were first developed by Utah climbers to prepare for the short but sustained routes at American Fork Canyon. JC Hunter's *Fantasy Island*, 5.14b, is a perfect example.   Andrew Burr

the ground and moves to the start of the next problem. This does not accurately simulate climbing and violates the imperative for specificity in endurance training. Extremely taxing, dynamic, powerful climbing, like that which often composes a route's crux, will rarely afford much more than a half-second of rest at a time as hands dart from one hold to the next. Therefore, the five or more seconds that pass as the climber drops from the end of one problem to start the next is a virtual eternity to battered forearms gasping for respite. These unrealistic rests reduce training stress and interfere with the desired adaption.

LINKED BOULDERING CIRCUITS

The first form of PE training described, the Linked Bouldering Circuit (LBC), is a form of high- and mid-intensity PE training that will improve the climber's ability to sustain a series of difficult moves. Based on the classic 4x4, a linked bouldering circuit is an unbroken chain of boulder problems or a long boulder traverse consisting of a premeditated number of moves, designed to mimic the goal route as closely as possible. If there isn't a specific goal route in mind, a reasonable target for mid-range PE training is about

24 total hand movements (about 12 per hand), with no rest stances or shakes — chalking up should not be possible. This type of training is designed for routes requiring about 20 uninterrupted high-intensity hand movements (like many of the "hard" routes in the US). The moves should be powerful and dynamic, requiring a boulderer's "go for it" mindset to complete. Thus the climber will be forced to conjure up this attitude in the face of debilitating fatigue, and will learn that such moves can be done even when pumped. This "attitude rehearsal" will transfer nicely to the goal route during the redpointing process.

A single LBC set will take one to four minutes to complete (averaging about six seconds per move), which is generally the time limit of the glycolytic energy pathway. Therefore, assuming the moves are the correct difficulty (more on this to come), the circuit will bring the climber to the limit of glycolysis, stimulating the release of the desired enzymes that trigger beneficial adaptations.

The circuit should be difficult but not desperate; easy enough that the climber can complete it most of the time when she is warmed up but not yet fatigued. It shouldn't have any "stopper" moves, but the

Linked Bouldering Circuits can be created in the gym by linking together existing boulder problems (often with some down-climbing in between). This LBC includes increasingly difficult problems, to train for a pumpy route with a high crux

difficulty can vary as needed to mimic a goal route. When in doubt, err on the side of making the circuit too easy. It's better to complete the sets with energy left over and add more sets at the end than to fall off too early, before sufficient fatigue is developed (which would yield little training benefit). Because of the way fatigue develops in the forearms, an appropriate LBC will not cause a debilitating pump during the first set or two. It may require three or four sets for the pump to develop. While a dizzying pump may not exist, the muscles are still fatiguing, resulting in a loss of power and coordination (which could cause failure without a deep pump). This is the necessary training stimulus to achieve the desired adaptation — the ability to sustain powerful, precise movement for 20 to 30 moves. This is consistent with the type of stress imposed by many limit redpoint routes.

Creating Linked Bouldering Circuits

Building a proper LBC is not trivial and requires some thought and experimentation, which is why the 4x4 framework is helpful. By building up the circuit from three, four, or five distinct boulder problems, it is easy to tweak the composition and difficulty of the overall circuit by manipulating characteristics such as the order in which the problems are climbed, or by substituting problems. For example, consider the three very different circuits constructed from the same pool of five boulder problems rated V2, V2, V3, V5 and V6:

Circuit No. 1	Circuit No. 2	Circuit No. 3
V5	V5	V5
V3	V2	V2
V2	V2	V3
V2	V3	V6

There are dozens of ways this circuit could be constructed, but these were chosen to illustrate a few key points. Assuming each problem is only climbed once, Circuit No. 1 is the easiest possible arrangement because the harder climbing is done early in the circuit, when the climber is less fatigued. By the same token, Circuit No. 3 is quite difficult because the hardest problem comes at the end, when the climber will be much more fatigued. Circuit No. 2 is slightly harder than Circuit No. 1, which was accomplished simply by swapping the order of two problems. This is a simple adjustment that can be used to fine-tune the difficulty of a circuit, or to make the training progressive throughout the season. Ideally, the order of difficulty will *eventually* mimic the goal route.

A further benefit of this circuit-construction method is that it allows the climber to select the appropriate style of problems (angle, hold type, etc.), and keep them constant. If all of the original five problems are of the desired style, rearranging or substituting them still creates a circuit of the desired style. These problems can be worked and rehearsed during the Limit Bouldering routine sessions of the Power Phase (as part of the Warm-Up Boulder Ladder or Hard Bouldering phases of those workouts). Thus, when it is time to include them in LBCs, they will be well-known problems that can be climbed on demand, with a low chance of failure.

Route Intervals

Route Intervals are a form of lower-intensity PE training that are usually accomplished by climbing a route or bouldering circuit repeatedly (also known as "route lapping"). Route Intervals are appropriate training for goal routes that are long and sustained, with less-distinct cruxes. Such routes will often include poor rests that provide enough recovery to allow climbing to continue beyond the two-to-three minute time limit that constrains "pure" PE climbing. This does not necessarily mean there are no hard crux moves, only that there are ample rests to allow the effort to continue beyond the typical PE limit.

A benefit of route lapping is that it can be done on lead, thus providing an opportunity to practice all of the challenging components inherent to lead climbing. Route Intervals also make better training for onsight climbing, because the lower-intensity and longer-duration efforts are more specific to onsighting. Therefore, it is common to begin the PE Phase with Linked Bouldering Circuits, then transition to Route Intervals later in the phase (especially when the climber is training for several goal routes with a variety of endurance demands). This coincides with the general decline in power that occurs through the Performance Phase.

Route Intervals can be performed on outdoor routes, indoor routes, or indoor traverse circuits, but route selection is critical. The difficulty should be about one letter grade above the climber's consistent onsight level. Therefore, the climber's goal route usually should not be used for this type of training. Instead, select a route that is less difficult than the goal route, but similar in terms of length, angle, hold type, etc. (refer to the previous section, "Specificity of Endurance Training," for more details). If practical, it is beneficial and not uncommon to use an outdoor

Route-Setting Considerations for PE Training

Specificity: PE Training is highly specific, so select or create routes that utilize similar hold types, steepness, and style as the goal routes you are training for.

Venues: PE Training circuits can be set in many locations, but some are better than others. A rotating climbing wall (aka a Treadwall®) is the ideal artificial tool for PE training. Problems can be set on these machines that cover one complete revolution of the tread, and start and finish at the same point so the climber can climb continuously from one problem into the next without interruption. Further, some models allow the angle and rotation speed to be adjusted to simulate specific terrain. The bouldering area of a quality climbing gym is great for LBCs (especially if you have route-setting privileges), while the lead wall is preferred for Route Intervals. Avoid lead routes for LBCs, so clipping isn't required. If route-setting privileges aren't granted, the gym staff may be willing to set problems specifically for training. It's always possible to create "unofficial" problems using existing holds or a systems wall, Campus Board, etc. A home bouldering wall is another great option for creating linked circuits that can be used for LBCs or Route Intervals.

Continuity: On bouldering walls, it is important to build a continuous linked circuit. That means downclimbing, and possibly traversing between problems. Use problems that are nearby, and avoid overly easy downclimbs that afford too much rest. Going down should be just as hard as going up. Alternatively, it may be easier to build a traversing circuit, but this type of climbing is less specific, so incorporate alternating sections of up- and downclimbing (not just horizontal movements) into the "traverse."

Rests: High- and mid-intensity PE training should not include resting or shaking within a set, and moves should be so difficult that chalking up isn't feasible. However, low-intensity sets may include chalking or resting, especially if it is possible to mimic a taxing rest position on the goal route. A good way to limit rest opportunities is to eliminate holds that allow matching (and avoid placing two holds side by side). To allow limited rest, set one jug for each hand, separated by a few moves, thus allowing one hand to shake briefly and chalk, but preventing alternating shakes with both hands. The number and duration of rests will impact the total duration of the set, which could push the set duration beyond ten minutes in the case of a long Route Interval.

Pacing: Beware that routes or circuits climbed in the gym will generally be climbed much faster than outdoor routes because the holds are easy to spot and have uniform surfaces, thus less time is required for analysis and precise movement. Climbing too fast can sabotage PE-training effects. As described earlier, time the duration of the goal route's crux section, or gather general data from several routes to guide future PE training (this is also a helpful analysis tool when projecting routes). It may be helpful to create technical, complex movements, with insecure footholds, to slow the climbing pace during PE training. Using pockets or other complex holds for footholds is one proven method for reducing climbing speed. Another method is to establish "time gates" at key holds; do not proceed past these gates until the specified amount of time has passed.

Adjustments: It is unlikely that you'll create your circuit perfectly the first time. Adjust holds and sequences as necessary to achieve the desired level of intensity, length, and level of pump. Be prepared to make changes throughout the season to maintain proper duration and intensity as the sequence becomes "dialed" and PE improves.

A rotating climbing wall is the ultimate tool for PE training.

route at the same crag. Such a route will mimic the goal route better than any gym route possibly could. The training route should be adequately rehearsed so that the climber can "send at will" when she is unfatigued. Therefore, a former project at the same crag that is similar to the current goal route would be ideal for Route Interval training. Strenuous rest and chalk opportunities should be included, but avoid "camping out" at easy stances.

Once the route is selected and adequately rehearsed, a Route Interval workout can be performed. The route will be climbed two to four times in succession, with a duty cycle of roughly 1:2 (time required to complete one lap is half the duration of the rest period), which should be reduced to 1:1 as the climber progresses. Therefore, time the duration of each lap and rest period.

As with all PE training, this is not a race; climb at the appropriate pace for the goal route, including pausing to rest and shake. While LBC training demands a boulderer's "go for it" attitude, Route Intervals should utilize the controlled, confident attitude of a redpoint climber. The pace should be slower than LBC training, especially if rests are involved. Concentrate on technical details such as breathing, relaxation, grip control, and precise movement. Laps should be climbed on lead if possible, in order to practice the unique elements of lead climbing such as clipping from the best stances, staying relaxed while clipping, climbing confidently through a runout, etc. Route Intervals can be performed on a bouldering traverse (which is easier to set and modify), but doing so sacrifices the benefits of lead-climbing rehearsal and upward movement.

It is common to wrap up a day of limit redpoint climbing with a Route Interval session. This is appropriate when the previous climbing for the day consisted of primarily working crux moves on goal routes (roped bouldering) and did not include taxing, sustained endurance efforts. This is common early in the redpointing process, when just beginning to learn the moves on the project and long "linkage" isn't yet possible. Beware that by tacking on this extra workload, more rest may be required before the next climbing day. Therefore, it is more advisable to perform these at the end of a climbing weekend. Nevertheless, this is a good way to incorporate some PE training into an otherwise-crowded training schedule. Follow the aforementioned guidelines, but only perform two or three laps at the most. Route Interval training is very similar to route projecting, so it can hasten "burnout" and result in accumulating fatigue that impacts overall climbing performance. Exercise restraint in performing this type of training.

PERFORMING THE WORKOUT

Once a training route or LBC is prepared, it should be rehearsed sufficiently that failure during training will result from muscle fatigue, not a botched sequence. If training in a public gym, aim for a low-traffic time slot to stay out of the way of other climbers. Each "lap" of the circuit or route is considered one "set." The duration of each set should be timed and recorded, but this isn't a race and the goal isn't to "speed up" each successive repetition. The goal should be to complete the circuit at the appropriate pace (simulating an outdoor route-climbing pace).

If the circuit is the right difficulty, simply completing it once will be quite difficult. As mentioned earlier, rest between sets will decrease from workout to workout as the climber progresses. Early in the PE Phase, aim for a duty cycle of 1:2. As fitness improves, reduce the work/rest ratio toward a 1:1 duty cycle.

Have a partner time your work intervals and rest periods to ensure progression through the PE Phase.

LINKED BOULDERING CIRCUIT (LBC) ROUTINE

WARM-UP PHASE 1:

- **Low-intensity ARC traversing (15 to 20 minutes)**
- Light, active stretching on the wall

WARM-UP PHASE 2:

- **Warm-Up Boulder Ladder (15 minutes)**
- Begin with "V-easy"
- 1 to 3 problems of each grade up to flash level
- No more than three attempts per problem
- Rehearse any problems incorporated in the LBC

WARM-UP PHASE 3:

- **Hard Bouldering (20 minutes)**
- 2 to 3 "realistic" problems — if necessary, rehearse problems that will be used in the LBC
- 3 to 4 quality attempts per problem
- 2 to 5 minutes rest between attempts

LINKED BOULDERING CIRCUIT:

- **Move Selection:** Powerful, dynamic moves that are specific to goal routes and are well-rehearsed, so the circuit can be completed most of the time when un-fatigued.
- **Duty Cycle:** 1:2 early in the phase, progressing to 1:1 late in the phase. (For example, begin the PE Phase by resting four minutes for a two-minute set, progressing toward two minutes' rest for a two-minute set.)
- **Sets:** 6 to 8 for sets of 20 moves or less; 4 to 6 for sets of 20 to 40 moves.
- **Pace:** It's not a race; climb at a pace similar to the goal route and focus on proper breathing, relaxation, grip control, pump management, and precision movement. Time the lap and record it.
- **Notes:**
    o If you fall but aren't too pumped, resume the circuit.
    o If you fall due to fatigue, end the set and note the time and number of hand movements completed.
    o During rest periods, focus on proper breathing and prepare for the next set.
    o Once you cannot complete 75 percent of a set due to fatigue, end the workout.

COOLDOWN:

- Low-intensity ARC traversing (15-20 minutes)
- Rest 10 to 20 minutes after Phase 4 before cooldown (stretch and massage forearms)
- Rehearse techniques
- Light, active stretching on the wall

161

Anywhere from two to eight sets may be accomplished in a given workout, depending on the climber's goals (which should determine the intensity). Typically, three to six sets are performed, and the last couple of sets will often not be completed successfully due to accumulating fatigue. If all sets are completed, continue the rest and work cycle until fatigue is reached, and then reduce the rest period accordingly for the next workout. There is little value in attempting more sets once fatigue has set in. If it isn't possible to complete at least 75 percent of a given set, end the interval workout and move on to the cooldown. See Table on previous page for more details on rest periods and numbers of sets.

In reality, it is not so easy to anticipate when fatigue will cause failure in the midst of a training session — or a season. Nevertheless, the goal is to create a circuit or route that imparts a massive, building pump and requires considerable effort to complete. Throughout the workout, it should be increasingly difficult to complete each lap, with failure almost certain on the last couple of sets. It is not necessary to fail at the end of every set. It is perfectly acceptable to complete a lap "with a little gas left in the tank," albeit this process should be hard and accompanied by a pump (high-intensity PE training may not last long enough to develop a debilitating pump). If a fall occurs midway through a set due to some factor other than severe fatigue, jump back on the wall and attempt to complete the set. If a fall occurs as a result of fatigue, end the set.

After each set, record its duration and note if the set was completed or where failure occurred. Focus on good breathing and recovery during rest periods. Sip water and/or pace slowly to aid recovery. Chalk up and be in position to begin the next set when the rest period ends. These are among the most physically exhausting work-

With a "kick plate", a campus or hangboard can be used for PE training in a pinch.

outs a climber will perform. Be prepared to suffer and produce tremendous effort during the last set or two.

While climbers are urged to perform PE training on rock or an artificial climbing wall, it can be done on a more compact apparatus such as a system wall, Campus Board, or even a hangboard. Follow the same protocols described above, and take extra care to ensure that the proper intensity and pace of "climbing" are used. For the Campus Board and hangboard, which would normally be used without feet, add a *kick plate* (a small panel plastered with footholds — see photo in last column) so that the hands can be weighted with realistic loads and you can simulate climbing movement. The hangboard can overhang the kick plate to simulate overhanging climbing.

FOCUS AND INTENSITY

During strength and power training, very high arousal is desired to produce maximum force and power. This high state of arousal and accompanying intensity level would lead to premature fatigue in PE training. Therefore, a lower level of arousal should be used, similar to that of a limit redpoint or onsight attempt. The intensity level must be high enough to complete the individual moves of the circuit, but no higher; thus it might be necessary for the climber to adjust arousal and intensity within a circuit. Though challenging, adjusting arousal on the fly is an important skill that is essential for difficult redpoints, and practicing it is one of the key benefits of PE training.

PE circuits are more similar to real-life redpoint attempts than any other training activity in the Rock Prodigy program. Therefore, treat them as rehearsal, practicing the desired behaviors required for performance efforts. Focus on climbing efficiently when *possible*, and turning up the intensity and effort when *necessary* to complete the moves. Use a relaxed grip when possible and focus on executing flawless technique. Maintain steady breathing and stay calm and relaxed. When difficult moves interrupt breathing, practice "Finding Calm" (See Chapter 3: Skill Development). For suggestions on good performance-climbing behaviors, see Chapter 13: Redpoint and Onsight Climbing.

COOLDOWN

A cooldown is critical after PE training, because such training leaves the muscles packed with harmful metabolites. Moderate cyclic contractions are known to aid blood flow through the muscles, which helps to replenish fuel and remove the waste products of muscle

ROUTE INTERVAL ROUTINE

INDOOR WARM-UP:

Phase 1: ARC traversing (15 to 30 minutes), or three to four warm-up routes
- Rehearse techniques
- Light, active stretching on the wall

Phase 2: Warm-Up Boulder Ladder or one to two routes (15 minutes)
- Begin with "V-easy"
- 1 to 3 problems of each grade up to flash level
- No more than three attempts per problem
- If route climbing, use routes up to flash level

OUTDOOR WARM-UP*:

Phase 1: Outdoor Mileage routes (two to three moderate routes)
- Rehearse techniques
- Light, active stretching on the rock

Phase 2: Outdoor route (15 minutes)
- Climb one more difficult route: either an onsight one to two letter grades below your OS limit, or a well-rehearsed route slightly above your OS limit — such as the interval training route
- Rest 30 to 45 minutes

__ NOTE:__ If performing Route Intervals at the end of an outdoor limit-redpointing day, skip the Phase 1 and Phase 2 warm-up activities and begin with Phase 3: Route Intervals.*

ROUTE INTERVALS:

- **Route Selection:**
  - One letter grade harder than your onsight level
  - Similar to the goal route in terms of length, angle, hold type, etc.
  - Well-rehearsed and can usually be climbed on demand when un-fatigued
- **Pace:** Climb at a pace similar to the goal route, including rests that would normally be used to redpoint the route. Time the lap and record it.
- **Duty Cycle:** 1:2 early in the phase, progressing to 1:1 late in the phase. (For example, begin the PE Phase by resting 16 minutes for an eight-minute set, progressing toward eight minutes' rest for an eight-minute set.)
- **Sets:** Complete two to four laps

COOLDOWN:

ARC traversing (15 to 30 minutes) or Outdoor Mileage (one to two routes)
- Rest 10 to 20 minutes after Intervals before cooldown (stretch and massage forearms)
- Rehearse techniques
- Light, active stretching on the wall

fatigue. Therefore, after a sufficient rest period of 10 to 20 minutes, each PE training session should finish with at least 20 minutes of ARC climbing (30 minutes is even better). Climbing moderate routes is also acceptable, but ensure that the continuous climbing time is at least 20 minutes, and avoid excessive difficulty (it may be necessary to climb back-to-back routes before swapping with the belayer). If excessive skin wear prevents ARCing, consider light upper-body circuit training as a cooldown.

PROGRESSION

Progression in PE training should not consist of performing the circuit more quickly — that would be regression, as the body is asked to perform shorter sets. In other sports, endurance progression would be indicated by performing the effort for a longer duration or at a faster pace, but neither of these make sense for climbing, in which the goal is to climb a fixed number of difficult moves. Therefore, in climbing, given that a specific goal route is being simulated, it is better to fix the duration and number of moves in the set, and progress in one of two ways (or both). The first option, and the easiest to implement, is to climb the same LBC or Route Interval and progressively reduce the rest period between sets. The second option is to progressively increase the difficulty of the moves, still aiming to complete the circuit before fatigue sets in.

A combination of these approaches is ideal. After analyzing the goal route and building a suitable circuit or training route, progression throughout the PE phase should consist of reducing the rest period and/or tweaking the circuit appropriately to increase the difficulty of each subsequent training session. Increase intensity by swapping out larger holds for smaller holds, adjusting rest points, or reordering the sequence of linked boulder problems as previously described.

SKILL DEVELOPMENT

As described in Chapter 3: Skill Development and Chapter 5: Base-Fitness, skill development and endurance training go hand in hand. Just as novel movements were learned during the Base-Fitness Phase, those same moves can be further refined and stress-proofed during the PE Phase. However, it requires deliberate attention to do so. A few specific skill-devel-

opment goals, which can be emphasized throughout the training program, should be set at the beginning of the season. By the time the PE phase is reached, these skills should be mature enough to include in LBCs and Route Intervals. If necessary, design the circuit or route to include opportunities to attempt these novel moves.

While performing PE sets, pay attention to these novel moves, but always keep in mind the other climbing fundamentals: proper breathing, relaxation, grip control, pump management, and precision movement. The nature of this training often compels climbers to "race" through the set, but it is not a race. Climb at a reasonable pace, identical to that used on similar redpoints (use time gates, if necessary). Relax, breathe, *think*, and maintain controlled, precise movement. Do not flail! That massive pump will set in whether you're climbing slow, fast, controlled, or flailing, so climb the right way and make it a habit that will transfer to redpoint attempts — when it really matters.

PE workouts are ideal for stress-proofing novel moves and skills.

Sunday	Monday	Tuesday	Wednesday	Thursday	Friday	Saturday
*WBL 60 min *Linked Bouldering Circ (LBC), DC=2:4	*Skin Care		*WBL 50 min *LBC, Duty Cycle (DC) = 2:3; SE	*Skin Care		*Redpoint (RP) attempts on bouldery routes
*Redpoint (RP) attempts on bouldery routes	*Skin Care		*WBL 50 min *LBC, DC = 2:2 *SE	*Skin Care		*RP Attempts *OM, 2 mod pitches
*RP Attempts *OM, 2 mod pitches	*Skin Care		*WBL 40 min *Intervals, DC = 4:4 *SE	*Skin Care		*RP Attempts on pumpy routes *OM, 2 mod pitches

Key:

ARC – Aerobic Restoration and Capillarity Training	LBC - Linked Bouldering Circuits	SE - Supplemental Exercises
OM – Outdoor Mileage	min - Minutes	DC - Duty Cycle (work-to-rest ratio)
OAE – Optional Aerobic Exercise	mod - Moderate	WBL - Warm-Up Boulder Ladder
	RP - Redpoint	

Sample PE training schedule integrated with outdoor climbing. This schedule assumes that Saturday and Sunday are the typical outdoor climbing days. If "three-day weekends" are possible, this can be modified to add a rest day between the RP days. Note: Duty Cycle (DC) is given in minutes (i.e., 2:4 means about 2 minutes of climbing followed by 4 minutes of rest).

> "The difference between getting to the last move and doing the last move could be a month of training"
> — Jerry Moffat[5]

SCHEDULING

PE training is performed near the end of the macrocycle, beginning immediately following the Power Phase, and continuing through the Performance Phase. Both LBCs and Route Intervals can and should be performed as part of a "healthy diet" of PE training. These are complementary exercises that will benefit different aspects of climbing performance. The importance of PE training exercises in any given season varies greatly, depending on the season's climbing goals. Very bouldery routes with ample rest might not require any PE training at all, while long, sustained routes without distinct cruxes, or with ample rests, may require only Route Intervals but no LBC training. These factors should be considered when scheduling PE training.

The muscles' enzymatic adaptations to PE training occur quite rapidly (within a few days), but they are short-lived, lasting only a few weeks. Therefore, training this way early in a season, well before the Performance Phase, accomplishes little and also interferes with more-beneficial activities. Furthermore, continuing PE training beyond about four weeks will likewise accomplish little. The muscles adapt quickly to this training, to a point, after which further training adds little new capability while extending the subsequent recovery time.

PE training should be started one to two weeks prior to the Performance Phase and continue for up to four weeks, into the Performance Phase. The process of projecting and onsighting goal routes is very similar to PE training, and will have similar training effects, so it is not necessary to perform a large volume of dedicated PE training if regular access to goal routes is possible. In the midst of the Performance Phase, if cragging two days per week, climbers should perform no more than one supplemental PE training session per week. As mentioned earlier, a modest volume of Route Intervals can be performed at the end of performance days at the crag by performing two to three laps on a familiar route or by attempting one or two sub-maximal onsights. Following a PE workout, 48 to 72 hours of rest will be required. An example three-week schedule for a climber incorporating route climbing with PE training is shown at the top of the page.

Projecting goal routes can be very similar to PE training, so allocate a significant portion of your PE Phase training time to outdoor climbing on goal routes. Paul Nelson working *8 Ball*, 5.12d, the Madness Cave, Red River Gorge, KY. Janelle Anderson

Projecting Fitness

The process of working a project route has PE-training benefits, so it's possible to use the projecting process to make endurance gains without any supplemental PE training. However, like any endeavor, the devil is in the details. The typical hangdogging process for learning and rehearsing moves is more akin to bouldering than endurance training, especially at first, when the moves are not yet familiar. However, PE training becomes possible as "linkage" improves. Once you're able to execute the individual moves regularly, try to link multiple moves together. Use the rope or fixed protection to "pull through" stopper moves if necessary. When falls occur, instead of resting, pull back on the wall immediately and continue climbing. Aim to perform a "set" of moves comparable to a LBC in terms of duration and number of moves. Once a set's worth of moves has been climbed, take the appropriate rest, then repeat for the desired number of sets. Used this way, two to three "working burns" can account for six to eight sets of PE training, and a very productive workout in terms of PE training and route rehearsal.

In the winter of 2009, I trained diligently for a trip to Smith Rock, but a month before going I severely sprained my ankle playing basketball (another good reason to limit extraneous cardio). I continued to train on the hangboard, and even did some ARCing, but hard bouldering was out of the question (due to the risk of ground falls), so I was unable to attempt LBC training. I ventured to Smith Rock as planned and set my sights on Rude Boys, one of my dream routes. With no PE training, I was a long shot to send this classic endurance testpiece. I utilized the strategy described above, trying to make long links, and pulling back on quickly after falls in order to cobble together PE "sets." Sure enough, after five of these "training" days spread across a week and a half, I had the endurance to make it through the redpoint crux and send my dream route.

— Mike Anderson

SUMMARY

- A forearm pump is caused by repeated intense contractions that limit blood flow and cause harmful waste to build up.
- PE training causes several enzymatic adaptations that improve the muscles' ability to continue activity beyond the maximum steady state level of effort. Intensity must be high enough to stimulate adaptations in the fast-twitch muscle fibers.
- Adaptations to endurance training are specific, so the training should closely mimic climbing in terms of :
  - Duration
  - Intensity
  - Pace
  - Terrain (hold type, size, wall angle, movements, rests)
- PE training is best performed with Linked Bouldering Circuits (LBC) or Route Intervals, which should be constructed specifically to simulate goal routes and may be designed to lie anywhere on the endurance spectrum.
- As set duration increases, intensity and number of sets performed should decrease. The duty cycle is consistent between PE training exercises, so the longer the set duration, the longer the rest interval.
- Endurance training should progress through a season by increasing the difficulty of moves and/or reducing the rest between sets.
- Skill-development activities should be incorporated into PE workouts.
- PE workouts occur just before and during the Performance Phase, and should be followed by 48 to 72 hours of rest.

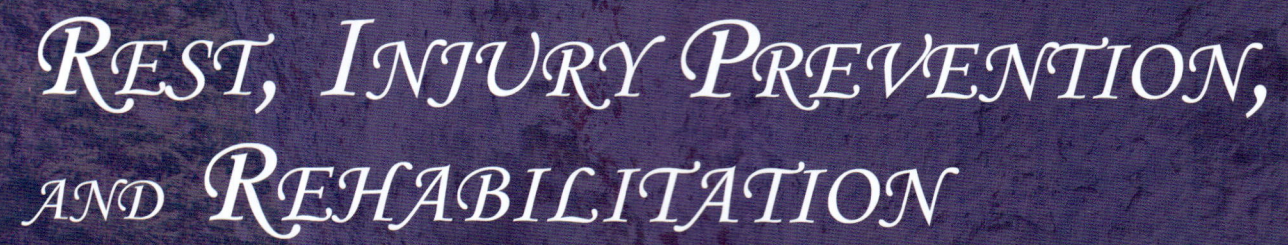

REST, INJURY PREVENTION, AND REHABILITATION

Jonathan Siegrist drinking in the fourth ascent of *Moonshine* 5.14d, Wild Iris, WY.　Mike Anderson

CHAPTER 9

"I think that one of the most important issues in one's training plan is to know when you need to take a rest." — Iker Pou[6]

It's been four months of hard work and self-denial: honing the body, learning new skills, and applying the right strategies and tactics to goal routes. This work has produced some impressive results, and maybe even a new personal best. The new strength and fitness that have been diligently created have boosted confidence and magnified the enjoyment of climbing's many pleasures. After several weeks of riding this performance peak it can be hard to say goodbye to a magical season and start over with the hard work to prepare for the next season. Your newfound level of mastery is well-deserved, and it is tempting to try to milk it for as long as possible. The reality is that doing so simply isn't possible. The body will eventually fall off the peak. Even worse, attempting to extend a performance peak can lead to serious injuries, impacting future climbing seasons.

The final phase of the periodic training program is Rest. This chapter will discuss the importance of rest — within a training phase, during performance, and between seasons — and how to get the most out of prescribed downtime. This is the final piece of the puzzle that will enable each climber to build his or her own custom training plan. Finally, a brief discussion on injury prevention is also presented, and though hopefully it isn't needed, a few words of advice on rehabilitation.

"Rest is very important....Only when I have given my body the right amount of food and rest do I feel authorized to use it to do what I want to do."
— Fred Nicole[7]

REST

REST DAYS

Rest days are critical to the recovery process, facilitating progression as well as successful performance. They provide the body the opportunity to adapt to training stress, thus enabling improvement.

Rest days are not days in which nothing happens. During training, rest days include any days that don't have specific climbing workouts planned, though other supporting activities should take place. The optional Base-Fitness training days that follow intense workouts (during the Strength and PE phases) are also rest days. This program incorporates many rest days because it is focused on *improvement*. Though improvement is stimulated by exercise, that improvement *occurs* while resting. Therefore, climbers using this program may feel like they are resting too much and are thus "not tired enough," but that is not the mark of an effective training program. There are infinite, useless ways to get tired that will do nothing to improve a climber's abilities. If long-term improvement at climbing is the goal, appropriate rest is essential.

First and foremost, a productive rest day should do no further damage. Don't engage in activity that will further tax the muscles being trained, overstress weary joints, or place further wear and tear on the skin (sheltering finger skin is especially critical during the Performance Phase). It is acceptable to perform optional aerobic exercise on rest days, so long as the volume is limited to ensure it does not interfere with sport-specific training.

During the Performance Phase, rest days are those not spent attempting limit routes at the crag, and should be even more restful than rest days during training phases. Avoid long bouts of manual labor, or other taxing activities such as endurance sports. Climbers should try to stay off their feet and out of harsh weather. Light activities, such as a hike to the crag to gawk at routes or belay a friend, are good Performance Phase rest-day activities. Set aside some time for quiet reflection to consider the previous climbing day, visualize the current project, and set short-term goals for the next day (see Chapter 2: Goal Setting and Planning for more details). Finally, perform any rehabilitation tasks such as skin care, stretching, massage, or icing.

Most climbers love being active, especially when visiting the outdoor playgrounds in which the great crags often reside. Climbers naturally want to explore with long hikes, bike rides, and so on, but this can be detrimental to climbing performance. Many sacrifices were made along the way to reach the performance peak, so the focus should be on maximizing climbing performance to the greatest extent possible. That said, it may be difficult to give up "rest-day activities," especially when visiting a new part of the world. Therefore, this tradeoff should be considered early in the seasonal planning process. If non-climbing activities are very important to you, make a decision to include them and accept that climbing performance will be less than maximal. Alternatively, consider scheduling particularly grueling rest-day activities early in the trip, making it possible to rest thoroughly later in the trip, when a redpoint is more likely. Any such tradeoffs should be discussed with traveling companions well in advance to establish expectations and avoid disappointment or potential conflicts.

SLEEP

Sufficient sleep is vital to recovery and athletic performance. Research shows that improving the quantity and quality of sleep directly improves reaction time, power, endurance, cognitive function, technical skills, mood, and qualitative energy levels. Lack of sleep can lead to ineffective recovery, reduced performance, and general feelings of lethargy or poor motivation. Many climbers exacerbate this problem by carrying "sleep debt" for weeks on end, making it very difficult to perform effectively. Adults should attempt to average seven to eight hours of sleep per night; teens and young adults should average nine or more.[1] Several tips for improving sleep include:

- Account for sleep in daily planning
- Minimize sleep debt by getting regular sleep for several weeks prior to important performances
- Go to bed and wake up at regular times
- Attempt to get extra sleep (up to 10 hours per night) during the week leading up to important performances

"Good strong skin is critical."
— Jerry Moffatt[11]

SKIN CARE

Skin care is an essential rest-day activity, demanding attention during both the training and performance phases. Skin on the hands and fingers is the primary interface between the rock and the climber, and many climbing trips (and even entire seasons) have been derailed by skin issues: (toe and heel skin is also subject to abuse from climbing, and may warrant similar attention for some climbers). Acute problems like bloody flappers or splits in the pads can be disastrous to project climbers. Even onsight performance can be hampered by worn-down finger pads that ooze moisture.

Every performance-oriented climber should have a simple skin-care kit. This kit should come along on every trip to the crag or training facility, and should be used regularly (daily during the Performance Phase of the season). At a minimum, this kit should have:

- Two rolls of athletic tape
  - Wide roll for taping wide swaths
  - Roll of narrow strips for finger taping
- Nail clippers
- Neosporin or similar antibacterial ointment
- Band-aids (variety of sizes)
- Tweezers
- Needle
- Cuticle cutters (found in the beauty department)
- Sanding block (found at a hardware store)

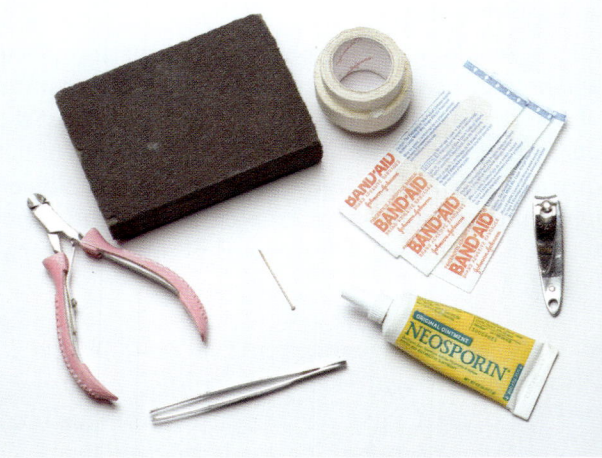

Assemble a Skin Care Kit such as this, and keep it handy when climbing or training.

The best way to manage skin is to keep it healthy. First, prepare the skin for battle well in advance. Ideally, each climber should begin preparing the skin for the upcoming season when she begins her Strength Phase. In these initial stages, cut away any rough areas with cuticle cutters, then sand the finger pads the day after each training session. Keep these tools handy during the workout in the event of an issue. Repeated climbing can cause *calluses* (hard layers of dead skin) to form on the fingers and palms. These can lead to bloody *splits* or *flappers*. Sand calluses down between climbing sessions and apply lotion to prevent these injuries.

Topical skin balms can be applied after each training session. Be cautious during non-climbing activities to avoid unnecessary wear and tear. Get into the habit of using leather gloves for any type of construction, maintenance, or landscaping activity. (Look before you leap: Don't shove your hand into a closed box and hope there aren't open scissors waiting to greet you!) Keep the hands dry in the few hours preceding a workout or crag session; moist skin is soft and more susceptible to damage. Avoid extended hot tub soaks, baths, or showers prior to climbing.

Once on the rock (or at the gym), realize that skin quantity is limited, so use your skin judiciously. Avoid flailing on textured holds. Instead, once the fingers are placed on a hold, don't allow them to slip or slide. Avoid blind dynos; the target hold might have a razor-sharp lip. Carry the narrow-strip tape roll on climbs (clipped to a carabiner) so that tape can be preemptively applied when a threatening hold is discovered. Better to tape in the early stages of working a route, with the option of removing the tape for a committed redpoint attempt, than to forgo taping early and be forced to tape over a bloody flapper when it's time to send. Most acute injuries like lacerations and minor flappers begin as abrasions. Caution is the better part of valor in these cases, so quit early and save some skin for the next climbing day.

Chalk can be a great ally in protecting a climber's skin. Extra chalk should be carried to the crag or gym in the event of a massive spill, and the chalk bag should be inventoried before each roped burn to ensure there is an adequate supply. Thoroughly coat every part of each hand before starting up a climb, and continue to chalk regularly, especially on warm or humid days. Chalk is used as a dry lubricant in gymnastics and weightlifting, so thick layers of chalk can be used to alleviate hot spots: (areas of weakened/abraded skin).

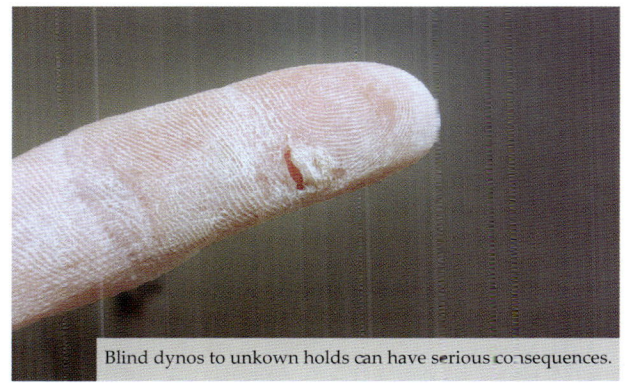
Blind dynos to unkown holds can have serious consequences.

Even with the best preventative measures, skin injuries are inevitable. Any emerging problem areas should be dealt with swiftly. Common climber skin injuries include abrasions, "flappers" (which can be caused by minor lacerations or shear stress), and blisters (including blood blisters and water blisters).

ABRASIONS

Most climbing abrasions are minor and can be left alone to some extent. Serious skin issues are more often caused by repetitively using a single rough hold than by using a particularly sharp hold once. Minor abrasions become problematic when the abuse is continued, resulting in a more serious injury. Tape abraded areas early in a climbing session if the intent is to continue climbing. At the end of the day, clean the affected area, then apply a thin layer of Neosporin. Severe abrasions (those that are oozing blood or other moisture) should be treated immediately with Neosporin, and then covered with a band-aid and several wraps of tape. Depending on the location and effectiveness of taping, it may be possible to continue climbing.

FLAPPERS

Flappers should be taped at the first sign of distress, particularly if you're still on the route. If the "flap" is minor (not oozing blood) and in an area that can't easily be taped, like a finger pad, simply continue to try other moves and save the sharp holds for the next burn. Once on the ground, first use cuticle cutters to remove any flaps of skin that have separated from the underlying layer. If not removed, these flaps can catch on sharp rock protrusions, thus causing further damage to the surviving tissue. If the newly exposed patch of skin is not tender, carefully sand the edges of the top layer of skin until they are flush with the newly exposed layer, to prevent these edges from catching on the rock. Ideally, this should be done without irritating

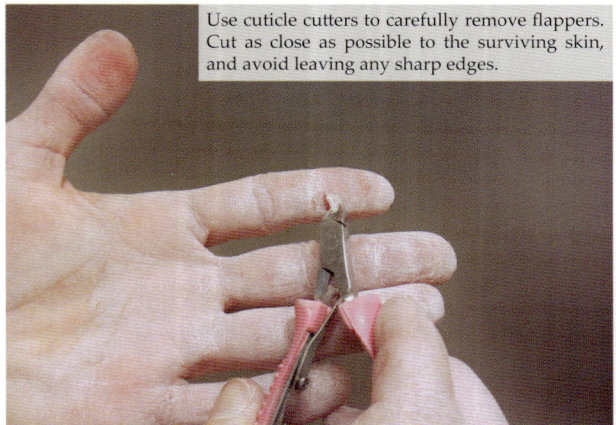

Use cuticle cutters to carefully remove flappers. Cut as close as possible to the surviving skin, and avoid leaving any sharp edges.

the newly exposed skin. If the skin is raw or sensitive, apply Neosporin, a Band Aid of the smallest size that covers the affected area, and then wrap the entire area with tape. If done correctly, it should be possible to continue climbing on all but the ugliest wounds. The affected areas should be washed and sanded every day. Raw skin should be treated with Neosporin and wrapped until it is no longer raw.

Once the flapper is trimmed away, use a sanding block or emery board to smooth the edges of the remaining outer layer of skin.

BLISTERS

Blisters are usually acute and can be slow to heal. A blister is basically a shear stress–caused flapper that hasn't opened up (yet). Eventually, the outer layer of skin will need to be removed, but in most cases the best bet is to keep the skin intact while draining any fluid with a sterilized needle. If a blister occurs mid-route, it may be possible to continue climbing with thorough application of tape. Once on the ground, use a lighter to sterilize a needle, let the needle cool, and then poke a tiny hole in the most distal (closest to the finger tip) end of the blister. The needle should be parallel to the finger when making the insertion. Remove the needle, drain the fluid (it may be necessary to reinsert the needle a few times to remove all fluid), and then re-tape the blistered area. It is often possible

to continue climbing once the blister is treated. Re-drain the blister periodically throughout the session and over the next few days. Eventually, the outer layer of skin will dry up and die. It's generally best to preserve this outer layer for as long as possible, since the underlying layer will be weak and sensitive. Once the blister opens up, treat as for a flapper.

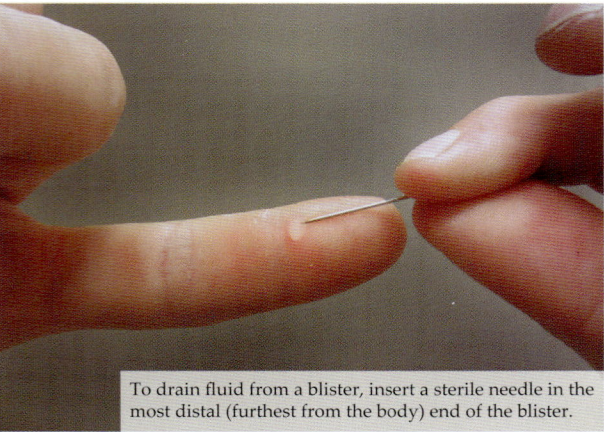

To drain fluid from a blister, insert a sterile needle in the most distal (furthest from the body) end of the blister.

GERMAN FOOSBALL CREAM

The blogosphere is abuzz with whisperings of mystery ointments from distant lands that will transform even the hands of a princess into callused leather baseball mitts overnight. Some of these creams are designed for farm animals, some for industrial applications. The notorious *Anti-hydral* (sold at www.foosball.com) is labeled entirely in German, making it difficult to discern exactly what's in it or its intended use.

In general, these creams do in fact work. Some of them work so well it's scary. Be warned, however: Excessive use of these creams will *cause* far more problems than it prevents, and that is to say nothing of the unknown long-term side effects. Even modest use can dry and toughen the skin to the point of cracking, resulting in a bloody mess that requires weeks to recover from. Even without acute side effects, these creams often create a glassy, smooth surface on the skin that reduces tactile sensitivity to the rock and can make friction grips (like slopers and pinches) more difficult.

I've experimented with these products and my conclusion is that they work, but they are often not worth the risk. Diligent use of a sanding block and cuticle cutters will produce thick, yet still supple skin on the pads without the potentially catastrophic consequences. Plus, your significant other won't recoil at your touch.

— *Mark Anderson*

"You can take it for granted that people will train; it's when and how much they rest that's variable. Too much training is as bad as not enough."
— Jerry Moffatt[11]

The Final Phase

At the conclusion of every performance peak, it is essential to rest briefly before beginning training activities for the next season. This rest period is the final phase in the Rock Prodigy program, and it is just as important as the other phases. The periodic training approach works best when used in its entirety, and the Rest Phase is no different. This Rest Phase should not include any climbing whatsoever, and can be as short as five days or as long as four weeks, but typically two weeks are planned.

Rest plays an important part in physical training by allowing super-compensation to take place after training. This effect is clear for short rest periods following individual workouts, but it also applies to entire seasons. Certain desirable adaptations to training, such as the reinforcement of bone, tendon, and ligaments, occur on much longer time scales than adaptations within the muscles. Therefore, a longer, less frequent rest period is needed to allow those structures to adapt.

Furthermore, the motor processes that are used to control a climber's movement and to develop new skills need rest as well. A brief rest period allows the central nervous system to reinforce the optimal neural networks for controlling movement, and clean up any less efficient commands that are leftover from the skill-acquisition activities. The improvement in skill execution that often accompanies a break from intense practice is known as the *reminiscence effect*, and is a result of this neural "housekeeping" process.

Time away from the all-encompassing pursuit of mastery over the complex sport of climbing also provides an opportunity to gain a new perspective. When mired in the details of daily workouts or cruxes, it is difficult to recognize the bigger picture and identify weaknesses in the larger process. A break from this minutia, especially if engaging in other, unrelated activities, may offer unusual insights about the overall process of climbing improvement that would be impossible to gain otherwise. Finally, resting restocks the motivational stores that are essential to the success of the coming training cycle. Use this time to enjoy other hobbies, spend time with neglected friends or family, or take a vacation to a non-climbing destination.

On the other hand, refusing to rest will lead to diminishing, and eventually evaporating, returns. Performance will stagnate, and then regress. While it is tempting to cling to the last drop of better-than-normal performance that characterizes the waning days of a performance peak, doing so stifles long-term progress. This is because sub-optimal performance days replace what would otherwise be productive improvement time. While performance climbing days are absolutely essential (they are the whole reason for training in the first place), performance days at the crag are not the most effective training for climbing. Performance climbing requires *avoiding* fatigue, thus the physical stimulus is not sufficient to trigger physiological improvements. Performance climbing utilizes well-mastered movements and skills in an urgent situation, thus it does not afford the time, motivation, setting, or novel sequences needed for effective skill development. Experienced climbers know that they get out of shape at the crag, and they get in shape with training — take it from Adam Ondra: *"You don't train while trying a hard route; you need 100 percent rest before every single try, hence you need to rest a lot in general, and within a longer period of time some sort of regress is bound to take place."*[5]

This is especially so for the last days of a Performance Phase when the climber typically makes fewer and fewer attempts on easier and easier routes, with more rest; call it garbage time. Trading effective training days for such garbage time is shortsighted. The climber may get lucky and add one or two more ticks to his list, but it's at the expense of future progress. Recall the discussion of the Time Value of Climbing Ability from Chapter 1: Introduction. That additional 5.1X redpoint is trivial compared to the value of the extra time it takes to achieve it, for as the climber improves, that route becomes easier and easier to "tick." Save it for a future season, and focus near-term efforts on long-term improvement.

The optimal strategy for climbers seeking long-term, lasting progress is to complete as many macrocycles as possible in his or her career. Tacking on four weeks of garbage time at the end of every season adds up to one fewer training cycle per year, and many lost opportunities for improvement. Instead of falling into this trap, be grateful for the season's sends. For those routes that remain undone, accept that prioritizing long-term improvement is the surest way to accomplish them. Move on to the next macro-cycle, make new goals, and hatch a new plan to achieve them.

WHEN TO CALL IT QUITS

It can be hard to decide when to end the Performance Phase, especially for those climbers who are new to periodic training (or any structured training, for that matter). Climbers experienced with periodic training can *feel* when their body is tiring and their performance is declining. They may also rely on past experience and simply terminate the Performance Phase after a given time period (say four weeks), based on the experience of previous seasons that went too long. Making this decision is more difficult for those using a structured training program for the first time. Often, the amount of improvement within the first few seasons of training is so great that even when performance declines, it is still higher than the previous baseline. This tempts the climber to extend the Performance Phase.

The Performance Phase should last at least three weeks (not including the Power-Endurance Phase), and in that time, every effort should be made to reap the benefits of the season's training. There are few long-term downsides to ending the phase too soon, however. Overextending the Performance Phase is much more problematic. To simplify the decision, start with this hard-and-fast rule: *Do not continue climbing beyond a six-week Performance Phase*. In general, the actual performance peak will be shorter than this. While this may seem like a brief payoff for months of hard work, keep in mind that the two-to-four week Power-Endurance Phase includes performance days as well, which provide ample sending opportunities, effectively lengthening the Performance Phase.

Besides temporal limits, physical indicators should be used to establish the end of the Performance Phase. Any serious injury, regardless of when it occurs, should end the season. These include:

- Finger-tendon or ligament tears
- Forearm muscle pulls
- Acute elbow or shoulder injuries
- Chronic upper-body aches or pains lasting more than two weeks
- Major bodily injuries (back, ankles, knees, broken bones, etc.)

When possible, end your season on a high note, such as after achieving a new personal best redpoint or onsight. Kristin Yurdin ready for a well-earned break after redpointing her first 5.14a, *Chemical Ali*, Smith Rock, OR. ☉ Mike Anderson

Tendonitis or tendonosis may or may not be season ending depending on several factors, including the severity of the inflammation, the extent to which it is aggravated by current climbing activities, prevention/rehabilitation actions, and your pain tolerance. A minor injury early in a Performance Phase might be worth climbing through, whereas the same injury near the end of the phase is likely a sign to cease climbing. A more complete discussion of injury prevention and rehabilitation is presented later in this chapter.

Besides injury, a decline in physical performance is a sure sign to end the season, but often such declines are not obvious. If the climber is on the verge of sending a difficult project, his growing familiarity with the moves may mask any decline in physical fitness. Therefore, if continuous steady progress is not being made on the project, it is likely time to move on and return to the project another season. Climbers shouldn't expect to reach a new high point on every go, but if three or more climbing days pass without additional linkage or a new high point, the route is probably unattainable *that season*. Power gradually decreases towards the end of the performance peak, and many experienced climbers use this as their cue to proceed to the Rest Phase. (Be very cautious about attempting "tweaky" or powerful routes after this power decline: Doing so often leads to injury.) Another indication of the end of the performance peak may be the need for longer and longer rest periods. If more than 48 hours of recovery is required between cragging days (which should be relatively low intensity, as explained previously), the peak has ended and so too should the Performance Phase.

Changing motivation or attitude can also warrant ending the season. Trying hard day after day on limit routes can be very mentally demanding, and climbers shouldn't feel ashamed or somehow less than committed if they lose motivation for this over several weeks. A lack of tangible success further exacerbates this problem. In such situations, it is critical to focus on the larger goal of long-term improvement over the career. The climber should embrace the learning opportunities that exist amidst the struggle of a hard project, but not affix his or her self-worth to the ultimate result. Doing so can lead to self-esteem injuries that are every bit as debilitating as physical ones. If necessary, move on to the next season, look forward to improving, and plan to come back another season, stronger and wiser.

REST PHASE ACTIVITIES

The Rest Phase should not be a time for all-out sloth and gluttony. While a break from climbing is necessary, other physical activities should be performed instead, making this a period of *active rest*. During the final phases of the season, non-climbing activities were reduced, so this is the time to pick them back up again. Go cycling, skiing, play tennis, or whatever it is that distracts from climbing and provides moderate exercise.

This is also a time for reflection, goal-setting, and planning. Review the last season and consider these questions:

- Were the goals appropriate (too easy or too hard)?
- Were the goals accomplished? If not, why?
- Were weaknesses improved? If not, why?
- How should the training plan be adjusted to:
  - Improve the chances of accomplishing the goals?
  - Increase the improvement of weaknesses?
- Did the performance peak occur at the right (expected) time?
  - How long did the peak last?
  - Can this timing be predicted, to aid the planning of trips, vacation time, etc. in the future?
- Did the season reveal any previously unknown strengths and/or weaknesses?
- Does the season's improvement warrant re-prioritizing your weaknesses?

Reviewing the previous season should occur simultaneously with planning the next (discussed extensively in Chapter 2: Goal Setting and Planning). Each climber should consider the progress that was made toward his overarching and long-term goals, and decide if any course corrections are required. Determine what the intermediate and short-term goals should be for the next season and build that plan, then get psyched for the next season!

INJURY PREVENTION AND REHABILITATION

Injuries are not a pleasant topic, but given the unusual and extreme loads that we climbers place on our bodies, they are likely to happen at some point in every career. The fingers and forearm muscles are the most susceptible to injury in climbing, and these injuries are also the most debilitating. Therefore, finger injuries (and the behaviors that lead to them) should be avoided at all costs. With restraint and discipline, much can be done to prevent finger injuries from occurring in the first place, and that should be every climber's strategy going-in. When injuries do occur, there are some deliberate approaches that can be used for rehabilitation. For more information on this topic, consult Hochholzer & Schoeffl's *One Move Too Many...*, which is an excellent resource for preventing, diagnosing, and rehabilitating climbing injuries that should be on every climber's bookshelf.[30]

"An ounce of prevention is worth a pound of cure." — Benjamin Franklin

175

PLANNING FOR ADEQUATE REST

The first rule of avoiding injury, which every athlete knows (but struggles to follow), is to ensure adequate rest. A significant advantage of the Rock Prodigy program is that rest is built in. The duty cycle for workouts is relatively conservative, because the overarching goal is long-term improvement over a career. Injuries are devastating to such a goal, so extra rest is built in to reduce the risk of overuse injuries. The onus is on the climber to follow the plan, avoid sneaking in extra workouts (like impromptu bouldering sessions at the gym, etc.), and back off when the body signals that additional rest is required.

TAKING CUES FROM THE BODY

While resting adequately will go a long way toward preventing injury, it is still essential for every climber to constantly assess the health of his or her body. One of the primary benefits of progressive resistance training is that it allows an athlete to push right up to her limit without exceeding it. However, that only works if the athlete pays attention to the body's response and adjusts training volume accordingly. While performing exercises, it is critical to pay close attention to feedback from the body, in order to avoid traumat-

ic or *acute* injuries. Hangboard, Campus Board, and Limit Bouldering exercises are the most likely to cause acute injury. For example, if a particular grip position on the hangboard feels too "tweaky," reduce the load applied, or better yet, skip the remaining reps/sets of that grip and move on. Take note of any such sensations so that the load can be reduced for the following workout.

Overuse injuries tend to develop slowly, so are harder to detect, but they can be just as debilitating as acute injuries. These are a result of the accumulation of repetitive microtraumas that occur over the course of repeated training or climbing. The progressive, near-limit training stimulus that eventually forces adaptation first causes this microtrauma (an important part of the super-compensation process). Overuse injuries can only be avoided if the body is able to heal these microtraumas sufficiently between each workout. This means taking any actions possible to encourage the healing process and allowing enough rest for healing, recovery, and super-compensation to occur. Varying the training stimulus from phase to phase also helps prevent overuse injuries by altering the repetitive stress before microtraumas can accumulate into a full-fledged injury.

Repetitive stress to the finger joints, such as that caused by pocket climbing, crimping, and fingerlocking, can culminate in severe overuse injuries. Sonnie Trotter taking a bite out of Stingray, 5.14a, Joshua Tree.　📷 Andrew Burr

Another good preventative measure is to ensure that your training tools are ergonomic. Such tools should align with the body's natural geometry. Any tool that forces the body into an awkward position, places torsional stress on a joint, or otherwise feels orthopedically uncomfortable should be banished. Hangboards are notorious for their poor ergonomics, forcing fingers into contorted positions or placing unnecessary strain on the shoulders. Climbers come in different sizes, while training tools often do not. Select properly sized tools, or make adjustments as needed. A small amount of effort up front preparing ergonomic training tools can save huge amounts of effort on rehabilitation.

If detected early enough and acted upon, overuse injuries can often be sufficiently managed such that the climber can continue training and climbing through the injury. Therefore, every climber should be highly motivated to listen to cues from the body and take action when any hint of injury develops. Specifically, climbers should watch for:

- Stiff/achy joints
- Swollen joints
- Acute pain in any climbing-specific joint (whether caused by climbing or not)
- Reduced joint flexibility/range of motion
- Unusual lumps or protrusions
- Intermittent twinges
- Tingling sensations in fingers, arms, elbows, or shoulders

Only YOU Can Prevent Repetitive Stress Injuries

Climbers often see chronic injuries approaching from a long way off. Yet they watch, transfixed as though observing a slow-motion train wreck, as their elbows/shoulders/fingers get worse and worse, failing to take any meaningful action. Our passion for climbing is so great that we can't accurately judge the obvious trade-off between a few weeks of preventative rest today in place of several months of rehabilitation down the road. Detecting oncoming injuries is less than half the battle; wisdom and action are necessary to make use of that foresight. Adjust training or climbing behavior at the first sign of distress, when small adjustments can pay huge dividends. Once the nagging ache has blossomed into a full-blown debilitating injury, far more effort (and time) will be required to correct the problem.

Climbers should not routinely take anti-inflammatory or pain-relief medications, because they mask these symptoms, allowing minor injuries to develop undetected into major injuries (in fact, research shows "Non-Steroidal Anti Inflammatory Drugs" (NSAIDs) actually hamper soft-tissue healing!).[1] If any of these symptoms arise, follow the measures suggested in the "Injury Prevention" and "Rehabilitation" sections that follow. If these do not control the injury, increase the rest intervals between workouts and see a doctor.

"Anybody can get strong. The trick is to get strong and not get injured!"
— *Wolfgang Gullich*[16]

Injury Prevention

Besides using a progressive training approach with adequate recovery, preventive maintenance is the next best way to avoid injury. There are several ways to encourage the healing of microtrauma between workouts. These include:

- Eliminating inactive joint stress
- Stretching
- Massage
- Icing
- Preventive bracing/taping

Inactive joint stress occurs when arms, legs, and/or fingers are placed in stressful orientations when not being used. Typically, this involves bending joints unnecessarily, to the limit of their natural range of motion, and maintaining the position for lengthy periods. Some examples of this include:

Elbows and wrists: Sleeping on top of bent arms (as in the fetal position) places unnecessary stress on the elbows (a common injury site for climbers). A climber dealing with *climber's elbow* could reduce this unnecessary stress by sleeping flat on his back with arms straight at his sides.

Back: Poor posture, especially while seated for long periods (while driving, watching TV, or at the office), can be harmful for the back muscles and spinal column. Sit up straight!

Fingers: Avoid clenching the fingers in a fist for long periods (sleeping especially), or other twisting motions.

Knees: Avoid squatting on bent knees, crossing the legs, or curling the feet under the chair when seated, which stresses the knee ligaments.

Shoulders: Sleeping on either side places substantial strain on the rotator cuff of the bottom shoulder and should be avoided. This is a common problem among big-wall climbers, who like to spoon on portaledges.

Many of the injuries that can be attributed to "muscle/strength imbalance," such as *lateral* and *medial epicondylitis* (climber's elbow), may actually be a result of a general lack of muscle flexibility, or

an *imbalance* of flexibility. A tight, inflexible muscle places constant stress on the points where the muscle's tendon attaches to the bone. Though these attachments are capable of withstanding tremendous loads, they are not intended to be loaded around the clock. A forearm muscle that is tight as a bowstring is constantly tugging on these attachment points, af-

fording little or no rest to the weary tendon. Simply stretching the forearm flexors *and extensors* regularly, and after training, can loosen these muscles and relieve this constant stress. Some useful stretches for climbers are shown in the Figures below. Stretch the joint up to a slight feeling of discomfort, or tightness, but not pain. Stretches should last 30 to 60 seconds.

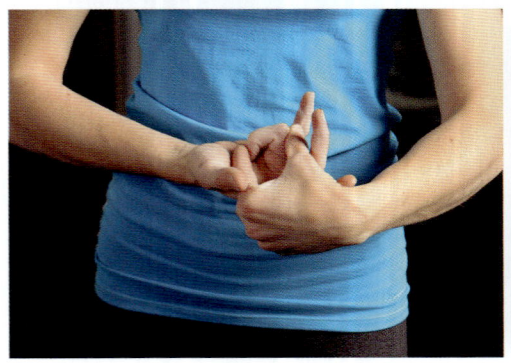
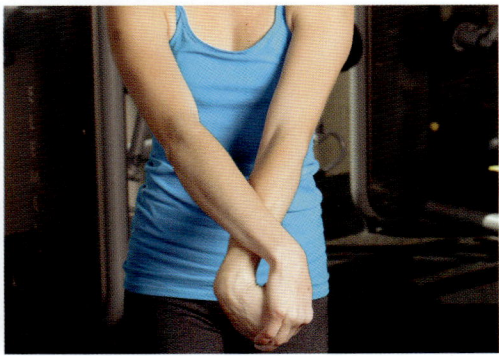

The forearm stretches illustrated here can help prevent elbow inflammation.

How to Beat Climber's Elbow

Climber's elbow (which includes both *medial* and *lateral epicondylitis*) is a very common overuse injury that can result from many climbing activities. It is rarely the result of an acute trauma; instead it usually develops gradually, making it hard to identify the root cause. If not corrected immediately, climber's elbow can develop into a debilitating *chronic* injury (consistent pain lasting more than three months). Chronic injuries require much more intensive rehabilitation and should be avoided. Treatment of such chronic injuries often includes re-creating a controlled inflammation sufficient to trigger the body's internal healing process. It is much easier to identify and treat these injuries at their first sign.

In some cases, these injuries are caused by a flexibility imbalance that results from neglect of the forearm muscles and elbows; in particular, most climbers simply don't know how to stretch their finger extensors, or even that they need to. I suffered from these nagging injuries for many years, but in 2006 I instituted a regime of stretching, massage, and icing that completely eliminated this injury. Occasionally I'll have a flare-up when I get lax with my stretching routine, but it's easily corrected with more diligence. Here's what I do to control the effects of climbing stress on my elbows:

Stretch: Stretch the forearm flexors and extensors thoroughly every day (whether I climbed or not, but especially after climbing workouts). See the Figure on the previous page for recommended stretches, which should include individually stretching each finger's flexor and extensor muscle.

Massage: Massage the forearm flexors and extensors frequently to keep them loose. Simply press into the muscles with the thumb and/or forefingers, and "kneed" the muscles. This can be done while watching TV, hiking to the crag, or meeting in the board room.

Ice: Ice the elbows by submerging the entire forearm in an ice-water bath for 10 minutes after any hard workout. Icing should be done last, after cooling down, stretching, etc. (generally one hour or more after exercising).

— *Mike Anderson*

Icing is a tried-and-true method for reducing inflamation after injuries, but it also aids in recovery from the micro-trauma of everyday training.

Massage plays a role in injury prevention similar to stretching, and generally is used to increase muscle flexibility and thus reduce stress on the tendon's attachment points. However, in addition to this, massage promotes blood flow to the affected muscles, delivering nutrients and removing waste products, thus improving muscular recovery between training or climbing days. While all muscles of the body will benefit from massage, climbers should make a point to massage the forearm flexors and extensors for 10 to 20 minutes within a few hours after any training session or climbing day. This massage should be repeated on rest days as well. In addition, very light massage of the fingers themselves can help promote blood flow to the finger joints (ligaments and tendons), which ordinarily receive very little blood flow. Many climbers find it beneficial to massage their forearms between climbing attempts at the crag, which seems to encourage short-term recovery between burns.

The three previously listed steps for injury prevention —eliminating inactive joint stress, stretching, and massage — all relate to eliminating unnecessary stress on the joints. Icing seeks to prevent injury by encouraging healing between climbing or training events. As Hochholzer & Schoeffl point out in *One Move Too Many...*, "invented over 4 billion years ago, this frozen combination of hydrogen and oxygen atoms has not yet been improved upon."[20] Though the chemical composition is irrelevant (the temperature is the key), they make a good point. Simply cooling an ailing joint does far more for rehabilitation than any manmade cure. Icing reduces swelling and temporarily restricts blood flow, which is beneficial for acute injuries. On the other hand, when the cold is removed, blood flow increases (called *reactive hyperemia*), which is especially beneficial for fingers, which suffer from lower-than-average blood flow, and for flushing tired forearms after a long day of pumpy climbing.

The virtues of icing after injury are well-known, but the scientific community is undecided on its effectiveness for general recovery from training.[2, 4, 15, 17] Nevertheless, many athletes swear by it, and anecdotal evidence supports its use, especially after very pumpy climbing. Icing can be done after every limit climbing day or intense climbing workout. The best method is to submerge your entire forearm in an ice bath (a tub of water filled with ice), from your fingers up to, and including, your elbow. Try to leave the fingertips out of the water to prevent frostbite and any softening of the fingertip pads. Ice each arm for 10 minutes, and then elevate each arm for another five to 10 minutes. Only ice well-after completing a workout, after performing the appropriate cooldown or supplemental exercises, and after stretching and massage. Stretching a muscle immediately after icing can cause injury! A good rule of thumb is to wait at least one hour following an intense workout (not including the cooldown) before icing.

Finally, some acute and overuse injuries can be avoided with preventive taping before training or climbing.[12] Tape is generally applied to the fingers to support the *pulleys*, which are ligaments that hold the flexor tendons in place and allow joint movement. These are often injured by overloading while in a crimp grip. The photo below shows a common method for supporting the A2 and A3 pulleys with tape. Tape must be very tight to be effective, and should be replaced between every burn, because it stretches. In general, taping should be avoided during training so that the finger ligaments are subjected to stress in a controlled setting (unless dealing with an existing injury). This allows the support structure of the fingers to strengthen, reducing the likelihood of injury in the future. On the other hand, it is not a bad idea to tape up for activities that will place an unknown and uncontrolled load on the fingers, such as dynamic, powerful bouldering at a new area, or the first few attempts on a difficult project.

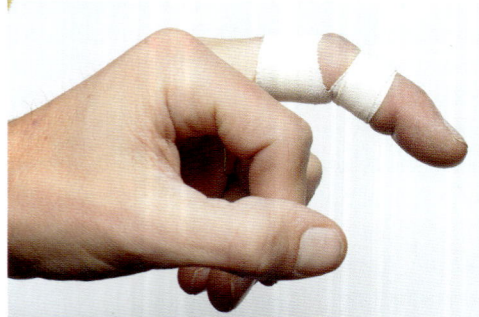

H-Taping has been shown to reduce crimping stress on the A2 and A3 pulleys. Tape must be tight and replaced regularly to be effective.

> "Going through the moves with confidence is difficult because you're just not sure when it's going to be too much. You don't know exactly what your fingers can take, and when you go too far, it's really bad." — BJ Tilden[8]

REHABILITATION

As discussed in the accompanying sidebar, "When to See a Doctor," the vast majority of climbing injuries are best treated with diligent *rehabilitation*.[13, 14] Rehabilitation (also known as physical therapy) is a process of restoring damaged tissue through methodical and controlled application of stress. If this sounds similar to progressive overload, that's because it is. The primary difference is that the loads involved must be vastly reduced during the initial stages of rehab. Furthermore, a rehabilitating athlete may require more rest than a typical healthy athlete in training. Rehab is typically not fun, but it is an extremely powerful method of injury treatment.

For climbers who train, rehab becomes a relatively simple matter. The tools and methods used for improving strength in healthy joints can be easily applied to injured joints. Of course, *this only works if the resistance applied is drastically reduced!* This is critically important and bears repeating. Initially, the resistance may be so low that assistance (from a partner

Shouldering the Burden

Shoulders are also susceptible to chronic injury caused by an imbalance of flexibility, poor posture, and poor technique when reaching. To avoid such injuries, stretch the pectoral muscles, stand up straight, and avoid the hunched-over, caved-in posture typical of many muscle-bound climbers. As noted earlier, avoid sleeping awkwardly or otherwise unnecessarily stressing the shoulders. In severe cases, a physical therapist ("PT") can help restore correct posture and joint motion. A PT will be able to prescribe numerous preventative maintenance exercises for the shoulders that use very low intensities while traversing the joints' range of motion. The supplemental exercises listed for shoulders in Chapter 6: Strength can also be used as a starting point to develop injury-resistant shoulders — just be sure not to push too hard. If experiencing nagging night pain in one or both shoulders, see a PT, as this is a symptom of a torn rotator cuff.

When to See a Doctor

Taking a climbing injury to a doctor can be a lot like taking a faulty iPad™ to a plumber. Most doctors simply have no experience with such injuries. It's not that doctors are *bad* per se; it's just that general practitioners are not trained to treat sports injuries. While an orthopedist (a doctor specializing in injuries to the skeletal-muscular system) may help diagnose them, sports injuries require rehabilitation to treat, and for that, you need a sports physical therapist. Doctors are trained to do one of two things: prescribe drugs and perform surgery. If you think one of those approaches will help you, a doctor might be just the right person to visit (note: those interventions are rarely helpful!).[13, 14]

There are many skilled, caring doctors who can help with invasive treatments. If you do decide to visit a doctor, see a specialist who focuses on your area of injury (for example, see a hand specialist for finger injuries, but keep in mind, a hand *surgeon* may be more biased toward performing *surgery*). Seek referrals from other climbers when possible. Arm yourself with information and be prepared to coach your doctor about climbing, the stresses involved, potential diagnoses, and recommended treatments. Bring a copy of Hochholzer & Schoeffl's *One Move Too Many...* and use it as a visual aid.[10] It's up to you to make the visit valuable.

One good reason to see a doctor for a typical climbing injury is that doctors have access to diagnostic tools like ultrasound, x-rays, and MRIs. If you have a nagging injury, and rehab is going slow, you might consider seeing a doctor in order to use one of these tools. Keep in mind, however, that the treatment is unlikely to change much, regardless of the diagnostic results. The primary value of the diagnosis is to rule out surgery. Another treatment doctors can offer is *cortisone*. Cortisone is a steroidal drug that can be injected into inflamed tissue (such as climber's elbows) to reduce inflammation and numb pain. While it is proven to reduce pain in the short term, recent research suggests it has no long-term benefits and may even be harmful, weakening connective tissue (if considering a cortisone injection, be sure to discuss these findings with your practitioner).[3]

At the end of the day, rehabilitation is the solution to the vast majority of climbing injuries.[13, 14] As such, the logical course of action is to start with rest and rehabilitation, then visit a doctor only if several weeks of these measures fail to produce results. In the case of severe acute trauma, where you feel surgery might be necessary, see a doctor immediately, but come prepared and take charge of your diagnosis and treatment.

or healthy limb) is required just to perform weightless range-of-motion (ROM) exercises. Climbers must listen to their bodies to determine how much resistance to use, and when or how much to increase that resistance. During rehab, the consequences of using too much resistance are much greater, so caution and patience are vital.

When rehabilitating chronic overuse injuries, it's important NOT to use NSAIDs like Ibuprofen or aspirin. First off, very high doses are required to achieve any anti-inflammatory effect (around 800mg every four hours). Second, these drugs interfere with the body's natural response to inflammation, hampering recovery.

STAGES OF INJURY REHABILITATION

Nearly all injuries will follow the same basic rehabilitation approach. Even in extreme cases requiring surgery or other invasive treatments, rehab is vital to complete recovery. The training tools and methods used may vary depending on the site and type of injury, but the following general stages of rehab apply to the vast majority of climbing injuries:

1. **Rest:** The purpose of this stage is to eliminate the source of the injury, reduce swelling, and allow any initial pain to subside before transitioning to more active recovery measures. Ice the injured area several times per day for the first three days following injury and also avoid heat; then, continue to ice after each rehab training session. Take advantage of any downtime by analyzing the events that led to the injury in order to avoid repeating any mistakes you made. Consider that acute injuries are often the result of several weeks or months of repetitive abuse. Finally, it's important to realize that little healing occurs during the rest stages. Many climbers rest too long after injury, then after many weeks of inactivity they are surprised to discover no improvement when they return to activity. Injured tissue requires frequent stimulation to promote healing, which can be as simple as pain-free stretching and range-of-motion exercises (more to follow). Rest periods can be as short as one week, but generally not more than four.

2. Alternative Training: The purpose of this stage is to find a productive use for the climber's time and energy that contributes to his long-term goals. A climber with an ankle injury might hangboard to improve finger strength, while a climber with inflamed elbows might toprope technical slabs to improve footwork. This type of training can be quite motivating. Even though one aspect of fitness has regressed, other aspects can be improving, suggesting that once recovered, the climber will be that much better than he was before the injury. Depending on the injury, this stage can begin concurrently with the rest stage and should continue until the climber is healthy enough to resume normal training activities.

3. Range-of-Motion (ROM) Exercises: Once the initial pain of injury has subsided, begin moving the joint within the available pain-free range of motion. In addition to restoring flexibility, these exercises will improve blood flow and stimulate recovery. Start by warming the injured joint (preferably through light exercise, but heating pads or warm water work too). Begin by exercising the joint within the comfortable range, gradually increasing the ROM as the joint warms up. Include some very light stretching once the joint is completely warm. It can take many weeks or even months to completely restore ROM, since any residual swelling will inhibit joint movement.

As more aggressive rehab activities are added, swelling may return, further hampering ROM. Be patient and continue using ROM exercises throughout the entire rehab process.

4. Progressive Rehab: Once major swelling has subsided and basic ROM is restored, it's time to accelerate the recovery process. Progressive rehab begins by performing the basic sport-specific functions of the joint with extremely low resistance (for example, no weight other than that of the limb may be an appropriate starting point). Perform progressive rehab just as you would perform progressive overload training, but consider performing more repetitions of each exercise. Push the injured area just beyond the comfort zone, then rest for several days to allow the tissue to recover, and repeat. The primary differences are that rehab resistance should be vastly lower than training resistance, and rest periods between rehab sessions should be greater (begin by taking three full rest days between rehab activities, then adjust based on the body's response). Pay close attention to the body's response to rehab and make adjustments as needed. Just as with progressive training, eventually the body may stop responding to progressive rehab. In these cases, a periodic approach may work. If sufficient recovery has occurred to permit safe climbing, consider a few weeks of mod-

Keep Fingers Looking Good

There are many ways to injure a finger in climbing, but A2 pulley strains and collateral-ligament strains are the most common. I've suffered both on numerous occasions. In 2012, I severely strained the A2 pulley in my left ring finger while working an open project at Shelf Road. This injury was a long time coming — the culmination of several years of intermittent tendonitis. This was the worst finger injury of my career, and at times I seriously doubted I would ever recover completely, writing in my journal: "*I think I really hurt my A2 pulley pretty badly. It's hard to imagine bearing down on a crimp any time in the near future. At this age, you can't help but wonder which injury will end your career. What makes me hopeful is that I've been in this position many times, and it always seems hopeless in the moment, yet I've always managed to come back stronger than ever.*"

I began my rehab with two weeks of complete rest, followed by a four-week course of conservative, progressive hangboarding. I began with extremely low weight (half my normal starting load) and took an extra rest day each week. At the end of this stage, my strength had improved considerably but I was nowhere near cured. I took three weeks off, then completed another four-week course of hangboard rehab. At the end of this regimen, the hangboard results indicated that my injured finger was at about 80 percent of its previous strength, so I spent the following month climbing moderates before beginning a third round of hangboard rehab. By the end of the third course, I had set new personal bests on the hangboard and was climbing as well as ever. The entire rehab process took six months, including several setbacks, and plenty of hard work. Still, it was well worth the effort: I am now 100 percent pain free, and considerably stronger than I was when the injury occurred. In February 2013, I returned to Shelf to complete the first ascent of Flight of the Phoenix, the route that pushed my finger past the brink.

— *Mark Anderson*

erate climbing before returning to more deliberate progressive rehab. Severe injuries can require three or more iterations of progressive rehab spanning several months of intensive work.

5. **Progressive Training:** The final stage of rehab is to return to normal training activities, albeit at a reduced volume initially. Again, additional rest may be required between training sessions, and you should expect some mild swelling to return following intense workouts. Continue to ice the injured area after training, and complete ROM exercises regularly. This stage will culminate in a return to climbing. Consider the circumstances that initially led to injury and strive to correct them going forward.

PSYCHOLOGICAL CONSEQUENCES OF INJURY

Injuries can feel overwhelming and highly demoralizing at the onset. In extreme cases, climbers end a salvageable career simply because the rehab process is too overwhelming. Therefore, a positive mental attitude and faith in the recovery process are essential to effective rehabilitation. It will require a great deal of time, hard work, and may involve a setback or two, but with perseverance, complete recovery is usually possible. Once injured, many athletes who diligently rehab come back to their sport even stronger than before. Use the rehab period as a time to re-focus on other physical weaknesses or improve movement skills.

While no climber would opt for a lengthy rehab, it's not all bad. Rehab can provide a good opportunity to explore other interests. Find something to put energy into that will distract from the disappointment of not climbing. Use these activities to replenish motivation, and then apply that energy to rehab.

Patience is critical to the rehab process; realize that rehab will take time and hard work. Expecting quick results often causes climbers to progress too quickly, risking relapse and a longer rehab period. Remain cognizant of long-term climbing goals; these can be powerful motivators when facing the long road to recovery. In the long run, the best way to overcome injury is to strive for 100 percent recovery and to achieve that state as quickly as possible. This may seem painfully obvious, but few climbers pursue this aim. The goal of achieving 100 percent recovery means a climber should not accept limping through life with a nagging injury that is constantly holding him or her back (or repeatedly relapsing). The best way to achieve recovery as quickly as possible is through conservative, steady (and therefore patient) progress. Pushing slightly too hard usually results in a setback that costs the climber many weeks of additional recovery and rehab. Go slow, consider the long view, and don't quit until complete recovery is achieved.

SUMMARY

- Resting is the final phase of the Rock Prodigy periodic training program. Intermittent rest days are also critical within the training and performance phases.
- Rest days are essential to allow recovery and super-compensation to take place during the progressive training process. There are numerous supporting activities that should be performed on rest days including skin care, supplemental exercises, preventative maintenance exercises, skill practice, and planning.
- Skin is the climber's connection to the rock, and caring for it is critical. The best way to avoid skin injuries is to prepare the skin for climbing in advance, and to use your skin judiciously.
- The Rest Phase is necessary for continued long-term improvement. The decision of when to start the Rest Phase should be based on past training data, signs of injury, or declining performance. Never climb beyond a six-week Performance Phase.
- It is much easier to prevent climbing injuries than it is to recover from them. Rest, preventative maintenance exercises, and monitoring the body's response to training and climbing are the best ways to avoid injuries.
- Injury rehabilitation follows a process similar to progressive training but uses exercises of a much lower intensity, with more repetitions and more rest. Mental toughness and perseverance are needed to see things through, but complete recovery is nearly always possible.

BUILDING A SEASONAL TRAINING PLAN AND OTHER TRAINING CONSIDERATIONS

Peter Vintoniv cruxing out on *Anabolica*, 8a (5.13b), Siurana, Spain.　　Andrew Burr

CHAPTER 10

The previous chapters explained in detail how to execute each phase of the Rock Prodigy training program, presenting a selection of effective training routines that each climber can use to propel his or her climbing performance to new heights. The last step is to synthesize that information into a practical, easy to follow, day-to-day training plan. This training plan will describe specifically which training routines to perform on each day of the season, from day one of the Base-Fitness Phase, through the last day of the Rest Phase. A well-conceived schedule will guide the climber through each phase of the training cycle, maximizing improvement opportunities, while ensuring sufficient recovery to optimize progression and reduce the risk of injury. Finally, a detailed Seasonal Training Plan can provide tremendous encouragement when motivation is lacking. Think of this plan as a coach, unphased by the discomfort of daily training efforts, and stubbornly demanding maximum commitment from the athlete.

Ideally, an individualized Seasonal Training Plan should be sculpted to fit the specific needs of each climber. This chapter presents a variety of sample Seasonal Training Plans, along with tips for personalizing them. Select the sample plan that best applies to you, examine it closely, and then make initial adjustments to tailor it to your goals and desires. After using this prototype plan for a season, make further adjustments as experience dictates and as your strengths, weakness, and goals change. Continue iteratively adjusting this plan from season to season, experimenting with different training volume, recovery periods, phase lengths, and phase timing to develop the optimal personal-training program.

Finally, this chapter briefly discusses a variety of alternative training approaches, including the pros and cons of each method. This information can be used to evaluate their suitability, and identify situations in which these approaches may be warranted.

BUILDING A SEASONAL TRAINING PLAN

Chapter 2: Goal Setting and Planning discussed the planning process in broad terms. Now with a comprehensive understanding of the purpose, theory, and application of each training phase, it's time to synthesize this information into a practical, individualized macrocycle. Seasonal Training Plans should vary from climber to climber, based on physical traits, strengths and weaknesses, and training experience. Furthermore, even for a single climber, the macro-cycle should vary from season to season as the climber progresses, and in accordance with the climber's season-specific goals. A macro-cycle geared toward a bouldering project will look much different than one aimed at free-climbing El Cap.

The following discussion will present two example macro-cycles, tailored to climbers of different experience levels, then explore various tradeoffs to consider when adapting such plans to one's own abilities, experience, and goals. The plans presented below are far more detailed than the conceptual plan presented in the Figure on p39. Such detail is not always necessary, but it can be extremely helpful, espe-

Week	Sunday	Monday	Tuesday	Wednesday	Thursday	Friday	Saturday
-	Last Week of Performance Phase of Previous Season						
-	Rest Phase of Previous Season						
-							Sa Day 1 *Outdoor Mileage (OM), 6 mod pitches *Skill acquisition

Base Fitness Phase

Week	Sunday	Monday	Tuesday	Wednesday	Thursday	Friday	Saturday
1	Su Day 2 *OM, 4 mod pitches *Skill acquisition	Mo 3 *Optional Aerobic Exercise (OAE)	Tu 4 *ARC 1: 2 x 20 min *Skill acquisition	We 5 *OAE	Th 6 *ARC 2: 2 x 25 min *Skill acquisition	Fr 7 *OAE	Sa 8 *OM, 7 mod pitches *Skill acquisition
2	Su 9 *OM, 5 mod pitches *Skill acquisition	Mo 10 *OAE	Tu 11 *ARC 3: 2 x 30 min *Skill practice	We 12 *OAE	Th 13 *ARC 4: 2 x 30 min *Skill practice	Fr 14 *OAE	Sa 15 *OM, 8 mod pitches *Skill practice
3	Su 16 *OM, 6 mod pitches *Skill practice	Mo 17 *OAE	Tu 18 *ARC 5: 3 x 25 min *Skill practice	We 19 *ARC 6: 3 x 25 min *Skill practice	Th 20 *ARC 7: 2 x 25 min *Stress-proofing	Fr 21 *OAE	Sa 22 *OM, 10 mod pitches *Stress-proofing
4	Su 23 *OM, 8 mod pitches *Stress-proofing	Mo 24 *OAE	Tu 25 *ARC 8: 3 x 30 min *Stress-proofing	We 26 *ARC 9: 3 x 30 min *Stress-proofing	Th 27 *ARC 10: 2 x 30m *Stress-proofing	Fr 28 *OAE	Sa 29 *Hangboard (HB) 1 *Supplemental Ex

Strength Phase

Week	Sunday	Monday	Tuesday	Wednesday	Thursday	Friday	Saturday
5	Su 30 *Optional OM, 4p *OAE *Skin care	Mo 31 *OAE	Tu 32 *HB 2 *SE	We 33 *Opt ARC: 2x20 min *OAE *Skin care	Th 34 *OAE	Fr 35 *HB3 *SE	Sa 36 *Optional OM, 4p *OAE *Skin care
6	Su 37 *OAE	Mo 38 *HB 4 *SE	Tu 39 *Opt ARC: 2x20 min *OAE *Skin care	We 40 *OAE	Th 41 *HB5 *SE	Fr 42 *Opt ARC: 2x20 min *OAE *Skin care	Sa 43 *OAE
7	Su 44 *HB6 *SE	Mo 45 *Opt ARC 1 x 30min (Begin Tapering) *Skin care	Tu 46	We 47 *HB7 *SE	Th 48 *Skin care	Fr 49	Sa 50 * Warmup Boulder Ladder (WBL) 60m * Campus 15 min

Power Phase

Week	Sunday	Monday	Tuesday	Wednesday	Thursday	Friday	Saturday
8	Su 51 *Skin Care	Mo 52	Tu 53 *Limit Boulder (LB) 90 min *SE	We 54 *Skin Care	Th 55 * WBL 60 min * Campus 20 min * SE	Fr 56 *Skin Care	Sa 57 *(Optional LB Outdoors)
9	Su 58 *LB Outdoors	Mo 59 *Skin Care	Tu 60 *WBL 60 min *Campus 25 min *SE	We 61 *Skin Care	Th 62	Fr 63 *LB 90 min *SE	Sa 64 *Skin Care

Power Endurance

Week	Sunday	Monday	Tuesday	Wednesday	Thursday	Friday	Saturday
10	*WBL 60 min *Linked Bouldering Circ (LBC), DC=2:4	*Skin Care		*WBL 50 min *LBC, Duty Cycle (DC) = 2:3; SE	*Skin Care		*Redpoint (RP) attempts on bouldery routes
11	Su 72 *Redpoint (RP) attempts on bouldery routes	Mo 73 *Skin Care	Tu 74	We 75 *WBL 50 min *LBC, DC = 2:2 *SE	Th 76 *Skin Care	Fr 77	Sa 78 *RP Attempts *OM, 2 mod pitches
12	Su 79 *RP Attempts *OM, 2 mod pitches	Mo 80 *Skin Care	Tu 81	We 82 *WBL 40 min *Intervals, DC = 4:4 *SE	Th 83 *Skin Care	Fr 84	Sa 85 *RP Attempts on pumpy routes *OM, 2 mod pitches

Performance Phase

Week	Sunday	Monday	Tuesday	Wednesday	Thursday	Friday	Saturday
13	Su 86 *RP Attempts (pumpy rtes) *OM, 2 mod pitches	Mo 87 *Skin Care	Tu 88	We 89 *WBL 40 min *Intervals, DC = 4:3 *SE	Th 90 *Skin Care	Fr 91	Sa 92 *RP Attempts (pumpy routes) *OM, 2 mod pitches
14	Su 93 *RP/On Sight (OS) Attempts *OM, 2 mod pitches	Mo 94 *Skin Care	Tu 95 *RP Attempts (pumpy routes) *OM, 2 mod pitches	We 96 *RP/On Sight (OS) Attempts *OM, 2 mod pitches	Th 97 *Skin Care	Fr 98 *RP/On Sight (OS) Attempts *OM, 2 mod pitches	Sa 99 *Skin Care
15	Su 100 *RP/OS Attempts *OM, 2 mod pitches	Mo 101 *Skin Care	Tu 102	We 103 *WBL 45 min	Th 104 *Skin Care	Fr 105	Sa 106 *RP/OS Attempts *OM, 2 mod pitches

Rest Phase

Week	Sunday	Monday	Tuesday	Wednesday	Thursday	Friday	Saturday
16	Su 107 *RP/OS Attempts *OM, 2 mod pitches	Mo 108	Tu 109 *OAE and/or Optional Cross-Training (OCT)	We 110	Th 111 *OAE and/or OCT	Fr 112	Sa 113 *OAE and/or OCT
17	Su 114	Mo 115 *OAE and/or OCT	Tu 116	We 117 *OAE and/or OCT	Th 118	Fr 119 *OAE and/or OCT	Sa 1 First Day of Next Season

Seasonal Training Plan for Novice Trainee *focused on sport climbing. This example is tailored toward climbers with little training experience, climbing below the 5.12 level. It emphasizes the Skill Development-rich phases of Base-Fitness, Power-Endurance, and Performance, while minimizing the Strength and Power phases, since novice trainees experience significant improvement in these areas with minimal training volume. Optional ARC workouts are prescribed throughout the Strength Phase to further promote Skill Development. This schedule offers more opportunities for outdoor climbing than the advanced schedules. The activities for each day should be performed in the order they are listed. The day's primary activity is underlined. Note that this schedule includes a weeklong climbing vacation during Week 14.*

Week	Sunday	Monday	Tuesday	Wednesday	Thursday	Friday	Saturday
-	Last Week of Performance Phase of Previous Season						
-		Rest Phase of Previous Season					
-							Sa Day 1 *Outdoor Mileage (OM) [illegible] mod pitches *Skill acquisition
1	Su Day 2 *OM, 6 mod pitches *Skill acquisition	Mo 3 *Optional Aerobic Exercise (OAE)	Tu 4 *ARC 1: 2 x 30 min *Skill acquisition	We 5 *OAE	Th 6 *ARC 2: 2 x 35 min *Skill practice	Fr 7 *OAE	Sa 8 *OM, 10 mod pitches *Skill practice
2	Su 9 *OM, 8 mod pitches *Skill practice	Mo 10 *OAE	Tu 11 *ARC 3: 3 x 30 min *Stress-proofing	We 12 *ARC 4: 3 x 25 min *Stress-proofing	Th 13 *ARC 5: 2 x 30 min *Stress-proofing	Fr 14 *OAE	Sa 15 *Hangboard (HB)1 *Supplemental Ex
3	Su 16 *Optional OM, 4p *OAE *Skin care	Mo 17 *OAE	Tu 18 *HB 2 *SE	We 19 *OAE *Skin care	Th 20 *OAE	Fr 21 *HB3 *SE	Sa 22 *Optional OM, 4p *OAE *Skin care
4	Su 23 *OAE	Mo 24 *HB 4 *SE	Tu 25 *OAE *Skin care	We 26 *OAE	Th 27 *HB5 *SE	Fr 28 *OAE *Skin care	Sa 29 *OAE
5	Su 30 *HB6 *SE	Mo 31 *Skin care	Tu 32 *OAE	We 33 *HB7 *SE	Th 34 *Begin Tapering *Skin care	Fr 35	Sa 36 *HB8 *SE
6	Su 37 *Skin care	Mo 38	Tu 39 *HB9 *SE	We 40 *Skin care	Th 41	Fr 42 * Warmup Boulder Ladder (WBL) 60m * Campus 25m; SE	Sa 43 *Skin Care
7	Su 44	Mo 45 *Limit Boulder (LB) 120 min *SE	Tu 46 *Skin Care	We 47 * WBL 60 min * Campus 30 min * SE	Th 48 *Skin Care	Fr 49	Sa 50 *LB Outdoors
8	Su 51 *Skin Care	Mo 52 *WBL 60 min *Campus 35 min *SE	Tu 53 *Skin Care	We 54	Th 55 *WBL 60 min *Campus 40 min *SE	Fr 56 *Skin Care	Sa 57 *LB Outdoors (on boulders or routes)
9	Su 58 *Skin Care	Mo 59 *WBL 60 min *Campus 45 min *SE	Tu 60 *Skin Care	We 61	Th 62 *LB 120 min *SE	Fr 63 *Skin Care	Sa 64 *Redpoint (RP) attempts on bouldery routes
10	Su 65 *Skin Care	Mo 66 *WBL 60 min *Linked Bouldering Circ. (LBC), DC=2:4	Tu 67 *Skin Care	We 68 *WBL 50 min *LBC, Duty Cycle (DC) = 2:3; SE	Th 69 *Skin Care	Fr 70	Sa 71 *Redpoint (RP) attempts on bouldery routes
11	Su 72 *Redpoint (RP) attempts on bouldery routes	Mo 73 *Skin Care	Tu 74	We 75 *WBL 50 min *LBC, DC = 2:2 *SE	Th 76 *Skin Care	Fr 77	Sa 78 *RP Attempts *OM, 2 mod pitches
12	Su 79 *RP Attempts *OM, 2 mod pitches	Mo 80 *Skin Care	Tu 81	We 82 *WBL 40 min *Intervals, DC = 4:4 *SE	Th 83 *Skin Care	Fr 84	Sa 85 *RP Attempts on pumpier routes *OM, 2 mod pitches
13	Su 86 *RP Attempts (pumpier rtes) *OM, 2 mod pitches	Mo 87 *Skin Care	Tu 88	We 89 *WBL 40 min *Intervals, DC = 4:3 *SE	Th 90 *Skin Care	Fr 91	Sa 92 *RP Attempts (pumpier routes) *OM, 2 mod pitches
14	Su 93 *RP Attempts (pumpy routes) *OM, 2 mod pitches	Mo 94 *Skin Care	Tu 95	We 96 *WBL 40 min *Intervals, DC = 4:2 *SE	Th 97 *Skin Care	Fr 98	Sa 99 *RP/On Sight (OS) Attempts *OM, 2 mod pitches
15	Su 100 *RP/OS Attempts *OM, 2 mod pitches	Mo 101 *Skin Care	Tu 102	We 103 *WBL 45 min	Th 104 *Skin Care	Fr 105	Sa 106 *RP/OS Attempts *OM, 2 mod pitches
16	Su 107 *RP/OS Attempts *OM, 2 mod pitches	Mo 108	Tu 109 *OAE and/or Optional Cross-Training (OCT)	We 110	Th 111 *OAE and/or OCT	Fr 112	Sa 113 *OAE and/or OCT
17	Su 114	Mo 115 *OAE and/or OCT	Tu 116	We 117 *OAE and/or OCT	Th 118	Fr 119 *OAE and/or OCT	Sa 1 First Day of Next Season

Key:
HB - Hangboard Workout
LB - Limit Bouldering
DC - Duty Cycle (work-to-rest ratio)
m/min - Minutes
LBC - Linked Bouldering Circuits
OAE - Optional Aerobic Exercise
M/mod - Moderate
OCT - Optional Cross-Training
OM - Outdoor Mileage
OS - Onsight
SE - Supplemental Exercises
RP - Redpoint
WBL - Warm-Up Boulder Ladder
ARC - Aerobic Restoration and Capillarity Training

Seasonal Training Plan for Experienced Trainee, emphasizing finger-strength training for sport climbing. This example is tailored to an athlete with several years of training experience, climbing at the 5.13 level. This schedule assumes the athlete has strong movement skills but performance-limiting finger strength. The schedule maximizes the Strength and Power phases (since advanced athletes require far more training volume to stimulate finger-strength gains) while minimizing Base-Fitness. This schedule requires greater commitment to indoor training. The activities for each day should be performed in the order they are listed. The day's primary activity is underlined.

cially for those new to periodic training. These plans can be followed exactly, and neophytes should do just that (after selecting the most suitable plan). However, eventually it will be in each climber's best interest to diverge from these examples as experience and knowledge evolve. Chapter 14: Traditional and Big Wall Free Climbing and Chapter 15: Bouldering each present additional example plans specific to those styles of climbing.

TAILORING THE SEASONAL TRAINING PLAN

Create a draft schedule *before* beginning the macro-cycle. A firm schedule serves as a virtual coach, committing the climber to the program, and minimizing indecision that often leads down the path of least resistance. Once the schedule is drafted, changes should be well-considered and implemented at a time of rest, when the desire to avoid near-term discomfort is less likely to influence the decision. The following tips will help climbers tailor the above baseline Seasonal Training Plans to fit their individual physical attributes, address strengths and weaknesses, and train for specific goals:

The Rockprodigy training program results in a predictable Performance Peak – the perfect time to attempt your goal routes. Sonnie Trotter's boltless ascent of *Prosthetics*, 5.13d, Mill Creek, UT. 　Andrew Burr

INDIVIDUALIZING YOUR PLAN:

- Less-Experienced Climbers: Use relatively longer Base-Fitness, Power-Endurance, and Performance phases to maximize opportunities for Skill Development. Furthermore, these climbers should maximize opportunities to climb outdoors (where Skill Development is most specific) throughout the macro-cycle.
- More-Experienced Climbers: Use relatively longer Strength and Power phases since a greater training volume is required to stimulate adaptation in

well-trained athletes. Furthermore, such climbers should minimize supplemental ARC workouts during the Strength Phase to facilitate maximum intensity during strength workouts.
- Skill-Dependent Goals (such as a difficult slab climb or technical testpiece): Use relatively longer Base-Fitness and Performance phases to maximize opportunities for skill acquisition, practice, and stress-proofing. These climbers should also increase outdoor skill practice sessions, especially later in the macro-cycle.

"I record everything in a training di-ary — you get stronger very gradually so it's useful to look back and see what you were doing in terms of quality and quantity in a set amount of time."
— Ben Moon [1]

- Finger Strength–Dependent Goals (such as fingery bouldering or short, bouldery routes): Maximize the Strength and Power phases while drastically reducing the Base-Fitness and Power-Endurance phases as they are detrimental to pure power.

TIPS FOR MACRO-PLANNING:

- Phase Lengths: Ideally, phase lengths should be adjusted so that a phase ends just as the climber begins to plateau. If a plateau arrives earlier than expected, consider transitioning to the next phase ahead of schedule. Likewise, if there is no sign of a plateau at the end of a phase, it may be prudent to extend the phase, if doing so aligns with the climber's goals.
- PE and Performance Phases: Note that these phases are similar in nature. In fact, they could be considered two halves of the same phase. Focus more on indoor training early in the PE Phase, and more on outdoor performance climbing later in the phase.
- Performance Peak Timing: The Rock Prodigy program typically results in a *power peak* at the end of the Power Phase, followed by an *endurance peak* late in the Performance Phase. Plan performance goals accordingly. For example, plan to attempt boulder problems or bouldery routes during the power peak, and long, enduro redpoints or onsights during the endurance peak. As noted previously, attempting tweaky or powerful routes late in the season often leads to injury, and thus should be avoided.
- Climbing Trips: Road trips or other opportunities for plentiful outdoor climbing should be planned for the first two weeks of the Performance Phase. Those with the flexibility to choose when to use vacation time should arrange climbing trips for periods of optimal weather at choice crags, then plan the macro-cycle around that trip. Those with fixed vacation periods should schedule macro-cycles such that the Performance Phase coincides with maximal free time (doing so will create a ripple effect that impacts other seasons, so take that into account when deciding

when to start a macro-cycle).
- Aerobic Exercise: As discussed in Chapter 8: Power-Endurance, general aerobic endurance training has little direct benefit to rock-climbing performance. Such activities should be limited to the early phases of the macro-cycle, and even then only performed at low intensity to avoid draining effort away from climbing-specific training. Swimming in particular can further stress elbow and finger joints, and is bad for the skin, so should be avoided.

TIPS FOR MICRO-PLANNING:

- Weekends: Example plans are designed assuming Saturday and Sunday are days off from work. Climbers with other off days should adjust according to these guidelines:
  - If possible, avoid back-to-back outdoor *performance* days (back-to-back outdoor days during Base Fitness are acceptable).
  - Take two consecutive rest days after two consecutive climbing days.
  - Take one rest day after single climbing days.
  - Take two consecutive rest days (~70 hours) between high-intensity workouts such as hangboard, campus, or interval workouts. At the very least, attempt to schedule two consecutive rest days at least once every two weeks during Strength, Power, PE, and Performance phases. A relatively low-volume ARC workout can be performed on the first "rest" day.
- Order of Exercises: When performing different types of training on the same day, perform the more intense activity first (after a thorough warm-up). For example, during the Power-Endurance Phase, perform the various exercises in this order: 1) Warm-Up Boulder Ladder (including Hard Bouldering), 2) Linked Bouldering Circuit, 3) ARC set.
- Order of Performances: When climbing outdoors on consecutive days (such as over a two-day weekend), plan to perform more intense or powerful activities on the first day, and more endurance-oriented activities on the second day. For example, boulder or attempt difficult redpoints on day one; then attempt onsights or climb a multipitch trad route on day two. Alternatively, if one objective is more valued than another, attempt that objective first.

OUTDOOR TRAINING

In general, the training activities that make up the Seasonal Training Plan should be performed on the terrain specified in prior chapters (typically on an artificial climbing apparatus, or optionally outdoors, when noted). However, in some cases it is appropriate to perform outdoor training instead of indoor training, though care should be taken to tailor such climbing to the goals of that particular training phase (and the specific workout being replaced). The merits of specialized training were described at length in Chapter 1: Introduction, so the primary disadvantage of choosing to train outdoors is the rejection of those merits. Outdoor workouts are less quantifiable, less controlled, less thorough, less intense, and generally less effective than the exercises they replace.

However, there are some advantages to outdoor training, and a few specific reasons for doing it. Primarily, training on rock is very climbing specific (but only specific to the chosen rock type and route characteristics). Additionally, it sometimes offers the opportunity to make progress on a goal route while simultaneously accomplishing training objectives. In some cases, an indoor gym is not available, so outdoor climbing is the only option for certain types of training.

Certain long-term or seasonal goals warrant additional on-rock time. A climber preparing for a goal on an unfamiliar rock type or climbing style may be better prepared by training on that rock type. For example, if the goal is to free-climb Yosemite's El Capitan, it is essential to be skilled at slab, face, and crack climbing on granite. It may be impossible to accrue the necessary practice time without replacing some indoor training days with outdoor crag days. Another good case for training outdoors is the climber who struggles to adapt to outdoor climbing (and has a large discrepancy between indoor and outdoor climbing performances). In this case, further indoor training is unlikely to produce results on the rock anyway, so every effort must be made to overcome this disconnect between rock and plastic before focusing further effort on physical improvement.

When used, outdoor training should not completely replace all of the training exercises of a given phase. Outdoor training should be used intermittently; alternate outdoor workouts with recommended indoor training activities. This approach avoids excessive layoffs between like workouts. For example, consider the two-week schedules shown in the Figure at the top of the next page. These schedules demonstrate two options for incorporating outdoor bouldering with hangboard training.

Some objectives demand specific skill development that can only be accomplished on real rock. Slabmaster Justen Sjong finessing his way up *Town Crier*, 5.12+, Index, WA.　　📷　Andrew Burr

	Sunday	Monday	Tuesday	Wednesday	Thursday	Friday	Saturday
	Su	Mo	Tu	We	Th	Fr	Sa *Limit Boulder Outdoors 1 *Supplemental Ex
	Su *OAE *Skin care	Mo *Hangboard 1 *SE	Tu *Opt ARC: 2x20 min Skin care	We *OAE	Th *Limit Boulder Outdoors 2 *SE	Fr *OAE *Skin care	Sa *Hangboard 2 *SE
	Su *Optional OM. 4p *OAE *Skin care	Mo *OAE	Tu *Limit Boulder Outdoors 3 *SE	We *OAE Skin care	Th *Hangboard 3 *SE	Fr *Opt ARC: 2x20 min *Skin care	Sa *OAE

4 Days — *4 Days*

	Sunday	Monday	Tuesday	Wednesday	Thursday	Friday	Saturday
	Su	Mo	Tu	We	Th	Fr	Sa *Limit Boulder Outdoors 1 *Supplemental Ex
	Su *OAE *Skin care	Mo *Hangboard 1 *SE	Tu *Opt ARC: 2x20 min Skin care	We *OAE	Th *Limit Boulder Outdoors 2 *SE	Fr *OAE *Skin care	Sa *Limit Boulder Outdoors 3 *SE
	Su *OAE *Skin care	Mo *Hangboard 2 *SE	Tu *Opt ARC: 2x20 min Skin care	We *OAE	Th *Hangboard 3 *SE	Fr *Opt ARC: 2x20 min *Skin care	Sa *OAE

6 Days — *2 Days*

Sample schedules incorporating outdoor training during the Strength Phase. The first plan is preferred because it uses a consistent four-day gap between hangboard workouts, while the second plan uses a six-day gap at times. Such a long gap makes it difficult to correctly progress the load between hangboard workouts.

The first schedule uses consistent four-day gaps between indoor hangboard workouts. The second schedule is less consistent, varying the spacing between hangboard workouts anywhere from two to six days. The latter approach makes it difficult to predict the proper training volume for each workout, reducing the chances of achieving progressive overload and reducing the effectiveness of the training.

Outdoor training days should not be random, "climb whatever comes to mind" cragging. Apply the same deliberate approach that is used for training; establish a goal for the day that supports the long-term season goals, make a plan to achieve the goal,

and execute the plan. Outdoor training days should be tailored to fit the training goals of the phase in which they occur. Follow the guidelines in the figure below for outdoor-climbing activities that are appropriate for each phase.

The timing of sets and repetitions of outdoor training can mirror those used in the recommended exercises (mostly applicable to the ARC and PE workouts), but this may be impractical. Given the general inefficiency of outdoor climbing, expect to spend more time at the crag to obtain a training volume similar to that accomplished during indoor training.

Phase	Typical Training Exercise	Comparable Outdoor Training
Base-Fitness	ARC	Outdoor Mileage (climb many, moderate-intensity pitches focusing on skill practice, breathing & relaxation)
Strength	Hangboard Training	Bouldering or "roped bouldering" (working powerful route cruxes). Emphasize longer cruxes with fingery holds.
Power	Campus or Limit Bouldering	Bouldering or "roped bouldering". Emphasize shorter cruxes with dynamic movements.
Power-Endurance	Linked Bouldering Circuits	Redpoint/onsight attempts on pumpy routes (similar in length to goal routes) -or- Interval Laps
Peak	Redpoint & Onsight Attempts	Same

Training Mediums: Rock vs. Plastic

In theory, any of the exercises described in this program can be performed outside on rock instead of on artificial structures. However, experience shows that indoor training is much more effective at producing physical improvements in strength and power (whereas outdoor training is more effective for Skill Development, mental training, and often power-endurance training). The reason for this is that strength and power training rely heavily on the willingness of the athlete to push right up against his or her physical limitations — an activity best performed in a safe, controlled environment. Plastic (and steel) training tools allow athletes to carefully control individual variables, ensuring that all the relevant principles of effective training are addressed. Rock is too random, unpredictable, and ultimately unquantifiable to facilitate optimal training.

For best results, maximize indoor training opportunities to the extent possible when focusing on strength and power. When focusing on Skill Development or mental training, seek opportunities to climb

The right outdoor crag, such as the Red River Gorge's Motherlode, can provide better Power-Endurance training than many gyms. ☐ Dan Brayack

on real rock. As an example, PE training can be accomplished successfully on either medium, so the choice hinges on the quality of the gyms *and* crags available. Crags with steep, tall, jug-filled walls, like those found at the Red River Gorge, are ideal for PE training. Likewise, a tall gym with good route-setting can be superior to many crags. Gyms also provide more variety, and thus options for hold type, training duration, and intensity. Either way, consider the tradeoff between specificity and the principles that rely on accurate quantification of training stress when selecting your training medium.

"In the early days of sport climbing, training was thought to be 'uncool' among the climbers in our circle. 'A good climber doesn't need any training,' was the expert opinion. And in truth, up until that time, all you needed was good technique and the right attitude. But times had changed. The difficult routes were increasingly overhanging, so climbers were forced to think much more about their sport and the training that was necessary for it." — Alex Huber [3]

OTHER TRAINING CONSIDERATIONS

OTHER COMMON TRAINING ACTIVITIES

The Rock Prodigy program is proven to raise the level of performance of climbers of varying experience levels, body types, and abilities. Therefore, we have high confidence that it will be effective for every climber, if it is followed sincerely. Nevertheless, there are numerous other training activities that have their own merits, and it's sensible to consider them. The following discussion is included to acknowledge these activi-

Roped bouldering on a fingery route such as this can be a reasonable substitute for indoor finger strength training. Steve Maisch working out on *Calamity Jane*, 5.13b, Wild Iris, WY.　📷 Brendan Nicholson

gertips and the toes."[3] System training can be used for strength or power training by adjusting the number of repetitions performed and intensity of each repetition (by adding weight to the climber or reducing hold size). This activity has several disadvantages including:

- Lack of muscle isolation
- Reduced ability to progress the load
- Reduced ability to quantify the load
- Reduced intensity

The primary disadvantage of this activity is the lack of muscle isolation. By including full-body movements, many potential failure points (finger flexors, biceps, latissimus dorsi, shoulders, core) are introduced. It is unlikely each of these links in the chain will achieve failure at the same point in the exercises. Physically, the fingers are the weak link for most climbers. Every effort must be made to improve this weakness, and that means the tools and methods best suited to improving finger strength should be used. Hangboarding isolates the finger flexors (and supporting structures) better than any other training tool, making it the best choice for those determined to improve finger strength. Campusing is more plyometric and dynamic, capitalizing on the stretch reflex to maximize muscle recruitment, while improving functional muscle speed, and thus power. Additionally, the campus board minimizes technical complexity, facilitating the enhanced arousal and commitment required of effective power training.

Furthermore, adjusting the resistance during system training is problematic. Weight vests can be used to add weight, but these cause unnatural movement, thus reducing specificity; meanwhile, predictably subtracting weight becomes virtually impossible, because the pulley system used to remove weight during hangboard training would be impractical on a tall, steeply overhanging system wall. Additionally, the load placed on the feet from rep to rep, set to set, and day to day can vary as technique varies, so it becomes difficult to control and quantify the load placed on the fingers (and the rest of the arm-shoulder-back-core chain). Therefore, it becomes impossible to carefully and regularly overload the finger flexors, and progressively increase that loading over time as the fingers adapt to training.

All of these detrimental factors combined make system training much less effective for improving finger *strength* than targeted hangboard training. On the other hand, for a climber who has adequate finger strength but lacks other strength for climbing move-

ties and present the reasons for excluding them from the program. Those climbers who find these activities beneficial can incorporate them into their individualized Seasonal Training Plan.

SYSTEM TRAINING

System training is a form of structured bouldering that uses complex movements to apply a climbing-specific, controllable, repeatable, and somewhat quantifiable load to the entire body. System training was developed by the Germans Alex and Thomas Huber along with their coach Rudi Klausner[3]. The exercise requires a specially designed "system wall" that has identical, regularly spaced holds, so that exact movements can be repeated up and down the wall. The climber then performs "sets" by climbing up and down the wall, utilizing one specific grip at a time until the desired number of repetitions is performed. This training was intended as an improvement to campusing because it involves the whole body, "*through a perfect interplay of all the muscles in the chain between the fin-*

ment, system training may be appropriate (this would be a rare problem indeed). Most climbers have the upper-arm and back strength to perform individual pulls between good holds, but lack the endurance in these muscles to perform them repeatedly. One solution to this problem is to perform lock-off laps (described in Chapter 6: Strength) during the Power-Endurance Phase, in addition to performing highly effective hangboard training. Lock-off laps are a form of system training that de-emphasizes finger strength to instead isolate pull strength.

A System Wall can be used to train sport-specific strength with complex movements.

Complex Training

Complex training is an approach to strength training that was buzzing around climbing circles in the mid-2000s (though it has been around much longer in other sports). It involves combining strength exercises with plyometric exercises, and has been shown to improve speed and power output in large muscle groups (the legs, primarily). Typically, a set of strength-oriented lifts is performed followed by a short rest, then a set of a comparable plyometric exercise. For example, a basketball player (who needs to jump high) would

perform eight reps of squats, rest 90 seconds, then perform eight box jumps. This would be repeated for three total sets.

While known to be effective for many sports, there has never been a logical application of complex training to climbing. It has been argued that campusing is a form of complex training, and it is the most likely candidate for a means to adapt complex training to climbing. In this scenario, a climber might perform one weighted basic ladder up the board at low speed, followed by an unweighted max ladder at high speed (See Chapter 7: Power for descriptions of these exercises). This would provide the combination of a low-speed/high-intensity exercise followed by a high-speed/low-intensity exercise. The authors have experimented with combinations of hangboard and campus exercises as a form of complex training, but concluded that the results were no better than when these methods are used separately. Still, for those who would like to try it, the "Combined Hangboard and Campus Board Maintenance Workout" presented at the end of this chapter is a good baseline complex training routine.

Muscle Confusion

Numerous fad training programs are sweeping the globe (Crossfit, P90X, Insanity, etc.) that all essentially follow the same concept, that of *muscle confusion*. This concept is based on the principle of variability — that the athlete should vary exercises regularly and substantially to avoid training plateaus. Many folks swear by these programs for general fitness, but these are not specific to rock climbing and should not be expected to improve climbing performance. While they can help improve general fitness, these routines siphon training time and energy away from climbing, while adding muscle mass where it isn't needed.

Still, many climbers argue that a similar approach could be adapted to climbing training, by using climbing-specific training apparatuses while varying the exercises much more frequently. This is not recommended. Climbing itself is already a form of muscle confusion. Routes and boulder problems bombard the climber with widely varying movements and intensities. Controlled, progressive, repetitive movement is extremely rare on the rock, or even on artificial walls. Climbing keeps the body in a constant state of confusion, so what it really needs is more regularity (another equally vital principle of effective physical training). The relatively few times within a climbing season that a climber performs targeted training is the only time that the body experiences controllable, repeatable, quantifiable, and progressive loading. It is essential that these "islands of sanity" be maintained in what is otherwise a season of madness, in order to ensure steady, reliable adaptation and improvement.

AEROBIC EXERCISE

Many climbers include some form of aerobic exercise in their training. Aerobic exercise can be extremely enjoyable, and in moderation, good for overall wellness. However, the direct benefits to climbing performance are debatable. General aerobic fitness has little direct impact to performance on the rock. As discussed at length in Chapter 5: Base-Fitness and Chapter 8: Power-Endurance, climbing endurance is nearly always limited by the ability of the muscles in the forearms to produce ATP and remove waste products. Enhanced cardiovascular capacity has little bearing on these processes. That said, aerobic exercise can be helpful to climbers for these purposes:

- Establishing a basic level of fitness prior to beginning sport-specific training
- Maintaining healthy body composition
- Preparing climbers for extended multipitch climbs or strenuous approaches
- Preparing climbers for shorter routes at high altitude
- Improving general well-being and sanity

Some have theorized that aerobic exercise can help flush waste products out of the muscles between intense climbing or training days by increasing heart rate and blood flow. This may be true to an extent, but low-volume sport-specific exercise is far better suited to this purpose (such as short-duration ARC training).

ALTERNATIVE TRAINING APPROACHES: NON-LINEAR PERIODIZATION AND MAINTENANCE PROGRAMS

The training program described in this book utilizes a combination of *Linear Periodization* (LP) and *Non-Linear Periodization* (NLP), as explained in Chapter 4: Foundations of Physical Training. Whether it is deliberate or not, many climbers elect to use a Non-Linear Periodization approach exclusively, in which

all components of climbing fitness (strength, power, endurance) are trained simultaneously rather than separately in relatively distinct phases. With this approach, a weekly training schedule would include assorted workouts that target each component at least once during the weekly micro-cycle. Drawing from the exercises described here, consider the representative NLP schedule shown in the Figure at the bottom of the page.

Each of the fitness components is trained regularly in an effort to maintain all of them at a high level indefinitely.

This approach is appealing to some climbers because it facilitates uninterrupted outdoor climbing, avoiding the periods of exclusive indoor training that accompany the LP approach. The downside of NLP is that it results in a somewhat reduced level of peak fitness than LP. The LP approach delivers relatively predictable performance peaks that are ideal for those with limited on-the-rock climbing time, so that they can plan climbing vacations, etc. to coincide with peak fitness. On the other hand, climbers who have the desire and means to climb year-round, and who wish to do so at a consistent level, might prefer NLP.

NLP is only recommended as a piece of a larger LP approach. For those who wish to climb at a high level all the time, the unfortunate reality is that the human body responds cyclically to all training, both LP and NLP. In other words, regardless of the *training*, all climbing *performance* will be periodic, whether climbers like it or not. Therefore, the athlete should decide if he or she would like to control the timing of that performance. Those that choose NLP are choosing to take performance peaks and valleys as they come (seemingly at random).

This unpredictability of climbing fitness may not greatly impact newer climbers, who will experience steady progress as their skill improves, regardless of the approach. However, over time, this can be very frustrating, as the athlete is unable to count or steady improvement or predictable performance, with the good days and bad days seemingly uncorrelated to her training efforts.

A form of NLP that can be beneficial is the so-called *maintenance program*, which is used to main-

Sunday	Monday	Tuesday	Wednesday	Thursday	Friday	Saturday
Su STRENGTH: *Hangboard	*Mo* BASE-FITNESS: *ARC	*Tu* *OAE	*We* POWER-ENDUR: *Linked Bouldering Circuits	*Th* *OAE	*Fr* POWER: *Campus Board	*Sa* *OAE

Representative Non-Linear Periodization training schedule.

STRENGTH AND POWER MAINTENANCE ROUTINE

WARM-UP:

- Low-intensity ARC traversing (20 to 30 minutes)
- Bodyweight (or less) dead hangs on the hangboard:
  Three reps for three grip positions, 7/3 rep timing

EXERCISE 1: HANGBOARD ROUTINE:

- Perform seven-second reps with three seconds' rest as prescribed below for one grip position.
- The load performed during the first set of each grip for the last hangboard workout of the Strength Phase is the baseline load for this workout.

Set	Reps	Load
1	6	Baseline
	Rest 3:00	
2	6	Baseline + 10 lb.
	Rest 3:00	

EXERCISE 2: CAMPUS BOARD MAX LADDER:

Set	Exercise
1	Max Ladder, Leading Right
	Rest 1:30
2	Max Ladder, Leading Left
	Rest 3:00

REPEAT:

- Repeat **Exercise 1: Hangboard Dead Hangs** for the next grip position
- Repeat **Exercise 2: Campus Board Max Ladder**
- Continue until six grip positions have been completed.

SUMMARY:

The entire workout will consist of six circuits, with each circuit consisting of two sets on the hangboard and two sets on the Campus Board, performed in that order. Three minutes of rest should be taken between every set and every circuit.

COOLDOWN:

- Low-intensity ARC traversing (20 to 30 minutes).

tain and extend peak fitness after it has been achieved through an LP macro-cycle. During the Performance Phase, the climber makes every effort to perform on the rock as much as possible. However, performance climbing is poor training, and it is quite possible to rapidly lose fitness, especially with limited climbing days. Near the start of the Performance Phase, strength and power are initially high, but they begin to wane by the fourth week. Therefore, regular strength and power training during the Performance Phase are needed to sustain performance.

The best exercise for maintaining strength and power during the Performance Phase is Limit Bouldering on problems that contain both fingery and dynamic elements. This will provide a combination of climbing-specific strength and power stimuli. An effort should be made to select problems that are similar to the climber's goal routes to further increase specificity. The Rock Prodigy program includes these maintenance exercises in the form of the Warmup Boul-

der Ladder and Hard Bouldering included within the Linked Bouldering Circuit and Interval workouts of the PE and Performance phases. However, it may be desirable to further increase these exercises' emphasis in one of the following ways: 1) Increase the volume of Limit Bouldering within these workouts to train for more-powerful goal routes, 2) Increase the number of Limit Bouldering workouts to extend the duration of the Performance Phase. To accommodate these situations, a representative two-week maintenance schedule is shown in the Figure below for a climber who is able to perform outside on the weekends.

Limit Bouldering is the preferred maintenance training activity, but you can use other exercises as well. A combination of hangboard and Campus Board training is also effective (especially for those who don't have ready midweek access to bouldering). See the Figure on the opposite page for details on this workout.

Sunday	Monday	Tuesday	Wednesday	Thursday	Friday	Saturday
Su PERFORM: *RP Attempts *OM, 2 mod pitches	Mo	Tu POWER *Limit Boulder	We	Th POWER: *Limit Boulder	Fr	Sa PERFORM: *RP Attempts *OM, 2 mod pitches
Su PERFORM: *RP Attempts *OM, 2 mod pitches	Mo	Tu	We POWER: *Limit Boulder	Th	Fr PERFORM: *RP Attempts *OM, 2 mod pitches	Sa

Representative maintenance training schedule for use during the Performance Phase.

SUMMARY

- Committing to a detailed Seasonal Training Plan is an essential part of the Rock Prodigy training program, and key to maximizing improvement.
- Ultimately, the Seasonal Training Plan should be tailored to each individual climber, and should vary from season to season as goals change. Initially, use one of the example plans provided, then make small adjustments as your knowledge and experience improve.
- Adjust the training emphasis of the plan in accordance with your training experience and the season's goals, by varying phase lengths and favoring indoor or outdoor training.
- Include performance events in the Seasonal Training Plan, accounting for periods of peak fitness, opportunities for maximal outdoor climbing, and optimal conditions.
- Typically, indoor training is superior for achieving physical improvements, while outdoor training is superior for achieving technical improvements. To be effective, outdoor training must be structured and tailored to the training objectives of the current phase.
- System training is another popular method for training strength and/or power.
- Aerobic exercise does little to benefit climbing performance in most cases, but it can be helpful in some situations.
- Complex training can be used as a form of Non-Linear Periodization or maintenance training, to extend a performance peak.

WEIGHT MANAGEMENT

Mathieu Fontaine stalking *Predator*, 5.13b, Rumney, NH. Lee Hansche

CHAPTER 11

"Nothing tastes as good as skinny feels."
— Supermodel Kate Moss[32]

THE CASE FOR CLIMBERS TO MANAGE WEIGHT

Controlling body weight is critical to maximizing climbing performance. Climbers go to great lengths to develop finger and upper-body strength, with the aim of improving their strength-to-weight ratio in order to resist the pull of gravity. They work very hard (and proud) on the "strength" side of that equation, so it would be foolish to ignore the "weight" side. For those still not certain of the relevance of body weight, a season's worth of quantified hangboard training should demonstrate the difference 10 pounds makes when hanging from a small hold. From a purely biomechanical standpoint, the steeper the climbing, the more significant body weight becomes — steeper climbs require the upper body to support more of the climber's weight. However, less-steep routes at one's limit will have small holds with limited capacity to support the climber's weight, so even slightly slabby to vertical routes will be easier for leaner climbers.

Do I Have To?

Don't be ashamed if you're not excited about this topic: Weight loss and dieting aren't fun (as former wrestlers, both Mark and I have seen the drawbacks of performance-motivated weight loss, and cringe at the thought of dieting). Weight management is a tolerable sacrifice, however, one of many you already make for climbing. It becomes more tolerable with these two realizations:

1) It is very effective at improving climbing performance
2) With periodic training, it's not necessary to deprive yourself constantly.

A "performance diet" can be periodic, just like training, producing periods of samurai-like self-denial and periods of relaxation, celebration, and all-out gluttony. Just like other physical attributes (strength, endurance, etc.), low weight cannot be maintained indefinitely, so it makes sense to cycle it up and down with your training. Many high-performance athletes do this in other sports, including professional cyclists and bodybuilders. The latter group in particular needs to be very lean for competitions, to achieve the "cut" look, but muscle builds more quickly with more body fat, so they bulk up during mass-building phases then work off the fat in the weeks leading up to the competition, precisely timing their diet to appear "sliced" in time to impress the judges.

   This approach provides a break from the stress and self-denial of maximizing performance while maintaining the benefits. Once the goal weight is reached, it's much easier to maintain it throughout the Performance Phase due in part to the added time spent at the crag. Dieting is also easier knowing that the self-deprivation is only temporary, and aimed at a motivating goal with a finite time limit. When the goal is achieved, you can return to some of those vices that make life worth living. To say it plainly, it's much easier to go without when you know it's not permanent.

— Mike Anderson

"I spent time with [Wolfgang Gullich] in 1991 and he told me he was trying a new climb, and although he made no mention of its difficulty, I could see it was pushing him. He was dieting... he was incredibly ripped. The skin around his stomach was like the skin on the back of your hand." — Jerry Moffatt[18]

HOW LEAN, AND WHEN TO GET THERE

Every body is unique, and some stay lean more easily than others. For many climbers (especially older ones), weight management can be very difficult, but it offers tremendous return on the investment. A climber might spend six years to increase his two-finger pocket strength by 15 pounds, or (depending on his body composition) he could lose 15 pounds in six weeks and achieve the same climbing-performance benefits! Of course, the potential for such weight loss is limited. There is a point of diminishing returns where the benefit of losing a few extra pounds through extreme calorie restriction does not make up for the resulting reduction in muscle mass and general lack of energy.

Athletes should strive to be generally fit, with body fat less than 10 percent for men and 20 percent for women. In most cases, exceeding these thresholds places excessive stress on the joints, increasing the risk of injury and reducing enthusiasm for exercise. During the Performance Phase of a training cycle, when striving to maximize performance, it is beneficial to *temporarily* trim down to as low as 5 to 6 percent body fat for men, and 12 to14 percent for women.[12, 30] (Body-fat percentage is difficult to measure in practice; therefore, find your optimal climbing weight by tracking performance, as described later in this chapter.) Each climber may need to experiment to determine where that point of diminishing returns is, or how lean he or she can be before the low-energy malaise that comes with dieting begins to overpower any strength-to-weight ratio benefits achieved. Record your body weight in a training journal, along with notes about the corresponding energy level and quality of performance, in order to determine an ideal "fighting weight."

At the end of each season's peak, it is acceptable (and even desirable), to relax dietary restrictions and bulk up by five to ten pounds throughout the Rest Phase and into the following Strength Phase. It is very difficult to add muscle and effectively build strength with restricted caloric intake, because it is very hard to determine the correct number of calories to consume each day, as well as the correct ratio of carbs, fat, and protein. Undereating after a workout will inhibit the body's ability to restore glycogen stores in the muscles, leading to reduced performance in subsequent workouts. Worse, insufficient nutrition could weaken connective tissue, increasing risk of injury. Therefore, it's best not to attempt dieting through the Strength Phase. Instead, a climber in training should eat freely through the Strength Phase, and start dropping weight during the Power Phase. Weight loss can continue into the Performance Phase, but the resulting lethargy may hinder performance. It's better to reach the goal weight before the Performance Phase, then increase consumption slightly to enjoy higher energy levels throughout the remainder of the season.

Low body fat is an advantage on difficult climbs, but excessive dieting can sap strength and lead to injury or illness. To determine your optimal "send weight", experiment and note the results. Mike Anderson

Weight Loss Is Not Cumulative

Body weight and strength are both closely related to climbing performance, but they have different characteristics. Though we cycle strength on and off through periodic training, it gradually builds over time. The work put in five to ten years ago contributes to your current level of strength, which is to say, strength training is cumulative over your lifetime, to an extent. Weight loss is not. The weight I lost in high school does nothing for me today. Therefore, if life's circumstances prevent you from climbing for an extended period, there is little long-term performance benefit to staying ultra-lean. On the other hand, you would be wise to continue strength training, because the strength gained during your hiatus will contribute to your strength when you return. For example, from 2005 to 2009, I was sidetracked by the adventures of parenthood, severely limiting my climbing time. Therefore, any effort to stay lean would have gone unrewarded. Nevertheless, I kept training. Once my kids were old enough for us to climb more, I was able to trim down to maximize performance, and I wasn't penalized for the years that I "let myself go." Once I lost the baby weight, I achieved new career bests in redpoint and onsight ability.

— *Mike Anderson*

The author in chubbier times, in the midst of a PhD progam and raising young children (left), and two years later, 25 pounds lighter, and two letter grades harder (right). 📷 (left) *Rude Boys*, 5.13b, Smith Rock, OR: Mark Anderson; (right) *True Love*, 5.13d, RRG, KY: Anthony Carco

THE FUNDAMENTAL DIET RULE: THE CALORIC DEFICIT

With the requirement for weight management firmly established, the question of how best to achieve it comes into focus. The merits of various weight-loss programs have been debated endlessly, with new "miracle" diets appearing on the scene regularly — low-fat, Atkins, low-carb, Paleo, Zone, South Beach, the list goes on and on. It can be confusing trying to sort through the pros and cons of these diets, and very difficult to reconcile the misleading marketing with sincere testimonials from trusted sources. To make matters worse, rigorous scientific evaluation of these diets is inconsistent. A few programs receive lots of attention from the scientific community (low-fat and Atkins, especially) while the others remain unevaluated.[2] Even when they have been rigorously studied, the results are often inconclusive or contradictory.

The basis for many of these diets is an oversimplified explanation of the body's metabolic processes, which is then wildly extrapolated to create seductive theories about how the body might respond to certain combinations of food. The result is a convincing explanation for why such-and-such diet will make you shed pounds with ease, which is really a hollow house of cards built on a foundation of assumptions and outright speculation. Without rigorous scientific study, any claims of efficacy should be viewed with ample skepticism. Among all of the false claims and pseudoscience trolling the diet world, there is one universally applicable and indisputable fact: If more calories are burned than are consumed, weight goes down. Vice versa, and weight goes up. There is no way around this fundamental principle. No matter the chosen diet plan, if this *caloric deficit* is accomplished, body weight will decrease. Most climbers should aim to consume 1,500-1,800 calories per day while dieting — depending on body size and metabolism, but it shouldn't be necessary to meticulously count calories, as discussed in Baseline Diet, below.

The traditional, "blue collar" method of dieting is to eat smaller portions of generally "healthy" foods (i.e., low fat, low sugar, and low sodium). This method is tried and true, and effective, but it can also be very difficult for many people, as it requires considerable willpower. These diets only work if close attention is paid to food labels and the nutritional contents are correctly identified (especially challenging when eating out). Otherwise it is nearly impossible to know if calories are being reduced. Just because something is described as "low fat" doesn't mean it is healthy, or will cause weight loss. Low fat does not mean low calorie! One problem with "low-fat" diets (which were all the rage through the 1970s, '80s, and '90s) is that when the food engineers set out to reduce fat in foods, they replaced it with sugar and other carbs, which lack the *satiety* (feeling of satisfaction) of fat, despite the fact that the body easily converts them into fat for long-term storage.[1] Such engineered low-fat foods cause blood-sugar spikes, which are worse than eating the fat in the first place, because they disrupt how food energy is burned, consumed, and stored by the body.

SKEWING THE CALORIC EQUATION TOWARD WEIGHT LOSS

Many of the recent innovative diets (such as Atkins, South Beach, and Paleo, among others) seek to control weight by accounting for the speed at which digested carbs affect blood sugar. Despite the marketing tag lines such as "you can eat until you're full" and "no counting calories," these diets still depend on the fundamental principle of caloric deficit to stimulate fat loss. Therefore, these diets still require personal restraint and discipline. However, they differ from the "blue collar" diet in that they seek to skew the fundamental caloric equation in the dieter's favor, and thus lessen the requirement for restraint and discipline. This is done by attempting to manipulate key processes in the body that control:

1. Metabolism
2. Appetite
3. Fat storage

These processes are fundamental to how the body digests food, converting it to usable energy. These control mechanisms are used by the body to maintain blood sugar at an optimal level as food is consumed.[5] However, climbers can use these control mechanisms in reverse to control their weight. *By carefully selecting the foods eaten*, metabolism, appetite, and fat storage can be controlled, making it *easier to achieve a caloric deficit and thus easier to diet*.[28] These dietary techniques help to:

- Increase metabolism — allowing dieters to burn calories faster
- Reduce appetite — making it easier to eat less
- Manipulate the mechanism for fat storage — reducing the body's calorie retention

These effects can be achieved by influencing the body's glycemic response.

Glucose present in the blood (*blood glucose*, or *blood sugar*) is the body's preferred energy source for muscular activity and brain function (as opposed to glycogen stored locally in the muscles, or energy stored as fat in cells). In fact, glucose is the sole energy source for brain function, and since the brain is the most important organ, the human body has a robust system for maintaining adequate levels of blood sugar called the *glycemic response*. Glucose is provided to the blood by carbohydrates, and some carbs digest more quickly than others. When blood sugar is low, the body craves carbs and attempts to conserve energy (resulting in lethargic feelings). If carbohydrates are not ingested, the body will initiate the process of *ketosis*, which breaks down stored fat into fatty acids that can be used as energy in place of glucose (except in the brain).[10] Therefore, some low-carb diets claim that this induced state of ketosis forces the consumption of unsightly stored fat — however, these claims remain controversial and generally unverified.[2] In fact, any diet that reduces fat must induce ketosis, but low-carb diets seek to do so without extreme calorie restriction.

When blood sugar is high, our pancreas releases insulin, which signals the cells to absorb and store glucose, thus lowering blood sugar. Muscle and liver tissue store glucose by converting it to glycogen, up to a point — the rest is used to convert fatty acids to stored fat. The body seeks to control blood sugar in a narrow, optimal range. Therefore, when a rapid increase is detected, the body overcompensates, releasing excess insulin and triggering the rapid absorption of glucose by the cells. This is helpful immediately after a workout, when local muscular glycogen has been depleted and needs to be replaced quickly to facilitate recovery. However, at any other time of day, it is undesirable.

This rapid absorption of glucose will quickly saturate the muscles' capacity to store it as glycogen, so most of it will be stored as fat. Furthermore, the body can remove this excess glucose from the blood quite rapidly, lowering the blood sugar below optimal levels before the pancreas has time to shut off insulin production. This, ironically, causes a *low*-blood-sugar state and a corresponding *lowering* of metabolism to conserve energy (the "sugar crash"), and induces cravings for more high-sugar carbs. If those cravings are consummated, the result is a vicious cycle of rapidly rising and lowering blood sugar that leads to reduced metabolism, increased appetite, and excess fat storage. This trifecta has a devastating effect on the caloric equation.

Ideally, blood sugar should be maintained at a relatively constant level, with only small fluctuations that occur slowly over many hours. This gives the pancreas ample time to detect changes and react with measured insulin production. Rapid, massive spikes in blood sugar overwhelm the pancreas' ability to control blood-sugar levels, and lead to the aforementioned vicious cycle. Therefore, many dieticians have reasoned that foods with a low *glycemic index* (GI) — i.e., those that require more time to break down into blood glucose — may be beneficial to weight management.[4, 21]

The Mistress of Fitness Alli Rainey, lean and mean on *F'd in the A*, 5.14a, Tensleep, WY   📷 Andrew Burr

Recovery Plan

Proper post-workout nutrition is critical for climbers, because of the reliance on local glycogen in the forearms and the need to stay lean. For up to two hours immediately after a workout, carbs are converted to muscular glycogen three times faster than normal.[3, 14] Therefore, carbs ingested during this period are more likely to end up as useful muscle glycogen rather than stored fat (so it's OK to eat high-GI foods during this two-hour window). Further, consuming foods with a 4:1 ratio (by weight) of carbs to protein is known to improve the glycogen storage process.[3] Quickly replenishing muscle glycogen sets you up for your next workout or climbing day.[14] That said, climbing doesn't exhaust the largest muscle groups, so massive glycogen loading (like that done by endurance athletes) is not required for climbing.

After intense strength-training workouts (hangboard, campusing, or bouldering sessions), I typically eat half of a Clif Builder's protein bar and a banana, and drink at least 16 ounces of water — total nutritional value: 42g carbs, 10g protein, 240 calories. This provides the perfect recovery ratio and plenty of calories for a climbing workout. (Many other products are available with optimal recovery formulations.) At the crag, I nibble on snacks after every burn, typically eating an apple, a banana, a protein bar, two to three granola or energy bars, and two liters of water throughout the day.

— *Mike Anderson*

Which will help you lose weight? That depends as the candy has a high GI of 70, but a low GL of 4, while the banana has a low GI of 48, but a high GL of 12. In terms of Glycemic response, the candy is better, if you stop at one. 📷 Fredrik Marmsater

GLYCEMIC INDEX AND GLYCEMIC LOAD

The glycemic index was developed to quantify how rapidly particular foods affect blood-sugar levels as a means to treat diabetes, but it can be used to inform dietary choices for healthy individuals as well.[15] GI is somewhat controversial because it is very difficult to measure, and initially there was no clear standard for how to measure it. As a result, many foods registered wildly different values in early testing. Currently the GI of a particular food is measured by feeding a specified portion to a fasting patient, then drawing blood and measuring blood-sugar levels every 15 to 30 minutes thereafter for up to two hours (see www.glycemicindex.com for more details).[9] Tests of multiple patients are required to establish the GI of a single food, and even then, the resulting GI measurement can vary sig-

nificantly for that type of food based on the selected portions and ingredients (i.e., how should "pizza" be defined?). The University of Sydney's Human Nutrition Unit has been performing GI testing for years and hosts the International GI Database. GI is assigned to foods on a scale of 0 to 100, relative to pure glucose, which by definition has a GI of 100. A list of GI values for common foods is given on p206-207. The measure of GI shattered some long-held beliefs about which foods are healthy. For example, white potatoes were long thought to be healthy, "complex carbohydrates," but it turns out they have an extremely high GI of 85![9]

Because of the lengthy testing process, only a small percentage of foods have tested GIs, so it is a limited tool for informing dietary choices. Instead of using laboratory-measured values of foods to decide what to eat, it may be more practical to develop dietary rules of thumb.

GI is essentially a measure of how long it takes the sugar in food to be digested and reach the bloodstream. Sugary foods have a high GI because the industrial processing they undergo at the factory accomplishes much of the digestion before they are consumed. The body is capable of digesting *natural* foods, including sugars that are trapped within fruits and vegetables beneath layers of hearty "packaging" (fiber). However, as carbohydrates are further refined in the manufacturing process, the job of digestion has been supplanted by machines. Highly processed carbs thus require very little digestion, and the sugars that were once difficult to access are now instantly available when they hit the stomach. These sugars enter the bloodstream in one big jolt, rather than gradually over a long digestive process. The result is an immediate blood-sugar spike, along with the aforementioned negative consequences.[4] This goes for any highly processed carbs — white flour, overly cooked vegetables, corn syrup, etc.

Contrast that with uncooked vegetables or whole grains, both of which require a lengthy digestive process before the sugars contained in them can be accessed. Such foods provide glucose to the blood gradually and thus will not cause the blood-sugar spike that initiates the vicious cycle. Therefore, any foods that are slow to digest into blood glucose, or combinations of foods that slow the breakdown of carb-rich foods, are advantageous. As a rule of thumb, *eat real foods*. Eschew highly processed food products in favor of fresh, uncooked vegetables and fruits, and whole *grain* (not whole wheat) foods. Also, some *combinations* of food help to slow digestion. Fat and protein in general slow the digestion of carbs, as well as acidic foods like vinegar, lemon, and even sourdough bread (that's why balsamic vinaigrette is the salad dressing of choice for healthy eaters).[1] Eating highly processed carbs on an empty stomach is especially harmful in terms of glycemic response, akin to drinking alcohol on an empty stomach. Eat these foods alongside low-GI foods to dampen their effect.

While GI is a helpful metric for evaluating foods, it is incomplete, because it doesn't take into consideration the quantity of food consumed. A piece of hard candy has a high GI (70), but is a small enough portion that it won't spike blood sugar as much as a banana, which has a lower GI (48) but more total carbs. To account for the portion size along with the GI, the glycemic load (GL) is used. GL is defined as:[9]

$$GL = \frac{GI}{100} \times \text{Net Carbs}$$

Net Carbs = Total Carbs - Dietary Fiber (*in grams*)

A serving of food with a GL lower than 10 is considered low, and over 20 is considered high. By definition, a 50g serving (a lot!) of pure glucose would have a GL of 50. In the example above, the 6-gram piece of hard candy has a GL of 4, while a 120-gram banana's GL is 12. A favorite snack, corn tortilla chips, has a GI of 63 and GL of 11 for a single 28-gram serving, or about 14 chips (of course, it's hard to eat *only one* serving). For two servings, the GI is still 63, but the GL is 22, etc. That baked white potato mentioned above has 33 net carbs and a massive GL of 26. The authors of the South Beach Diet recommend consuming a running total of fewer than 100 GL points per day for effective weight loss, but their diet is geared toward inactive

folks with heart conditions, not athletes.[1] Instead, use GL as a guide to making healthier choices and learning about food. For those who are right-brained and must count and add, use 100 GL points per day as a baseline, and experiment — climbers in training will likely need more. The application of GL is much more practical than GI when it comes to making dietary choices, and represents a more moderate approach to dieting. Instead of ruling out all sweet and starchy foods, it empowers dieters to consume smaller, more reasonable portions without guilt.

A helpful resource for researching different foods is the *Nutrition Data* website (nutritiondata. self.com),[22] which has a large database of foods with nutritional data, including many fast foods and commonly available grocery store items. This interactive resource allows users to input overlooked foods. Because of the difficulty and expense of measuring the GI and GL of foods, they have developed an Estimated Glycemic Load™ or eGL that is a formula for predicting GL based on regression analysis of a given food's known nutrient contents (the formula is compared to lab-tested values on their website, and they demonstrate reasonable agreement). While these estimated values are not perfect, they offer a means of analyzing foods that lack laboratory tested values. They also offer a way to evaluate novel recipes.

Finally, GL is not a panacea. For example, many high-calorie, fattening foods have a low GI/GL (such as a 15-ounce T-bone steak — 1000 calories, 64g fat, GL = 0). Furthermore, recent research indicates that certain *types* of sugar, specifically fructose (and especially high-fructose corn syrup) and sucrose (table sugar), are worse than others. According to researchers, these sugars cannot be absorbed by muscle tissue, so go directly into stored fat.[25] Also, beware that GL only measures how *carbohydrates* affect blood-sugar levels, which is only one piece of the dietary puzzle. Understanding and capitalizing on this process skews the caloric equation, but the resulting caloric deficit must be considered as a whole. This is where many fad diets blow it, and why they've been so heavily criticized and often debunked. Absurd amounts of steak and eggs may prevent blood-sugar spikes, but they still make people fat!

Food Table

Nutrition data is shown for some common foods, ranked by GL. Many vegetables have virtually no GL, and aren't listed. GI and GL values are based on clinical trials by the University of Sydney.[9] Fullness Factor™, calories per serving, and Estimated Glycemic Load™ were calculated using the Nutrition Data website and are included to demonstrate how eGL may be used in place of clinical trials.[22] Fullness Factor estimates a food's satiety — the higher the number, the more full you'll feel. Pay attention to serving size when comparing foods.

Food Description	Glycemic Index	Fullness Factor ™	Serving Size (g)	Calories Per Serving	eGL ™ Per Serving	Glycemic Load Per Serving
Sugars						
Fructose	19	1.4	10	28	4	2
Honey	55	1.4	10	30	5	4
Lactose	46	-	10	-	-	5
Sucrose	68	1.3	10	39	7	7
Glucose	99	-	10	-	-	10
Maltose	105	-	10	-	-	11
Fruits						
Strawberries	40	4.3	120	40	2	1
Cherries	22	3.4	120	52	4	3
Grapefruit	25	4.5	120	32	3	3
Plums	24	3.5	120	52	4	3
Apples, Braeburn	32	3.3	120	65	3	4
Pears	33	3.1	120	64	4	4
Watermelon	72	4.5	120	32	4	4
Oranges	48	3.5	120	52	4	5
Pineapple	59	3.3	120	64	4	7
Grapes	46	2.8	120	76	8	8
Bananas	48	2.5	120	105	10	12
Raisins	64	1.6	60	168	26	28
Vegetables						
Carrots	47	3.8	80	32	3	3
Pinto Beans	14	2.7	150	214	13	4
Black Beans	30	2.8	150	198	12	7
Sweet Corn	60	2.4	80	83	8	11
Yams	37	2.2	150	114	16	13
Sweet Potato	61	2.5	150	138	14	17
Instant Mashed Potato	97	2.2	150	169	9	19
Baked Potato	85	2.5	150	145	16	26
Breads						
Barley flour bread, whole meal	43	-	30	-	-	5
Rye, Whole-grain, pumpernickel	46	-	30	-	-	5
Sourdough Rye Bread	53	2.0	30	83	8	6
Healthy Choice 7 Grain Bread	55	-	30	-	-	8
Wheat Tortilla	30	1.8	50	146	15	8
Old Elpaso Corn Taco Shells	68	1.5	20	98	8	8
Healthy Choice 100% Whole Grain Bread	62	2.2	30	74	6	9
White Bread	70	1.9	30	101	14	10
English Muffin	77	2.0	30	64	8	11
Wheat Bread	58	2.0	30	74	8	12
Corn Tortilla	52	-	50	-	-	12
French Baguette, White	95	2.0	30	92	11	15
Bagel, White	72	2.0	70	190	22	25

Food Description	Glycemic Index	Fullness Factor ™	Serving Size (g)	Calories Per Serving	eGL ™ Per Serving	Glycemic Load Per Serving
Breakfast Foods						
Yogurt	36	3.2	200	126	8	3
Oatmeal, Plain	25	2.1	30	106	11	5
Oatmeal, Apple & Cinnamon	37	1.9	30	128	15	8
Kellog's All Bran	38	3.2	30	81	8	9
Kellog's Raisin Bran	61	2.1	30	90	12	12
Grape Nuts	75	2.1	30	101	14	13
Kellog's Corn Flakes	92	1.6	30	101	18	24
Mixed Meals						
Pizza Hut Super Supreme, Thin Crust	30	2.1	100	209	10	7
Bean Burrito with Tomato Sauce	39	2.3	100	211	12	9
Pizza Hut Vegetarian Supreme, Thin Crust	49	2.1	100	175	11	12
Spaghettie, Whole Meal	32	-	180	-	-	14
Pizza, Cheese, Thick Crust	60	2.0	100	272	17	16
Spaghetti, White	42	2.1	180	284	29	20
Couscous	61	2.3	150	176	18	21
Peanut Butter Sandwich	59	-	100	-	-	26
Snacks						
Peanuts	14	1.5	50	297	1	1
Ice Cream, Low-Fat (1.2% fat)	47	2.2	50	69	7	5
Peanut M & M's	33	1.5	30	144	10	6
Chocolate Pudding	47	2.2	100	119	9	7
Ice Cream, Regular	61	1.8	50	103	6	8
Popcorn	72	2.2	20	78	8	8
Ironman PR Bar	39	-	65	-	-	10
Potato Chips, Plain	51	0.9	50	280	13	12
Pretzels	83	1.8	30	113	16	16
Rice Cakes	78	1.7	25	108	15	17
Tortilla Chips	63	1.5	50	246	20	17
Twix Bar	44	1.3	60	291	24	17
Chocolate Cake, Betty Crocker	38	1.5	111	367	30	20
Snickers Bar	68	1.5	60	271	21	23
Pop Tarts, Double Chocolate	70	1.5	50	201	25	24
Power Bar	56	2.0	65	247	29	24
Skittles	70	1.2	50	202	32	32
Beverages						
Tomato Juice	38	-	250 mL	-	-	2
Skim Milk	32	4.2	250 mL	86	9	2
Soy Milk, Low Fat (1.5% fat)	44	-	250 mL	-	-	8
Chocolate Milk	34	3.1	250 mL	157	13	9
Apple Juice	40	3.5	250 mL	114	6	12
Gatorade	78	4.5	250 mL	63	1	12
Orange Juice	57	3.6	250 mL	110	9	15
Coca Cola	63	3.7	250 mL	117	5	16
Cranberry Juice	68	3.2	250 mL	137	8	24

WHAT TO EAT

This dietary trifecta of metabolism, appetite, and fat storage are all affected by the body's response to carbohydrates. A perusal of nutrition labels will quickly reveal that carbs pack a lot of calories into popular foods. While fat has the highest caloric content by weight (nine calories per gram of fat vs. four per gram for carbs or protein), the fact is, modern foods have significantly more carbs than fat, so the majority of calories consumed come from carbs. This is by design. To meet the demand for low-fat foods, manufacturers replace the small portions of fat with loads of processed carbs, generally *increasing* calories and disrupting the glycemic response.

It should by now be obvious why commercial diets shun carbs. However, the real key is to eliminate highly processed carbs (refined sugar, refined flour, corn syrup, etc.). Naturally occurring carbs such as those locked within vegetables, fruit, and whole grains are much less harmful than refined sugars. It is not necessary to completely eliminate food groups. Such approaches are impractical, and typically lead to failure. Instead, eat a little of everything, and a lot of the right things.

VEGETABLES, FRUIT, AND WHOLE GRAINS

A healthy, high-performance diet should consist of large portions of fresh vegetables — the rawer, the better. Salad is perfect, and can be eaten in nearly unlimited quantities while dieting, as long as it's not

What I Eat When I'm on a Diet

Taste is personal, so take this list with a grain of salt....

- *Always*: Water...I never drink calories when I'm dieting.
- *Mostly*: Salad — tons of it; two to three salads *per day*, with lots of fresh veggies and olive oil–based balsamic vinaigrette dressing. I often top it with light tuna fish or grilled chicken. Salad comes in many varieties. If the typical garden salad sounds boring, taco or mango salads are just the tip of the iceberg; there are countless tasty salads to try.
- *Occasionally*: Low GI fruit — grapefruit, cantaloupe, apples, strawberries, and when I want to feel "full," watermelon!
- When I want *meat*: Grilled and seasoned fish and chicken breast (with fat removed).
- When I want *bread*: Whole grain breads (rye) and crackers (Wasa® Light Rye) — topped with tuna salad, salsa, guacamole, hummus, or bruschetta for protein and flavor.
- When I want *crunchy*: Quaker® Multigrain Fiber Crisps and Popped Rice Snacks (miniature rice cakes in both sweet and savory flavors), and pickles, carrots, celery sticks, etc.
- When I want *dessert*: Mango or peach salsa on a rice cake or Crisp 'N Light Wasa® cracker, pumpkin pie sans crust, dark chocolate–dipped strawberries, or Breyers® low-sugar ice cream.
- When I *road-trip*: Subway® grilled chicken salad with all the veggies; no cheese, croutons, or creamy salad dressings.
- When I want to *prevent mindless snacking*: Sugar-free chewing gum and Tic-Tacs®.
- When I *train or climb*: Trader Joe's "Power Crunch" protein bar, Clif Builder's Bar, Fiber One® granola bars, and/or Kellog's® Fiber Plus granola bars.

— *Mike Anderson*

An assortment of Mike's go-to diet foods: plenty of greens, lean protein, and fiber. 📷 Mike Anderson

"I went on a strict diet for about a week. Salads only....This wasn't hard. I was keen to lose the weight to give me an edge on that first move and I was so excited about doing [The Dominator, V13] that I could hardly eat anyway." — Jerry Moffatt[18]

smothered in bacon bits, croutons, ham, and fatty ranch dressing — again, raw vegetables should dominate. In general, fruits have more sugar and therefore calories than vegetables, but they provide numerous vitamins and minerals. Dieters can eat almost as much fruit as they want, but realize it can add up. Some fruits are better than others; refer to the GL data in the table on pp.206-207 (Grapefruit, cantaloupe, and berries are better than bananas, tomatoes, and watermelon.)

Besides slowing digestion and glycemic response, another great benefit of fruits and vegetables is that dieters can eat enough of them to feel full without ingesting excessive calories. This is because they contain mostly water and dietary fiber that isn't absorbed by the body. Researchers at the University of Sydney, who have been responsible for the lion's share of GI and GL research, and at Penn State University (responsible for the popular *Volumetrics* diet) have sought to identify satiating food properties that stave off hunger.[13, 23] *Nutrition Data* (nutritiondata. self.com) has extended that idea in an effort to identify foods that are the most filling per calorie. Their *Fullness Factor* ™ is an analytically derived satiety metric calculated based on the nutritional contents of a given food, and correlates well with lab-tested data.[22] Use this resource as a guide to learn about foods and identify diet-friendly choices. Not surprisingly, bulky fruits and vegetables top their list of low-calorie, filling foods.

Finally, foods high in processed carbs, such as most bread and crackers, should be limited. Opt for foods that are made from whole grains (not whole *wheat*). Rye bread, Wasa® whole grain rye crackers, Ezekiel bread, steel-cut oats, and whole grain pastas, to name a few, are good options. Highly refined breads, breakfast cereals, oatmeal, chips, and crackers have the detrimental combination of high GI and high net carbs. These should be eaten sparingly, and preferably in conjunction with low-GL foods like vegetables, protein, or fat to slow the glycemic response.[1]

LEAN MEAT

With a plate mostly full of veggies, the remaining space should contain lean protein: fish or chicken. Protein is essential for everyone, but especially athletes. The body relies on it for numerous functions. In the context of weight management, the challenge is always to get sufficient protein without excessive calories; enter lean meats. These will ideally pack a lot of protein into few calories. Tuna fish (canned, in water) may be the ultimate climber protein source, being cheap, lean, and non-perishable. Bodybuilders eat so much tuna that they can often be picked out of a dark room by their "tuna breath." A three-ounce serving has only 100 calories, almost all of which come from a whopping 22 grams of protein! For those with more refined tastes (and income), fresh fish and chicken breast are generally better tasting, while a so good sources of protein. Fish has beneficial omega-3 oils, but can be expensive. In case it's not obvious, these meats should be served grilled or baked, not deep-fried.

Pork is not a lean protein source and should be avoided when dieting. Soy-based protein bars are a convenient protein fix, but they will generally pack in more calories, with lots of sugar added to improve taste as well as fat. Clif's protein bar requires nearly 300 calories to get the same amount of protein as a 100-calorie serving of tuna. That's because these bars are also designed to replenish carbs and fat after a hard workout. Soy protein in general is very controversial, and government regulatory bodies have recently stripped some soy products of previous health claims.[6] Those who eat a lot of soy products are encouraged to research its safety to form their own opinion. Beans are a good source of protein, but some beans (black and refried) are packed with fat and carbs as well.

FATS

Fats are necessary, and should be consumed in moderation to maintain strong tendons, ligaments, and cartilage. When eaten together with high-GI carbs, small portions of fat can slow the digestion of these carbs (as explained above) and they can be satiating, making it easier to stick to the diet. Foods naturally have a combination of saturated, monounsaturated, and polyunsaturated fats. The healthiest foods have the highest proportion of poly- and monounsaturated fat and the least proportion of saturated fat. Monounsaturated fats are known to lower LDL (bad) cholesterol, thus benefiting heart health, and they have an anti-inflammatory effect — of great benefit to climbers.[1, 19]

Common food sources of monounsaturated fat that are also low in saturated fat are safflower oil, olive oil, canola oils, avocado, and some nuts (macadamia, almonds, cashews, and pecans).[26]

Omega-3 fatty acids, a form of polyunsaturated fat,[27] are also known to reduce inflammation. Omega-3s are mostly found in fish and other seafood, as well as flaxseed oil, kiwifruit, and certain supplements.[16] Omega-6 fatty acids are also a type of polyunsaturated fat that may be *detrimental* to climbers, because they are known to *increase* inflammation and negate the benefits of omega-3s. Government bodies recommend consuming a 1+:4 ratio of omega-3s to omega-6s (eat one gram or more of omega-3s for every four grams of omega 6s).[24] Most vegetable oils have low ratios of omega-3 to omega-6, but the worst are peanut oil and sunflower oil (no omega-3), corn oil (1:46), and palm oil (1:25). All of these should be limited or avoided, if possible.[20] Foods with high proportions of omega-6 include eggs (1:15), avocado (1:15), and most nuts (ratios vary).[22] Except for fish-gobbling grizzly bears, it is nearly impossible to avoid high ratios of omega-6s in any diet. Therefore, omega-3 fish-oil supplements are highly recommended to boost omega-3s, thus improving the overall ratio.

As usual, the best fat sources are those that are least processed. Olive oil has numerous health benefits, and should be the first choice for cooking and dressing foods (especially salad and bread). Extra-virgin olive oil is the healthiest (and most expensive), being highest in monounsaturated fat and with the highest omega-3 to omega-6 ratio, and has been shown to displace the negative effects of omega-6s.[11, 24] Olive oil is also known to lower blood sugar, so it can be used to dampen the impact of other, high-GL foods.[8]

Saturated fat and trans fat should be reduced or avoided. Saturated fats are mostly found in animal-based products, but also in some vegetable oils (common sources are fatty red meats, cream, cheese, butter, lard, coconut oil, palm seed oil, and chocolate). Saturated fat raises cholesterol, and the American Heart Association recommends restricting intake to less than 7 percent of total calories (around 15g per day).[17]

Trans fat occurs naturally, but in the modern diet it comes primarily from hydrogenated oils (margarine) — another "miracle" product invented in a food lab. Trans fat raises LDL cholesterol (bad) and lowers HDL (good), delivering a double-whammy to the heart. Trans fat is common in fast food, snack foods, fried foods, and highly processed baked goods. It is used because it is cheap, increases shelf life, and decreases refrigeration needs — all benefits for the food industry, but not the consumer. Experts recommend eliminating all trans fat, and some government bodies have outlawed it.[7] The best way to know if a particular snack has trans fat is to parse the label for ingredients containing the word "hydrogenated."

Dietary choices can affect the body's ability to fend off inflamation. For example, Omega 3 oils improve joint health and may help climbers recover from tweaky moves. Chris Hirsch chugging through mono country on *Big Train*, 5.13a, Spearfish Canyon, SD. Andrew Burr

Reducing Inflammation

Some foods have been shown to reduce inflammation, which is a must for rock climbers in training. Here are some dietary ways to reduce inflammation:

- Eat monounsaturated fats — safflower, olive and canola oils, avocado, and some nuts
- Eat omega-3 fatty acids — fish (such as herring, salmon, mackerel, sardines, and tuna), algae, and fish-oil supplements
- Avoid omega-6 fatty acids — found in vegetable oils such as peanut, sunflower, corn, and palm oil
- Eat certain spices — ginger, curry powder, garlic, onions
- Maintain stable blood sugar (high blood sugar aggravates inflammation)

DAIRY PRODUCTS

Dairy products are somewhat controversial, and whether or not to include them in a healthy diet is a matter of taste and personal choice. In moderation, dairy products aren't overly harmful, and they can be a good source of protein. Cheese may be the worst form of dairy (with lots of saturated fat and calories), and the easiest to reduce or eliminate. The average American eats 33 pounds of cheese a year, three times the level of the 1970s. This meteoric rise in cheese consumption is due in part to a concerted effort by "Dairy Management" (a partnership between the dairy industry and the USDA) to get Americans to eat more cheese, in order to help dairy farmers make more money. Therefore, whatever subconscious impulse is compelling people to include lots of dairy in their diet was likely surreptitiously placed there by the false advertising machine of a real-life conspiracy. These "public servants" are responsible for such gems as stuffed-crust pizza, Burger King's Cheesy Angus Bacon Cheeseburger, and the "Got Milk?" ad campaign. If pizzas or burritos are a must, ask the kitchen for "half" or "light" cheese.

Skim chocolate milk has been promoted as the ultimate post-workout recovery drink because of its mix of lean protein and medium glycemic index. It is clearly superior to protein-free beverages like Gatorade, but a protein bar eaten with plenty of water will also do the trick.

SNACKS AND TREATS

Clearly, snacks and treats are not diet foods, but realistically, people are going to cheat from time to time. The trick is to cheat in the best possible way. There are a number of healthier snacks that are sweet enough to provide the necessary fix without initiating hypoglycemic shock and derailing the diet.

Generally, it is best to eat sweets along with foods that slow the glycemic response (fiber, fat, or acid). Fruit is a good starting point, but also consider fruit salsas, or berries dipped in dark chocolate. Fatty deserts like pudding, frozen yogurt, ice cream, and pumpkin pie have relatively lower GIs so they are better choices than cookies, cakes, and candy bars. The first couple bites are the best, so keep the portions small.

For salty and savory snacks, avoid fried chips and crackers, which have lots of saturated fat and calories. Light popcorn with little or no butter can provide similar satisfaction, but don't eat an entire bag in one sitting — a little goes a long way. Also, Quaker makes miniature rice cake snacks in several flavors that provide the sensation of eating flavored corn or potato chips, but without the saturated fat and calories. Cut vegetables like carrots, cucumbers, cauliflower, and celery sticks sprinkled with salt and other seasoning are the best choice for a savory fix. Pickles have almost no calories, and make a nice quick snack.

If you have a sweet tooth, select sweets such as these that will scratch the itch without wrecking your diet. 📷 Mike Anderson

Dealing with a Sweet Tooth

I have a vicious sweet tooth, so I struggle with excluding sweet treats when it's dieting time. Nevertheless, I've found that if I go cold turkey for two weeks, my cravings are markedly reduced, and I can be satisfied with less-sweet foods than I would otherwise want. This conditioning is well-known; we become desensitized to flavors over time, necessitating richer and richer foods in order to get the same satisfaction. Therefore, as you eliminate the most egregious refined sweets from your diet, you should be able to satisfy the cravings with real, less-processed sweet foods such as fruit. In fact, after many weeks of omitting refined sugar, I find rich deserts like chocolate cake to be downright unpalatable. If you're also a slave to desert, have a small piece of fruit after dinner instead — before long you won't miss the other stuff.

— Mike Anderson

VITAMINS

When dieting, it is especially important to take vitamins and omega-3 fish-oil supplements, because it is unlikely that they will all be obtained naturally in 1,500 to 1,800 calories of food per day. Nutrient content varies by brand names and growing locations (in the case of fruit and vegetables), so it is very difficult to definitively know what is and isn't included in a given diet. It is much easier to take a multivitamin supplement and be certain. In addition to a multivitamin, climbers should consider taking a *glucosamine with chondroitin* supplement, which contains the building-block materials needed to repair joint cartilage. While the effectiveness of this supplement has not been proven, many orthopedic surgeons and injury-prone athletes swear by it. In the same vein, an omega-3 supplement is a must for its cardiovascular and anti-inflammatory benefits.

Super Subs

For most people, the hardest part about dieting is giving up your favorite foods or snacks. However, if you are willing to experiment, you can often find substitutes for your favorite foods that are much healthier, but provide similar satisfaction. For example, my Achilles' heel is chips and salsa. Salsa is actually a very healthy food (except for the sodium content), but tortilla chips are awful. A paltry 14-chip standard serving has 140 calories, and an eGL of 11. The problem is, I can't stop at 14 chips, and it's easy for me to consume an entire jar of salsa and half a bag of chips in one sitting. Frankly, the main purpose of the chips is to deliver salsa to my mouth. Recently, I discovered that whole grain Wasa® crackers can do that just as easily, and with a much lower GL and better feeling of satiety (a spoon works too). Some other good substitute foods include:

- Low-sugar ice cream over high-sugar ice cream
- Dark chocolate over milk chocolate
- Apple over banana
- Oatmeal-raisin cookie over chocolate-chip cookie
- Snickers marathon bar over [insert your favorite high-sugar energy bar]
- A taco salad or burrito bowl over tacos or burritos
- Fish/chicken/turkey over red meat
- Rice cakes over chips/crackers

Mike Anderson

An easy way to shave calories is to make a few substitutions. Identify the worst GI/GL offenders in your current diet and find a tasty alternative.

Sample Daily Meal Plan

This is a potential baseline meal plan for weight loss. It's only 1600 calories (appropriate for a 140-pound climber), but provides regular snacks throughout the day. Many items can be easily substituted to account for taste (i.e., chicken vs. fish, protein bar for breakfast, etc.). If weight drops too quickly, add calories with simple substitutions, such as a granola bar instead of an apple.[22]

Food	Portion	Cal (%Total)	Fat	Protein	Carbs	FF	eGL
BREAKFAST (9:00)		**229 (15%)**	**11 g**	**13 g**	**19 g**	**-**	**6**
Hard-boiled Egg	Qty: 2.0 x 1 large (50g)	155 (10%)	11 g	13 g	1 g	2.5	2
Grapefruit	Qty: 2.0 x 1/2 fruit (3-3/4" dia) (123g)	74 (5%)	0 g	1 g	18 g	4.5	4
SNACK 1 (10:30)		**95 (6%)**	**0 g**	**0 g**	**25 g**	**-**	**5**
Apple	Qty: 1.0 x 1 medium (3" dia) (182g)	95 (6%)	0 g	0 g	25 g	3.3	5
SNACK 2 (11:30)		**49 (2%)**	**0 g**	**3 g**	**10 g**	**-**	**3**
Carrots	Qty: 8.0 x 1 strip large (3" long) (7g)	23 (1%)	0 g	1 g	5 g	3.8	2
Cauliflower	Qty: 2.0 x 1 floweret (13g)	6 (0%)	0 g	1 g	1 g	4.5	0
Celery	Qty: 8.0 x 1 strip (4" long) (4g)	5 (0%)	0 g	0 g	1 g	4.5	0
Broccoli	Qty: 1.0 x 1/2 cup, chopped (44g)	15 (1%)	0 g	1 g	3 g	4.5	1
LUNCH - Mixed Green Salad with Tuna Fish (1:00)		**232 (14%)**	**10 g**	**24 g**	**13 g**	**-**	**2**
Tuna Fish, light, in water	Qty: 1.0 x 3 oz (85g)	99 (6%)	1 g	22 g	0 g	3.4	0
Romaine Lettuce	Qty: 3.0 x 1 leaf outer (28g)	15 (1%)	0 g	1 g	3 g	4.5	0
Cucumber	Qty: 0.5 x 1/2 cup slices (52g)	4 (0%)	0 g	0 g	1 g	4.5	1
Green Bell Peppers	Qty: 1.0 x 10 strips (27g)	5 (0.5%)	0 g	0 g	2 g	4.5	0
Onions	Qty: 0.5 x 1 slice, 1/4" thick (38g)	8 (0.5%)	0 g	0 g	2 g	3.8	0
Tomatoes	Qty: 2.0 x 1/4 wedge (31g)	11 (1%)	0 g	1 g	2 g	4.5	1
Dressing, Bals. Vinaigrette	Qty: 1.0 x 2 Table Spoons (30g)	90 (5%)	9 g	0 g	3 g	1.2	0
SNACK 3 (3:00)		**123 (8%)**	**1 g**	**1 g**	**32 g**	**-**	**10**
Grapes	Qty: 2.0 x 1 cup (92g)	123 (8%)	1 g	1 g	32 g	2.8	10
SNACK 4 (4:30)		**192 (11%)**	**0 g**	**7 g**	**42 g**	**-**	**17**
Light Rye Wasa Crackers	Qty: 2.0 x Custom Food (17g)	120 (7%)	0 g	4 g	28 g	3.0	14
Salsa	Qty: 2.0 x 100 grams (100g)	72 (4%)	0 g	3 g	14 g	4.1	3
DINNER - Baked Fish with Salad & Buttered Bread (6:30)		**513 (30%)**	**17 g**	**55 g**	**32 g**	**-**	**12**
Baked Grouper (Fish)	Qty: 1.0 x 1 fillet (202g)	238 (15%)	3 g	50 g	0 g	3.3	0
Romaine Lettuce	Qty: 2.0 x 1 leaf outer (28g)	10 (1%)	0 g	1 g	2 g	4.5	0
Spinach	Qty: 1.0 x 1 cup (30g)	7 (0%)	0 g	1 g	1 g	4.5	0
Cucumber	Qty: 0.5 x 1/2 cup slices (52g)	4 (0%)	0 g	0 g	1 g	4.5	1
Green Bell Peppers	Qty: 1.0 x 10 strips (27g)	5 (0.5%)	0 g	0 g	2 g	4.5	0
Onions	Qty: 0.5 x 1 slice, 1/4" thick (38g)	8 (0.5%)	0 g	0 g	2 g	3.8	0
Banana Pepper	Qty: 1.0 x 1 ounce (28g)	8 (0%)	0 g	0 g	1 g	4.5	1
Dill Pickles	Qty: 1.0 x 1 spear (35g)	4 (0%)	0 g	0 g	1 g	4.5	0
Dressing, Bals. Vinaigrette	Qty: 1.0 x Custom Food (30g)	90 (5%)	9 g	0 g	3 g	1.2	0
Bread, rye	Qty: 2.0 x 1 slice, thin (20g)	103 (6%)	1 g	3 g	19 g	2.0	10
Butter	Qty: 1.0 x 1 pat (1" x 1/3") (5g)	36 (2%)	4 g	0 g	0 g	0.5	0
Snack 5 - Desert (8:00)		**172 (11%)**	**1 g**	**3 g**	**43 g**	**-**	**6**
Watermelon	Qty: 2.0 x Slice, ~ 1/16 melon (286g)	172 (11%)	1 g	3 g	43 g	4.5	6
TOTAL		**1605**	**50 g**	**106 g**	**216 g**	**-**	**73**

BASELINE DIET

It should by now be clear that slow-digesting, low-GL foods help control appetite, keep metabolism high throughout the day, and discourage fat storage. However, that is only part of the equation. In order to lose weight, the burden remains to take in fewer calories than are burned. Some diets ensure that this is accomplished by counting calories or tracking points. This can be tedious at best, often impossible, and nearly always short-lived. A more common-sense approach is to begin with a baseline diet that can be replicated every day. A dieter can eat this consistently for a week, track his weight, and evaluate if it's working. For example, a typical daily meal plan is shown on the previous page. If the weight loss is too slow, gradually reduce certain portions (such as the amount of salad dressing at lunch, the daily allotment of fruit, or the serving of meat for dinner) until the desired weight loss occurs. If the weight loss is too rapid, increase portions slightly. After a few weeks of experimentation, it will be evident what the right diet plan is to achieve the desired rate of weight loss. Once determined, the baseline diet can be used season after season to lose weight.

CARDIO CONUNDRUM

Increasing exercise volume to boost weight loss (and avoid sacrificing food) is a common strategy that can be detrimental to climbers. First, the Rock Prodigy program provides ample exercise already, so additional exercise will hamper recovery and interfere with climbing-specific training. Second, it can be easier to lose weight by *reducing* the volume of cardiovascular exercise. Long, moderate-intensity cardio substantially increases food cravings, and often adds lower-body mass that isn't needed for climbing. This is a classic blunder, on par with getting involved in a land war in Asia.

Many dieters feel they *deserve* a good meal after a hard workout, but they often *deserve* too much, completely wiping out the weight-loss benefits of the workout. For example, it takes one 270-calorie donut to wipe out the benefits of a three-mile hike. Therefore, climbers opting for aerobic exercise must avoid overeating after hard workouts. Eat the minimum needed for recovery (half a protein bar or glass of chocolate milk) and drink plenty of water (at least 16 ounces), and then move on to another distracting activity. Most climbing workouts described here target the forearms, a very tiny muscle group with minimal glycogen requirements. A massive post-workout binge is not necessary to ensure adequate recovery.

Keep in mind, most diet and fitness plans aren't intended to cause *weight* loss; rather, they are intended to cause *fat* loss by increasing muscle mass and decreasing adipose fat. In other words, these plans may actually *increase* weight. This is fine for most people, but not climbers. Climbers need to be lightweight — leanness is just a side effect. Furthermore, pop diets are intended to change lifestyles in order to lose weight gradually over time and keep it off, without yo-yo-ing. This is nearly the opposite of what a peaking climber desires, which is to quickly lose 10 pounds or so for the Performance Phase before returning to the ideal body composition for training a few months later.

The Road-Tripping Dilemma

Maintaining a diet while on the road is hard for anyone, and climbers tend to be on the road a lot. Unfortunately, easily transportable, nonperishable foods are almost always unhealthy (high in sugar and trans fat), while the restaurant menu options are loaded with extra calories and unhealthy ingredients. Here are some simple tips to purify your next road trip:

Bring a cooler and pre-pack it with healthier snacks like baby carrots and other veggies, apple slices, watermelon slices, strawberries, etc.

For a very long trip, go online and scope out the locations of grocery stores near the highway so you can restock any perishable, healthy snacks en route. Also, search for healthier casual-dining restaurants like Quizno's®, Qdoba®, Panera Bread®, etc. A little pre-planning like this may prevent you from caving in to the Golden Arches.

When fast food can't be avoided, look for restaurants that provide choices (and nutrition data) like Subway®, which are co-located in many gas stations. Just be careful — it's very possible to overeat at a healthy restaurant. Stick to the salads and forgo the fatty meats, cheese, heavy dressings, sodas, chips, and cookies.

In the car, set time goals for eating. For example, have a small snack no more than every hour or 90 minutes. Don't leave that bag of pretzels propped open within arm's reach; pack it up tightly or put it in the trunk after you've dished out the right portion.

Despite Lena Moinova's beta for gaining the start holds on *Toker* at the Red River Gorge, KY, it's a rare climb indeed that demands much leg strength, therefore, rock climbers generally don't need large, muscular legs. 📷 Mike Anderson

GENERAL STRATEGIES & TACTICS FOR CONTROLLING DIET

In addition to knowing *what to eat*, successful dieting requires habitual lifestyle changes. These are proven methods for successful dieting:

ENVIRONMENTAL ADJUSTMENTS TO PROMOTE WEIGHT LOSS

• *Track progress:* Get a good bathroom scale and weigh in at the same time each day (weight fluctuates throughout the day). Tangible weight loss is highly motivating. The experts recommend losing no more than two pounds per week, but those recommendations are for people who want to keep the weight off permanently and are accounting for converting fat to muscle. Climbers are merely trying to quickly drop down for four to six weeks before returning to a higher training weight, so up to four pounds a week is reasonable.

• *Keep food out of sight and hard to access:* Tuck food safely away behind a cupboard door or in a desk drawer, and don't leave tempting snacks around the house. Every time you see food, you are tempted. Better to keep it out of sight, out of mind. One study recorded that folks ate 70 percent more out of a transparent candy dish than a solid-opaque one.[29] If you have family or roommates who aren't dieting, store your food in a separate cupboard and keep out of the others' so you won't be tempted by their treats. Make whatever food is around hard to get to — in one clever experiment, secretaries ate more than twice as many chocolates throughout the day when a bowl was placed on their desk rather than across the room.[29]

• *Motivate the right choices:* Hang a picture of your goal route or other motivational materials at the "gates of temptation," be it the fridge door, pantry, or on that box of cookies. At your moment of weakness, this will remind you of the big picture.

• *Dress skinny:* Wear your tight-fitting, "in shape" clothes to remind you of your goal, and discourage yourself from overstuffing at mealtime.

BEHAVIORAL ADJUSTMENTS TO PROMOTE WEIGHT LOSS

• *Graze:* Instead of eating two or three massive meals a day with forced fasting in between, try grazing, or eating numerous small meals and snacks throughout the day. Aim to eat something every one and a half to two hours, be it a piece of fruit, bowl of vegetables, or a small-portion meal.

• *Distract yourself:* Engage in activities that take your mind off food or make it difficult to eat altogether. Climbing is the ultimate distraction, because you are nearly always climbing or belaying, and eating becomes an inconvenience. When that isn't practical, engross yourself in your work or a personal project. Even playing a demanding video game can help; it's hard to spoon ice cream while pushing "A-A-B-Square."

"How hard it is to lose weight when you're overweight! That's where the mental process is interesting, because you face your choices: Do I really want to do harder routes or do I content myself with my cushy routine? At what point do I make the effort to climb harder?" — J.B. Tribout[31]

- *Use your head:* The brain needs as much as 20 percent of your daily caloric intake. Activities that keep you thinking hard will speed up your metabolism, and may be why mindless activities like watching TV are so closely linked with obesity.

- *Read labels and learn about food:* You can't expect to lose weight while remaining ignorant about nutrition. Spend some time in the grocery store reading labels, and do the shopping yourself. All the junk food is usually in the middle aisles, so stick to the perimeter of the store where the fresh food is. Healthy food takes more work to prepare than convenient junk, but it's worth the effort. Don't bring foods into the house that don't support your goals, and learn how to cook healthy, tasty meals.

- *Work as a team:* If you can, surround yourself with like-minded folks. Studies have shown a direct correlation between the number of people at a meal and how much is consumed, which is to say, if other people are eating a lot, you will too. On the other hand, if you are surrounded by supporters with similar goals, you can encourage each other to stick to the plan.

- *Be careful eating out:* Restaurants are traps, designed by cunning geniuses to encourage overeating. Also, the food is usually very rich, with way too much butter, lard, and sugar. Ask the waiter to skip the bread bowl or take it back early. Put half your meal in a to-go box or split an entrée with someone else. If dessert is unavoidable, share it with the whole table.

Learn about the foods you eat, and use that information to make smart choices at the grocery store. 📷 Mike Anderson

TIPS FOR CONTROLLING PORTIONS

Sometimes the hardest part of sticking to a diet isn't the fasting between snacks and meals, but controlling the portions eaten during meals. People often use illogical, external cues to tell them when they are full, rather than listening to their own bodies, as documented by Dr. Brian Wansink, author of *Mindless Eating: Why We Eat More Than We Think*. As a behavioral psychologist and professor, he has performed numerous experiments to explore these phenomena.[29] The following techniques will help control portion sizes:

- *Plate food in the kitchen:* Serve food onto plates in the kitchen, then retire to the dining room to eat. If you eat next to the leftovers, you'll likely eat more.

- *Use smaller dishes:* Numerous studies show that, given the exact same portion size, we feel more satiated and consume less when food is served in a smaller dish that creates the illusion of a full plate.[29]

- *Eat voluminously:* The authors of *Volumetrics* have clinically proven that people judge satiety by the visual size and weight of food, not calorie content or cues from the stomach.[23] Therefore, add volumizing food to every meal — high-bulk fruit and vegetables, especially salad. It creates the look of a full plate that subconsciously triggers satiety.

- *Seal containers:* To prevent repeated snacking, dish out the food and then put away the bag — tape it shut and place it in a hard-to-reach spot...or the garage or basement.

- *Repackage big-box food:* The "Grande" bag of tortilla chips is more economical, but studies show that bigger bags encourage overeating every time. The moment it comes home, separate the contents into smaller Ziploc bags of more appropriate portions. When it's time for chips and salsa, even if you blow through multiple Baggies, you will eat much fewer chips than if you were eating from the "Grande" trough.

- *Slow down:* Eating quickly increases the chances you will overeat. Put your fork down after every bite, chew and swallow before taking the next bite, and if eating with others, try to be the last one to finish.

- *Reduce variety:* Familiarity breeds contempt, which can be used to your advantage. A wide variety of foods will compel you to eat more of each type. If your dinner plate only has two courses on it, you're likely to eat less than if you had four.[29]

• *Don't extend meals:* After dutifully controlling portions during a meal, don't waste the effort by returning to the kitchen to snack. Before the meal starts, plan an activity to immediately follow it — a casual bike ride, a movie, etc. Make it a time crunch — you won't linger in the kitchen if you're running late for *Star Wars 8: The Return of Interesting Dialogue.* Another technique is to eat a breath mint, chew a stick of gum, or brush your teeth as soon as the meal is over (while you are still "full").

DIETARY CHOICES TO PROMOTE WEIGHT LOSS

• *Don't drink calories:* Sugary drinks, exotic coffees, and alcohol all pack in calories with little satiating benefit. Drink plenty of water, and spare those calories for foods that provide essential nutrients and satisfy hunger. If you must drink, studies show that using a tall, skinny glass will result in drinking 20 percent less than if using a short, wide glass.[29]

• *With treats, a little goes a long way:* The first few bites of a sweet treat or savory snack are the most satisfying, and then the law of diminishing returns kicks in. You'll feel just as satisfied after eating two cookies as you will after eating a dozen, with the minor difference being the self-loathing associated with the latter case.

• *Retain some comfort foods:* Eliminating *all* of your favorite foods is very difficult and often leads to failure. While many comfort foods are health nightmares (like pizza and fried chicken), most people have comfort foods, *or versions of them,* that are perfectly reasonable. Watermelon, salsa, or even a thin-crust vegetarian pizza with light cheese can satisfy a comfort-food craving without the guilt.

• *Don't be fooled by "healthy" advertising:* Labels such as "low-fat," "low-carb," "all-natural," etc. are misleading. For example, so-called "low-fat" granola has only 10 percent fewer calories than regular granola because the fat's been replaced with sugar. Pay attention to the label on the back of the box, not the one on the front, and always take note of the suggested serving size — for example, a 20-ounce soda contains 2.5 servings.

• *Create food policies:*[29] Many times, it is easier to rule out certain food options than it is to allow them in moderation. For example: no cheese, no beef, no liquid calories, no exceptions. There is no ambiguity, and it's an easy policy to enforce. Another example of an easy-to-follow policy might be to eat only "on the hour." Such policies will become habits after a few weeks, and habits are hard to break.

SUMMARY

• Climbers should strive for general fitness, but only need to be extremely lean during their Performance Phase.
• Excessive calorie restriction is counterproductive during the Strength Phase.
• A weight-loss diet doesn't need to exclude entire food groups (i.e., carbs). Numerous studies show dieters are more likely to stick to a diet that is inclusive.
• All things in moderation: Snacks may be eaten occasionally, but don't eat the whole piece of cake.
• Eat plenty of salad and raw veggies, and fruit within reason — they are filling and aid digestion.
• Regardless of the diet strategy, carbs must be limited in order to keep calories down. GL is a good way to evaluate foods, track calorie intake, and make dieting less difficult.
• Olive oil, fish, fish oils, and some nuts are good sources of satiating fat.
• Eat plenty of lean protein, preferably fish and chicken.
• Be careful not to overeat after workouts.
• Supplement the diet with a multivitamin, glucosamine with chondroitin, and omega-3s.
• Stay busy, don't think about food, dish out reasonable portions, and stop at the right time.
• Be mindful of the nutritional contents of foods, and take charge of the food-preparation process
• Keep goals in mind and post them prominently to stay motivated.

Preparing to Perform

Brent Perkins proving he's worthy of *Proper Soul*, 5.14a, New River Gorge, WV.　Dan Brayack

CHAPTER 12

INTRODUCTION

Ten weeks in the gym. ARC sessions, countless hangboard workouts, a blur of campus rungs. Pints of sweat, perhaps a few ounces of blood, and sore and peeling fingers. The training has been difficult, even monotonous, but the results have been dramatic — at least on paper. Now it's time to test this newly improved machine on the real thing. Your body is finely tuned, and the only remaining variable is the effort applied to the next redpoint attempt. Or is it?

While the majority of this text — and the majority of your training time — has so far focused mostly on physical, technical, and mental preparation for difficult sport climbing, there are *many* other factors that contribute to (or inhibit) performance. Climbers tend to obsess over two primary components of performance, *ability* and *effort*, but it is essential to understand the other relevant factors as well, and learn to manipulate them in your favor. While attending to details such as weather conditions won't catapult a climber through the grades, ignoring them will certainly sabotage him, unnecessarily delaying progress and preventing him from attaining his potential. On meaningful, at-the-limit climbs, such details will be the difference between success and failure.

This chapter begins with a discussion of the *external* factors that affect an ascent, and how to influence them to facilitate success. These factors include environmental conditions and equipment. Next, route rehearsal strategies are discussed, including methods for maximizing physical and mental readiness prior to a performance. Finally, techniques are presented for effectively executing the performance process.

EXTERNAL FACTORS

External factors can have a tremendous impact on performance. Factors like weather may seem impossible to control, but with good planning, the climber can increase the odds of encountering favorable conditions. Other external factors are well within the climber's control, but are often ignored. The following techniques will stack the deck in your favor.

ENVIRONMENTAL CONDITIONS

Climbing performance is greatly affected by outdoor environmental conditions, including temperature, humidity, wind, and precipitation. The time of year and time of day are both important factors as they directly affect the temperature and humidity of the performance environment. Because of finger perspiration, friction between the rock and fingers is best when the rock is cold and the air is dry, but not so cold that it causes the fingers to go numb during the ascent. This ideal temperature varies considerably between climbers, so experiment with different conditions and note the temperature, humidity, and effect on performance. Many climbers will find that after a bone-chilling warm-up, the fingers can tolerate continued cold conditions without subsequent numbing. This is usually the ideal state for difficult redpoints. Plan the training season and any climbing trips to increase the chances of encountering good *sending temps* for the most important performance objectives.

"Climbing is often best done in cold conditions, as cold as you can stand."
— Jerry Moffatt[4]

Certain regions — such as the American Southeast — suffer from extreme humidity most of the year, making the routes at these crags significantly harder during these periods, so plan trips to these areas for the fall and winter. Generally, across America, spring and fall are considered the ideal climbing seasons, but spring is much less stable than fall. Many of the Western Desert and Rocky Mountain crags experience high wind in the spring. This is beneficial in the late spring, keeping crags relatively cool, but a showstopper in early spring. Exposed routes like multipitch towers or protruding arêtes can become unclimbable in severe wind. Furthermore, crags that receive large amounts of winter rain or snowfall tend to seep in the spring. With a bit of research, it is usually possible to determine if a specific goal route is likely to be dry at a given time of year.

Temperature and humidity vary significantly within a single climbing day. Often crags are much colder in the morning, but more humid. Humidity is actually a function of temperature, so it will decrease throughout the day as temperature rises. A breeze can also reduce humidity.

Thoughtful planning will reduce the chances of visiting a crag when it's out of condition. 📷 Mike Anderson

Sun exposure and shade are important considerations. Virtually all performance climbing should be done in the shade. Direct sunlight will significantly heat the rock, while also making it difficult to see certain features and chalk marks. When it is extremely cold it may be sensible to climb in direct sunlight; however, this radiant warming is unreliable because it is dependent on wind and cloud cover. Most routes receive shade at some point in the day. A key element of the planning process should be to ascertain the times of day when the goal route is shady, and thus when it should be rehearsed and climbed.

Note the changing parameters (temperature, humidity, wind, sun/shade) and identify the optimal times for performance attempts. Calculate backward from your target redpoint window to establish times to wake up, arrive at the crag, begin the warm-up, etc. For popular routes, budget extra time to wait in line.

EQUIPMENT

The tools and apparel used during a challenging ascent should be carefully considered. Shoes are the single most important piece of performance equipment. Despite what the ads say, no shoe is perfect for all terrain. Ideally, each climber will have a few different models of shoe that perform differently, and perhaps even a few different pairs of certain models that are sized differently or in differing states of decay. Extensively loved (aka "worn out") shoes tend to be much more flexible and sensitive, allowing them to excel on low-angle slabs, or on steep terrain that requires toeing in and hooking. Vertical thin edging demands stiffness and precision, so new shoes with thick rubber and a tight fit are ideal.

Crack climbing presents its own list of shoe requirements, depending on the crack size and rock type. If the route has plentiful footholds, select a shoe to match them. Cracks with few footholds outside the crack will require foot jamming — use stiffer shoes for wider foot jams, and thin, sensitive shoes for thin cracks. Some climbers believe loose-fitting shoes minimize discomfort with extensive foot jamming. For difficult multipitch climbs, consider bringing two pairs of shoes, one that excels on face climbing and another that excels on cracks.

Regardless of shoe selection, each pair should be treated with care. Do not walk around in climbing shoes! Do not belay in climbing shoes! Clean the soles after each burn (simply wipe any debris off on a piece of cloth). In order to maintain fit and performance, avoid cramming shoes in the bottom of your pack. Do

Darkness at Noon?

Smith Rock is famous for its striking vertical walls and the brilliant edging routes that line them. These routes are notorious for their viciously sharp holds, so good redpoint conditions can make the difference between a successful ascent and a forced two-week layoff (to allow skin to heal). Many of the best climbs face southeast, so it's common to start late each day, in anticipation of ideal evening conditions. Patience is rewarded with tacky rock and fewer crowds, as the impetuous hang their heads late in the day, lamenting their throbbing fingertips.

This aspect of Smith climbing is woven into the fabric of Smith's history. The classic testpiece *Darkness at Noon* was so named because the route gets shade precisely at noon. Climbers flock to this spot at noon each day, waiting as long as possible for the rock to cool off, but not so long that someone sneaks in first, not unlike the boarding line for a Southwest Airlines flight. Of course, you will need to adjust your alarm clock for the summer months; during daylight saving time, it's *Darkness at One*.

not leave shoes in the sun or near other heat sources. This goes for between burns as well. On especially cold days it may be prudent to zip shoes inside your down jacket to keep them warm, but most of the time shoes perform better cold, so find a shady alcove to store shoes between burns.

Extensive walking and high heat cause feet to swell, so avoid walking around too much on climbing days that require the use of tight performance shoes. If climbing in the sun in August, consider up-sizing to a worn-out pair of shoes. Generally, it's a good idea to bring at least two pairs to the crag in case something happens to the primary pair or they're just not working well for whatever reason. A pair of older or needing-to-be-broken-in shoes can be used for warming up to spare the wear and tear on the primary pair. Warm-up shoes should still fit and perform well, as discussed in Chapter 3: Skill Development

The climber's harness should be well-fitting and built for the task at hand. A wall harness features many bells and whistles that add weight but aren't needed for a simple redpoint attempt. Use a harness with sufficient padding to provide comfort throughout a thorough working burn. Remove any extraneous objects like belay devices, locking carabiners, or belay-certification cards. Carry a small toothbrush at all times to clean holds and remove tick marks. A small

roll of tape should be carried on reconnaissance burns for preventative taping.

The climber's rope is a matter of preference, but the bottom line is to select a cord that inspires confidence, allowing the climber to commit 100 percent to difficult or runout moves. There are numerous lightweight varieties on the market, but these are more prone to slipping through some belay devices. Ensure that the rope is compatible with the belay device, and that the belayer can provide a safe catch. Thicker (and so, heavier) ropes are generally more abrasion resistant. Keep the rope clean to prevent contaminants from greasing up the hands.

Quickdraws can also affect performance. Use draws that are easy to clip, such as a wire-gate or bent-gate carabiner on the rope end of the nylon sling, secured to the nylon with rubber or tape so it cannot accidently rotate into an unclippable position. Try different quickdraw configurations to determine which you prefer, then practice with those draws. Many climbers take clipping for granted, but it is not trivial. If clipping is a weakness, practice clipping while vegging out in front of the flat screen: Hold the bolt-end biner of your preferred style of quickdraw at arm's length, and then clip a length of rope into the rope-end biner 100 times with your other hand. Now rotate the quickdraw so the clipping gate horizontally faces the opposite direction. Clip 100 times. Now switch arms and repeat. Move the quickdraw around in space to increase the difficulty of this drill. Usually only a few repetitions will cure even the most flustered clippers.

Considering the amount of money spent on clothing, it's amazing how little emphasis is placed on its performance qualities. Frankly, the rock jocks of the 1980s had it right: The ideal outfit is stretchy Lycra on the bottom and a loose tank top up above. Unfortunately, if men were to dress this way now, nobody would ever take their picture or kiss them (women, on the other hand, will be kissed more than they want if they dress this way), so a compromise is essential. Wear loose-fitting pants, preferably with stretchable fabrics, that shroud your knobby knees and tan lines yet do not inhibit flexibility. Leave keys, wallets, and smartphones in the backpack; they won't be needed at the fourth bolt. Some form of belt is usually helpful, but keep weight and bulk in mind and go with an integrated design or a simple piece of cord.

Upper-body clothing choices are purely personal. A shirt of some type is usually a good idea because it protects skin from rope burns and other abrasions, while providing a place to wipe sweat off the brow. Avoid tight-fitting shirts that can restrict blood flow or even pinch nerves in extreme cases. Bulky jackets or sweatshirts are almost always a bad idea. In extreme cold, consider wearing two or three T-shirts, or a vest. Most climbers will warm right up soon after they start climbing, but if it's really cold it may help to jog uphill for a few minutes just before tying in and then ditching any unneeded outerwear.

A hat or beanie should always be on hand. When in doubt, start up the climb with a beanie; it can be easily discarded once warmed up. Bracelets, necklaces, rings, etc., present a significant safety hazard so should never be worn while climbing.

ROUTE REHEARSAL

Route rehearsal is a significant part of the redpointing process that comes into play on every route that is not climbed successfully on the first attempt. The process of identifying the most effective sequence, internalizing this information, and preparing the mind to execute it under pressure is critical to realizing your climbing dreams. Mastering these skills takes practice and experience, but the following strategies will help jump-start the learning process.

"To climb hard routes, it's better to try every conceivable option...It'll save you time in the long run."
— Ethan Pringle[5]

DISCOVERING AND REFINING BETA

Determining the optimal sequence of moves on a difficult route is not trivial and often involves a bit of luck. However, there are tactics that can be applied to virtually any climb to expedite this process. These methods will help identify an effective sequence in short order, facilitating a quick ascent and saving time and energy for other objectives.

POSITIONING FOR OPTIMAL LEARNING

The first tactic is to utilize the modern conveniences of sport climbing that our Lycra-clad forefathers fought and dieted for. Work out sequences while hanging from the rope, and ensure that the rope is in the optimal position for working those moves. For slabby to vertical routes, that might mean a toprope. On steeper terrain, the rope should usually be clipped to the next bolt above the climber (though on terrain steeper than 45 degrees, the next bolt at or below the climber may be better). If necessary, use a quickdraw or carabiner to clip (aka *tram*) your belay loop into the belayer's side of the rope to stay close to the rock. As progress is made up the route, continually reposition the rope clip-in point to enable optimal learning.

A stick clip is an essential tool for rope management during the beta-discovery process. The stick should be used not only to keep the climber safe, but also to aid in positioning the rope. If unable to climb

On steeper terrain, clip a quickdraw from your belay loop to the belayer's end of the rope to stay within reach of the rock. 📷 Mike Anderson

onsight from bolt-to-bolt on the first go, clip in directly to the nearest bolt and use the stick clip to advance the lead rope to the next higher bolt. This is especially helpful for exploring dynamic or blind sequences, which can cause unnecessary skin wear. Instead, by advancing the rope above the crux section, each hold can be closely inspected to find the best grip posi-

Like a samurai with his katana sword, Rain Murphy uses his stickclip to slice up his project. 📷 Dan Brayack

tions and aim points, or to decide if tape or other preventive measures are required to avoid a skin injury.

THE BELAYER COACH

An engaged belayer can be extremely helpful, acting as a surrogate coach. In addition to providing moral support, a soft catch, and encouragement, an attentive belayer will note body positions during the execution of a difficult move and can help remind the climber of the successful sequence. Sometimes a third-person perspective can help identify potential options that the climber did not consider. The belayer should pay particular attention to the feet, as the climber rarely forgets which handholds were used. The climber and belayer should keep a running dialogue during this process to keep both parties on the same page and to help reinforce memorization of the correct sequence. An engaged belayer will learn from this sequence problem-solving as well (even if she has no immediate intention of climbing the route), improving her ability to read sequences and decipher cruxes. Keep this in mind when you are belaying.

In addition to utilizing the belayer's wisdom and perspective, it can help for the climber to imagine himself completing the move from a third-person perspective. The climber should attempt each move in his mind's eye before attempting it on the rock, including visualizing the movement of the hips, shoulders,

and each limb. This method can be used to brainstorm movement options, and will preserve the skin and muscles for the most promising possibilities.

ASSESSING THE OPTIONS

Actually unlocking the ideal sequence can be difficult, and the solution will vary greatly between routes. Think of every route as a series of boulder problems, and tackle each problem individually before considering the route as a whole. Use these steps to solve each individual problem:

- Identify all the potential holds and consider the useful attributes of each hold individually. Once the inventory is complete, consider how lesser holds might be used together (for example, two sidepulls in opposition).
- When examining potential handholds, consider every possible way the hold might be gripped. A hold may be used multiple times — perhaps as a gaston, and then later as a sidepull or undercling. Closely inspect potential footholds at eye level, identifying positive surfaces that can be hooked or used to pull the lower body into the rock.

Clues in the rock: a thumb print to the right of a hold indicates a left handhold and vice versa. Black marks or tick marks with no other chalk indicate popular footholds. 📷 Mike Anderson

- Assess the distances between the largest holds, and consider the pros and cons of making larger moves between the best holds versus smaller moves between lesser intermediate holds (or a combination of the two). Ace French climber Tony Lamiche advises to never underestimate the value of a big hold — even if it seems to be facing the "wrong" direction.

- Leftover chalk and rubber marks can provide clues to the most popular sequence (thumbprints below holds can hint at whether to use the right or left hand on a given hold), but don't assume previous climbers discovered the most efficient sequence. If it's possible to determine the correct hand for a given finishing hold, it's often easier to work backwards from that point. Often the key to a particularly puzzling sequence is a "shuffle" move where both hands use a single hold (though not at the same time, as when matching hands).

- Lynn Hill suggests that footholds exist wherever they are needed — simply determine the correct location for your foot, and then place it there. The rubber will do the rest.

Consider every possible option for completing a difficult move, even if it's already been climbed successfully. Often the first successful sequence is *not* the most efficient. Subtle changes in foot position or hip movement can make significant differences, so leave no stone unturned. If crux sections were worked when relatively fresh, return to them once you are fatigued to ensure your chosen sequence is executable when you are pumped or powered-down. Time spent dialing the moves is almost *never* wasted time. An extra 10 minutes of poking around at the crux can save days of unneeded redpoint attempts.

REST

Rest stances should be identified and evaluated. Any rest that the climber can sustain below the maximum steady state can be used indefinitely, as the climber should not incur more fatigue by remaining there (identifying this point comes from practice during base-fitness training). A poor rest may require substantial concentration to maximize weight on the feet while minimizing forearm grip effort. Some rests, such as kneebars or reachy stems, place physical demands on other parts of the body, and may become counterproductive after several minutes. Practice each rest during working burns — many climbers make the mistake of resting on the rope too much during working

burns, missing the opportunity to rehearse rest stances. Next, develop a plan for which rests will be used and for how long. It is wise to remain at very good rests for one to two minutes *after* you have completely relaxed, de-pumped, and your breathing and heart rate have settled down.

CLIPPING

Once the general climbing sequence is solved, consider each clip. Many will be trivial, but specific clips before, during, or after crux sections can be decisive. Position each quickdraw so that the rope-end carabiner is positioned for easiest clipping, keeping in mind also that your biner should face *away* from your direction of travel, especially on traverses. Identify the most efficient body position for clipping, which may be above or below the existing bolt placement. Extended draws can be used to allow clipping from a good stance below a crux. Sometimes a particular clip can be the hardest move on the route, and such clips are often skipped (in fact, certain mid-crux "dogging bolts" were placed with the intention that they would be skipped during redpoint attempts). Other times a clip is skipped just to save energy on a pumpy route. Whatever the rea-

Extend the length of fixed quickdraws so they can be clipped from the most efficient position, or to minimize rope drag. 📷 Mike Anderson

son, keep your belayer in the loop when considering skipping clips. Discuss the strategy for difficult clips and the pros and cons of skipping clips to ensure that your belayer can provide a safe catch in the event of a fall. Consider taking a few shorter practice falls to evaluate the consequence of a fall before committing to a longer runout.

LOWERING

Once at the top of the route, examine it closely while lowering slowly. Note any areas that are still unclear, and try to recall the sequence for each section of the route (going from bolt to bolt or rest stance to rest stance). Pause while lowering if necessary. Once on the ground, discuss the beta and the quality of your attempt with your belayer.

LINKING THE ROUTE

Once the individual boulder problems are known, it's time to put them together. Often the easiest way to get from point A to point B makes it significantly more difficult to get from point B to point C. Reconcile these

conflicts by identifying the most efficient sequence between obvious rest points or clipping stances. As soon as you begin to link individual sections, identify any moves or sequences that require further beta refinement. Moves that require extensive grunting, inhibit breathing, or leave one of the four limbs unused are ripe for further analysis. Once the route can be climbed with only three or four hangs, consider the proper pacing for the route. This varies widely depending on the climber and the characteristics of the climb (including length, angle, relative move difficulty, and availability of rests, among other factors). Also, this pacing will change for different segments. Generally, it's wise to climb as quickly as possible without fumbling a sequencing or becoming frantic. Some pure power-endurance sequences are best climbed as an all-out sprint, while technical endurance sequences may best be climbed slowly, with precision, taking lots of rest between moves. Finally, remember to place extra emphasis on dialing the sequences at the end of the route, or other places where a building pump or anxiety will hinder movement execution.

The Beta

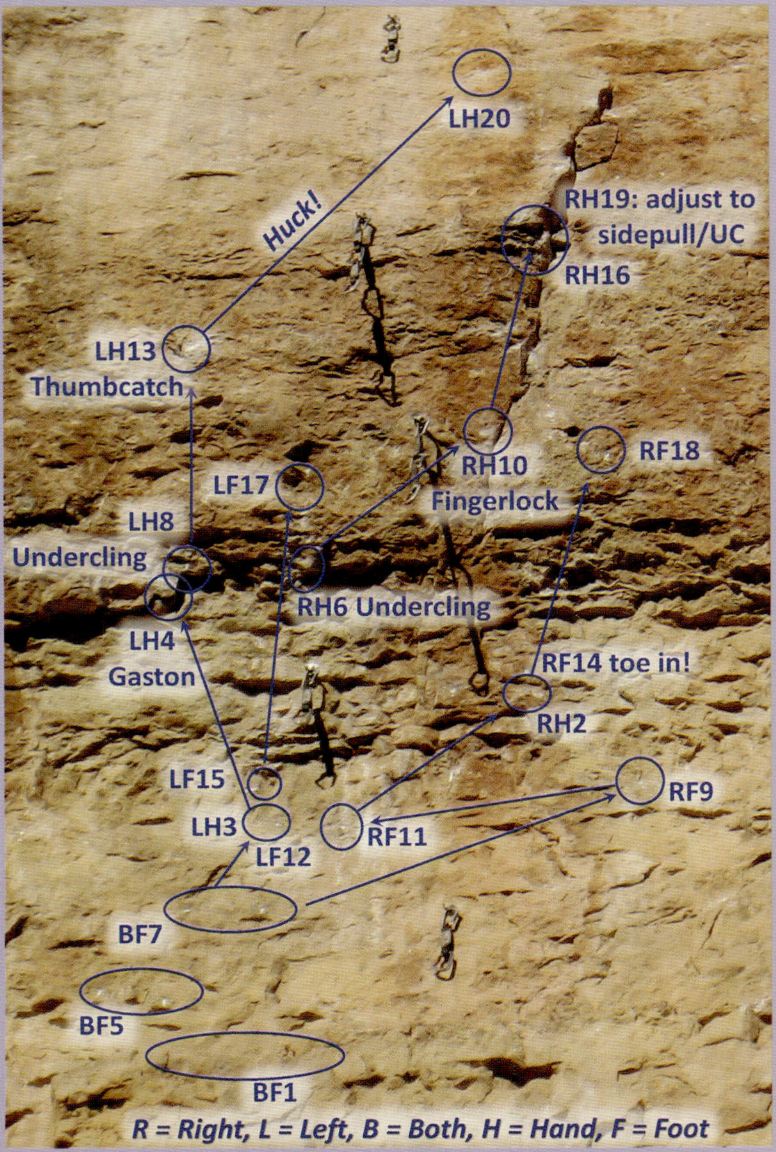

There are many ways to document route beta, including videotaping the sequence to review later — a blow-by-blow record of the route's moves that inspired the coining of the term "beta," for the now-defunct Betamax videotape format. Modern point-and-shoot cameras and phones, coupled with a cheap tripod, make it easy for anyone to film a climbing sequence. The goal is not Oscar-worthy cinematography, but rather a broad, stable shot that captures the sequences in a consistent manner so that one day's sequence can be easily compared to the next.

In addition to video, it's a good idea to create a beta sheet or beta map. These tools can be reviewed at the crag before an ascent, or even carried on the route during a redpoint burn (only review them after a fall!). Beta maps provide a visual representation of the route, and can be hand-drawn, or based on a photo like the one shown. Photo-based maps often capture the spacing and orientation of holds more accurately than hand-drawn maps.

In my experience, text-based beta sheets are the most effective, because they force the climber to think critically about every single move, and insert key reminders

R = Right, L = Left, B = Both, H = Hand, F = Foot

about effort, pacing, hip position, and other abstract or subtle factors that affect the ascent. A detailed beta sheet will describe how to grip each hold, when to clip, how to generate momentum, and when to relax. Below is an example of a detailed description of the opening moves of a different route (than the one pictured above). Note the details on hand position and pacing:

"Begin at Horizontal Break (HB), RF up on HB, RH to undercling/pinch diagonal plate along crack, cross LH over and MRP crimp diagonal edge just above slopey pod. RH go out right, avoiding rope, to crimp. Match LF to spike on HB, flag RF, LH to vertical slot, w/ pinkie in constriction. RF to highest part of diagonal ramp, then bump RH to Sidepull undercling (furthest right part, more of a sidepull than undercling). LF to triangular pod, then dyno/karate chop LH to next pod, walk LF, then RF, then LF to good chip out left, slap RH up to bad slopey sidepull, RF toe on spike at L edge of crimp, then pop RH up to gaston, stand a little & LH to mono. Don't rest, just keep trucking…"*

*RH = right hand, LF = left foot, MRP = middle, ring, pinkie fingers, etc

– Mark Anderson

REMEMBERING THE BETA

The perfect sequence is useless if it's forgotten. Ascents of limit routes require exhaustive memorization of the entire sequence. This includes not only which holds to use, but exactly how to use them, how to move the hips and shoulders, and the timing of dynamic lunges. There are many ways to help this memorization process.

Key locations or hard-to-see target holds can be highlighted with subtle chalk marks, but be judicious, and thoroughly brush them away after each session. Alternatively, get in the habit of noting subtle features in the rock itself that can be used as reminders of key holds. It's important to note the location of hard-to-see holds, but also to note exactly how to position the hands and feet on every hold. Sometimes success hinges on securing a crux hold exactly right, so note any peculiarities in the feel of the hold's surface for future reference — for example, that minute spike that sticks up between the middle and ring finger-pads when a certain edge is held correctly.

As soon as possible after the ascent, write down the beta. Consider creating a visually descriptive *beta map*, with a rough sketch of the features of the route, indicating the correct sequence for moving between holds. These maps are popular, but often result in confusing spaghetti lines that are hard to follow. Beta maps are suitable for visual learners, while verbal learners may prefer move-by-move text descriptions which can be recalled as an internal dialogue. Text descriptions also allow for unlimited detail and capture subtleties like hip shifts or the perfect hand placement on a key hold. If possible, consider shooting simple video of the climbing for later review — it certainly doesn't hurt to use all three tools.

The beta map, beta sheet, and/or video should be reviewed regularly (at least three or four times per day) between climbing days. It's not uncommon for climbers to conjure up potential alternative sequences during the review process. Jot these down for future evaluation, but stick with the tested beta for the redpoint go, and then try the new option if you fall, once hanging from the rope.

> "I remember all the moves of every problem I've ever done. This is what keeps me up at night."
> — Dave Graham[2]

Some holds require precise placement of each individual finger. Include this information, and other subtle beta, when documenting your sequence.

VISUALIZATION

Visualization is a technique athletes have used for decades to improve confidence and motivation. In the case of choreographed performances, like a gymnastics routine or rehearsed redpoint attempt, visualization is also a powerful method of memorizing the sequence of moves. It provides opportunities for the mind to rehearse the moves when the body's physically separated from the project, or too worn out for additional hands-on repetitions.

With visualization, the climber imagines successfully climbing her project in her "mind's eye." This process can help eliminate doubts in the climber's mind, opening it to the possibility of success. Confidence is essential to any successful athletic performance, but it's even more important in redpoint climbing, because it helps maintain motivation over the course of an extended project. It's difficult to commit complete-

---

Discovering and Refining Beta: Key Takeaways

- Use a toprope or stick clip to position the rope for optimal learning
- Keep chalk marks to a minimum
- Get your belayer involved
- Consider all available holds
  - Consider holds in combination
  - Get the most out of the best holds
  - Footholds are everywhere
- Note clipping positions
- Review the beta while lowering and between burns
- Reconsider moves that require extensive grunting, inhibit breathing, or leave one of the four limbs unused
- Document the beta

ly to a challenging goal when the result is constantly in doubt. Imagining what success will ultimately "look" and "feel" like provides a bridge for the mind to transition from a state of skepticism to one of sincere belief. This realization that the goal (which often seems inconceivable at the outset) is truly within grasp can fuel the final surge of effort necessary to succeed.

With practice, visualization can be performed anywhere, but first-time practitioners should set aside a short block of time free from noise and distractions. Sitting or lying down in a darkened room is a great place to start. With eyes closed, imagine the goal route. Some find it easier to imagine a *third-person perspective*, envisioning their performance as though they were a member of the audience rather than the leading character. Ultimately, strive to imagine events as they will eventually be observed in real life: from a *first-person perspective*. While visualizing, breathe deeply, as if on the climb. Establish the setting, including the crag scene, the weather, and the audience. Imagine stepping through the typical preparations: warming up, miming the moves below the route, tying in and booting up. Imagine a safe, secure belay from a trusted partner.

Imagine starting up the route, and then climbing each individual move. Envision every single hand and foot movement, as well as key hip or shoulder movements. Initially the hand moves are easiest to remember, but on more challenging projects internalizing the foot beta will eventually be essential. Whenever possible, mime each move as you progress up the route in your mind. Imagine all the subtle intricacies of the route—particular ways of grasping uneven handholds, hip shifts, variations in pace, clips, rest, and relaxation points. Imagine battling through a difficult crux, including shouts or grunts if these will likely be part of the final performance. Imagine a building pump, but fighting that extra bit harder to reach the next rest. Finally, imagine clipping the rope into the anchor after the send, and the euphoric feelings that accompany success.

A common mistake is to imagine "floating" up the route with ease. Occasionally, this does indeed happen, but it is rare. More often, successful performances are extremely difficult, requiring tremendous effort. Expect to struggle, but imagine trying very hard and overcoming these difficulties. Expect to have moments of doubt, but imagine reassuring yourself with positive self-talk. Embracing these challenges and preparing for them, rather than ignoring them, will provide comfort at the moment of truth. You knew it would be hard, so prepare to try hard.

Once the method is learned, visualization should be performed regularly throughout a project campaign. Take advantage of peaceful moments (such as when riding in a car or on a walk) to visualize. When time is limited, imagine the performance in sections. If possible, sit below the route while visualizing, to help you recollect any forgotten sequences. Video of the route can also be used to stimulate the visualization process, but the third-person perspective is not ideal. Use video to help refine the beta early in the campaign, but also take time for old-fashioned imagination.

CONFIDENCE

The expectations that a climber harbors about her potential ability to climb a given route contribute significantly to determining if she will. While this concept of the *self-fulfilling prophecy* is a cliché in many sports, in climbing it is very real. The climber's attitude directly affects her physical execution in several critical ways, including breathing, physical relaxation, grip control, and movement analysis and execution. With the right

A broad base of climbing experience will help breed the confidence needed to succeed on your limit routes. Megan Howk boosting her pyramid on *Bare Metal Teen*, 5.12a, Red River Gorge, KY. Dan Brayack

attitude, the climber's mind becomes a tremendous asset, able to perform the very demanding task of properly controlling these critical functions. With the wrong attitude, the mind will restrain an otherwise capable body. It becomes a burden that must be hauled up the route, tugging on the climber with every move.

A confident climber can relax and climb efficiently because she expects to overcome the challenges that arise, rather than bracing for retreat. Confidence that her feet won't slip allows her to relax her grip; confidence that the next hold will be adequate allows more-flowing movement; confidence that she will recover allows her to commit decisively to a crux; and so on. Achieving this mindset is fundamental to onsighting, so it is discussed further in Chapter 13: Redpoint and Onsight Climbing. However, confidence also has significant and distinct implications for redpoint climbing. During the initial route-rehearsal process, the climber must believe the send is possible eventually; otherwise her doubts will prevent maximum effort on the hardest moves. The mind will magnify these doubts to convince the climber that the moves are "impossible" and that such a lofty goal is a waste of time.

The confidence needed to combat the mind's meddling must spring from actual ability and achievements. Therefore, confidence must be cultivated and nurtured over a career. A *route pyramid* (described in Chapter 2: Goal Setting and Planning) is the perfect tool for building the broad base of experience needed to instill confidence for future projects. It helps identify chinks in the climber's armor, focusing her training effort to solidify her skills. Thus, by building diverse and thorough pyramids, the climber will have indisputable evidence that she is capable of achieving the next goal. It can be helpful to review these pyramids occasionally to reinforce this belief, especially at the outset of a new project or during moments of doubt. If she has done the work needed to complete the pyramid, and the pyramid leads logically to the goal route, then the climber has no reason to fear the route or doubt her ability to succeed. Instead, she should believe that she will find a solution and succeed on the route eventually — the proof lies in the stone foundation that is her pyramid.

THE PERFORMANCE PROCESS

There are several proven methods for preparing the body and mind to perform at their best when it counts: on the most cherished goal routes. In climbing, each route is unique, and so is each performance. However, the same basic process can be used to prepare for any climbing performance. This process can and should be tailored to each climber and the demands of each route, but the fundamental components remain universal. Once a suitable routine is established, repeating it will provide comfort on high-anxiety performance days.

WARMING UP

A thorough warm-up is critical to any performance — it can literally make or break a climbing day. The best warm-up for a given climbing day can vary dramatically depending on the performance objective, but there are some common characteristics. An effective warm-up will increase circulation throughout the body, clear out any residual waste products in the muscles, raise the heart rate and breathing, and activate the neurologic processes that control motor movement.

Warm-up activities should begin relatively easily, and then gradually increase in difficulty until a moderate pump is achieved. Err on the side of selecting warm-up climbs that are too easy in order to avoid the dreaded flash pump. The warm-up climbs should depend on the intended activity for the day, the climber's skill, and her familiarity with the warm-ups, so grades are not a good indicator of suitability. Duration is a better indicator. Thirty to 45 minutes of on-route climbing time should be set-aside for warm-

A complete warm-up is mandatory. Kate Anderson preparing to crush at Wild Iris, WY. 　Mike Anderson

ing-up, which can include as many as four warm-up burns for skilled climbers at a familiar crag. Don't rush through the warm-ups either, especially if climbing familiar routes; climb at a pace similar to the goal route. Try to select routes that are sustained, have comfortable holds, and are enjoyable to climb, so that they elicit a positive mood. Most popular crags have well-traveled warm-ups that fit the bill — ask locals for guidance and arrive early to get in the queue. If the best available warm-up is too easy, skip a few holds or linger on marginal holds to achieve the desired intensity.

Include some range-of-motion activities and active stretching while on route. Warm-up climbs should be done on lead to warm-up the "lead head" as well. Breathe steadily and intently throughout the warm-up to habitualize the best behavior for later performances. The nervous system requires a thorough warm-up as well, in order to optimize balance, motor control, and muscular recruitment. Disproportionally powerful efforts require a more intense warm-up to get all of the muscles firing effectively. Once the warm-up is complete, allow ample time to recover before moving on to the day's objective (30 to 60 minutes of rest is common). On occasion, it may be necessary to re-warm-up at times throughout the day if too much time passes between burns. One moderate pitch should suffice.

Mental focus can make or break challenging performances. Clay Cahoon keeps his eye on the prize on *Hellion*, 5.13b, Ten Sleep, WY. 📷 Andrew Burr

"As soon as I think to myself 'I'm so tired,' then I am instantaneously so much more pumped. The trick is to distract your mind. Think of the sequences in front of you, sing a song to yourself, or keep a mental rhythm going — a lot of methods work but through personal experience, telling yourself that you are pumped or that the next move is hard while you are on the wall definitely does not help. Instead, by focusing your attention on the sole movement in front of you, you can breathe easier, maintain attention, and climb much more precisely."
— Sasha DiGiulian[1]

FOCUS AND INTENSITY DURING PERFORMANCE

Finally, after countless hours of preparation, the moment of truth has arrived. When it comes time to attempt the redpoint of a limit route, many of the aspects that affect success (physical strength, body weight, technical ability, environmental conditions, etc.) have already been determined. What remains is to summon maximum focus and effort, and then sustain them throughout the duration of the effort.

The first order of business is to ensure that the playing field is properly prepared. This will reduce the chances of some minor detail distracting your attention from the ensuing performance. Are all the quickdraws in place? If not, what gear is required and how should it be racked? Verify that the rock is dry and free of other obstacles. If not, develop a plan for dealing with the annoyance so it's not a surprise when encountered on route. If stick-clipping, lay out the rope bag first thing, rig the rope through the stick, tag the clip, and then discuss your climbing strategy with your belayer, including:

- Rest locations and durations
- Potential fall locations
- Strenuous clips, runouts, or other locations where the belayer's attention is especially critical
- Locations where extra slack is needed (long dynos or reachy clips)
- Points where verbal encouragement or technical reminders are desired

Once all the trivialities are dealt with, it's time to get "in the zone" for the ensuing performance.

Manifesting intense focus is not trivial, but it does become easier with practice. Fortunately, the weeks of training leading to this point should have provided ample experience with focusing. Each climber will have a slightly different process for getting into the proper *zone* (the mental state of focus and concentration required for optimal performance), and many climbers have different ideas on what that zone should be. For example, some folks prefer complete silence, while others want their mates shouting encouragement. Each individual should determine the best zone for himself, by recalling moments in his past when everything clicked and he climbed confidently. What attitudes and thoughts were present during those moments, and what preparation led to them? Often these factors are difficult to control, but here are some effective methods for entering the zone:

- **Breathing.** Breathing is the key to the mind-body connection, in that it is a subconscious activity that can be controlled consciously.[3] Utilize this link to keep the mind calm and attentive, and the body relaxed and supple. Deep breathing will also reduce the likelihood of over-gripping during the climb, since it's difficult to squeeze really hard while breathing from the diaphragm. Start the breathing routine while booting up and tying into the rope. It's much easier to maintain good breathing once it is already started, not to mention that it helps to initiate any strenuous activity with fully oxygenated blood. Rhythmic breathing during final preparation helps calm the nerves, and sends a signal to the belayer that the climber is entering her zone. Breathe in through the nose so that the belly expands completely and causes the chest to rise. Hold the breath for a split-second, and then audibly exhale slowly and smoothly through the mouth while listening for a consistent rhythm. Effective deep breathing will slow your heart rate and relieve pre-climb jitters.

- **Be Consistent.** The order of final preparation is somewhat arbitrary, but each climber should keep that order consistent, and try to get deeper and deeper into the zone with each step. Simple rituals can be relaxing and put the climber's mind at ease, allowing him to focus completely on the task at hand. They also reduce the chances of forgetting a critical step (like tying in!). Identify a point during the preparation where chit-chat with the belayer should cease so you can get down to business.

- **Use Mental Cues.** Review any last-minute beta cues that are key to the ascent. Go over the general strategy for pacing and note any spots that require extra effort or commitment. Reminders like "shift hips to the right before slapping left hand" can be especially helpful. Finally, perform one last round of visualization, miming the moves while looking at the route. Chalk up one last time, check your knot, harness, and belay, and then go for it.

Once on the route, the climber's inner voice should narrate the moves, making sure to point out key reminders (such as hip shifts, etc.). While primarily focusing directly on the details of the moves in front of him, the climber must also regulate pace, ensure steady breathing, and avoid over-gripping. Fixed mental break points (like good rests or clipping stances) should be used to re-establish a deep, relaxed rhythm. Habitually reset breathing and relaxation each time such points are reached, even during route rehearsal.

Vision can influence thought patterns, so keep your eyes directed on objects that will reinforce mental focus. Depth perception should be limited to seeing no more than five to ten feet ahead, unless you're at a rest. Even at good rests, keep your eyes on the route, and only on the route. Visualize an upcoming crux or recall the locations of important holds. Often during a redpoint or onsight ascent, a looming roof or other distinct crux can be distracting. Obsessing over that particular section won't help you fire the slab 30 feet below it. Keep your eyes focused on the climbing immediately in front of you. During an onsight it is necessary to plan ahead somewhat, but generally long-range planning should be done from the ground or from a good rest stance.

Looking down much beyond the feet should be avoided. The only thing the climber needs to see when looking down is the last piece of solid pro and an attentive belayer. Everything else is a potential distraction. Granted, it may be prudent to downclimb during a challenging onsight, but at that point, the way up is down.

Verbal comments can be extremely helpful or extremely distracting, depending on the climber. These preferences should be discussed with the belayer, and any assembled onlookers, before leaving the ground. The climber shouldn't be afraid to ask for silence if that is his preference (or he can ask his belayer to do so on his behalf once he's left the ground). If verbal feedback is desired, specific cues or reminders should be requested, such as key beta points or reminders to relax and breathe. Ideally these comments should be provided at specific points along the route where the climber is inclined to hold his breath or over-grip. Finally, simple encouragement can be extremely helpful for powerful or committing moves requiring high arousal. Coordinate this encouragement in advance if it is desired.

Remain keenly relaxed throughout the performance. Avoid over-gripping, but be prepared to give maximum effort when the crux is reached. Have confidence that success is possible. If the preparation was thorough, there is a fighting chance. Believe in the beta that was so meticulously developed, believe in the plan, and believe in the training. Maintain an optimal pace, taking care not to rush intricate sequences. Stick to the sequences that were prepared. Rarely do spontaneous sequence changes pan out. There will be ample time to try all sorts of alternate sequences if the planned beta doesn't work out.

Expect the cruxes to feel hard. Don't hesitate unnecessarily. Instead, the climber should move steadily toward the crux and allow his momentum to carry him through. Remain mentally calm even if a desperate effort is required. Once past the crux, attempt to return to a relaxed physical state as quickly as possible by re-enforcing (or reinstating) proper deep-breathing habits and consciously relaxing the grip. Don't act surprised to have made it through the crux. That was the plan all along, so make sure the plan includes confident, cautious optimism once the crux is passed.

Smarter, Not Harder

One of my favorite expressions is "smarter, not harder." Advice to the effect of *try hard* is often misinterpreted to mean *squeeze as hard as possible as you scream like Sharma WHILE YOU ARE CLIMBING!!!* However, most of the time, it turns out that squeezing harder is not the answer. Discovering a new body position, distributing weight perfectly between fingers and toes, rehearsing the accuracy and timing of dynamic movements, pacing the effort correctly — these are often the keys to overcoming a challenging route. Rather than trying hard to execute a move by applying 100 percent of your crimping power, try hard to find a body position that allows you to do the same move with 80 percent exertion!

Furthermore, those that try hard only when they're literally on the rock — climbing — are missing out on countless opportunities to improve their climbing while on terra firma. Try hard to follow your training plan, schedule adequate rest, stick to a healthy diet, and get enough quality sleep. Try hard to wake up on time so that you can get to your project when the conditions are ideal.

At times, *physically* trying hard can be counterproductive, increasing the risk of injury or wearing down skin that could be saved for the next climbing day. Here are some guidelines for working smarter, rather than trying harder:

- Dose your efforts with a preference for quality over quantity
- Listen to your body; if you're too tired to give a quality effort, save it for tomorrow
- Don't climb frustrated, which is a sure path to regret
- Say "Take!" during a too-hard warm-up to avoid a flash pump
- While hangdogging, take a break to tape up before hucking for that sharp, gnarly jug yet again
- Consider new beta before doggedly trying the same move the same way for the tenth time
- Don't feel compelled to perform for the gallery.

When you are on redpoint (or onsight), on a meaningful climb, that is the time to go for it. If you're already in dogging mode, don't be a hero. Use that seemingly useless blob of ballast above your shoulders to do what makes sense in the long run.

– Mark Anderson

It's doubtful everything will unfold flawlessly, so be prepared to overcome some adversity during the ascent. Do not say "Take!" at the first sign of trouble. Keep fighting to the next clipping stance or jug and attempt to regroup by returning to deep, steady breathing and a relaxed mental and physical state. Remain focused on the moves immediately at hand, rather than on anxiety regarding success or failure. If the climber follows through, stays focused, and gives each attempt an honest effort, chances are he will come out on top eventually.

Performance Review

After any difficult performance, whether it results in a send or not, the climber should spend a few minutes debriefing the effort (preferably with the belayer or a coach). This is an opportunity to learn and increase the odds of success in the future. Discuss the aspects of the ascent that went right or wrong. The "Performance Review" sidebar recommends a few questions worth considering after any performance event. One purpose of this review is to identify possible triggers that brought about a lack of confidence, lack of resolve, or otherwise prevented you from focusing on the important tasks of breathing properly, climbing efficiently, and executing the plan. Once these triggers are identified, active measures can be used to overcome their influence. A great example of a trigger is dynamic movement, which causes many climbers to hold their breath. With practice and conscious effort, climbers can learn to restart breathing at the conclusion of such moves. Each climber must seek out these triggers in his or her own climbing, and develop a plan to overcome them.

Cooldown

Throughout the climbing day, encourage quick and thorough recovery by refueling and hydrating regularly. Food should be consumed in small, regular doses rather than singular heaping meals, so nibble on energy and protein bars every hour and save the sub sandwich for dinner. Pace climbing effort over the course of the day, limiting the length of working burns to avoid excessive fatigue. While resting between burns, stay out of the sun. Once the hard climbing is done for the day, and the performances have been analyzed for lessons learned, perform a cooldown to hasten the recovery process for the next climbing day. Climb one or two easy yet slightly pumpy routes, which will force blood through the forearms, flushing waste products and delivering blood glucose to the muscles.

Performance Review

Here are some key questions to consider when conducting a post-performance review:
- What went right or wrong?
- Was the warm-up adequate?
- Was there a point at which you started holding your breath or over-gripping?
- Did you maintain a positive attitude?
  - If not, at what point did it break down, and why?
  - If the breakdown was avoided, how did you do it? (Perhaps it was a shout from the belayer to "breathe deep," or a drill used in training that reminded you to relax your grip at the pivotal moment.)
  - Can something be learned from the tenor of your "Inner Dialogue"? Did it start out positive and devolve at a certain point?
- Did you stick to the plan? If not, why not?
- Did you attempt crux moves differently from how you rehearsed them, or did rehearsed sequences feel untenable when or redpoint?
- How did cumulative fatigue affect the performance?
- How did you feel physically (lethargic or energetic, strong or weak)?
- How did the committing (dynamic or scary) moves go?

The mind needs a cooldown as well. Most redpoint burns end in defeat, so finishing off with a couple laps on a favorite moderate or an easy onsight ends the day on a high note and instills positive memories of the crag and the day. After climbing, thoroughly stretch the forearm flexors and extensors as described in Chapter 9: Rest, Injury Prevention, and Rehabilitation. If practical, ice the forearms after any climbing session that causes a deep pump, in order to continue the muscle-flushing process throughout the rest period (a cool stream can be used when camping). See Chapter 9 for details on icing.

End each crag day with one or more moderate cooldown pitches, like *Moondance*, 5.11b, at Smith Rock, OR. John Borland www.morffed.com

SUMMARY

- External factors can make or break climbing performances.
- Be cognizant of environmental conditions affecting your goal routes, and plan your visits to coincide with periods of stable, predictable weather.
- Climb in the shade whenever possible.
- Ensure that you're familiar with your climbing equipment, that it inspires confidence, and that is in good working order.
- Be creative and exhaustive when discovering beta. Consider every possible option, and ask your partner to participate in this process. Consider clip and rest stances as well.
- Document your chosen sequence on video, paper, or both.
- Visualization is a powerful tool for improving performance. Visualize your sequence several times per day when working a difficult project.
- A thorough warm-up is essential for optimal performance. Warm-up the body *and* the mind.
- Stay focused during the performance. Practice getting in "the zone," use good breathing habits, and keep your attention on the task at hand.
- A broad and thorough route pyramid will provide the needed confidence to believe you will succeed on your goal route.
- Review each performance with your partner to identify any opportunities for improvement.
- End each climbing day with a cooldown. A cooldown will speed recovery between climbing days and ensure that each day ends on a high note.

The biggest adventures all start with the smallest of things.

Tommy Caldwell on the Dawn Wall, Yosemite

REDPOINT AND
ONSIGHT CLIMBING

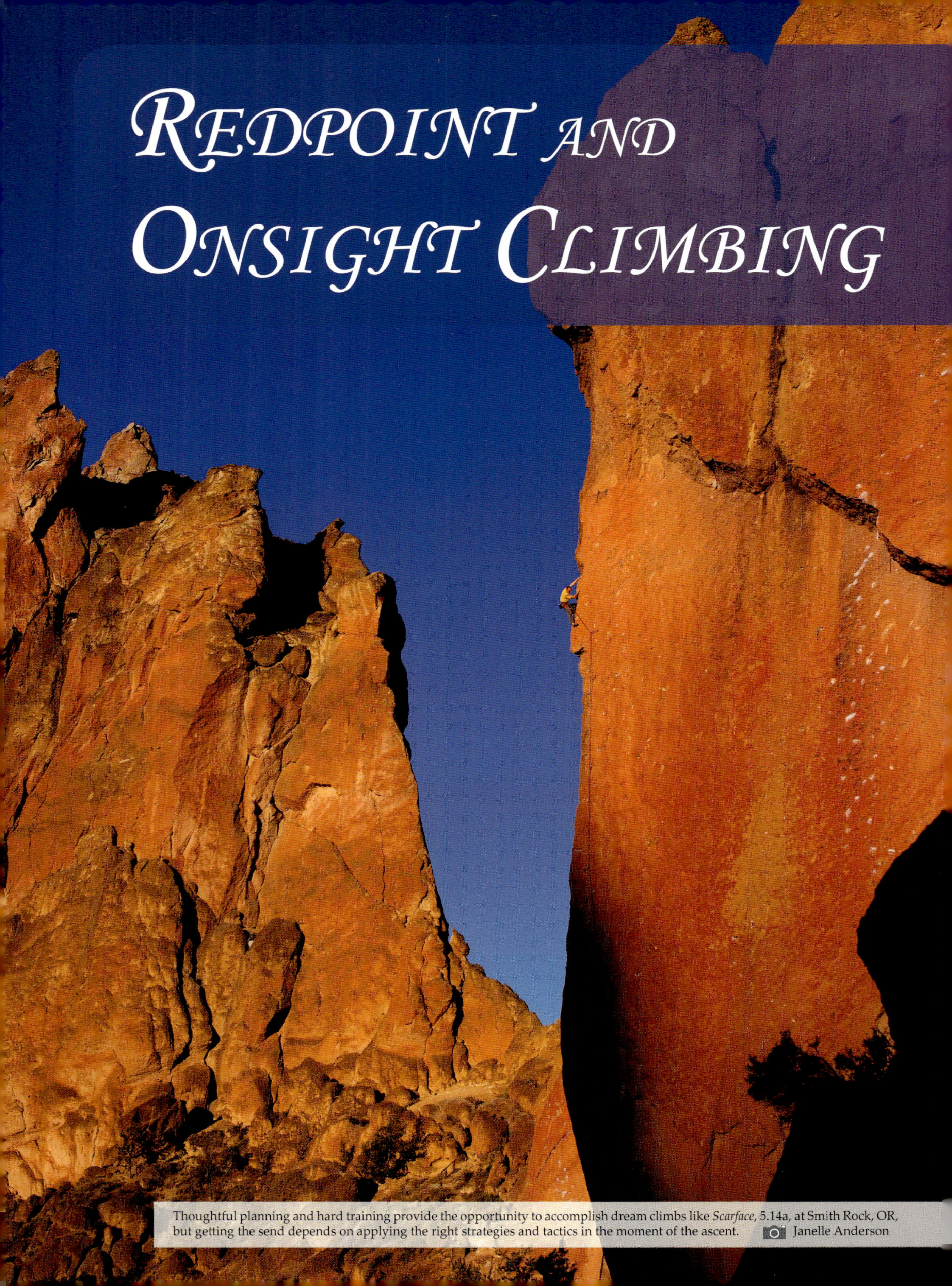

Thoughtful planning and hard training provide the opportunity to accomplish dream climbs like *Scarface*, 5.14a, at Smith Rock, OR, but getting the send depends on applying the right strategies and tactics in the moment of the ascent. Janelle Anderson

Chapter 13

"Long and successful climbing careers are like wars. Few people get to the other end without giving up or slowing down because they can't get past the many small failures and get back up and keep going until the success finally arrives."
— Dave MacLeod[6]

By the time a climber boots up at the base of his dream route, the outcome has largely been determined by the work he accomplished to prepare for that attempt. The route choice itself and the timing of the moment reflect this preparation — both are the result of careful research and planning. Crafting an effective plan and working hard by following through with the training are the most effective ways for a climber to achieve future success. Training effort is like compounding interest, multiplying its value over time, producing long-term improvement that could never be realized otherwise.

Nevertheless, for a climber to reach his highest potential requires the appropriate application of effort in the moment of the ascent. Not the *maximum* effort — the *appropriate* effort, because success usually hinges on the ability to ration effort along the climb, reigning in strength and power whenever possible so that both are available to unleash where they are most needed. This applies to the route-projecting process as much as it applies to the eventual redpoint. Careful application of physical effort, time, skin, and belayer patience is required to discover the keys to the route in time for a worthy redpoint attempt. In this chapter, this delicate and critical balancing act will be explored in detail for short-term redpoints, long-term redpoints, and onsight ascents.

STRATEGY FOR A SHORT-TERM REDPOINT

Not every route worth climbing requires a long, protracted siege to send, and there are numerous reasons for climbers to pursue routes below their absolute limit. Recall from Chapter 2: Goal Setting and Planning and Chapter 3: Skill Development that long-term improvement is best achieved through the pursuit of near- limit, *short-term redpoints* that can be sent in three to four days. In addition, the length of a road trip may dictate a short-duration project. The perfect example is a quick trip to a faraway crag with a particular classic route on the agenda that is unlikely to be onsighted, but may be completed in one to three days, if all goes well. Finally, not every goal route is at the climber's absolute limit, but sending it in personal record time can be a worthy challenge.

PLANNING THE CAMPAIGN

Short-term, near-limit redpoints pose unique challenges, so the strategy and tactics used should be modified accordingly. With limited time, energy, and even skin, each burn becomes more precious, so good planning is essential. First consider how many days are available and develop a plan for which days to climb, the time of day to climb, and when to rest, taking into account the weather, shade, sunrise, and sunset. The primary calculus when developing this plan is the tradeoff between working the route to learn and refine moves, and resting sufficiently to execute the redpoint. Working the route is very taxing, especially on a new project in which the climber can expect to consume energy and skin repeatedly attempting moves incorrectly before refining the beta. The "Weekend Plans" sidebar details how to make the most of a short trip.

237

Weekend Plans

The best way to optimize a climbing weekend is a classic debate among climbers, on par with *"Did Mallory reach the summit of Everest?"* This is a no-brainer for many, who just climb until failure every day, but the wily veterans know better. Climbing straight through a long weekend typically results in deteriorating performance, with the best day (the first one) "wasted" on learning the beta for the project. Over many three-day weekends my partner has ridiculed me for resting on the second day, only to burn himself out early on the third day, citing wrecked skin and overwhelming fatigue. We both wound up climbing the same amount (two days), but I had the advantage of a rest day between my climbing days.

For difficult climbing, the goal should be to fit in as many *high-quality* climbing sessions as possible. Sessions stacked atop each other without rest are not high quality. Also, working burns early in a campaign are more taxing because the most difficult moves are climbed repeatedly and often inefficiently at first. Therefore, more rest is called for early in the process. To maximize a weekend, take into consideration how much time is available, and the travel time to the crag. The coveted three-day weekend will afford two high-quality climbing days and a full rest day, while a two-day weekend may require climbing two days consecutively. If an early Friday arrival is possible, consider a Friday-evening climbing session, followed by a Saturday rest day, thus enabling a high-quality climbing day on Sunday (with beta) to send.

Breaking the days up into early-morning and late-evening sessions (so, resting midday) is a good strategy in the summer when days are long and midday heat is an issue. An effective strategy for a two-day summer weekend is to climb Saturday morning and Sunday afternoon (assuming shade is available), which allows for 24-plus hours of rest. Alpine starts aren't just for mountain climbers — don't be afraid to wake up *early* for the best conditions. Some of my most memorable sends came after a 4 a.m. wakeup call! A midday siesta will let you catch up on the rest you missed, and make better use of the entire weekend. Four-day weekends are like gold, and climbing on days one, three, and four will yield the highest-quality sessions.
— *Mike Anderson*

LEARNING THE ROUTE

Once on the route, a different calculus occurs: determining how much effort and time to spend learning each move, and what mysteries to save for the redpoint. A primary assumption is that the route is *near* the climber's limit, but not *at* the limit, which implies that a flawless effort is not required to send; the climber can afford to make a few mistakes or figure out certain moves on the fly. With unlimited time, a climber would do well to ruthlessly rehearse every move, but that is neither practical nor necessary for a short-term redpoint. Considering the entire route, the climber should assess each section and prioritize them by difficulty. Plan to spend the majority of rehearsal time and effort on the hardest sections while assuming some risk on the easier sections by under-rehearsing them.

THE FIRST BURN

On the first burn, it is imperative to attempt every move on the route, clear to the chains. The goal of this burn is primarily to understand the nature of the route: where the cruxes are, how difficult they are, where recovery will be possible, and ultimately if a redpoint is feasible in the time available. Besides that, the climber just might send on the second burn, and a minimal survey of every move gives him a fighting chance. Making it to the chains may require working moves less thoroughly, but there will be plenty of time for a more in-depth reconnaissance while lowering from the anchor or during the next burn. This first-burn "recon" helps the climber characterize the route and its challenges (a distinct crux, multiple cruxes with rests, or an endurance test), and informs his strategy going forward.

THE SECOND BURN

On a short-term redpoint, every subsequent burn (and possibly the first as well) should begin as a redpoint attempt, because you never know what might happen — you just might send! Once a fall occurs, the climber can lower and pull the rope if necessary to work the route properly. A possible exception to this rule would be a route with a high crux or one that features very pumpy, draining climbing that the climber clearly needs to rehearse before he is ready to redpoint. The second working burn should focus primarily on deciphering the cruxes. Work the hardest moves early in the burn, when most fresh, so you can apply maximum effort. Avoid doggedly repeating a single move over and over, especially on routes with small holds and/or sharp rock. This focuses wear and tear on the skin, and risks a devastating flapper in a location that coincides with a critical crux hold — apply tape proactively to prevent these injuries. If the move is troubling and tape won't solve the problem, come back to it later in the burn or later in the day, allowing your skin a chance to recover.

LEARNING THE MOVES

Lower cruxes require less refinement because a fall low on the route during a redpoint attempt is not devastating — the climber can quickly lower to the ground and restart. On the other hand, a fatiguing redpoint burn that fails high on the route will require lengthy recovery. Therefore, spend more effort dialing higher cruxes, including *redpoint cruxes* (cruxes high on the route that wouldn't otherwise be limiting, but become so because they are reached when you're already highly fatigued). With the upper sections wired, the lower cruxes can be approached with a boulderer's mentality — attempting low cruxes from the ground on redpoint, lowering back down between attempts, and continuing to the top when you eventually overcome these cruxes. This approach balances the effort between rehearsal and performance, so that during the redpoint attempts, the higher the climber gets

and the more fatigued he gets, the more practice and confidence he should have with the remaining moves.

The easiest sections of the route need not be ruthlessly wired, but they should be rehearsed in a manner that doesn't expend energy unnecessarily. The warm-up or cooldown can be spent lapping easy sections of the project rather than using that effort and skin on an unrelated route. Easier sections near the ground would be best for the warm-up, while higher stretches would be best to rehearse as a cooldown (sometimes it is possible to hang a toprope from an adjacent route in order to warm up on a high, easy run to the chains, or the climber might stick-clip up to that point). If there is any possibility whatsoever of blowing a redpoint attempt on the "easy run to the chains," it must be rehearsed thoroughly, including rest positions. The propensity to fail high on a route varies by climber, so if this is a common problem for you, pay extra attention to the final sequence of moves.

MENTAL REHEARSAL

Mental rehearsal and visualization are powerful tools that are essential for conserving energy and skin during short-term projects, when beta must be memorized quickly. When lowering after every burn, pause often to recall, visualize, and memorize sequences

The challenge of a short term redpoint campaign is to learn the moves quickly. Pause regularly to mentally rehearse the sequences while lowering after each burn. 📷 Andrew Burr

(remember, when climbing, the handholds will be viewed from below, so visualize them from a similar angle). Utilize the downtime between burns and rest days to mentally rehearse the project from the base of the route. See Chapter 12: Preparing to Perform for recommended visualization techniques.

RECOVERY

Because of the time constraints facing short-term redpoints, it is critical to recover quickly between burns and between climbing days. Good recovery begins early, by adequately refueling throughout the climbing day to restore muscle glycogen supplies. Eat recovery foods, and examine and treat skin between each burn throughout the climbing day. Once the hard climbing is done for the day, enhance the recovery process by performing a thorough cooldown, stretching, and then icing as described in "Cooldown" in Chapter 12: Preparing to Perform.

GOING FOR THE REDPOINT

Once the sequences are unlocked, it is time to attempt a redpoint (actually, it's not uncommon to attempt a redpoint on the first try). When a redpoint burn ends in a fall, the climber faces another decision of whether or not to work the route, or lower immediately to conserve resources for the next burn. *In general, the climber should work the route after each unsuccessful burn, continuing to the chains to ensure that the climb's highest, most fatiguing sections are also the best rehearsed.* Adopting an attitude that the climber will surely send on the "next try," and then lowering to the ground without additional practice, usually prolongs the project. This approach is rarely justified, unless it is the last burn of the trip.

Immediately after a fall, analyze the attempt. Don't focus solely on the point where the fall occurred; often, falls result from errors made lower on the route. Instead, review the entire performance, noting all sequences that were climbed inefficiently, or points of hesitation or uncertainty about the proper sequence. A simple mental rehearsal with miming may be adequate for sequences that were unclear or climbed hesitantly. On the other hand, the climber must physically rehearse cruxes that depend on subtle details, such as how the holds are gripped, foot location and placement, hip position, and the timing of movements. If any of these details are unresolved, lower down and rehearse them (reposition the rope if necessary). Finally, be sure to brush or otherwise clean any key holds while lowering off the route.

If all goes well, you'll soon be sipping champagne around the campfire, but don't use this metric to judge the value of the experience. Whether or not the effort results in a send, working through the process will expand your sphere of experience and knowledge, increasing the likelihood of success on the next campaign.

STRATEGY FOR A LONG-TERM REDPOINT

A *long-term redpoint* is any project that takes more than a week's worth of climbing days to complete. Some such projects can take entire seasons, multiple seasons, or even multiple years to complete. Projects of this length can be intimidating, but they can also be extremely rewarding. These campaigns test the boundaries of one's physical and mental abilities, requiring extreme fitness, commitment, and perseverance.

Generally speaking, long, protracted sieges should be used sparingly. They can be the ace card for ascending a lifelong goal route, but they are normally not the best path to steady improvement. Imagine two climbers, one who spends three straight seasons working one 80-foot route with 50 moves. His buddy works and sends three routes per season of roughly the same length. The climber who chose shorter-term projects will be exposed to roughly nine times more sequences, a wider variety of rock types, and many different styles of climbing. The climber who chose to invest the entire year on one project will learn a great deal about the strategic and mental aspects of climbing performance, but he won't learn many new moves, and will be exposed to a relatively narrow selection of climbing styles and physical challenges over the same time period.

By this point it should be apparent that, for the purpose of achieving continuous improvement, training is preferable to climbing. Eventually every protracted project devolves to a point of training on the route. While this strategy may result in a send in the fewest number of calendar days, it wastes countless climbing days — days that could be spent sending other quality lines, while fitness and skill continue to steadily improve. In the long run, it usually makes more sense to stay on the path of continuous improvement and return to the lifelong goal route when it can be climbed in fewer days.

Regardless, sooner or later most climbers will benefit from working a route that is a reach for their climbing ability. Such experiences are tremendously inspiring, require the climber to raise her game through dedicated training, and can produce substantial personal growth, humility, and, ultimately, improved confidence.

PLANNING

Committing to a project that could span multiple years is no simple matter. This leap should be well-considered. A cavalier attitude usually results in a lack of commitment. A long-term project requires uncommon determination and perseverance, which are difficult to apply without a strong commitment to the process. The first step is to decide if such a project is desirable. Good reasons to make the leap are a lack of inspiring shorter-term options within the climber's target zone (routes that can usually be sent in six days or less), or proximity to a particularly inspiring line that is barely within reach (such as a lifelong goal route). Err on the side of spacing such campaigns too far apart, allowing at least a year's worth of near-limit (short-term) projecting in between. Consider how this project might affect potential partners. Are they willing to visit the same crag day-in and day-out for multiple seasons? Discuss this with the affected parties and make sure the entire team is supportive.

Selecting the objective is a big decision, one to be taken after careful consideration. This route will be the object of obsession for a long time, so it should be worthy of your full attention. If possible, reconnoiter the potential candidates to determine which line is most suitable. This is usually not the time to work weaknesses, but rather to favor routes that play to your strengths. The route should be fun and enjoyable to climb on. A move that feels a bit painful on day one will feel downright gnarly on day 20. Geography can be a big factor — a nearby route can be worked more frequently. Also, consider the general weather conditions — routes with narrow windows of good weather will lead to frustration. Ultimately, the line must be inspiring. The ensuing effort to climb this route will put all previous accomplishments to shame, so the route must produce unequaled amounts of motivation to get the climber through the months (and sometimes years) of training that will be required to succeed.

Once the objective is defined, the fun can begin. If an initial recon was not conducted, do some research on the route to uncover as much information as possible about the style of climbing, physical attributes and abilities required to send it, and the best times of year to attempt the route. Develop a long-term plan for the campaign, including a rough estimate of how long it is expected to take. Count the days out on a calendar to get an idea of how many weeks or seasons will be required, but don't expect everything to turn out according to the plan. (While it varies considerably by climber, a good rule of thumb can be to triple the amount of time spent on a project for each letter-grade increase in difficulty. Thus if 13a takes three days, 13b might take nine, and 13c, 27!)

The Seasonal Training Plan should be developed such that the Performance Phase coincides with the

Genetic Drifter, 5.14c, Wild Iris, WY, was the ideal long-term project for BJ Tilden, being a dream route at his local crag. He made the second ascent in 2009 after many years of concerted effort. 　Chuck Fryberger

ideal climbing conditions for the goal route. For a geographically distant project, it may make sense to make an initial visit early in the year to learn the character of the route, followed by another season of training dedicated specifically to that route, and then finally a return trip to send. If specifics about the crux moves are known, consider augmenting the training plan to target these moves, particularly if they exploit a known weakness (for example, if the crux requires the use of a mono pocket, incorporate this grip into the Strength Phase). If possible, construct boulder problems on a home wall that replicate crux moves.

Where to Begin?

A long-term project will begin much like any other: with the climber confident the send will materialize much sooner than it actually does! These efforts are ultimately a test of will. Like any project, with sufficient rehearsal, the moves will eventually become familiar enough that they can be linked on redpoint. The real question is whether the climber can sustain motivation long enough to see the process through to the end. It may help to begin each season with one or two short-term projects to inspire confidence and provide a pseudo "insurance policy" on the season, because the gratification of sending the long-term project could be a long time coming.

A beyond-limit project will be intimidating upon initial inspection. While strategies for short-term redpointing demand previewing every move on the first burn, the climber will be lucky to attempt every move of a long-term project on the first *day* (and many of the moves will likely feel impossible). Begin by separating the route into sections that can be dealt with individually. Have faith that eventually the sequences can be linked, but first focus on simply identifying the most efficient way to climb the individual sequences. Consider each section like its own boulder problem, with the initial goal to send ten (or however many) individual boulder problems.

Focus on the Process

When working a long-term redpoint, focus on the process. The detailed process of discovering and refining beta is not much different than for any other project; the difference is that these steps will take much more time, so it will be necessary to set modest goals for each burn or climbing day. Every crag day should begin with a clear set of goals for that day. These should include some performance goals (for example, "attempt to climb from the ground to the chains with two hangs or less" or "send the crux on lead"), but also some goals that are achievable regardless of performance (such as, "rehearse the moves between the fourth and sixth bolts" or "find a better clipping stance for the seventh bolt"). Weekends, or sets of climbing days, should begin with clear goals as well. For a multi-season project, the goal for the first season might simply be to climb all of the individual moves.

Climbers will want to focus most of their energy and attention on the crux sequences initially. These sequences will require the most time to "learn down," so get an early start. It makes little sense to dial the moderate entry moves if the crux is impossible. That said, small victories can go a long way, so save some time each day to enjoy the easier moves. Attempt the most powerful sections earlier in the day (or burn), and save the easier moves for later. As the moves come together, explore how best to exploit the rest stances, then spend time rehearsing the easier moves to save energy for the cruxes.

Long-term projects require repetitive use of specific body positions and holds, so repetitive stress injuries are possible. Limit the number of attempts per day on moves that use tweaky or otherwise threatening body positions, and limit the use of extremely sharp holds to avoid damaging skin. Often the early days of a limit project will be completely exhausting, as the moves are rarely climbed in the most efficient manner, and must be attempted repeatedly. Early in the process you should plan extra rest days and limit the length of burns (use a stopwatch if necessary). As the beta starts to come together, there will be ample time to run to the chains on every burn.

Maintaining Motivation

The difference between success and failure often boils down to motivation, because the desired result (a redpoint ascent) is often too distant to be motivating. To the contrary, simply contemplating the redpoint, as far off as it feels, can be overwhelming and demoralizing. If the climber can stay psyched long enough to see the process through, success is likely. The best way to maintain motivation is to enjoy the process of learning and embrace the present challenge. Unfortunately, many projecting climbers develop a vague schedule for their project, which then becomes a cruel source of frustration. As soon as the rate of progress exceeds this arbitrary schedule, the climber is elated; and whenever it lags behind, he is disappointed. Rather than obsessing over imaginary deadlines, focus on making progress each day. Be satisfied with each new

Motivation is essential for any long-term project, including that of the belayer(s). A faraway route, and/or a long approach will increase the pressure, as Jason Haas learned on his remote route *Question Your Progression*, 5.14a, South Platte, CO. 📷 Ben Schneider

opt to work a long-term project concurrently with other short-term projects or onsights in order to spread out the physical and mental wear and tear, and hedge their bets. Mixing in other climbing can buoy self-esteem, prevent de-training, and relieve belayers, but there are downsides. At a minimum, this approach extends the length of the project, but even worse, the lack of commitment often leads to a loss of focus and eventual abandonment of the long-term project. Consider these factors when deciding how to approach a long-term project.

THE END GAME

Once the redpoint is within sight, it may be beneficial to alter your mindset slightly. By this point, the best warm-up climbs should be identified — those that are enjoyable, don't aggravate skin or other ailing body parts, and prepare the mind and body to perform at their peak. Professional athletes often describe *the grind* as a consistent routine that can reliably produce peak performance while minimizing stress. Climbers can use this approach by accomplishing every task in the same order, using this routine to build a sense of calm confidence in anticipation of the impending challenge.

At this point, it's common for anxiety to build up as a result of all the hours and days that have gone into the effort. Remain focused on the learning process, approaching each day as another opportunity to learn and improve,

bit of information that is discovered, and revel in every new high point or improved link.

In addition to setting intermediate goals that provide opportunities to achieve periodic success, strive to make the process fun. Climb with friends who keep the mood light, savor the hike to the cliff, and take time to climb fun moderates every now and then. There will be plenty of time to stress out over the outcome down the road, so enjoy the growth process for as long as possible. Watch inspiring climbing videos, or read a hero's autobiography on rest days to maintain psych.

It may be helpful to take a break from the project occasionally to onsight routes at another crag, climb a multipitch route, or enjoy some non-climbing recreation. Find an activity that breaks up the routine and gives the mind a chance to reset. A well-timed break will have the climber itching to get back to her project at the next possible opportunity. Many climbers

rather than hoping that today is the day. Take every step as it comes, and eventually the right opportunity to send will present itself.

Most successful long-term projects involve one or two near misses, where the climber fails on a relatively easy move when it seems the ascent was in the bag. While not ideal, these near successes are not the end of the world either (if the climber reached that point once, he can do it again). Entering the process with an acceptance that this may happen can reduce the immediate stress that comes when the climber finally sends through the crux, or surpasses a previous high point. Be pleased with the new progress, rather than worried about the coming sequence. Either way the day has proven successful, so continue with focus and the knowledge that there is "nothing to lose." Overconfidence can sour the experience and distract the climber from focusing on the climbing at hand.

Live to Fight Another Day

Occasionally the selected project is simply too hard (for now). Endlessly persisting under such conditions is no fun, but even worse, it won't help the climber improve. Sometimes it makes sense to "cut bait" and focus energy on other routes or additional training. One method of informing this decision is to consider how much time is budgeted for the total campaign, and then strive to hit certain milestones within a percentage of that time. The specifics will vary depending on the nature of the route (powerful vs. pumpy, etc.), but generally one might expect to have done all of the individual moves by the end of the first quarter, linked the route in three or four sections by halftime, and one-hanged the route by the end of the third quarter. If the climber is five days into a ten-day trip and still can't do several moves, it might make sense to move on (or start planning a return trip).

External influences can provide additional decision points. Shifts in weather, significant skin issues, an aching joint, fatigue of partners and family, or waning fitness can all provide opportune moments to re-evaluate the strategy. Once all the moves are known, steady progress should come in the form of increasingly longer links and fewer hangs on the rope. As long as the climber is still making progress (at least every other day) and remains motivated, it often makes sense to continue. When in the throes of a long-term project, climbing efficiency typically improves as physical fitness wanes. Once waning fitness outpaces efficiency, progress will stagnate or even regress. If the climber is consistently failing in the same locations,

Two Years and 14 Days

I first attempted Scarface in the spring of 2005. I spent five days working the route, and at the end of the week there were still several tweaky pocket moves I couldn't do. Clearly I was not strong enough for the route, but I was inspired by this thrilling line and determined to climb it someday. I added a few more pocket grips to my strength-training program, but otherwise went about my normal business of working and sending projects closer to home. Scarface remained in the back of my mind, providing inspiration during monotonous training sessions.

In spring 2006 I returned to Scarface, and this time I did all of the moves on the first day, despite the twelve-month hiatus. I was stunned. I made much more progress that week (including several "two-hang" ascents), but now that I had the strength to do each move, it became clear that I lacked the power-endurance to link them.

Again I returned home, and focused on improving. That year I sent several memorable routes, including my hardest redpoint to that point. Early in my preparations for the spring 2007 season, I created a Linked Bouldering Circuit (modeled after the moves on Scarface) to improve my power-endurance. On my first day back on Scarface I matched my previous best, and three days later, I sent it — my first 5.14. It was nice to tick Scarface, but the redpoint was insignificant compared to the improvements that were inspired by my desire to climb it.

A dream route like *Scarface* can inspire us to elevate our climbing. Like a distant beacon, it guides our training, and motivates us daily to work harder. Mike Anderson

— *Mark Anderson*

day after day, it may be a sign that he has reached this threshold of declining performance. When tangible progress on the route reaches this plateau, it usually makes sense to reconsider the approach.

As discussed above, attempting to train on the project route to regain waning fitness is not ideal. A better long-term strategy is to return to the optimal training venue (usually the gym), redouble your efforts to improve as a climber, and then return to the project in a few months or a year. The knowledge gained during the process is equally valuable whether it results in a redpoint or not. Many times a climber returning to a route after a long layoff will discover more-efficient sequences that had previously gone unnoticed. Approaching the project a second time, with fresh energy, skin, and fitness, is often the quickest path to success. Finally, one of the great aspects of this sport is that the route will always be there to climb. The knowledge discovered during the initial campaign, along with the realization that a valued send is close at hand, can be used to inspire the next round of training, resulting in significantly improved fitness and a much more productive campaign the next time around.

ONSIGHT CLIMBING

To many, onsighting represents the pinnacle of climbing mastery. An onsight ascent is one in which the climber leads a climb successfully without prior rehearsal on the route, or specific information about the climbing. An onsighting climber will not know where a route's cruxes lie, or what moves are typically used to surmount them. He won't know anything beyond what he can presume from the ground. An onsight is the purest form of ascent, with no stylistic compromises — no hangdogging, rehearsing, or borrowing beta. Onsight climbing transcends the sub-disciplines of climbing. Be they trads, rads, or pebble-wrestlers, all climbers respect the onsight ascent because it is the ultimate test of climber versus the rock.

"To me onsight climbing is the ultimate, the perfection; it's putting it all together and making the best ascent you can on a route." — Lynn Hill[4]

In many ways, onsight climbing demands the most from the climber, and the most preparation. An onsight ascent is to a redpoint as a street fight is to a choreographed Hollywood fight scene. The onsight climber must react to the situation as it unfolds, bobbing and weaving, if you will, to navigate the punches thrown by his opponent in real time. Without prior knowledge of the route ahead, the onsight climber has little time to contemplate strategies and engineer the perfect sequence. The onsight climber must immediately execute whichever to-be-determined movement skills are required for the ascent, so whatever skills he needs, he must carry with him — hanging from the rope to acquire new ones is not an option. As such, the wise onsight climber will cultivate a broad set of climbing skills and the ability to deploy them at a moment's notice, ideally as a subconscious reflex. While a redpoint climb can be (and often is) selected to hide a climber's weaknesses, that tactic is unreliable for onsighting. An onsight climber with a glaring weakness might get lucky a few times by happening upon climbs that don't expose it, but he cannot rely on this good fortune to continue forever.

Is it an Onsight or a Flash?

Opinions vary on how much prior-knowledge about a route is acceptable for an ascent to earn the lofty title of *onsight*. Some hardliners argue that even knowing the grade is TMI (too much information), but most climbers accept that it is reasonable to know the grade and path of the climbing. Many modern guidebooks give away more details than that, such as the location and relative difficulty of crux sections, or even specific moves or rests ("kneebar at the fifth bolt..."). My own rule of thumb is that any information about a route that appears in the printed guidebook (that is generally available to anyone) is fair game. I've made this decision because it's impractical for me to ignore an entire guidebook to a favorite area merely to avoid reading route descriptions or viewing topos of routes I may want to onsight someday. However, I will avoid reading lengthy Internet-posted route descriptions such as those found on MountainProject.com or similar websites. In the end, unless the international media is logging your ascents, it's likely that only you and your crew really care about what you call an onsight. Therefore, as with all stylistic "rules" of sport climbing, each climber must define his or her own standards.

— *Mike Anderson*

When onsighting, the climber must be prepared to execute any move the route throws at him, as Greg Kerzhner discovers on *Ride the Lightning*, 5.13b at the New River Gorge, WV. 📷 Dan Brayack

Obtaining the physical fitness and broad repertoire of skills is one challenge to mastering onsight climbing. The other, more elusive skill is developing the ideal samurai-like state of mental arousal needed for difficult onsights. This preferred state is a mix of calm relaxation and heightened awareness that allows the climber to control the unconscious workings of his body and absorb a mass of information from the environment. It enables the climber to retrieve any skill that might be required or to generate a sudden herculean effort. While the challenges of onsight climbing are largely mental, there are key physical demands that are distinct from redpoint climbing. The following section will address these unique challenges, and how to develop the skills (mental and physical) to overcome them.

> "What makes climbing so great is that its rules are not given from human beings, they are given from nature, so there are as many possibilities as there are rocks on this planet."
>
> — Fred Nicole[3]

SKILL DEVELOPMENT FOR ONSIGHT CLIMBING

The most fundamental step to improving at onsight climbing is to develop a repertoire of climbing skills, as discussed in detail in Chapter 3: Skill Development. In redpoint climbing, any necessary skill that a climber lacks or is deficient in can be learned or improved during the route-rehearsal process. For onsight climbing, a wide array of climbing skills must be developed in advance. While it is best to acquire completely new skills in a low-stress gym environment, the goal of the onsight climber should be to strengthen existing skills such that they can be applied to various outdoor climbing situations, and eventually the high-stress environment of an onsight. Proven methods for strengthening these skills are presented in Chapter 3.

PHYSICAL TRAINING VARIATIONS

Onsight climbing places different physical demands on the body than redpoint climbing does. A potential limit onsight route will be of an easier technical grade than a limit redpoint, thus the holds will generally be larger or closer together, the route less steep, etc. The largest difference may be the length of time it takes to climb the route. A well-rehearsed redpoint may last a few minutes or less, while a lengthy onsight could take dozens of minutes. A redpoint may contain less demanding sections that are climbed at a slow pace, but the crux sections will nearly always be climbed at a much faster pace than is possible during an onsight. Onsight climbing will generally involve these physical variations:

- Slower pace
- Larger holds
- Climbing more statically
- Longer duration
- Recovering from difficult climbing at poor rests
- Downclimbing difficult moves

While this may sound overwhelming, the good news is that many of these traits can be developed through training exercises that are already part of the Rock Prodigy program. Most of these traits relate to local forearm endurance, and thus are best trained through the same exercises used to develop forearm endurance for redpoint climbing, with slight adjustments to better suit the unique demands of onsight climbing. The ultimate physical training for onsight climbing is Base-Fitness Training, where many of the necessary skills can be developed concurrently. As a matter of necessity, the lion's share of climbing during an onsight attempt will take place below the Maximum Steady State (MSS), with only short, infrequent bursts above it to surpass crux moves.

The standard ARC workouts described in Chapter 5: Base-Fitness can be used to train for onsighting, but emphasis should be placed on climbing at a slower pace and with a less-dynamic style. Lock-off exercises can be used, such as hovering over each handhold for one to two seconds before grabbing it to simulate searching for holds on an onsight attempt. In addition, downclimbing can easily be practiced while ARCing, but you should emphasize downclimbing more difficult moves than might otherwise be downclimbed in your typical ARC session. The terrain used for ARCing should match, as nearly as possible, the terrain of the onsight goal routes in terms of angle, hold density, and type. It is essential to develop the ability to rest at poor stances and recover by actively climbing, which can also be trained while ARCing.

The following *recovery drill* is a good exercise for onsight training. Begin the drill as for a standard ARC workout, with at least 10 minutes of moderate-intensity traversing to ensure that the MSS has been reached. Once in the ARC zone, climb a more difficult boulder problem that forces you beyond the MSS, but without spitting you off the wall. After completing this crux, assume a demanding rest position and then shake out as necessary to return below the MSS. Once recovered, continue ARCing for a period of time, and then repeat the drill. Alternatively, rather than shaking out at a stationary rest stance, the climber may continue climbing on easier terrain and practice recovering through the act of climbing — an essential skill for overhanging climbs. Typically this *moving recovery* will involve climbing quite slowly with forced breathing, shaking each arm briefly between each move. Moving recovery requires a loose grip — as loose as possible without falling off — so intense concentration should be focused on relaxing the grip as much as possible and placing maximum weight on the feet. Breathe deeply to slow the heart rate and restore the calm that may have been lost during the crux section. The recovery terrain for this exercise may need to be easier than typical ARC terrain for the climber. Alternate between stationary and moving recovery during onsight-training sessions.

The Rock Prodigy program can be tailored to favor onsight climbing performance by adjusting the training in terms of pace, hold size, and duration, as well as by practicing crucial onsighting skills like recovering at taxing rest positions. ◉ Mike Anderson

Initially, these exercises should be done on a bouldering wall, where easy and hard terrain can be easily identified, crux sections can be pre-rehearsed, and tricky rest stances can be created. Rests should place significant strain on the arms, so avoid stems, ledges, or good kneebars. Instead, rests should be on steep terrain with positive handholds that require the climber to recover under load by using a relaxed grip, weighting the feet as much as possible, and alternately shaking each arm.

As the climber progresses, these exercises should be performed in lead-climbing situations, adding an element of stress that better simulates real-world onsighting scenarios. It may require some pre-planning and trial and error to locate the desired terrain. In a climbing gym, where routes of varying difficulty are set on top of (or very near) each other, consider using parts of multiple climbs. For example, on a gently overhanging wall, you might up- and downclimb the "blue route," a juggy 5.10, for ten minutes to get established at the MSS, then (without switching ropes or moving) climb the crux of the "yellow route," a crimpy 5.11+, before switching back to the "blue route." This approach multiplies the route-climbing options available. This technique can be used to a lesser extent on the rock. Two closely spaced routes can be mixed and matched to add or remove cruxes, or an easier route can be climbed as an eliminate — deliberately skipping certain holds — to modulate the difficulty of the climbing as needed for the workout.

While a majority of onsight climbing will take place below the MSS, on limit onsights the climber will inevitably call on his power-endurance (PE) for portions of the climb. Therefore, PE training such as Linked Bouldering Circuits (LBCs) or Route Intervals should be used to train for onsighting. Again, to improve the specificity for onsighting, PE exercises should be performed at a slower pace, on holds and angles similar to the climber's onsight limit, rather than redpoint limit terrain. Thus, while an LBC geared for redpointing may last one and a half to two minutes and include three boulder problems totaling 20 intense hand moves, an onsight-focused LBC might aim to complete 20 slightly easier moves in two and a half to three minutes The selected LBC might even offer the possibility to shake out at poor rests. If possible, perform the LBCs on problems you don't know well (which can complicate the problem-selection process).

Many of the physical skills necessary for limit onsights can be obtained within the confines of a red-point-centric training program, but if onsight climbing is the highest priority, the training program should be adjusted to favor these desired outcomes. Others place the highest priority on redpoint climbing, mixing in onsights occasionally. When following the Rock Prodigy training program, the ideal fitness for onsighting typically arises near the end of the Performance Phase. This is when endurance, technical skill, and familiarity with lead climbing and falling are all at their peak — ideal for most limit onsights. However, onsights of short, powerful routes (or routes with short cruxes split by excellent rests) should be attempted in the first two weeks of the Performance Phase, when power is highest.

MENTAL PREPARATION

For a climber who has decent fitness for redpointing, onsighting is primarily a mental test. Forearm endurance can easily be undermined by a poor mental state, leading to poor breathing, tunnel vision, misreading sequences, inefficient movement, over-gripping, and eventually pumping out. This can't be overstated: Great endurance only helps the climber who is able to climb efficiently, without over-gripping! A well-trained climber who panics on a climb, stops breathing, and over-grips will fail every time.

These behaviors generally result from the climber's own assessment that the route is too hard for him and failure is likely. This makes the climber tense, causing him to over-grip throughout the climb, wasting energy and exacerbating the pump. His movements will be rigid and static rather than flowing and smooth, because he is constantly anticipating retreat or afraid of what is to come. He doesn't believe there will be rests so he's in constant fear of pumping off. When a crux arises, he's likely to rush through it too quickly because he's certain climbing slower will make him pump off. If the climber attempts a sequence incorrectly, he is likely to doggedly persist, assuming that it is the correct sequence and he is simply not strong enough to climb it. Instead of this attitude of "impending doom," climbers should seek a mental state in which they are relaxed and confident enough to remain calm when faced with adversity, but ready to spring into action with decisive effort when needed — call it "cautious optimism."

"Mountains have a way of dealing with overconfidence." — Hermann Buhl[‡]

Onsight Climbing with a Fear of Falling

Climbers who struggle with a fear of taking lead falls must address this issue before utilizing the other techniques discussed in this chapter. All of the challenges of onsighting pale in comparison to dealing with a fear of falling. The calm mental state needed for difficult onsights cannot be achieved by someone who is pre-occupied by a fear of falling. That is not to say that such climbers should not attempt onsights, but they should realize that the set of challenges facing them on an onsight is different than what is addressed here. Climbers who fear leading and taking lead falls would do well to read Arno Ilgner's groundbreaking *The Rock Warriors Way*,[5] and then return to the subject of improving at onsight climbing when they are not handicapped by anxiety over falling.

Onsight climbers must be willing to go for it at any moment, without regard to falling anxiety. Cheryl Pirozzi feeling the heat on *Tacos Diablos*, 5.13a, Alta, UT. Brendan Nicholson

Cautious optimism describes an attitude in which the climber feels that there is a high likelihood of success on the route, but also understands that it will be hard and a great effort will be required. Still, he believes that he will rise to the occasion and succeed. Therefore, the climber must have the confident belief that he is skilled enough to send the route, something a climber can't lie to himself about. This confidence imparts several advantages during an onsight. It imparts a belief that the climber can recover if a mistake is made, and a belief that he will find the correct sequence through the crux. This relaxed mental state makes it easier to take the climbing as it comes and solve movement problems as they present themselves. In a sense, it is a self-fulfilling prophecy: If the climber believes that the onsight is possible, or even likely, then it just might be. That belief enables the climber to remain calm and relaxed, climb most efficiently, and thus handle the physical challenges. On the other hand, when a climber believes the onsight is not possible, or even unlikely, it most certainly will be.

Unfortunately, there is no easy road to acquiring this confidence. It is a result of your self-image, and thus a result of your true accomplishments (not including whatever "fish tales" you may relate to your mates). A climber builds that confidence by building his accomplishments through an onsight-specific route pyramid (see Chapter 2: Goal Setting and Planning). A climber contemplating a 5.12a onsight attempt has tangible confidence if he has onsighted other 5.12a's, or many 5.11d's, especially if they are of similar styles and at the same crag as his target onsight route.

Onsight pyramids should begin humbly, with routes well below the climber's limit, because there is only one shot to onsight each route. Work to build a substantial base at each grade before moving up to the next. Therefore, an onsight pyramid should be flatter than a redpoint pyramid, and it should only be composed of outdoor routes on real rock. The nature of gym climbing eliminates most of the challenges of onsighting, so these routes will not build the necessary skills for onsighting on rock. Given the variety of climbing styles, it is also advisable to build pyramids for each rock type or crag; for example, a climber might track separate route pyramids for granite, sandstone, and limestone sport climbing. You shouldn't expect your onsight prowess to immediately transfer to a new crag, so again, start humbly with a route pyramid to learn the peculiarities of the new crag (e.g. weather conditions, unique techniques, rock friction and foothold confidence), then gradually ratchet up the difficulty as familiarity grows and confidence builds. This will be the best use of time on a road trip and will set the climber up for success on limit onsights later

Replacing Your Misplaced Calm

One thing I've learned through experience and careful observation is that I tend to hold my breath during strenuous moves, especially dynamic moves. While this by itself isn't too terrible, the real problem is that I forget to restart breathing after the tough move or dyno ends. My breathing throughout the climb will dramatically shift from slow, deep breathing before the move, to shallow, inadequate breathing after — up until the point where I over-grip, get pumped, and fall off. I've had success overcoming this with a simple drill I call *Finding Calm* (see Chapter 3: Skill Development). This drill is easy to practice during ARC sessions.

Plan your ARC terrain to incorporate several dynamic moves. Take some time to perform these dynos during each ARC set. Consciously force yourself to pause after every dyno and re-start your breathing with slow, deep breaths. Also deliberately relax your grip, force weight onto your feet, and if possible shake out. It is very helpful to have a partner observe you because it is so easy to forget to do this after *every* hard move. As with any new skill, you must transition it to real rock climbing for it to be useful. Therefore, as the drill gets easier during your ARC workouts, incorporate it into more realistic scenarios: PE training exercises, outdoor warm-up routes, and eventually difficult redpoints and onsights. With directed practice, the bad habit of breath holding can be reduced or even eliminated.

— *Mike Anderson*

in the trip, when success is most likely. For onsights of a specific route you highly covet, it would be prudent to log several onsights at that grade before the pivotal attempt. Still, be certain to try eventually — failure is guaranteed if you never give it a go.

PREPARING FOR AN ONSIGHT ATTEMPT

After all of the training and preparation, it is time to go for the onsight. The first step is to select an appropriate route, but which routes make for good onsight opportunities? While climbers often joke about routes that they are "saving for an onsight," some do hold climbs in reserve for many years without an attempt, hoping to onsight them at some time in the future. Climbers do this because ideal onsight routes are often few and far between, especially at certain crags or on certain rock types. The best candidates for onsights are heavily chalked routes, preferably sporting fixed draws. Routes with low crux sections are also a good choice, because they are easy to scout from the ground. A good onsight candidate is of consistent, sustained difficulty, and thus lacks tricky, hard-to-read, stopper crux moves. Routes like these are generally very popular, and are thus easy to spot at most crags. Most of all, the ideal onsight routes are brilliant, magnificent routes that beg to be climbed and will inspire a great performance.

Once a route has been earmarked for an onsight attempt, very specific preparations should take place. It's best to set aside climbing days specifically for onsighting. The preparations for limit onsights and limit redpoints are distinct enough that combining both in the same day will leave the climber inadequately prepared for one or both. First, be clear with yourself and your partners that the intention is to onsight the route. Commit decisively to that goal. If the attempt is unsuccessful, you can return for a redpoint, but at least commit that first attempt to an all-out effort for the once-in-a-lifetime chance at the onsight. Anything less than total commitment to that attempt will lead to indecision once on the route and less than 100 percent effort when it is needed. The belayer should be in the loop about the onsight attempt to give the correct encouragement, and notify bystanders that the climber doesn't want beta shouted from below.

Warming up for a limit onsight should be slightly different than that for a redpoint. Perform a warm-up that's slightly longer than normal to dial in balance and footwork, because onsight climbing depends so heavily on movement skills. While the warm-up should include a standard progression of increasingly difficult routes to prepare the body, the mind needs preparation too. Therefore, if possible, the warm-up should include easier onsights so that you can practice the unique physical and mental skills required for onsighting. This will gradually build the climber's confidence, and create an opportunity to assess whether or not he or she is ready for the goal route.

Finally, just before an onsight attempt, the climb should be reconnoitered, as described below. A reconnaissance may go on for years before climbing a particular route, but at a minimum, it should be scouted throughout the warm-up, leading up to the attempt, with a final, thorough recon just before tying in. The climber should have a general strategy for the route, with specific plans for navigating the seeming crux sections. Discuss these with the belayer so he or she will know when to expect rests, when falls are more likely, and when maximum encouragement will be appreciated.

Routes that are heavily chalked, with fixed draws make good candidates for onsighting. Mike Anderson defying the laws of gravity to onsight *40 Oz of Justice*, 5.13a, at the Red River Gorge, KY. Dan Brayack

ROUTE RECONNAISSANCE

The ability to anticipate the necessary climbing movements, or to *read* the climb, is a critical skill for onsighting. This process occurs on the ground, before an onsight attempt, but it also goes on continuously throughout the ascent. Climbers read routes from the ground routinely in the climbing gym, especially while bouldering, where it is typically easy to see all the holds. Generally a climber begins by visualizing the starting hand positions, and then imagining the sequence of hand movements leading to the top. Depending on the complexity of the route-setting, this may be very straightforward in a climbing gym, but it is much more difficult on real rock, where there are many more holds to choose from, they are more difficult to see, and they often look very similar. Bring a cheap pair of binoculars to the crag, and use them to help identify holds from the ground. Furthermore, the holds on a real climb do not necessarily follow a logical, manmade pattern, so the moves may be much more complex. Additionally, reading an entire route requires analyzing an order of magnitude more movements than what you encounter on a gym boulder problem. Fortunately, there are a few techniques to simplify the process.

Hot Flashes

This chapter focuses mostly on onsight climbing, so if attempting a flash ascent (climbing a route first try with beta from other climbers), consider these tweaks:

- When receiving beta from another climber, be cognizant of physical differences such as reach, as well as strengths and weaknesses. Bubba's beta may not fit Suzie.
- Consider the pros and cons of using beta from a long-term projector vs "second-try guy." The long-term projector probably knows the best sequence, but unless he can boil it down to a few easy-to-remember sentences, the information may be overwhelming.
- If a running "spray-down" is available, take it! If you disagree on the suggested sequence once on the route, just bear down and execute the moves as instructed. Let the mind focus on breathing and relaxation.
- If nothing else, learn the *locations* of cruxes and rest positions. Beyond that, the most useful information to obtain is the proper *sequences* for the cruxes.
- The Internet is full of climbing videos. Just about every route worth climbing has been filmed. Find some video footage and study it before the ascent if possible.

Before an onsight attempt, carefully inspect the route and anticipate the climbing sequences. Fred Gomez anticipating a *Wild Gift*, 5.12c, RRG, KY.

The first step is to break the route into sections that can be more easily digested (or *chunk* it). Routes vary, but it's often logical to chunk the route by bolt locations, or apparent rest stances. Start by simply judging if each section will be easy or hard. Easy sections should be simple to identify — e.g., those that are less steep or those that are densely packed with good holds. Don't be fooled by easy-looking sections high on a route, where it can be difficult to judge the distances between holds. Two good holds that seemed a short span from each other when looking up from the ground could turn out to be part of a difficult crux. Sections of difficult climbing will have smaller holds, and generally fewer of them. Other cues, such as the quantity of chalk, may reveal where cruxes are. An increase in tick marks or a heavily chalked rest hold just before a thin-looking section may indicate a crux. On a route with fixed draws, an especially worn carabiner (indicating the site of many falls) or extended draws may hint at hard climbing to come.

Once the route is chunked, identify the sections that appear easy enough to be climbed onsight without detailed reconnaissance. These sections should be scanned for potential rest stances and superficially sequenced (hands only, perhaps) to catch any potential "gotchas." Otherwise, don't expend much effort meticulously sequencing these sections. The sequences are likely to be forgotten anyway, and that memory will be put to better use elsewhere on the route. Note the rest opportunities, and move on to the crux sections.

For crux sections, the goal is to create potential sequence options. The most basic planning is to decide which hands will use which holds, and in which order. Spend time analyzing each handhold. The locations of tick marks or thumbprints on the rock can be critical clues as to how best to use a given hold. This information will help decipher a sequence. For example, a horizontal edge with a prominent thumbprint to the lower left is used by most climbers with their right hand. Thumbprints are especially pronounced near pockets. Next, consider how each hold will be gripped: Is it a crimp, a pinch, or perhaps an undercling or sidepull? Identify if certain holds would be used best from certain angles, as not every hold is best used in a straight-down pull. Pockets in particular lend themselves to use as sidepulls and underclings.

Finally, identify the footholds that will be necessary to execute the crux moves. Remember, the merit of a particular foothold has more to do with its location than its size or shape. Opposition holds, such as underclings and sidepulls, require opposing footholds, so locate these and imagine using them. If these footholds aren't apparent, perhaps the assumed opposition sequence is not correct.

Once the holds are assessed individually, imagine the movements between them in an unbroken sequence. If a particular handhold combination can be identified, such as the right-hand edge mentioned above, work backward and forward from that point to fill in the gaps. Matching or shuffling moves may be required if a viable sequence can't be identified. Considering the hand and footholds together, determine if any unusual body positions will be necessary, such as backsteps or drop-knees. Recalling the chunks, ensure that a clear sequence is identified from the beginning of the chunk to the end. Preferably these chunks would end at a rest hold, or at a minimum, a hold large enough to match on, so that the sequence used for the next chunk is independent of the preceding chunk.

Once each section has been assessed and visualized, create a strategy for the route as a whole. Decide on a climbing pace for each chunk: Easier sections should be climbed more slowly, to conserve energy and cultivate the desired calm mental state, while hard sections will dictate a faster pace, to avoid pumping out. Identify where you'll rest and how you'll clip each bolt. Identify the most likely failure points on the route. These may be the hardest chunks, or moderately hard chunks high on the route where fatigue is a factor. Identify the rest positions immediately before and after each apparent crux, and assess the possibility of downclimbing to a rest if a planned sequence turns out to be incorrect. Focus on these crux sections last so that the planned sequences will be freshest in your memory.

Finally, the last step should be to completely visualize and mime the climbing of the route from bottom to top, including clipping. The climber should do this at the same pace intended for the climb (rests can be abbreviated), while practicing good breathing — slow and deep. If done right, the climber's heart may race as she mimes the crux sections. This is great — it's an opportunity to practice breathing deeply and relaxing to regain the calm state that will be needed at the same point on the climb. At the top of the route, visualize clipping the chains and the gratification that will bring.

PERFORMING DURING AN ONSIGHT

Once on the route, the real mental challenge begins: managing the flow of effort to conserve energy throughout the climb, while poised to conjure superhuman effort to overcome cruxes. During a well-rehearsed redpoint, many climbers seek an *autopilot* state in which they robotically execute the moves, sparing their conscious mind to focus on relaxation and breathing. Onsighting is not that simple.

> ## Onsight Literacy
>
> Keep this checklist in mind (or better yet, in hand) when reading a route at the crag prior to an onsight attempt:
>
> - Chunk the route into manageable sections, preferably separated by good rests.
> - Sort the chunks into easy and hard categories. An increase in tick marks may indicate a crux, while a heavily chalked jug may signal a rest.
> - In the easy chunks, look out for "gotchas" and identify rests, but don't otherwise over-analyze these sections.
> - Spend your time and memory on the hard chunks; locate and assess the handholds — chalk patterns, such as thumbprints and tick marks, can give away sequences.
> - Identify the crux footholds, focusing on those that are in the best location.
> - Connect the holds to develop sequence options through the hard chunks, ensuring a continuous sequence from the start of the chunk to its end.
> - Once the chunks are planned, create a strategy for the route as whole, including pacing, resting, likely falls, and possible downclimb points. Discuss these with the belayer.
> - Finally, mime the route from bottom to top, with appropriate pace and breathing, and make sure to clip the chains when you send!

"Absolute strength is less important in climbing than the ability to unleash your strength at the right time...When Elie Chevieux onsighted the first 5.14 I do not think he could do a one-arm pull-up, but he knew how to read the rock and anticipate the moves with incredible intuition." — Fred Nicole[2]

Along with route-finding and sequence problem-solving, the onsighting climber must consciously ration effort throughout the climb, and adjust the pace of climbing through each section. The climber should already have a plan for this, but the route may dictate real-time adjustments. When a rest comes, the climber will need to explore and assess the quality of it in order to decide how long to spend there (use the MSS as a guide). When first arriving at a rest on route, look for ways to improve the rest (various hand positions, hidden holds, thumb catches, scumming other body parts, etc.). After four to five shakeout cycles, pick the best, most relaxing rest position and stick with it, because rests often become more restful with practice, as confidence in the footholds grows and the grip relaxes.

While actively engaging in problem-solving, it is essential to keep an emphasis on relaxation ongoing in the background. Accomplish this primarily through deep breathing, which should begin *before* the climb starts — while tying in. Deep breaths will keep the heart rate low, force slower climbing, and encourage a relaxed grip. The belayer should monitor the climber's breathing throughout the climb (requiring loud breathing on the part of the climber!), reminding her to "breath deep," especially after dynos or crux sections when the climber is likely to tense up and lose focus.

Recall the desired attitude of cautious optimism. As challenging sections materialize on the climb, be confident that a solution will present itself. If a move feels overly difficult, perhaps you've missed something: a key foothold, a different way of grabbing a handhold, a different body position — don't automatically assume that the move should be as hard as it initially feels. Some moves, such as long dynos, are irreversible, and thus very committing. Only make such moves as a last resort. These moves can often be completed with a lock-off, or a slow dyno or dead-point that gives the climber a chance to remain on the rock and try again in the event the dyno fails. Dynoing to an unknown hold gives the climber very little time to assess the best way to grip the hold, so if the move can be slowed at all, the chances of successfully latching the hold increase significantly.

In many cases, when faced with a perplexing crux, it is best to downclimb to the closest rest rather than forge ahead with a poor plan and weakening body. It's not unheard of for a skilled onsight climber to downclimb past multiple bolts to reach a good rest, resulting in a successful onsight. Whether and how far to downclimb always depend on the situation, but take into account the desperation of the current perch, the quality of any available rest, and the likelihood of making it there. Downclimbing to a good rest that is likely to be reached is never a bad choice, because a well-trained climber can achieve nearly full recovery, with patience, and will cultivate a better mental state in the process.

Generally, an onsighting climber should seek to approach the style of climbing used on hard redpoints: flowing movement that is not too static but also not out of control. Novel moves will be encountered, but they should be similar to moves the climber has done hundreds of times. Don't overanalyze them; the body remembers how to climb these moves, so let it do so. Intensive, conscious pre-analysis of moves should be a last resort, reserved for the most perplexing cruxes, and preferably only performed from a good rest position. Consider a trail runner: She doesn't pre-plan every foot placement and muscle movement; she flows along the trail, calling on years of practice to make thousands of subconscious decisions on the fly, only thinking consciously when faced with extraordinary obstacles like a large rock or downed tree. Throughout the climb, use deep, regular breathing, slow but flowing (not jerky) movement, and a relaxed grip. The conscious mind should be reserved to focus on the pressing issues of pacing, rationing effort, and active problem-solving.

Inevitably, a limit onsight will require a decisive moment, when the moves are too difficult to climb in this flowing, Zen-like state. These are the make-or-break moments when the climber must bust out some hard moves. In these cases the climber should not expect easy climbing, but should be confident that he has a good shot at sticking the moves. He should then investigate all of the possibilities to flow past the crux before deciding to go for it. Realizing there is only one chance, the climber should resolve to climb in a manner he won't regret later — and to try hard! When engaged in a desperate crux section, don't dillydally.

When onsighting, the tremendous mental challenge is to remain calm and relaxed while reserving the ability to spring into action to execute any unanticipated cruxes. Cheryl Pirozzi chills the *Lemon* 5.12, the Hoop. 📷 Brendan Nicholson

There should be a plan before setting out, so execute the plan as quickly as possible. Don't try to milk every hold to get a better grip; if you stick the hold, move on to the next one and get through the crux. It's going to feel awkward and hard (especially during an onsight), but this is what makes the route challenging — deliberately savor the challenge, and don't try to avoid or delay it! Once past the crux, it is critical to return back to the state of calm efficiency in order to complete the remainder of the route and cruise to the chains.

PERFORMANCE REVIEW

A difficult onsight attempt should be reviewed and evaluated immediately after the effort, just like a difficult redpoint attempt (see "Performance Review" in Chapter 12: Preparing to Perform). Due to the unique mental requirements of onsighting, there is an even greater opportunity for improvement by conducting a thorough, honest evaluation of how your mental state evolved during the climb. Most of the evaluation criteria used for redpoints apply to onsight attempts. In addition to those, also consider:

- How did your mental state, and its evolution during the climb, differ from what is typically experienced on a limit redpoint?
- How did you react to uncertainty or deviations from the plan?
- How did the actual movements compare to the planned sequences developed during the reconnaissance?
- How can those differences inform future recons?

After every onsight or redpoint attempt, take time to evaluate the effort, review the moves, and note any lessons learned.
Mike Anderson

No Purchase Necessary, but Must Be Present to Win

Not to sound like a know-it-all, but you will never onsight the route you never try. It sounds painfully obvious, yet climbers make this mistake all the time. They assume they aren't capable of onsighting a certain grade, so they simply never try. This frequently happens with a route the climber has decided will be a redpoint project. They declare their first attempt a "working burn," and thus *plan* on hanging on the rope at the first opportunity. Why not forfeit one burn (there will be more) and give an all-out try for the onsight? Are you reluctant to "waste" a burn on an unlikely onsight attempt? Keep in mind, even if you fall, you're likely to gain critical knowledge that may be the key to eventual success. Maybe you'll get "lucky" — more accurately, maybe your low expectations and "nothing to lose" attitude will enable you to climb better than you normally would on a high-stakes onsight. Maybe you'll succeed; you'll never know if you don't try.

SUMMARY

- Structured training is the most effective use of time and effort for continuous improvement, but it's also necessary to apply effort at the crag, during performances, to realize those improvements.
- For the fastest and surest long-term improvement, it is best to select redpoint projects that can be completed in five climbing days or less. This approach exposes the climber to more routes over the long term, and thus a wider variety of climbing styles, movements, and challenges.
- During a short-term redpoint, the challenge is to learn the moves quickly and move on to redpoint attempts. Therefore, it isn't necessary to perfect every move — focus on learning the cruxes and the final pumpy run to the chains (when applicable).
- Long-term redpoint projects should be attempted only rarely (such as when a dream route is within reach). Consider the location, your strengths and weaknesses, and level of inspiration when selecting a mega-project.
- A long-term redpoint will have very hard cruxes, so work on these moves early in the process, early each day, and early each burn. It's also helpful to target training to the route.
- Once committed to a long-term project, see it through to a logical conclusion and enjoy the process. Split the route into believable segments, set achievable goals for each day, and try to make tangible progress each day. Take a break or a long hiatus once progress stagnates.
- Onsighting is the ultimate expression of climbing mastery. There is only one chance for success, so it requires the climber to be completely prepared before the ascent. Developing a broad repertoire of climbing moves and techniques is the best preparation.
- Onsighting generally requires more endurance than redpoint climbing, to allow time for the climber to discover the moves as he climbs. Rely on the body's natural climbing instincts and don't try to analyze every last, trivial move.
- The climber's mental attitude is critical to onsight climbing. Be cautiously optimistic and have confidence that success is possible, but be ready to exert great effort when needed. Evaluate and learn from every onsight attempt, and use the experience to develop as a climber.

TRADITIONAL AND BIG WALL FREE CLIMBING

Traditional climbing can take you to magnificent locations. Mike Anderson on the upper reaches of Half Dome during the First Free Ascent of *Arcturus*, 5.13b, Yosemite, CA. 📷 Andrew Burr

CHAPTER 14

"The magnificent beauty and historic significance of [The Nose], as well as my own efforts to free it, then later freeing it in a day, made this ascent the most meaningful achievement of my entire climbing career." — Lynn Hill[1]

Traditional climbing skills provide access to some of the most spectacular and inspiring features on the planet. From soaring shields of flawless Sierra granite to gravity-defying towers of Wingate sandstone, the ability to perform on gear-protected terrain opens the door to a magnificent world of limitless adventure. While the intricacies of gear placement are beyond the scope of this book, there are technical climbing skills and physical-fitness requirements unique to traditional (trad) climbing that can make a significant difference on the sharp end. Furthermore, besides its intrinsic value, trad climbing can also reveal gaps in a climber's capabilities, and thus provide an excellent means to improve general climbing weaknesses.

THE UNIQUE REQUIREMENTS OF TRADITIONAL CLIMBING

Due to the differences that often exist between sport and trad climbs, a slightly modified training approach should be used. While traditional routes can take nearly any form, this discussion focuses primarily on the most archetypical trad routes: granite and sandstone gear-protected climbs that are not very steep. These types of trad climbs differ from the typical sport climb in many important ways. Training adjustments can be made to better prepare for such a goal trad route. These general differences include:

Trad routes can be much longer than the typical sport pitch, requiring modified training. Rob Pizem high over the fjord on Steind, Norway. Andrew Burr

- Length: A sport pitch rarely exceeds half a rope length (30m) and is usually much shorter, while some trad pitches go for an entire rope length (60m) and can be much more physically repetitive.
- Duration: Regardless of the pitch length, trad routes often require more time to recpoint due to the need to place protection and the

intricate hand placements required for jamming cracks.

- Angle: Trad climbs are generally vertical to slabby (step back from the cliff and it's clear that most of those Indian Creek splitters are less than vertical).
- Pace: The need to place protection and fiddle with jams slows the trad-climbing pace.
- Hold type and size: The jams afforded on a trad climb require specialized techniques to exploit, and may be painful, or even injurious.
- Duty cycle: Handholds will generally need to be gripped much longer than those on a typical sport climb, but they're usually better holds. The rest period between holds is also longer owing to the need to carefully place intricate jams.
- Rests: The occasional "bomber" jam means that rests will likely be more frequent, but they may be more complex and less amenable to alternating-hand shakeouts.
- Gear: Removable protection adds weight to the climber and slows him down. It may also increase leading anxiety and (justifiably in some cases) reduce the willingness to go for it.

- Onsight: Because of historical practices, some climbers emphasize a ground-up or onsight-preferred approach to trad climbs. Big walls or multipitch climbs often necessitate such an approach.
- Shoes: Certain trad climbs may call for specialized climbing shoes (such as a very stiff-soled shoe) that otherwise hamper general footwork.
- Conditions: Trad climbs are often located in extreme environments with imperfect conditions. Furthermore, on multipitch climbs, it may not be possible to time the climbing so that the hard pitches are climbed under the best conditions.

Trad climbs generally share many traits with vertical face climbing, which makes them good substitutes for each other for training and/or practice. Trad and face climbing both benefit from strong, precise footwork by allowing the feet to support a large portion of the climber's weight. They both tend to have small face holds that require precision and power to exploit. Additionally, with the obvious exception of the perfectly continuous enduro cracks of the Colorado Plateau,

Trad routes typically hinge on the climber's ability to execute short, technical boulder problems, where power and footwork are paramount. Jean-Pierre Ouellet finding a *Home on the Range*, 5.13, Vedauwoo, WY. 📷 Andrew Burr

most trad climbs consist of one or more bouldery cruxes separated by generally good rests. While endurance is a factor on these climbs, they rarely require a *power-endurance* sprint typical of many overhanging sport climbs. Instead, the redpoint most often hinges on the ability to execute boulder-problem cruxes above gear, and recover at the intermittent rests afforded by a good jam or large foothold. These critical characteristics dictate how best to train for these types of trad climbs.

TRAINING ADJUSTMENTS FOR TRAD CLIMBING

To maximize trad-climbing performance, the Rock Prodigy program should be adjusted to account for the unique requirements of trad climbs. The training should be tweaked to improve the climber's ability to execute technical, vertical boulder problems and to sustain long-duration redpoint or onsight efforts. Therefore, notwithstanding a specific goal route with more definitive characteristics, a climber training for a generic trad-climbing goal should increasingly empha-

Hard Trad...Or Is It Sport?

"I haven't learned nearly as much from cracks that I can apply to face as I have from face that I can apply to cracks. Sport climbing gives you a new repertoire of moves and ways to position your body. For me, faces used to be the crux — now they're an opportunity." — Steve Petro[4]

As routes increase in difficulty, the apparent distinctions between trad and sport climbs begin to fade. With few exceptions, as cracks get more difficult, they become narrower, incipient, and less secure. The crack becomes less useful for upward progress so the fundamental jamming skills that are essential on a moderate crack climb become less critical to success. Instead, difficult cracks rely more on face holds and face-climbing techniques, and the crack itself, rather than being the star of the show, is just another member of the supporting cast, contributing its poor features for face climbing. It is also common for so-called "trad" routes to sprout more fixed protection (which may include fixed pins, nuts, cams, bolts, etc) as the difficulty increases, further blurring the line between "sport" and "trad."

As routes increase in difficulty, the line between "trad" and "sport" becomes blurred. The standard-setting *East Face* of the Monkey, 5.13d at Smith Rock, OR is the perfect example. 📷 Mike Anderson

These distinctions can be left to the media for now, but as goal-oriented athletes, our focus should remain on what, if any, changes should be made to our training to prepare for a difficult trad goal route. Fortunately, this merger of climbing styles toward the top of the grade scales actually simplifies the job of selecting and accomplishing the proper training. As you rise through the grades, it becomes more likely that your typical training approach to sport climbing will be effective for that occasional trad project. Whether you call it "sport" or "trad," it's helpful to commit to your goal route (sport or trad) at the beginning of the season, identify the relevant characteristics of the climb (length, angle, difficulty and duration of cruxes, etc.), and adjust your training accordingly to prepare for the specifics of the route.

— Mike Anderson

Good footwork is a tremendous advantage in trad climbing. Tommy Caldwell using his feet on *Vital Transformation*, 5.12c, Squamish, British Columbia, Canada. 　Andrew Burr

size hangboarding, ARCing, Route Intervals, and skill practice (especially outdoors, on relevant rock types). Linked Bouldering Circuits, Campus training, and over-hanging indoor climbing should be deemphasized.

Trad climbing is very technical, both in terms of movement and protection skills, and thus more responsive to improvements in technical skill. There-fore, when training for trad goal routes, it is appro-priate to emphasize technical skill practice by setting aside extra time for practice. This may necessitate re-placing typical indoor training activities with outdoor training, or reducing the volume of indoor sessions to allow for supplemental outdoor sessions, which per-mit more specific technical skill practice. Base-Fitness training is the easiest to accomplish outdoors. Indoor ARCing should be replaced with Outdoor Mileage (OM) on relevant rock types whenever possible. To maximize the effectiveness of the practice, set skill-development goals, make a plan, and be mindful of these throughout the climbing day. Don't let it de-volve into unstructured cragging. Vary the fear and/or risk elements as necessary to stress-proof new skills as they develop.

Regardless of the climbing style — sport or trad — the fundamentals of good climbing technique al-ways apply: weighting the feet, precise and efficient movement, grip control, breathing, remaining calm, etc. In some cases — when difficult, insecure protec-tion is involved — some of these factors may be *more* important than in sport climbing. Every aspiring trad climber should re-emphasize the learning and prac-tice of these critical abilities. To tailor indoor practice sessions to trad climbing goals, select vertical, or near vertical terrain, and limit footholds to small screw-on holds (aka jibs) and/or sculpted features. It is a com-mon mistake to learn and practice these techniques on indoor face climbs, where the footholds are unre-alistically large and positive; then, struggle to apply them later where it counts, on often-slabby outdoor trad climbs with micro-footholds. Therefore, *specifi-cally emphasize transferring these skills to outdoor trad climbs*. This can be accomplished in two ways; first, by utilizing realistic terrain for indoor practice (near-vertical with tiny holds), and second, by setting aside specific outdoor climbing days (such as the OM climbing sessions suggested below) for deliberate practice and stress proofing, as described in Chapter 3: Skill Development.

A seasonal training plan is shown on p262 that has been tailored for trad climbing goals. This sched-ule prescribes more outdoor climbing than the sport climbing–oriented training plans because indoor climbing gyms are generally not very specific to trad climbing (the typical gym terrain of steep/juggy/slopey doesn't adequately simulate typical trad climbing terrain, rock, and hold types). The following adjustments have been made to tailor this plan to a trad-climbing goal:

- During the Base-Fitness Phase, many of the standard indoor ARC training sessions have been replaced with OM climbing, scheduled to coincide with the weekend. Climbers may adjust as necessary to capitalize on their typical outdoor cragging days.
- The Strength Phase has been lengthened to accommodate outdoor training activities in addition to the nine hangboard workouts. Roped bouldering on hard trad routes or a Limit Bouldering session may be used for these outdoor strength exercises. Also during the Strength Phase, additional Base-Fitness training sessions have been added in the form of OM or ARC training on the days following intense strength training. These adjustments are prescribed in order to enhance the *potential* for trad climbing–specific skill development. That development will only occur if the climber diligently and thoughtfully applies the principles described in Chapter 3: Skill Development toward his or her specific trad-climbing skill weaknesses.
- The Power Phase has been reduced accordingly.
- The Power-Endurance Phase can be absolutely essential or completely superfluous depending on the training goal. This example includes a substantially reduced PE Phase, which exclusively consists of longer-duration Route Intervals to develop the type of fitness required for pumpy trad climbs. Instead of short-duration PE, trad climbers will generally rely on long-duration PE and an increased Maximum Steady State (MSS) resulting from the numerous additional ARC workouts in the season. This modification is suitable for an athlete training for a long enduro crack (climbed mostly below the MSS) or a big-wall free climb with long pitches sporting short, bouldery cruxes.
- The "optional" tag has been removed from many of the Aerobic Exercise workouts to prepare climbers for the workload of multipitch climbing. However, there is at least one full rest day per week.

Where there's a will...Alex Honnold on *No Way Jose*, 5.13c, North Wash, UT.   Andrew Burr

Week	Sunday	Monday	Tuesday	Wednesday	Thursday	Friday	Saturday
–	*Last Week of Performance Phase of Previous Season*						
–		*Rest Phase of Previous Season*					
–							Sa — Day 1 *Outdoor Mileage (OM), 8 pitches *Skill acquisition
1 (Base Fitness)	Su Day 2 *OM, 8 pitches *Skill acquisition	Mo 3 *Aerobic Exercise (AE)	Tu 4 *ARC 1: 2 x 20 min *Skill acquisition	We 5 *OAE	Th 6 *ARC 2: 2 x 25 min *Skill acquisition	Fr 7 *Optional Aerobic Exercise (OAE)	Sa 8 *OM, 12 mod pitches *Skill acquisition
2	Su 9 *OM, 12 pitches *Skill acquisition	Mo 10 *AE	Tu 11 *ARC 3: 3 x 30 min *Skill practice	We 12 *ARC 4: 3 x 25 min *Skill practice	Th 13 *ARC 4: 2 x 30 min *Skill practice	Fr 14 *OAE	Sa 15 *Outdoor Roped Bouldering (ORB) 1 (hard trad routes)
3 (Strength Phase)	Su 16 *OM, 8 mod pitches *Stress-proofing *Skin care	Mo 17 *AE	Tu 18 *Hangboard (HB) 1 *Supplemental Ex	We 19 *Opt ARC: 2x20 min *AE *Skin care	Th 20 *OAE	Fr 21 *HB 2 *SE	Sa 22 *OM, 8 mod pitches *Stress-proofing *Skin care
4	Su 23 *OAE	Mo 24 *HB3 *SE	Tu 25 *Opt ARC: 2x20 min *AE *Skin care	We 26 *AE	Th 27 *HB 4 *SE	Fr 28 *Opt ARC: 2x20 min *AE *Skin care	Sa 29 *OAE
5	Su 30 *ORB 2 (hard trad routes)	Mo 31 *Opt ARC: 2x20 min *AE *Skin care	Tu 32 *AE	We 33 *HB5 *SE	Th 34 *Opt ARC: 2x20 min *AE *Skin care	Fr 35 *OAE	Sa 36 *ORB 3 (hard trad routes)
6	Su 37 *OM, 8 mod pitches *Stress-proofing *Skin care	Mo 38 *AE	Tu 39 *HB6 *SE	We 40 *Opt ARC: 2x20 min *AE *Skin care	Th 41 *OAE	Fr 42 *HB7 *SE	Sa 43 *OM, 8 mod pitches *Stress-proofing *Skin care
7	Su 44 *AE	Mo 45 *HB 8 *SE	Tu 46 *Opt ARC: 2x20 min *AE *Skin care	We 47 *AE	Th 48 *HB 9 *SE	Fr 49 *Opt ARC: 2x20 min *AE *Skin care	Sa 50 *OAE
8 (Power Phase)	Su 51 *LB Outdoors (boulder or routes)	Mo 52 *AE *Skin care	Tu 53 *LB 105 min *SE	We 54 *AE *Skin care	Th 55 *LB 105 min *SE	Fr 56 *OAE *Skin care	Sa 57 *LB Outdoors (boulder or routes)
9	Su 58 *OM, 8 mod pitches *Stress-proofing *Skin care	Mo 59 *AE *Skin care	Tu 60 *LB 105 min *SE	We 61 *AE *Skin care	Th 62 *LB 105 min *SE	Fr 63 *OAE *Skin care	Sa 64 *RP Attempts *OM, 2 mod pitches
10 (PE)	Su 65 *RP Attempts *OM, 2 mod pitches	Mo 66 *OAE *Skin Care	Tu 67 *WBL 60 min *Linked Bouldering Circ (LBC), DC=2:4	We 68 *OAE *Skin Care	Th 69 *WBL 50 min *LBC, Duty Cycle (DC) = 2:4; SE	Fr 70 *OAE *Skin Care	Sa 71 *RP Attempts *OM, 2 mod pitches
11 (Performance Phase)	Su 72 *RP Attempts *OM, 2 mod pitches	Mo 73 *OAE	Tu 74 *OAE	We 75 *WBL 40 min *LBC, Duty Cycle (DC) = 2:3; SE	Th 76 *OAE *Skin Care	Fr 77	Sa 78 *RP Attempts *OM, 2 mod pitches
12	Su 79 *RP Attempts (pumpy rtes) *OM, 2 mod pitches	Mo 80 *Skin Care	Tu 81 *RP Attempts *OM, 2 mod pitches	We 82 *Skin Care	Th 83 *RP Attempts *OM, 2 mod pitches	Fr 84 *Skin Care	Sa 85 *RP Attempts (pumpy routes) *OM, 2 mod pitches
13	Su 86 *Skin Care	Mo 87 *RP Attempts *OM, 2 mod pitches	Tu 88 *Skin Care	We 89 *RP Attempts *OM, 2 mod pitches	Th 90 *Skin Care	Fr 91 *RP/On Sight (OS) Attempts *OM, 2 mod pitches	Sa 92 *Skin Care
14	Su 93 *RP/OS Attempts *OM, 2 mod pitches	Mo 94 *Skin Care	Tu 95	We 96 *WBL 45 min	Th 97 *Skin Care	Fr 98	Sa 99 *RP/OS Attempts *OM, 2 mod pitches
15	Su 100 *RP/OS Attempts *OM, 2 mod pitches	Mo 101 *Skin Care	Tu 102	We 103 *WBL 45 min	Th 104 *Skin Care	Fr 105	Sa 106 *RP/OS Attempts *OM, 2 mod pitches
16 (Rest Phase)	Su 107 *RP/OS Attempts *OM, 2 mod pitches	Mo 108	Tu 109 *OAE and/or Optional Cross-Training	We 110	Th 111 *OAE and/or Optional Cross-Training	Fr 112	Sa 113 *OAE and/or Optional Cross-Training
17	Su 114	Mo 115 *OAE and/or Optional Cross-Training	Tu 116	We 117 *OAE and/or Optional Cross-Training	Th 118	Fr 119 *OAE and/or Optional Cross-Training	Sa 1 First Day of Next Season

Key:

LBC - Linked Bouldering   RP - Redpoint

m/min - Minutes

OCT - Optional Cross-Training

SE - Supplemental Exercises

DC - Duty Cycle (work-to-rest ratio)

M/mod - Moderate

OS - Onsight

ARC - Aerobic Restoration and Capillarity Training

LB - Limit Bouldering

OAE - Optional Aerobic Exercise

HB - Hangboard Workout

WBL - Warm-Up Boulder Ladder

Key:
HB - Hangboard Workout   LB - Limit Bouldering
Circuits   OAE - Optional Aerobic Exercise
OM - Outdoor Mileage
WBL - Warm-Up Boulder Ladder

Seasonal Training Plan for trad route climbing. This example allocates time for outdoor skill development throughout the entire season while emphasizing the Base-Fitness, Strength, and Performance phases and deemphasizing the Power and Power-Endurance phases. Additional Base-Fitness workouts are prescribed through the Strength Phase to further reinforce trad climbing–specific skill development. This schedule offers more opportunities for outdoor climbing than sport climbing–oriented training plans because indoor climbing gyms generally don't simulate trad climbing very well. The activities for each day are listed in chronological order, but the day's primary emphasis is underlined. Note: This schedule includes a two-week-long climbing vacation during weeks 14 and 15 — the ideal time to attempt a trad goal route.

BIG-WALL FREE CLIMBING

Big-wall free climbs and long multipitch climbs entail a whole host of challenges beyond the typical half-pitch crag route. Common characteristics such as scale, remoteness, rock quality, protection, weather, and inaccessibility of crux pitches all conspire to heap difficulties on aspiring climbers. Accordingly, the inherent reward is equally massive, and if success is achieved, it is always worth the effort.

Free big walls are climbed in a wide range of styles, even more so than single-pitch sport climbs. Walls are climbed in every manner from ground-up, onsight, in a day with each team member free-climbing each pitch, to well-rehearsed, weeks-long redpoint sieges (and even topropes) with each pitch free-climbed by only one team member. The choice of style is personal, and won't be debated here. It is only mentioned to point out that the chosen style has an enormous impact on the preparation necessary to execute the climb and time spent on the route. As always, it is best to clearly establish the goal far in

"I have forgotten the monumental amount of work [of the "Free Salathé" campaign]: the painful fingers and hands; the heavy, heavy burden of what, especially at the time, was an awfully tall stack of difficult pitches.... The climb was the greatest breakthrough of our climbing lives. The Salathé experience proved to Toad and me that these walls could actually be free-climbed." — Paul Piana[5]

advance, along with the chosen style, and discuss it honestly between partners in order to properly prepare to achieve the goal. Consider these two similar goals: "to redpoint every pitch of *Moonlight Buttress*" or "to onsight *Moonlight Buttress* in a day." There is a big difference in the training and practice required to prepare for each goal, not to mention the very different logistical options afforded by them.

In addition to the unique characteristics associated with trad climbing in general, the scale and inaccessibility of long multipitch wall routes create several more difficulties that aspiring climbers must overcome. These include logistical and physical challenges, as well as more abstract and unpredictable factors that are part of the game.

LOGISTICAL CONSIDERATIONS FOR BIG-WALL FREE CLIMBING

There are a number of logistical challenges facing aspiring big-wall free climbers that arise from the sheer size and complexity of enormous cliffs. These considerations generally require mental preparation in addition to physical preparation, and range from intricate planning, to fostering the right habits and attitudes, to practicing wall-climbing skills (such as belay setup and gear hauling). These logistical considerations are less dependent on the climber's physical and technical climbing ability, but inattention to them can very easily sabotage an ascent.

Todd Skinner and Paul Piana during the first free ascent of the *Salathe Wall*, VI 5.13b, El Capitan, Yosemite, CA. 📷 Bill Hatcher

Multipitch Free-Climbing Styles

"I believe people should always strive to do climbs in the best style they think possible, but never criticize others for what they choose to do.... As long as you are not harming the rock or the route for future ascents, and you are honest about what you have done and your style, you should be able to climb in whatever fashion you want." — Tommy Caldwell[2]

The chosen style of ascent of a big wall is a very important variable that has far-reaching implications on the likelihood of success and the requisite preparation and training. Therefore, it is important to select your style of ascent at the time the goal is established to facilitate further planning. Some relevant characteristics of style that should be considered are given below. At the end of the day, big-wall free climbing is always a team effort, regardless of the chosen style, so agree on the approach and standard of success as a team to avoid wavering commitment or other complications. The various styles generally form a spectrum of possible options that permit a great deal of latitude for creating an achievable plan. *(The format of the list below is not intended to imply a hierarchy of virtue.)*

- What is the standard for "free" climbing (redpoint, pinkpoint, yo-yo, toprope)?
- Must every team member free every pitch?
- Must every team member lead each pitch, or is it acceptable to follow free?
- Are fixed ropes permitted to commute to and from the ground or bivy sites?
- Must the route be climbed in a single push, or is it acceptable to bivy on the ground?
- Must the pitches be climbed in order?
- Is it permissible to pre-rehearse the route?
- Is it acceptable to approach from the top down?
- In the event of a fall, must the entire wall be repeated, or just that pitch?
- Can gear (water, snacks, bivy gear, key pieces of protection) be strategically pre-placed before the climb, or must the climbers carry it on the final ascent?
- Is support from non-climbing team members permitted (belays, gear hauling, etc.)?

There are a wide range of acceptable styles for free climbing a big wall, so don't fall victim to peer pressure or the judgment of armchair critics. The only opinions that matter are those of the climbing team. I've climbed walls in almost every style possible, and I'm reluctant to proclaim one as superior to another — each has its own rewards. Maybe this makes me "unprincipled," but I would instead say "un-fanatical." Personally, I enjoy the variety, and believe each climb warrants a tailored approach. The accessibility of the wall and the amount of time you are able to commit to it are important factors in the decision-making process.

Whichever style you choose, agree on it well before the ascent. Deferring these choices until you are on the route, under pressure in the moment of struggle, is a sure path to later regret. During the goal-setting process, ask yourselves: "What style of ascent will we be satisfied with when the climb is over?" That is the only relevant standard.

— Mike Anderson

LOGISTICAL PLANNING

In the big-wall free-climbing game, logistics can make or break the ascent, so they deserve significant attention. Typically, there will be a limited amount of time for the entire wall-climbing campaign (limited by weather, if nothing else). A lot of work must be accomplished in this time, so upfront planning is critical. The flow of events varies depending on the chosen style, but in general, common steps include:

1. Scout, assess, and plan the route
2. Move gear to the climb
3. Move onto the wall, assess the climbing, and rehearse the crux pitches
4. Prep the wall for an ascent (clean any loose debris; stash food, water, and other supplies)
5. Make the redpoint attempt
6. Repeat steps three through five, as necessary
7. Remove any gear from the wall

Scouting the route is essential to designing a good plan. A high-powered spotting scope like this can reveal useful details that you might otherwise miss. 📷 Andrew Burr

Juggernaut

Ascending fixed ropes, or *jugging*, can be an essential skill in the sport of big-wall free climbing. While none of us got into the sport to climb ropes, it's another element that can torpedo an ascent if the climbers don't have a minimum level of competency. Though it is physically exhausting, jugging is a skill that can be learned and improved. The ultimate goal should be to jug efficiently, so as to save precious energy for free climbing. If done properly, the legs should do the majority of the work, especially on less-than-vertical terrain. Much of this comes down to correctly setting up your jugging equipment with tethers and foot stirrups of the proper length. Consult a big-wall instructional book for more details, then get out and experiment with your own gear. Practice jugging over roofs, in corners, along traverses, wearing a pack, or saddled with a heavy rope — all of which may require different tethering arrangements. Jugging on a big wall is rarely straightforward, so be prepared for anything.

The logistical planning challenge is to complete all of this work in the allotted time, while preserving enough energy, fitness, and motivation for the eventual redpoint. Consider these factors when creating a plan:

- Equipment (haulbags, portaledges, static ropes, etc.)
- Specialty protection (offwidth gear, thin-crack gear, etc.)
- Shoes and clothing (are multiple pairs of shoes or outfits required?)
- Sun/shade exposure and hours of daylight or moonlight
- Optimal time of day to climb crux pitches
- Bivy and rest locations
- Optimal schedule for climbing, hauling, and resting
- Optimal gear-caching sites

One planning approach is to start by estimating how much time will be needed for the final ascent, then budget time for the initial preparation of the climb (i.e., ferrying gear). Any remaining time is allotted for route rehearsal and rest. Finally, prioritize the route's difficulties and plan to spend the most time rehearsing the hardest sections. Factor in the time it will take to reach specific pitches on the wall in order to rehearse them. Utilizing fixed lines, rappelling in from the top, or traversing from an adjacent route should all be considered as means to access the route for rehearsal (in accordance with your chosen style). Keep in mind that route prep, load ferrying, and gear caching can all occur simultaneously with rehearsal, but budget sufficient time for rest amongst these potentially exhausting activities.

"A difficult 5.13 climb thirty feet off the ground is technically no harder than one 3,000 feet off the ground, but tell that to your pounding heart and sweaty palms." — Todd Skinner [6]

PERSONAL GROWTH OPPORTUNITIES

There are certain aspects of big-wall free climbing that can't be controlled. These factors are rarely welcomed by the climbers in the heat of battle, but in the framework of long-term improvement, they can be optimistically thought of as *personal growth opportunities*. They are part of the game — part of what makes it difficult and part of what makes it rewarding. Through careful planning and preparation, it is possible to avoid or mitigate the consequences of these factors:

- Weather: Almost by definition, big cliffs come with heightened environmental challenges, including the threat posed by extreme weather. Preparing for the weather is critical because the length of a wall increases the climber's exposure to it, while reducing her ability to react to it. Wall climbers won't have a full arsenal of clothing, and extreme weather conditions (hot or cold) will have more time to wear on the climbers. If the weather turns dangerous, it won't be easy to retreat either. Simple tasks like belaying or setting up a rappel can become onerous in a stiff wind. Try to avoid these issues by planning far in advance to schedule the climb for the best conditions for the chosen cliff (but be flexible once you arrive on the scene). Seek advice from local climbers on the best seasons, and spend some time scouting out the climb and area, if it is unfamiliar to you. Always have an escape plan, and be willing to abandon gear to get down in a hurry. Develop a pitch-by-pitch plan that accounts for sun exposure and time of day to ensure that the hardest pitches can be climbed in the best available conditions.

- Exposure: Exposure — the vertical drop below your feet — is another environmental condition brought on by the size of the wall. It can be crippling for some folks, and motivating for others. Frequent, repeated experience is the best way to overcome a negative reaction to exposure and feel more at ease on the high stone. If a specific pitch's exposure interferes with the climber's ability to relax and climb effectively, it can be helpful to reinforce trust in the protection system with progressive *practice falls*. Start by ensuring that the belay is solid, along with the highest piece of protection — and/or the pieces below it too, if necessary. The leader should then hang on the high piece to take the stretch out of the rope and verify the placement, then lower off of it a few feet and take a

Safely navigating poor rock requires attention, patience, and communication. Jason Haas on the first free ascent of *West Side Story*, 5.12c, Fisher Towers, UT. 📷 Andrew Burr

short "toprope" fall. Continue with increasingly longer falls, progressing to short lead falls until you're comfortable with the protection and the exposure, and able to climb freely.

- Rock Quality: Big cliffs tend to have worse rock overall than most single-pitch crags. This can contribute to poor protection, the risk of longer falls, and deadly rockfall. Try not to disturb obviously loose rock. This includes avoiding placing protection near loose rock, and making every effort to route the rope away from it. Alert the belayer to any potential for rockfall, and, if possible, wait for him to move under cover before proceeding. A haulbag or pack can be used as a shield if rockfall is inevitable. When faced with a pitch of poor rock, there is no substitute for experience, and some climbers are better than others at managing such chaos. The timid might argue that this is a natural-born talent (or mania) that some climbers have and most do not, but this explanation is simplistic and incomplete. Composure in the face of poor rock is an *intangible* mental skill that can be developed. The following section presents strategies for developing this and other such intangible attitudes that are useful for big-wall free climbing.

"Ultimately, the hardest part of big-wall free climbing is not the exposure, but the acceptance that there is no instant gratification... to gain what we set out to gain, we had to accept our gratification in small parcels and take joy in the process." — Todd Skinner [6]

Big wall free climbing demands a lot from climbers, including the ability to deal with poor rock, execute unusual moves at a moment's notice, and work closely as a team. Mike Anderson and Rob Pizem on the first free ascent of Angel Hair, V 5.13a, Zion, UT . 📷 Keith Ladzinski

ATTITUDES FOR SUCCESSFUL BIG-WALL FREE CLIMBING

Success in big-wall free climbing depends on several intangible abilities. These can be loosely described as the collective mental faculties for persevering through the numerous hardships inherent to wall climbing. These hardships include exposure, loose/dirty/wet/icy rock, vegetation, poor or insufficient protection, mounting fatigue, insufficient sustenance, poor weather, route uncertainty, and non-ideal sending conditions (among many others). The abilities needed to handle these hardships are intangible n that they can't be measured, but it is possible to develop them. Successful big-wall climbers are *robust* — able to perform well under different (often poor) conditions. Like any skill, it is possible to increase a climber's robustness through practice. However, robustness is really a collection of very fundamental *attitudes*, so it's not as simple as learning a new movement skill, like a dropknee. Attitudes are a result of our past experience and repeated practices, or habits, which must be cultivated over a lifetime. Therefore, to develop the most robust attitudes, climbers can adopt these habits and reinforce them throughout their career:

- Urgency: On a long climb, there is never enough time. The climber can always expect to be under pressure to climb, *and send*, quickly, whether rehearsing pitches in preparation for an eventual redpoint or on the final ascent itself. The team must be highly efficient with all of the logistical tasks such as placing gear, establishing belays, hauling, rappelling, route-finding, and even hiking to the cliff (among many other chores). The more moderate pitches will generally need to be onsighted, in order to save time, so climbers must be competent at onsighting on the given rock type. Crux pitches will need to be assessed, rehearsed, and sent much faster than a pitch at ground level, so climbers can't count on getting complete rest between burns. To improve urgency, climbers should individually practice efficient climbing whenever possible (at the gym and crag, and even in preparation for those activities), and partners should work to develop efficiency as a team. It may be beneficial to practice speed climbing together to develop and refine the logistical systems. To speed the rehearsal and redpointing process, borrow techniques from the sport-climbing game — instead of a stickclip, be prepared to aid a crux pitch or pull on gear to expedite the route-rehearsal process. See "Strategy for a Short Term Redpoint" in Chapter 13: Redpoint and Onsight Climbing for more tips on quick redpointing.

- Team Work: Unlike single-pitch cragging, big-wall climbing is a team sport, regardless of the style of ascent. A good team is essential, and can be built through practice, training, and mutual suffering. Start with a likeminded partner of similar ability, and honestly discuss the team's mutual goals as well as each climber's commitment to them and his ability to spend time to accomplish them — few things are as frustrating as a supposedly "committed" partner with no free time to train or practice. Use the processes outlined in Chapter 2: Goal Setting and Planning to honestly assess each team member's strengths and weaknesses, assess the weaknesses of the team as a whole, and then make a plan to improve the team. Often the best partnerships include teammates with complementary, rather than overlapping, strengths. In many cases, it can be helpful to explicitly define a division of labor or otherwise clearly establish roles and responsibilities, especially on large teams. Very experienced teams will often fall into these roles automatically through habit, but it's always smart to air these subjects in advance. Remember that compatibility and devotion to the team (and its goals) beat physical strength every time.

- Be the Leader: While mentors are needed to learn the proper safety systems for climbing early in a career, they can easily become a crutch over time. A more experienced climber who is always picking the routes, leading the harder pitches, hanging the draws, or otherwise "bailing out" the pupil is only stifling the pupil's growth. Once a climber is competent at lead climbing, it's time to step out of the mentor's shadow. An aspiring wall climber should establish her own goals and plans to accomplish them. She should be driving the conversation about which routes to climb, and volunteering to take the sharp end at every opportunity. If she gets in over her head and can't finish a pitch, she should deal with the consequences of dogging, aiding, or leaving gear behind. She should not call in for reinforcements from the former mentor, who won't be available to help on the wall. Instead, she should seek to become self-reliant, push herself on difficult climbs, and practice risk management.

- Learn to Learn: Another critical aspect of becoming self-reliant is to personally develop the skill of solving boulder problems. On unfamiliar routes, take the time to experiment with the holds and moves, to solve the problems and learn the beta. Don't take beta from others who won't be there to lend it when it really matters, high on a wall.

- Get Uncomfortable: The masses flock to crags that have great rock, inspiring routes, well-textured holds, perfect conditions, and lots of convenience... and why shouldn't they? Climbing is

Chris Lindner enjoying unusually calm weather on *El Nino*, 5.13c A0, Yosemite, CA.
Brendan Nicholson

supposed to be fun, after all. However, these amenities are uncommon or at least unreliable on a big wall, so special effort should be made to seek out crags and climbs that will expand the climber's tolerance for imperfect conditions. The popular crags that are "nice" to climb at are not the best venues to develop robustness. Instead, seek out the opposite: obscure crags and routes that are generally avoided because of these imperfections. These unpopular, "old school" crags may have stiff grades, runouts, and cobwebs, and they may require unfashionable techniques such as wide jamming and slab climbing. These are the skills needed for big-wall mastery, and the lack of crowds will also require the climber to be self-reliant in terms of route-finding, beta, and general climbing logistics.

- Climb Exhaustively: Every crag has certain routes that are "classic" and receive nonstop attention. These crags also have anti-classics that never get climbed. Strive to climb every route, wherever you are climbing. A big-wall free climb will not afford the option of cherry-picking only the cleanest, most enjoyable pitches. The process of ticking every route at a crag will force the climber to develop a broad repertoire of techniques and confront any weaknesses. It will also help develop route-reading and route-finding skills, both critical to success on a big wall. Furthermore, it will help cultivate an attitude of exploration and a willingness to tread boldly where few others would.

- Love to Suffer: The plethora of poor environmental conditions that can arise on a wall are hard to deal with if you're inexperienced. Rotten or imperfect rock (including wet, icy, dirty, loose, or vegetated stone) is the ultimate example, but poor weather, dehydration, lack of sleep, and fatigue can be equally debilitating. Suffering through similar conditions is the best way to prepare to do it on a wall. Alpine rock climbing* is the best way to get a concentrated dose of all these environmental imperfections, as well as a great way to learn to accept conditions as they are and then deal with them. Wet rock *can* be climbed, and scaling a snowy cliff is a good way to prove it to yourself. In the alpine realm, bad rock is unavoidable, so this is a great place to hone the mental and physical skill of moving past it (just be sure to use a toprope and a helmet for the first forays into the delicate art of "chossaneering"). The beauty of alpine climbing as a training tool is that it is very complementary to sport rock climbing. The typical season for alpinism (late summer) rarely interferes with the prime sport-climbing seasons in North America, and the physical demands don't overlap with rock-climbing training. Therefore, pile on as much alpine climbing as possible — there is very little reason not to. (*Side effects may include death and dismemberment.)

- Keep Your Chin Up: Good morale is essential to any committing adventure. A positive attitude and high spirits can overcome any number of challenges. Cultivate this positive spirit by finding joy in simple things, like the incredible view or the camaraderie of the team. Endeavor to be habitually upbeat when at the crag or on training climbs. Don't be a pessimist. Remember that regardless of the situation, you *chose* to be there, and you made that choice because you truly love that type of climbing. Keep your love of climbing at the forefront and embrace challenges as they arise. Big-wall free climbing is often transformative, and such experiences are rarely easy (or completely carefree). Embrace these factors and expect to encounter a few unforeseen obstacles on each adventure. Refer to Ilgner's *The Rock Warrior's Way* for more strategies on cultivating a positive mental attitude[3].

While transforming one's climbing attitudes may at first seem overwhelming and impossible, it is possible to make minor day-to-day changes that will add up in the long run. Simply accepting imperfection in daily cragging or training sessions is a good place to start. Don't be the person at the crag who needs absolute silence, perfect weather, and aligned planets in order to even attempt a redpoint. If the margin of error is that slim on a big wall, failure is certain because all of those factors cannot be controlled and will inevitably be less than perfect on any given day. Instead, resist the urge to control every situation; embrace the chaos, and use it to develop a mental buffer that can eventually be applied on the big wall of your dreams.

PHYSICAL CONSIDERATIONS FOR BIG-WALL FREE CLIMBING

To free-climb an entire wall requires the ability to meet the physical demands of any given pitch, anywhere on the wall. This is a great challenge that is distinct from single-pitch rock climbing. The challenges presented by a big wall may necessitate additional physical training, skill practice, or shrewd planning to improve the body's coping ability on the route. Some of these considerations are listed below, along with tips climbers can use to better prepare for them. These physical factors should be considered in the context of the specific goal route to determine their relative importance, as well as their likelihood of impacting the climb. If these factors are identified early, a plan can be developed to minimize their impact. In many cases, variations to the training plan may be appropriate, in order to, for example, improve total-body stamina or add/improve a particular movement skill.

- Stamina: The volume of climbing required by a big wall is nearly impossible to simulate in training, and would likely be injurious or counter-productive in the long term. Therefore, during a big-wall ascent, the overarching strategy must be to conserve energy at all times. Logistics will contribute to this, so careful planning is a key coping strategy. On longer climbs, avoid carrying any unnecessary gear, and consider pre-placed caches to conserve energy during the send. Optional cardio work can be added to the training program to prepare for the extra workload of big-wall climbing, without risking overuse injuries to the climbing musculature. Climbing training must take priority, so perform these workouts on climbing rest days, or after the climbing workout on training days.

- **Warming Up:** The crux pitches on long routes must be taken as they come, not necessarily when the climber is ready for them. Often a hard pitch or move will need to be dispatched with little or no warm-up, such as when it is the first pitch off the ground, or the first pitch of the day on a multi-day route. To mitigate this, the climbers can warm-up on the pitch itself, by pulling through the hardest moves. High on a route, it may be possible to lower down and toprope the previous pitch as a warm-up, or jug a fixed line to get the big muscles firing, if nothing else.

- **Movement Variety:** The sheer amount of rock that the team must overcome guarantees that a wide variety of skills will be needed, while the time urgency imposed by the climb will prevent learning these skills on the spot. Therefore, the climbers need to arrive at the climb already equipped with the preponderance of techniques needed. There is no shortcut to developing a large technique library; it takes a lifetime of climbing. The general strategy of racking up mileage on a wide variety of rock types and styles is the best bet — never pass up an opportunity to learn a new move or address a weakness. For a specific big-wall route, study the route or talk to other climbers to determine if any unique skills are needed — e.g., the ability to jam a certain size crack. If such a skill happens to be a weakness, make time in the training program to improve it.

- **Fatigue:** The demands of multipitch climbing tend to fatigue climbers much differently than the relatively sedentary crag scene. Count on being hungry and dehydrated, then add the whole-body *logistical fatigue* that results from all the ancillary tasks such as:
  - Hiking to the wall
  - Hauling gear
  - Belaying a second from above
  - Hanging belays
  - Rope drag
  - Rappelling
  - And, in the case of a first ascent;
    - Cleaning
    - Drilling bolts

Big wall chores contribute to a level of fatigue unlike that of crag climbing. Mike Anderson hauling gear on Angel's Landing in Zion, UT.
Andrew Burr

Although food and water are always limited on a long climb, try to stay hydrated and fueled throughout the day, and consider rationing a little extra for the moments leading up to the crux pitches — a favorite snack can be emotionally uplifting in addition to raising blood sugar. Limit sun exposure as much as possible throughout the climb, and don't get too cold either — shivering wastes energy. Budget time for a brief rest immediately before a redpoint attempt on a crux pitch. During this time, spare the leader from any strength-sapping logistical chores, such as hauling gear (to the extent possible). When the time comes, the ability to compose yourself in the face of this fatigue and muster the necessary effort to succeed on a critical pitch is as much mental as it is physical. Logistical fatigue generally doesn't affect the primary climbing muscles, so just because the body *feels tired* doesn't mean it's incapable of cranking on poor handholds. Therefore, try to ignore this tiredness. Apply the same mental techniques that are used for any redpoint and focus on the climbing, not the shouts of protest from your tired body.

PROGRESSIVE LONG-ROUTE TRAINING

Just like any feat, athletes can develop the ability to handle the physical demands of climbing long multi-pitch routes. The same training principles that were discussed in Chapter 4: Foundations of Physical Training apply to long-route training as well. They are:

- Specificity
- Overload
- Recovery
- Reversibility
- Regularity
- Progression
- Variation
- Individualization
- Transfer

To build up to a particular goal route, t can be very beneficial to set intermediate multipitch goal routes that provide physical training, mental training, and skill practice, while also serving as an evaluation of the team's progress. Carefully select intermediate goal routes of appropriate difficulty that mimic the goal route or address key weaknesses, in order to satisfy the principles of effective training. If possible, strive to climb routes on the same rock type or same cliff as your final goal route, and try to tune the length and difficulty of intermediate goal routes to ensure the appropriate progression. Recall that climbing *volume* — the product of intensity and duration (pitch difficulty and overall route length, respectively, in this case) — is the best way to chart progression. Gradually increase the total volume of each intermediate multipitch route throughout the season to build up to the goal route.

The constraints of everyday life will prevent most climbers from regularly climbing long multipitch routes as training for a big wall; in fact, many climbers are lucky to sneak in one long route per season. However, the physical efforts can be simulated at the crag or in the gym by doing climbing mileage days, in which many single-pitch routes are packed into a single day. Using landmark routes as a template (i.e., doing an

Training for a Big-Wall Free Climb

In spring 2004, while living and climbing at Smith Rock, I had the good fortune of meeting the legendary Lynn Hill — the first person to free *The Nose,* and then the first to free El Cap in a day, not to mention her stack of international competition victories. With plans to attempt *Freerider* later that season, I asked what the secret to her big-wall success was, and the answer surprised me.

Lynn relayed that she spent most of her preparation time in France, climbing limestone sport routes. To develop the superhuman endurance necessary for Grade VI-in-a-day free climbing, she would climb 10 to 15 moderate pitches ("moderate" for her, so 5.11 to 5.12), and then finish each day by attempting a few 5.13 pitches once she was already powered down from all the mileage climbing. It was hard to imagine completing such a regimen myself, but I could see how a climber like Lynn Hill, with flawless technique and phenomenal fitness, could pull it off.

In track and field, this would be called "negative split" training, starting off with relatively low-intensity intervals, then progressively dialing up the intensity as fatigue mounts. I applied Lynn's advice to the technical, near-vertical sport routes and stellar cracks of Smith Rock. After several weeks of this training, I set off to meet Mike below the towering walls of Yosemite Valley. Thanks to the solid technical skills I'd developed at Smith, and my newfound levels of stamina, Mike and I walked away a few days later with a team redpoint of *Freerider.*

— *Mark Anderson*

"Astroman," "Moonlight Buttress," "Half Dome," or "El Cap" day) is a common technique that vastly increases the fun factor and motivation. For example, during a "*Moonlight Buttress* Day" the climbers might try to complete 10 pitches, including at least six pitches of 5.12- or harder. Include a variety of pitches (in terms of difficulty, style, *and* quality), just as the goal route will require. The calendar shown in the Figure on p262 includes numerous Outdoor Mileage and indoor ARC training sessions. These workouts can be replaced with progressive long-route training; just be sure to include adequate rest (increasing as the volume increases throughout the season).

Get a Leg Up

Single-pitch rock climbing doesn't require substantial leg strength or endurance, so many sport climbers avoid activities that might beef up their legs and reduce their strength-to-weight ratio. However, multi-pitch and big-wall projects typically involve plenty of hiking with heavy loads that can cripple you if your legs and lungs are not prepared. Rob Pizem and I learned this the hard way in 2006 when we attempted a first free ascent on Yosemite's Half Dome — a cliff that *starts* 3,000 feet above the valley floor. In the first three days of the trip alone we logged 12,000 vertical feet (and countless miles) of hiking and another 3,000 feet of jugging. The *down-hiking* was the most devastating, and by the fourth day we were absolutely trashed. We had expected to be fatigued, but we were anticipating fatigue of the upper-body and skin variety. Instead, the climb was hinging far more on our ability to ferry loads to the cliff.

We didn't complete the climb that summer for several reasons, so when we made plans to return the following year, we prepared more thoroughly. In addition to my normal climbing training, I made a point to hike up nearby peaks once or twice a week, carrying additional weight in a backpack as I progressed (I hauled rocks or water, and then discarded them for

If unprepared, the physical toll of big wall free climbing logistics can sabotage an ascent. [O] Andrew Burr

the hike down — a rare geologic phenomenon known as "reverse erosion"). We also carefully planned the climbing and route-prep schedule so that, once in Yosemite, we could get by with less hiking and load hauling in the first few days (we only hiked 7,000 feet of vertical the first three days of the 2007 trip). This two-pronged attack of training and planning solved this key logistics problem, and three weeks later we made the first free ascent of *Arcturus* (5.13b).

— *Mike Anderson*

SUMMARY

- Traditional climbs differ significantly from most sport climbs, but they *do* often resemble vertical face climbs, making such routes good training for trad climbs and vice versa.
- For trad goal routes, climbers should adjust their training to emphasize outdoor-skills practice climbing, Base-Fitness, Route Intervals, and strength training, while deemphasizing Limit Bouldering Circuits and Campus training.
- Long multipitch or big-wall free climbs add a number of challenges that result from the scale, remoteness, and complexity of the climbs. Learn to manage these logistical considerations, and practice good planning on a regular basis.
- For big-wall routes, clearly establish the team's goals well in advance, to include matters of style and the logistical approach. Doing so will clarify the training process needed to achieve the goal.
- Success on a free big wall requires the right attitudes, which can take many years to cultivate. These are habitual, so start early and constantly reinforce them in day-to-day climbing situations.
- Progressive training can be used to prepare for the physical rigors of wall climbing. Develop a plan that produces a steady progression of physical, technical, and mental training.

Melissa Love on *Snake Watching*, 5.13a, Flatirons, CO. 📷 Adam Sanders

BOULDERING

Jake List on *A Maze of Death* V12, The Buttermilks, CA. Dan Brayack

CHAPTER 15

"I originally perceived bouldering as the distilled essence of the climbing experience, free of extensive paraphernalia and practiced close to the ground." — John Gill [6]

Bouldering is climbing in its simplest form. By eliminating equipment, belayers, and exposure, climbing is simplified to movement over stone. With this freedom, climbers can commit completely to a handful of moves and pursue their true limits. Bouldering is an essential training tool that should be used by all climbers in pursuit of continuous improvement, but it's also an extremely popular and worthy endeavor in itself. This chapter explains how to modify the Rock Prodigy training program to maximize bouldering performance for its own sake (details on utilizing bouldering as part of a larger training program are provided in Part II: Physical Training). In addition, the unique mental aspects of bouldering will be discussed, along with strategies for maximizing performance out on the *blocs*.

Bouldering differs from roped route climbing in several important ways, and many of these differences should be accounted for when developing a bouldering-specific training plan:

- Length: Short boulder problems require little to no endurance.
- Hold Type: Bouldering typically involves more slopers and compression holds than roped climbing.
- Intensity: Bouldering moves are much more intense, increasing the importance of strength and power.
- Duty Cycle: The work-rest schedule is greatly compressed. Bouldering attempts are much shorter than route attempts, as is the rest period between attempts. Also, when actually climbing, the duty cycle for hand movements is often much faster because of the more dynamic nature of bouldering, and the ability to easily identify and rehearse sequences from the ground.

- Movement: Bouldering is often more dynamic than roped route climbing, and many problems entail strenuous opposition moves that require greater core and shoulder strength.
- Arousal: The emphasis on powerful and dynamic movement requires high levels of arousal, and the ability to cultivate such a mental state quickly and frequently.
- Style: The ability to *hangdog* on routes simplifies the process of discovering and refining beta. This tactic is not typically used in bouldering — you climb from the ground or partway up the problem every time — increasing the effort (and skin) required to unlock sequences.
- Exposure: The height and landing area of a boulder problem will affect the consequence of a fall from the problem. These variables produce a spectrum of danger that can range from extremely safe to life threatening.
- Accessibility: Proximity to the ground permits many more attempts on a boulder problem per session. This allows difficult sequences to be sent in less time, but also increases the repetitive stress on joints and skin.
- Group Size: Roped climbing requires exactly one partner. When bouldering, more is almost always merrier, and a bigger crew means more crashpads, more spotters, and more beta, resulting in a greater willingness and ability to go for it on committing moves.
- Conditions: The temperature-sensitive interactions between skin, shoe rubber, micro-crimps, and friction holds are ever magnified in bouldering. Cold is almost always better, and a sub-freezing day on which route climbing would be impossible may be ideal for bouldering. On these days, it takes extra effort to warm up and remain warm throughout the day.

Recall that, according to the principles of specificity and transfer (Chapter 4: Foundations of Physical Training), training is more effective when the training conditions most closely mimic the performance conditions. Therefore, each of the above characteristics should be considered, and the training adjusted appropriately, to prepare the boulderer to perform at her very highest level. In many cases, training exercises can be easily modified to increase specificity. Such modifications include selecting comparable hold types, training intensities, rep and set durations, duty cycles, and movement skills.

TRAINING VARIATIONS FOR BOULDERING

There are two primary differences between the physical demands of bouldering and roped route climbing. Bouldering requires maximum power, due to the intense and dynamic nature of the movement, and minimal endurance, due to the brief nature of most problems. (One exception: Training for long bouldering traverses should mimic training for routes of a similar length.) While roped climbing typically calls for a balance between these two somewhat mutually exclusive attributes, bouldering typically does not. For boulderers, this simplifies matters tremendously. If not for the importance of skill development (which is emphasized during Base-Fitness training), a climber who boulders exclusively could eliminate most forms of endurance training.

On the other hand, the importance in bouldering of strength, power, and dynamic movement calls for greater emphasis on strength and power training. Furthermore, any training activities that interfere with the cultivation of power should be reduced or eliminated, such as long-duration, low-intensity climbing. The suggested Seasonal Training Plan shown on the next page employs the following bouldering-specific adjustments:

- Shortened Base-Fitness Phase
- Bouldering-specific Outdoor Mileage workouts added
- Optional ARC workouts eliminated
- Power-Endurance Phase eliminated
- Power-specific training extended through the Performance Phase
- Shortened Performance Phase

Bouldering emphasizes dynamic movement, and often involves the use of unusual holds like slopers. Chuck Fryberger, Baja Norte, Mexico. Andrew Burr

Week	Sunday	Monday	Tuesday	Wednesday	Thursday	Friday	Saturday
-	*Last Week of Performance Phase of Previous Season*						
-	*Rest Phase of Previous Season*						
-							Sa Day 1 *Outdoor Mileage (OM), 20+ M probs *Skill acquisition
1 (Base)	Su Day 2 *OM, 10+ moderate problems *Skill acquisition	Mo 3 *Optional Aerobic Exercise (OAE)	Tu 4 *ARC 1: 2 x 30 min *Skill acquisition	We 5 *OAE	Th 6 *ARC 2: 2 x 30 min *Skill practice	Fr 7 *OAE	Sa 8 *Handboard (HB) 1 *Supplemental Ex
2	9 *OAE *Skin care	10 *OAE	11 *HB 2 *SE	12 *OAE *Skin care	13 *OAE	14 *HB3 *SE	15 *OAE *Skin care
3	16 *OAE	17 *HB 4 *SE	18 *OAE *Skin care	19 *OAE	20 *HB5 *SE	21 *OAE *Skin care	22 *OAE
4	23 *HB6 *SE	24 *Skin care	25 *OAE	26 *HB7 *SE	27 *Begin Tapering *Skin care	28	29 *HB8 *SE
5	30 *Skin care	31	32 *HB9 *SE	33 *Skin care	34	35 *HB10 *SE	36 *Skin care
6 (Power Phase)	37	38 *Warmup Boulder Ladder (WBL) 60m *Campus 25m; SE	39 *Skin Care	40	41 *Limit Boulder (LB) 120 min *SE	42 *Skin Care	43 *WBL 60 min *Campus 30 min *SE
7	44 *Skin Care	45	46 *LB 120 min *SE	47 *Skin Care	48 *WBL 60 min *Campus 35 min *SE	49 *Skin Care	50 *LB Outdoors
8	51 *Skin Care	52 *WBL 60 min *Campus 40 min *SE	53 *Skin Care	54	55 *LB 120 min *SE	56 *Skin Care	57 *LB Outdoors
9 (Performance)	58 *Boulder Attempts *OM, 5 mod problems	59 *Skin Care	60	61 *WBL 60 min *Campus 45 min *SE	62 *Skin Care	63	64 *Boulder Attempts *OM, 5 mod problems
10	65 *Boulder Attempts *OM, 5 mod problems	66 *Skin Care	67	68 *WBL 60 min *Campus 45 min *SE	69 *Skin Care	70	71 *Boulder Attempts *OM, 5 mod problems
11	72 *Boulder Attempts *OM, 3 mod problems	73 *Skin Care	74	75 *WBL 60 min *Campus 45 min *SE	76 *Skin Care	77	78 *Boulder Attempts *OM, 5 mod problems
12	79 *Boulder Attempts *OM, 3 mod problems	80 *Skin Care	81	82 *WBL 60 min	83 *Skin Care	84	85 *Boulder Attempts *OM, 5 mod problems
13 (Rest)	86	87 *OAE and/or OCT	88	89 *OAE and/or OCT	90	91 *OAE and/or OCT	92 First Day of Next Season

Key:
ARC - Aerobic Restoration and Capillarity Training
HB - Hangboard Workout
LB - Limit Boulder
M, mod - Moderate

OAE - Optional Aerobic Exercise
OCT - Optional Cross-Training
OM - Outdoor Mileage
SE - Supplemental Exercises
WBL - Warm-Up Boulder Ladder

Seasonal Training Plan for an Advanced Boulderer. This program emphasizes strength and power for bouldering, while purposely avoiding endurance training (which reduces power). The activities for each day are listed in chronological order, but the day's primary emphasis is underlined. This schedule results in a significant Power Peak during the tenth and eleventh weeks of the cycle.

A noteworthy consequence of emphasizing power and excluding endurance is that the resulting performance peak is shortened. The standard route-focused Rock Prodigy training program generates a longer peak because the various fitness components peak at slightly different times — creating a power peak early in the performance peak, and an endurance peak late in the peak. Route climbers can emphasize powerful but less sustained climbing early in the Performance Phase, and then gradually transition toward less powerful but more sustained routes as their performance evolves throughout the phase.

Bouldering: The Weakness Magnifier

Being short, boulder problems distill difficulty into very few moves. Sometimes a problem boils down to only one move, in essence. If the move in question coincides with your personal strengths, the problem may seem a bit easy for the grade. However, if the move exposes a personal weakness, the problem will feel quite hard or even impossible. Esoteric moves or problems can be humbling, but they also provide the rare opportunity to confront a weakness head-on.

The legendary Southern bouldering mecca of Horse Pens 40 is a great example. Many of the problems at Horse Pens consist of very slopey holds used in compression and opposition. This climbing style is almost never encountered elsewhere, let alone on routes. When I first climbed there, I was captivated by the setting, but bewildered by the climbing style. I was tempted to drive the two hours north to Little Rock City, a crimpier area that suited my technical style, but instead I accepted the opportunity to explore a potential weakness. I revised my expectations and replaced my V-grade-focused goals with the resolution to learn this unique climbing style.

I'm still no sultan of slopers, but since that first trip I have vastly improved my skills on friction, compression, and tenuous mantles. When you stumble upon a problem (or in my case, an entire climbing area) that seems outrageously difficult, be humble; consider that the issue might be your own lack of skills (not the "blankety-blank guidebook author"), and then take the opportunity to learn something new — and improve.

— *Mike Anderson*

Horse Pens 40, AL - Sloper Heaven! Dan Brayack spanking *Bum Boy*, V5. 📷 Dan Brayack

For those emphasizing strictly power, it makes little sense to extend the Performance Phase once the power peak has waned. The result is a shortened Performance Phase; however, the power peak experienced with this bouldering-focused plan will last substantially longer than the power peak produced by a route-focused plan. This is because the additional high-intensity bouldering activities prescribed throughout the Performance Phase will sustain the power peak. Also note that there is little practical difference between the latter weeks of the Power Phase and the Performance Phase, so goal boulder problems can and should be attempted at any time during weeks seven through 12. Keep these factors in mind when scheduling road trips or otherwise deciding when to attempt goal boulder problems.

In addition to the adjustments to the Seasonal Training Plan described above, consider these additional training adjustments:

- Add sloper and/or pinch grips to strength-training routines if you're not already using these grips. Pockets are unusual for boulder problems, so depending on your goals, these grips can be de-emphasized.
- During finger-strength training, consider using shorter repetitions, longer rest between repetitions, and fewer repetitions per set. These adjustments will make hangboard training more specific to bouldering. An example of such a routine is provided in the "Max-Recruitment Training with a Hangboard" sidebar found in Chapter 7: Power.
- Emphasize dynamic movement while training, including during indoor bouldering and Campus Board training.
- Supplemental exercises should receive extra attention, particularly exercises that train shoulder, upper arm, and core strength. Lock-off laps and other exercises targeting muscular endurance can be reduced.

AROUSAL

Bouldering demands the very highest level of intensity. Often a problem right at a climber's limit will require 100 percent effort merely to complete a single move. However, applying every ounce of determination and will to each attempt is not a simple matter. The key to unleashing maximum effort is *arousal*. Arousal is a psychological state of alertness and readiness to react to challenging situations. It is a primary driver in the

"Lately, I have given 100 percent for every try I take... no half-assing anything... The only way that I can try hard is if I am pushed to try hard, and this comes from self-motivation."
— Daniel Woods [1]

"fight-or-flight" response common to all creatures. High arousal increases muscular tension and focus (among other effects), making it an essential tool for motivating athletic performance [10].

The *Yerkes-Dobson Law* states that arousal directly affects performance, and each person has an ideal level of arousal for the performance of different tasks. Intellectual tasks that depend on high amounts of concentration and receptiveness (such as delicate slab or technical endurance climbing) require relaxation and low arousal [5]. Tasks that depend on tremendous physical strength and narrow focus (like powerful bouldering) require high arousal, which explains why grunts and even screams regularly escape from bouldering caves. Aside from the spectacle, such brutish behavior can actually improve performance. Optimal arousal levels vary from person to person, so note the levels of personal arousal that produce the best results in each situation [8].

Chemicals in the brain called neurotransmitters regulate a person's arousal level, but arousal can also be influenced externally. Learning to manipulate this command pathway can allow an athlete to regularly unleash tremendous power. Several methods for increasing arousal include:

- Listening to upbeat music
- Visualizing the ensuing performance
- Physical activity
- Vocal encouragement from spectators
- Positive self-talk
- Reviewing performance goals

These influences will have a different effect on each climber's arousal level, so experiment with each to find an effective combination. Whatever the combo, apply more energy and zeal to these activities to achieve a higher state of arousal. Competitive athletes in power sports (and even some boulderers) often find it helpful to yell encouragement to themselves, flex their muscles, jump up and down, or even slap themselves in the face to achieve the highest state of arousal. It is possible to overdo it, however. An Incredible Hulk–like state of maniacal rage will impair technical abilities and judgment.

GET AMPED!!!

"When you do hard routes, you have to try hard. They're not easy routes. You have to give everything you have. You have to get totally animalistic.... It's like martial arts. When Bruce Lee threw a punch, he had to mean it. Haahhh! Like that. When you're doing a hard move, there is this excess energy you have to let out. Air explodes out of you." – Chris Sharma[3]

I'm known as a very reserved, unemotional person. However, that personality, and its accompanying low level of arousal, is not ideal for bouldering. I'm unlikely to access the very zenith of my physical potential while remaining calm. It's a biological fact that all of us are stronger and faster when we're "crazy," and there are many examples of regular folks conjuring superhuman strength in life-or-death situations.

To access this fight-or-flight state for the hardest moves, you must manufacture an adrenaline surge. I do it by subtly and momentarily getting angry. This is a far cry from my typical demeanor, and very different from the appropriate arousal for route climbing; therefore, it's not easy. I might think of something that bugs me (like starving children in Africa or my boss tasking me on Friday afternoon), then I exhale rapidly, grit my teeth, and "growl" or grunt quietly. In the moment of the move, I might even scream.

Don't be ashamed to use these techniques. It may sound ridiculous, and many climbers think they are above such antics, but this is a *technique* for improving climbing performance just like other more physical tools such as hand jams or drop-knees. It has been used in the martial arts for centuries to access greater power, and new trainees are coached to scream "Kia!" with every blow in practice. Considering that martial arts involves an opponent literally trying to pummel you, it hardly seems necessary to artificially amplify arousal! Absent an impending physical beating, climbers must be much more deliberate to reach an equivalent state of arousal, so don't be afraid to go ballistic, unleash your *GRRR face*, and get amped!!!   — Mike Anderson

Bouldering demands high intensity and arousal. Melissa Lipani sticks *Bu Shi*, V5, Fry Canyon Boulders, UT.   Andrew Burr

Once on the problem, extremely high intensity should be maintained throughout the ascent. Boulder problems do not require the steady, efficient movement that facilitates successful route climbing, because accumulating fatigue is rarely limiting in bouldering. Therefore, don't be afraid to go all out on every move. Often climbers who excel on routes struggle with boulders because they have trained themselves to climb within their limits in order to ration their energy for a redpoint. While this approach is critical for route climbing, it can be detrimental on a limiting boulder problem, leading the climber to fidget in search of comfort after each move, when maintaining upward momentum would be more prudent. Give each attempt maximum effort until you fall — don't jump off voluntarily because you botched a sequence or a handhold doesn't feel perfect. As long as you are still clinging to the boulder, there is still a fighting chance, so keep fighting.

Bouldering can be as much about "letting go" as holding on — letting go of your control over the situation. Many climbers have "wobbled" their way up extreme boulders, just barely latching each move with wild desperation. This state is sometimes referred to as "going squid;" perhaps bungling sequences, flailing haphazardly, but inconceivably sticking just enough to make the next unlikely move. This style may seem careless, but it defines some of the best boulderers in history.

Influence your arousal prior to attempting a limit boulder problem, and then once in "battle mode", give each move every ounce of your effort. There are no style points, and there is no looming crux to conserve energy for. If necessary, think of yourself as falling upward, using your commitment and momentum to stick moves you never would otherwise. If you never let go, this intensity has the power to carry you to the top.

"I love the feeling of getting shut down, then discovering subtle tricks that make the problem possible. The test is seeing how small of a hold the body can pull down on or how crazy of a position you can put yourself into."
— Daniel Woods [1]

STRATEGY AND TACTICS

The convenience of bouldering, and the often playground-like venues involved, tends to discourage in-depth planning. Meanwhile, the necessary high density of difficult movements can take quite a toll on the body, both in terms of the pulling muscles and joints but also key junctures in your lower body, like feet, ankles, and knees, which must absorb the shock of each fall to the ground. Fortunately, sound strategy and tactics can help ensure optimal, injury-free performance out on the blocks just as it does with other styles of climbing. Here are some approaches to make bouldering more efficient and productive:

SAFETY FIRST

Many neophytes assume bouldering is relatively safe since the climber is never very far off the ground. In fact, bouldering is the most dangerous form of climbing in terms of injuries per participant. Boulderers hit the ground every time they fall, and these countless impacts result in many injuries, to every body part imaginable. Furthermore, even those falls that don't cause acute trauma can cause debilitating repetitive-stress injuries over the years, including permanent arthritis. A climber can't perform if he is injured, but equally important, he can't commit to difficult moves if he's scared. To perform optimally, boulderers need a reassuring spot and a tall stack of crashpads, so join up with a good-sized crew and take advantage of their strength in numbers. Bouldering in large groups also has many other advantages, including the free flow of beta and plentiful encouragement.

Before attempting a problem, assess the landing zone carefully. Remove any rocks, logs or other obstacles — in accordance with the landowner's policies, and with consideration for other visitors and the environment. Consider where the climber might roll if she loses her balance when she lands. Arrange the pads tightly, so there are no gaps between pads. If possible, stack multiple layers of pads, and overlap any seams or soft spots in the padding. If not making a flash attempt, take a few practice falls from low on the problem to ensure that the pads are properly aligned. Inspect the descent before starting up the problem, or use it as a warm-up if possible.

Have a spotter (or several) positioned to guide the climber to the crashpad in the event of a fall. The spotter's job is primarily to redirect the climber's center of mass (near the hips) to a safe landing zone, but

Establishing a safe environment is essential for facilitating complete commitment. Jimmy Webb feeling secure on the *Dune Aréte* (V9), Hueco Tanks, TX. Dan Brayack

also to ensure that the head and neck do not contact the ground (especially critical on steeply overhanging or horizontal terrain). The spotter should not attempt to "catch" a falling climber.

WORKING A PROBLEM

From a technical perspective, working a problem is much like working a route crux, though the tactics used are much different. In bouldering, it's usually necessary to climb up to each move before trying various options, and it may not be possible to thoroughly feel each hold (a consequence of not having a rope or fixed protection points). This is rooted in tradition and style. Historically boulderers have embraced the *ground-up* ethic, and eschewed aids like toprope inspection. However, these former taboos are rapidly fading. For example, a stepladder was famously used to facilitate the second ascent of *The Mandala*, a classic V12 in the Buttermilks[2]. Consider the advice of John Gill:

"When I did most of my bouldering, in the late 1950s through the 1970s, I used topropes sometimes and at other times avoided any type of protection. Toproping was acceptable for most climbers who bouldered — until the relatively recent introduction of pads... Don't be reluctant to put on a rope if you think you may come off from more than a few feet above the ground — thirty or forty years from now your back, knees, ankles, and feet will thank you."[6]

With this in mind, consider every practical option when struggling to unlock a challenging problem. Take a few steps back from the boulder and examine the problem from various angles, to evaluate each hold as well as potential sequence options. Stack pads, use a power spot, or get a boost from your partner to inspect each hold and attempt individual moves. Use the descent route to reach the top of the boulder in order to examine and clean potential finishing holds. It may even be possible to downclimb a few moves to inspect crux holds from another point of view. Considering the effort it requires simply to *arrive* at the crux on many problems, good pacing is essential. If working a problem in a group, skip a turn every now and then and let others put their energy and enthusiasm (and skin!) into unlocking the sequence. Visualize all possible sequence options before wasting an attempt on a dead end. Whenever possible, seek beta from others or on the Web to save precious energy for more attempts.

The P-Spot

It can be quite frustrating to learn a limit move: It's often a binary proposition in which the move either seems to be very clearly climbable or very much not so! In other words, there is no way to ease into such a move or to learn it progressively. In fact, limit moves *can* be attempted progressively with a *power spot*, a critical tool for advancing on the hardest boulder problems. With a power spot, the spotter places his hands on the climber just above the hips and removes weight as the climber moves. The spotter should press upward, against gravity, not into the rock, and should attempt to permit the climber to move naturally in the case of dynamic moves. The spotter should provide as much assistance as necessary for the climber to complete the move, with said assistance reduced progressively over subsequent attempts as the climber imprints the move. Implemented in this way, the power spot provides a means for slowly but surely learning to complete moves that otherwise feel impossible.

Power spotting is as old as bouldering. While some look down on it, myriad bouldering legends have used the technique throughout the decades. A case in point is Jerry Moffatt's first ascent of *The Dominator* in Yosemite's Camp 4, one of the world's first V13s. As described in his autobiography *Revelations*, Moffatt used a power spot from Kurt Albert while working out the crux moves:

"I had to see if I could hold these features and support my weight. I got Kurt to help me. He was six foot two of solid German muscle, so he would pick me up and hold me onto the rock while I figured out the positions... With that, Kurt would release me and I would struggle to keep my body in contact with the rock for a moment before falling off... In this way, I worked right along the boulder, trying various ways of getting to this hold."[9]

Finally, when trying to learn the moves on a new problem, it's easy to climb too much and rest too little — spurred on by your enthusiasm for the novel moves and the deceiving feeling that you've *almost* stuck it. Don't fall into this trap; when working a hard problem — or going for the send — patience is vital. Rest at least five minutes between each attempt. Take a longer break after five or so good attempts. Slip on a pair of tennis shoes and go for a short walk, eat a snack, and drink some water. Frantically hammering away on a single problem again and again will only hasten fatigue and frustration.

BRUSHING

Bouldering often involves the use of big slopers or other friction-dependent holds. For this reason, the stone must be clean and free of any loose dirt, chalk, or other debris. Brush holds regularly (between each attempt) when friction is a factor. Consider mounting a toothbrush to the end of an extendable pole to brush out-of-reach holds. Different brushes may be preferable for various tasks. Lapis horse or boar's-hair brushes are ideal for cleaning the rock without polishing it. Large soft-bristled nylon brushes should be used for big slopers, and stiff-bristled brushes like the Metolius M16 should be used for tiny holds on harder metamorphic rock types like granite. Finicky climbers can also attach a blow tube, allowing them to blow on distant holds.

The same applies to shoes, hands, and crashpads. It's easy to dirty shoes while bouldering, so brush or wipe them off before each attempt. Start

Consider creative ways to inspect out-of-reach holds. Jon Glassberg feels the grips on *Defying Gravity*, V15, in the South Platte, CO while Rich Crowder and Rob D'Anastasio support. 📷 Jason Haas

each problem by stepping off a pad to keep shoes clean, or use a small section of tarp or carpet if pads are limited. Keep the pads clean by regularly lifting them up and shaking off loose debris. Keep hands clean, and wipe away any excess chalk before starting up, to avoid caking the holds.

SKIN MANAGEMENT

Since bouldering is akin to climbing crux-like moves over and over, it's easy to quickly wreck your finger skin. As always, prevention is far more effective than treatment. Pace bouldering efforts throughout the day and examine your finger pads between each attempt. Tape sensitive areas preemptively to avoid skin injuries. Be cognizant of any sharp or irregular handholds, and avoid attempting such moves too frequently. It's best to attempt particularly sharp problems on colder days, when the skin is hard and resilient. Rest frequently, and allow the skin to cool and dry between each attempt. Bring a skin-care kit to the blocks and use it as needed. Details on skin care are provided in Chapter 9: Rest, Injury Prevention, and Rehabilitation.

PACING AND VARIETY

Adequate rest is necessary to generate maximum power. Rest at least a good five minutes between attempts, and avoid the urge to jump back on a problem immediately after an unexpected fall. Consider the rest intervals used in the Power Phase of training (between Campus Board sets, for example), and apply that pacing to performance-bouldering sessions. A duty cycle of 1:20 is perfectly reasonable (i.e., for a 15-second effort you'd allow five minutes of rest). Wear a jacket or sweater between attempts to stay warm — the simple act of donning and removing clothing and shoes between attempts can help slow the pace of a bouldering session. Consider the beta and the quality of the previous attempt during each rest period. Analyze what worked and what didn't and consider alternate sequences. Take frequent breaks throughout each session, and take several long breaks during the day.

One pacing strategy is to equate the bouldering day to a route-climbing day, where each effort to solve a problem is equivalent to a route attempt. Spend 45 to 60 minutes unlocking the moves, taking minutes to rest between each "knowledge burn." Then take an extended break after you send the problem or the hour is up, whichever comes first. Use this time to have a snack or watch other climbers, or move on to another boulder if you failed to send your project. A single problem should not be worked for longer than an hour — including rest breaks — at a time, lest you risk injury.

Another way to prolong a bouldering session is to vary the route style. For example, spend some time on pocket problems, transition to crimpy problems, and then finish on open-hand sloper problems. Vary steepness as well. Steeper routes will emphasize physical strength and large muscle groups, whereas vertical or slabby routes will emphasize footwork and finger strength.

GRADES

It's easy to get hung up on numbers, regardless of climbing style. However, bouldering grades are even more subjective than route grades, since strengths and weaknesses tend to average out over a greater number of moves. A problem's difficulty often depends on the physical characteristics of the climber, like height and reach, so take grades with a grain of salt, and take pleasure in the quality and novelty of the movement whatever the rating.

Savoring the experience on *So High,* V5 R, Joshua Tree.　Brendan Nicholson

Matt Bosley cranking *Esperanza*, V13, Hueco Tanks, TX. Dan Brayack

Flashing a Problem

Sending a problem on the first attempt is the most prized style of ascent. In route climbing, first-try sends are distinguished between *onsights* (where the climber has little to no prior knowledge of the route) and *flashes* (where the climber receives *beta* by watching or talking to other climbers). While the definitions are constantly evolving and open to personal interpretation, boulderers generally do not make this distinction[4]. Every first-try ascent in bouldering is called a "flash," whether external beta was used or not. Furthermore, the consensus among leading pebble wrestlers is that groping any holds within reach of the ground does not invalidate a flash[4]. The point being, when bouldering get all the beta you can before a flash attempt.

To begin, video of most well-known problems is available online, so do a little research beforehand. Then visit the area on a busy day, when you can observe several other climbers on the problem, and discuss the intricacies of the beta with them: how to grasp each hold, where to position hips, and key footholds. Place special emphasis on learning which features to aim for when making dynamic moves — the hardest moves to flash. Attempt the problem after a thorough warm-up that includes working a few harder problems. Wait until a plethora of pads and spotters are available so you can climb with complete confidence and commitment. Flashing at your limit requires an aggressive attitude, so get fired up before your attempt, and ask your spotters to shout encouragement.

SUMMARY

- Bouldering differs from route climbing in a number of key ways, including: length, intensity, movement, arousal, hold type, exposure, style, group size, accessibility, conditions, and duty cycle.
- Training can be tailored to maximize bouldering performance, but doing so may temporarily hamper route-climbing performance (i.e., reduce endurance).
- To emphasize bouldering performance, minimize Base-Fitness training while maximizing Strength and Power training. Train on representative hold types, such as slopers, pinches, and crimps.
- Emphasize dynamic movements in skill development and training. Place extra emphasis on core, upper-arm, and shoulder strength training.
- Bouldering benefits from high arousal. Learn how to influence arousal and practice these methods regularly.
- Ensure a safe bouldering environment in order to stay healthy and apply maximum commitment to each attempt.
- Be creative when attempting to unlock sequences. Get different perspectives and watch other climbers.
- Pace your efforts throughout each session, and vary the style of climbing to prolong bouldering sessions.
- Monitor your skin, and address any potential issues preemptively. Keep holds, shoes, and hands clean.
- Bouldering grades are especially inconsistent, so avoid fixating on them. Instead, focus on the opportunity to develop as a climber.

GLOSSARY

4x4 – A power-endurance training exercise in which four (or any number) boulder problems are climbed in quick succession, followed by a rest period, then repeated until a total of four (or any number) sets has been completed.

Actin – Thin filament proteins within the muscle's Sarcomeres that myosin proteins bind to in order to contract the muscle.

Action Potential – An impulse from the central nervous system that initiates muscle contractions.

Active Rest – Non-climbing exercises performed during the Rest Phase that promote general health and well-being.

Acute Injury – An injury resulting from a specific event or trauma, as opposed to an Overuse Injury.

Adaptation – The body's process of growth and change in order to improve physical, technical or mental abilities.

Aerobic Respiration – A very efficient, but slow, energy metabolism process that requires oxygen.

Anaerobic – A less-efficient energy metabolism process that does not require oxygen.

Aerobic Restoration and Capillarity (ARC) – A form of base-fitness training consisting of continuous climbing for 20 - 45 minutes, right at the climber's Maximum Steady State level of intensity.

Arousal – A psychological state of alertness and readiness to react to challenging situations.

Adenosine Di-Phosphate (ADP) – A byproduct of ATP Hydrolysis during muscle energy metabolism that contributes to fatigue.

Adenosine Tri-Phosphate (ATP) – The primary fuel for many bio-chemical functions in the body, especially muscle contractions.

ATP Hydrolysis (aka ATPase) – The chemical reaction that converts ATP and water into ADP, P_i, and H^+, while releasing energy for cellular functions, such as muscle cell contractions.

Base-Fitness – The body's capacity to fuel muscle contractions for sustained activity.

Baseline – An athlete's standard ability at the beginning of any training season, phase, or exercise. The baseline changes as the athlete improves or de-trains over the course of a career.

Calcium Ions (Ca2+) – Minerals in the muscle cells that trigger cross bridge cycling by the actin and myosin (muscle contractions) when released from the Sarcoplasmic Reticulum.

Campus Board – A ladder of finger edges (typically wood) fixed to a slightly overhanging wall.

Campusing – A climbing movement that is performed without the feet touching the rock. It requires power and momentum to move the hands dynamically from one hold (or wooden rung on a campus board) to the next while the feet hang free.

Caloric Deficit – The condition needed to cause weight loss that is created by consuming fewer calories than are burned.

Capillarization – The density of capillary blood vessels in a muscle, particularly the forearms.

Cardiovascular Exercise (Cardio) – Relatively low intensity exercise that stresses the body's systemic aerobic metabolism, especially the heart and lungs' capacity to supply oxygenated blood to the muscles.

Center of Mass (COM) – The point in space around which the climber's body is perfectly balanced.

Climber's Elbow – See Medial or Lateral Epicondylitis.

Closed Crimp – A hand grip position in which all the fingers are bent at ~90 degrees at the PIP joints. The thumb may or may not wrap over the index finger nail. See photo on p55.

Complex Training – A method that combines strength and plyometric exercises to improve speed and power output.

Concentric – A muscle contraction where the muscle shortens.

Contact Strength – The amount of force the fingers can generate during the period of initial contact with a given hold; which is critical to latching a target hold during dynamic moves.

Cross-Bridge Cycling – A process in which the actin and myosin proteins interact and repeatedly pull on each other to contract the Sarcomeres, and muscle fibers.

Cross Sectional Area (CSA) – The sum-total area of contracting muscle fibers in the plane orthogonal to the direction of contraction. A primary factor in muscular force production.

Cytoplasm – Fluid within the cells (particularly the muscle cells). Allows chemicals for muscle contractions to diffuse around the cell to various locations where they are needed.

Dab – When a free-hanging body part incidentally contacts the ground or other "off-limits" supporting structure.

Deadhang – A static, isometric hang from a hangboard (or similar) involving virtually no motion, in which arms are straight and elbows and shoulders are slightly flexed.

Deadpoint – A dynamic move in which the climber catches the target hold at the highest point of flight, with no overshoot, or extraneous motion of the COM. Deadpoints are used to conserve energy, and are required for latching non-positive target holds.

De-Training – The process through which trained muscles revert back to un-trained levels of fitness.

Duration – A quantitative measure of the time required to complete a training activity.

Duty Cycle – The ratio of work time to rest time (a 2 second effort with a 1 second rest, is a duty cycle of 2:1).

Eccentric – A muscle contraction where the muscle lengthens.

Estimated Glycemic Load (eGL)™ – A metric provided by Nutrition Data (http://nutritiondata.self.com) that estimates a food's effect on the body's blood sugar level based on its nutrition contents.

Failure (training) – The point at which the body can no longer perform a given exercise.

False Grip – A hand grip in which the hand is wrapped around a protruding hold. See photo on p55.

Fast Twitch Fibers (aka Type IIa and IIX/d or IIb) – Muscle fibers that contract relatively quickly and with great force, but fatigue quickly.

Finger Board – Another term for "Hangboard" (see "Hangboard").

Flapper – A skin injury in which the skin of a finger pad is cut deeply and a portion of the pad is peeled away.

Flash Pump – A rapidly developing and debilitating pump that typically results from an inadequate warm-up.

Focus – Attention to the task at hand. Essential to effective training and performance.

Fullness Factor ™ – A metric provided by Nutrition Data (http://nutritiondata.self.com) that estimates a food's satiety based on its nutrition contents.

Functional Hypertrophy – AKA Sarcomere hypertrophy. Growth of the contractile tissues within the muscle, as opposed to non-functional (AKA) sarcoplasmic hypertrophy, which is growth of the energy supply tissues surrounding the muscles.

Gap Analysis – The process of comparing the attributes of a goal climb to the climber's strengths & weaknesses in order to identify areas in need of improvement.

Gaston – A vertical hand grip that lies above, and facing the climber, requiring a thumb-down hand orientation to utilize. See photo in Chapter Three: Skill Development, p55.

Goal Route – A specific climb the climber desires to complete. Ideally the climb is selected in advance of training so it can be used to guide training efforts.

Grip Control – The conscious process of relaxing the forearm flexors as much as possible while climbing or resting, in order to delay the onset of fatigue.

Glucose – An energy-dense sugar, derived from carbohydrates that is the preferred fuel for generating ATP to power muscle contractions.

Glycemic Index – The quantitative measure of how quickly blood sugar level rises after consuming a particular food.

Glycemic Load – The cumulative effect of eating a given portion of a particular food that accounts for the food's glycemic index, and its total amount of net carbohydrates.

Glycemic Response – The body's change in blood sugar level as a result of consuming a particular food. This response is measured by the Glycemic Index.

Glycogen – Stored chemical energy that resides in the liver and muscles, and is derived from Glucose through the glycogenesis process. It can be quickly converted to Glucose to support muscle activity.

Glycolysis/Glycolytic Pathway – A complex process for quickly converting glucose and/or glycogen to ATP without oxygen (anaerobically). It eventually leads to accumulating metabolites and muscle fatigue.

Half-Crimp – See Semi-Closed Crimp

Hangboard – A device used for training finger strength in which athletes perform static hangs from various hard grips while adjusting resistance by adding or removing weight from body weight.

Hangdog – A technique for learning the movement sequences on a route by using the rope for support between learning attempts, as opposed to lowering immediately after a fall.

Hard Bouldering – A training activity in which the climber attempts boulder problems that are too difficult to flash, but can usually be completed in a single session of effort.

Hydrogen Ions (H⁺) – A byproduct of muscle energy metabolism that contributes to fatigue.

Hypertrophy – The volumetric increase of a particular organ or tissue. In strength training, this term s used to describe growth in muscle tissue volume.

Individualization – The deliberate tailoring of a training program to address the specific strengths, weaknesses, and response to training of a given athlete.

Inorganic Phosphate (P$_i$) – A byproduct of muscle energy metabolism that contributes to fatigue.

Intensity – The level of effort that must be applied to complete a given exercise. For some exercises, intensity is easily quantified in terms of the resistance used. For other exercises, intensity cannot be easily quantified, but it can be qualitatively estimated.

Isolation – The principle of training muscle groups individually.

Isometric – A muscle contraction in which the muscle length remains constant.

Isotonic – A muscle contraction in which the force remains constant while the length of the muscle changes.

Jib – A tiny artificial foothold that is so small it must be screwed onto the wall (rather than bolted on). See photo on p50.

Ketosis – A condition of low blood sugar level in which stored fat is broken down into fatty acids that can be metabolized in place of glucose to fuel muscle function.

Kick Plate – A small panel covered with footholds that is fastened beneath a hangboard or campus board, allowing mock-climbing. See photo on p162.

Kipping – Swinging the lower body to generate momentum for a campus movement.

Lateral Epicondylitis – (aka Tennis Elbow) A common overuse injury manifesting as acute pain at the point in the elbow where the finger extensor tendons attach to the lateral epicondyle.

Limit Bouldering – Climbing short boulder problems that feature 1 - 2 crux moves (preferably dynamic moves) that are right at the climber's limit.

Limit Route – A route or boulder problem barely within the climber's ability, that requires multiple days of rehearsal and attempts to climb successfully.

Linear Periodization – An approach to periodic training in which various attributes of physical ability are trained in distinct phases or meso-cycles.

Linkage – Successfully climbing sub-sections of a route in one continuous effort during the route rehearsal process.

Linked Bouldering Circuits (LBC) – A high- and mid-intensity form of power-endurance training in which several near-limit boulder problems are linked together to create a circuit of 10 – 40 hand movements requiring 45 seconds to four minutes to climb.

Load – The amount of weight (or resistance) applied to a given exercise.

Logistical Fatigue – Fatigue that develops during multipitch climbs as a result of ancillary, non-climbing tasks.

Macro-Cycle – AKA "Season" A period of time selected by the climber (typically 3 - 4 months) in which periodic training, rest and performance activities are planned.

Maintenance Training – A form of Non-Linear Periodization used to extend the length and quality of a Performance Peak.

Mantel – A hand grip in which downward pressure is placed on a hold with the palm of the hand. See photo on p55.

Maximum Recruitment – A type of physical training designed to encourage the activation of the greatest proportion of motor units for a given contraction.

Maximum Steady State (MSS) – The level of effort that can be sustained by the muscle indefinitely by primarily utilizing aerobic respiration (aka Anaerobic Threshold, Aerobic Threshold, Lactic Threshold).

Medial Epicondylitis – (aka Golfer's Elbow) A common overuse injury manifesting as acute pain at the point in the elbow where the finger flexor tendons attach to the medial epicondyle.

Meso-cycle – AKA "Phase." A period of time within a Macro-Cycle (typically 2 - 4 weeks) focused on a particular type of training (such as Base-Fitness, Strength, Power, or Power-Endurance).

Metabolites – Byproducts of muscle energy metabolism that interfere with muscle function and cause fatigue (including H^+, P_i, NADH, ADP).

Mitochondria – An organelle found in many cells that aerobically supplies energy (ATP) for cell function (especially muscles).

Mono – A pocket hold that admits only a single finger.

Motor Neuron – Nerve cells that carry signals from the Central Nervous System to the muscles to initiate muscle contractions.

Motor Unit – The smallest functional unit of the neuromuscular system, composed of bundles of one or more muscle fibers, and controlled by a single Motor Neuron.

Muscle Fiber – A long tubular cell composed of numerous myofibrils.

Myofibrils – The smallest individual contractile units in the muscle.

Myosin – Thick filament proteins within the muscle's Sarcomeres that bind to Actin proteins to contract the muscle.

Near-Limit Route/Redpoint – A route or boulder problem that is one or two letter grades easier than a Limit Route, and can typically be climbed successfully in two or three days of effort.

Net Carbs – The portion of a food's total carbohydrates that will be absorbed by the body, calculated as the number of grams of total carbs minus grams of dietary fiber.

Non-Linear Periodization (NLP) – An approach to periodic training in which various attributes of physical ability are trained concurrently, in a single training session or in week-long micro-cycles.

Non-Steroidal Anti Inflammatory Drugs (NSAIDs) – Drugs commonly used for temporary pain relief that are known to delay healing of soft tissue.

Occlusion – Reduced flow of blood to the muscles during muscle contractions.

Open Grip – A hand grip in which the PIP joint is only slightly flexed. See photo on p55.

Outdoor Mileage – A form of base-fitness training, much like ARC training, in which a high volume of climbing (typically 6 - 12 pitches in a day) is performed at a moderate intensity (approximately two number-grades below onsight level).

Overload – Training stress must exceed the body's baseline capability in order to stimulate physical adaptation.

Overuse Injury – An injury that develops gradually over time from excessive stress, as opposed to an Acute Injury.

Oxydative Phosphorylation – An aerobic process that occurs within the mitochondria for converting the metabolites NADH, H^+ and P_i, along with oxygen, into ATP.

Pace – The rate at which a sequence is climbed. Pace can vary within a given ascent, i.e., climbing faster or slower.

Performance – The act of climbing on rock or during competition, for the purpose of achieving a goal.

Performance Peak – The period during which the athlete expects to experience optimal performance. The length and timing of the Performance Peak is determined by the timing and effectiveness of the training cycle, and can be difficult to precisely control.

Performance Phase – The scheduled mesocycle within a macro-cycle in which the athlete attempts to perform outdoors on rock as much as possible. The length and timing of the Performance Phase is determined by the athlete.

Periodization – A strategy for physical training in which different training activities are performed in accordance with a carefully designed schedule to achieve a synergistic effect on overall performance that results in a *performance peak* at a predictable time.

Phase – A period of time (typically 2 - 4 weeks) within a periodic training program focused on a particular type of physical training.

Pinch – A hand grip in which the thumb is used. See photo on p55.

Phosphagen Pathway – The fasted method for ATP production, used by the muscles for immediate action, and in the first few seconds of muscle activity. Uses the creatine kinase reaction to break creatine phosphate into ATP.

Plyometrics – Dynamic exercises that require the muscles to exert maximum force quickly in order to increase speed and power.

Proximal Interphalangeal (PIP) Joint – The knuckle joint between the two finger bones of each finger that are nearest the palm of the hand.

Plateau – Stagnation in performance caused by the Law of Diminishing Returns.

Power – The ability to quickly exert high force on a set of holds.

Power-Endurance – The ability to perform multiple near-maximal climbing moves without rest (typically in bouts lasting 30 - 180 seconds). During power-endurance climbing, the intensity of the moves is sufficiently high that recruitment of fast-twitch muscle fibers is required.

Power Spot – A spotting technique in which the spotter places his hands on the climber's hips and/or low back and pushes gently to remove weight from the climber to assist in learning difficult moves.

Practice Falls – Progressively longer falls used to condition the lead climber to exposure and reduce falling anxiety.

Project – A goal route that requires more than one attempt to send.

Progressive Overload – The systematic and iterative application of incremental training stress and subsequent recovery to gradually improve the body's capabilities over the previous baseline.

Progression – Improvement over time.

Pulleys (finger) – The ligaments that hold the finger flexor tendons in place to facilitate finger joint movement.

Quantification – The process of measuring training intensity and duration in order to document and control volume and progression.

Range of Motion – The distance a joint can freely move.

Reactive Training – A method of shock-loading the muscles in order to activate their inherent stretch-shortening injury-defense reflex and maximize muscle fiber recruitment.

Recovery – A period of rest following physical training during which supercompensation occurs.

Recruitment – Describes the proportion of active motor units contributing to a given muscular contraction.

Regularity – Training must be performed repeatedly at reasonable time intervals in order to avoid de-training.

Rehabilitation – The process of recovering injured tissue to a healthy state through methodical and controlled application of stress and rest.

Repetition – A term used in physical training to denote a single exercise cycle, such as lifting and lowering a weight.

Resistance – The quantity of weight (or load) applied to a given exercise.

Reversibility – Physical adaptations achieved through training can be lost just as easily as they are gained, if training stimulus is not maintained or increased.

Robust – Able to perform well under various (often poor) conditions.

Roped Bouldering – Working individual crux moves on a difficult route, in preparation for an eventual redpoint. The intensity, duration of effort, and duty cycle are similar to that of bouldering, but the climber is *hangdogging* on a rope to allow access to the most critical moves.

Route Intervals (aka laps, or lapping) – A lower-intensity power-endurance training exercise in which a pumpy route is climbed several times in succession, with a specified rest period between laps.

Route Pyramid – A visual representation of a climber's "resume" of single pitch rock climbing ascents; an approach to climbing progression that emphasizes building a broad base of experience on routes that are below the climber's maximum ability.

Sarcomeres – The segmented units of the muscle's myofibrils that shorten in a contraction.

Sarcoplasmic Reticulum (SR) – An organelle within the muscle cells that stores and provides calcium ions for muscle contractions.

Satiety – The feeling of satisfaction, or fullness from eating.

Season – AKA "Macro-Cycle" A period of time selected by the climber (typically 3 - 4 months) in which training, rest and performance activities are planned.

Self-Talk – The internal dialogue a climber engages in while climbing. Typically, *positive* self-talk is most beneficial.

Semi-Closed Crimp – AKA Half Crimp, a hand grip position in which the Index and Pinkie fingers are straight, and the Middle & Ring fingers are bent ~90 degress at the PIP joint. See photo on p55.

Set – A term used in physical training to denote a group of repetitions performed consecutively, such as lifting and lowering a weight five times in quick succession.

Sidepull – A vertically-oriented hand grip that faces away from the climber. See photo on p55.

Size Principle – During muscular contraction, smaller, slow twitch motor units tend to be activated first, and the larger and stronger fast twitch units tend to be activated last.

Skill Development – The process of acquiring new technical movement abilities, refining them through practice, and finally stress-proofing those abilities for use during performance.

Slow Twitch Fibers (aka Type I) – Muscle fibers that contract relatively slowly and with less force, but are able to sustain contractions for a longer duration.

Specificity – An athlete will primarily achieve physical adaptations in the systems that are stimulated by the training activity.

Stamina – The body's ability to endure multiple difficult climbing efforts, or pitches, throughout a climbing day.

Strength (physical strength) – The body's ability to exert high force on a climbing hold.

Strength (performance strength) – A skill or ability required for climbing that the climber performs well (relative to other skills and abilities).

Stress-Proofing – A progressive process for improving the ability to perform a new skill in high-pressure situations.

Super-Compensation – The body's adaptive response to physical training stress.

Supinate – Outward rotation of a limb. For example, an arm rotating from a palms-down position to palms-up.

Systemic – A condition that affects the entire body as a whole.

Tapering – Steadily reducing the total volume of exercise near the end of a season in order to augment a performance peak.

Time Under Tension (TUT) – The duration of a training activity spent under load (total exercise time, minus the duration of any rest intervals).

Time-Value of Climbing Ability – Time invested today in training, will pay off with more sending power in the future.

Transfer – Train in a manner that replicates the conditions of performance to the extent possible.

Training – An approach to improve climbing performance that is systematic, disciplined, and science-based.

Training Stress – The cumulative fatigue resulting from a climbing workout or performance day.

Treadwall® – An artificial climbing wall that rotates as the climber climbs, like a vertically-oriented treadmill.

Tweaky – A hold or move that qualitatively feels likely to cause injury.

Twitch – A mechanical response in the motor unit caused by an action potential from a motor neuron.

Undercling – A downward-oriented hand grip, on which the climber must apply upward pressure. See photo on p55.

Variation – Adjustments to training methods and stress to avoid performance plateaus.

Volume – The product of training intensity and training duration.

Warmup Boulder Ladder – A warmup activity in which the climber completes a series of boulder problems beginning with V-Easy, and progressing up to the climber's flash limit.

Weakness – A skill or ability required for climbing that the climber performs poorly (relative to other skills and abilities).

Workload – The total volume of training stress applied to an athlete during a given time period.

Wunderkind – A phenomenal climber who began climbing regularly as a child.

Zone – The mental state of focus and concentration required for optimal performance.

REFERENCES

CHAPTER 1 - INTRODUCTION

1. Juul, A, Holm, K, Pedersen, S, Michaelsen, K, Scheike, T, Rasmussen, S, Muller, J, Skakkebaek, N, "Free Insulin-Like Growth Factor 1 Serum Levels in 1430 Healthy Children and Adults," *J Clin Endocrinol Metab*, 82(8): 2497-2502, 1997.
2. Neumann, U, and Goddard, D, *Performance Rock Climbing*, Stackpole Books, 1993.
3. Petro, S, Yaniro, T, Gnade, L, and Yaniro, K, *Fingers of Steel*, Excalibur Distribution, 1990s.
4. Caldwell, T, Black Diamond, blackdiamondequipment.com/en-us/climbersskiers/global/detail/username/tommycaldwel, accessed Feb 2013.
5. Drozdz, P, "Iker Pou on the Training in Sport Climbing," *Climb and More*, www.climbandmore.com/climbing,700,0,1,training.htm , accessed Mar 5, 2013.
6. Gresham, N, "Bouldering & Power Training – Malcolm Smith," Neil Gresham's Climbing Masterclass, http://climbingmasterclass.com/training/protips.asp?article=2, accessed Aug 2013.
7. Trotter, S, "Sonnie's Simple Training Tip of the Week," *Sonnie Trotter Blog*, http://sonnietrotter.com/2009/03/09/sonnies-simple-training-tip-of-the-week/, accessed Aug 2013.
8. Trotter, S, "Sticky Fingers," *Sonnie Trotter Blog*, http://sonnietrotter.com/2008/07/29/sticky-fingers/, accessed Aug 2013.

CHAPTER 2 - GOAL SETTING AND PLANNING

1. Barnett, C, *The Swordbearers: Studies in Supreme Command in the First World War*, Eyre & Spottiswoode, 1963.
2. Lawrence, TE, *Seven Pillars of Wisdom*, Doubleday Doran & Co, 1935.
3. Moffat, J, *Revelations*, Vertebrate, 2010.
4. Skinner, T, *Beyond the Summit*, Penguin, 2003.

CHAPTER 3 - SKILL DEVELOPMENT

1. Acrimowicz, M, "Josune Bereziartu Interview," *Climb and More*, www.climbandmore.com/climbing,493,0,1,interviews.html, accessed Aug 2013.
2. Acrimowicz, M, "Josune Bereziartu on Training," *Climb and More*, *www.climbandmore.com/climbing,266,0,1,training.html*, accessed Aug 2013.
3. Dawes, J, "About Johnny," Johnny Dawes Blog, www.johnnydawes.com/about-johnny/, accessed Aug 2013.
4. Ericsson, A, Krampe, R, and Tesch-Romer, C, "The Role of Deliberate Practice in the Acquisition of Expert Performance," *Psychological Review* Vol 100 (3), 363-406, 1993.
5. Hague, D, and Hunter, D, *The Self-Coached Climber*, Stackpole Books, 2006.
6. Lueoben, C, *Rock Climbing: Mastering Basic Skills*, The Mountaineers Books, 2004.
7. Mlodecka, M, and Szymik, J, "Listen to the Master: Francois Legrand," *Climb and More*, www.climbandmore.com/climbing,345,0,1,training.html, accessed Aug 2013.
8. Mlodecka, M, and Szymik, J, "Listen to the Master: Lynn Hill," *Climb and More*, www.climbandmore.com/climbing,411 0,1,training.html, accessed Aug 2013.
9. Moffat, J, *Revelations*, Vertebrate, 2010.

CHAPTER 4 - FOUNDATIONS OF PHYSICAL TRAINING

1. Baker D, Wilson G, and Carlyon R, "Periodization: the effect on strength of manipulating volume and intensity," *Journal of Strength and Conditioning Research*, 8:235 – 242, 1994.
2. Baurock.ru, "Ahead of Time: Interview with Adam Ondra," http://www.baurock.ru/interview2/ondra_eng.htm, 2010, accessed Nov 16, 2012.
3. Hoffman, JR, "Physiological aspects of sport training and performance," *Human Kinetics*, Champaign, IL, 131 – 142, 2002
4. Lieferman, J, Jones, N, Dangelmaier, B, and Dedrick G, "Temporal specificity in exercise training," *Medicine and Science in Sports and Exercise*, 27(5), Supplement abstract 124, 1995.
5. Mann, JB, Thyfault, JP, Ivey, PA, and Sayers, SP, "The Effect of Autoregulatory Progressive Resistance Exercise vs. Linear Periodization on Strength Improvement in College Athletes," *J Strength Cond Res*, 2010.
6. Moffat, J, *Revelations*, Vertebrate, 2010.
7. O'Bryant, HS, Byrd, R, and Stone, MH, "Cycle ergometer performance and maximum leg and hip strength adaptations to two different methods of weight-training," *Journal of Applied Sports Science Research*, 2:27 – 30, 1988.
8. Stone, MH, O'Bryant, H, Garhammer, J, "A hypothetical model for strength training," *Journal of Sports Medicine*, 21:342 – 351, 1981.
9. Stowers, T, McMillian, J, Scala, D, Davis, V, Wilson, D, Stone, M, "The short-term effects of three different strength-power training methods," *National Strength and Conditioning Association Journal*, 5:24 – 27, 1983.
10. Willoughby, DS, "A comparison of three selected weight training programs on the upper and lower body strength of trained males," *Annals Journal of Applied Research in Coaching Athletics*, March:124 – 146, 1992.
11. Willoughby, DS, "The effects of meso-cycle-length weight training programs involving periodization and partially equated volumes on upper and lower body strength," *Journal of Strength and Conditioning Research*, 7:2-8, 1993.
12. Acrimowicz, M, "Josune Bereziartu Interview," *Climb and More*, www.climbandmore.com/climbing,493,0,1,interviews.html, accessed Aug 2013.
13. Alstrin, C, "Making Tommy," *Vimeo*, http://vimeo.com/57701693, accessed Aug 2013.
14. Trotter, S, "Sticky Fingers," *Sonnie Trotter Blog*, http://sonnietrotter.com/2008/07/29/sticky-fingers/, accessed Aug 2013.

CHAPTER 5 - BASE FITNESS

1. Allen, D, Lamb, G, and Westerblad, H, "Skeletal Muscle Fatigue: Cellular Mechanisms," *Physiol Rev*, Vol 88: 287-332, 2008.
2. Barcroft, H, and Millen, JL, "The blood flow through muscle during sustained contraction," *J Physiol* 97: 17–31, 1939.
3. Enoka, R, and Duchateau, J, "Muscle Fatigue: What, Why and How it Influences Muscle Function," *Journal of Physiology*, 586.1, 2008.
4. Goddard, D, and Neumann, U, *Performance Rock Climbing*, Stackpole Books, 1993.
5. Humphreys, R, and Lind, A, "The Blood Flow through Active and Inactive Muscles of the Forearm During Sustained Hand-Grip Contractions," *J Physiol*, Vol 166: 120-135, 1963.
6. Lind, A, and Williams, C, "The Control of Blood Flow Through Human Forearm Muscles Following Brief Isometric Contractions," *J Pysiol*, Vol 288:

529-547, 1979.

7. Moffat, J, *Revelations*, Vertebrate, 2010.

8. Roberg, R, Ghiasvand, R, and Parker, D, "Biochemistry of Exercise-Induced Metabolic Acidosis," *Am J Physiol Regul Integr Comp Physiol*, Vol 287: 502-516, 2004.

9. Scott, W, Stevens, J, and Binder-Macleod, S, "Human Skeletal Muscle Fiber Type Classifications," *Physical Therapy*, Vol 81, No 11, 1810-1816, 2001.

10. Stackhouse, S, Reisman, D, and Binder-Macleod, S, "Challenging the Role of pH in Skeletal Muscle Fatigue," *Physical Therapy*, Vol 81: 1897-1903, 2001.

11. Wright, J, McCloskey, D, and Fitzpatrick, R, "Effects of muscle perfusion pressure on fatigue and systemic arterial pressure in human subjects," *J Appl Physiol* 86: 845–851, 1999.

12. Yang, B, Prior, L, Taylor, J, Li, Z, Laughlin, M, and Terjung, R, "Training-Induced Vascular Adaptations to Ischemic Muscle," *J Physiol Pharmacol*, Vol 59, 2008.

13. Mlodecka, M, and Szymik, J, "Listen to the Master: Ben Moon," *Climb and More*, www.climbandmore.com/climbing,19,0,1,training.html, accessed Aug 2013.

CHAPTER 6 - STRENGTH

1. Aagaard, P, Simonsen, EB, Andersen, JL, Magnusson, P, and Dyhre-Poulsen, P, "Neural adaptation to resistance training: changes in evoked V-wave and H-reflex responses," *J Appl Physiol* 92: 2309–2318, 2002.

2. Allen, D, Lamb, G, and Westerblad, H, "Skeletal Muscle Fatigue: Cellular Mechanisms," *Physiol Rev*, Vol 88: 287-332, 2008.

3. Anderson T, and Kearney, JT, "Effects of three resistance training programs on muscular strength and absolute and relative endurance," *Res Q Exerc Sport* 53:1–7, 1982.

4. Andrews M, "How Does Exercise Make You Stronger?" *Scientific American*, October 27, 2003.

5. Butt, C, "Muscle Growth Part 1 & 2: Why, And How, Does A Muscle Grow and Get Stronger?" *The Weight Trainer*, 2007.

6. Campos, G, Luecke, T, and Wendeln, H, "Muscular adaptations in response to three different resistance-training regimens: specificity of repetition maximum training zones," *Eur J Appl Physiol*, 88: 50–60, 2002.

7. Carpinelli, R, Otto, R, and Winnet, R, "A Critical Analysis of the ASCM Position Stand on Resistance Training," *Journal of Exercise Physiology* 7 (3), 2004.

8. Duchateau, J, and Hainaut, K, "Isometric or dynamic training: differential effects on mechanical properties of a human muscle," *Journal of Applied Physiology* 56 (2): 296–301, 1984.

9. Fleck, S, and Kraemer, W, *Designing Resistance Training Programs 3rd Edition*, Champaign, IL: Human Kinetics, 2004.

10. Kitai, TA, Sale, DG, "Specificity of joint angle in isometric training," *Eur J Appl Physiol Occup Physiol*, 58(7): 744-8, 1989.

11. Lieber, R, *Skeletal Muscle Structure, Function, and Plasticity*, Lippincott Williams & Wilkins, 2009.

12. Moffat, J, "Listen to the Master: Jerry Moffat," *Climb And More*, www.climbandmore.com/climbing,18,0,1,training.html, accessed Nov 16, 2012.

13. Schoenfeld, B, "The use of specialized training techniques to maximize muscle hypertrophy," *Strength and Conditioning Journal*, 33(4): 60-65, 2011.

14. Stanfield, C, and Germann, W, *Principles of Human Physiology*, Benjamin Cummings, 2008.

15. Smith, J, "Seven Requirements for Building Functional Hypertrophy," http://www.ericcressey.com, Jan 31 2008, accessed Nov 16, 2012.

16. Stone, WJ, and Coulter, SP, "Strength/endurance effects from three resistance training protocols with women," *J Strength Cond Res*, 8:231–234, 1994.

17. Thepaut-Mathieu. C, Van Hoecke. J, and Maton, B, "Myoelectrical and mechanical changes linked to length specificity during isometric training," *J Appl Physiol*, Apr; 64(4): 1500-5, 1988.

18. Young, K, McDonagh, M, and Davies, C, "The Effects of Two Forms of Isometric Training on the Mechanical Properties of the Triceps Surae in Man," *European Journal of Physiology*, 405(4): 384-8, 1985.

19. Mlodecka, M, and Szymik, J, "John Gill on Training," *Climb and More*, http://www.climbandmore.com/climbing,242,0,1,training.html, accessed Aug 2013.

20. Trotter, S, "About Us – Sonnie Trotter," Black Diamond, http://webdev.bdel.com/en-eur/climbersskiers//detail/username/sonnietrotter, accessed Aug 2013.

21. Vecchiato, D, "Freak Legends – Ben Moon," Freak Climbing, www.freakclimbing.com/modules.php?name=People&rop=showcontent&pid=11, accessed Aug 2013.

CHAPTER 7 - POWER

1. Drozdz, P, "Iker Pou on the Training in Sport Climbing," *Climb and More*, www.climbandmore.com/climbing,700,0,1,training.html, accessed Mar 5, 2013.

2. Fioravanti, R, "Hot Seat: Gentle Giant Fred Nicole," *Climbing*, 200, 2001.

3. Frohlich, M, Emrich, E, and Schmidtbleicher, D, "Outcome Effects of Single-set Versus Mutiple-Set Training – An Advanced Replication Study," *Research in Sports Medicine* 18(3), p. 157-175.

4. Hepp, T, Wolfgang Gullich: *A Life in the Vertical*, Menasha Ridge Press, 1995.

5. Mlodecka, M, and Szymik, J, "Listen to the Master: Ben Moon," *Climb and More*, http://www.climbandmore.com/climbing,19,0,1,training.html, accessed Aug 2010.

6. Mlodecka, M, and Szymik, J, "Wolfgang Gullich," *Climb and More*, http://www.climbandmore.com/climbing,471,0,2,climbers.html, accessed Mar, 2013.

7. Moffat, J, *Revelations*, Vertebrate, 2010.

8. Moon, B, "Campus Boarding," http://www.moonclimbing.com/blog/school/campus-boarding/, accessed Feb 28, 2013.

9. Petro, S, Yaniro T, Gnade, L, and Yaniro, K, *Fingers of Steel*, Excalibur Distribution, 1990s.

10. Scott, W, Stevens, J, and Binder-MacLeod, S, "Human Skeletal Muscle Fiber Type Classifications," *Physical Therapy Journal*, 81(11): 1810-1816, 2001.

11. Stanfield, C, and Germann, W, *Principles of Human Physiology*, Benjamin Cummings, 2008.

12. Yessis, M, *Explosive Plyometrics*, Ultimate Athlete Concepts, 2009.

CHAPTER 8 - POWER-ENDURANCE

1. Hepp, T, and Mailander, L, *Wolfgang Gullich: A Life in the Vertical*, Menasha Ridge Press, 1995.
2. Holloszy, J, and Coyle, E, "Adaptations of skeletal muscle to endurance exercise and their metabolic consequences," *J Appl Physiol*, Vol 56:831-838, 1984.
3. MacDougal, D, Hicks, A, et al., "Muscle performance and enzymatic adaptations to sprint interval training," *J Appl Physiol*, Vol 84:2138-2142, 1998.
4. Mlodecka, M, and Szymik, J, "Mental Training Quotes, " *Climb and More*, http://www.climbandmore.com/climbing,20 0,1,training.html, accessed Mar 5, 2013.
5. Moffat, J., *Revelations*, Vertebrate, 2010.

CHAPTER 9 - REST, INJURY PREVENTION, AND REHABILITATION

1. American Academy of Sleep Medicine, "Extra Sleep Improves Athletic Performance," *Science Daily*, June, 2008.
2. Burke, D, MacNeil, S, Holt, L, Mackinnon, N, and Rasmussen, R, "The effect of hot or cold water immersion on isometric strength training," *J of Strength & Conditioning Research*, 14(1), 2000.
3. Coombes, B, Bisset, L, and Vincenzino, B, "Efficacy and safety of corticosteroid injections and other injections for management of tendinopathy: a systematic review of randomized controlled trials," *The Lancet*, 376:1751-1767, 2010.
4. Crowe, M, O'Connor, D, Rudd, D, "Cold water recovery reduces anaerobic performance," *Intl J Sports Med*, 28(12):994-8, 2007.
5. Drozdz, P, "Adam Ondra on Bouldering," *Climb and More*, http://www.climbandmore.com, accessed Feb 4, 2013.
6. Drozdz, P, "Iker Pou on the Training in Sport Climbing," *Climb and More*, http://www.climbandmore.com/climbing,700,0,1,training.html, accessed Mar 5, 2013.
7. Fioravanti, R, "Hot Seat: Gentle Giant Fred Nicole," *Climbing*, 200, Feb 2001.
8. Fryberger, C, *Core*, Chuck Fryberger Films, 2010.
9. Greene, J, "Cost-conscious prescribing of non-steroidal anti-inflammatory drugs for adults with arthritis," *Archives of Internal Medicine*, 152:1995-2002, 1992.
10. Hochholzer, T, and Schöeffl, V, *One Move Too Many...*, 2nd ed., Lochner Verlag: Ebenhausen, 2006.
11. Moffat, J, *Revelations*, Vertebrate, 2010.
12. Schoffl, I, Einwag, F, Strecker, W, Hennig, F, and Schoffl, V, "Impact of taping after finger flexor tendon pulley ruptures in rock climbers," *J Appl Biomech*, 23(1):52-62, 2007.
13. Schoffl, VR, Einwag, F, Strecker, W, and Schoffl, I, "Strength measurement and clinical outcome after pulley ruptures in climbers," *Medicine and Science in Sports and Exercise*, 38(4), 637-643, 2006.
14. Schoffl, V, Hochholzer, T, Winkelmann, HP, and Strecker, W, "Therapy of injuries of the pulley system in sport climbers," *Handch.ru-gie, Mikrochirurgie, plastische Chirurgie*, 36(4), 231-236, 2004.
15. Vaile, J, Halson, S, Gill, N, and Dawson, B, "Effect of hydrotherapy on recovery from fatigue," *Intl J Sports Med*, 29(7):539-44, 2008.
16. Ward, M, "Wall Warriors: A History of Training for Climbing," *UK Climbing*, http://www.ukclimbing.com/articles/page.php?id=3393, accessed Mar 4, 2013.
17. Yamane, M, Teruva, H, Nakano, M, Ogai, R, Ohnishi, N, and Kosaka, M, "Post-exercise leg and forearm flexor muscle cooling in humans attenuates endurance and resistance training effect on muscle performance and on circulatory adaptation," *Euro J Appl Physiol*, 96(5): 572-80, 2006.

CHAPTER 10 - BUILDING A TRAINING PLAN AND OTHER TRAINING CONSIDERATIONS

1. Gresham, N, "Masterclass Secrets: Bouldering and Power Training with Ben Moon," *Climber*, November 2000.
2. Hepp. T, *Wolfgang Gullich: A Life in the Vertical*, Menasha Ridge Press, 1995.
3. Huber, A, *The Mountain Within: The True Story of the World's Most Extreme Free-Ascent Climber*, Skyhorse Publishing, 2010.
4. Ramsey, W, "The Pain Box," unpublished.

CHAPTER 11 - WEIGHT MANAGEMENT

1. Agatston, A, *The South Beach Diet*, St. Martin's Press, 2003.
2. Astrup, A, Larsen, T, and Harper, A, "Atkins and other low-carbohydrate diets: Hoax or an effective tool for weight loss?" *The Lancet*, 364 (9437): 897–899, 2004.
3. Baty, J, Hwang, H, Ding, Z, Bernard, J, Wang, B, Kwon, B, and Ivy, J, "The effect of a carbohydrate and protein supplement on resistance exercise performance, hormonal response, and muscle damage," *Journal of Strength and Conditioning Research*, Vol 21(2), 321, 2007.
4. Brand-Miller, J, and Foster-Powell, K, *The Low GI Diet Revolution: The Definitive Science-Based Weight Loss Plan*, Marlowe & Company, 2005.
5. Ebey, S, "Regulation of Glucose by Insulin," *Science-ay*, May 4, 2009.
6. Fallon, S, and Enig, M, "Newest Research on Why You Should Avoid Soy," *Nexus*, Vol 7, No 3, April, 2000.
7. European Food Safety Authority, Panel on Dietetic Products, "Scientific Opinion on Dietary Reference Values for Fats," *EFSA Journal*, 8(3):1461, 2010.
8. Ferrara, L, Raimondi, A, d'Episcopo, L, Guida, L, Dello Russo, A, and Marotta, T, "Olive oil and reduced need for antihypertensive medications," *Archives of Internal Medicine*, 160 (6): 837–842, 2000.
9. Foster-Powell, K, Holt, S, and Brand-Miller, J, "International table of glycemic index and glycemic load values: 2002," *American Journal of Clinical Nutrition*, 76 (1): 5–56, 2002.
10. Gasior, M, Rogawski, M, and Hartman, A, "Neuroprotective and disease-modifying effects of the ketogenic diet," *Behavioural Pharmacology*, 17 (5–6): 431–9, 2002.
11. Haban, P, Klvanova, J, Zidekova, E, and Nagyova, A, "Dietary supplementation with olive oil leads to improved lipoprotein spectrum and lower n-6 PUFAs in elderly subjects," *Medical Science Monitor*, 10(4): 49-54, 2004.
12. Hochholzer, T, and Schöeffl, V, *One Move Too Many...*, 2nd ed., Lochner Verlag: Ebenhausen, 2006.
13. Holt, S, Brand Miller, J, Petocz, P, and Farmakalidis, E, "A Satiety Index of Common Foods," *European Journal of Clinical Nutrition*, pg. 675-690, September, 1995.

14. Ivy, J, "Effect of a carbohydrate-protein supplement on endurance performance during exercise of varying intensity," *International Journal of Sport Nutrition and Exercise Metabolism*, Vol 13: 382-395, 2003.

15. Jenkins, D, Wolever, T, and Taylor, R, "Glycemic index of foods: a physiological basis for carbohydrate exchange," *American Journal of Clinical Nutrition*, 34 (3): 362–6, 1981.

16. Kris-Etherton, P, William, S, and Harris, L, "Fish Consumption, Fish Oil, Omega-3 Fatty Acids, and Cardiovascular Disease," *Circulation*, 106 (21): 2747–2757, 2002.

17. Lichtenstein, A, Appel, L, and Brands, M, "Diet and lifestyle recommendations revision 2006: A scientific statement from the American Heart Association Nutrition Committee," *Circulation*, 114 (1): 82–96, 2006.

18. Moffat J, *Revelations*, Vertebrate, 2010.

19. National Heart Foundation of Australia, "Dietary Fats, Dietary Cholesterol, and Heart Health," www.heartfoundation.org.au/sitecollectiondocuments/dietary-fats-dietary-cholesterol-and-heart-health.pdf, 2009, accessed Nov 2012.

20. National Institute of Health, "Essential Fats in Food Oils," http://efaeducation.nih.gov/sig/esstable.html, accessed Nov 2012.

21. Nordic Council of Ministers, *Glycemic Index: From Research to Nutrition Recommendations?* Copenhagen, 2005.

22. Nutrition Data, http://nutritiondata.self.com/, accessed Nov 2012.

23. Rolls, B, and Barnett, R, *Volumetrics: Feel Full on Fewer Calories*, Harper, 1999.

24. Simopoulos, A, "The importance of the ratio of omega-6/omega-3 essential fatty acids," *Biomedicine and Pharmacotherapy*, 56 (8): 365-79, 2002.

25. Taubes, G, "Is Sugar Toxic," *The New York Times*, Apr 2011.

26. "Unsaturated Fat," http://en.wikipedia.org/wiki/Unsaturated_fat, Wikipedia, accessed November 5, 2012.

27. Wall, R, Ross, R, Fitzgerald, G, and Stanton, C, "Fatty acids from fish: the anti-inflammatory potential of long-chain omega-3 fatty acids," *Nutrition Review*, 68 (5): 280–9, 2010.

28. Walker, R, and Rodgers, J, *Type 2 Diabetes – Your Questions Answered*, Dorling Kindersley, 2006.

29. Wansink, B, *Mindless Eating: Why We Eat More Than We Think*, New York, Bantam Dell, 2006.

30. Watts, P, "The Physiology of Difficult Rock Climbing," *European Journal of Applied Physiology*, 91:361-372, 2004.

31. Zoutte, L, "Jibe Tribout Just Did It Again!" *8a.nu*, http://www.8a.nu/?IncPage=http%3A//www.8a.nu/articles/ShowArticle.aspx?ArticleId=383, accessed Mar 2013.

32. Wardrop, M, "Kate Moss: 'Nothing Tastes as Good...'," *The Telegraph*, www.telegraph.co.uk/news/celebritynews/6602430/Kate-Moss-Nothing-tastes-as-good-as-skinny-feels.html, accessed Aug 2013.

CHAPTER 12 - PREPARING TO PERFORM

1. DiGiulian, S, "Don't Get Pumped," *Five-Ten Website*, http://fiveten.com/community/blog-detail/13797-dont-get-pumped-sasha-digiulian, accessed Feb 2013.

2. Drozdz, P, "Quotes," *Climb and More*, http://www.climbandmore.com /climbing,0,10,0,quotes.html, accessed Mar 2013.

3. Ilgner, A, *The Rock Warrior's Way*, Desiderata Institute, 2003.

4. Moffatt, J, *Revelations*, Vertebrate, 2010.

5. Pringle, E, "What I've Learned," *Rock and Ice*, 208, Mar 2013.

CHAPTER 13 - REDPOINT AND ONSIGHT CLIMBING

1. Buhl, H, *Nanga Parbat Pilgrimage*, Hodder and Stoughton, 1956.

2. Fioravanti, R, "Hot Seat: Gentle Giant Fred Nicole," *Climbing*, 200, 2001.

3. Fryberger, C, *Core*, Chuck Fryberger Films, 2010.

4. Hill, L, "Patience with Lynn Hill," *Pro Tips*, Vol 9, Climb X Media.

5. Ilgner, A, *The Rock Warrior's Way, Desiderata* Institute, 2003.

6. MacLeod, D, *9 Out of 10 Climbers Make the Same Mistakes*, Rare Breed Productions, 2010.

CHAPTER 14 - TRADITIONAL AND BIG-WALL FREE CLIMBING

1. Ament, P, *A History of Free Climbing in America: Wizards of Rock*, Wilderness Press, 2002.

2. Caldwell, T, "The Dihedral Wall," *Climbing*, 234:48, 2004.

3. Ilgner, A, *The Rock Warrior's Way*, Desiderata Institute, 2003.

4. MacDonald, D, "A Hard Crack is Good To Find," *Rock and Ice* 71: 46-56, 1996.

5. Piana, P, "Todd Skinner The Renegade," *Rock and Ice*, 2006.

6. Skinner, T, *Beyond the Summit*, Penguin, 2003.

CHAPTER 15 - BOULDERING

1. Achey, I, "15 Questions with Daniel Woods," *La Sportiva.com*, www.sportiva.com/live/live-archive/climbing-archive/daniel-woods-interview, accessed Feb 2013.

2. Ament, P, *A History of Free Climbing in America: Wizards of Rock*, Wilderness Press, 2002.

3. Cahall, F, "Chris Sharma: King of Kings," *Climbing.com*, http://www.climbing.com/climber/sharma-king-of-kings/, accessed Mar 2013.

4. Drozdz, P, "Adam Ondra on Bouldering," *Climb and More*, http://www.climbandmore.com, accessed Feb, 2013.

5. Easterbrooke, J, "The effect of emotion on cue utilization and the organization of behavior," *The Psychological Review*, 66: 187-201, 1959.

6. Gill J, "Reflections and Commentary," *John Gill: A Climbing Memoir*, http://www.johngill.net, accessed Mar 2013.

7. Laeser, L, "Jorgeson Sends Insane 45-foot Highball," *Climbing.com*, http://legacy.climbing.com/news/hotflashes/jorgeson_sends_insaine_45-foot_highball/, accessed Mar 2013.

8. Lashley, K, "Basic Neural Mechanisms in Behavior," *The Psychological Review*, 37 (1): 1–24, 1930.

9. Moffatt, J, *Revelations*, Vertebrate, 2010.

10. Schachter, S, and Singer, J, "Cognitive, Social, and Physiological Determinants of Emotional State," *The Psychological Review*, 69(5): 379–399, 1962.

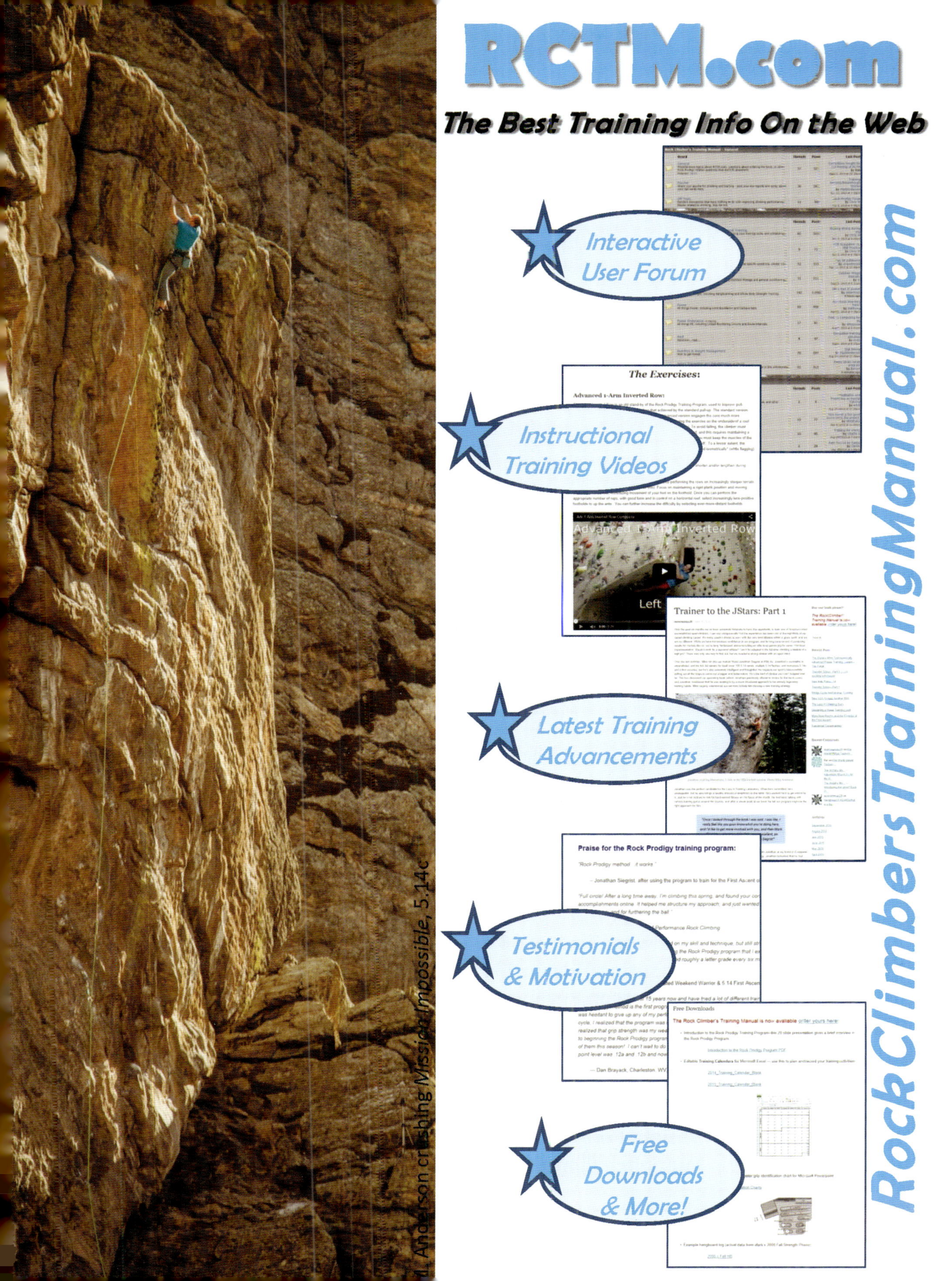
RCTM.com
The Best Training Info On the Web
Interactive User Forum
Instructional Training Videos
Latest Training Advancements
Testimonials & Motivation
Free Downloads & More!
RockClimbersTrainingManual.com
The Exercises:
Advanced 1-Arm Inverted Row:
Trainer to the JStars: Part 1
Praise for the Rock Prodigy training program:
Free Downloads
Anderson crushing Mission Impossible, 5.14c

APPENDIX

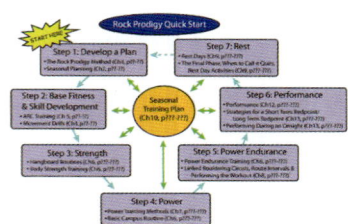

**Quick Start
Guide – p.21**

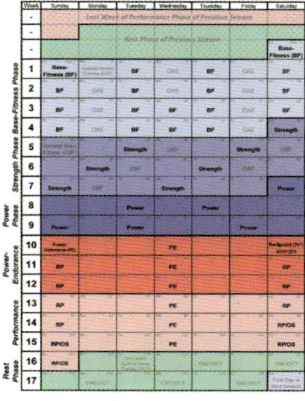

**Basic Seasonal
Training Plan – p.39**

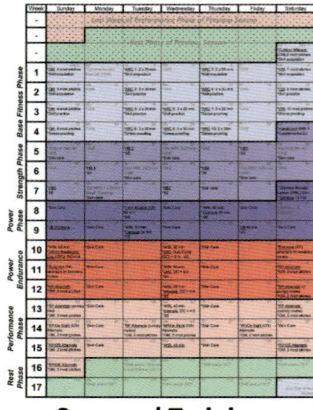

**Seasonal Training
Plan for Novice – p.186**

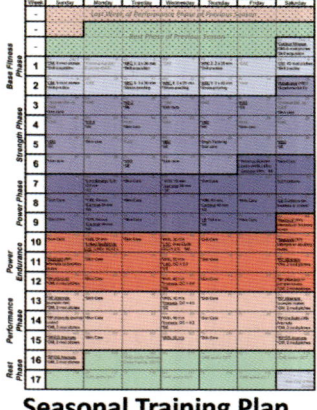

**Seasonal Training Plan
for Experienced
Trainee – p.187**

**Seasonal Training Plan
for Traditional
Climbing – p.262**

**Seasonal Training Plan
for Bouldering – p.277**

INDEX OF SELF ASSESSMENTS, CHECKLISTS, AND TIPS

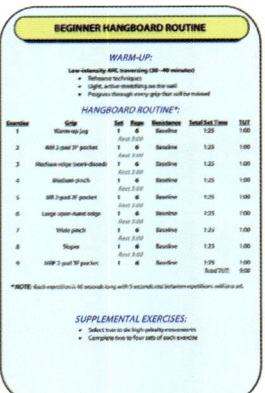

Beginner Hangboard Routine – p.119

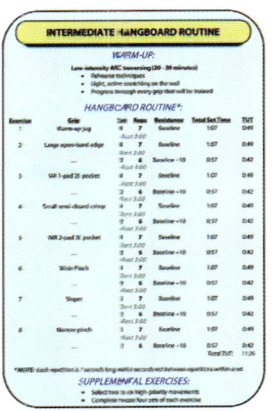

Intermediate Hangboard Routine – p.120

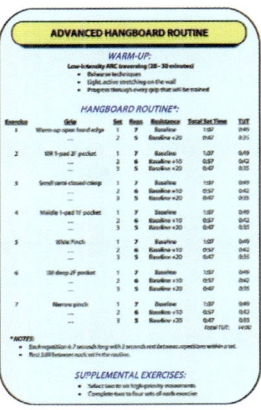

Advanced Hangboard Routine – p.122

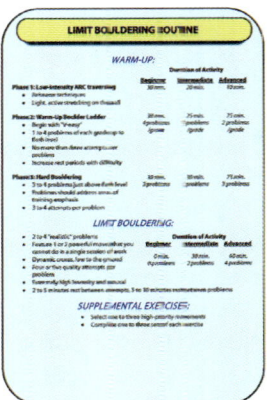

Limit Bouldering Routine – p.134

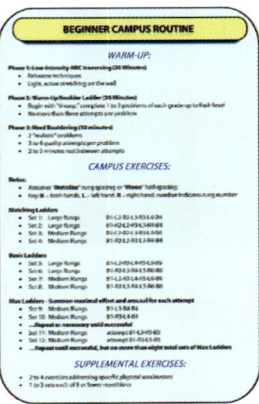

Beginner Campus Routine – p.142

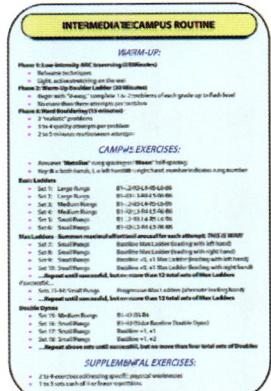

Intermediate Campus Routine – p.144

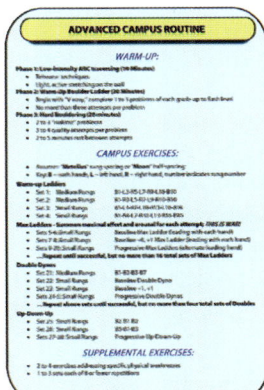

Advanced Campus Routine – p.145

Max-Recruitment Hangboard Routine – p.148

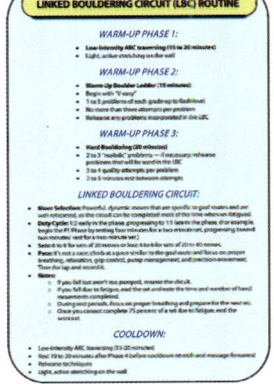

Linked Bouldering Circuit (LBC) Routine – p.161

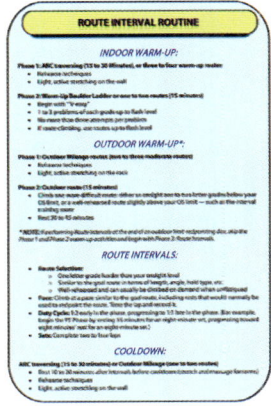

Route Interval Routine – p.163

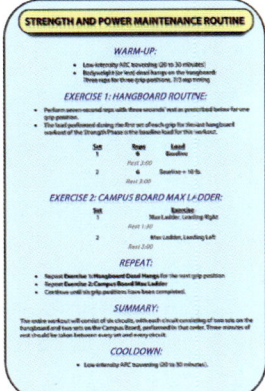

Strength and Power Maintenance Routine – p.196

MODEL BIOS

PAIGE CLAASSEN

For me, training is all about mental dedication. I have to be both motivated to work hard and confident in my abilities. With these two things, I can push my body to new limits. It's quite amazing the work our bodies are capable of, if only we can set aside the pain and mental barriers of training. With practice, I think training can actually be quite fun, and even addicting. Once I put in that effort and see the results afterward, I understand the payoff of my hard work, and this pushes me to keep training harder and harder.

There's also an important balance with training. Sometimes it's important to push yourself through lack of motivation. It's easy to be lazy at times and skip workouts or not try as hard. Having a specific goal to work towards is helpful when motivation is low. That said, it's important to rest as well. For me, lack of motivation is often my body's way of telling me to back off. Hard training can be rough on your body, and it's important to allow yourself time to heal.

NOTABLE ACHIEVEMENTS:

- 2007 USA Climbing SCS National Champion
- Repeats of *Grand Ol' Opry* (5.14b/c), *To Bolt or Not to Be* (5.14a), *Zulu* (5.14a), and *Motley Crux* (5.14a)
- Flashes of Flour Power (5.13b), and Gracias Fina (5.13b)
- First ascent of *Digital Warfare* (5.14a)

TOMMY CALDWELL

Training is central to achieving any athletic goal. It gives an outlet for our drive, and provides the strength and technical practice we need to improve. The way we go about our training, and the intensity in which we are able to bring to our climbing are what make us our best.

NOTABLE ACHIEVEMENTS:

-Established *Flex Luther*, first 5.15 in North America
-First Free Ascent of El Capitan's *West Buttress* (VI, 5.13c), *Lurking Fear* (VI, 5.13c), *Dihedral Wall* (VI, 5.14a), and *Magic Mushroom* (VI, 5.14a)
- First Free Ascent of *Dunn-Westbay* (VI, 5.14a) on The Diamond, Longs Peak CO

ABOUT THE AUTHORS

MICHAEL ANDERSON

Mike lives in the United States with his wife Janelle and boys Lucas and Axel. A dedicated climber since the early 1990s, he bought his first hangboard in 1997 as an occasional 5.11 redpointer and immediately began researching and experimenting with training. From these humble beginnings, Mike has progressed steadily to 5.14 redpoints and 5.13 onsights. Mike is a strong proponent of expanding the horizons of free climbing, especially on long multi-pitch routes. Some of his First Free Ascents include *Touchstone Wall* (5.13, IV), *Space Shot* (5.13 IV) and *Thunderbird Wall* (5.13 VI) in Zion, and *Arcturus* (5.13, VI) on Yosemite's Half Dome. Mike's favorite crags are Smith Rock, Zion, the Red River Gorge and Lander, Wyoming.

MARK ANDERSON

Mark lives in Evergreen, Colorado with his wife Kate and their children Logan and Amelie. Mark has been an avid climber for more than 20 years, and enjoys all types of climbing, from bouldering to high-altitude alpinism. While he is a world-traveling sport climber with numerous 5.13 onsights and cutting edge 5.14 repeats, Mark has also established numerous first ascents, including the First Free Ascent of Zion's *Spaceshot* (5.13a, IV), and all three of Shelf Road's 5.14 sport climbs. Mark is the author of the *Lazy H Climbing Club* training blog, and designed the Rock Prodigy Training Center as a member of Trango's Pro Team.

The authors Mike (Right) and Mark Anderson were destined to be among the mountains.

FIXED PIN

FP promotes climbing ethics that benefit the long-term sustainability of the climbing community by hosting trail days, replacing manky hardware, partnering with local climbing co-alitions, and collaborating with government agencies to improve policies from raptor closures to opening of formerly closed crags.

FP conducts business in a socially, economically and environmentally sustainable fashion by printing in the U.S. on recycled paper whenever possible, donating to the Access Fund and the American Alpine Club, and continuing to stay involved with the preservation of areas for which we publish guidebooks.

Looking for a New Place to Test Your New Fitness Level?

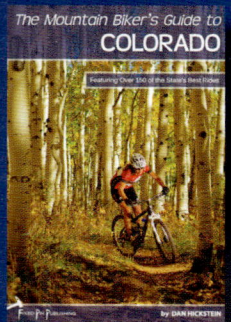
Mountain Biking Colorado

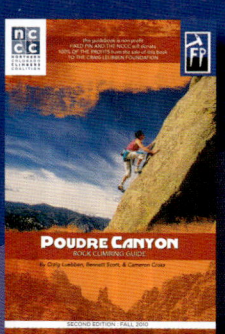
Poudre Canyon (CO)

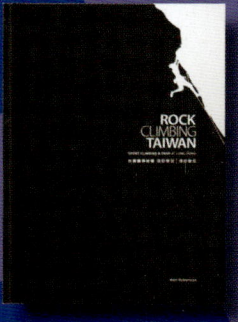
Taiwan

The Virgin Islands

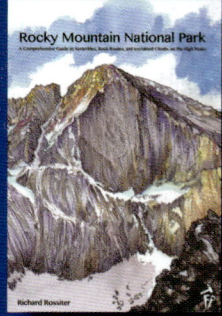
Rocky Mountain National Park (CO)

The Needles of Rushmore (SD)

South Platte (CO) - Volume 1

Jackson Hole (WY)

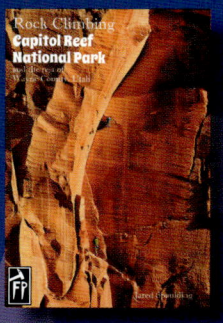
Capitol Reef (UT)

Horseshoe Canyon (AR)

Clear Creek (CO)

Rock Climbing Arkansas - 2nd Ed

Table Mountain (CO)

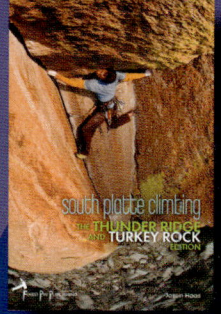
South Platte (CO) - Volume 2

Crack Climber's Tehnique Manual

www.FixedPin.com

Visit our website to learn about new titles, get free downloads, get free books, and contact us with your idea for a new guidebook you're interested in writing.

facebook